Electronic Marketing

Integrating Electronic Resources into the Marketing Process

Electronic Marketing

Integrating Electronic Resources into the Marketing Process

Joel Reedy
University of South Florida

Shauna Schullo
University of South Florida

Kenneth Zimmerman
Chateaux Software Development

The Dryden Press
Harcourt College Publishers

Fort Worth Philadelphia San Diego New York Orlando Austin San Antonio
Toronto Montreal London Sydney Tokyo

Publisher Mike Roche
Acquisitions Editor Bill Schoof
Market Strategist Lisé Johnson
Developmental Editor Bobbie Bochenko
Project Editor Colby Alexander
Art Director Biatriz Chapa
Production Manager Angela Williams Urquhart

Cover Image by Lamberto Alvarez

ISBN: 0-03-021107-7
Library of Congress Catalog Card Number: 99-64779

Address for Domestic Orders
The Dryden Press, 6277 Sea Harbor Drive, Orlando, FL 32887-6777
800-782-4479

Address for International Orders
International Customer Service
The Dryden Press, 6277 Sea Harbor Drive, Orlando, FL 32887-6777
407-345-3800
(fax) 407-345-4060
(e-mail) hbintl@harcourtbrace.com

Address for Editorial Correspondence
The Dryden Press, 301 Commerce Street, Suite 3700, Fort Worth, TX 76102

Web Site Address
http://www.harcourtcollege.com

Printed in the United States of America

0 1 2 3 4 5 6 7 8 066 9 8 7 6 5 4 3 2

The Dryden Press
Harcourt College Publishers

Dedication

For my parents, Melissa and Edward, whose faith in me, steadfastness, and love carried me through times of turbulent health. JER

To my husband, Scott, his loving patience and support was, as always, my anchor. SJS

For my personal cheerleading squad: Monica, Karen, Michael, Mom, and Dad. KRZ

The Dryden Press Series in Marketing

Assael
Marketing

Avila, Williams, Ingram, and LaForge
The Professional Selling Skills Workbook

Bateson
Managing Services Marketing: Text and Readings
Third Edition

Blackwell, Blackwell, and Talarzyk
Contemporary Cases in Consumer Behavior
Fourth Edition

Boone and Kurtz
Contemporary Marketing^WIRED^
Ninth Edition

Boone and Kurtz
Contemporary Marketing 1999

Churchill
Basic Marketing Research
Third Edition

Churchill
Marketing Research: Methodological Foundations
Seventh Edition

Czinkota and Ronkainen
Global Marketing

Czinkota and Ronkainen
International Marketing
Fifth Edition

Czinkota and Ronkainen
International Marketing Strategy: Environmental Assessment and Entry Strategies

Dickson
Marketing Management
Second Edition

Dunne and Lusch
Retailing
Third Edition

Engel, Blackwell, and Miniard
Consumer Behavior
Eighth Edition

Ferrell, Hartline, Lucas, Luck
Marketing Strategy

Futrell
Sales Management: Teamwork, Leadership, and Technology
Fifth Edition

Grover
Theory & Simulation of Market-Focused Management

Ghosh
Retail Management
Second Edition

Hoffman/Bateson
Essentials of Services Marketing

Hutt and Speh
Business Marketing Management: A Strategic View of Industrial and Organizational Markets
Sixth Edition

Ingram, LaForge, and Schwepker
Sales Management: Analysis and Decision Making
Third Edition

Lindgren and Shimp
Marketing: An Interactive Learning System

Krugman, Reid, Dunn, and Barban
Advertising: Its Role in Modern Marketing
Eighth Edition

Oberhaus, Ratliffe, and Stauble
Professional Selling: A Relationship Process
Second Edition

Parente, Vanden Bergh, Barban, and Marra
Advertising Campaign Strategy: A Guide to Marketing Communication Plans

Reedy, Schullo, and Zimmerman
Electronic Marketing: Integrating Electronic Resources into the Marketing Process

Rosenbloom
Marketing Channels: A Management View
Sixth Edition

Sandburg
Discovering Your Marketing Career CD-ROM

Schaffer
Applying Marketing Principles Software

Schaffer
The Marketing Game

Schellinck and Maddox
Marketing Research: A Computer-Assisted Approach

Schnaars
MICROSIM

Schuster and Copeland
Global Business: Planning for Sales and Negotiations

Sheth, Mittal, and Newman
Customer Behavior: Consumer Behavior and Beyond

Shimp
Advertising, Promotion, and Supplemental Aspects of Integrated Marketing Communications
Fourth Edition

Talarzyk
Cases and Exercises in Marketing

Terpstra and Sarathy
International Marketing
Seventh Edition

Weitz and Wensley
Readings in Strategic Marketing Analysis, Planning, and Implementation

Zikmund
Exploring Marketing Research
Sixth Edition

Zikmund
Essentials of Marketing Research

Harcourt College Outline Series

Peterson
Principles of Marketing

About the Book

As the world of marketing information becomes more and more complex, marketers should strive to simplify their decision making processes. Over the last twenty-five years, marketing data have grown by volumes to the point of intimidation, and this overflow of data has been fanned by computer resources, either PC, mini, or mainframe machines. Fortunately, these same computer tools are being harnessed by marketers to assist in the analysis, planning, and implementation of marketing programs, in both consumer and business-to-business situations. Improved communications and enhanced corporate memory are the results of the marketer's electronic environment, whether the business comprises of two employees to two thousand employees. Any enterprise benefits from improvements in operational efficiency and effectiveness, and the marketing function is now embracing more electronic resources as computing costs go down and computing utility goes up. It has been said that a successful marketer's career depends on two qualities—the ability to organize and the ability to persuade. The purpose of this textbook is to assist marketers and marketing students in recognizing the value of electronic marketing resources and to demonstrate how to integrate these electronic tools into each stage of the marketing process. Better organization through improved segmentation strategy or better database management as well as enhanced execution of online communications channels leads to better management of the marketing function that, of course, leads to better performance. The ability to organize, be it marketing research, prospect profiles, segmentation or media strategies, customer communications systems, or database arrangements, allows the marketer to stay on track with firm direction. Likewise, knowing the shortest distance between two points, say from the marketing concept to market consumption, is worth its weight in gold to any company. While this textbook does not deal with the second marketing quality of persuasion, well-designed and carefully considered marketing programs can be quite persuasive to the marketer's superiors and peers. Concise strategies do speak volumes.

The content of this textbook and the experiences and examples of marketing activities have been drawn from the collective business backgrounds and education of its three authors. Their experience spans three decades of marketing history. As they all have specialties within the applied marketing arenas, the authors stand united in their approach to harnessing electronic resources to improve the steps of the marketing process. The stages of a traditional marketing approach, specifically engaging in a situation analysis that leads to the marketing planning and then advances a pattern of marketing implementation, are carefully followed. The authors believe the methods by which marketing success is attained can be made more accurate and timely. The book proposes to introduce and integrate the best practices for the contemporary marketing process. The reader will note that the content of the text is ultimately directed toward enhancing decision making among promotional tools, primarily advertising and other forms of communications. In traditional marketing, the promotional element is a costly portion of the marketing budget. Can the promotional effort become more cost effective and efficient?

This leads to the applications for the Internet, more specifically the World Wide Web. The Web is recognized as a tremendously flexible medium that is well suited to the marketing function. The Web will be used in several manners in this textbook: as a research tool, as an exposure tool for advertising and other promotional activities, as a customer contact vehicle, as well as a customer feedback vehicle. The Web performs admirably in all of these research and communications tasks, but it is wise to remember that currently the World Wide Web can muster household penetration of less than 25 percent. Other traditional media such as newspaper or television are still needed to reach the maximum of consumer groups. In other words, the net of the Web is still not sufficiently big enough to use online communications exclusively. World Wide Web usage is growing, but it still needs more time to mature. Most communicators compare the household penetration to that of cable television. Cable took more than twenty years to become a viable advertising vehicle, and marketers believe that Web usage will outstrip the acceptance levels of cable television.

The textbook's writing style stresses a clear, concise, and interesting treatment of electronic marketing and electronic commerce subjects, and up-to-date examples and situation vignettes are employed abundantly in every chapter. The organization of the material within each chapter follows a critical thinking path of *who, what, when, why*, and *how* in developing the marketing processes. This direct and repetitive approach keeps the processes on target. In the narrative text, frequent references are made to the marketing or communications cycle for products and services. To avoid a horrendous repetition of these two elements, many times the text will read "products," with no restatement of the equal marketing position of services. Therefore, when products are being discussed, the student should read the reference as "products and services" unless otherwise disclaimed.

Electronic Marketing is divided into four parts, organized according to the planning and implementation from concept to special topics of the marketing process. The first part, "The Concepts of Electronic Marketing," explains the foundations of online research and marketing and draws parallels to the stages of the traditional marketing process (situation analysis, marketing planning, and marketing implementation). The second part, "Integrating Electronic Marketing Resources," develops the substituting electronic tool for the traditional tool and provides examples of the online execution. Section three, "Implementing the Commerce Concept," covers the actual activities of establishing and promoting a virtual storefront with attention given to ongoing responsibilities of the e-marketer and Web master. The fourth part, "Special Topics," addresses the unique opportunities that the Web presents such as a direct business-to business channel, international e-commerce, the ethics of e-marketing, and the commerce-expanding possibilities in the future of electronic marketing. The textbook includes appendices of an outline for creating an online marketing and promotional program, geo-demographic data analysis, a list of current electronic marketing resources and Web addresses, and a survey format for interviewing businesses that are online.

One last comment about Web navigation: Understand that Web addresses continually change and sometimes are abandoned by their creators. While the authors have diligently tried to include current and active Web site addresses by publication time, some addresses may have changed or have been deleted by the information source. Sometimes a posted notice on the Web page you have been routed to may be included informing the viewer of changes; sometimes this new address is a hyperlink to an active location. In these cases, follow the hyperlink to see if your desired information resides on that site, or double-check the address that you originally typed.

Supplemental Material

To assist the marketing or communications instructor, the authors have assembled a variety of teaching tools. The first edition of *Electronic Marketing* is accompanied by an Instructor's Manual that has been class-tested for over two years at the time of publication. It contains suggested course content, a schedule (for both a fifteen-week semester and a ten-week summer term), and a discussion of appropriate teaching tips.

The Test Bank contains questions for both midterm and final examinations. They are multiple-choice questions and are arranged by chapter chronology, thus giving the instructor the choice of cumulative or noncumulative exams. One last but very timely resource is the text Web page (www.embook.com) which is designed to present new and relevant Web marketing activities and online points of interest. The Web site will be reviewed and revised twice monthly, so it is hoped that instructors will consult the site to obtain fresh teaching materials as well as updated information. The authors encourage instructors to share and e-mail any suggestions or anecdotal information to Joel Reedy at reedy@coba.usf.edu to aid the instructional materials and Web resources.

In addition to the textbook's Web page, an *Electronic Marketing* site has been created by Eric Sandburg and The Dryden Press. Using this site, students and professors can gain additional information and resources using the Net. This *Electronic Marketing* page is located on The Dryden World Wide Web site at www.harcourtcollege.com

Acknowledgments

Chapter after chapter we have benefited greatly from the insightful comments and suggestions of an outstanding group of reviewers. They have provided perspectives, shrewdness, and constructive criticisms that are vital in planning and writing a comprehensive textbook on such a new marketing topic and discipline. Therefore, we would like to express our appreciation to the following colleagues who participated in the review process for the first edition of *Electronic Marketing: Integrating Electronic Resources into the Marketing Process.*

Catherine Campbell, University of Maryland

Patrali Chatterjee, Rutgers University

Anne Forte, Walsh College

Ellen R. Foxman, Bentley College

Carolyn E. Predmore, Manhattan College

Many thanks to The Dryden Press for assembling a staff so professional, skillful, and congenial that they made the first edition's writing process smooth and complete from the book's conception to publication. Bill Schoof, acquisitions editor and baseball aficionado, picked our diamond from the rough, provided us steady direction, and offered great encouragement throughout the project. Bobbie Bochenko, our developmental editor, made improvements at every turn and displayed exceptional patience as we wrote and rewrote. She jumped in and assisted, prodded, and praised our team to produce the best manuscript we could. Sandy Mann, copy editor, polished our copy masterfully, while Colby Alexander, project editor, ran the production schedule with the expertise of a train conductor, eyes glued to the details. Also, thanks are extended to the following team members: Linda Blundell, picture and rights editor; Angela Urquhart, production manager; April Eubanks and Biatriz Chapa, art directors; Kim Samuels, manufacturing manager; and Lisé Johnson and Marcia Masenda from the marketing department.

Thanks also to the Val-Pak marketers, especially Lynn Johnson who produced the GIS data analysis according to my expectations. Associates Lisa Berry and Steve Egge of National Decision Systems in San Diego gave us permission to use the company data files for the Tampa Bay and metro Orlando areas for use in the geo-demographic exercise; NDS executive Bob Giest has shared the segmentation data with us since 1995. An old friend, Tom White with E-Com Systems shared with us the latest news in electronic catalog and payment systems.

Thanks from Joel Reedy

Defining and describing the dynamics of a new marketing process and medium are difficult tasks but a rare opportunity for the marketing practitioner. I would like to thank my Department of Marketing chair, Bill Locander, my good friend Paul Solomon, and all my marketing colleagues, including our former office manager Lori Wilder, for encouraging and supporting my efforts during a trying year of ill health. Thanks also to Rosemary Ramsey, marketing chair at Eastern Kentucky State University at Richmond and ex-colleague, for suggesting back in early 1996 that I develop an electronic marketing course. From this course framework emerged this marketing textbook.

I sought out the best professionals and interviewed them extensively for insights into the Internet and online marketing. Thanks to Christopher Steinocher, Susan Cook, Christopher Akin, Kristy Funderburk, Hugo Toledo, Sara Suarez, and Russell Tewksbury for outstanding contributions to the course development; each added his or her expertise in the course materials development. Doctoral student Rich Gonzalez demonstrated to me great appreciation for electronic processes of information management and showed me something new every class period. He shared his insights on the future of information, and shortly some lucky undergraduates will benefit from his understanding of electronic marketing. I have a great admiration for the work of a former student, Sonal Mehta, who assisted me night after night with graphics selection and preparation and text assembly. Her excellent academic prowess I knew, and I am benefiting greatly from attitude, computer skills, and an upbeat enthusiasm for online marketing. Another former student, Chris Bilotta now a marketing professional with Val-Pak Direct Marketing Systems, contributed the geographic mapping segmentation information and map graphics. Thanks also to the Val-Pak marketers, especially Lynn Johnson who produced the GIS data analysis according to my expectations. An old friend, Tom White with E-Com Systems, shared with me the latest news in electronic catalog and payment systems. Rose Stambaugh, my nurse, provided tremendous support during the entire process. Thanks and love to my sister, Mary Ann Mason, who tackled the tedious task of typing interview transcripts for case histories.

I teamed up with two professionals from different industries. Shauna Schullo, an expert in software applications and teaching software applications, teaches at the University of South Florida. Shauna served as a guest speaker on HTML, Web site, and forms design as I launched the electronic marketing course. Her knowledge and facility in the software of marketing systems immediately impressed me, and I proposed that she contribute the Web tools instruction to the textbook. She agreed.

The other industry professional is Ken Zimmerman, a software systems wizard and twenty-first century information technologist, whom I have known since 1985. He is a software and systems visionary, and I wanted his participation in writing the textbook. He knows communications, database, and e-commerce business issues. His knowledge of newness is legendary, and each of his Chateaux Software Development clients benefit from Ken's vault-like mind. I am proud to have Ken's and Shauna's wisdom and experience in coauthoring this timely and classroom-tested textbook for college and professional readers.

Lastly and most importantly, my wife and children have been extremely patient and supportive as I neglected them over the last nine months, ignoring e-mails from and meals with them. While writing my portion of the textbook, I gave my wife Shirley and children Chandler and Chanel a serious scare with a three-week hospitalization and a two-month recovery during which they pushed the medical establishment and pulled me back to steady health. No three persons have ever cheered more for a dad.

Thanks and love to my sister, Mary Ann Mason who tackled the tedious task of typing interview transcripts for case histories.

Thanks from Ken Zimmerman

First, and foremost, I would like to recognize the unstinting comments and sage advice that have flowed from two of my very best friends for the past fifteen years: Joel Reedy and Hugo Toledo. We are only human, but Joel is probably the only superhuman I know. He has for years pushed me to achieve more by showing me what people are really capable of, while Hugo has always been, well, the smartest person I know. But his wisdom has certainly been superseded by his kindness to all the people close to him, and I count myself fortunate to be one of them. Hugo is a master of reliable sources of information, and during the formulation of my contribution to this book, I frequently referred to Hugo's sources—and they have not failed me!

Sherlyn Celone, in her capacity as friend and advisor, lent her considerable expertise in helping to document case histories of the e-commerce systems she proposed and executed during her management position at Bayer Corporation. Russell Madris, the founder of Corporate Buying Service, provided excellent commentary on the opportunities and pitfalls of creating his CBSdirect.com web-enabled sales system as he had envisioned it to be—years before the Internet became the center of commerce it is today. Denise Carreau worked nights to research and write about many topics that later became material for this book, while Zolton Varszegi, Mike Mcleish, Sean Jacobs, and George Ackerly provided terrific service and support as Chateaux Web masters. And although they did not contribute directly to content for the book, John Bartsch, George Ballantoni, and Michael Cantone provided excellent technical review of relevant material while helping to guide the ship of Chateaux Software during my "writing days."

Kudos go to my father, who in former years ran a marketing and publishing institute of his own, for his advice about writing to a marketing audience that has changed in many ways—but not in others—with the advent of the electronic age.

Thanks from Shauna Schullo

The writing of a textbook is an enormous endeavor that I have come to realize takes time, energy, and enthusiasm throughout the long haul. Having never attempted such a feat, I was not completely prepared for the road that lay ahead. However, the experience has been a good one that has taught me many lessons. Most importantly, I can now proudly say that the job is complete and I am exuberant about the quality of work that has come together in this book. On this note, I would like to take a moment to pass on some thanks for the experience that I have gained from being on this team of writers. First and most importantly, I would like to thank Joel Reedy for his steady hand and encouragement throughout the writing of this book. Joel is an amazing man whose stamina is truly unbelievable. Through all his tribulations, he always remained positive and enthusiastic. Thanks Joel for allowing me the opportunity to begin my writing career and to work with such a great bunch of people. Second, I would like to thank my friends and family for always believing that I can do anything, even when sometimes I do not believe it myself.

About the Authors

Joel Reedy, BS in advertising from the University of Florida and MBA and marketing instructor at the University of South Florida in Tampa, has proven credentials in the planning and execution of effective marketing programs. Before beginning his teaching career at USF (http://coba.usf.edu/Reedy) in 1990, he worked as an advertising agency principal and marketing strategist for twenty years. His planning specialties included account planning, media planning, and process evaluation. While at USF, his attention has been directed toward segmentation and promotional strategies for more effective marketing performance, and he is an active user of electronic marketing tools as well as interactive technology. During his eight years of full-time teaching at USF, Reedy has won four undergraduate teaching awards. In 1993, he published a marketing segmentation strategy book, *Marketing to Consumers with Disabilities*, through Probus Publishing (now McGraw-Hill) in Chicago.

Kenneth Zimmerman is the founder and president of Chateaux Software Development, Inc., and has over fourteen years consulting experience, specializing in enterprise-wide, mission-critical systems. His work is particularly geared toward producing highly efficient systems, primarily in tuning databases, developing compact code, well-designed data structures, and a user-oriented architecture. During recent engagements on projects for domestic and international companies, such as Pepsi, Bayer Pharmaceuticals, and Dannon, he has focused on the design, development, and implementation of client/server systems. Ken holds an undergraduate degree in geology from Duke University, and a MS degree in petrochemical geology from the University of Southern California. He also was honored as an Arco scholar in 1983. Ken currently serves as a member of the Oracle Corporation's Developer Program Advisory Council. Chateaux Software Development (www.chatsoft.com) is headquartered in Stamford, Connecticut.

Shauna J. Schullo (shauna@usf.edu) is currently the computer programmer analyst manager of academic computing at the University of South Florida. She holds a BS in chemistry, a MS degree in chemical engineering, and is pursuing her doctoral degree in instructional technology. Schullo has worked in the private industry and understands the application of online technology to commerce. She also brings classroom teaching experience and training in online and Web-related tools; she is an expert in many software packages including Lotus Notes, Excel, Access, Web browsers, electronic mail programs, HTML, and survey/forms design. Schullo is proficient in Authorware, multimedia packages, networking software, and graphics programs such as Adobe Photoshop and Adobe Premiere.

BRIEF TABLE OF CONTENTS

TABLE OF CONTENTS

Chapter 9

Chapter 10

Chapter 11

Chapter 12

Chapter 13

Chapter 14

Chapter 15

PART FOUR

Chapter 16

Chapter 17

PART ONE

The Concepts of Electronic Marketing

All successful marketing programs are founded on good product or service qualities, good pricing strategies, good distribution planning, and good promotional activities. Underlying the marketing plan is good research on the prospect's needs and wants. These motivating factors are uncovered through a thorough and expansive effort called the *situation analysis*, the initial step of either the traditional marketing process or the online marketing process. Electronic marketing resources bring into sharper focus the profiles and behaviors of targeted market segments.

CHAPTER 1

Introduction to the Resources of Electronic Marketing

Retrieving information from the Internet is like trying to drink from a fire hose.

Anonymous

LEARNING OBJECTIVES

- To introduce and explain various electronic marketing resources that can be integrated into the **traditional marketing process** to cultivate the ultimate goal of successful electronic commerce systems
- To demonstrate how electronic marketing resources increase **value added** uses and perceptions to the products and services of e-commerce
- To differentiate the strategic and tactical uses of electronic marketing resources

Introduction

Huge enterprises are being created using electronic commerce, the practice of satisfying consumer and business wants and needs through online procurement. Facilitating electronic commerce is the processes of electronic marketing, which has been greatly enhanced by online technology. In recent years, an electronic communications and information medium called the **Internet** has spawned software and hardware innovations designed specifically to aid the convenience of online shopping. Collectively with the Internet, electronic marketing resources such as online customer research, **e-mail,** Web sites, **intelligent shopping agents,** self-identifying online surveys, and **online customer service** among other electronic tools are being integrated into traditional marketing programs, improving reach, effectiveness, and efficiency of contact to targeted audiences. Online marketing is a high-tech, strategic and tactical extension of information gathering, direct marketing, and customer feedback, all important activities of the **Integrated Marketing Communications (IMC)** program. Therefore, in perspective, we will be investigating the processes of electronic marketing, augmented in many communication, transaction, and decision areas by electronic marketing resources that smooth the path to successful and timely electronic commerce.

The Marketer Enters the Online Age

Technology has entered just about every business except the barber shop. Technological advances are now enabling the marketer to identify specific prospects to deliver specific products for consumption by specific markets using **narrowcasting** (rather, mass broadcasting) and online messages using electronic tools such as **listservs, discussion groups,** hotspot advertising, online press releases, or online conferences to mention a few electronic tactics. Electronic marketing has the personalizing capacity for remembering the customer's preferences—ordering what flavor, scent, or texture and how often; in what quantities; whether for a gift or personal use; and by what method of delivery the consumer is partial to in her shopping habits. Electronic marketing helps you, the marketer, in determining the segmentation strategy before taking the products or services to the market by online marketing research and in analyzing aftermarket reception by consumers through online customer service and surveys. All of these qualities and considerations are influenced by electronic marketing, the online execution of delivering customer benefit and satisfaction enhanced through electronic marketing resources.

- **Electronic commerce** is the conducting of business communications and transmissions over networks and through computers, specifically the buying and selling of goods and services, and the transfer of funds through digital communications. Electronic commerce can also include all intercompany and intracompany functions (such as marketing, finance, manufacturing, sales, and negotiation) that enable commerce and that use electronic mail, **EDI (Electronic Data Interchange),** file transfer, **fax,** video conferencing, workflow, or interaction with a remote computer. Electronic commerce can include buying and selling over the **World Wide Web** and the Internet, **electronic funds transfer, smart cards, digital cash,** and all other ways of doing business over digital networks.
- **Electronic marketing** is all the online or electronic-based activities that facilitate manufacturing goods and services by the producer to satisfy the wants and needs of the consumer. Electronic marketing draws heavily on networks' technology to coordinate market research, aid product development, develop

strategies and tactics to persuade consumers to buy, provide for online distribution, maintain customer records, conduct customer satisfaction services, and gather customer feedback. Electronic marketing advances the overall marketing program that in turn supports the corporate objectives of electronic commerce.

- **Electronic marketing resources** are those technological or electronic marketing tools that are used to complete the marketing directives. Electronic marketing resources are primarily implementation-oriented for communications, information processing, or commerce transactions. Typical technology marketing resources involve the World Wide Web, interactive Web sites, shopping agents, **avatars** representing people or objects in virtual reality environments, cyber shopping malls, **fax-on-demand** information, or CD-ROM presentations. Many electronic marketing resources feature multimedia; the purpose of each tool as it enhances electronic marketing will be discussed.

Listening to the Consumer Speak

What are the most precious commodities that a consumer values in today's marketplace? If you read business periodicals, the recurring answers are saving money, saving time, and enhancing convenience. All of us lament that we as consumers are time poor and errand rich. Life and work move at an alarmingly brisk, almost breakneck, pace, and we should expect only a faster, information–rich lifestyle in the future. Various electronic online devices as personalized news editors, decision support software, or self-service parcel tracking or shopping systems are now influencing the methods in which we gather necessary information, improve our decision-making processes, shop for necessities or convenience goods, communicate with a company's customer service department, and check on delivery schedules. The list of online communications or transactions systems can go on and on.

Communications, transactions activities, information research are all parts of traditional marketing, but can marketers improve or streamline these traditional marketing processes? If you look toward and apply some of the ubiquitous electronic communications facilities, such as e-mail, online discussion groups, and the World Wide Web readily at hand, and investigate some of the more esoteric electronic marketing resources, these processes can be improved or streamlined. With these tools, you can better research your product's or service's industry, better research environmental trends, better target your markets, maintain better knowledge of and communications with your current and prospective customers, and receive almost instantaneous feedback on new products or services. In short, by employing electronic marketing tools, you can become better marketers to serve your customer constituents more effectively. Distance as in distribution becomes almost inconsequential. Electronic marketing resources introduce previously unheard-of speed and accuracy as well as help to build a person-to-person relationship unavailable through mass media such as television, radio, or newspaper messages. New marketing aids to explain how to better plan and execute marketing programs will be investigated later, and current and relevant industry examples will be looked into.

The following is a specific and overriding statement of principle concerning electronic marketing resources. The logic and consistency of the marketing process, namely **situation analysis, marketing planning**, and **marketing implementation,** are firmly endorsed; following these standard steps will provide success more often than failure. The *what*, or the objectives setting of the marketing process, is important to define, but the *how*, or the implementation stage, can be better executed with newly-available marketing tools. As the telegraph was replaced with the analog telephone, which is being replaced by digital telephony complemented with pagers, personal digital assistants, video conferencing, or handheld voice mail devices, regardless of the instrument's capability, all of these innovations led to progress in the function of communications. People still talk, gossip, or complain to one another; the only difference is the type of communications equipment they use. The payoffs of each stage of innovation were related to saving time, saving money, and improving the ease and convenience of use. After the innovation was established, the execution of product or service delivery was continually enhanced, even if the improvement was minuscule. With this train of thought, this book's goal is to improve the execution stage of the marketing process, in some ways minor and in some instances momentous, at least in a marketer's eye. While the consumer will probably not notice or not care about the differences of marketing techniques, it is the marketer's mission to improve the marketing process, hopefully as in breakthrough fashion or in incremental steps, so that it delivers as much customer benefit or satisfaction as possible.

As we explore electronic marketing resources, it will be wise and more fruitful to switch back and forth between a consumer's mindset and a marketing student's mindset to fully appreciate the workings of electronic marketing tools, those applications that were unavailable just ten short years ago. These electronic marketing means are proving to be both a boon and a bane within the marketing industry. Using electronic tools is a wonderful window to the world of information-gathering for the knowledgeable techno-consumer. However, this same consumer is probably bombarded with computer-generated direct mail pieces and possibly unwanted e-mail offers. One of the foundational premises of electronic marketing is to provide the inquirer with information that he *wants*, not the unsolicited junk mail that many advertisers push at him. So in keeping with the abundance of techno-consumers, this book will attempt to introduce materials and sharpen your skills as a techno-marketer. The following discussion delves into the potentials of the future, those marketing opportunities that you will face during your marketing career.

The Importance of Electronic Marketing Resources in Business Today

Simply put, the better you know your customers, the better you can serve, and hopefully, anticipate their needs. You can hopefully satisfy, as well, their needs and desires before a competitor does. It is wise for you to keep up with customer interests because as customers' knowledge grows, marketers should have a matching knowledge curve. Further, many consumers demand instant gratification, which means that speed of delivery and accuracy in fulfilling the order are crucial. In other marketing courses, you the student probably have been exposed to stories of unexpected technology shifts or fierce competition highlighted by price wars or expensive sales promotion tactics. Slugging it out with competitors is a costly and dangerous strategy. With electronic marketing resources, marketers can be forewarned to these unproductive and costly competitive strategies by introducing the premise of ***added value*** services to each and every one of your clients or customers. Customers expect you to know their personalities, likes and dislikes, or whims as well as you know your immediate family's personalities and the such. By adding value to your product or service, you can achieve a higher, perhaps more predictable brand equity and reputation that none of your competitors can match. Say, for instance, your customer base numbers in the thousands, even millions, how can you acquaint yourself with them? Perhaps, on the other hand, your company is expanding, and it is your job to select the locations for new stores or maybe a new production facility. How can you select a site that matches your demographic profile with some degree of certainty? One of your responsibilities, however, could be to initiate an employee feedback system to handle positive or negative criticisms of company policy or management activities. Each of these situations can be enhanced by electronic marketing or communications systems that are readily available. It is your job now to recognize expedient solutions to business problems and opportunities and to know when and how to bring these resources onto your playing field. Specifically, here are some business situations for which online marketing resources are very appropriate.

- **Company communications,** for both internal and external messages, is a good example where online marketing resources could be utilized. Now considered an old workhorse, something close to plain vanilla in excitement, electronic mail, or e-mail, is an inexpensive and wide-reaching communications tool. Whether you need to e-mail a message to the next building, the next block, or across the border, e-mail is a simple and permanent (until you choose to delete the message) vehicle. As people ask you for your telephone number, their follow-up question usually is, "And what is your **e-mail address?**" E-mail can connect groups of people with a touch of a single key using an e-mail list of designated names and addresses. With e-mail, you can communicate twenty-four hours a day, and on your own timetable. E-mail waits until you open it, and you can get many more deliveries than with the U.S. Postal Services' one drop each day. The corporate culture has been infected with e-mail, and it seems that associates prefer sending e-mail to talking on the telephone. E-mail eliminates telephone tag because messages are received while you are in meetings, on the road, or while you sleep at night. E-mail is a positive performance-enhancing resource that has worked its way throughout the corporation. It has been said that e-mail is responsible for bringing back the lost art of correspondence because the writer actually has to think and compose his or her messages before he or she presses the Send key. People are making a more conscious effort in what they write because the e-mail message is a hard copy reflection of their own mental processes. Written messages are usually better composed than hasty sound bites. While spoken words may rarely be recorded, an e-mail printout has our names written all over it. Hasty, ill-composed messages also have our names written on them.
- Another previously dreaded chore (at least to some persons), that of **marketing research,** has been enriched by online communications. The market researcher can test attitudes, maintain dialogues with various market constituencies, and record opinions that can be monitored over long periods of time. Web site measurement, such as the number of visitors to a site or how long the visitor lingered on the site or on a particular page, will provide many interesting revelations as well as stoke some mysteries on how, when, and why people use the Internet. This book will be investigating some of this measurement software shortly. Marketing organizations are frequently polling viewers or listeners on their preferences using Web addresses. Very common are sports programs asking trivia questions to viewers and awarding prizes to the first person to log-on to the program's Web site or e-mail address with the correct answer. Local and national news broadcasts that sponsor opinion polls on current events, as well, are becoming common. Polling activities such as this is reminiscent of the "grass roots" politicking when every man (of course before 1920) had his own vote. This one-to-one response mechanism is the marketer's answer to building samples of various sizes and of various geographical locations. An example might be an owners' discussion group devoted to a particular make of automobile; this informal forum could review the likes, dislikes, and wished-for improvements in future models—the ultimate give and take of outflow and inflow of marketing research rich in information. Pinpointing attitudes and beliefs has never before been as timely or accurate as now.

- **Marketing planning** and sales support are other business situations in which online marketing resources are appropriate. As more and more people are exposed to the Internet, more people will look to that medium for marketing information. Again, this method of dissemination can be either internal or external audiences. While certain persons are hesitant to purchase over the Internet, countless millions are willing to shop for information using this vehicle. With the completion of Secure Electronic Transaction (SET) protocols, people will be more confident in putting their credit card numbers over the Internet. Marketing efforts will be further augmented by consumers who are being spoiled to the turnaround speeds from order placement to front-door delivery. Until recently, merchants would promise delivery in three to six weeks after order placement; now merchants routinely ask if you would prefer overnight or two-day delivery.

- **Productivity innovations** are still other situations that utilize online marketing resources. Salespeople in the field are benefiting from online resources because, once again, electronic tools speed salespeople's response time to customer questions such as inventory levels, product details, and other business inquiries. Fantasy items such as wireless faxes, e-mail on the run, and laptop order placements now exist, and the most productive performers have become adept at scooping the competition. This is business innovation at its best.

- For the immediate future, online marketing and sales usage will be much more conducive for **business-to-business exchanges.** In 1998, analysts estimated that electronic commerce was comprised of approximately 85 percent of business purchases with the remaining 15 percent accounting for consumer expenditures. Online transactions business of just three companies—Cisco Systems, Inc. (www.cisco.com), Dell Computer Corp. (www.dell.com), and General Electric Co. (www.ge.com)—totaled about $3 billion in 1997. The combined Internet commerce of these three companies will grow to $17 billion a year within three to five years, and the Commerce Department expects the U.S. total to top $300 billion. (Wysocki 1998) As business departments pave the way, consumers will begin to embrace online transactions with more trust and greater expectations. Personal computer banking, financial transactions online, seems to be the next hurdle for banking marketers to overcome. If consumers are comfortable in transferring their hard earned assets online, activities such as ordering videos, purchasing automobiles, even purchasing residential homes will not be far behind.

- Looking from the consumer's viewpoint, **time and access to commercial sites** become less hectic. In essence the store or service you are trying to contact is never closed. You may have to leave a voice mail, but your order should be on its way to be processed the very next business day. An automated **audiotext** response system can reply to questions, technical sheets, specifications, or technical support most likely generated from a fax-back system. Contacts with your suppliers or vendors can also be maintained in a similar manner. Smart businesses allow for several order methods such as toll-free numbers with operators standing by or acceptance of mail or fax orders, as well as supporting a field sales staff. The easier you make it for the consumer, the more frequently she will return for more business transactions. An added benefit to managers is that electronic ordering systems allow better management in labor scheduling since orders can be archived to smooth out the peaks and valleys of fulfillment of orders. Operations such as these are advantageous for maximized resource allocation of the entire corporate entity.

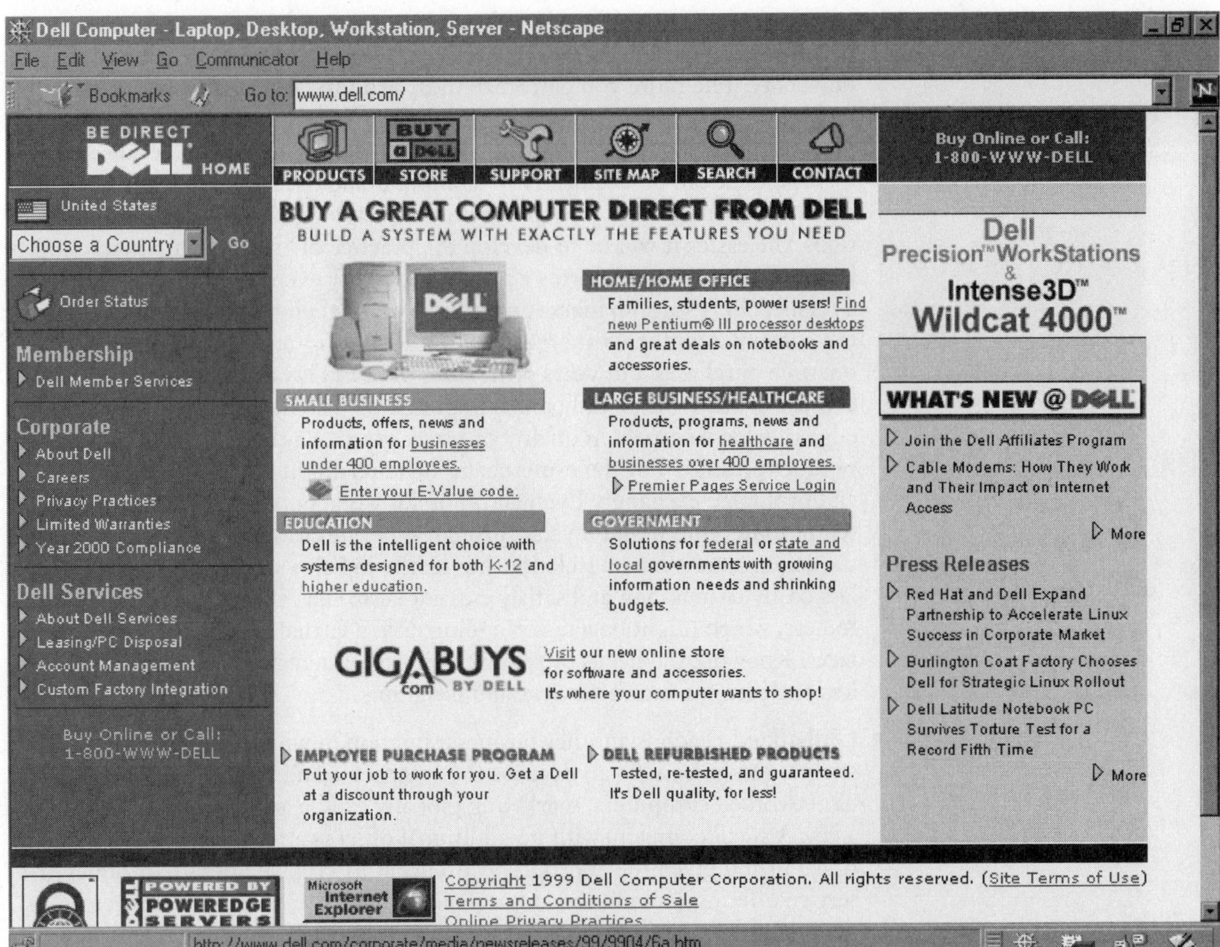

Dell Computers (http://www.dell.com)
The Dell site appears to be an online catalog of vast information. Informational hyperlinks lead to more informational hyperlinks and all the information about Dell that an online shopper might want.

- **Customer loyalty** is another business situation in which electronic marketing resources can come into play. Many companies are interested in their customers' purchase habits and preferences and are developing detailed databases to track purchase activities. Usually past behavior will predict future actions, and information such as this can help managers plan future sales or merchandising events, manage inventory levels, or track brand movement. Behavior patterns such as expenditure amounts, brand or item preferences, day or hour of the week when shopping occurs, type of payment method, and many more similar segmentation questions take much of the guesswork out of merchandising decisions. Also popular are customer loyalty programs in which retailers track customer purchases to reward them with points or discounts toward future purchases. The frequent flier miles program is a good example of how a particular airline can encourage the business flier to concentrate his air travel to one airline. Similarly, Pepsi (currently www.pepsiworld.com; www.pepsi.com has been used in the past) and Marlboro cigarettes have created bonus programs based on purchase points. These programs add interest to mature products as well as encourage larger purchase quantities to increase product sales. Further promotional efforts can be targeted to loyal customers in the form of new product or discount coupons or online announcements or newsletters that treat these buyers as special. **Affinity marketing,** a grouping of customers with similar interests, is another example of loyalty programs. Examples of the loyalty program might be a T. J. Maxx Visa card with a rebate program (www.tjmaxx.com) or a MasterCard (www.mastercard.com) issued by your university. The more you patronize these vendors, the greater your reward will be.

Customer loyalty and affinity programs are popular today because the management can be overseen by a computer and database infrastructure; the easier it is to manage loyalty programs and ongoing customer communications, the easier it will be to develop the practice of "relationship marketing," in which the consumer forms a preference for or even a bond with a brand or a retailer. Relationship marketing is built on the belief that mutual benefits for the consumer and the e-merchant will lead to long-term relationships—not onetime purchases, but years or decades of brand loyalty and frequent repurchase. For the consumer, benefits might be the product consistency, a knowledge of what to expect in quality or price, product availability, and purchasing product prestige. For the e-merchant, benefits might be recurring revenues and profitable exchange. Even automobiles while purchased infrequently attempt to develop brand loyalty through superior customer service long after the acquisition is made. Relationship marketing also stresses the fact that it is less costly to maintain and satisfy current customers than to acquire new customers, which might be a never-ending task, a virtual revolving door of new faces. Knowing the needs or requirements of past customers helps the marketer to plan for future services and programs.

- **Globalized reach** is another business situation in which online marketing resources can be beneficial. Because the Internet is an international connection of networked computers, marketing globally can be achieved with the touch of a key. A small company with no additional offices can appear to be a multinational firm if given the appropriate attention to Web site design, product or service offerings, and linking to complementary sites to extend this reach. As the history of advertising has demonstrated time and again, image (reality or not) can be everything in building a successful company. Random surfing of the Web will bring you to many colorful, content-laden sites that might impress you. Because of the anonymity of the Web, however, you will have no indication if the owner of the Web site is real or not. Certainly this phantom appearance is not consigned only to U.S.-based sites. Other than perhaps knowing the country of origin, global exposure is quite blind. Marketers, therefore, must consider carefully how they will address an international presence. For modest enterprises, a worldwide audience may be of little benefit because of the economics involved. The smaller firm might lose money shipping a minuscule order to New Zealand—the delivery costs might outweigh the price of the contents. Language differences might also pose problems with customer service or technical support. A Catalonian-speaking person might be disappointed if she cannot understand the timetable for delivery after talking with an operator who speaks American-spoken Spanish. All businesses should consider the consequences of international marketing via the Internet because there are advantages and disadvantages. After all, the purpose of marketing is to create a good relationship or experience with prospects and customers.
- In order to have **competitive intelligence,** a company must utilize the online marketing resources. The World Wide Web site is an open book for your competitors to investigate your product or service offerings, and you can do the same. In fact, some organizations have convened a *techno-watch,* delegating different people within a department to track specific areas of technology that are important to their company. Perhaps the company is computer-oriented. One staff member might be responsible for reading trade magazines, monitoring discussion lists, or attending industry conferences solely about servers.

Another person might oversee information on networking or areas of emerging technology. Still yet another employee might observe a close competitor's actions or innovations. Taking the pulse of a close and aggressive competitor might assist you in developing your next strategic marketing plan.

- Employing online marketing resources can help a company utilize **cost management.** Marketing departments today feel the budget crunch just as much as any other department; there appears to be too many people chasing too few budget dollars within the organization. E-mail is an excellent substitution for long-distance telephone charges or the cost of a postage stamp and stationery. Electronic tools such as video conferences or Electronic Data Interchange (EDI) can replace expensive travel and lodging costs. Any marketing manager will confirm that given equal levels of effectiveness, the cheaper of two methods will likely be chosen. After initial equipment installation, electronic marketing resources are most cost efficient; in many cases even with the installation costs, the introduction of electronic marketing resources is very cost effective compared to customer marketing benefits achieved.

- **Partnering and logistics** become easier to maintain through online marketing resources. Corporations like to think of themselves as lean and mean. Electronic marketing resources add to that perception and reality because people can act more decisively and quicker by being electronically linked. Linkages may include internal intranets, or extranets, and external partnerships or **collaborations** with outsourced companies. These networks are lean because many departments, staff, and activities that were previously considered an in-house requirement are handled now by companies outside the lean company. To operate effectively, communications among companies must be quick and accurate, with each hand knowing what the others are doing. These collaborations must be able to share data quickly, hence the need for EDI. Huge amounts of data are exchanged within or among companies or branches, and your local bank is an excellent example. Daily transactions must be routed to a central bank, both quickly and accurately. It is not to imply that people are no longer part of the exchange, but in recent years, more people are working remotely, away from the central office. This work arrangement is called **telecommuting,** which gives the staff more options for work environments, such as at home, at the soccer field, at the library, or just about anywhere above water where a personal computer can be interfaced. Another important communications aspect is the **asynchronous** nature of information transmission, which allows a difference between the time a message is sent and received. An example of an asynchronous transaction could be the purchase of bicycle parts at 2:30 A.M. in which the order is processed at 8:30 the next morning. Remember that the Internet is *anywhere, anytime,* so you can conduct business in Tokyo or London at your convenience.

- Online marketing resources can be used as well for **corporate recruitments.** Technology workers are in short supply. Recruiters, therefore, should think with their mind-sets. Since technological whizzes spend their waking hours in front of a color monitor, they are probably accessible through online discussion lists or responses to Usenet postings. Companies can locate potential employees, as well as search for consultants, government documents, specialty trades, or general contractors. Texas Instruments recently announced an update to its corporate Web site to offer career development tools for "Net-savvy students." New to the site is "Ask a Cyber Recruiter," an interactive area where students can ask for career advice, post questions about Texas Instruments, and learn how to use the Web for job searches. (Bellinger 1999) If you, the employer, set aside one-half hour each day to look for trained associates

> and post your employment opportunities, you will find the people who have the necessary electronic skills. You will be talking with them on their own turf, as well. Be prepared, however, to present a consistent and professional interviewing process.

There are additional benefits that can be exploited as electronic resources expand, which, in turn, eases the cost of technology. With **intranets,** a company can share resources or educate its workforce regardless of time or distance or the department in which the associate works. Activities such as company seminars, technical updates, company policies, or calendars of events can be published and readily accessed by customers, intranet employees, or vendors. Training can also be accomplished, eliminating travel and lodging costs, through Internet and intranet postings or by video conferencing sessions. **Extranets,** communications networks maintained for outside suppliers or other external groups, also efficiently disseminate privileged information.

Is E-Commerce for Large or Small Companies?

There are no parameters yet for fitting e-commerce into traditional marketing and sales programs, only the commitment to thorough and appropriate use of marketing strategy. A smaller firm, such as SoBe Beverages (www.sobebev.com) of Norwalk, Connecticut, employs its Web site to maintain distributor communications and expand consumer awareness of its healthy beverages, which bear exotic names such as "Black Tea," "Elixir," "Zen Blend," or "Power." The Web site is simple, displaying the bottled drinks with links to a merchandise page and a United States map depicting the sales territories. No persuasive copy rests on the site; the lizards of SoBe are the stars of the site.

On the other hand, the Coca-Cola and Pepsi sites are quite elaborate, featuring contests, merchandise, historical information, demonstrations of pop culture, even love letters from devoted fans. Again, these Web sites do not encourage online product sales; the entertaining sites are devoted to supporting the Coke (www.coke.com) and Pepsi brands. Is the objective of supporting brands, distributors, or sales outlets part of the concept of e-commerce? Absolutely. While online sales of products and services are growing, the traditional retail and wholesale sales channel is fully mature. In the opinion of CBS MarketWatch (www.marketwatch.com):

> The value of online retail sales will increase to six percent within five years, according to a Forrester Research (www.forrester.com) market study; Forrester predicts "a rapid growth spiral in online retail sales" will produce revenues totaling $108 billion in 2003. The Boston Consulting Group (www.bcg.com) estimated online sales [in 1998] could total $13 billion which it said would be about one percent of North American retail sales. Forrester interviewed 100 North American online merchants across 11 retail categories. (Barnako 1998)

The question, therefore, is not about appropriate sales volumes or number of employees but rather an intense interest of a company to participate in e-commerce. **"Online retailing** has left the experimental phase and is accelerating into the mainstream," said James L. McQuivey, an analyst in Forrester's Online Retail Strategies service. "Merchants are reporting dramatic growth in both sales and site traffic over the past 12 months. This pattern will become a self-perpetuating cycle—as more consumers come online to shop, retailers will compete more aggressively for sales, in turn drawing still more consumers and merchants to the Web." (Barnako) Quotes and predictions are easily enough made, and the student will see many concerning e-commerce because this topic is popular to discuss. However, talking about

SoBe (www.sobebev.com)
Refreshing products are the stars of this colorful, simple and hip Web site. It is a dual purpose site featuring Lizard products and a promotional racing sponsorship with Cannondale Corporation, makers of motorcycles and bicycles.

e-commerce is not practicing the same. Take in the rosy forecasts, but be prepared to follow the traditional marketing process to expand sales, increase awareness, service customers, or compile databases through e-commerce. The Web is merely another vehicle to be integrated into the marketing makes to achieve these ends of electronic commerce.

What Electronic Marketing Tools Are Shaping the Future

Speed, accessibility, accuracy of information, and competitive advantage are four of the major forces driving business, from a two-person lawn care enterprise in which the owners carry beepers and cell phones to a Fortune 500 pharmaceutical firm that institutes sophisticated fax-back system to support field representatives in answering client questions about possible side-effects or dangerous interactions of prescription drug ingestion. Add to these forces the ability to personalize the message with the product or service order, the payment system, the delivery date, and even the hour of the day, and the marketer, the retailer, and the wholesaler can offer the consumer an unprecedented package of convenience. These electronic methods take on various forms, and their purposes usually are to aid the speed of communications or to improve corporate memory. Never before has the cliché, time is money, ever been so true. Think of the

E-MARKETING CASE HISTORY: SOUTH BEACH BEVERAGE COMPANY

SoBe Beverages, Herbal-Enhanced Beverages That Are Good for the Mind, Body, and Spirit

"Tastes good and better for you." That was a powerful concept of wellness developed by John Bello, 52, a marketing veteran who has worked with beverage divisions of Maxwell House, Pepsi, and Arizona brand teas. A long-time trend spotter, Bello read article after article and watched TV news reports about the health benefits of ancient herbs such as ginseng and Echinacea; he also monitored the booming sales of herbal products by General Nutrition and Rite Aid retailers. Then he wondered about a beverage application for "refreshing, wellness" products, and after testing, SoBe Beverages were born in 1995. To date the Yang and Yin lizard logo has found its way into thirty-five states, Bermuda, the Bahamas, and the Virgin Islands. Quite an accomplishment as the New Age teas and fruit drinks were becoming stale with sales flattening out.

South Beach has tapped into an herbal niche of nutriceuticals, tagged as functional foods, and has created a unique and exotic use for them as "old-fashioned curatives going into new-fangled foods." The herbs are mixed in very small amounts to the elixirs and teas. There is no definitive medical evidence that any of the herbal supplements actually do what they purport to do, but hope is a powerful motivator. (Bundy 1998) According to Bello, "We are tapping into three very important trends that are driving consumer behavior today. The first is the universal desire to live a longer, healthier, more active life and the understanding that what you put in your body can help achieve this goal. The second is the high level of awareness of the contributions that natural herbal supplements can make to overall wellness and improve mental and physical performance. And the third is the growing interest in exotic teas and juice blends that have proven their long-term health benefits over centuries of use." (Lenderman 1997)

In crafting the SoBe marketing strategy, Bello drew from his experience working at NFL Properties, the marketing and merchandising arm of the National Football League, to produce a memorable logo, packaging and image maintenance. As a fashionable, arguably nutritional beverage with trendy, stylish marketing, Bello created a "healthy hedonism," positioning the SoBe products as an interactive beverage brand. Some of the interactive examples that Bello cites are:

> The package itself is an important interactive component. The clear bottle with 38 millimeter printed twist cap sports an embossed "twisted lizards" logo in the wide-mouth neck. The colorful bottle is silkscreened according to the exotic flavor names, such as "Wisdom" (orange and mango juices mixed with ginkgo and St. John's wort), "Power" (fruit punch mixed with creatine and taurine), or "Black Tea" (a dark beverage brewed with ginseng, ginkgo and guarana). SoBe's lizard icon is more than a graphic element. It opens a range of promotional efforts such as T-shirts and hats.
>
> Another interactive components is the company's 800 phone line. The SoBe Lizard King answers, but you can't appreciate the communication's "flavor" unless you call the number, 800-588-0548, yourself. The phone message promotes the brand and gives callers the opportunity to leave messages. Hundreds do. (Peters 1998)

A colorful yet simple Web site supports the interactive theme, featuring product and merchandise as distributor territories within the United States. The Web pages introduce the various flavors in full color highlighted by the imaginative, lizard-etched bottle. Also the names and addresses of vendors throughout the country are posted as well as the available sales territories. Lizard merchandise such as T-shirts and bumper stickers are displayed on another page; this merchandise is available through redemption of bottle caps. A simple customer loyalty program.

Consistent with the interactive philosophy, a primary marketing tool used to promote the beverage is sampling. Prime prospects are introduced to the SoBe line efficiently through the sampling method.

For all these promotional activities, Bello pronounces the bottom line. "SoBe tastes great and our Lizard icon projects fun, image and an attitude that consumers relate to in a lifestyle brand."

capital cost, the lost revenue, even the loss of goodwill among your patrons if excessive time delays your online marketing program. American management wants status reports or intelligence information yesterday. You should, therefore, gear your operations with speed in mind. Best of all, customers will come to expect this special treatment, and they will come back to this organization that promises and delivers speed, accessibility, and accuracy of information, all personalized to their needs.

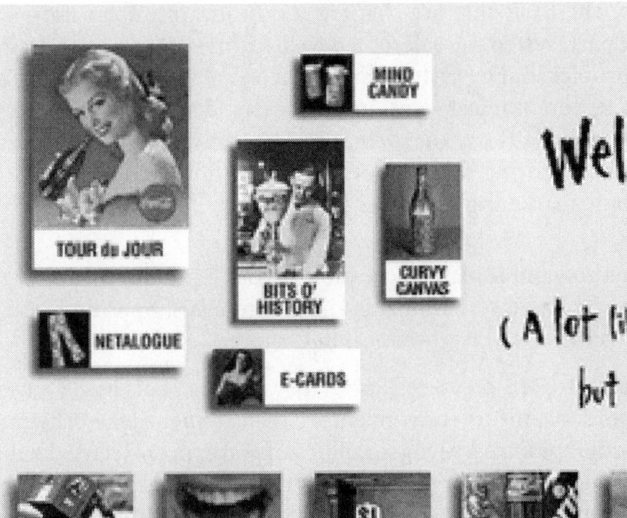

Welcome to The World of Coca-Cola.

(A lot like the real thing in Atlanta but no standing in line.)

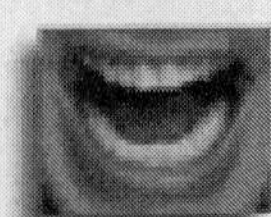

Today we're dropping you right into our virtual museum, so you can learn more about the historical significance of our favorite beverage than anyone on your block. Of course, if there's someplace you'd rather be (and we can't imagine that there is), you've got several other choices:

The Coca-Cola Company. From Investor Relations to Coca-Cola Scholars, you can learn about the company behind the brands at The Coca-Cola Company site.

Speak Your Mind. Pontificate and ponder. Grab a gif. Forward some fun to a friend.

Trading Post. The place to be for collectors, traders and shoppers.

Refreshment. As more of The Coca-Cola Company brands from countries all over the globe become Web-wise, this spot will really heat up. In the meantime, quaff some mental refreshment.

It's a Mystery. People cruise the Web because they're looking for someplace to go. Someplace Cool. Someplace Refreshing. Someplace Fun. Someplace...Else. Here are a few of our pixels.

Sports and Entertainment. The Coca-Cola Company has a loooooong association with all sorts of sports and entertainment. Here's a diving board into some diggable spaces.

Digital Workout. Let your mouse fly — here's the place to play some of our whacky, wild, never-seen-before in stores, games.

Coca-Cola (www.coca-cola.com)
Coke introduces you to this site with a bit of trivia about the product and where it's served. Clicking on the hyperlink takes you to a menu of products, collectibles, quizzes, feedback, investor and public relations programs, and more.

What exactly are the tools that are shaping the future of information and commerce? For the most part, systems are designed to distribute information to solve specific organizational problems. The systems are electronically based to supplement the organization's ability to communicate with its customers, dealers, representatives, and suppliers. Some tools provide the *what*, such as to improve corporate memory; others provide the *how*, such as storing and retrieving data within the database functions. Categories of electronic marketing resources include:

- Online information and research accessible through public and private databases for domestic and international information needs. Specific research strategies and vehicles will be discussed in Chapter 2.
- Computer- and software-based resources that include Web-based advertising and sales promotions, proprietary inventory management networks and software, geo-demographic and psychographic software, proprietary database management, online customer service and fulfillment, customer and prospect surveys, **videoconferencing,** "smart cards," and virtual reality environments.
- Telephony resources that include **fax** and fax-back systems, pagers, beepers, and **telemarketing.**
- Network-based resources such as the Internet, World Wide Web sites, intranets, extranets, news release networks, Electronic Data Interchange, and transactions and authentication networks. Many technologies, such as the use for the Web for communications and transactions, can overlap.
- In-store resources such as optical scanners, electronic coupon dispensers, electronic kiosks, low frequency radio broadcasting, electronic price shelf tags, and video shopping carts.

Many useful applications have been derived from other forms of new technology; all are fast and expensive. Some systems you may already be familiar with; all can be factored into marketing programs as appropriate. The following various operatives will be discussed in more detail as their places in the marketing process are reached in the book: fax-back systems, customer tracking methods such as Access database programs, customer surveys and order forms using **HTML (Hypertext Markup Language)** editors, smart cards, optical readers, **cybermalls,** and efficient communications systems.

Electronic Marketing Resources, Strategic or Tactical?

The answer to the above question is yes. Electronic marketing tools can be utilized in strategic planning and in tactical execution. In the strategic aspect, a marketer can hone the longer term direction of the marketing plan by using electronic databases of government statistics, trade association information, investigating competitive Web sites, or geo-demographic software to profile selected market areas. An excellent argument for strategic planning and the Internet is made by Mary J. Cronin, a management professor at Boston College:

> Every company needs to work through a process of assessing its particular environment, identifying opportunities, overcoming barriers to electronic commerce, and designing and implementing online programs that will add value to both the organization and the customer. Establishing this

> strategy-building process, and fine-tuning it frequently, are essential for continued success. The first step is a realistic assessment of the current barriers to commerce on the Internet, together with an overview of emerging solutions. The second step is an evaluation of the Internet's core capabilities, examining how companies are using the features of the global network in different corporate settings. This grounding in network obstacles and capabilities sets the stage for analyzing how the Internet can enhance internal information management. Finally a model for integrating Internet applications, which places interactions with the customer at the center of a networked information management system, provides a framework for redesigning traditional business functions for maximum advantage. (Cronin 1996, 8)

For example, perhaps the marketer is working within a franchise organization, and it is his assignment to select new store locations. Electronic resources can be employed in several strategic areas of planning. In store site selection, the marketer might require situation assessment data on household growth, population profiles, income and occupation figures, traffic counts, or psychographic characterizations to compare the potentials of different market locales. Decision making is enhanced when hard data is introduced in strategic planning, and information sources or databases are utilized, such as the Census Bureau (www.census.gov) or the Bureau of Labor Statistics (www.bls.gov), Stats USA (www.stats-usa.gov), National Decision Systems (www.natdecsys.com), Claritas' Prizm (www.claritas.com), or similar data repositories that are available on the Internet. These systems provide more certainty in the decision making and direction setting stages of the situation analysis and marketing planning efforts. These tools are particularly helpful if the marketer is unfamiliar with the environmental forces and idiosyncrasies of the market areas. Financial analysis on corporate performance is readily available as well. A most comprehensive resource is Hoover's Online (www.hoovers.com), an information service that contains helpful profiles, financial data, and industry newsletters in electronic form.

As in the Hard Rock Cafes' example, captains of industry, otherwise known as CEOs, are eyeing how the Internet might affect their companies' way of doing business. In a recent survey sponsored by PricewaterhouseCoopers of 377 chief executive officers, 20 percent indicated they believe electronic commerce will completely reshape the manner in which their companies do business. An additional 59 percent stated that it will lead to significant changes in their business strategies. This vote of confidence is mirrored by a study prepared by Deloitte & Touche Tohmatsu International, a consulting firm, which predicted electronic commerce will grow by 300 percent over the next two years. In 1998 consumer e-merchants were prospected at ringing up $2.6 billion in sales according to a consensus estimate by the electronic newsletter Iconocast (www.Iconocast.com). (Iconocast newsletter 1998)

Think of the tactical application, those shorter term activities that make the marketing implementation come alive by putting the strategic ideas into action. At this stage in the marketing process, the World Wide Web is the medium for stimulating innovative development, gaining awareness by prospects, keeping in touch with current customers via surveys or e-mail, improving corporate memory with prospect or customer databases that catalog purchase characteristics such as product categories, seasonal selections, amount spent, preferences of all kinds, or supporting network systems. These tactical offenses provide speed, accuracy, and convenience for the customer; the benefits to the marketer include building customer loyalty, timely execution of marketing programs, and organizational efficiencies that contribute to the bottom line profitability.

EXHIBIT 1.1 **REVENUE FIGURES FOR PUBLICLY-TRADED E-COMMERCE SITES**

Schwab announced that retail investors now buy and sell more than $2 billion in securities weekly via its site, far surpassing any other e-commerce outlet. According to Schwab, the top publicly-traded e-commerce sites list:

Ranked Company	Web Commerce, First Quarter 1998 (in dollars)
1. Schwab	26 billion
2. Auto-By-Tel	1.5 billion
3. AOL	694 million
4. Dell	450 million
5. Amazon.com	87 million

Schwab also announced it reached 1.74 million active online accounts and $120 billion in online customer assets in May 1998, an increase of more than 500,000 active online accounts and $40 billion in online assets since December 1997.

SOURCE: Charles Schwab & Co, June 1998.

Navigating through a World of Change

The world of marketing is being tested to handle continual and momentous change. One element of the marketing mix that needs to be addressed is promotions. Promotions entail comparing traditional media with complementary (or perhaps,

HARD ROCK CAFE MAKES A STRATEGIC COMMITMENT TO THE WEB

Hard Rock Cafe International, Inc., the global music entertainment and original theme restaurant company, announced that it will crank up the volume by launching its music-oriented Internet site at www.hardrock.com. Created by Hard Rock and developed by USWeb (www.usweb.com), a leading strategic Internet services firm, recently merged with CKS interactive advertising agency, hardrock.com will be multifaceted: featuring information and imagery of Hard Rock Cafes, Hard Rock Hotels & Casinos and Hard Rock concert venues worldwide; displaying daily rock industry news and concert webcasts; offering visitor incentives, promotions and sweepstakes; and presenting five online retail shops, including a Gallery for purchasing never-before-offered iconic rock photographs taken by legendary photojournalists. Said Jim Berk, President and CEO of Hard Rock Cafes, "In teaming up with USWeb, we have built a site that not only acts as an information resource but links our holdings worldwide, and for the first time, takes the Hard Rock brand into the realm of online commerce."

The launch is strategically integrated into Hard Rock's ambitious effort to extend its brand and core business worldwide. In a year when Hard Rock profits have already experienced a 15 percent increase, the company continues its efforts to offer more to its customers through new ventures and strategic brand extensions, from hotels and performance venues, to records, concerts and a weekly televised music program, and Hard Rock beer. "Because Hard Rock is starting from scratch, hardrock.com will be a showcase for a truly strategic use of the Internet," said Toby Corey, President and COO of USWeb. "This will be substantially more than a promotional site. It will foster a greater level of interaction with customers, offer high-profile opportunities to reach out to new customers and, above all, provide an online experience every bit as enjoyable as the cafes, hotels and performance spaces themselves."

"Hard Rock Cranks Up the Volume by Launching Its Music-Oriented Internet Site 'www.hardrock.com'" PR Newswire [Online] Wednesday, November 18, 1998, Orlando, Fla.

EXHIBIT 1.2

The Postal Service Fights Back with Point, Click = Stamps!

The latest way to send a letter or package through the U.S. Mail requires little more than a click of your mouse—and it's coming soon to a computer near you. Several firms including E-Stamp Corp.'s Internet Postage were the first online postage systems to get the nod of approval from Uncle Sam. The technology enables consumers to securely purchase postage online—printing "digital" stamps on envelopes, labels or any other document—with a personal computer and standard printer. The cost of the postage gets deducted from a prearranged account, which can be "filled" with payments from a major credit card. The companies have worked closely with the U.S. Postal Service to develop their respective technologies, ensuring that universal security and implementation standards are met. Postage finds 24–7 at last.

"Point, Click = Stamps!" New York, November 19, 1998, CNNfn wire.

replacement medium). What is largely driving this change is the need for segmentation because that is what advertisers are demanding. The largest advertising expenditure is placed in America's 1500 daily newspapers, of which the leaders (the interactive edition of *The Wall Street Journal*, www.djinteractive.com, is a good example) are turning to online versions of their printed format. The traditional hard copy news and business magazines such as *Fortune*, *Time*, or *Money* (www.pathfinder.com) offer online Web sites designed to extend their currency from weekly to fortnight issues to daily coverage. Broadcast television networks facing households using television (HUT) levels of 50 percent, down from the low 90 percent range in the early 1970s, are trying to bring technological viewers back to their flock using Web addresses and Web sites featuring late breaking news, sports updates, and national weather information. Even radio stations try to keep up with listener relations by maintaining Web sites with pages of archived program transcripts or listener polls on national or local current events. (An example is WCBS-AM Newsradio, www.newsradio88.com, in New York City.) Traditional media are trying to embrace online media as an extension of traditional media's capabilities. There is much confusion, and possibly timidity, among established media on the objectives and strategies in either embracing or blunting these online competitors.

Summary

All told, utilizing electronic marketing resources equates to competitive advantage in the marketplace. Following the objectives of speed, accessibility, and accuracy is the best way of staying close to the customer. Electronic media give the marketer a dual ability: first to reach the marketer's customers and, secondly, to react quickly to the customers' needs and desires. Electronic marketing resources also enhance the strategic and tactical advantages of online marketing with speed and accuracy that lead to better decision making. Customers expect special treatment from the management of the products and services they buy. These marketing tools that have been introduced are enabling marketers to be better equipped for the information age that surrounds us all. E-commerce also provides consumer convenience enhanced by speed, accessibility, and accuracy. Retailers, as well, can easily encourage the consumer to buy from their company by establishing a well-researched, well-executed Web presence.

Key Terms

Affinity marketing

Asynchronous

Audiotext

Avatars

Business-to-business exchanges

Collaboration

Company communications

Competitive intelligence

Corporate recruitments

Cost management

Customer loyalty

Cybermall

Digital cash

Discussion groups

E-mail

E-mail address

EDI (Electronic Data Interchange)

Electronic commerce

Electronic funds transfer

Electronic marketing

Electronic marketing resources

Extranet

Fax

Fax-on-demand

Globalized reach

HTML (Hypertext Markup Language)

IMC (Integrated Marketing Communications)

Intelligent shopping agent

Internet

Intranet

Listserv

Marketing implementation

Marketing planning

Marketing research

Narrowcasting

Online retailing
Online customer service
Productivity innovations
Partnering and logistics
Situation analysis
Smart cards
Telecommuting
Telemarketing
Time and access to commercial sites
Traditional marketing process
Value added products and services
Videoconferencing
World Wide Web

QUESTIONS AND EXERCISES

1. Within the framework of the traditional marketing process of situation analysis, marketing planning, and marketing implementation, in which step do you think electronic marketing resources are most valuable and best suited? Write a short paper justifying your answer.

2. Every technological advancement has its advantages and disadvantages over the previous systems in place. What are the advantages and disadvantages of using electronic marketing resources in the marketing process? Be prepared to discuss these points in the next class.

3. Interview a businessperson who is involved with electronic marketing or electronic commerce. What has been his or her experience in integrating electronic tools into the present company systems? Has this integration met success or failure compared to traditional marketing efforts? Is it too early in this businessperson's opinion to make a judgment? What are the performance criteria used to judge success or failure? Write a short news release for the local newspaper to announce your findings.

4. Discuss why a company would choose *not* to employ electronic marketing resources throughout the enterprise. Should certain departments always be equipped with electronic marketing tools, or should certain departments always be excluded from them? Prepare an outline of your thoughts.

5. Many marketing situations are tradeoffs between the optimal and actual choices. If you were required to make an either/or choice, which would you the marketer select, a good product with bad online promotion or a bad product with good online promotion. Write your stockholders a short memo justifying your position.

6. Go to your college library or access the library online to investigate the stories of five companies that have recently announced the establishment of its first Web site. Print out the news story and write a one-page report summarizing the purpose for the new company Web site.

7. Online communications cover a broad marketing spectrum of customer contact, from customer characteristics databases to interactive Web activities to online customer service after

purchase. In which category of the promotional mix (advertising, sales promotion, public relations, direct marketing, or personal selling) do you feel the World Wide Web is best classified? What would be the second best fit of promotional element? The third best? Write a one-page memo to your boss explaining your thoughts on the promotional mix and the World Wide Web.

8. Web sites can be used for various purposes. Access various sites with the following purposes; print out the home page or supporting page. Write a paragraph explaining the purpose (new product announcement, general image awareness, specific product sales, publicity support, product or service relationship, employment, and customer survey page) of each site or page.

9. What is relationship marketing? How can electronic marketing resources assist in developing or supporting ongoing relationships with customers? E-mail your answers to your professor.

10. Access the Internet either from your college's computing lab or from your online service at home to research the five largest online business-to-business vendors' sales volume over the last three years. Use a resource such as www.deja.com to check various vendors' sales figures. Record the performance of these five companies and hand in at the next class.

Bibliography

Barnako, Frank. Net retailers to gobble up market share. CBS MarketWatch [Online]. 20 November 1998.

Bellinger, Robert. TI taps cyberrecruiting to attract net-savvy students. CMP Net [Online]. 12 February 1999.

Bundy, Beverly. 1998. Eat, drink and be happy with popular herbal foods. *Houston Chronicle*, 25 April, 3F.

Cronin, Mary. 1996. *The Internet Strategy Handbook.* Boston: Harvard Business School Press.

Iconocast newsletter. 10 June 1998, 1.

Lenderman, Max. 1997. South Beach change yields healthy products and results. *Periscope*, 31 October, 8.

Peters, James W. 1998. Lizard logo leaps beyond new age beverage positioning. *Brandpackaging*, April/May, 28.

Wysocki, Bernard, Jr. 1998. Internet is opening up a new era in pricing. *The Wall Street Journal*, 8 June, A1, A18.

CHAPTER 2

Concept of Electronic Commerce and the Traditional Marketing Process

"Today we are passing through a technological discontinuity of epic proportions, and most are not even remotely prepared. The old paradigm, a system of mass production, mass media, and mass marketing, is being replaced by a totally new paradigm, a one-to-one (1 : 1) economic system. The 1 : 1 future will be characterized by customized production, individually addressable media, and 1 : 1 marketing, totally changing the rules of business competition and growth. Instead of share of market, the goal of most business competition will be share of customer–one customer at a time. The 1 : 1 future business will focus less on short-term profits derived from quarterly or annual transaction volumes, and more on the kind of profits that can be realized from long-term customer retention and lifetime values." (Peppers and Rogers 1993, 5)

LEARNING OBJECTIVES

- To examine the audiences and potentials of electronic commerce
- To describe how the e-marketing process affects electronic commerce
- To explain how the situation analysis can be monitored by electronic marketing resources

Introduction

There is a parallel between the processes of online or electronic marketing and the traditional marketing process. Both first call for a situation analysis to establish the benchmark of the past and present marketing situation; from this foundation of opinions and facts the ensuing steps, marketing planning and marketing implementation, can be established. Electronic marketing resources assist the situation analysis in providing more readily accessible research resources in a more timely and convenient manner for the marketer; in essence the statistics of government and private research offices come to you wherever you may be. Searches for opinion studies, international trade figures, or consumer behavior characteristics can be conducted online, and the findings can be integrated into the online marketing planning process. Knowing where you have been and where you are today is essential in planning where you wish to go tomorrow.

Think about the electronic marketing process as a loop. Activities start with the situation analysis, and then the discoveries forge the future strategies of marketing planning. Planning leads to action, the marketing implementation step, and from the implementation, results of the program are learned, either positive or negative. These results loop back into the next year's situation analysis as an important factor to be integrated into future programming. At each step, electronic marketing resources add a unique feature over the traditional marketing process, that of interactivity. Interactivity is the ability for a two-way communication between the consumer and the e-merchant or e-marketer. You might say it reduces the need for mind reading. A strong electronic marketing program enables the successes of electronic commerce.

The estimates of electronic commerce are substantial, yet among general consumer goods, such as housewares, clothing and accessories, or appliances, success remains to be proved. The first solid indications of electronic shopping came with the Christmas holidays of 1998. "It really was America's first Internet-driven Christmas. When all the mouse clicks and money get counted, consumers will have spent about $4 billion buying goods and services (excluding travel) online during the fourth quarter of 1998, and nearly $10 billion throughout the year, according to the Boston Consulting Group (www.bcg.com). E-commerce sales more than tripled from the e-year before. With mouse and **modem,** consumers in more than eight million households voted that they'd rather buy online than fight for Furbys and parking places at stores." (Sellers 1999, 71)

Is Anybody Out There?

Before the discussion of electronic commerce begins, just who is using the World Wide Web (which is the commercial component of the Internet) for shopping or buying purposes? The estimates of the number of Internet users vary widely, and given the nature of this youthful communications vehicle, it is easy to understand. A recent survey by Matrix Information and Directory Services (MIDS, www.mids.org) estimates that presently 57 million consumers are using the Web, and by the year 2000, more than 700 million persons will have Web access. (MIDS study 1997) Another study by the respected research company, FIND/SVP (http://etrg.findsvp.com/features/newinet.html), reports that in the United States, 8.4 million adults and 1.1 million persons under the age of 18 use the Internet. The research company further states that 7.5 million persons use the World Wide Web, and that 7.3 million use the Internet at home. The company estimates that 700,000 of 1.1 million children use the Internet at their schools. Only to complicate the estimates further, Mediamark Research (www.mediamark.com) reports that 62 million U.S. adults ages 18 years plus now have access to the Internet, up 13 percent from the 55 million reported last year. (Mediamark Research 1998) A respected online newsletter, Iconocast, heralds that the Internet is growing by 1.3 million U.S. users each month. Which estimate is right? Anywhere from conservative to outlandish estimates are generated by respected research compa-

ICONOCAST is the definitive resource for facts, figures, trends and rumors in the Internet marketing industry. Here's what the press thinks of ICONOCAST: A "must for intense Net marketers," Computer Currents called it. And the Atlanta Business Chronicle said: "There's a lot of marketing information on the Internet, but most of it is not user friendly like ICONOCAST."

Besides great Internet market analysis, ICONOCAST also features a weekly column called "The Jacobyte," which is packed with insider information. In fact, Wired wrote: "ICONOCAST is a fantastic gossip source." ICONOCAST is written by Michael Tchong, the founder of CyberAtlas, a market research site recently acquired by Mecklermedia, and MacWEEK. Subscribe today!

Tell Jaco a rumor **and also check out:**

Iconocast (www.iconocast.com)
This online newsletter covers marketing intelligence on the Web. Issued weekly, the marketer can stay abreast of marketing information technology.

nies as well as "pseudo futurists" waving prediction papers with numbers containing six to nine zeros as user universes. There probably is no accurate figure for Internet users by which to build a marketing plan to take to the bank. At this point there is no sure-fire resource for delineating exact numbers of users, buyers, or shoppers. Suffice it to say, the Internet is a difficult medium to measure because users have the ability to access it from a number of different locations—work, home, school, dormitories, libraries, and so forth. For this book's purpose, only the best logic will be used in determining Internet usage.

If the number of Internet users cannot be quantified, can the user in general be profiled? Yes; the ninth survey of **Georgia Tech's Graphics, Visualization, and**

Usability (GVU) WWW User Survey (www.gvu.gatech.edu/user_surveys) reports the gender imbalance is quickly equalizing. (GVU Ninth User Survey 1998) In this April 1998 survey of more than 10,000 Web users, 38.7 percent of Web users are female, an increase of 5 percent from the 1997 survey and up from 5 percent female users in 1994. Forrester Research (www.forrester.com), a highly regarded online consultant, estimated the female population on the Web accounted for 43 percent of the Web traffic during 1998, with 45 percent projected for 1999. (O'Connell 1998) In a similar survey prepared by CommerceNet/Nielsen in March 1996, 21.8 percent of adults 16 years and older had access to the Internet, up from 14.1 percent the year before. Of the 21.8 percent adults, 17 percent have accessed the Internet within the last six months. If marital status is important to the marketer, the GVU Ninth Survey estimated the largest category of respondents (41.1 percent) is married, and the next largest is single (38.7 percent). According to the GVU Ninth Survey, the Internet populace remains a well educated group with 80.9 percent having at least some college and 50.1 percent having obtained at least one degree. Those persons who have been on the Internet for four years or more are likely than newer users to have an advanced degree such as a master's or doctorate. Because of its research and educational origins, the linkage to postgraduate work is very logical. *Fortune* magazine reports that 70 percent of e-commerce shoppers live east of the Mississippi. (Sellers 1999, 73)

Education-related occupations are the largest category of GVU respondents at 26.2 percent, followed closely by computer (22.3 percent) and professional (21.7 percent) employment. Educational attainment is reflected by income levels; the average annual income for the GVU Ninth Survey is $52,500. Household annual incomes of more than $50,000 were reported by 46.2 percent of respondents. It is interesting to note the value of privacy in that the largest percentage (16.9 percent) of respondents chose not to answer the income range question.

Usage patterns in the home are also telling. The reach of online services is growing; through 1997, the percentage of households with Internet service was estimated at 23 percent by Decision Analyst, Inc. (www.decisionanalyst.com) of Fort Worth. This number is up from 12 percent the year before and up from 5 percent in 1995. According to ZD Market Intelligence research firm (www.zdintelligtnce.com), Internet growth is being propelled by the home environment. From its last survey, which measures a 12,000-member home panel, the number of U.S. personal computers that accessed the Internet reached 45 million, a 43 percent jump from the first quarter of 1997. While e-mail continues to be the most popular Internet activity at 85 percent, an increase in Internet shopping is noteworthy. A new category, shopping on the Internet but buying using normal channels, is described by ZD Market Intelligence as 40 percent of Internet households. More than one quarter of the United States are buying via the Internet, states ZD. Further, the research company reports that the average Internet personal computer was connected to the Internet 4.5 hours a week, a full hour more than in 1997.

U.S. INSTALLED PERSONAL COMPUTERS WITH INTERNET ACCESS BY ENVIRONMENT

Period	Home (in Percent)	Self-Employed (in Percent)	Workplace (in Percent)
First quarter 1996	23	26	17
First quarter 1997	37	43	26
First quarter 1998	48	52	33

SOURCE: ZD Market Intelligence, May 1998.

Consider the consumer of tomorrow. Iconocast newsletter reported that a Simmons study called STARS (Simmons Teenage Research Study) discovered that 28 percent of all teens ages 12 through 19, or 8.6 million, accessed the Internet in the past thirty days. According to Media Matrix, the top sites preferred by teens are virtually identical to that of adults. When the news and information sites are analyzed, interesting patterns emerge. While male and female teens both like entertainment sites, boys prefer a dash of spice.

TOP WEB SITES VISITED BY TEENAGERS IN MARCH 1998

Boys, Ages 12–17			Girls, Ages 12–17		
Rank	Site	Reach (in percent)	Rank	Site	Reach (in Percent)
1	ESPN	8.2	1	Eonline	6.8
2	Playboy	6.9	2	Pathfinder	6.2
3	Sony Online	6.0	3	*Titanic*, the movie	6.0
4	Comedy Central	5.9	4	Warner Bros.	4.3
5	*Titanic*, the movie	5.9	5	Disney Online	4.3

SOURCE: Iconocast, issue 3 June 1998; Media Matrix, May 1998.

European respondents continue to be predominantly male, at 78 percent. For European respondents, 44 percent report English is their primary language with 12 percent speaking the German language and 10.5 percent speaking Dutch. In another study sponsored by Visa (www.visa.com), worldwide users were projected into the year 2000. Web usage was estimated by a Singapore research firm as follows:

Geography	1995 (Usage in Percent)	2000 (Usage in Percent)
USA	76	50
Europe	12	17
Asia/Pacific	9	25
Rest of world	3	8

SOURCE: IBC Research, 1996, http://infobase.s-one.net.sg.

The number of Web users worldwide has been estimated by Nua, one of Europe's leading online consulting agencies. Presently Nua estimates the number of Internet users worldwide to be 100.5 million persons. By the end of the year 2000, analysts predict the number will jump to 200 million. A computer intelligence report predicts a continued 30 percent growth rate for 1998. (CyberAtlas/Nua report 1998) These figures demonstrate what a truly international communications vehicle the Web has become.

Estimates of electronic commerce volume are elusive at best. Another respected research firm, Forrester Research, estimates consumers spent $3.3 billion via electronic commerce in 1998, with a rise to $7 billion projected for the year 2000, only a small percentage of the $7 trillion U.S. economy. *The Wall Street Journal* had the following to say about Internet usage.

> Thousands of merchants are trying to sell everything from Rachmaninoff to radish seeds on the Internet. Some of the companies are offshoots of

> traditional retailers, but many are closely held startups. They are spurred on by optimistic forecasts from Internet analysts and even the Commerce Department, predicting that online merchandising will soar from almost nothing in 1995 to tens of billions of dollars a year soon after the millennium. These vendors' business models are almost identical: easily searchable catalogs on the Internet, payment by credit card, and home delivery by shippers such as United Parcel Service of America. (Anders 1998)

Why Should Companies Consider Using Electronic Marketing?

You should recognize by now that Internet marketing requires efforts for more situations than one standard approach. Decisions to embrace the Internet can be made by long-established companies looking for fresh approaches. Other entrepreneurs might use the Internet to jump-start a startup business or one that has some history but no money. Another possible option is that an ongoing domestic company sees a product or service that fits to a selected market within a selected country or region, such as superb jams for jellies or quality candy that might appeal to the tastes of Southern European palettes. In each case, the marketer must realize a new kind of intelligence is necessary, that of e-information to match e-marketing. Wide-ranging information searches should include timely online resources.

Before any company decides to jump onto the Internet bandwagon, it would be smart to review the reasons why electronic commerce is right for the firm. Is the exploration of the World Wide Web fashion or folly for your industry? Does the company have a solid strategic plan and implementation process for its primary marketing offensive? Would plunging onto the Web be putting the cart before the horse? Is initiating a Web presence merely a boss directive? There are many questions a marketer should ask herself before any electronic media actions are taken. Too many organizations have pounced on the Internet medium without setting specific goals or plans or without a method of measuring performance. Before wasting a large amount of money and time, ask yourself these simple questions about online marketing:

- What is the company's purpose for engaging in online communications? What are appropriate goals? Is the company striving for profits or prestige? Is it serious about making an online presence?
- Why should the company go online? To introduce new products? To reduce distribution costs? To reach new prospects? To improve technical support? To enhance dealer relations?
- What do we hope to achieve with an online presence? Different companies have different expectations. Within a company, different departments may have different needs of an Internet site, or an intranet system. The engineering department may require extensive data exchange, whereas the human resource department is hoping to use the site for employment or as a personnel records repository, while the public relations people may wish to use the site for incoming media questions.
- How will the communications departments integrate this Web presence and address throughout the appropriate promotional materials? Who will be in charge of this identity transformation? Who will make sure this checklist is completed?
- Similarly, who will be in charge of the Web site creation? How will various departments provide information as to their expectations for the site? Who will be the final arbitrator on appropriate Web site content? Who will be the ongoing **Web master?**

- Who will set the budget for Web site production and implementation? From which department or departments will costs for online activities be drawn? Does the company have sufficient resources to produce an outstanding online representation?
- Does the company have the talent and patience to allow the Web site to grow into a mature and productive communications vehicle? Does your company operate with a long- or short-term focus? Online activities benefit from a long-term perspective.

Understand that simple questions may require complex answers. If your superiors cannot give you sufficient, well composed answers to these marketing and operations questions, it may not be advisable to pursue the Internet project. Internet efforts, like other promising but untested programs, may not generate success for a year or more. Further, the marketer must continue to coddle and tweak the project amid uncertainty and even derision from other people within the company. Therefore, be prepared to take criticisms and advice as the Internet project begins.

Now that some objectives and expectations for Internet activities have been established, the following discussion will move toward an understanding of electronic commerce. You will encounter many different definitions of electronic commerce, but usually the difference is only industry-deep. Simply defined, **electronic commerce** is a system of online shopping and information retrieval accessed through networks of personal computers. Electronic commerce can be considered the *end* results; electronic marketing resources are the means, the tools by which electronic commerce or e-commerce is executed more efficiently and effectively. This method of commerce usually is a direct transaction—which can be goods or services and can also include information, video or sound clips, or motion sequences—from the manufacturer to end consumer. The exchange can involve ordering goods from a retailer, and most aggressive retailers have introduced online presentation and ordering systems. Most any retailer, manufacturer, or distributor will feature either a Web site address or an e-mail address or both. You might think of the Internet as an additional promotional faucet to tap into the flow of customer and prospect purchases. Other faucets emanate from traditional promotional vehicles such as newspaper, television, radio, or direct mail. Marketers develop their own recipe of promotional tactics to fit the product lines or industries in which they compete. Now electronic communications tools are and will continue to be an important ingredient in the promotional mix.

How is business using the Internet? Approximately 47 percent of businesses use the Internet for gathering information, with 14 percent of business Web users purchasing products or services in 1996. (CommerceNet/Nielsen Internet Demographics Recontact study) A proposed 46 percent of businesses are using the Internet for communications purposes; 20 percent use the Internet to **download** software. MRI estimates that 20 million people access the Internet from their work locations. Interestingly, of the businesses using the Internet frequently, 16 percent of the firms are selling products while 30 percent are purchasing products and services. Specifically of business Web users, the following table outlines the five activities that are most common to businesses. (CommerceNet/Nielsen Internet study)

Gathering product information	77 percent
Researching competitors	49 percent
Collaborating	43 percent
Vendor support	42 percent
Internal communications	39 percent

Enter the Virtual Retailer

The opportunity for vast exposure all day and all night long has led to the emergence of virtual retailers, virtual storefronts, and virtual shopping malls. Do these entities exist? Yes, but not in bricks and mortar but as electronic representations of stores, warehouses, or shopping centers. The front door, roof, and back door of a virtual store are the flat surface of your monitor. For example, one of the largest book sellers, with 6.2 million customers as of early 1999, Amazon.com (www.amazon.com) is a virtual bookstore with no physical location (in late 1998, however, Amazon did build a real 80,000 square foot distribution center in south Seattle), no salespeople, and no books arranged neatly on any shelf. As you search and order books, audiotapes, or videos, the ordering system alerts the publisher or the wholesaler to ship directly to the ordering party's address. Most books and similar merchandise are never touched by the Amazon company. If, however, you look closely around the Web, you will see a very large presence of Amazon advertising on search engines, on various home pages, and on many hyperlinks back to Amazon. On the other hand, the traditional retailer Barnes & Noble (www.barnesandnoble.com) maintains a chain of retail outlets as well as hosting a large visibility on the Web. What drives different strategies between the two companies? Probably one of the main driving forces includes the fact that each retailer serves customers with different demographic, **psychographic,** and behavioral characteristics. They use different distribution strategies as well, but each sells the same product—books and printed matter. There is further divergence of sales strategy in that Amazon has recently decided to sell CDs via the Web while Barnes & Noble has chosen to sell CDs in its stores and not over the Internet. The two bookstores use dissimilar differentiation strategies—Amazon boasting of large price discounts and a list of 2.5 million book titles while Barnes & Noble creates a coffee bar atmosphere with smaller discounts—but both have embraced the Web as an important communications and sales vehicle.

Who are the other participants in the online sales operation besides the seller of the goods or services? Marketers hire communications specialists such as in-house designers or Web masters to create and maintain the company's Web stance. The company may, however, opt to engage an outside company to develop and implement the Web assignment in a **turnkey** manner. This outside company might be a one-person operation or a national **interactive advertising agency,** and the marketer's selection of the appropriate supplier depends on his department's plans or needs. The third participant is the **Internet provider (IP)** or **Internet service provider (ISP),** which arranges for the necessary equipment (the servers, the Internet connection, and the system maintenance) to handle the client's daily placement. These three parties must keep in close contact so that the site is attractive, up to date, and operating properly. The marketer's job is to monitor the site's performance as well as the ISP's delivery of uninterrupted service.

Comparing the Traditional Marketing Process Model

It is possible, and certainly advantageous, to introduce electronic marketing resources in each of the steps of the marketing process. Why? Because electronic resources provide more accurate data, with greater speed, and at both the micro and macro levels of the marketplace. The World Wide Web, as well, is perfect for communicating on a one-on-one basis that allows, with proper service standards, for a mutually beneficial relationship between the marketer and the consumer. You probably have bookmarked—the practice of saving useful addresses in a special directory—several sites on your Web browser, and you have done this because these sites yield information or entertainment that you want. Perhaps the bookmarked sites are ESPN Sports

Amazon.com (www.amazon.com)
Amazon.com is the marketing operations and financial model for launching online enterprises. It is now encouraging independent retailers to place an Amazon search engine on the retailer's site to earn additional commissions.

PRICELINE CEO SEES NET DRIVING CAR SALES

Internet-commerce entrepreneur Jay Walker, chairman of the privately-held Priceline.com, says that he hopes to cash in on the fact that many consumers abhor car dealers. Priceline's new service eliminates pain and stress of car shopping by cutting out the main irritant in that process—the salesperson. "Cars, unfortunately, are the one item consumers feel is the most distasteful in terms of the [shopping] process," Walker told Reuters in an interview. Stamford, Connecticut-based Priceline.com, which has 100 employees, launched this summer a "name-your-own-price" service for new cars and trucks on the company's Web site. The service, initially offered only in the New York City area but is slated for expansion across the United States, had 20,000 visitors on its first day, Walker said. "Priceline's initial service, airline tickets, was launched in the spring, and chalked up sales of 30,000 tickets in the first three months," said Walker.

SOURCE: Lewis, Matthew. Priceline CEO sees Net driving car sales. [Online]. Reuters, 10 July 1998.

(http://ESPN.SportsZone.com), the White House (www.whitehouse.gov), the *X-Files'* episode guide site (www.thex-files/episodes.com), or *South Park* (www.comedycentral.com). These are Web sites that you enjoy, and over the months or years have become your friends, something you can readily dial up and interface with. That is a relationship, as you know, in which someone will be home when you call.

How do the steps in the process compare, and what tools can be integrated to create an even richer dialog with the customer? It has been said that without a direction, any road will get you there. But with planning, you can arrive at your destination more directly. The traditional marketing process model will be discussed here first before the new electronic resources will be introduced. Whether you are introducing a brand new product or service or if you are planning the next year's marketing program for an existing product or service, marketers must understand the current dynamics of the marketplace. What has changed since last year? Have new competitors invaded the marketplace? What are the environmental factors that face you today? Are interest rates up? If so, higher interest payments might push some of your audience out of the market. What are the demographic trends that affect your product's sales? Are birth rates up, or are marriages or divorces down? If you are selling to a children's market, you may be talking to a smaller audience than before. If your service is health care oriented toward the maturity market, what are the trends in retirement today, and are retirees moving to your area? All of these examples are environmental issues that you, the marketer, cannot control. It is wise, however, for you to be aware of shifts in the marketplace *before* you start making your marketing plans and spending your marketing budget. Is information tracking environmental trends available to the marketer? Yes, and with electronic tools, the trends can be studied more fully, and with more speed. Below is an illustration of the traditional model.

Marketing process model

Situation analysis → Marketing planning → Marketing implementation

The first step in your marketing overview is to initiate a situation analysis. This practice is particularly important since you will be basing the remaining two steps on this situation analysis foundation. Much like a rocket on a trip to the moon, the smallest error in trajectory at the launch will result in greatly missing a target over a long distance. The greater the error, the farther away the goal will be. Therefore, take particular care in establishing your facts and opinions, or your marketing program may have a foundation built upon sand. Following is an outline for establishing the online marketing process steps and corresponding electronic resources.

I. Situation Analysis

   A. State the objective(s) of your marketing investigation

B. Relevant market research/input	*Industry or associations Web sites, discussion groups,* **Usenets,** *government data sources, electronic newsletters,* **CD-ROM** *storage*

1. Define what information you require.
2. Is that information available?
3. Where can you obtain this necessary information?

C. Proposed prospect/market description	*Company databases, industry Web sites, government sources, survey e-mail, CD-ROMs*
D. New product or service explanation	*Customer databases, survey e-mail, discussion groups, industry newsletters*
E. Environmental factors and market trends	*Government data sources, survey e-mail, industry sites*
F. Demographics and other characteristics	*Demographic software, industry Web sites, government data sources*
G. Company history and/or competencies (if applicable)	*Internal documents, employee interviews*
H. Competitive analysis and evaluation	*Competitive Web sites*
I. Assessment of niche opportunity	*Analysis of all factors*

Evaluating the Online Marketing Situation

By beginning with the situation analysis, you are likely to uncover unexpected changes in the marketplace, regardless if you are a seasoned marketing executive or a summer intern. Demand for your product or service may shift slightly (or greatly) because of external factors that sneak up on you or your department. Relentless competition may be undermining your distribution channels, attacking dealer relationships, or preparing for a new product introduction supported by large advertising expenditures. It is extremely easy to become lazy when you are on top as it is equally easy to forget how your company got to the top. Those little efforts, such as staying in contact with your salespeople or your dealers on a weekly basis, doing competitive pricing studies, shopping your rivals' new super stores, interviewing consumers on a quarterly basis, checking economic indicators for your market area, and preparing training programs for your employees, are probably some of the methods that put your company at the top. There is no finish line when you, the marketer, are among the leaders in your industry.

As with any marketing effort, online or otherwise, the marketer must know where to begin to know where to finish. There can be two different places to start, depending on if the online marketing program is originating from scratch, or if the program is a continuation or a supplement of an ongoing agenda. If the program is ongoing, results of the previous year's performance should be carefully reviewed to judge how well the online resources worked. Knowing at what point to start is always the key to successful marketing efforts; the stalwart queries of *who*, *what*, *when*, *where*, and *why* are the conventional, tried embarkation concepts for the investigation. This measurement of ongoing performance will be discussed shortly. Meanwhile, the immediate discussion will assume the online marketing program is in its initial planning stages. Where should you start? The marketer should decide what are the objectives for an online presence. There are several objectives that could be chosen for marketing online.

- Initiate an online awareness as an extension of the product's or service's promotional program. In this case, copy and graphics would adhere to existing advertising or sales promotion themes. In the early days of Web promotion, advertisers merely reproduced a print advertisement into an online version. This mirroring of existing print ads held little gratification for the interested viewer because few sites contained interactivity such as hyperlinks within the site or accommodated any unique content from which the viewer could learn more about the product. By the mid-nineties, Web site marketers and designers were creating sites with user-friendly, memorable graphics, sound, and motion. While not quite as entertaining as a video game, Web sites have become unique vehicles in which consumers can exercise control over the information they choose to access or to disregard. Now hardly a consumer or business-to-business ad is produced without a Web address or e-mail address.

- One purpose of a Web site could be to assist the overall media plan, targeted either to a consumer or a trade group, with an online product or service introduction. The media planner can use online advertising as a primary vehicle with traditional media support or choose to use online advertising as a support medium for traditional media awareness. Depending on the industry—such as in the computer or other high-tech commerce where online exposure is the primary media vehicle—online advertisements reinforce messages carried by the primary media such as broadcast or print vehicles. An advantage of Web messages is the ability of encouraging interactive response—the Web allows the newspaper or magazine reader, the television viewer, or the radio listener to immediately type in a Web address and take part in the content of interest. Traditional advertising has always been a monologue of the advertiser communicating with the consumer, but not vice versa. With the advent of the online medium, a true dialog can be nurtured, hopefully resulting in a long-term relationship between both parties. Not only do Web resources produce a two-way dialogue, the Web performs its functions with great speed. Therefore, many of the members of the Generation X who are accustomed to a high-speed world are impatient or rushed to provide instant solutions to their business needs, and, depending on the type of connection—telephone modem, T-1, fiber optic, **ISDN** (Integrated Serial Digital Network), or other connection service provided—none never seem fast enough. Marketers should recognize the "need for speed" as they plan the communications or logistics of the marketing plan.

- Another facet offered by online communications is the capability to improve the dialog and react quickly to customer service inquiries. An e-mail address for customer comments or complaints is an excellent companion to the steadfast toll-free telephone number. A well considered set of **frequently asked questions (FAQs)** can oftentimes substitute as an answer key, saving time for all customer service representatives. The prospect or customer can look at the organization's list of FAQs, select the question, and receive the answer that is relevant to her inquiry. Certainly some questions will require a customized response, but a good FAQs list can field the most commonly requested information.

- Similar to customer service abilities, technical support can be enhanced by e-mail communications. Customers can e-mail hardware or software questions such as configuration problems to the technical people who can guide the caller through the anticipated problem. The assumption is that written, meaning e-mail, responses can be collected through the evening and overnight periods to be later handled in batches such as on the day shift. This asynchronous strategy can reduce labor costs by eliminating the need for technical specialists on call twenty-four hours a day and thus distributing the workload evenly. Another benefit is that technical information can be dispensed with a greater quality of consistency if fewer people are dealing with customers. Consistency of information dispensed will result from customer service staff training in which the marketing department should actively participate. More and more companies are realizing customer contact is largely a marketing function and are charging the marketing departments to develop a training agenda that will mesh with corporate missions and visions.

- The Web is conducive for testing new product or service concepts among friends such as current customers or dealers or even with new prospect groups. Since the Web site address can be passed around quietly, the marketer can gather input in private, and then a new iteration can be tested again and again. In introducing the new Beetle in 1998, Volkswagen (www.vw.com) conducted eighteen months of intense product design and consumer reaction activities via Web response. The effort proved worthwhile because consumer reaction placed new Beetle deliveries on back order. Volkswagen also had to limit dealers to initial allocations of only eighteen vehicles each month. Carefully researching consumer opinions and then incorporating the research into the design and production of the renovated Beetle are significant examples of being in tune with the Volkswagen customer constituency.

- Customer tracking has become much easier and more accurate as companies have instituted database development programs that automatically update buyer activities over time. Frequency of purchase and types of products begin to form distinctive patterns from which online retailers can start offering customized menus of merchandise, such as specific kinds of outdoor wear or sporting goods, CDs by a favorite composer, or literary works by a favorite author. Several online merchandisers such as Amazon.com or Columbia House (www.columbiahouse.com) employ e-mail announcements when new products or services are available that fit previous purchase patterns. Databases record customer interests, purchasing habits, preferred credit cards, expenditure levels, and other selected shopping activities; drawing on the database parameters, targeted promotions can be tailored to each customer grouping. The benefit can be mutual to the customer and the retailer since offering selected merchandise saves the purchaser time and aggravation while the retailer hones its marketing communications to qualified and interested purchaser lists.

- Another opportunity online marketers are discovering is that of employee recruitment for various departments or facilities throughout the company or the world. Companies can post job openings, develop résumé banks, or assist employees with relocation information concerning community amenities, schools, homes, apartments, shopping centers, or other living accommodations as is the charter for economic development groups as Tampa Bay Partnership (www.tampabay.org). New or prospective companies or newcomers are presented with extensive information on the Tampa Bay region by the seven-county coalition. The employment site for Clorox (www.clorox.com) posts job openings for the experienced professional and for recent college graduates. It also encourages applicants to paste their résumés to an employment dialog box within the site. This method of submitting résumés is an excellent idea since knowledgeable workers with electronic skills are likely to apply.

Defining the Information Search

In any marketing effort, the marketer should devise a shopping list of relevant market research and input to help set direction for the future marketing plan. Again, the better the foundation of factual information, the better the results will be. The shopping list may consist of primary or **secondary research** or both. **Primary research** is commissioned to collect specific information about a product or service that is used (or proposed to be used) by target markets. Primary research could be considered a custom investigation in that the information derived is proprietary, that is owned by the company that commissioned the study or survey. Large consumer-oriented companies such as Procter & Gamble (www.pg.com) or Gillette (www.gillette.com) supervise ongoing consumer research to keep in touch with their customers' wants and expectations. Consumer opinions can change rapidly and with little notice. This is particularly true in the fashion and cosmetics industries where brand image and assumed loyalty can change overnight. In recent times, pharmaceutical companies, especially those that deal with consumer groups, have seen their fortunes wax and wane because of the findings of government studies—the diet pill Redux—or of the introduction of new products—the male impotence drug Viagra, www.viagra.com. Primary research can uncover unexpected facts and opinions that might greatly alter marketing strategies. An example of unforeseen opinions could be that of Jewish backlash to the merger of automobile giants, Chrysler Corporation and Daimler-Benz (www1.daimlerchrysler.com). Jewish interest groups remember the role that Daimler played with its use of forced labor during World War II. Sentiment ran so high in some Jewish circles that a boycott of Chrysler products was demanded. Attitudes and opinions surveys, properly constructed, can be an early warning system to foresee potential problems and, thus, trigger specific marketing and public relations programs to mitigate possible negative situations.

Budget constraints may limit the feasibility of conducting primary research, and the marketer must utilize secondary research sources that are comprised of data collected by outside sources, usually from public documents such as the Census Bureau (www.census.gov) or the Bureau of Labor Statistics (www.bls.gov). Data from public resources are often excellent in detail but can become out of date by the time it is released. Secondary research can be obtained from government records for domestic and international trade; industry associations, such as the American Association of Advertising Agencies (www.aaaa.org), the Food Marketing Institute (www.fmi.org), or the National Association of Broadcasters (www.nab.org), may have research or library departments or may commission research studies on behalf of their membership. Oftentimes these studies are available to the public. There are also companies that offer for sale research reports that were conducted as primary research and that after six to twelve months are sold as secondary research. One respected company is FIND/SVP (www.findsvp.com); at any given time FIND/SVP has an inventory of research reports for sale. These reports are usually very specific in scope with topics such as grocery shopper consumption of diet cola beverages or preferences of auto mechanics for motor oils. Occasionally a marketer will find secondary research reports like these that fit his industry. Secondary research is less costly than primary research, but secondary research is available to all competitors. If you, the marketing student, price these reports listed on the FIND/SVP home page, you will probably find these reports too expensive for the student. A basic document, "Finding business research on the Web," is $175.

Perhaps the marketer would like an answer to a single question. To save the aggravation of Web research or to avoid contacting a full-service research company, the marketer might use an online research company such as Answers.com (www.answers.com); Answers.com will field single questions much like the public library of old. Answers.com, however, charges a fee for its search service. After opening an account with a credit card number, the marketer can type in a question and select a level of difficulty (simple, medium, or extended research). The site charges $1.79 to answer simple factual questions while it charges $11.99 for difficult, extended research questions. Answers.com promises to reply within twenty-four hours. This service is an anomaly to typical Internet information since Answers.com charges for Internet content. Yet this research source provides all relevant Web sites in its responses, showing users how to handle similar questions on their own. It is a good research source, but with frequent use, this service could become expensive. (Weber 1997)

Perhaps your information need is much more complex. There are Web sites with expert and extensive information throughout the world, so it is your job to locate them and understand these various data sources. For example, perhaps you are the marketing director of a Midwestern grain grower, and the summer has been extremely dry to the point of creating wildfires among your wheat and corn crops. The entire company is anxious and uncertain about getting the crops harvested and to market, and you might be charged with investigating the wildfire phenomena, perhaps contributing conditions, prevention, extinguishment, productive regeneration, or future fire management, or charged with locating a wildfire expert or becoming an expert yourself overnight. In Freiburg, Germany, Johann Goldammer operates the Fireglobe Web site (www.ruf.uni-freiburg.de/fireglobe), which provides near-time (actually same day) satellite information on prescribed and uncontrolled fires globally. His organization in Southwest Germany is at the center of a global movement to combat the surge of uncontrolled fires on the planet during the last decade. Both fire warnings from the United States to Southeast Asia to Australia and educational materials are offered on the Fireglobe Web pages. On this particular day, Fireglobe has issued alerts for northern Mississippi and Alabama and has posted photographs of actual forest fires and wildfires in progress in these areas, but Fireglobe has not issued any warnings in your upper Midwestern areas. With this timely reassurance, Fireglobe becomes a valuable intelligence resource, and you can begin briefing your managers in several states as to the current conditions. As far as information retrieval, it is as easy as Web access on a daily basis. (Zachary 1999)

After the relevant research is defined, the second step in the research process is to ascertain if and where the information can be obtained. Most state universities and many private institutions have extensive marketing research resources for demographic, psychographic, and behavioral investigations. The U.S. census (taken every ten years) and labor, international trade, and industrial and service performances are just a few of the wealth of secondary research available online or in hard copy at a university library. Psychographic or lifestyle information is usually available through publications such as Simmons Market Research Bureau (www.smart-mktg.com), Mediamark Research, Inc., or Standard Rate and Data Service's Lifestyles Market Analyst (www.srds.com); these research sources provide extensive and behavior profiles of target market areas, lifestyle activities, and media usage patterns. The electronic database resources will be addressed in more detail shortly.

Why engage in primary or secondary research in the first place? The better the information factors, the better the decision process. The personnel of a marketing department can become lax or stale, going through the motions of meeting customer demands and environmental changes. Further, a marketer's individual likes and dislikes can subjectively shade decisions that should be made in austere objectivity. Also, supporting the marketing program with pages of black and white facts demonstrates the diligence and preparation of new market ventures. More marketing programs fail because of subjectivity (as in what the boss likes) than those that fail due to objectivity; marketing research can assist the marketer in walking away from an unsound proposition if the facts and opinions of the populace are heeded.

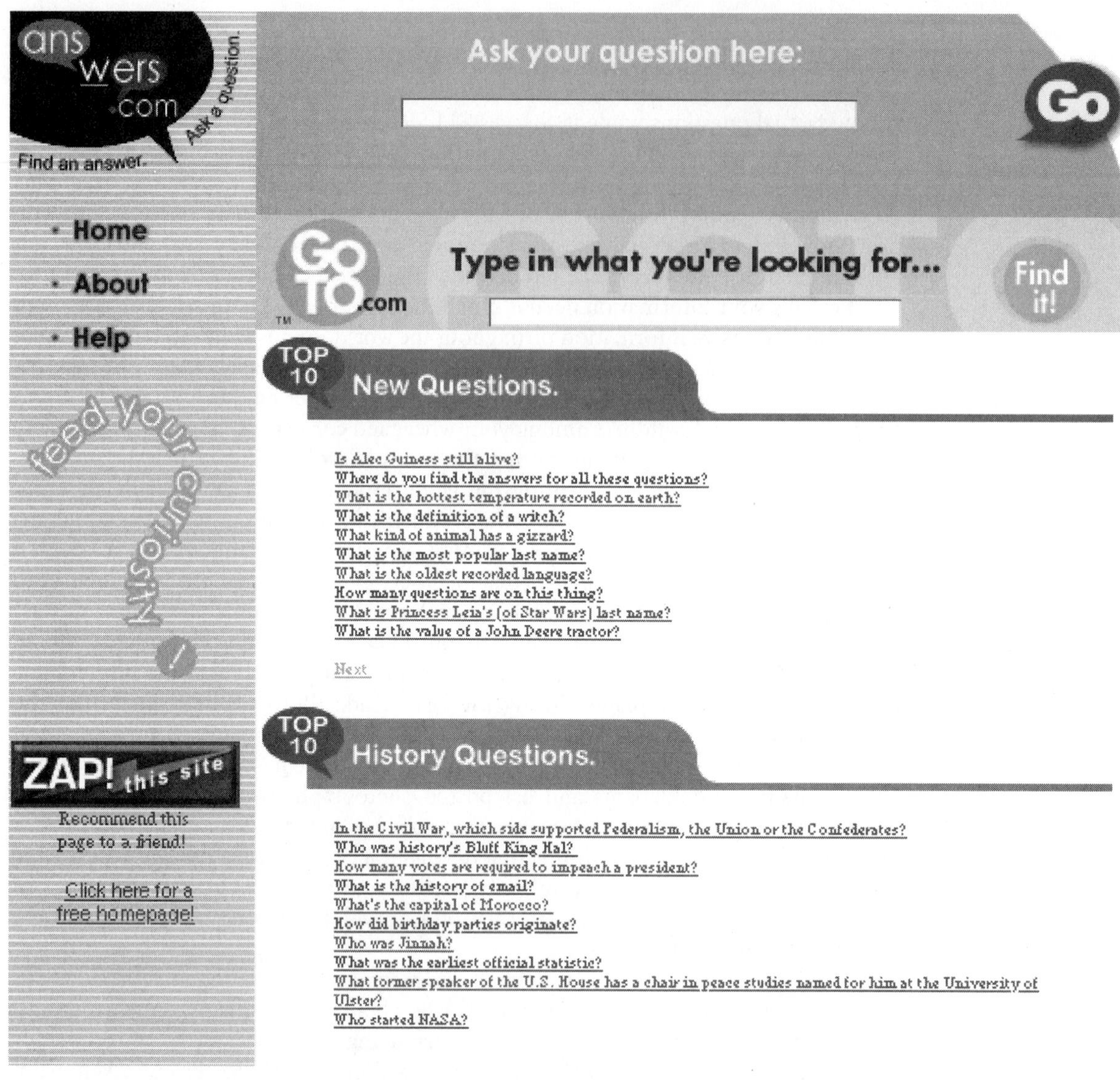

Answers.com (www.answers.com)
Simple to complex questions can be asked to Answers.com. This resource points you to relevant Web sites so you can obtain your own solutions.

Proposed Market Description

Which comes first, the product selection or the prospect selection? Most savvy marketers will posit that until consumer needs or desires are identified, there is no proverbial hole to fill. Many products and services have languished on store shelves because they offered no benefit to any market segment. After the environmental factors are defined, a prospective market should be described—perhaps two or three market segments could be appropriate for communications and consumption targets. From experience, sometimes painful, the seasoned marketer should begin to paint a picture of the target audience, largely in broad terms. Perhaps the prospect is a college educated male, ages 25 to 49 years of age, married with young children, earns between $30,000 to $49,000 annually, lives in a comfortable suburb, works as a manager or professional, and owns a personal computer at home with Internet access. This profile sounds like a perfect fit to the typical online prospect. Setting expansive prospect parameters allows the marketer to begin construction of the marketing strategy, and as the marketing planning evolves, more narrow and clearer profiles will start to emerge.

New Product or Service Definition

The marketer must be able to concisely describe the concept of the new product or service; if the marketer cannot, it is unrealistic to expect the audience to work to understand. It has been said that if a manager cannot write her idea on the back of a business card, the concept is too ambiguous and unwieldy. As with the traditional marketing model, the product or service must satisfy some need or desire of the target market, yet the prospect is not buying the tangible object alone. The prospect is buying, renting, or leasing the benefits that the product delivers. A marketer must think in terms of expected benefits that are attractive to the intended audience. The product or service is a bundle of benefits, not just a tangible good or a primary service function. A businessman does not purchase a new suit for its cloth and thread; he purchases an Armani suit because of its style, its fit, its panache. The brand name speaks highly of the businessman's own good taste. In framing the product or service concept, there are several facets to consider: general utility of the good, convenience of procuring the good, timely delivery of the good, and the sales environment where the good is purchased. As the marketer assesses the marketplace, these attributes are important to include as benefits to the end consumer, and the practice of satisfying consumer demands is called consumer-oriented marketing. Many new products are developed as marketers keep tabs on market trends within their industry. Product suggestions can be obtained from customer recommendations, industry publications, or online industry resources.

A new service is more difficult to establish, either online or otherwise, because most services must be consumed before any judgment of satisfaction can be made. The typical service is a promise of performance, an intangible substance that offers further intangible benefits such as saving time, improving appearances, providing security, or conveying convenience. Services can be solutions to either needs or wants. Think of a simple service such as a haircut. It can be the answer to a need—"I have an interview tomorrow for a terrific new job"—or a want—"I'm getting a haircut to look like Chandler Bing from *Friends.*" The product or service must deliver satisfaction, and it is the marketer's job to gain notice from the target market that the product did indeed satisfy. Pleasing attributes must be carefully and creatively described to keep the product's or service's name in memory, and descriptions that appeal to the senses—taste, smell, touch, hearing, or sight—are most memorable. At this point of the marketing investigation, the marketer should be thinking in highly descriptive terms as to the benefits delivered by the new product or service concept. As in defining the prospect profiles, think broadly about the promised benefits.

Environmental Factors and Market Trends

No organization operates in a vacuum today. Status quo in industries no longer exists, and the only thing certain is change. So many factors influence consumer behavior, and it is the marketer's responsibility to foresee and manage the environmental and market forces to the benefit of the brand. There are four major categories of environmental factors that the marketer must monitor. He must recognize that environmental forces cannot be controlled by one company, or even one government, but marketing plans can be developed to minimize the disruption of change or to cash in on market trends. These four watch guard categories are the economic environment, the cultural environment, the legal environment, and the political environment. A strategic marketing program is by definition long-term, and the macro focus should anticipate change from year to year.

Each of these four environments is equally important since an imbalance in one area can create unexpected tremors in others. Recently the United States has seen an economic crisis in Asia, which has led to an ever-widening trade deficit because Asian firms and consumers are buying fewer imports that cause U.S. companies to pare back expansion plans, that then reduce new job creation, and that finally constrict local economies. This chain reaction is unavoidable, so the marketer must look ahead, observe the various opportunities and threats, and then act accordingly to preserve the company's marketing equities. What are the telltale symptoms in the environmental sectors? Following are some of the environmental factors that might face a company that is conducting business both domestically and internationally.

- What is the trend in interest rates, rising or falling? What is the trend in inflation, rising, falling, or stabilized? How are the major stock exchanges performing, both in the United States and abroad?
- What is the trend in producer prices—one of the best indicators of the general direction of the economy? Again, is the index rising, falling, or stabilized?
- What is the trend in wages as well as the unemployment rates?
- Concerning international trade, what are the exchange rates and the dollar's stability?
- What is the balance of trade status within the company's major foreign markets?

While these points are not inclusive of the economic horizon, the direction of the stock and bond markets usually foretell the mood of public confidence in the economy. Higher levels of the Dow Jones index (www.dowjones.com) encourage small and large investors alike.

Following are some of cultural factors that might face a company both domestically and internationally.

- Is there any change among the various lifestyle segments? Is there a movement among younger persons toward the conservative or the liberal mindset?
- What is the content of popular entertainment, particularly among the television programming and motion pictures?
- What is the national collective conscience, pessimistic or optimistic, indulgent or altruistic, active or passive?

- Who are the current cultural icons or intellectual, spiritual, athletic, or business leaders?
- What are the morals and values that the public aspires to?
- Are taboos changing among the generations?

A specific example of changing cultural taboos is being noticed through the increase in teenage smoking. As parents, the media, and the government discourage smoking and other tobacco use, this perceived ban makes tobacco a forbidden practice. This implied taboo is thought to enhance a rebellious, on-the-edge image among teens. Other examples are the increase of tattoos seen (and unseen) among young women or earrings worn by males of all ages.

Following are some political factors that a company might face when doing business both domestically and internationally.

- What is the general opinion of public leaders? Are they held in high or low regard?
- Are national or local elections to be held soon? Are there significant differences between major parties, particularly in business issues?
- What in general is the public opinion of business within society?
- In international ventures, what is the stability of the government? What is the attitude toward foreign investment?

As a result of the Asian economic crisis, the leader of Indonesia, President Suharto, was forced to resign from the post he held for thirty-two years. Public confidence was lost, the currency was in shambles, business was at a standstill, even food was being hoarded because of uncertainty in all sectors.

The following legal factors need to be considered when doing business domestically and internationally.

- What is the position of the government toward business in general, supportive or restrictive?
- How do laws or regulations affect your industry? Is there pending legislation that will change the way business is conducted?
- In international commerce, what is the method of settling business disputes? Is local legal counsel or lobbying necessary?

In the legal arena, the Microsoft company (www.microsoft.com) led by Bill Gates continues to be held to close scrutiny by the Justice Department (www.usdoj.gov) of the federal government. One of the biggest investigations has occurred over the forced inclusion of the Internet Explorer Web browser that caused great confusion about the release date for Windows 98. Questions of monopolistic practices by Microsoft are not new to industry behemoths, as AT&T (www.att.com) and IBM (www.ibm.com) can testify. Both came to agreements with the Justice Department, as did Microsoft.

Demographic and Other Characteristics

There is a fifth dimension of environmental factors to consider. This is the area of change that applies to the people portion of the marketing equation. Demographic information comes from the ten-year census initiated in 1790, and with each new census, demographers scramble to interpret the data, looking for large or small changes or important shifts in population trends. It takes the Census Bureau about one and one-half years to process the data, which are then released on tapes to the public. Private companies with statisticians and analysts then take the raw data and model it to approximate the American demographic and psychographic representations. These interpretations are important in many marketing decisions, and those analysts that prognosticate closely toward the American market estimates are valuable professionals. Demographic information is fairly straightforward in gathering and manipulating numbers. The psychographic projections require qualities of both art and science because psychographics are attitudinally constructed, and many attitudes are difficult to quantify. For example, one market data company divides all American households into fifty clusters of specific characteristics, while another company profiles households into forty-eight clusters of similar but different characteristics. However households are divided up and whatever modeling technique is used by each company, one is probably just as good as the other. Geo-demographic software application will be discussed shortly.

In segmenting populations into similar groups, a marketer can analyze many factors as supplied by the Census data. Some of the more enlightening features can include the following.

- Population totals and percentage changes from previous periods can be useful tools to use in segmenting populations. Many companies may also project expected future population figures. These percentages can be positive (growing) or negative (shrinking) numbers; most marketers are searching for growth markets, therefore, positive percentages.
- Other interesting information to consider using is the number of households and expected percentage changes. Households can be described in several ways such as total number by county, zip code, Census tract, or radius in miles or by heads of households.
- Age profiles are important, as are the demographic data reports on several age formats such as male and female age clusters, females with children clusters, and general population age clusters. These composite percentages are valuable in deciding product or service potentials.
- Income clusters are important too, and median household and individual incomes are estimated. Some programs estimate future income totals as well.
- Educational levels may be important to your marketing program; educational achievements such as high school graduate, some college, undergraduate degrees, and graduate degrees can be estimated.
- Occupational status, such as executive, sales, managerial, trade, or laborer, is estimated for each geographical area that you choose. Depending on the target market, you can search the database for areas with higher concentrations of the desired occupational profile.
- Psychographic or lifestyle analysis accompanies the demographic profiles and usually presents lifestyle clusters in a matrix fashion of high to low income against urban to rural housing. These lifestyle cells sport cute but informational descriptors such as "backyards and barbecues," or "tuition and braces." Solid segment knowledge builds as psychographic data are overlaid with demographic information.

Locating the geographic prevalence of market segments or the demographic composition of target market areas proves beneficial in cost efficiencies and program effectiveness. Psychographic analysis can uncover lifestyle characteristics for which the marketer is searching, or assist in substantiation of market potential suspicions. The better the marketer knows her market's characteristics, the better the communications will be.

Company History and Competencies

What made the company successful? Behind every successful business lies skills or competencies that sets the enterprise apart. Customers come to recognize these competencies, such as dependability, vast selection, convenience as in multiple offices, or creativity in providing solutions to client problems. The marketing manager can perform an internal audit (or external audit among suppliers, current customers, or past customers) to evaluate perceived and real strengths and weaknesses; these competencies should be reflected as benefits derived in dealing with your company. All eminent corporations have formed their marketing prowess on one or two user benefits, and after careful study, a demonstrable and consistent promotional program was initiated. Think of these examples. FedEx (www.fedex.com) promises to "absolutely, positively" deliver the package overnight for its two million customers each day. Merrill Lynch (www.ml.com) boasts with "the difference is Merrill Lynch" as being the premier

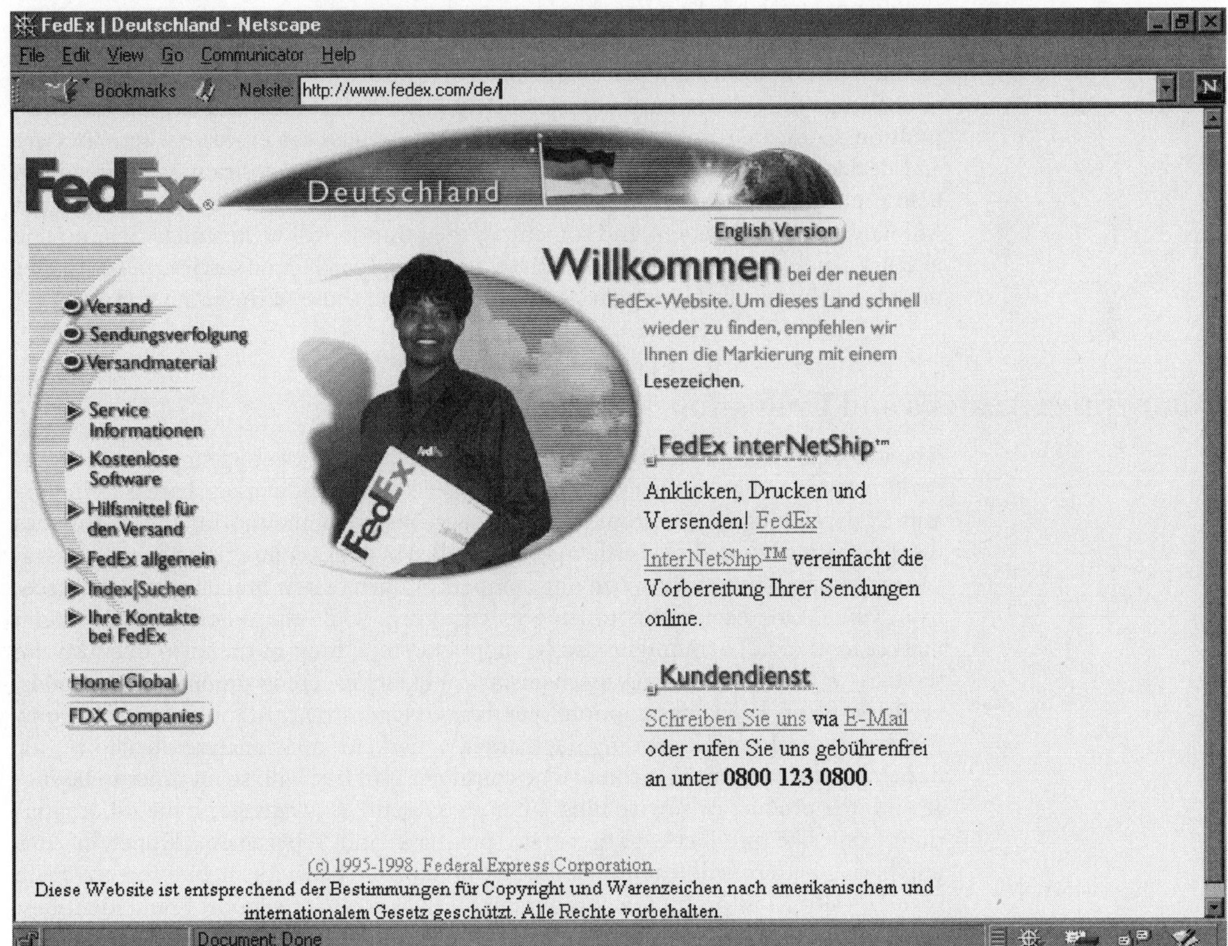

Fed Ex (www.fedex.com/de_english/)
Federal Express travels the world delivering packages and, as such, many sites overseas are translated into the host country's language. Here is the German presentation of FedEx's services.

financial adviser. Projecting a friendly, comfortable image, Nabisco (www.nabisco.com) welcomes you to "the Nabisco Neighborhood," which offers the viewer to participate in games and contests on its home page. Each company has isolated its consumer benefits—its reason for being—in concise and compelling imagery. FedEx is serving the business market that values speed and accuracy in all of its dealings; FedEx's performance makes it a valuable business partner. Merrill Lynch with its powerful bull logotype tries to stand apart from the herd as it promises to be different from the others. Portraying itself as a friendly member of a small town, Nabisco creates its own "neighborhood" where kids can play and the main street shopping area is a collection of old-fashioned storefronts. The family-friendly Nabisco image is appropriate since its brands, Lifesavers, Oreos, and Chips Ahoy!, are appealing to the family market. All are samples of positioning strategy, which is an awareness technique for selecting the correct image by which the company or brand wishes to be perceived.

This concept of positioning was developed in the early seventies by Jack Trout and Al Ries in their influential books *Marketing Warfare* (Mass Markets Press, 1986) and *Positioning: The Battle for Your Mind* (Mass Markets Press, 1993). Their contention was that every competitor, either company, brand, or service, vies among like rivals in product categories, and each is ranked by the consumer on a product ladder. At the time, IBM was at the top rung of the computer category ladder, Hertz (www.hertz.com) was on top of rental cars, and Coca-Cola (www.coke.com) was the top player in soft drinks. If the top competitor was well entrenched, the smaller brand should not attack head-on but should try to flank the leader or create a new positioning ladder or category. Avis (www.avis.com) "tried harder" than Hertz and moved into second position from sixth place in its category; Seven-Up (www.7up.com) chose not to challenge the cola leaders but instead created a new soft drink ladder, the "un-cola" position. Companies with customer-valued competencies can evaluate where they are and decide where they wish to go; a logical and consistent positioning strategy can help the company achieve its promotional goals. Sometimes the company's position will flank other contenders, and sometimes the position will be in a niche that no one else has claimed or created. To accurately position a product or service, the marketer must know his product strengths and weaknesses and those of the competition.

Competitive Analysis and Evaluation

The marketer must be vigilant in his or her research and marketing strategies, as competitors come and go in the marketplace. Protecting current market share is as important as developing new customer shares; everyone is competing for the consumer's discretionary income. This battle may materialize as direct competition encroaches on your territory; for instance, a banking competitor opens a new branch across the street from yours. One bank fights to keep its customers while the other works to gain a market foothold. There might also be indirect competition in the form of substitute services (or products). Savings mechanisms could include credit unions, mutual funds, or 401(k) plans. Even consumption, spending dollars earmarked for savings, is a competitive threat. In understanding the market, a marketer must analyze the choices for dispersing the consumer's income. The consumer is of free will, so, in order to be successful, the product or service must offer a competitive advantage, some differentiation from like products, to generate purchase and repurchase. Hopefully this purchasing pattern will lead to habitual or predictable behavior in an effort to create brand loyalty. Most promotional programs work to create or support brand identities. Consumers come to expect certain benefits from the products or services they select, and a strong brand identity helps to set the product apart from others within the product category.

Conducting research on competitors' products or services has been facilitated by Web usage because so many Web sites contain so much information. Without a stretch of the imagination, surely Music Blvd. (www.musicblvd.com), one of the Internet's most popular online music stores, keeps tabs on the activities and offerings of close competitors such as Tower Records (www.towerrecords.com), who boasts of its speedy deliveries. Specifications, pricing, inventory availability, dealer or retailer locations, shipping options, even financing information give valuable details that were very difficult to obtain in the past. Marketers must be careful in the amount of information that is published on the Web site. There is a fine line between intriguing a prospect and telling your competitors everything there is to know about your company. If a Web site answers all questions, future contact may be minimal. However, surfing for competitive information is a good idea, particularly if the marketer is entering new fields or new territories. Printing Web pages from a competitor's site is as good as having the sales brochure. Just type in a name in the Web browser, and you will be surprised what a wealth of competitive data comes up.

Assessment of the Niche Opportunity

After this careful analysis of the marketing factors and forces, the marketer will be able to establish the product's or service's niche of opportunity for creating the ensuing marketing plan. The emphasis is on a **niche,** a narrower rather than broader market segment that the company is well suited to serve. The idea that no company can tend to all markets since an array of market segments will have an array of needs is generally understood. Probably the best balance in a marketing relationship is derived as a market segment's needs are met satisfactorily while the company's operation is profitable and efficient. The market opportunities can come from existing customer bases, such as extending current offerings into new products—Classic Coke to Diet Coke to Caffeine-free Coke—or creating new demand or uses for existing products or services—Arm & Hammer baking soda (www.armhammer.com) as a refrigerator deodorant or Southwest Airlines' expansion (www.iflyswa.com) into eastern routes)—or new products for new markets—Tommy Hilfiger clothes for women (www.tommyhilfiger.com). In each case, marketing managers studied market trends—cola drinkers concerned about gaining weight or wanting to reduce caffeine consumption, Southwest Airlines' saturation of western air travel, or the traditional look of Tommy for women. Environmental factors pointed toward positive demand trends from which market segment penetration could be established. The retailer the Limited (www.limited.com) has successfully segmented its markets and offered to each market a differentiated product—the Limited, for casual attire; Express, for more contemporary fashion; Limited Too, for toddlers and children; Lerner New York, for more business attire; Victoria's Secret, for lingerie; Abercrombie & Fitch, Henri Bendel, Bath & Body Works, for bath and beauty products; Structure, Galyan's Trading Company, and Lane Bryant; for full-size figures. The Gap (www.gap.com) has differentiated offerings as well, the Gap, GapKids, babyGap, Old Navy, and Banana Republic. Each catering to a different market with different product benefits.

Summary

All successful marketing programs are constructed from a careful evaluation of market conditions; this evaluation is the situation analysis. This analysis reflects the current marketing factors facing the company, its brands of products or services, and the competition in each product category. From the situation analysis, the marketer gains an understanding of the marketplace and the opportunities that it affords. Market opportunities, usually a selection of target markets called niches, result from studies of market trends and from market segments that are being underserved. All of this marketing information becomes the foundation of the marketing plan, which will be examined in the next chapter.

Key Terms

CD-ROMs

Download

Electronic commerce

FAQ (frequently asked questions)

Georgia Tech's Graphics, Visualization, and Utilization (GVU) WWW User Survey

Interactive advertising agency

IP or ISP (Internet Provider or Internet Service Provider)

ISDN

Modem

Niche

Psychographic research

Primary research

Secondary research

Turnkey

Usenets

Web master

QUESTIONS AND EXERCISES

1. Your boss says in a meeting, "Always keep sights on our customers. They continue to be moving targets." What did she mean by this statement? Translate this remark into an e-mail message to the staff reporting to you.

2. Evaluate and expand upon the statement, "Electronic marketing resources are the means to the end of electronic commerce." Write a one-page memo, with examples illustrating your points, to a basic marketing class explaining this concept.

3. How does the traditional marketing process differ from the electronic marketing process? What elements of the processes are the same and which are different? Write a one-page memo to your boss explaining this concept.

4. In the text discussion, the recommended starting point for a marketing review is the situation analysis. Many marketers deal with their products and companies for years and years. Given this long experience, is it even necessary for the seasoned marketer to pursue the situation analysis, often reaffirming what he already knows, or should he skip this stage to begin with the marketing plan? Be prepared to discuss your thoughts in class.

5. As the three stages of the marketing process are discussed in the text, which step, the situation analysis, the marketing planning, or the marketing implementation efforts, is most

important? Write your response as an e-mail to a colleague who is starting her first marketing management assignment.

6. You are the head strategic analyst for a newly-established division of a hundred-year-old candy company. Many of your brands lead in the categories important to the consumer. For the last six months, you have been gathering market intelligence that will be crucial in launching a new upscale brand in department stores. Much of the information, however, is contradictory, such as the target market's interest in quality chocolate while at the same time dismissing high-priced goods. Which data source should you pay most attention to—industry statistics, company statistics, consumer opinions, or customer survey opinions? Prepare your response as a speech outline that you will be giving to a stockholder meeting.

7. You are the customer satisfaction manager, and you are reviewing customer comments sent to you by e-mail. You know that one in ten prospects purchase your product, which means that nine leave your store without purchasing. Prepare a proposal that would survey those nonbuyers leaving your stores, and project what you would expect to learn from this study.

8. The various influences that shape the competitive environment in which businesses must operate is discussed in the chapter. In your opinion, rank from most important to least important those environmental factors—economic, cultural, legal, political, and demographic trends. Write a memo to your boss explaining why these influences are important and in what order should they be studied.

9. Using the tactic of positioning, many brands have created unique images for themselves. Either watch television commercials, read a popular consumer magazine, or walk through a department store or supermarket to pick out ten examples of successful products or services and their positioning lines. Write a brief paragraph identifying the positioning and explain the benefit or benefits being offered by the brands.

10. As a brand becomes more and more successful, often marketing managers begin to reduce marketing efforts and expenditures. This seems to be sensible in saving valuable monetary resources in the near-term. Considering electronic marketing activities, do you support or reject this line of thinking? Compose an e-mail to the chief financial officer stating your position on the proper strategy and level of marketing expenditures.

Bibliography

Anders, George. 1998. Comparison shopping is the Web's virtue—Unless you're a seller. *The Wall Street Journal,* 23 July, A8.

CommerceNet/Nielsen Internet Demographics Recontact Study. 1996. Executive summary for March/April [Online].

CyberAtlas/Nua Report. 1998. [Online] [cited 13 January 1998].

GVU Ninth User Survey. 1998. [Online]. Atlanta, GA.

Mediamark Research. May 1998. [Online].

MIDS Study. January 1997. [Online] Austin, Tex.

O'Connell, Vanessa. 1998. Soap and diaper makers pitch to masses of Web women. *The Wall Street Journal,* 20 July, B-1.

Peppers, Don, and Martha Rogers. 1993. *The One to One Future.* New York: Currency-Doubleday.

Sellers, Patricia. 1999. Inside the first e-Christmas. *Fortune,* 1 February, 71, 73.

Trout, Jack and Al Ries. 1986. *Marketing Warfare.* New York: McGraw Hill.

———. 1993. *Positioning: The Battle for Your Mind.* New York: Warner Books.

Weber, Thomas E. 1997. Watching the Web. *The Wall Street Journal,* 27 February, B5.

Zachary, Pascal G. 1999. A scientist tracks the world's fires. *The Wall Street Journal,* 8 February, B1.

CHAPTER 3

Marketing Planning Stage for Online Activities

"The Internet was not built with commerce in mind; it was built by scientists for publishing and sharing information. These purposes were not afterthoughts; they were built into the very architecture of the system. Precisely what constitutes 'marketing' in this new environment remains one of the least understood challenges to what a business seeking to use the Internet as a channel for sales. While a definitive answer to this question is unlikely to emerge for some time, it is possible to describe some general strategies that businesses can use to address the issue of how to market on the Internet." (Gonyea and Gonyea 1996, 80–81)

LEARNING OBJECTIVES

- To define the e-marketing mix elements of product, price, promotion, distribution, and measuring performance
- To introduce the methods of market segmentation
- To explain how electronic marketing resources can enhance the traditional marketing activities of effective and efficient marketing planning strategy.

Introduction

Electronic marketing has become synonymous with information, and only good information will do. Today's marketers polish their online research skills by accessing deep and rich information from a variety of public and private sources, skills which were discussed in Chapter 2 as the situation analysis. Research from the situation analysis provides the input on the market conditions, potential competitors, or economic factors that impact decisions concerning the marketer's planning toward goals' feasibility, timing, and ultimately marketing success for the product or service. Creativity puts personality onto the flat landscape of cold analysis, and electronic marketing resources put an edge on the construction of an imaginative marketing mix. Electronic components could include computer-aided prospect selection or customer database familiarity, pricing models that allow forecasting of the effects of situational changes, and distribution software to project optimal delivery routes and workflow practices. One last and important strategic planning aspect is promotions, and new electronic capabilities of the World Wide Web—the accessibility, the appearance, and the usability of Web sites—provide fresh dimensions in interactivity and customer communications for marketers. Web sites offer a previously unavailable combination of graphics, color, motion, sound, and virtual reality environments to support customer interactivity. This novel interactivity, a two-way communication between the marketer and the customer, adds speed and accessibility to e-commerce transactions. By using Web communications and transactions systems, marketing planning will never be the same activity for retail or business-to-business marketers.

Planning with Electronic Ps

In the next two chapters, the last two steps of the marketing process—marketing planning and marketing implementation—will be discussed. Because they are last steps discussed in the marketing process, this does not minimize their importance. Many people think they can take the facts and opinions set forth in the situation analysis and create a fail-safe marketing plan based unfortunately on their own misinterpreted data. They may also think they can make the bridge from marketing planning, the future-oriented program, to the marketing implementation program, the action-oriented stage. In reality, these supposed marketers lack the knowledge and skills necessary to initiate a marketing program because they are overwhelmed with marketing data and become confused as to the next step to take. The logic of the marketing planning and implementation is quite clear. In marketing planning, the marketer draws upon the findings of the situation analysis and constructs future activities according to structuring the marketing Ps. The situation analysis indicates what market segments are being ignored or underserved, and within the marketing planning module, a specific group (or groups) is selected. The promotional aspects of the marketing plan will be explored in detail because many electronic resources match the communications requirements. The implementation activities also tap into the strengths of electronic resources, specifically for customer feedback and opinions as well as prospect profiling and record keeping or for enabling exchange transactions. These terms should be familiar to the marketer. After all, the process of marketing on the Web parallels traditional marketing; as was stated earlier, only the tools change—from traditional to electronic resources. The findings of the situation analysis beget the market niche to be filled, which begets a product need and definition, which in turn leads to manufacturing a brand by fashioning image parameters, and which lastly beget the identity elements. Thus, a new product offering is formed with new image and identity benefits tailored to the perceptions of a new target market segment. If the situation analysis indicates a void among men's shoes, what is the shoe's purpose? Walking, hiking, bowling, dress, work? If it is a hiking boot and you worked for the Timberland company (www.timberland.com), you might want to introduce the shoe under the Timberland brand and give it a rugged outdoors look. That would be the **image** benefits sought. What is the difference between image and identity? The image is what the marketer wants the audience to think and remember about the product—the *what* about the product—and the **identity** is comprised of the tools that carry the image—the *how* the image will be delivered. In the current American Express (www.americanexpress.com) image advertising, the flexibility of use is championed by the positioning line, "Do more." The identity materials that carry this image are television commercials, newspaper and magazine ads, statement stuffers, office signs, and even the design of the credit card itself. The coordination between image and identity is critical since all marketing materials should speak with **one voice.** Attention to detail is a telltale indication to the company's commitment to its marketing program. While implementation might be the most tedious of the marketing processes, timely and carefully executed identity elements speak highly of first class marketing. Therefore, possibly the first aspects to be developed for consumption by the target segment is setting the image of the product or service.

Crafting a Unique Online Image and Identity

What is the essence the marketer's product or service does for his clientele? Many volumes of marketing advice have suggested a successful marketing strategy be based on a simple proposition from which the user will benefit. With an attractive concept and solid product execution, hopefully the offering cannot be easily duplicated by a competitor. Given a perceived or real uniqueness, the marketer can build a niche strategy online that is designed to set the product or service apart from competitors. Establishing a singular benefit, whether it be a great barbecue sauce or outstanding pest control service, sets some companies in an exclusive position. Usually there is a difficult-to-match quality found in the product or service delivered that fuels its desirability. Any product in just about any industry can be positioned to offer special qualities; it takes understanding of the general purchaser's buying motives and an understanding of how the product or service fills the consumer's void. Strong brands have established benefits propositions that through promotions are well known. Take Kentucky Fried Chicken's (often known as KFC) slogan, "We do chicken right" (www.kfc.com); KFC has successfully beat back competitors over the decades. Since 1952, those "eleven different herbs and spices" have created an image mystique, and as the markets have matured, the food itself has been updated to changing consumption patterns. Competition from Church's Chicken, Scott's, and even powerful McDonald's have all taken punches at KFC with less than overwhelming success. The consistent uses of the Colonel and uniform restaurant design are strong identity elements; the menu features familiar and innovative products to please family tastes. Even commodities such as oranges (Sunkist brand, www.sunkist.com) or potatoes (Idaho brand, www.potatoes.org or www.idahopotato.com) have been promoted as superior to a typical orange or potato. Typically, as well, a perceived superior product can command a higher price thus leading to increased profit margins.

Similar strategic planning can be applied to online marketing programs, and the concept of niche marketing melds well with the ability to customize World Wide Web offerings and sites. Electronic marketing considerations start with the product name, of course, and considerable attention should be given to the URL address name so that it is distinctive and readily reminds the user of the product name. What will be your server name, that of your ISP or your own server? What is the proper domain designation? Will you use the prefixes www in your address? Will you choose to hyperlink to other sites, and will you reciprocate? What types of hyperlinks will you

Sunkist Growers (www.sunkist.com) presents a healthy and informative picture of its oranges, lemons, navels, and grapefruit as the fruit dissolves into a photo of light salads, dessert dishes, and refreshing drinks. The links are varied and range from recipes to nutrition to a teacher's corner. News releases such as crop availability and freeze damage can be accessed through a "Special Update" hyperlink.

allow on your pages? Various search engines have varying degrees of visibility; with what types of search engines will you register your Web site address? Will you print-block your Web pages so that the viewer cannot print your page? These considerations add up to an online image, and you should be sure that this image is yours and yours alone.

If the marketer's strategy is to introduce an existing product to the Web, she can prepare an audit of the advantages and disadvantages of the product to compare with the advantages and disadvantages of Web exposure. What has made your brand what it is today, and for what reasons do you have a product following? What attributes does your audience value and why? If you were a customer, why would you buy from you? Which of these benefits do your customers value? Quality as in durability or reliability? Faster and friendlier service? Technicians with high levels of expertise? On-time service? Twenty-four hour convenience? Money-back guarantiees? Twenty-four hour tracking service? Perhaps well trained and caring store personnel? Knowing which of these attributes the marketer's customers value and which of the benefits are considered marginal to unimportant, contributes to a well developed marketing program. Now which of these competencies can you leverage into your online marketing efforts? Accurate product prices on your Web site, quick replies to e-mail inquiries, correct policies posted to frequently asked questions, responsive modem connections, up-to-date product offerings? If the market segment covets these qualities offline, should not the segment be equally receptive to online marketing vehicles?

Building the Marketing Plan

Before becoming distracted with *how* marketing problems will be solved, you the marketer should first direct your attention to the *what* is to be achieved, the objectives of the online marketing effort. No different from traditional marketing, the objectives are usually set as numeric goals, but these numeric targets give no direction as to how these objectives should be attained. Examples of numeric goals could be measures such as a percent of market share, a dollar sales volume, a dollar sales quota per sales representative, a percentage or dollar return on investment or asset, a dollar sales volume per territory, and so forth. From industry to industry these measures might change depending on management expectations, so there is no rule of thumb. However, comparing each measure to another allows for no marketing direction. To solve

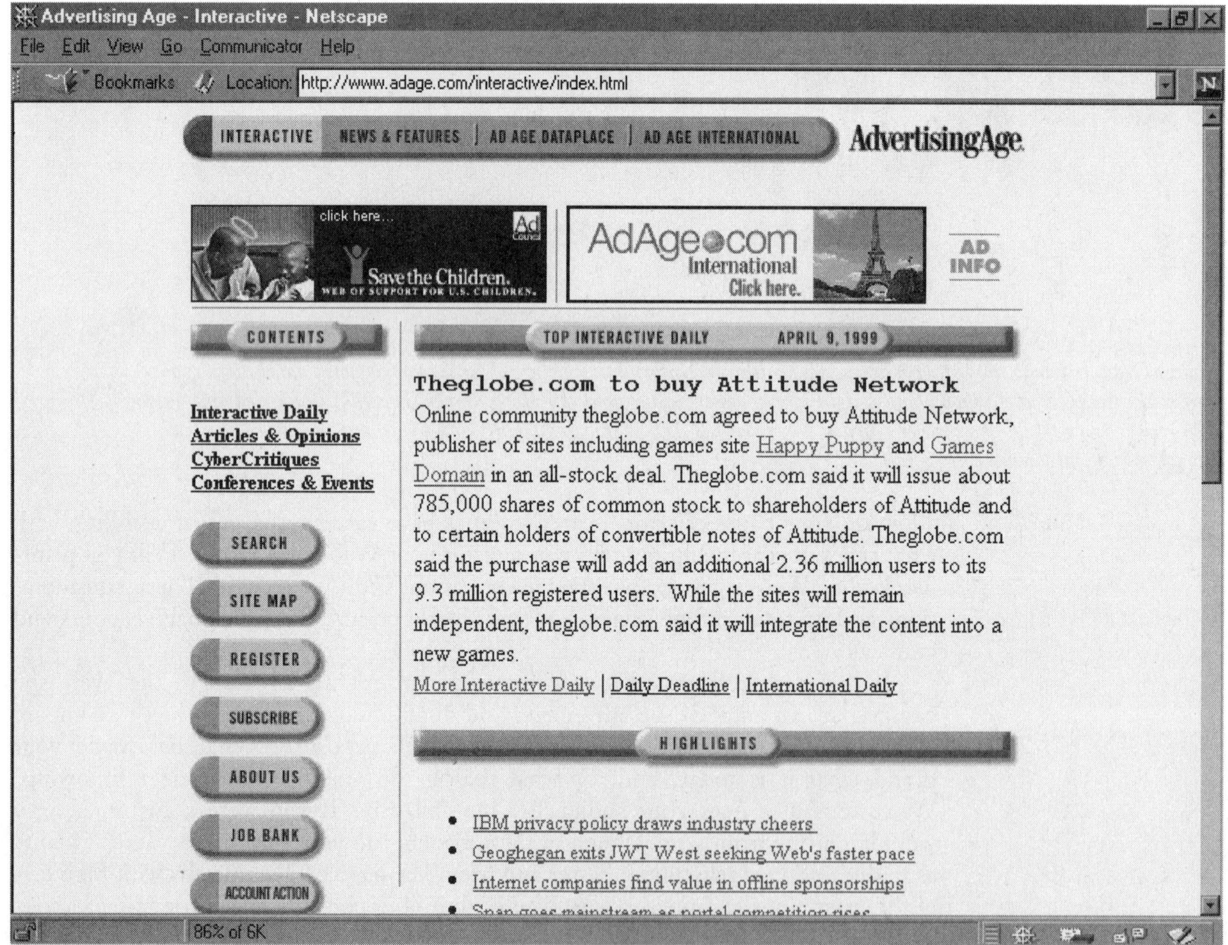

Advertising Age (www.adage.com)
An interactive version of the symbol of the advertising industry, Advertising Age produces daily coverage through this informational Web site. The internal search engine assists in locating marketing subjects and past articles.

this impasse, additional sets of objectives can be established, objectives such as market target descriptions, communications objectives, sales, media, or public relations objectives. The more detailed the planning, the less guessing those that execute the program will have. Further, having established numeric objectives, the marketer will be able to compare the program's performance at year's end. This review will provide input into the next year's planning, answering the questions on whether to expand those activities that worked well or to eliminate the activities that were unproductive.

How do you initially establish goals? There is no clear-cut answer to this. Clever marketers will consult current literature such as *Tire Review* or *Advertising Age* (www.adage.com) magazines, interview fellow staff members, check with industry associations, and even contact competitors to develop realistic program parameters. Marketing programs will differ depending on the stage of the product life (new or mature stages of the life cycles, when promotional efforts are critical in establishing an awareness and position for the new product), the level of competition, the size of the sales territory, the type of product entry (luxury good, shopping item, or convenience purchase), and whether the product is a seasonal good or service; the factors affecting marketing objectives and subsequent performance are numerous, with some impossible to predict within the scope of the marketing plan. Inquiring among the experienced marketers within a company certainly assists in establishing realistic program predictions. Because in marketing, trial and error is a powerful instructor.

Selection of Prospect Groups Is Critical

A thorough investigation of prospect clusters begins now. With the target marketing method, the marketer should evaluate all possible segments within the product's or service's prospect universe. Also important is the manner in which the marketer segments these prospects or customers. Which is most logical for segmenting the market: by geography, by demographics, by psychographics, or by behavioral characteristics? Perhaps the product being marketed is upscale rental apartments; what would be the best way to isolate the various possible segments? Research might help the marketer identify prospect segments such as area residents and newcomers to the area. This is not particularly helpful since area residents already have a home, and newcomers are relocating to the area without a predictable out-of-state origin. Therefore, out-of-state newcomers might form promotionally-inefficient markets of one. Another **segmentation** method alternative might be segmenting by demographic clusters. For any given area, the Census data is reported by age, sex, number of households, ethnicity, and other numeric categories. The number of persons in age groupings such as 18 to 24 years, or 25 to 30 years, with other combinations of age groups, could be overlaid to the occupancy of rental units in a certain area such as one zip code. However, with this strategy, identifying upscale prospects is almost impossible because age and income frequently go hand in hand, yet most older persons would prefer to own their residences rather than rent an apartment. Pursuing an older market, therefore, would produce a smaller, less interested audience.

The marketer can then look to psychographics as a segmentation strategy. Psychographics, the study of lifestyles and self-concepts, could help in identifying the market areas populated by individuals whose own egos are upscale. There could be several lifestyle segments to quantify—young professionals, either singles or couples; young managers or salespeople; middle-aged professionals probably without children; or mature singles or couples who dislike the chores of home maintenance. Each segment has different reasons for choosing rental apartment living, but from a self-concept expectation, these dissimilar groups all desire a comfortable to luxurious apartment home in a rental community that is perceived as elegant and classy. Dividing the market by psychographic clusters may achieve your goal of lifestyle differentiation. Research tools such as geo-demographic and psychographic data analysis will be discussed in Chapter 8. One last method of segmenting market groups is by investigating the behavioral and usage patterns, such as heavy users, moderate users, or light users of the product or service. This approach does not provide an accurate segmentation method because apartment renters can consume only one unit at a time. Therefore, all prospects would fall into one group that is not differentiated. Yet many industries live and die by marketing to behavioristic tendencies such as beer consumption (in a beer company's eyes, heavy drinkers are best) or within the toothpaste business (frequent users, brushing more often than during the morning's hygiene, should be the target market). Picking the correct segmentation approach comes by experience. For this study, psychographic segmentation appears to be the best solution, with promotional appeals directed toward the prospect's ego or pastimes.

From the segmentation of the renter universe, the marketer now must select one or two prime clusters as the primary markets in which promotional efforts, probably online advertising or discussion groups tools, will be directed. At this point, a market profile, delineating the demographic and psychographic characteristics of the market area, is most helpful and illuminating. Is the market comprised of young professionals, middle-aged families, or active retirees? What other cluster groups might you encounter? Does one cluster group dominate in numbers over all other segments? If so, what marketing strategy, probably heavily dependent on advertising and sales promotion, is appropriate for the target segment? The advantages and disadvantages of the online promotional mix will be discussed in Chapter 9. It is well for the marketer to recognize that different market segments react differently to different promotional activities; also, different market segments have different media preferences, so one promotional plan does not fit all. Many of the marketing efforts are quite obvious and common sense, but some differences between market groups are subtle. For instance, all market groups are concerned about security as they select their rental apartments. Generally, the maturity market values covered parking over recreational amenities; the young professional is more interested in a prestige address that offers social activities. Both market groups will pay the same amount for their apartment, but each group has its own motivations as they shop for shelter.

At this point, you will have prepared a market segmentation strategy and will have developed a measure by which to compare the population of each segment. These measures can be drawn from online or offline geo-demographic and psychographic databases for the area. The measure could be the amount of household growth; the percentage of rental apartments as a part of residences; the various income level percentages; the population of various age segments such as the 18 through 34 group, the 35 through 49 group, the over 50 group, or other combinations of age segments; or the population of various occupations groups. The measure of segment size will give some direction as to the target groups of highest potential, and with this ranking method, more portions of the marketing plan will be clearer to you the marketer. Depending on the target segments, decisions on the product offering, the pricing strategy, the promotional mix, and the distribution strategy can be made with more certainty. The better the information, the better the decision.

With a better understanding of the target market, the next step is to develop a benefits analysis, a statement of benefits chosen. It has long been said that people do not buy electric drills; they are really buying holes. That is a good way to establish the corollary between products or services and the derived benefits. A good marketer knows what benefits her customers are purchasing. The basketball enthusiast buys a ticket, not for the paper or printing, but for the entertainment that admission to the arena provides. A person with a toothache does not visit a dentist just to be cordial or chatty; the purpose of the visit is to be relieved of pain. Now, different market segments may have different reasons to purchase the same product, so it is well for the marketer to comprehend the various consumer motivations that move his markets. For example, sunglasses are a popular consumer item. They can be purchased for several reasons: for eye protection, either from the sun or flying objects as someone mows the lawn; for fashion apparel, to be stylish from year to year; or for special purposes such as being shatterproof or being capable of flipping up as a baseball player's sunglasses often are. Likewise, buying a watch could represent different motives: simply to tell time accurately; as a fashion accessory like the Swatch (www.swatch.com) watch fad some years ago; for prestige or self-esteem reasons as Rolex (www.rolexes.com) or Patek Philippe (www.patekphilippe.com) brands; or for special purposes such as a stopwatch for runners or swimmers to time their intervals or as a timer for scuba divers. An objective evaluation should be prepared by the marketer to better understand purchase motives, and the marketer must keep her own subjectiveness from clouding the process. Many marketing failures have resulted in the marketer's insistence on creating products that he liked, regardless of what the marketing research (if any was commissioned) stated. Not everyone likes tuna-flavored potato chips or chocolate styling mousse. Products such as these, however, have made it to the marketplace, but not for long.

From this benefits analysis, the marketer has derived excellent direction to develop the product or service positioning strategy that will be reinforced throughout the e-communications program. From the earlier discussion, positioning strategy establishes the image or highlights the benefits valued by each segment. It is the task of the marketing manager (or the advertiser if no formal marketing function exists) to develop the positioning concept that may consist of a few key words or perhaps a phrase. The marketer devises the essence of the buyer benefits and then turns these precious few words over to the advertising manager or advertising agency to craft a memorable **positioning line,** a creative statement that includes the benefit delivered to the market. These positioning lines should be integrated into all online activities. Most large advertisers hire advertising agencies to handle creative development because of their experience and staff's skills in communications. Some strong and memorable positioning lines have been: "Always Coca-Cola"; Chevrolet trucks' "Like a rock" (www.chevrolet.com); Intel Pentium II's "The computer inside" (www.intel.com); British Airways' "The world's favourite airline" (www.britishairways.com); and United Parcel Service's "Moving at the speed of business" (www.ups.com). The stronger the creative execution, usually the longer the line will survive. While advertising campaigns come and go according to the situation, strong positioning lines should endure, such as "Snap, crackle, pop." Who needs to mention the product's name? Some positioning lines might work even better with the Web's color, motion, or sound. Under the marketer's watchful eye, the positioning line as well as Web and e-mail addresses should be sprinkled on every external and internal document, site, advertisement, publicity release, sign, stationery, and every item big enough to maintain legibility. This continuity of message and identity is a large portion of the implementation stage and, through proper care, leverages the continuing investment in corporate image and identity.

Framing the Ps of the E-Marketing Plan

It seems the situation analysis has left parts lying all over the floor. The marketer's next task is to add order to the process by defining the electronic marketing strategy according to the marketing Ps. The prospect profile has been selected because of some proclivity in matching the customer to a motivation or set of motivations. Demand is expected to be satisfied by creating a product or service, either a primary or substitute good, or enhancing an existing product or service; the marketer must now delineate the characteristics of what the goods or services should be comprised.

Defining the Product or Service

Referring to the strategy of filling an unfulfilled niche of opportunity, there may be several possibilities for the marketer to explore. Certainly consumer research among

E-MARKETING CASE HISTORY: BAYER PHARMACEUTICAL

Information On Demand: Faxback

Bayer Pharmaceutical is one of the world's leaders in pharmaceutical drugs. In particular, Bayer's Flagship product, Cipro, represents almost half its revenue. When Bayer determined that Pfizer's Pharmaceutical was gearing up for the launch of its new anti-infective product, Trovan, Bayer knew it had a problem. According to Sherlyn Celone, Bayer's Manager of Marketing Communications, "we were very worried. Pfizer's new product was about to hit us hard, and we knew we'd have to fight back just as hard." Therefore, Bayer decided to launch a "challenge strategy" whereby it would attempt to counter the direct attempt by Pfizer to steal market share in this important market segment.

As part of the challenge strategy, Bayer recognized that its Clinical Communications Department needed to be able to respond to physician requests for information. Bayer in fact already had a *system* for this in place. The sales force would instruct the medical specialists to call Bayer directly and speak to a product specialist. The product specialist would then give instructions to the support staff. The support staff would then collect the information in hard copy out of filing cabinets, make copies, fax the information to the medical specialist, and finally create a record of the transaction. It quickly became apparent that this method, while fine for many requests, was clearly not sufficient to meet Bayer's need in this instance. Web sites and e-mail were considered but ruled out; even though all the information was considered FDA-approved, a physician signature, electronically transmitted at a minimum, was still required. A FaxBack solution was therefore deemed to be the only alternative, and it had to achieve the following objectives:

- Respond to requests for information within an hour
- Provide an automated processing and response to physician requests
- Provide high volume input (2,200 incoming one-page requests per day)
- Provide high volume output (33,000 outbound faxes per day)
- Reduce administration to a single Bayer member

When a request for proposal (RFP) was issued to companies interested in providing this service on behalf of Bayer, the company was stunned to learn that three months of service would cost about $300,000—about the same as creating a system from scratch. Therefore, after a thorough analysis of available options, Bayer took the decision to use a combination of custom designed forms written in Lotus Notes, plus a bundled shrink-wrapped software solution from two partnering companies, Cardiff Software and RightFAX Corporation. An additional benefit would be that Bayer would own the system upon completion.

Today, this solution allows Bayer, through its toll-free number, to accept incoming fax requests for information from physicians anywhere in the United States, twenty-four hours a day, seven days a week. A special fax form specially designed for Bayer enables a computer to use Optical Mark Recognition technology to decipher the physician's request, including the ability to figure out if the physician signed it. The system creates a customized letter based on the letter and faxes it back to the physician in minutes, of course accompanied by the requisite product information and other literature. According to Ms. Celone, "our FaxBack solution is terrific. It has enabled us to decrease the response time for requests to only a few minutes, and reduced our staff overhead for this task to one."

As it turned out, Bayer's Clinical Communications Department was not the only beneficiary of this marketing solution. It quickly became apparent that there was a gold mine of information at its fingertips. So the system was modified to capture the information from physicians, match it up to other information in Bayer's data banks, and then forward it to Bayer's marketing department, where staff could go to work on this new source of demographic data. And more! Bayer has even begun to recruit this FaxBack to broadcast press releases and other information of vital interest to its medical community, using . . . the data gathered from the original FaxBack endeavor!

the prospect group members is well founded, particularly if there is a concrete product for the group to touch, taste, or otherwise experience. Research findings can take a product or service through several iterations of improvement, and good marketers should always listen carefully to the reactions and opinions of her users. Markets are continually changing, adding and subtracting households each day. Over the period of years, market composition and consumption can turn upside down as beef, fish, and poultry producers have experienced. By assuming nothing and continually listening, the marketer may investigate one or more of these new product ventures. One application for electronic commerce could be to launch a new product or service for sale or for rent or lease. Some of the pioneers of online selling have taken a traditional, probably less than dazzling, consumer product or service, repackaged for convenience, and then produced a strong promotional program to expose (or perhaps overexpose) it to online audiences. Consumer products such as compact discs, videos, books, software, or similar entertainment products sell well because the trial aspect has very little risk since the consumer has long experience with the medium. Success in selling on the Web is still governed by exposure to the correct target market. The Iconocast newsletter makes these observations:

> Like bricks and mortar retailers, e-merchants rely on traffic to create sales opportunities. Media Matrix says that visits to shopping sites rose 55 percent in 1997, commensurate with the growth of the Net population, which must be up 60 percent in the past year. Much the same way that shopping malls changed the face of retailing, the Internet is slowly seeping into the psyche of shoppers worldwide. And it's doing so through pockets of shopping activity. (1998, 1)

Iconocast continues its report with a focus on products and services that were purchased over the Internet from June of 1997 to June of 1998.

Top Items Purchased Online in the Past Twelve Months

Item	Millions/Purchasers	Percent
Software	25.8	38.9
Books	10.0	19.4
Computers	10.0	15.1
Travel	7.5	11.2
Music	6.7	10.2
Food/Gifts	6.4	9.7
Clothing	6.1	9.2
Investments	4.2	6.3
Consumer electronics	3.0	4.5
Auto/Accessories	2.3	3.5

SOURCE: Iconocast newsletter, June 1998. Consensus of estimate of seven research studies conducted in 1997; buyer universe estimated is based on a current U.S. Internet user population of 66.3 million.

What are some of the categories that are being sold on the Web? In general, guidelines for products and services of interest revolve around the qualities of better, faster, more convenient, or more unique. First, consider what has met with success in the traditional channels of direct marketing; what has made the company successful? Next, ask yourself if this success can be transferred to online tools or activities. Then blend in one or more of the qualities previously mentioned. Your most significant reward is for the customer or prospect to bookmark the enterprise's Web address. Can the marketer achieve these processes and promises?

- Offer an outstanding variety of a single product with the tactic of narrow focus and deep selection as the Web proposition. That is the strategy of the housewares store, Lechters (www.lechters.com), with particular attention to kitchen and bath items.

- Offer a product that will last longer or feature a better warranty. Sears' Craftsman tools have long been recognized for their lifetime guarantee; these tools as well as other retail items can be found at www.sears.com. The Sears' site is also presented in Spanish.
- Add convenience to the company's distribution channels. That is why the cap store, Lids, is reachable on the Web (www.lids.com), by toll-free telephone (1-800-LIDS-INC), or by e-mail (info@lids.com). This company also offers a narrow product selection (caps) but features caps of all manners of colleges, professional sports teams, and special interest items.
- Offer more expertise (remember narrow focus and deeper knowledge), and demonstrate this commitment on the Web pages. Take the folksy Vermont Sign School at Stowe site (www.signschool.com) that sticks to its knitting, instruction, education, and consulting on creating carved and routed dimensional signs. The proprietor Jay Cooke has established a school, a bulletin board, an information repository, and a gallery dedicated to art in wooden signs; the school crest reads, "Skill, Pride, Profitable Business." The school demonstrates its instructional success by displaying students' work on the Gallery page.
- Faster service to customers or prospects should be obvious. Answer e-mails within twenty-four hours and return telephone calls the same day. While a pledge to customer service sounds nice, customer service action speaks louder than a promise. In some businesses, the president or owner of the enterprise asks for all customer contact records or replies at the end of the day. Taking the time to review customer service correspondence demonstrates to customers and employees alike that customer communications are important in the eyes of management. For two hours each day, Andy Grove, ex-CEO of Intel, answered his e-mail from employees, customers, and friends at each day's end, and he felt this effort kept him in touch with the tides of the company. (Grove 1996, 156)
- Display the awards, certifications, or industry affiliations the company has earned. These blessings contribute to the credibility the company must build to be a partner in online commerce. An example of credentials disclosure is on the Web site of Product Safety Engineering, Inc. (www.pseinc.com), which includes the Underwriters Laboratory seal as a certified agency.
- If the site is consumer-oriented, incorporate a guest book of site visitors' names and telephone numbers, or publish letters of praise on various aspects of the consumer purchase experience. These testimonial letters might speak of the excellent product performance, the convenience of ordering, the speed of delivery, or whatever aspects the customer deems extraordinary. Retailers and manufacturers might also use this customer recognition tactic if buyers do acknowledge their performance. Telephone numbers are helpful for further contact, which can be risky since the contact is not moderated. Perhaps your customers are so enthusiastic and satisfied that you can create a discussion group about your products or services. Customer participation in a news group can be the ultimate compliment.

Specific categories can include new or existing products or services; an experienced marketer's imagination can add many more. To focus attention, an entrepreneur can peruse the yellow pages in the telephone directory to review various business categories. After looking at the categories of interest, the marketer can compare the above business attributes with the product or service concept. Consider these topics for commerce; remember, the more specialized or unique, the better.

- Advertising-direct marketing
- Amusement places
- Animal hospitals
- Aquariums and supplies
- Astrologers
- Autograph collections
- Balloons—advertising
- Bed and breakfast lodgings
- Beer home brewing equipment
- Billiard equipment
- Books—new, used, antique
- Bowling supplies
- Business consultants
- Career counseling
- Cigar/tobacco and supplies
- Coffee specialties and supplies
- Collectibles of all kinds
- Comic books
- Compact discs
- Computer consultants
- Dancing Schools—adults and children
- Desktop publishing equipment
- Diamonds—retail/wholesale
- Diving supplies and equipment
- Doughnuts
- Drug abuse services
- Educational consultants and services
- Employment agencies and services
- Engineering services
- Environmental services
- Equipment for disabled persons
- Executive search services
- Exercise equipment
- Financial advisory services
- Fire alarm and security systems
- Fishing guides and parties
- Flags and banners
- Florists and floral supplies
- Formal wear
- Gold and silver dealers
- Golf equipment
- Gourmet shop
- Graphic designers
- Guitars
- Gymnastics instruction
- Handwriting experts
- Hats
- Health care services
- Health clubs
- Hot tubs
- Hotels and motels
- Ice cream shops
- Insurance
- Interior design and decorators
- Internet consultants and services
- Jewelers—retail and wholesale
- Laboratories
- Leather goods and supplies
- Limousine services
- Mailing lists—e-mail or postal
- Maps
- Marketing consultants
- Mortgage service
- Motion picture equipment
- Museums
- Needlework
- Newspapers or news services
- Night clubs
- Nursing services
- Office furniture or furnishings
- Optical services
- Party planning
- Pharmaceutical supplies
- Photo supplies
- Playground equipment
- Popcorn and popcorn supplies
- Psychics
- Quilting instruction and supplies
- Recording studio equipment
- Recreational vehicles

- Recycling service
- Religious goods
- Research consultants
- Rubber and plastic stamps
- Saddles
- Satellite systems and equipment
- Security systems—computers
- Sound systems and equipment
- Sports cards and memorabilia
- Stereo and hi-fi equipment
- Stocks and bond brokers
- Tax return service
- Telemarketing service
- Ticket sales and events
- Trademark consultants
- Translators and interpreters
- Trucking transportation brokers
- Uniforms
- Vending machines—retail
- Video equipment
- Video games—retail
- Video production
- Vintage clothing
- Vitamin and food supplements
- Watches—retail
- Water skiing equipment and supplies
- Wedding and party services
- Weight control services
- Wigs and hairpieces
- Wine-making equipment and supplies

Again the more specific, harder-to-find products sell well on the Web. Retail sales are easier to consummate since manufacturer or wholesaler transactions are usually negotiated for larger amounts, quantities inappropriate to most individual consumers. The marketer also knows the majority of Web exchanges are for discretionary purchases, so the product selection and promotional presentation are geared to wants, some perhaps whimsical such as collectibles of Beanie Babies or football trading cards, unusual sunglasses or sandals, or vintage jukeboxes. This might require the site to be able to handle large amounts of information in many different classifications such as the eBay auction site (www.ebay.com), growing from a site searching for Pez dispensers to now offering 1.4 million items at auction daily in over a thousand classifications. Further, the Web's capability for searching makes the unique and one-of-a-kind easier to find, as eBay has proven. Items have a much greater audience and a better marketability through online exposure. Perhaps a customer is interested in finding a color, eight-by-ten, autographed photograph of Ted Williams from his 1959 baseball season; she could access an autograph collectors' site such as Joe Wasson's Autograph Auction (www.autografs.com) to check current autograph availabilities. Perhaps an enthusiast, to satisfy an interest in Native American pottery by Fannie Nampeyo, could find a Hopi wedding vase by Ms. Nampeyo at the site address www.indart.com, complete with descriptions and photographs.

Now is the time for the marketer to consider how well the Web as a delivery vehicle fits to the product's or service's logistics. Obviously, information services such as software, income tax preparation, legal advice, and library search services are well suited for online delivery. But what about tangible products with weight and dimensions? As a general rule, tangible products should be contained within compact packaging (square is best) and be handled in one hand. Since convenience is highly regarded among consumers, the marketer should also offer overnight or two-day delivery that further encourages smaller, compact packaging. Shipping perishable or fragile items is not a good idea because the marketer cannot guarantee the condition of the goods received. More likely the consumer will be disappointed if the New York cheesecake has been turned upside down. Also, to reduce aggravation, the product should arrive with as few installation steps as possible. Telephone call centers may be necessary to staff, but telephone explanations are many times harder to follow and,

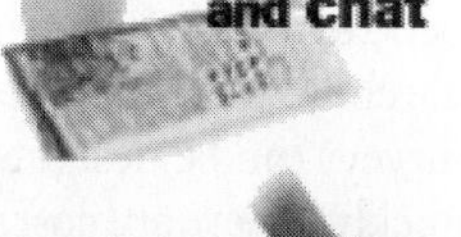

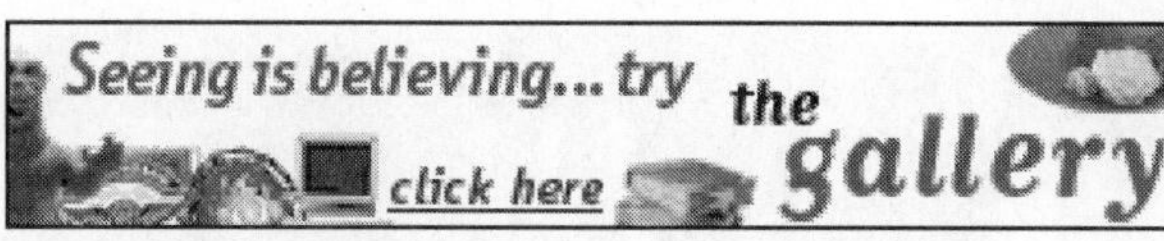

eBay (www.ebay.com)
The premier auction site on the Web. Enthusiasts can buy, sell, trade, or just browse over 2 million items in over 1,600 categories.

therefore, can be frustrating. The marketer, therefore, should keep installation as simple as possible. One last point on product appropriateness needs to be made: Online exposure is applicable for private or for-profit companies, and it is equally acceptable (and probably more cost efficient) for use by nonprofit organizations. The mission of many charitable groups is to disseminate information about their cause, and an online presence is an excellent vehicle to support other means of communication.

Information services are popular; some equally mundane dispatches are soaps and scopes, as in soap opera summaries or horoscopes, and these services probably have benefited the market's experimentation with 900 audiotext numbers. Information such as counseling and other authoritative advice can be easily and widely distributed along the Internet. Probably the most awkward Internet aspect of information for sale is language translations, although the lingua franca is English; at present 80 percent of Web sites are in English. (Wysocki) There is a possibility commercial Web sites may gravitate toward totally visual, rather than heavily textual. The following international advertising sites are examples in which the communications method relies on visual persuasion and intuitive site navigation: Levi's (www.levis.com), Nike (www.nike.com), and Joe Boxer (www.joeboxer.com). Another form of commercial Internet traffic is that of research; market researchers are quickly recognizing the interactive usability of the Internet as a research tool. Surveys can be designed, administered, and tabulated among diverse or like samples very quickly. There are cost savings associated with online research because printed surveys, envelopes, and postage are eliminated. Using listservs or discussion groups, population samples are easier to generate. Of course, the researcher must be careful to contain his samples to the appropriate universe because more than 75 percent of households are not online. A famous blunder in opinion surveying was that of the *Literary Digest*, which polled individuals by telephone and subsequently declared Alfred Landon would beat Franklin Roosevelt in the 1936 presidential election. The sampling methodology, that of interviewing households with telephones, was ill-conceived since affluent households with telephones were in the minority, many times leaning toward Republican candidates. Needless to say, many

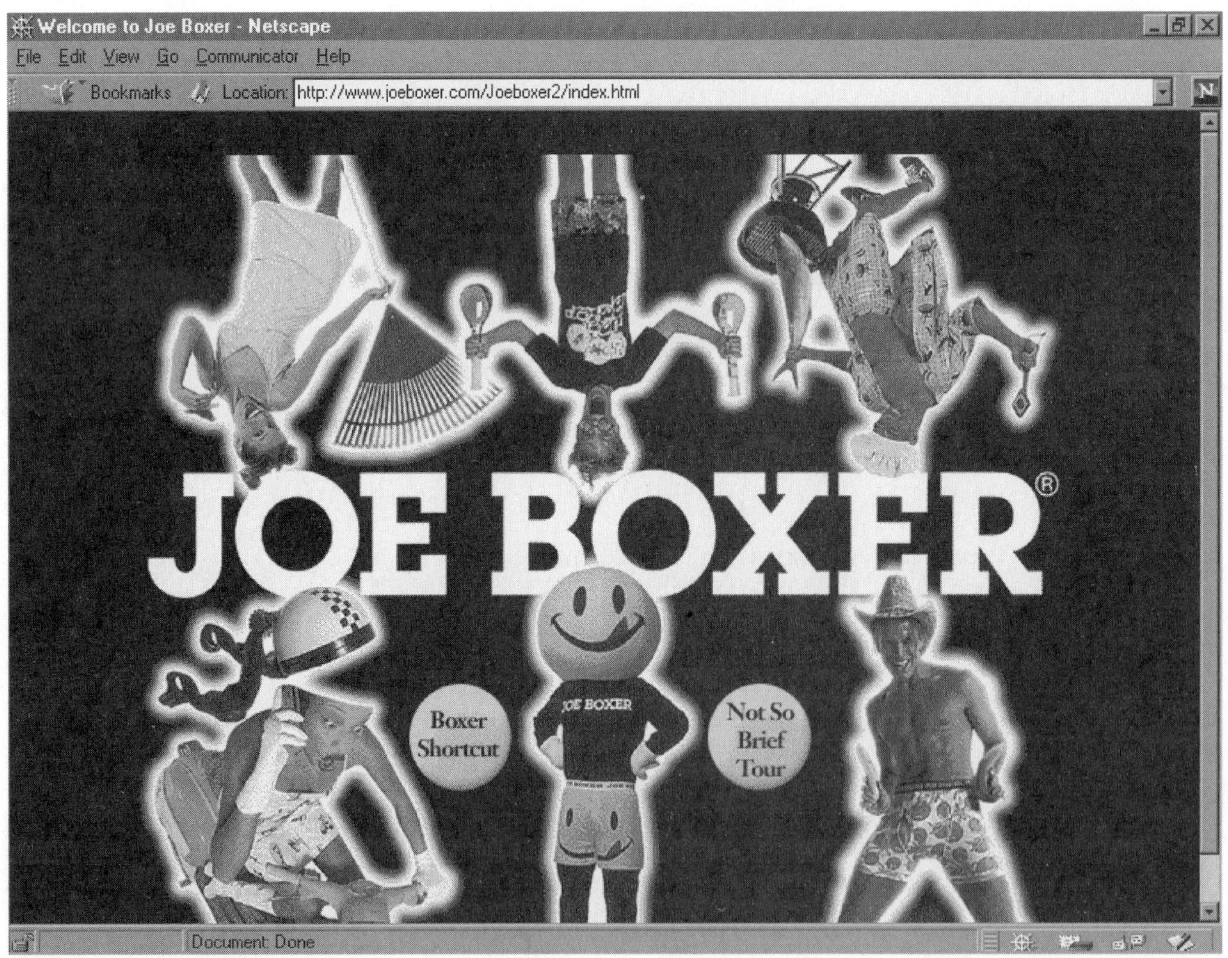

Joe Boxer (www.joeboxer.com)
Attitudes at Joe Boxer are anything but stuffy. Their imaginative products are demonstrated by males, females, and even a cowboy. If you click on the home page, you can try on Joe Boxer's Virtual Underwear Processor.

Democrats without phones voted Roosevelt into office. The *Literary Digest* subsequently folded in humiliation.

More than likely, marketers will employ the Internet to announce new enterprises as part of the promotional plan. One reason is the lower cost of media introductions compared to traditional media, and many entrepreneurs often work on shoestring budgets. As will be discussed in Chapter 9, simple Web site design can be produced for less than $1,500. Measured against traditional media such as television, newspapers, or magazines, the cost of traditional media is much greater, and most Web sites are operating twenty-four hours each day, every day of the year. Compare the costs of a thirty-second local news television commercial, which runs once and only for a fleeting half minute, or a full-page, black-and-white local newspaper ad, which generally is tossed out the next day, to the costs of an Internet site, and the maintenance cost of an Internet site appears inexpensive. Web exposure rivals that of television with color, motion, sound, and channel selection. A Web presence bests conventional television because of the interactive capability of dialog between the viewer and the marketer. On closer examination, however, there are additional costs the Web marketer must sustain. The advertiser will need to register the site address with appropriate search engines and may have to consider advertising banners, sponsoring discussion groups, or participating in conferences, all at additional charges.

A second reason online media may be selected over traditional media campaigns is that the product or service may be electronic in nature and, therefore, be attractive to the technological crowd. Using discussion groups, new product or service announcement sites, or Usenets, can create a buzz within narrow interest market groups and can result in a positive, word-of-mouth information source that is passed along from group to group. Internet messages are easily forwarded to new addresses as are Web sites bookmarked for future reference. The culture of the Internet supports sharing of information, and news of entertaining sites spread quickly among faithful Net users.

Another likely scenario in distribution channel selection is that of availing an existing product or service to an online presence, thus producing another distribution method and advertising vehicle to tap into the online audience. This form of product or service promotion may hold unexpected promise because many of the Internet users have abandoned traditional news media, turning instead to round-the-clock news sites such as CNN (www.cnn.com), NBC Nightly News (www.nbc.com), or sports on the Fox Channel (www.foxsports.com). Viewers can select the news topic of their choice, when they wish to access the information (more or less frequently than a 6 P.M. or 11 P.M. time slot), and where they want to access the site (at the office or at home), and viewers can frequently download the file for future reference in an asynchronous fashion. Consumer marketing thought is moving toward the consumers' terms. This program power appeals greatly to many independent-minded, technological-viewers. Web usage as a news media vehicle is just underway, and user media habits are yet to be defined. For the immediate future, the wise marketing manager will continue to engage in traditional and new media as methods of contacting customers or prospects. As track records are established on the desirability or performance of various media mixes, more effective and more efficient communications programs will result.

In this strategy of online exposure for established, existing products, more purchasers will be more familiar with Web addresses to the point of suspicion for those advertisers who do not feature a Web address. Much like an advertiser that twenty years ago did not provide a toll-free telephone number, the consumer has come to expect the manufacturer or retailer to shoulder the burden for communications. If a customer constituency wishes to communicate with a marketing function, the marketer should make every effort to create easy-to-use, cost-free message systems for the consumer to access and use. Certainly e-mail fits these criteria, being low cost to the company and accessible twenty-four hours each day. The system can be automated to respond with a fax-back reply, or the sender can check for her information reading the FAQs that apply to the question. Marketers should encourage customer contact to the point of being flattered by the consumer's communication. If the consumer is contacting the marketer's call center, the consumer is not contacting the competition.

Allied to customer communications is the ability of a company to perform better and faster customer service. Some years ago there was a cry that the customer is king (or queen, as appropriate), and with this new level of buyer interaction, the customer can be treated royally. Face it, not every transaction or service experience is performed perfectly, even with the greatest of effort and intention. Online communication allows a fast response and a genuine apology to those customer service snafus that should be righted. Companies can increase the speed of delivery of technical support that has created a black eye in the computer industry. Horror stories abound about the amount of time and the cost of the long-distance call, usually across the nation, that computer purchasers were forced to incur. Truly customer-oriented companies will mandate that customer communications should take priority over all communications company-wide. Purchasers are educated to read the packaging labels for nutritional content, then for company contact addresses, and lastly for price information. Marketers must decide what paradigm suits their company vision: higher information value and higher margins versus lower information value and lower margins. As never before, price and value go hand in hand.

Pricing Knowledge Will Become Universal

Price levels are rather vexing since most consumers are happy to shop online but hesitant to purchase online using their credit cards. They would rather purchase offline for safety's sake. The practice of electronic commerce may require the retailer to rethink traditional pricing models because the consumer will have perfect knowledge of the marketer's price structure. No longer will the seller have the upper hand in the mysteries of price setting. No longer will management agonize over the advantages of price skimming for new products versus penetration pricing to gain market share. Pricing strategies should become simpler for the retailer to set and for the consumer to decipher. At issue are savvy consumers armed with up-to-the-minute price information, most at suggested manufacturers' retail price, and thus Web pricing creates a more level playing field when dealing with retailers or manufacturers. Over time, the Internet may turn out to be more of a price equalizer than a price cutter. To economic theorists, perfect market knowledge tends to make prices converge. *The Wall Street Journal* observed:

> The story of the Internet's role in pricing goods and services is just beginning to unfold. More than a new way to take orders or delivery, the Internet is emerging as a paradise for comparison shoppers. The past couple of years have brought a slew of Web sites and online services that put more information about prices into the hands of buyers. With vastly better data on prices of golf clubs, airline tickets, and cars, consumers are cutting better deals. (Wysocki)

Knowledgeable consumers are arriving at auto dealerships with complete manufacturers' costs every day, and it is estimated that 30 percent of all traffic has downloaded the bottom line information, thanks to pages such as "Make Your Own" pricing information by Chevrolet. Salesperson posturing and sales manager price haggling may be ancient history in the future. One site, Auto by Tel (www.autobytel.com), will provide the consumer with manufacturers' prices, then contact some of the 3,000 competitive dealers (by region) to inquire about the availability of the automobile, and furnish the prospective buyer with the quotations. The site features inventories of new and used cars; the information is available nationwide by clicking on a new versus used button and then entering the make and the model of the car you are interested in and your zip code. The regional dealers pay a commission to the company. The prospect can apply online for financing or leasing or insurance dealing directly with the finance company. As credibility statements, Auto by Tel promises a 100 percent, seventy-two-hour, money-back guarantee on its certified used cars and displays a small vignette of a couple from Pasadena, California with the following testimony: "Great experience. No hassle. The easy, only way to go." Auto by Tel positions itself as having "better deals—better dealers."

There is an alternative strategy for protecting quality and profit margins against cutthroat pricing. Online shoppers value two deliverables that e-marketers can protect: 1) quality-related information about the product or service and 2) differentiating brands within a category. Online shopping can produce less price sensitivity at a brand level and more sensitivity to search attributes associated with quality than does traditional shopping. A study in the *Journal of Marketing* concluded:

> This is a critical point for manufacturers that offer differentiated merchandise with superior points attributes. Similarly, retailers that carry unique merchandise and/or provide superior information about merchandise could face less rather than more price competition. Perhaps this is why vendors cooperating with multiple-category search agents such as Fido the Shopping Doggie (www.shopfido.com/Vendors.html) are predominantly manufacturers and retailers selling highly unique merchandise such as arts and crafts, alternative music, hot sauces and spices, and gourmet foods and wines. Conversely, manufacturer of the "me-too" brands competing on cost can expect more intense price competition with the infusion of interactive home shopping (IHS), and retailers carrying nationally branded merchandise with limited service also will face increased price competition. Therefore, the introduction of the IHS channel will intensify the competitive environment, but this need not shift the emphasis from quality to price. By providing more information to customers with minimal search cost, manufacturers and retailers with differentiated offerings will have a greater opportunity to educate consumers about the benefits they offer, and consumers will find it easier to access and compare the offerings of firms competing on price. (Alba et. al. 1997)

This portion of the Ps strategy is potentially the most recast of all the marketing functions. Logistics is the universal thread or pipeline that plans and coordinates the delivery of products or services to customers all over the world. Many of the logistics activities include: strategic planning, transportation, purchasing, warehousing, materials handling, inventory control, and forecasting. Logistics is involved every time a product is purchased, whether it is food, medicine, or clothing. It does not matter how the customer shops—at a store, by mail order, through direct sales, or via the Internet—the customer is being served by the logistical interactions of several companies. From a marketing viewpoint, logistics facilitates market exchanges, provides a major source of employment, and is a major purchaser of assets and materials. (Council on Logistics Management 1998) Logistics, also called distribution, the *place* element of the marketing Ps, has become an offense weapon more so than its past role of mere fulfillment. Direct contact with the customer has opened many new opportunities for distribution and sales channels. The World Wide Web is the first mass targeted communications, mass distribution, and mass consumption vehicle that can be monitored by the purchaser at all times. This ability for keeping close to the consumer is due to online resources that will continue to mature with e-commerce. While distribution has always played a strategic and tactical role in the marketing process, the distribution function

Note: Fido hasn't been maintained for over two years. We only keep it around for demo purposes. Feel free to play with it, but don't expect much. If you want some shopping links, try the shopping topic at *Links* 2 Go .

FIDO: the Shopping Doggie!

by Continuum Software, Inc.

Featured vendors:

Spice Merchant	Chinese, Thai, Indonesian, Indian, and Japanese spices, teas, noodles, rice, flours, grains, cookware, cookbooks, servingware, etc.	Fido doesn't know about any 'sake sets,' but why not search for some 'saki sets.'
Lands' End	Clothing galore.	Get some sports shorts for the summer.
Radar City	Discount home electronics.	A new boom box would be perfect for the beach.

To use Fido, just enter a brief product description in the form below, and press the *Submit* button.

Product description :

With price between: 0.00 *and* 100000.00

Submit | Clear Product Description

☒ My browser supports tables. ☒ Match parts of words. ☒ Strip suffixes. ☒ Terse results.

New Feature (Under Construction):

Try browsing Fido's products by category (10307 out of 151964 products are currently classified).

- 900 Lines (2)
- Arts And Crafts (151)
- Business Resources (20)
- Clothing (234)
- Collectibles (207)
- Computers (1479)
- Educational Items (9)
- Hardware And Tools (9)
- Health And Beauty (195)
- Housewares (25)
- Infant Care (2)
- Jewelry (81)
- Music (21)
- New Age (83)

Fido: The Shopping Doggie (www.shopfido.com)
This shopping site encourages the viewer to input product descriptions and a range of price. If the product is available on the Web, Fido will retrieve the information.

now requires more attention and a different perspective. In deploying electronic tools, the marketer should break the logistics function into smaller, more manageable steps.

Consider the distribution function as an input and an output system in which customer communications is the initial input (or order) that leads to an output (product or service delivery) with continual customer contact to start the process over again. How do online tools improve the distribution cycle? The thread of speed, accuracy, and efficiency runs through the logistics strategy, from package delivery to hamburger sales to retail clothing stock reorder. The key to any distribution plan is to remove bottlenecks, either internal or external in nature, from information registration to finished, delivered product. In fact, an excellent distribution program will anticipate bottlenecks or broken links before production ever starts. Companies such as FedEx or United Parcel Service have created an industry in the improvement of distribution methods, with UPS originally providing ground transportation and FedEx, the skies. Both companies' efforts have enabled marketers to expand the geography of the enterprise, and expansion in turn has satisfied new customers' wants and needs. This expansion has also fueled economic growth of many regions of the United States Simple pleasures such as Ben & Jerry's ice cream (www.benjerry.com) might have been limited to a small radius of its Waterbury, Vermont production facility had a distribution infrastructure to serve all fifty states not been created for this perishable product within the last twenty years. Similarly, the prospects of the Limited were broadened as the company purchased its own Boeing 747, which is dedicated to flying clothing reorders from the Far East factories to the Limited's distribution centers in Columbus, Ohio. An immense effort was undertaken by the Limited to capture popular fashion trends by eliminating the proverbial slow boat from China. National retailers who best knew how to track sales movements have tackled the problem of inventory levels versus sales. Wal-Mart (www.wal-mart.com), for example, monitors daily sales by product categories through interconnection of optical scanners at the checkout point with transmission via rooftop dishes transmitting information to its satellite reporting system. Wal-Mart inventory and buyer personnel can read the merchandise movement to know what to buy or what to reorder or ship to the stores from regional warehouses. Fast food purveyors like Burger King (www.burgerking.com) are also using electronic sales tracking of its 9,500 restaurants worldwide, replenishing its ingredients from the sales of 4.6 million Whopper sandwiches each day. As a point in passing, Burger King has changed its counter distribution system to accommodate the motorist. Burger King reports that 60 percent of its sales are derived from drive-through traffic; just think about the lost revenues should the restaurant management have fought consumer preference to buy through the drive-through. Another online company, Travelocity (www.travelocity.com), has established itself as the premier virtual travel source as its distribution plan bypasses the traditional travel agency. The site dispenses information on four-hundred domestic and international airlines through search engines that hunt for customer parameters of lowest fare, or airline choice, or convenient departure and arrival times. The traveler enters his selection, and the preferences are listed, such as low fare rates, in ascending order. Travelocity can assist with rental car or hotel reservations, as well; weather information on the destination is also presented. Needless to say, travel agents dislike this direct distribution opportunity, but the travel consumer works in his best interest, becoming actively involved in the information retrieval and decision making. These are examples of logistics creativity that count as much as advertising creativity, operations innovations, or customer service breakthroughs. Definitely the pressing (or oppressive) force in distribution is time, but not a breakneck rush to minimize the minutes, hours, or days, but a controlled crash that follows a preordained plan of what the steps should be. Charting the distribution activities is one more process that the marketer coordinates with the operations or production managers. Foresight saves time and effort in the controlled crash of getting products to market. What are the distribution tools that the marketer must manage and the consumer can easily access? Here is where the World Wide Web shines. From the promotional materials that showcase the product or service of interest, the consumer places an order, either online or offline, and the Web site can be set to acknowledge the order and predict a delivery date. This procedure saves the problem of postal delay; by electronic transmission, the order is entered into the production schedule. Depending on whether the order fulfillment is short, such as mailing or shipping overnight delivery, or longer, such as the days necessary to contact a wholesaler, manufacturer, or perhaps publisher, the time schedule can be determined and reported to the customer. FedEx's tracking system assigns a tracking number, and using proprietary software, the customer can learn just where the package or shipment is located. These confirmations are important because the software reports produce a tangible representation of an elusive service. The Web, through its communications capability, adds an accuracy dimension previously unreliable. This is a valuable business quality for the customer and for the shipping agent. Again, the level playing field metaphor arises with equal information held by both parties. The consumer can be an even greater participant in online shopping. According to the logistics council:

> Consumers perform a major portion of the distribution function when purchasing from stores. They transport merchandise from stores to their homes and bring unsatisfactory merchandise back to the store. In an interactive home shopping system, these substantial costs of home delivery and returns will be fully borne by the seller and must be factored into the price. Because these costs are substantial, IHS players that can select and package multiple items for delivery to individual households will have a competitive advantage over IHS competitors that lack such skills. The importance of this advantage naturally is greater when the preparation for shipping constitutes a large fraction of the overall price of the product. (Council on Logistics Management 1998)

The logistics program employs communications aspects of the Web to disseminate marketing information, placement and receipt of the order, update the production schedule, and choose the most efficient shipper of the goods to the customer. If the goods are computer software or textual or graphical information, the transaction can be completed almost instantly.

Online tools also create interactive resources for the existing sales staff, particularly to support field sales representatives. Growing in popularity is the fax-back system in which a salesperson queries her company's repository for, say, information on the availability of a certain product in stock (usually designated by its stock keeping unit number or SKU). The request is faxed to a central database, and the data is faxed back to the inquiry party. Again, speed in response is the tactical weapon for the salesperson. Often an answer can be supplied to the sales representative while he sits in the client's office. E-mail is also used for communications with the home office or the MIS or inventory departments, but this contact requires a designated e-mail receiver to be on duty and alert. Dialing into the company's inventory page on their Web site is another option; however, the information on inventory must constantly be updated as products move in and out of the company's stock.

A Targeted Promotional Strategy

With many marketing decisions now in place, such as the intended prospect group, the components mix of the product or service, the pricing strategy, and the distribution plan, the marketer can turn his attention to the online promotion strategy. The promotion mix selections include advertising, sales promotion, public relations, direct marketing, and personal selling, each of which have strengths and weaknesses, advantages and disadvantages. Online media does offer a tremendous advantage of selectivity over the traditional mass vehicles of advertising, sales promotion, and public relations, and the Web is powerful both in delivering messages to large audiences via browser and banner advertising or in delivering messages to esoteric, low profile listservs. Online media fits best into the direct marketing category—in the future, direct marketing may be renamed interactive marketing to highlight the dialogue potential—since many of the consumer or business transactions are carried out as direct sales, largely eliminating the retailer or wholesaler. As a matter of course, direct marketing entails direct relationships with customers, thus making unnecessary mass advertising or extensive sales promotions. Electronic exposure contributions include Web presence, e-mail, listservs, electronic bulletin boards, sponsorship of discussion groups, Usenets, FAQs, and .sig files. Each of these resources has specific uses and advantages and disadvantages. Knowing in what situations to use each is important to the marketer; also knowing how to complement traditional media such as print (newspapers and magazines), broadcast (television and radio), or even support media (signage, specialty advertising, or product placement) is vital to an integrated marketing communications program. This textbook is focused on the online capabilities of electronic marketing resources, and full explanations of electronic promotional strategies will be presented in Chapter 9.

Formulating the Marketing Budget

One last planning activity is to prepare a master marketing budget and rationale for the proposed activities. Too often little attention is paid to the budgeting process with omissions popping up throughout the marketing path. The budget development should not be a casual undertaking, sometimes delegated to junior marketing members. In competent, precise corporations, the approved budget will serve the marketing function for a full year. Thus, corporations, like individuals, cannot operate beyond their means. The budget for online marketing is a component of the comprehensive marketing program, and marketers should be held accountable to perform the marketing effort within the approved allowance. To accompany the marketing budget, a solid rationale should be prepared to explain where the money is to be spent. This rationale exercise assists the marketer (and probably her superior) in anticipating the myriad of activities to be faced and in establishing criteria that the marketing program is to achieve. Frequently, lofty expectations are voiced only to be dashed by insufficient funds. Foresight in detailed planning can avoid being blindsided by budget problems.

The best method of budgeting, regardless of online or traditional programs, is the **objective and task method** in which the marketer delineates the marketing tasks for the period and then calculates a cost for each task. This process assumes all programs will be carefully scrutinized as to cost efficiency, and those programs that are productive will be carried over to the next budget period, while new program objectives are set. This objective and task discipline is also called **zero-based budgeting** since all programs begin anew with a zero budget. This is much more difficult and time-consuming since all pieces of the puzzle are carefully inspected; the easier method would be to take last year's budget and add an arbitrary 10 percent. This is an unjustified, wasteful use of company resources, however. The marketer should substantiate all phases of the marketing function to demonstrate his control of and expectations for the marketing effort. The marketing plan will be executed in phases, and these phases comprise the actions stage of the marketing process. The actions, or marketing implementation, should also be carefully delineated so that the appropriate marketing staff members understand what actions are her responsibilities. Remember, nothing happens until actions are put before the target audience. The most elegant marketing plan is merely a collection of ideas; marketing implementation puts the rubber to the road. Thus, things begin to happen.

Summary

Formulated from the facts, attitudes, and opinions of the situation analysis, marketing planning is founded on the prospect segment or segments that the marketer finds underserved or neglected. This market segment is designated as the target group, and the planning process is initiated using the traditional paradigm of the marketing Ps. With an eye to the targeted segment, the marketer begins the design of a product or service that satisfies the market void, structures a pricing strategy, develops the appropriate distribution system, and oversees the creation of traditional and electronic promotional programs. Apart from the traditional marketing program, the strengths of the electronic marketing program are the speed, accuracy, and the interactive capabilities that help to create a long-term marketing relationship with the customer or prospect. This level of intimacy that the marketer can achieve with electronic marketing tools can grow and produce a mutually beneficial relationship.

Key Terms

Branding

Identity

Image

Objective and task method

One voice

Positioning line

Segmentation

Zero-based budgeting

QUESTIONS AND EXERCISES

1. Bill Gates has said, "Everyone will have access to most of the world's information." From a marketer's point of view, is this a positive or negative occurrence? Or does it depend on the situation? Justify your answer in a three-paragraph statement to your company's CEO.

2. What is the difference among branding, image, identity, and positioning as a marketer creates a perception for a new business-to-business product or service? Which tactic is the most important in setting a public perception for the new product? Write a one-page strategy statement reporting your division's new product plans for your company's annual report.

3. The coordination between image and identity is critical since all marketing materials should speak with one voice. Marketers generally accept this statement as true. Can you think of special circumstances in which online vehicles might take a different voice? Write a one-page memo advising your public relations director of your deviation in the marketing plan and why this change makes sense.

4. Much of the promotional strength of online communications comes from word-of-mouth endorsements through Usenets or discussion groups. Consumers can also post their dissatisfactions about products using Usenets. Select a product you either strongly like or dislike and log onto a discussion group site such as Deja.com (www.deja.com) to monitor what other people are saying about your product. Write an e-mail to your professor summarizing public opinion about your selected product.

5. Perhaps a disgruntled ex-employee—fired from your company for stealing supplies—stated in a newspaper interview that your spring water company was actually selling tap water drawn from the city water supply. This allegation was false, but to combat rumors, you commissioned a product testing study that confirmed the purity of your water from a natural source. To reach your better educated, technological-savvy consumers, what would be the best tactic to state your case and findings: posting the study on the company Web page,

placing online ads, sponsoring online conference, or employing Usenets? Write an action strategy to submit to your marketing director.

6. There is a second method of segmentation, product differentiation, that focuses on offering products or services with different features but within the same category. Think of General Motors' array of differentiated brands such as Saturn, Chevrolet, Pontiac, Oldsmobile, Buick, and Cadillac, with economy to luxury features that have made the brands famous. In your opinion, which strategy, market segmentation or product differentiation, is more customer-oriented and, therefore, more attentive to delivering customer benefits? Prepare your thoughts as a five-minute talk with basic marketing students.

7. Market identification strategies of demographic, psychographic, geographic, and behavioristic segmentation are each very different ways to profile your market segments. Define the bases of differentiation for each method such as numeric, and state the advantages and disadvantages of each strategy. Be prepared to support or defend each method in a class discussion.

8. Distribution/logistics has long been overlooked as a promotional element to create competitive advantage. Name the electronic marketing resources that have produced tactical advantages in the marketing plan, and how these tools attained cost or time efficiencies. Write a memo to your chief financial officer.

9. In the *Journal of Marketing* article about interactive home shopping, the authors stated a considerable amount of distribution costs is borne by the consumer when unsatisfactory merchandise is returned. Within the distribution scheme, how can electronic marketing resources prevent these costs to the consumer? Assuming no one buys a product merely to return it, formulate five distribution policies that could be used in conjunction with electronic ordering and transactions systems.

10. Given that company operating policies are usually driven by either budgetary efficiencies as in being low cost producers or benefits bundling to enhance effectiveness for products of less price sensitivity, in which scenario, cost efficiencies or marketing effectiveness, do you think electronic marketing resources perform better? Are your thoughts an either/or answer, or must other factors be considered? What are these factors? Be prepared to present your thoughts in a class discussion.

Bibliography

Alba, J., J. Lynch, B. Weitz, C. Janiszewski, R. Lutz, A. Sawyer, and S. Wood. 1997. Interactive home shopping: Consumer, retailer, and manufacturer incentives to participate in electronic marketplaces. *Journal of Marketing* 61 (July): 46.

Council on Logistics Management. 1998. *Careers in Logistics.*

Gonyea, James C. and Wayne M. Gonyea. 1996. *Selling on the Internet.* New York: McGraw-Hill.

Grove, Andrew S. 1996 *Only the paranoid survive.* New York: Doubleday.

Iconocast newsletter. 10 June 1998. Consensus of estimate of seven research studies conducted in 1997; buyer universe estimated is based on a current U.S. Internet user population of 66.3 million. San Francisco, distributed by Message Media, Inc. (Online.)

CHAPTER 4

The Actions of Marketing Implementation

"Interactive marketing is far more than multimedia used to entertain or engage a customer. It is a higher level of strategic marketing, made possible by sophisticated technology and intelligent databases that can respond to interactive relationships. The Internet has brought into a real-time arena and has dramatically impacted the clout of traditional advertising. Today's technology allows us to capture, measure, compare, and analyze the consumer's input, then intelligently sort this information and strategically allocate traditional and interactive resources. Businesses willing to balance risk with knowledge and understanding of this new electronic marketplace stand to reap great benefits. Those that don't are taking an even greater risk. This is the age of true pioneers, and the gold is in the relationships made possible through interactive technology." (Komenar 1997, 87–88)

LEARNING OBJECTIVES

- To describe the tactical issues that face hands-on execution of the electronic marketing mix strategies
- To explore the tasks, advantages, and disadvantages of engaging outside suppliers
- To establish performance objectives to determine whether marketing progress achieved corporate objectives

Introduction

This implementation stage means action, the carrying out of the design plans to execution. Implementation skills are critical to a successful marketing program; while communications designs can produce memorable impacts for products and services, unless these designs are placed on television or in magazines, no one will see them. With no media exposure for your product, prospects will buy other products. Therefore, marketing planning points out direction, and marketing implementation gets the train to stop at the right stations. Implementation tasks can be complex or simple; many times it is the marketing implementation specialist that sees a new, easier way to get the same job done, and with better results.

Individuals with strong implementation talents are rare. Sometimes through lack of experience, marketing planners might suggest a Web site design that cannot be produced within the allotted budget or time. The implementation specialist steps in, and delivers the assignment on spec (specification), on budget, and on time. Everyone wins. Implementation actions take both creativity and critical thinking skills of logic: asking the *who, what, why, where,* and *when* to decide on *how* the electronic marketing assignment such as a World Wide Web design should be produced. Marketing implementation covers more than Web communications; equally important are the electronic tools for collecting and recording customer preferences and for staying in touch with the client. Execution of database retrieval and analysis, maintenance of electronic data collectors such as optical and digital readers, Web site feedback and e-mail systems, electronic surveys, or transactions systems **fulfillment** all fall under marketing implementation. These are the pieces that touch the consumer and often frame his impressions of the product or service experience.

Sometimes because of needed expertise or short time frames, outside suppliers are called in to assist with program implementation. There are advantages and disadvantages for the marketer to engage outside vendors for systems completion. How the supplier can be of assistance, how to evaluate the supplier's credentials, and how to keep the in-house staff and the outside supplier working well together will be discussed in more detail.

Adding another marketing P should be considered for measuring performance, questioning whether the marketing efforts and expenditures are producing cost-efficient results. Some marketers might be afraid of the answers, but without measurement, ineffective or inefficient programs might be continued for years and years. Electronic marketing resources such as Web site traffic statistical packages produce straightforward, easy to understand analysis of site performance. Electronic ordering systems also allow for understanding the activities of buyers and nonbuyers. Smart marketers would rather know than guess.

Minding the Details

In the marketing profession, how many times has it been said, particularly with well planned, well executed marketing programs, that success was because "God is in the details"? Planning may be a more exciting, higher profile marketing function, but successful implementers, those people who know how to negotiate thirty-second radio spots when a station is sold out, how to locate the specialty packaging supplier in twenty-four hours, or know where to find a cool biohazard suit for the afternoon's television commercial shoot are a particular, relentless breed that make things happen regardless of the circumstances (and sometimes regardless of the budget) in their achieving the marketing and promotional tactics. These people may have titles such as marketing assistant, production manager, production assistant, media buyer, or traffic supervisor, and each has tasks and responsibilities that are integral in making the marketing program gain momentum and fly. While luck is a marvelous circumstance, it is an elusive occurrence to depend on when people's careers or millions of dollars swing in the balance of marketing success. Good marketers prepare workable and realistic implementation plans, and should luck visit their program, all the better. The fact that marketing planning is future oriented, taking information on market segments and transforming this data into product benefits and promotional programs (along with strategies for the other marketing Ps) that then becomes the elusive substance for marketing action, has been discussed previously. Marketing implementation is based in the present, perhaps today, certainly no longer than thirty days into the future. Planning is tomorrow, maybe months away, but implementation, putting plans into action, is now.

If plans are close to dreams, how can reality within the marketing fantasy be produced? The marketer forges reality with the five simple words, *who, what, when, where,* and *why,* which were addressed in the evaluation of the online marketing situation discussed earlier. Since most of the programs involved in marketing activities are processes, a series of decisions or steps that are built on decision after decision, these five words, *who, what, when, where,* and *why,* are critical in strategic and tactical decision making because marketing actions must be logically ordered to achieve efficiency and effectiveness. As in situation analysis and marketing planning, the five Ws plus a helpful *how* assist in setting direction among the abstract or vague strategic options facing the marketer. A clearer understanding of logical marketing benefits the entire company or organization because the different departments know what parts they are to play and why, when to play, and where to play. The objective is toward full disclosure because when associates or staff try to read minds, they are prone to misreading every time. Therefore, implementation activities are set as mileposts for tracking timing and performance goals. The charting of implementation actions is every bit as important as the findings of the situation evaluation or the creative formulation of the marketing Ps, but often the details of advertising campaign execution, direct marketing fulfillment such as counting coupons, responding to telephone or e-mail requests, or even training for operators in a call center, go unnoticed or unsupervised for long periods. This portion of the marketing process is particularly important and sometimes sadly ignored because, at this point, the customer or prospect has responded to the company's offer and expects consummation of the sales cycle. In other words, the company's functions are in close scrutiny by the consumer, and fumbling the fulfillment will, at the least, disappoint the buyer, or, at most, enrage a snubbed customer who might in turn tell a dozen of her friends about the shoddy practices of the company. Getting close to the customer is a popular business platitude these days, and successful implementation policies make the encounter pleasant. Can electronic marketing resources aid in this adage of closeness? Certainly, and probably with more adroitness than in the two previous process steps.

During marketing implementation, much of the interest and communication has been established by the tools of the promotional mix (advertising, sales promotion, public relations, direct marketing, and personal selling), so the marketing emphasis now falls to fulfillment and ongoing customer contact or feedback. Electronic resources are exceptionally well suited for communications and record keeping, which is also defined as improved corporate memory. The marketing department must provide the information services department with its database requirements, develop the logistics plan (as previously discussed, logistics such as distribution or packaging can be a decidedly important competitive advantage; as of this writing, Wal-Mart is suing Amazon for hiring a former Wal-Mart logistics specialists away from the company), explore outsourcing opportunities, and establish lines of customer communications, ordering, or possibly future opinion gathering. All of these activities fall under the implementation umbrella that can be tightly bound by electronic tools. If the marketing department decides the *who,* what implementation functions can be facilitated by electronic resources?

Consumer Tracking Strategies

After the prospect is identified and the customer is acquired, marketing programs designed to retain and expand the commercial relationship should be entertained; most marketers attempt to gain as much profiling data or consumer habits as possible without invading the privacy of the customer. Many marketing relationships are based on mutual benefits, and if the customer wishes to review items or services of interest to him, relevant preferences usually are readily divulged. Here the marketer will develop a customer tracking system (or prospect tracking since many purchases have long decision cycles such as home buying or recreational vehicle acquisitions) to record individual purchasing habits or special interests. The marketer may create a database using a simplified software package that might double as an inventory tracking device, or in medium to large companies, the marketing department might work with the MIS personnel to collaborate on a custom generated database program. The marketer must define what characteristics should be recorded such as name, address, age, gender, or similar selections. Other information might include purchase dates, length of warranty, categories of merchandise, gift or personal use, or payment preference; different characteristics are important to different industries. The experienced marketer will know what features to capture in database design. While predetermining these customer qualities seems obvious, database design and formatting begin before the data collection program is built. Database design usually evolves from a list of characteristics compiled by the marketing or sales department; savvy marketers know the proper sequence is rough design, finished input formatting, and lastly database construction.

At the same time as data input is being considered, equally important is forethought to the reporting formats. Will the marketing information be used as formal reports to other managers for supporting data for program evaluation? Will the marketing information be formatted for mailing lists to customers, dealers, wholesalers, or prospects? Will the information be maintained for customer service or maintenance records? Each of these situations may require different formats, depending on communications purposes. In marketing program reviews, sales movements for products or services, especially those featured in newspaper, radio, or Web advertising, might be a deciding factor in planning future advertising expenditures. The various ad placements might bear some identification code or key, such as different telephone numbers or different addresses or post office boxes, each for a different television station, magazine, or newspaper. These **coupon keys** on mass media vehicles require careful attention to keep the vehicles' performance, or pulling power, differentiated. Inquiries or orders on the World Wide Web are easier to document since the e-mail or the order form address appears on the transmission. With Web sites, statistical software packages can monitor the site, disclosing answers for virtually any question the marketer can formulate; this reporting software registers time, date, domain names, days of the week, weeks of the month, type of inquiry such as page views or specific views on the page, and length of time spent on the Web site. Different packages offer different reporting information and many allow the marketer to customize the reports according to her information needs. Tracking software also will organize the information into easy-to-read and understand reports with color graphs or charts. This close consultation with Web commerce, user data, and site performance provides excellent feedback for designing marketing parameters for future online activities. Attentive efforts to trace advertising or other communications' performance should not be confined to Web activities; all advertising vehicles should be measured as to the cost per inquiry, the cost per thousand, the cost per rating point, the cost per sale, or whatever evaluation criteria makes sense to the marketer's company, geography, competitive situation, or industry. The assessment criteria are available in most cases, and marketing efforts measurement is a wise stewardship for every company or organization.

E-MARKETING CASE HISTORY:

CBSdirect's TRAXX System

Talk about timing. Corporate Buying Service (www.cbsdirect.com), a direct marketing site selling personal computers and accessories headquartered in Boca Raton, Florida, was launched in 1992 to sell hardware and software to the business market. Initially, the sales plan called for direct selling efforts via a telephone center taking orders and mail orders generated through company product catalogs. The previous year, 1991, saw the World Wide Web become available to consumers and business customers alike. Says Russell Madris, president of Corporate Buying Service, "The transformation in our business has been phenomenal by our inclusion of Web marketing. Eighty percent of our orders are processed electronically, and we're open 24 hours each day, 365 days a year." Declares Madris, "I'm ecstatic about the benefits that the Web has brought my company." In 1998, eighty percent of company sales were Web generated with the remaining twenty percent developed through telephone sales from companies without Web access.

As a sophisticated corporate procurement source, CBS soon recognized that it must offer more services and conveniences than telephone ordering to its thousand-member enrollment and in April 1993, introduced the software procurement system called TRAXX. Resolving to build its business around TRAXX, CBS enhanced the software to become a complete purchasing system, not just a Web page. To deliver fuller information to its members, TRAXX:

- allows the comparison of prices from wholesale distributors that resellers purchase from;
- its design permits all buyers to share and track all order information;
- its system retains a complete history of orders for over five years;
- can maintain standard repetitive orders within the system to be ordered at anytime;
- can create proposals, then edit, and subsequently convert to orders; and
- allows the tracking of orders by city, state, date, carrier, and tracking number.

Other marketing benefits besides the sales and logistics strengths are that CBS has eliminated all brochures and other collateral items. If the viewer wants specific information, he can print from the Web page. As Madris noted, "If you want to learn about CBSdirect, it's all on the Web page."

As a result of the automated buying system, CBSdirect can now offer its customers a selection of over $2 billion of inventory from major distributors and over 80,000 products with competitive pricing. CBSdirect has established inventory control, inventory comparison pricing, inventory timing, inventory specifications and all without inventory. CBS seems to have found the database and communications balance for the twenty-first century buying service.

Keeping in Touch with the Customer

Marketing practitioners have estimated that it is seven times more costly to attract new customers than selling to and servicing a company's existing customer base. To reduce marketing costs even further, successful marketers recognize that happy, satisfied customers tell their friends and relatives about their purchasing activities. This word-of-mouth endorsement leads to low-cost referral opportunities. Generating referrals is a low-cost function, not a no-cost activity, because keeping customers contented still requires excellent marketing execution with an eye toward responsive customer communications. There are many ways to remind the customer who trades frequently or infrequently with a business. E-mail notices are used in both situations. From the customer profiles, the marketer can create segments of similar product or service interests and can match promotional offers to be delivered by e-mail. A company can ask the patron for his e-mail address to send an electronic newsletter with subject matter of interest to the customer or can create a coupon mailer featuring action videos, for example, from video rentals preferences. Perhaps the action video fan has not visited the store in the last sixty days; an electronic coupon or direct mailing piece featuring free microwave popcorn, as Blockbuster (www.blockbuster.com) has done, could entice the video renter to stop by. How does Blockbuster know the

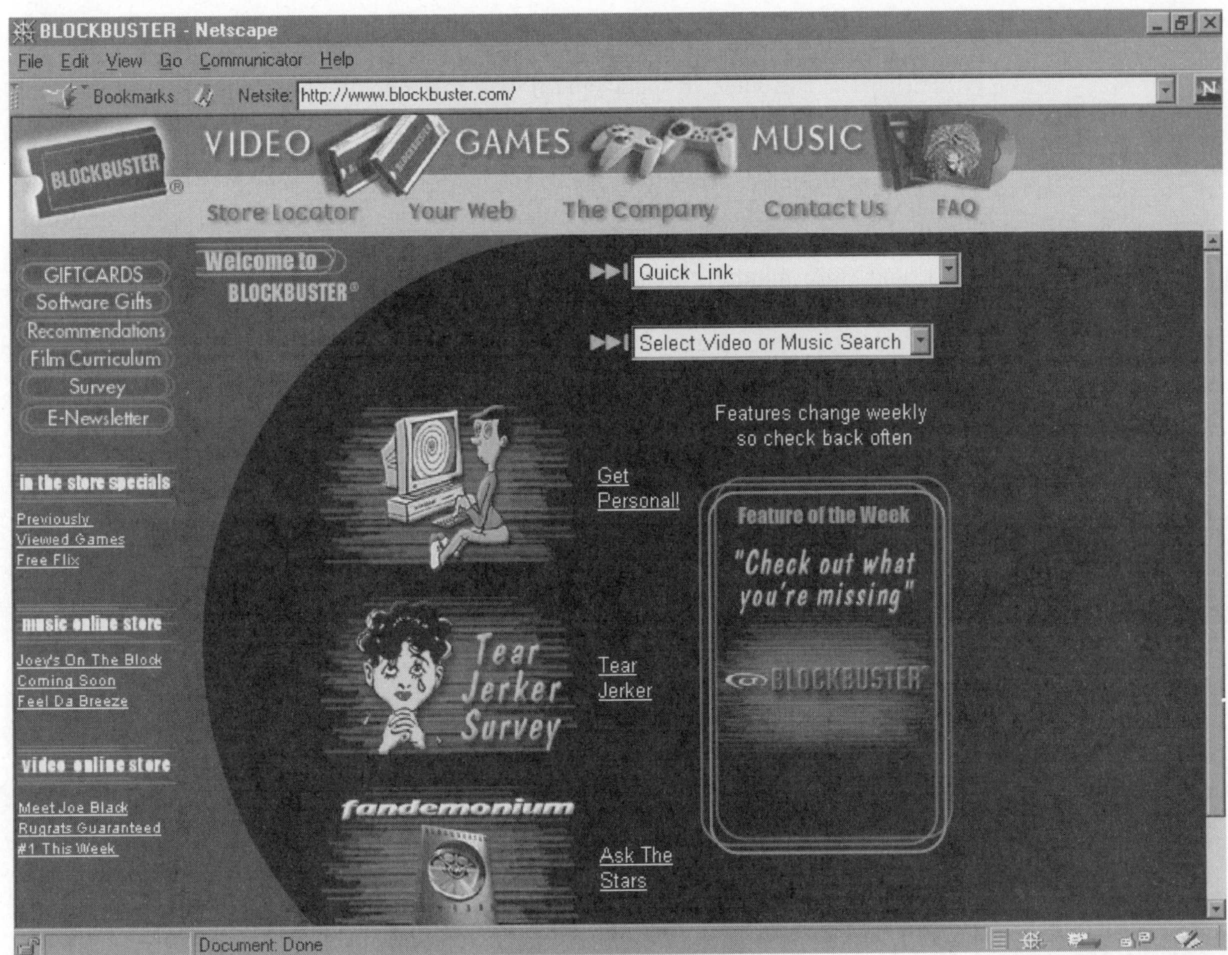

Blockbuster (www.blockbuster.com)
With such a wide selection of videos and video games for sale or rental, along with a large music selection, the viewer can shop for his or her entertainment choices before visiting the store, or even order online. Notice the "trip-a-day" giveaway promotion as an added Web site incentive.

individual likes action, romance, thriller, or comedy videos? Companies like Blockbuster or Tower Records produce preferred customer identification cards, and as the renter or buyer checks out movies, this card is swiped, recording the genre of video, day of the week rented, purchased with cash or credit card, multiple rentals, coupon used or not, and other appropriate information. Purchases on the Web (or by telephone) can be confirmed by e-mail; if a customer buys books from Barnes & Noble, an e-mail confirmation is sent within the hour. This service is most helpful for the customer in knowing that the order was entered properly and for the online company in that the correct items were shipped and replacement stock was noted for inventory purposes. The confirmation, with a thank-you line, is appreciated by the customer as a goodwill gesture.

New products or services can be announced by e-mail, as Amazon Books recently did when it began selling compact discs from its existing Web site. Building an accurate customer database is the link in sharing information of interest in which advertising or sales promotion could then invite new sales opportunities. This scenario of announcing new products or services is perfect for sponsoring sneak previews for preferred customers who arrived at that status by database tracking. Another customer-oriented tool is a customer feedback system in which the clientele can post an inquiry to a message page, often titled "Contact us." Customer service personnel then research the question or status of the order and reply to the customer via e-mail. Many marketers learn much about customers' concerns by studying their compliments and complaints to the point of having these comments routed through the marketing department. A sample criticism might be that customers on the west coast cannot reach an east coast service representative because of the three-hour time difference. Perhaps a customer dropped all of her merchandise because the shopping bag tore apart. While these problems are easy to solve, it requires the attention of an alert manager who takes the initiative to read and respond to customer comments. Many of the best service ideas come from the customer who notices or is affected by service breaches. Simple and quick solutions also head off larger problems that become compounded over time. Business-to-business operations can also benefit from mindful, proactive customer service. Sophisticated tracking programs that reassure the customer of the package location twenty-four hours a day are already in use by parcel delivery companies, and a **global positioning satellite system (GPS)** is a valuable differentiation factor in transportation alternatives, such as car rentals and ships and recreational craft usage; trucking firms can use a global positioning system to monitor and locate shipments throughout the country. The bottom line is that customers want to know the facts even though they might not like the answers.

Marketers often dictate how the customer service reporting system is to work. Hundreds of customer communications might build up with no resolutions if no one is appointed to the job of responding to these communications. Ownership, with the ability to make decisions to rectify inequities, should be awarded to those persons that interact with customers. A routing system can be devised in which a representative sample of customer inquiries (better yet, all inquiries) is electronically forwarded to the marketing department every day. Follow-up questions or replies can be issued within a time standard, such as a twenty-four-hour turnaround regardless if the problem originated in-house or through an outside supplier. Reports from customer feedback are only helpful if they are read and resolved, and this resolution is best handled through the marketing department.

Setting Priorities for Action

As was discussed previously, marketing implementation can be simple or complex; it can require national, regional, or local efforts. It may bring together manufacturers, wholesalers, and retailers, and the marketing details may seem overwhelming. Good marketers, however, will agree that each program is fulfilled in a linear fashion—one step at a time. To do everything at once is to do nothing at all. Experience being under fire teaches the importance of organization and delegation to achieve the expected results. Many marketers start every implementation effort by outlining the tasks and determining who will implement these tasks. This is another case of breaking down the big program into bite-sized portions, to orchestrate the *who, what, when, where,* and *why* activities. After several implementation assignments, the marketing assistant will recognize that a detailed checklist helps to order these questions, and that most all implementation actions begin to resemble the last program and the next program. The checklist of people, supplies, merchandise, display materials, or support media is an excellent method of organization and helps to ensure as little as possible will not be forgotten. Rarely does any promotional event, electronic or otherwise, escape some oversight, but planning well early reduces excessive worry later.

The marketer has to coordinate internal personnel and tasks as well as external resources for e-commerce. An outline of online tasks should be prepared so all players know who is doing what and when. Online implementation can be complex since longer lead times are required by telecommunications or hardware suppliers. For example, setting up a call center or initiating a fax-on-demand program entails such contractual responsibilities for hardware, support equipment, dedicated telephone lines,

EXHIBIT 4.1 CHECKLIST OF VARIOUS TASKS OF EVENT IMPLEMENTATION

Roberts Communications Special Events Checklist

Event: ______________ Client: ______________

Date: ______________ Time: ______________

Location ______________________________

Item	Due Date	Responsibility
■ Press kit		
Press kit cover		
General release		
Biographies		
Fact sheet		
History		
Activities		
Photographs		
Business cards		
Maps		
■ Press release		
■ Online release		
■ Invitations		
Mailing list		
E-mail addresses		
Copy		
Layout		
Mechanical		
Printing		
RSVP		
Invite mailing		
E-mail release		
■ Agenda		
■ Program		
■ Mementos		
■ Signage to event		
■ Parking instructions		
■ Security		
■ Rehearsal		

Roberts Communications. Tampa, Florida. (www.robertscommunications.com)

A checklist of various tasks of event implementation/Roberts Communications, Tampa (www.robertscommunications.com)

hiring and training of operators, software development systems, and ISP (Internet service provider) supplier. Suppliers can be of great help, and many marketers will outsource some crucial activities, such as software development or personnel training duties, usually because the marketer does not have internal resources or the creation of these resources might be expensive and time-consuming. Dependable suppliers can be a blessing, but the marketer must realize that he has to provide direction on the project—to explain the entire situation and marketing strategy to be implemented. This indoctrination may take several months of meetings and many project plans to bring everyone to the same understanding. There are several effective software planning applications such as BusinessObjects that help to identify tasks, set time frames, and pinpoint mileposts for judging progress.

A discussion on suppliers, those key people or organizations working outside the company, is now in order. In working with a nonemployee, it is wise to delineate what final outcomes are expected, a "what might happen" frame of mind, how the work or systems are to be designed and how progress is to be measured, who the people that comprise the supplier's staff are and what qualifications the staff has, what the length of the engagement is expected to be, how ongoing maintenance of the Web site is to be performed, and how or when the supplier is to be paid (such as prepayments, installment payments, or milestone payments). Many times the client will insist on interviewing and personally selecting the members of the supplier's team. E-commerce is a young industry in which many grandiose promises are made to clients, but after starting the assignment, promises end in nonperformance. Thus, great care is exercised in selecting the analysts, designers, or technicians that constitute the supplier group; care should be applied by the marketing client and with the supplier's team leader. Experience, understanding of the task, and good personal chemistry between the client and supplier are the foundation qualities that almost always result in marvelous marketing successes. There are mixed opinions on the value or flexibility in using outside suppliers. Supporters pose that engaging outside software developers adds fresh thinking and objectivity, introduces experience gained from other assignments, and pushes overhead costs to the consulting firm. Fresh thinking, many times unfettered by corporate restrictions or bureaucracy, is probably the most valuable quality procured because the client firm receives the best, most current, and most logical electronic marketing resource experience available in the marketplace. An old saying, which is very appropriate here, is that you are learning on someone else's nickel. To verify the supplier firm's credentials, the marketer can telephone other companies the supplier has worked for; requesting, as well, a detailed written explanation of the expected project plan in proposal form is a wise precaution since some communications may be lost or misunderstood in the project briefings. Asking for another written document, the statement of qualifications, or SOQ, in which the supplier details how the proposed project meshes with the supplier firm's strengths and experience is also a good thing for the marketer to acquire. Well thought out and well constructed proposals assist the marketer in understanding the supplier's attention to detail and its communications abilities, and in judging the care in which a company listens. Based on written documents, samples of previous work, and the intuitive feelings on both parties, the road to success or possibly failure begins.

Opponents of hiring outside the firm have much ammunition too. Many nationally recognized consultants in systems development, consumer or business-to-business marketing, or public relations counsel charge large up-front retainers, and it is difficult for the marketing manager to justify what these funds are buying before any work has been performed. Sometimes flashing résumés or passing around project plans does not give the hard-core skeptics the necessary proof or promise of successful completion, and keep in mind many people have trouble visualizing the end product or service. Often it is well that this cynical person's presence helps to sharpen the marketing manager's presentation skills and supporting materials preparation. Simply asking for trust does not fly well among professional managers. The marketer should provide as accurate as possible projections that weigh anticipated costs versus anticipated benefits. Critical opinions can be swayed by using detailed and realistic financial forecasts buttressed by imaginative marketing approaches. A frequent worry in engaging outside suppliers is that the supplier staff is incompetent, better suited for telling tall tales than actually producing the work, or that the in-house staff is also incompetent to handle the online assignments, which may be true in judging online experience. The supplier firm's credentials are easily checked by calling current and past clients, speaking with suppliers that have done business with the company, and pulling a financial inquiry report such as Dunn and Bradstreet financial profiles. Companies in financial trouble are desperate to maintain their businesses to the point of deception, and many innocent people and businesses can be direly injured by unscrupulous operators. The more the marketer learns about the supplier's business practices, the better. Some marketing people have complained about seeing the superstars of the supplier firm, and after the contract is signed and a prepayment is processed, junior people become the liaison to the client. To assure that equal attention is paid to the client before and after the marriage, the client marketing representative can write into the business contract who will be the company contact and the software design team and who in each firm will be the arbitrators should problems or misunderstandings arise.

More and more often clients and suppliers are concerned with confidentiality and security issues. Both concerns are real, damaging, and difficult to recover from. Careful screening of the software firm and its associates is an operational imperative, and nondisclosure agreements should be signed by all parties including supplier and client interests. Recently, a concern for physical building security as in fortifying buildings with tasteful but secure parameter barriers, escorts by security personnel for building visitors from check-in to checkout, as well as careful scrutiny and verification of authenticity with credible companies of companies that supply services to the building such as janitorial services, delivery people, or building repair or telephone installers has been gaining more exposure. There is a fascination by television and movie viewers of action programs that are based on undercover operations or government spying or similar conspiracies, and many program plots are not too far from the truth. Marketers must separate the good guys from the bad guys before the supplier can steal plans or technologies. One last caution on using outside suppliers is that the marketer should be suspicious of liaisons such as hiring the brother-in-law's software company or his advertising agency, or employing an old college chum of the CEO or other ranking official, or retaining the president's wife to decorate the new corporate offices. Time and again this inner-circle member has the connections to land the marketing or information technology positions but not the knowledge or decisiveness to effectively lead the company to higher levels of success. Occasionally, this insider does succeed because of previous years of experience in the industry; however, the CEO may view marketing as low priority or a necessary evil, so placing his brother-in-law in the marketing position will not harm the company. There are legitimate hesitancies to heed in hiring suppliers, and the best approach is to employ the best qualified, balancing the monies required with the completion of the work in the allotted time frame. The independent supplier, therefore, has to perform to her best ability because no relative will be available to bail her out. Respect tempered by distrust is the best way to engage superior supplier services.

Assigning Program Responsibilities

Again in applying logic, the marketer decides who is best to implement the various elements of the program and why they are best suited to carry out the marketing actions. By now you should be comfortable in asking yourself the standard *who*, *what*, *where*, *when*, and *why* questions at every important milestone. The marketer can also add two additional qualities—those of efficiency and effectiveness concepts introduced in the last chapter. There is a significant difference between these two concepts. Efficiency is often described as doing a task right and can be determined by the numbers. Comparisons of two media alternatives can usually be measured relatively by numeric means, such as a **cost per thousand (CPM)** for newspaper or radio vehicles or a cost per rating point (**GRPs, gross rating points,** or **TRPs** as in **target rating points** for more narrowly defined audiences) for television. Unfortunately, Web site measurement criteria are still in the formative stages with many online gurus still arguing about what should be counted and how the data should be compiled and reported. Some camps insist that page hits, an initial viewing of the home page, are equal in value as **clickthroughs,** the number of Web pages viewed in one site visit. The more often a page is hit upon by Web surfers is considered better, and the deeper into a particular Web page these surfers drill down is also considered better. Others conjecture that the length of time spent on the Web site is the most telling statistics, while others postulate that the number of return visitors is most important. The concept of **unique visitors,** one viewer is counted once no matter how many times she visits the site, is also considered the most reliable number. Somewhere between the unique visitor count and the undifferentiated page hit totals, a reasonable and realistic measurement technique will arise. Many efforts to quantify performance have been developed. Ways to measure performance may include gauging the individual salesperson through monthly sales volume, sales by product line, or territory sales totals; gauging the retail store through the amount of sales per square foot, the sales per square foot for every department, or monthly sales volume; or gauging the particular industries by measuring the amount of billing volume by employee to determine each account's profitability, such as in the advertising agency business. Largely, business can be measured and placed under the efficiency microscope. However, those that cannot be quantified are judged in other ways.

The second concept, effectiveness, is doing the right things and is qualitative in explanation, distinctive within a defined spectrum with soft parameters. Questions concerning effectiveness might be similar to the creative problem solving presented to the young Alexander the Great as he studied enigmatic Gordian knot; however, marketers still face modern day queries on effectiveness such as How much is enough? or How low is low without compromising the campaign? as in budget preparation or in levels of media expenditures. Unfortunately, there is no cut and dried answer since all the corners have rounded edges. For example, two graphic artists may bid on the same Web page project, and the amounts of the bids may be very dissimilar. Should the marketer take the lowest bidder (the more efficient) and proceed with the project? Or should be quality of each artist's work be the deciding factor (the more effective)? Or how good does good have to be (a question that produces total confusion on the marketer's part)? Qualitative judgments can be most difficult in deciding the best selection, and sound marketing choices come with experience. Research can also be devised to place numbers on creative ideas or campaign approaches. In this approach, a ranking is developed usually rating ideas on a one-to-ten basis in which a rating of one could represent the feeling or reaction of strongly dislike or strongly disagree. The ten level could represent the feeling of strongly like or strongly agree. Less distinctive emotions or reactions fall between one and ten with a neutral or sometimes stated neither like nor dislike position hovering between five and six. Some, even strong, reaction of either liking or disliking the marketing approach is hoped for to give a definitive response to guide qualitative development.

This discussion of efficiency versus effectiveness (the best outcome would be a direction or solution that is equally efficient and effective) is very relevant in the decision by a marketer to provide a service or produce a good in-house rather than purchasing this service or product from an outside vendor. The marketer should establish expectations for cost and quality of marketing programs, such as an impressive Web site (costly), an attractive three-color sales brochure (moderate), or a one-color publicity kit (inexpensive), and establish whether these costs entail Web resources, equipment, advertising and other promotional elements, customer service personnel and training, or shipping guidelines. A judgment criterion might be to consider the audience for which the promotional piece is intended—the more important the audience, the more effort and budget are allocated to that marketing program. In short, the list is long and complicated as tradeoffs, such as lower quality but lower cost, come into play. This is a reoccurring situation in which the marketer must either turn to his in-house staff to execute the marketing program, work with outside suppliers that requires in-depth expertise, such as CD-ROM production, or that proves to be extremely time-consuming in coordination, such as database creation and records entry, or preferably, do some of both. Different staff members will have different strengths as will different marketing suppliers. Good suppliers know their strengths and limitations as do good marketers, and professionals will confirm or deny their abilities in program execution. As a confident marketer, you will probably choose to delegate some communications management duties to in-house staff and purchase some specialty programs and materials from qualified, reliable suppliers. Using outside resources can give a novel, fresh appearance or personality to a familiar, perhaps tired product or service. Intuitively, most marketers know the abilities of all of her associates, inside and outside the organization, and will match the checklist of tasks to the best able parties. The most important insight for marketing managers to recognize is that unless someone is specifically handed and takes ownership of the assignment, no one is responsible for its completion. Orphan assignments become no one's responsibility.

It is being found that many online or electronic systems require high levels of expertise and hands-on experience on the practical problems encountered from previous engagements. These high technology applications appear best handled by knowledgeable suppliers who might cost more in the short term but could save dollars, reputations, time, and probably prevent customer defections as new marketing communications and fulfillment services are added over the long term. Training in-house staff in complex database software such as Oracle (www.oracle.com) or communications systems such as Lotus Notes might cause excessive work delays, production shortages, and overly stressed staff who may not be capable of developing software applications. Weekly news in *The Wall Street Journal* chronicles the demise of companies, large and small, attributed to ineffectual billing, inventory, shipping, and even sales tax collection software systems. In most cases, marketers can sidestep many of the common but complicated electronic resource applications such as Web page development, e-mail collection, online ordering, company intranet development, and other marketing elements by hiring trained suppliers to perform the work. In commissioning a onetime assignment to start the application, the marketer can request a detailed description of the assignment, set a realistic time frame, and have a not-to-exceed budget estimate. If satisfied, the marketer can continue to issue project assignments quarter after quarter to keep the systems going strong and the budget in line.

It is the supplier's job to specify the equipment and infrastructure needed to market and operate online. Again, a checklist is a necessary planning tool, and the supplier should know the ingredients that comprise the assignment. The marketer must, however, realize that in using outside suppliers, the individual supplier sees only part of the whole marketing picture but may perform the assignments admirably anyway. The marketing endeavor is a series, possibly hundreds, of little steps or links that lead to a successful finish. It can be quite confusing and frustrating as suppliers (and in-house people as well) drop the ball during the implementation stage. From these outages, a seemingly life-or-death scramble begins. Imagine you are setting up a display booth at a consumer computer trade show. The show managers have rented to you a

ORACLE

Home | Site Map | Site Index | Search

Try & Buy   Free Download   Support   News   Events   Contact Oracle

Oracle Store™

Welcome to the Oracle Store!

Save up to 20% on Oracle Software and 10% on Oracle Support only when you buy online

Trial Software
Servers
Tools
Business Intelligence
Support Services
Documentation
Publications
Education

Product Spotlight

Oracle8i Personal Edition

Oracle8i Personal Edition is the most powerful desktop database available on the market today. By bringing the award-winning functionality of Oracle8i to the personal computer, Oracle offers a database that combines the power of the world's most popular database with the ease of use and simplicity you'd expect in a desktop product.

Especially popular with consultants, developers and students, Oracle8i Personal Edition is the full-featured version of Oracle8i, for use by individuals who require full compatibility with the entire Oracle8i database family. Oracle8i Personal Edition's superior ease of use enables efficient harnessing of the ever-increasing power of PCs for development, by using advanced replication and distribution features to easily deploy work in an Oracle enterprise environment.

Buy online today and save!

- Get Your Purchasing Dept. Involved NEW!
  Fax in a P.O. for payment.
- Customer Satisfaction Survey
  Complete the survey for a chance to win an Oracle Store t-shirt.
- Oracle Technology Network - OTN
  Developers - Join today!
- IOUG-A
  Become a part of the Oracle User Group Community.
- Newsletter
  Stay informed! Subscribe to our monthly newsletter.

Site Information

We accept purchase orders and the following credit cards:

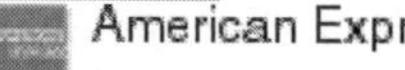

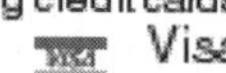

[Home Page | Hot Deals | Site Information | Help Desk]
[Trial Software | Servers | Tools | Business Intelligence | Support Services | Documentation | Publications | Education]

Can't find a product you're looking for? Call 1-800-Oracle1 to speak with a sales representative.

Oracle Store (http://oraclestore/oracle.com)
Shop online and save 10% on Oracle software at the Oracle Store. This relationship marketing site offers featured product, trial software, "hot deals," decision support, an online newsletter, and many other services and products of interest to Oracle users.

twelve-foot-by-twelve-foot display area that contains three walls and a concrete floor, which is to be transformed into an attractive, informative, memorable representation of a product or service. All displays are portable since there is a circuit and schedule of consumer events that will provide excellent exposure for the product. When you arrive at your bare cubicle at about 5 A.M., the convention hall has not provided electrical power to the booth that was stipulated in your reservation/contract, and worse, the air conditioning in the hall is not working. Because your product is home sales in central Florida in a picturesque residential community that has been equipped with the latest communications infrastructure such as fiber optic land lines and satellite uplinks, and the consumer sales exhibits are targeted to a suburban, technological, home show audience, it is important to depict the lifestyle of your client' s community using photo displays, a PowerPoint slide show, and an interactive kiosk that portrays the surrounding amenities such as shopping, golf courses, medical facilities, and the regional airport. The kiosk highlights the location of various conveniences as the prospect presses a menu button. There is a computer with a database that has compiled names and hometowns so that when the executive prospect inputs his current hometown, names of residents, possibly ones he knows, will pop up. To showcase the beauty of uncrowded, open landscapes, you routinely paint the display walls in a deep blue to highlight the stellar photography of the community's residents, homes, and rolling terrain dotted with pristine lakes. After painting the walls, the paint will not dry, and worse yet, the photo murals are beginning to peel away from their frames because of the humidity. The air conditioning is finally repaired about noon. You begin to repair the photo frames with a dry adhesive because a wet adhesive will not set in time, even with the help from a hair dryer, still affected by the moisture in the monstrous hall. During this time, your marketing assistant learns he forgot to pack the heavy duty extension cords that run to the power source that was turned on at 2 P.M., and the show begins at 6 P.M. The marketing assistant remembers seeing a Wal-Mart along the way and is dispatched to buy extension cords that he pays for on his Visa card. As the electronic marketing displays are being readied, you realize the PowerPoint display in the center of the display area will block traffic from seeing the photo displays. You, therefore, decide to move the PowerPoint display to the corner by the structural column. You then learn there is no electrical power in that corner, so you ask the convention manager to drill a hole in the raised wooden floor (it is elevated about twenty inches above the concrete floor to allow the power cords, speaker cords, or other substructures to be out of the way of prospect traffic). The convention hall manager will have a maintenance person there about 5:30 and will charge you $650 (union minimum) for drilling the hole and running power to it. The pace is hectic, and the marketing staff and suppliers must be well prepared and flexible to handle these last minute changes or surprises. Many times in trade shows, the marketer should thoroughly preplan for contingencies that may arrive. At trade shows, overlooked incidentals such as a roll of electrical or duct tape may cost $20. In using supplier talent, the longer the marketing team works together, the smoother promotional programs can be implemented.

The Disadvantages of Implementation

Some marketers believe that marketing implementation is like foul-tasting medicine. Because it tastes bad, it must be good for you. This attitude of avoidance will never lead to complete success within the marketing world. If plans are well designed, marketing implementation is not a difficult activity. Success is in the follow-through. As marketer Komenar comments:

> One of the places where many companies fail is in a stage just following implementation. If they do not have a thorough understanding of what they have created and how to maintain and evolve it, their investment can result in unnecessary loss. Using skilled and well-rounded talent, respecting the experience of [interactive] agencies that have managed the big picture for clients, while equally heeding the knowledge and direction provided by

> those design firms specializing in new media development and implementation all will increase the probability of success. Making educated use of the vast resources available today and observing the successes and failures of competitors will provide a needed advantage in this electronic marketplace. (Komenar 1997, 87)

Excellent implementation requires understanding, observation, and patience to complete the marketing process. With experience, marketers learn there are hard ways to do easy tasks, and there are easy ways to do hard tasks. Asking questions and receiving thoughtful answers make the next task of implementation much easier.

Planning for the Entire Year

Marketers plan new products and new services with great diligence and enthusiasm; they also use time or timing as a competitive tactic to maximize marketplace opportunities. Time, of course, is available to everyone, so to create competitive advantage, the marketer must be ingenious and decisive to employ time as a marketing weapon. The starting place for new product or annual planning is not in counting days or months; the starting place is gathering accurate and realistic information about the design, production, and distribution of the intended new product entry or new versions of an existing product. Without accurate and realistic data, promotional calendars are worthless, dealer incentives are inconsequential, and publicity activities are futile. Realistic expectations for the various production sequences are important as well because no marketer can create product introduction miracles given inadequate time allowances. While marketers are some of the most positive people on this planet, no one can produce product out of the thin air. As has been discussed, marketing programs are a series of steps or decisions that are inextricably linked but not necessarily with product inventory, services delivery, or marketing actions.

That said, the most effective manner of bringing the marketing process to life is through planning—using the objective and task method that sets out specific tasks that must be performed, such as creating the logotype or packaging, setting objectives for various exposure vehicles such as Web page design or newspaper or allied traditional media, developing the copy and graphic approach for the media, selecting and budgeting for media support, planning the distribution, training the retailer and salespeople, and many other potential objectives. With so many tasks and so little time (while it has been said that time pressures grow or shrink according to the time allowed for each activity, in other words, the further away the deadline, the longer you can procrastinate), careful and logical time planning is the best way for setting an accurate twelve-month, roll-out calendar. The marketer should identify each task and speak with the appropriate managers within the company such as the managers for the design, production, legal (if there are federal or state government approvals as in pharmaceutical or alcohol content requirements), shipping (for example, any customs or container specifications for other countries that are markets for distribution), retailer relations (as in the automotive business, dealer personnel training is an important link in new models' introduction, or in the fast food industry, bringing new menu items to the public requires franchisees' endorsement as well as product preparation training), or customer service departments. These are all matters important to internal stakeholders in which common objectives and communications should be readily understood since each party has mutual benefits in working together. Benefits for in-house personnel might be increased salary, bonuses, promotions, stock options, industry recognition, or personal satisfaction in seeing a difficult job made simpler. For people outside the manufacturing or service company, such as franchisees, key suppliers, government officials, or the financial industry, the rewards could include increased

EXHIBIT 4.2

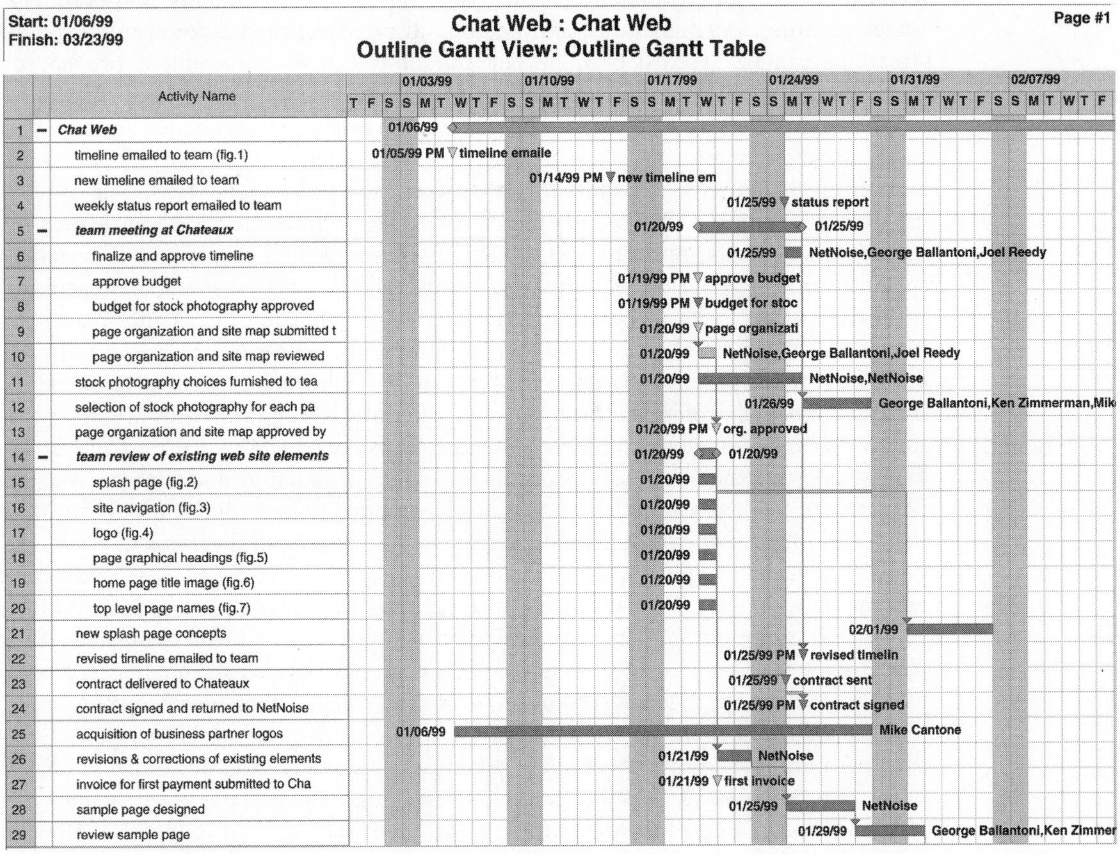

Start: 01/06/99
Finish: 03/23/99

Chat Web : Chat Web
Outline Gantt View: Outline Gantt Table

Page #1

Weeks: 01/03/99, 01/10/99, 01/17/99, 01/24/99, 01/31/99, 02/07/99

		Activity Name	Chart label
1	–	***Chat Web***	01/06/99
2		timeline emailed to team (fig.1)	01/05/99 PM timeline emaile
3		new timeline emailed to team	01/14/99 PM new timeline em
4		weekly status report emailed to team	01/25/99 status report
5	–	***team meeting at Chateaux***	01/20/99 – 01/25/99
6		finalize and approve timeline	01/25/99 NetNoise,George Ballantoni,Joel Reedy
7		approve budget	01/19/99 PM approve budget
8		budget for stock photography approved	01/19/99 PM budget for stoc
9		page organization and site map submitted t	01/20/99 page organizati
10		page organization and site map reviewed	01/20/99 NetNoise,George Ballantoni,Joel Reedy
11		stock photography choices furnished to tea	01/20/99 NetNoise,NetNoise
12		selection of stock photography for each pa	01/26/99 George Ballantoni,Ken Zimmerman,Mik
13		page organization and site map approved by	01/20/99 PM org. approved
14	–	***team review of existing web site elements***	01/20/99 01/20/99
15		splash page (fig.2)	01/20/99
16		site navigation (fig.3)	01/20/99
17		logo (fig.4)	01/20/99
18		page graphical headings (fig.5)	01/20/99
19		home page title image (fig.6)	01/20/99
20		top level page names (fig.7)	01/20/99
21		new splash page concepts	02/01/99
22		revised timeline emailed to team	01/25/99 PM revised timelin
23		contract delivered to Chateaux	01/25/99 contract sent
24		contract signed and returned to NetNoise	01/25/99 PM contract signed
25		acquisition of business partner logos	01/06/99 Mike Cantone
26		revisions & corrections of existing elements	01/21/99 NetNoise
27		invoice for first payment submitted to Cha	01/21/99 first invoice
28		sample page designed	01/25/99 NetNoise
29		review sample page	01/29/99 George Ballantoni,Ken Zimmer

An excerpt of a project chart of annual planning activities. The activities and tasks to be completed are listed in the vertical columns, and the dates and times allotted are placed in the horizontal rows. Adjustments are made according to tasks completed, tasks behind schedule, or tasks ahead of schedule.

Chateaux Software, Stamford, CT.

profits for the franchisees, increased sales for key suppliers, economic growth for local government interests, and loan repayments or increased loan activities for the lenders.

Working with accurate and realistic time frames cannot be emphasized too strongly. Some marketing managers (as well as their superiors) cheat on time segments given to other departments, to marketing or communications assistants, and to outside suppliers. In this game of issuing false deadlines, some marketers assume they will be given inaccurate time frames, and that the production department or the software developer is also supplying exaggerated time estimates. What results is that an inferior, possibly underdeveloped product or service is rushed to market; necessary refinements are being disregarded, and the subsequent poor performance of the product becomes a company embarrassment and, most probably, a waste of company resources. This deception frequently occurs when the marketer is unsure of her abilities in process management, or when the marketer is suspicious of associate or supplier performance. Hopefully, respect for each party and its abilities is established before the manufacturing and marketing operations begin so that everyone has the greatest and fairest platform to create company masterpieces. If not, the ensuing struggle will lead to service lapses, production snafus, distributor disappointments, and eventually finger-pointing, incriminations, and possibly dismissal of the marketing staff. These situations can be avoided with proper and honest time-management procedures. Time-management procedures should begin with the planning calendar.

The objective and task method establishes the task and its sequence among other tasks; sets the months, days, or hours each task will require; and then steps backwards away from the targeted introduction date given these parameters. This issue of tactical timing is critical at the middle management and supplier levels because after the marketing managers approved the big idea, the strategic direction to be followed for a specified campaign period, the implementation tasks, are now divided among the appropriate parties, both in-house and outside the organization. Certainly marketing managers are briefed daily or weekly on the program progress, and linear and **concurrent activities** are compared to the timeline to determine those tasks on schedule, those behind, and preferably those ahead of schedule. **Linear activities** are those that follow a specified sequence of development, such as the situation analysis that leads to Web site design, then to pages design, then to pages production, and lastly to Web site publication. Concurrent activities are those assignments that can be produced independently of the sequence schedule, such as commissioning illustrations or photography (in-house or supplier source) for use on the final iteration of page production before publishing live, specialized attention-getting graphics employing Java scripts, a specialized programming language that can give motion to an otherwise static Web page production with colors, sound, or other special effects, or applying statistical packages, automatic e-mail responses, or other off-the-shelf electronic packages. These production elements can be composed at the same time (thus, described as concurrent) and inserted into the work in progress as the marketing personnel in charge of the assignment or the supplier staff chooses. In other words, the linear sequence of job production can go forward as these assignments are worked on without slowing the tactical marketing time frame.

The marketer becomes more and more familiar with the amount of time required for each step of the various marketing process elements. Overall, some steps take much longer (program strategy and creative platform for ensuing campaign elements), and some steps require less time (integrating a standard statistical package into the home page instructions with embedded HyperText Markup Language [HTML, the instructions that will be used frequently in this textbook in ensuing electronic resource development]). Marketers also learn which suppliers are quick in turning around design or production assignments and which labor should be used extensively in conceiving their portions of the master plan. Of course there will be delays, even disasters, as the marketing implementation effort rolls along. Computer programs can be erased or damaged, in-house personnel or suppliers might misunderstand their roles or assignments, campaign elements shipped overnight might become lost, and other unimaginable perils can raise their ugly heads. In each case of success or adversity, the marketing manager is responsible for continuing accomplishments or for shouldering the setback. Cautious planning has spawned more achievements than failures; the more attentively the marketer monitors these implementation steps, the more effectively he can guide the speed, accuracy, and cost efficiency of the marketing rollout.

Measuring Performance

There is one invisible marketing P that more and more marketers are bringing into the light. This is the P in performance, and as accountability is the measurement of all company, corporate, or organizational resources, performance goals are being built into all marketing programs. In fact, any marketing plan that does not estimate acceptable goals and the time and budget allocated to reach the goals is an incomplete marketing plan. This is a very sensible effort because for many decades marketers and companies were accused of throwing money at the problem. Accounting for the marketing program performance was rarely required by the corporate managers. Beginning in the late 1980s and throughout the 1990s and beyond, however, professional marketers have developed measuring sticks or goals for performance to include in each product's or service's marketing program. Whether one marketing effort achieved its goals or fell short is an important factor in the situation analysis for the next year. The consequences could be to redesign the product from feedback of past users or to discontinue the product or service entirely. How would the marketer approach the best decision? Asking why the product is not selling and from marketing sales data collection, the marketer can form an appropriate go–no go informed decision. If the marketing results were underachieving, was the root of the problem that of ineffective advertising or not enough spending in the media budget? Was the distribution plan poorly executed, or were the retailers' salespeople ill-trained or underachievers? Perhaps the product packaging was defective, and retailers' returns were exceptionally high in which case the marketing program might have reached all performance expectations, but the product malfunctioned to no fault of marketing. The Japanese have a penetrating management practice of questioning the lagging manager about the disappointing sales activities; the higher ranking officer poses a general question of why the product or service is not meeting the performance goals. The ranking marketing official asks *why* five times, and generally the problem is uncovered. Questioning might go something like this: Ranking manager asks the product marketer a generic question such as, "Sales projections are not meeting introduction sales expectations. Why?" Marketing manager responds, "We are receiving merchandise to the stores too late in the season." Senior marketing manager probes further, "Why?" "Because the designers are taking much too long to anticipate the fall, spring, summer fashion." "Why?" "Because the key account managers are not reporting information from each account input in a timely fashion to our design and production people." "Why?" "Because we are lacking strong leadership among the product managers since two of the four managers resigned about three months ago, and we have no replacements." "Why?" "Because the new shop personnel does not perform well without direction." If performance measurements are set at the beginning of the year, monitored all year long, and compared at the year's end (preferably at each quarter's end), questions such as these can be answered, and the results factored or adjusted to future programs. Granted, there are factors that pop up infrequently that will demand unusual compensation to achieve estimated performance. (El Niño has produced unusual and sometimes threatening weather patterns over the past years, wreaking havoc in the agricultural, construction, and tourism industries.)

Depending on the results, the resourceful marketer will analyze the symptoms and the effects to prescribe correcting actions for future plans. If the cost per sale was too high (meaning the planning measure was set for a range of $10 to $12 per unit for advertising), and the resulting measure was $15.50 average per unit, did the advertising create sales traffic, but the sales force was ineffective in making projected sales volumes? Or were there too few retail outlets for the national advertising programs, thus spending too much advertising for fewer than projected sales volumes? Or was manufacturing and distribution sixty days late in delivering the product to the franchisees while the two Super Bowl thirty-second television commercials advertising this product could not be canceled, therefore, the advertising ran even though the shelves were empty? There are so many scenarios to research that the marketing manager must understand and be able to parse the underlying causes to the success or failure effect. The program performance is usually traced to one or more of the following factors: budget, time, or people. The magazine *Communication Arts* once featured a graphics design shop for its outstanding work, and on the front door hung a tasteful sign reading, "Quality, Speed, and Price: Pick any two." This tongue-in-cheek admonition supports the comparison of budget, time, or the human ability to produce quality work. As the marketer researches program smashes or stumbles, probably the best sequence for review is evaluating the budget expenditure (too much or too little for support of each product or service, too early or too late, too much to trade partners or too little to consumer audiences, or how much was spent on each element of the promotional mix), then consider the timing of the program (too early or too late for the industry's selling seasons, ill-timing of distribution channels, or ill-timed promotions according to various regions), and then consider the people/ quality issue (effective and efficient task performance, which sums this query very well). It is wise to investigate people performance issues last since this investigation can be intimidating or insulting if the true cause of underachievement is either in the budget or in timing parameters.

Different companies and different industries set different performance measurement criteria. This book has addressed the measurement parameters for judging the salesperson's performance in either volume or probability by product or service or by client account. The retail industry has developed its own measurement criteria, generally thought in terms of real estate, such as sales per square foot, sales per counter, or sales per store. Service businesses have become very creative in relatively new measurement systems that entail measuring service, the very reason the company is in existence. Performance among certain companies can be measured by the number of customer complaints per thousand transactions, the percentage of customer complaint resolutions within twenty-four hours, the percentage of resales to current customers, or the length of time a customer or prospect spends on hold while telephoning the company. As stated, measurement criteria can be creative, but more importantly, these criteria should measure those steps that lead to customer satisfaction. Those special steps, as well, are usually generated by research, asking the customer what she values most from the company's product or service consumption. Customer feedback and surveys will be discussed in more depth in Chapter 13.

Summary

This chapter completes the groundwork for understanding the three steps of the traditional marketing process: 1) situation analysis, 2) marketing planning, and 3) marketing implementation. Emphasis is placed on actually doing the steps that link the planning stage to the implementation stage as well as minding all the internal and external linkages, large and small, within this action section that brings the marketing program to its public. An important overview of this marketing phase is a conscience balancing of the primal questions of *who*, *what*, *when*, *where*, and *why*. Each action of marketing implementation should be evaluated according to these five considerations, the marketer then should investigate that element further to either continue or disregard the issue.

A thorough discussion was presented on the value of using suppliers outside of the company to extend the marketing capabilities of the firm without hiring seldom-used marketing or communications' specialties. There are advantages and disadvantages of engaging suppliers that should be carefully considered within the corporate security policies as well as the cost/benefit value to the marketing effort. The chapter closed with a review of the importance of planning and execution time frames to optimize the company's resources. The better managed the marketing process, the more likely the success of product or service introductions. Lastly performance measurement could be considered the fifth marketing P; all important marketing outputs should be measured and compared to last year's performance and as information to the next year's program. Many times marketing underachievement can be traced to specific marketing actions, and if identified by measurement, the marketing implementation can be streamlined for future activities.

Key Terms

Clickthrough

Concurrent activities

Coupon keys

CPM (cost per thousand)

Fulfillment

GPS (global positioning satellite system)

GRP (gross rating point)

Linear activities

TRP (target rating point)

Unique visitor

QUESTIONS AND EXERCISES

1. You are hiring an assistant marketing director to help you run a two-person marketing department. What are the five most important personality characteristics you will be looking for in your new hire, and why are these characteristics important? Make a written list to refer to as you interview.

2. You are a production manager working on producing a new Web site for your company. You have the designs for various Web pages, but you have no further input about the assignment. The marketing director of your company is on vacation for two weeks, and she expects the site to go live the week after she returns. What questions would you e-mail her if you needed more information in implementing this assignment?

3. In implementing an e-mail order confirmation system, you recognize that the primary purpose of the system is to acknowledge order receipts to customers. What are other benefits, some psychological, that comes with this type of customer contact? Prepare a one-page memo on system benefits that will be used in training customer service representatives.

4. You are in charge of implementing a large proprietary database system that will contain all company financial, client project, and employee records; your publicly-traded construction company has sales of over $3 billion. You report to the chief operating officer, and he is extremely nervous and paranoid about losing control of this data. For certain phases of the transition from integrating three databases of the old system to your new consolidated information network, you will need to use an outside firm that specializes in data warehousing and holds proprietary software that could make the whole system operate 25 percent cheaper in processing costs, run 35 percent faster, and produce construction estimates in half the time with 15 percent better estimating accuracy. Your boss, however, has declared that no outside consultants or suppliers will be considered for this assignment. You have spoken with the data warehouse supplier and it is willing to sign nondisclosure agreements that your firm will draw up for signature. With what arguments can you approach your boss with to change his mind to produce a better system for the company? Cost arguments? Performance arguments? Staff inexperience in certain phases? Other logical considerations? Prepare a list of

situation points to discuss with your superior so persuasive that he can only say yes. Develop at least five argument propositions and counter arguments to discuss with him.

5. Implementation planning requires an organized, logical mindset to be able to think both in linear and concurrent time frames You keep notes from meetings, double-check your figures, and write progress reports highlighting weekly developments. Over coffee one morning, you describe your activities to a marketing assistant in another division, and he laughs at your diligence. "Can't you keep this in your head?" he taunts. What is your answer to him? Prepare six scenarios that might occur to you as you organize your work on paper and in spreadsheets and what might occur to him as he keeps everything in his head.

6. The text spoke of completing implementation projects on spec, on budget, and on time. As a marketing manager, which objective do you feel is most important to the benefit of your job? Which is most important to the benefit of your division? To the benefit of your company? Are there conflicts? Write a one-page outline summarizing your thoughts on achieving goals at these various levels of personal and company interests.

Bibliography

Komenar, Margo. 1997. *Electronic marketing.* New York: John Wiley & Sons.

CHAPTER 5

An Introduction to the Internet

"One of the virtues of a virtual place is that it can be whatever you want it to be. For much of its history, that was the charm of the Internet—a cross between a swimming hole and a cosmological worm hole, a secret place where nerds, geeks, and others in the know could gather, and then, collapsing time and distance, travel anywhere in the world, often to the electronic inner sanctum of institutions that would have turned them away if they had shown up in person and knocked at the door. Everyone was equal on the Net. It operated outside the tariffs and rules that governed the rest of telecommunications, even as the Net became the Web and commercial interests began to encroach on it, and Web addresses appeared on magazine covers and movie ads and business cards. The Net took hold of the popular imagination as a way to connect with others and to hide behind a screen of anonymity."

(Kupfer 1998)

LEARNING OBJECTIVES

- To offer insight into how and why the Internet was developed
- To introduce and clarify the operation and technology of the Internet
- To discuss the Internet resources that will be most vital for use in the process of electronic marketing and e-commerce

Introduction

The world has begun to discover and utilize resources that merely a few years ago were only being used by government, university researchers, and a few adventurous souls. These resources consist of many tools, but by and large the Internet is the fastest growing of these tools. The Internet encompasses many components of which the now popular World Wide Web is only one. To truly understand the power of the Internet and the resources available to the marketer, the Internet as a whole *must liken* to a tool kit containing multipurpose gadgets with many useful innovations. An overview of these innovations explaining where they began and how they evolved should prove useful to understanding the potential of the Internet for enhancing electronic marketing.

At its simplest description, the Internet is a worldwide network of networks, enabling millions of smaller computers to share information with each other and to share various communications, database, and transactions resources. Each individual that is connected to the Internet can contact anyone else on the Internet, can trade or publish ideas, and can sell products with minimum overhead costs. In the future, the Internet may have a dramatic impact on business and higher education as more companies offer goods and services and universities offer courses online. (Internet Introduction 1998)

With deepening complexity and diverse applications growing daily, the e-marketer and e-merchant are learning more about the commerce characteristics and promise of the World Wide Web. These experiences are facilitating customer shopping and satisfaction with each transaction, as well. From the wizardry of color graphics and sound bites that were novel to the Web landscape, to the initial uncertainty of online purchases, to the ongoing and informative customer e-mails and newsletters, and to the expanding familiarity of loyal customer shopping habits, commerce on the Web is maturing. The power of interactivity is allowing this to happen; the power of ingenuity is pushing the envelope of the Web at breathtaking speeds. Never has a medium grown so fast.

The Internet as a Whole

In order to make the best use of technology, it is often important to know how certain technologies have evolved. The Internet began as a federal government project and is still growing because of the support of the government, and more recently, the Internet has evolved to satisfy the demands of commercial interests. Although many organizations have increasingly started to make use of the World Wide Web (WWW or Web), the Internet was a very quiet, small network merely a few years ago. This chapter discusses how the Web evolved into what it is today—an elegant, dynamic, utilitarian resource—and how it is revolutionizing information distribution and retrieval on the Internet.

The invention of the telegraph, telephone, radio, television, and computer set the stage for an innovative integration of technologies, namely, the Internet. With this integration of vehicles, the Internet revolutionized the computer and communications world. So, what is the Internet exactly? There are many definitions from the ambiguous technical description to one that can be readily understood by everyone. Here are a few that may help clear up a bit of confusion. The Internet is a worldwide computer network accessed via modem, special communication lines, or even satellite. The Internet connects universities, government laboratories, businesses, and individuals around the world. In 1998, this global system connected an estimated one hundred million users, and more than one hundred countries were interlinked to share information, largely at no cost to the user. To give a more general understanding of the purpose of the Internet, it is a worldwide communication technology, a vast mechanism for information dissemination, and a medium for collaboration and interaction between individuals and their computers without regard for geographic location. It can be thought of as a virtual community of cooperation, which covers the entire globe, spanning political, economical, and cultural spectrums. The Internet is virtual in that it has no physical home or dimension, weight, or texture. Users of the Internet can communicate with each other, sending electronic mail, transferring files, and accessing information at speeds that a few years ago were not even imaginable.

There is a significant difference between the Internet and commercial online services. The online services are centrally controlled and programmed to serve the likes of the subscribers; the Internet is decentralized with little control by any party. Thought to be a rogue in nature by some, the Internet was intended to be decentralized by design. Think back to the redundant communications system that would never be silenced. Specifically in case of war or disaster, the Internet's connections might be broken in one place yet pop up reconnected in another location equally serviceable. Described as anarchy, the Internet has proven to be a system that works with surprising reliability and order. In this textbook's discussion of electronic marketing resources, the text will interchangeably use online and electronic to describe the accessibility and delivery of communications and transactions. However, these references are not expressing the characteristics of control or chaos, only that the systems are networked among participants.

History of the Internet

In order to understand the speed at which the Internet has evolved, a history lesson is in order. This is intended to be a brief and incomplete history. There is information about the history, technology, and usage of the Internet available in other books and on the Internet itself. After reading this abbreviated history, you may want to investigate further with your own readings. Much has been written about the Internet phenomena, and you can find excellent information at these web address references:

www.pbs.org/internet/timeline/index.html

www.isoc.org/guest/zakon/Internet/History/HIT.html

www.isoc.org/internet-history/brief.html

Besides online sites, books and magazines abound about Internet history and new exploits to be enjoyed. While the Internet's history spans approximately thirty years, its utility and potential lie in the future, not in the past.

In the Beginning

The first recorded description of interactions through **networking** was in a series of memos written by J. C. R. Licklider of MIT in August 1962 (just two months before the Cuban missile crisis that placed a nuclear threat ninety miles from the American mainland), which discussed his "Galactic Network" concept. He envisioned a globally interconnected set of computers through which everyone could quickly access data and programs from any location. In spirit, the concept was very much like the Internet of today. Licklider, a psychologist who was considered the foremost authority on psychoacoustics, was named the first head of the computer research program at the **Department of Defense Advanced Research Projects Agency**. **(DARPA,** www.arpa.mil/); it is there that the Internet originated.

EXHIBIT 5.1 A QUICK OVERVIEW OF SOME IMPORTANT EVENTS IN THE HISTORY OF THE INTERNET

1969	The ARPANET began
1971	E-mail was developed
1974	Telnet and FTP (File Transfer Protocol) were developed
1976	Queen Elizabeth II sends first e-mail
1982	Desktop computer revolution begins
1984	Number of hosts breaks 1,000
1985	First registered domain on the Internet
	Symbolics.com (http://stony-brook.scrc.symbolics.com/www/index.html)
1987	Number of hosts breaks 10,000
1988	**Internet Relay Chat (IRC)** developed
1989	Number of hosts breaks 100,000
1992	Number of hosts breaks 1,000,000
1993	NSFNET backbone upgraded to T3 (44,736 Mbps)
1994	U.S. White House comes online (http://www.whitehouse.gov/)
1997	71,618 mailing lists registered as Liszt (http://liszt.com)

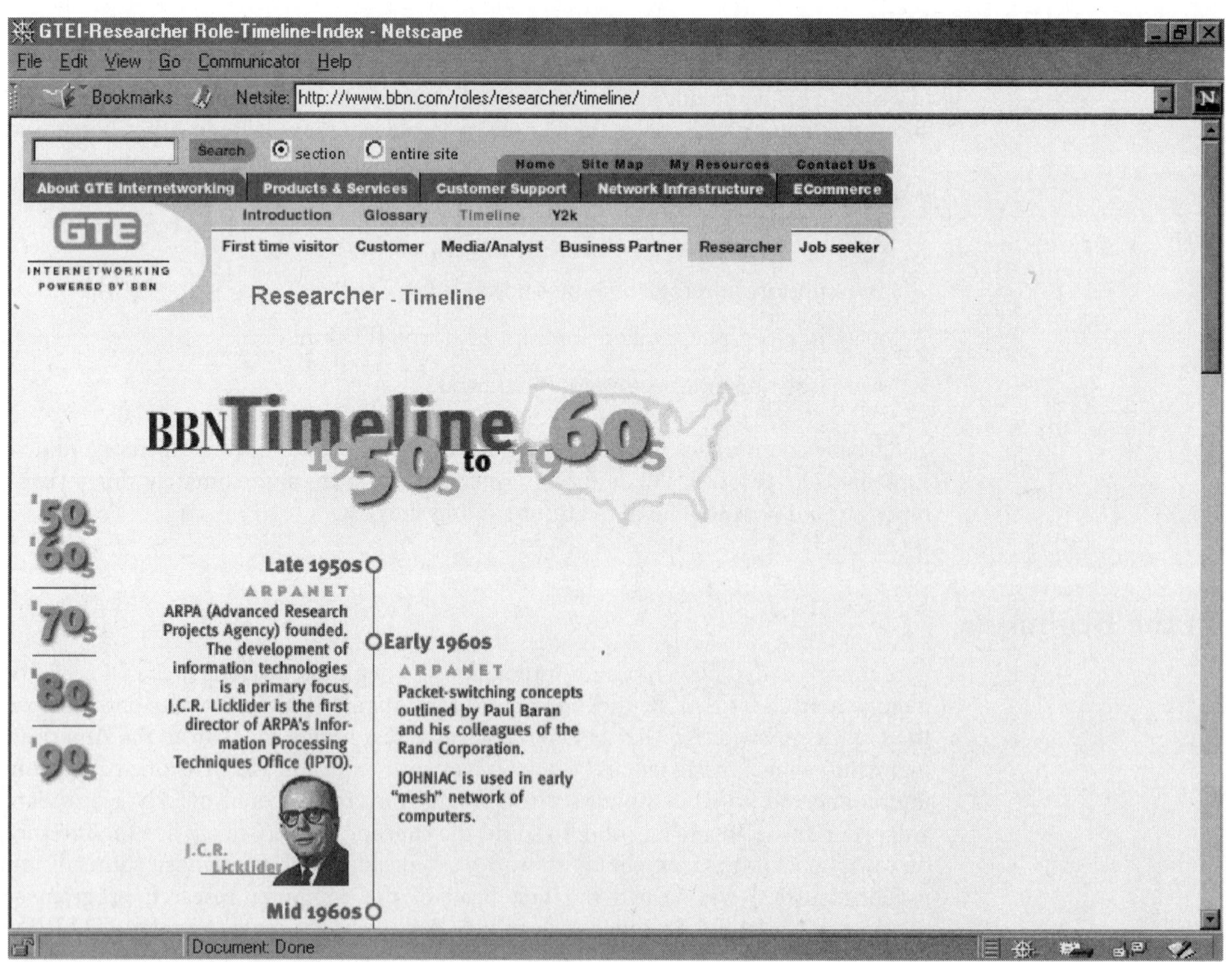

An example of an Internet timeline from BBN (www.bbn.com/timeline/).

EXHIBIT 5.2

A Popular Diagram That Represents the NSFNET and Its Connections to the World

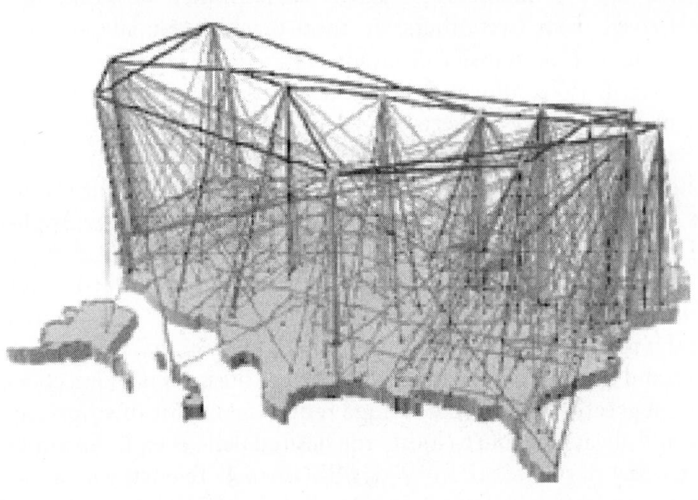

A popular diagram representing the NSFNET and its connections within the United States.

In 1969, DARPA created an experimental computer network called **ARPANET,** to provide a test-bed for emerging network technologies. The original ARPANET connected four universities (UCLA, Stanford Research Institute, University of California at Santa Barbara, and University of Utah), thus enabling scientists to share information and resources across long distances. ARPANET continued to expand, growing to connect many more sites, mainly in the research and academic arenas throughout the 1970s and 1980s.

In 1973, Bob Kahn of ARPA posed an Internet problem that initiated the Internetting research program at the Advanced Research Projects Agency (ARPA). This program investigated techniques and technologies for packet networks of various kinds. The objective was to develop communication protocols or agreed-upon standards, allowing networked computers to communicate transparently across multiple, linked packet networks. By making the analogy to **packets,** information would be broken into many smaller units that would be easier to route through the network; long streams of information could choke the system, much as railways are often stopped to wait for the opening of the single tracks. Called **packet switching,** the information, be it a text message, a photograph, or illustration, motion, or sound, would be disassembled at the origin of the message into smaller packets. Some packets would travel north, some south, all directions that the interlinked network physically covered. When the packets reached their destination, they were reassembled into a complete and intelligible message. The original ideas of a gateway architecture were sketched by Vinton Cerf on the back of an envelope in a hotel lobby in San Francisco. Later that year, Cerf and Kahn presented their basic Internet ideas at the Internet Network Working Group (INWG). The system of protocols, which was developed over the course of this research effort, became known as the **TCP/IP Protocol Suite** after the two initial protocols: Transmission Control Protocol (TCP) and Internet Protocol (IP). These communications protocols are used to link host computers on the Internet; TCP/IP is built into the **UNIX** operating system, making it the default standard for transmitting data over networks. Setting these standards was a major step for programmers, systems designers, and software developers to work with a common understanding of how the network was to perform. This standardization, as well, led to the creation of many communications applications that proved to increase the accuracy and speed of business.

Internet Tools Are Invented

In 1971, Ray Tomlinson of Bolt Beranek Newman (BBN, www.bbn.com) invented the first e-mail program that could send messages across a distributed network. His original program was derived from two others: an intra-machine e-mail program (SNDMSG) and an experimental file transfer program (CPYNET). He continued to improve the e-mail program in 1972, allowing the sender to use the software to send and receive mail. Also in 1972, Larry Roberts, an MIT researcher, wrote his first e-mail utility to list, selectively read, file, forward, and respond to messages.

Other major steps in the creation of the Internet, as is known today, were the evolution of **Telnet** that was developed by the National Center for Supercomputing Applications (NCSA) and FTP (File Transfer Protocol). Telnet allowed for remote log on, or access, making it easier to connect to a remote computer. FTP standardized the transfer of files between networked computers; for example, a student or marketer could search for a specific subject, find it residing on a host computer across the country, use FTP to dial into the remote host, and transfer the file to the student's or business person's computer. This transfer system greatly reduced the storage requirements for the everyday user because the user would always be able to locate the desired data, even if the information resided in another part of the world. In 1974, BBN opened Telenet, which was the first public packet data service (a commercial version of ARPANET).

An Online Community Begins

Network development continued to heat up. During 1980 through 1981, two other networking projects, BITNET and CSNET, were initiated. BITNET (www.cren.net/index.html), the "Because It's Time NETwork," started as a cooperative network at the City University of New York, with Yale University in Connecticut as its first connection. The original acronym stood for There instead of Time in reference to the free protocols provided with the IBM systems. BITNET provided electronic mail and listserv servers to distribute information, as well as file transfers. A listserv is a communications list to which participants sign on or subscribe to a common interest list usually at no charge; the subscriber has his messages forwarded to the user's e-mail. Today, BITNET and its parallel networks in other parts of the world have several thousand participating sites.

Many important government agencies contributed to the Internet during this nascent period, such as DARPA, the Department of Defense (DoD), and the **National Science Foundation (NSF).** Some of these organizations were sponsored by the federal government because of the enormous capital outlays and the highly specialized, technical staff required to develop the Internet network. Among these, none has made more significant contributions than the NSF (www.nsf.gov/), an independent agency of the U.S. government, established by the National Science Foundation Act of 1950. The mission of the NSF is to promote the progress of science; to advance the national health, prosperity, and welfare; and to secure the national defense. While these objectives may seem lofty, the development of the Internet is a concrete example of performance by the NSF. Many equally successful programs were sponsored by the NSF; in fact, the NSF must be careful and selective in the programs it underwrites. For example, Computer Science NETwork (CSNET) was initially funded by the National Science Foundation to provide networking services for university, industry, government, and computer science research groups with no access to ARPANET. The CSNET name server provided an early example of a white pages directory service, and this software is still in use at numerous sites. At its peak, CSNET had approximately two hundred participating sites and international connections to approximately fifteen countries. CSNET later became known as the Computer and Science Network, and

EXHIBIT 5.3 GROWTH OF THE INTERNET AS PORTRAYED IN HOBBES' TIMELINE

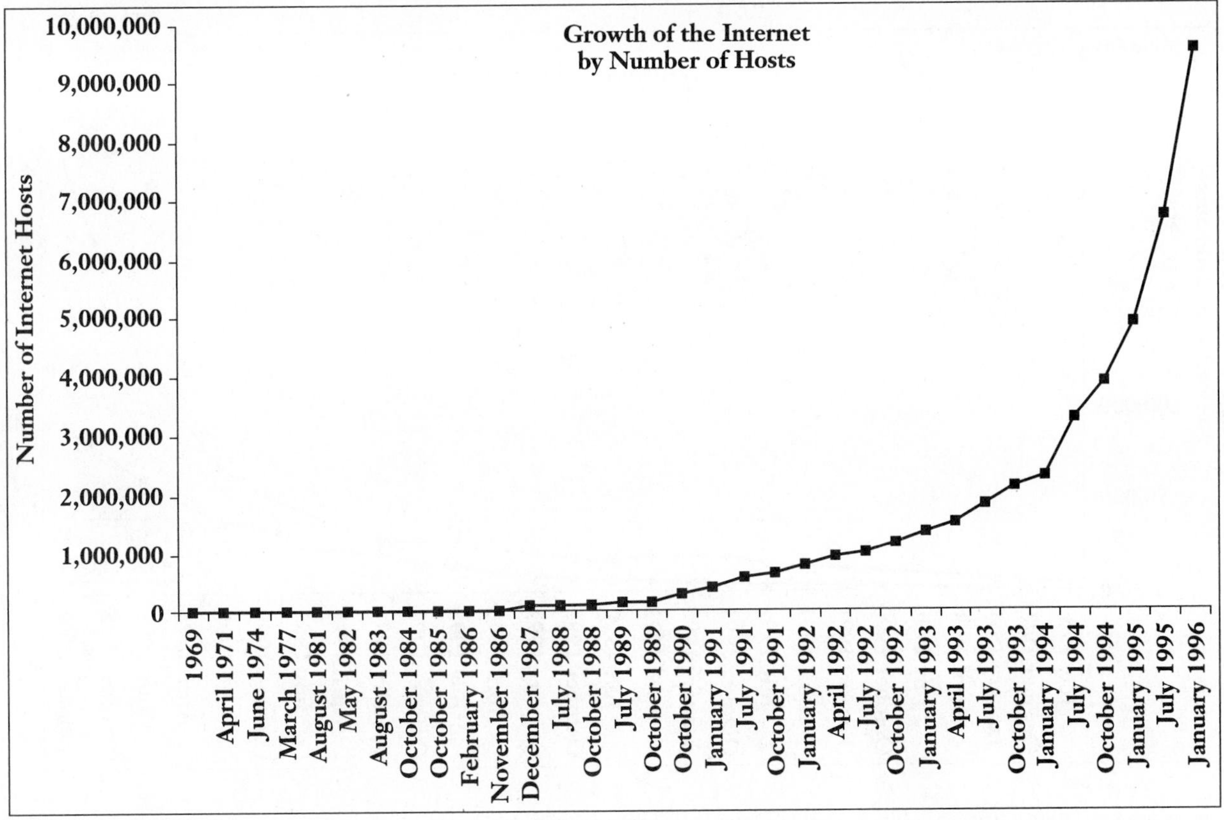

(www.isoc.org/zakon/Internet/History/HIT.html) Source: Internet Society

in 1987, BITNET and CSNET merged for cost savings to form the Corporation for Research and Educational Networking (CREN). In the Fall of 1991, CSNET service was discontinued and dismantled, having fulfilled its important early role in the provision of academic networking service. On the commercial front, the first relays between a commercial electronic mail carrier and the Internet were developed with MCI Mail through the Corporation for the National Research Initiative (CNRI) and CompuServe through Ohio State University. Business was beginning to discover, utilize, and embrace the merits of the Internet. As commercial applications expanded, businesses found more and more ways to exploit the speed, accuracy, and cost savings of Internet communications.

The Revolution Starts with the Explosion of Personal Computers (PCs)

In 1982 and 1983, the first desktop PCs began to appear. Many were equipped with an operating system called Berkeley UNIX, which included networking software. This software provided for relatively easy connections to the Internet using Telnet. The personal computer revolution continued through the eighties, making access to computer resources and networked information increasingly available to the general public. Also in 1983, a name server program was developed at the University of Wisconsin

EXHIBIT 5.4 EXPANSION OF THE INTERNET BY INCREASE IN NETWORKS AND DOMAINS AS PORTRAYED BY HOBBES' INTERNET TIMELINE

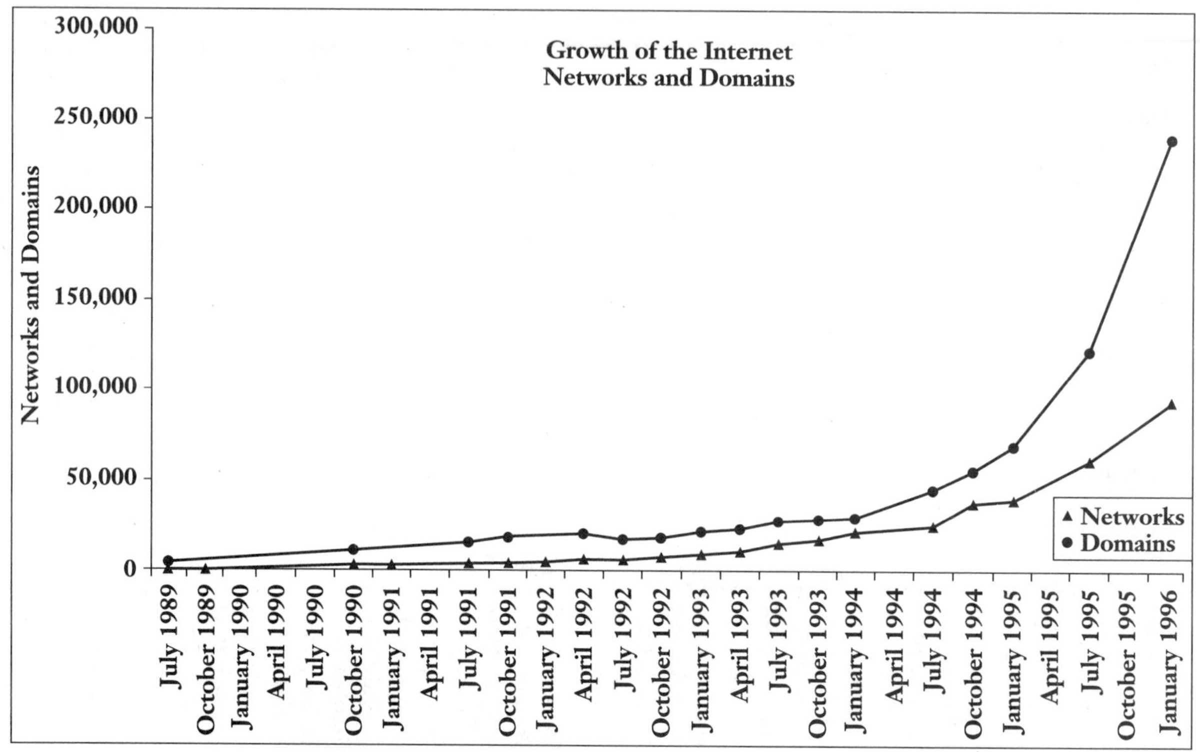

(www.iso.org/zakon/Internet/History/HIT.html) Source: Internet Society

that no longer required users to know the exact path to other systems. Computer programs were previously very unforgiving, requiring addresses to be input to the exact letter, number, or symbol. Now, the name of the machine a user wants to contact to connect to is the only information that is needed. Along with the name servers, networking needs of users switched from having a single, large time sharing computer connected to the Internet at each site to connecting entire local networks. During 1985 through 1986, the U.S. National Science Foundation connected the nation's six supercomputing centers together. This network was called the **NSFNET,** or NSFNET **backbone,** and today provides a major backbone (the main carrier) communication service for the Internet. To expand access to the Internet, the NSF supported the development of regional networks, which were then connected to the NSFNET backbone. In addition, the NSF supported institutions, such as universities, in their efforts to connect to the regional networks. Commercial network providers in the U.S. and in Europe began to offer Internet backbone and access support to any interested parties on a competitive basis.

To maintain some control and standardization with the vast growth of the Internet, the Internet Activities Board (IAB, www.isi.edu/iab) was established. In 1986, the Internet Engineering Task Force (www.ietf.cnri.reston.va.us/home.html) and Internet Research Task Force (IRTF) came into existence under the IAB to assist in the organization and standardization of the Internet. The first **Freenet** (Cleveland) came online in July. Later, Freenet program management was assumed by the National Public Telecomputing Network (NPTN) in 1989. Each of these moves expanded awareness

EXHIBIT 5.5 GROWTH OF THE WORLD NETWORKS AS PORTRAYED IN HOBBES' TIMELINE

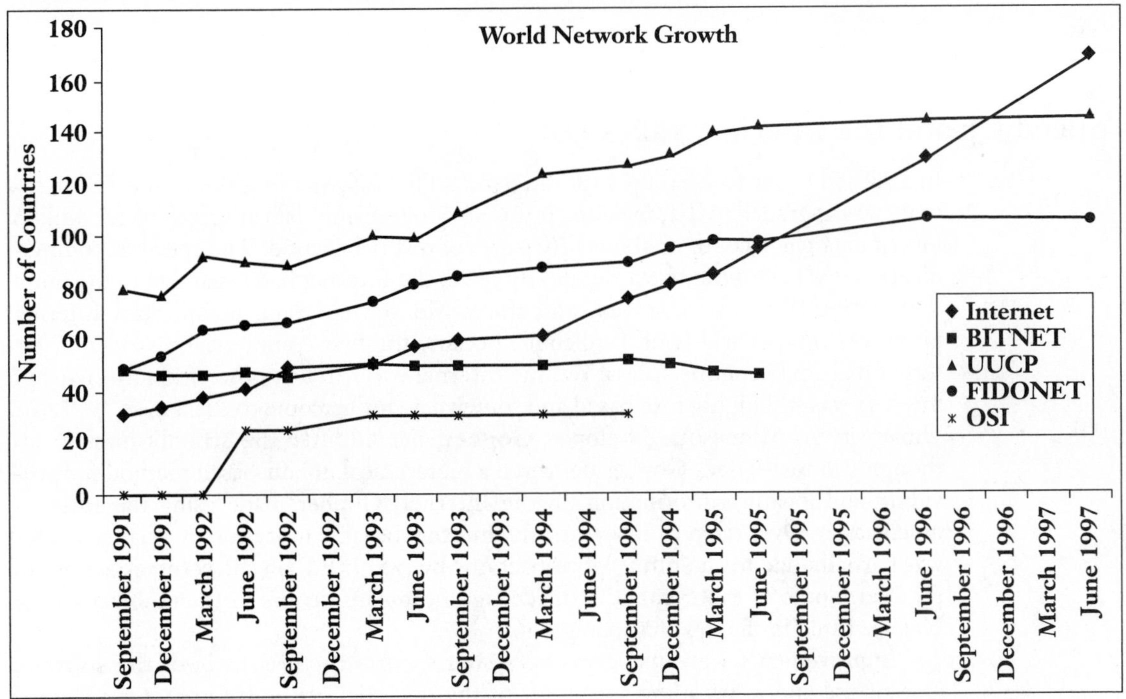

(www.iso.org/zakon/Internet/History/HIT.html) Source: Internet Society

for the Internet and brought businesses and the public closer to knowing the why and what of the flourishing network.

Problems and Solutions

One of the first hard times (and resulting negative publicity) for the Internet came in 1988 when an Internet **worm** burrowed through the Net, affecting approximately 6,000 of the 60,000 host computers. On the evening of November 2, a self-replicating program (the worm) was released upon the Internet. This program invaded large computer systems running versions of Berkeley UNIX and used their resources to attack still more computers. Within the space of hours, this program had spread across the United States, infecting thousands of computers and making many of them unusable due to the burden of its activity. Soon after the worm inci-dent, DARPA formed the Computer Emergency Response Team (CERT, www.cert.org/) to respond to issues such as the worm incident by issuing advisories and help. While virus attacks are still frequent, and new viruses are released on the Internet every day, damage has been limited because of the experience and rapid response by the CERT personnel. There are many forms of computer viruses and even more Internet hoaxes that can cause fear for the Internet user. Being aware of how to protect against viruses and where to get information on hoaxes is a useful strategy. Information on these topics can readily be found on the Internet with a simple search. Try going to Yahoo and searching for Internet hoaxes to see what you find. Although computer hoaxes will continue to be a problem as long as technology continues to advance, because of the government's, and more recently businesses', investments in the Internet infrastructure, system vigilance will continue to grow.

Things Speed Up and the Internet Takes Off

In 1989, in order to keep up with the demand for information, the NSFNET backbone was upgraded to **T1,** meaning it was able to transmit data at speeds of 1.5 million bits of data per second, or about fifty pages of text per second. The speed of communication was beginning to accelerate. By 1990, the Internet had expanded to the point that ARPANET was dissolved, and the world started using commercial Internet providers. The World (world.std.com/) became the first commercial provider of Internet dial-up telephone access. Yet, the Internet was still not a user-friendly environment. It was still highly text-based and somewhat cumbersome to use. So, in 1991, the University of Minnesota developed **Gopher,** named after the school's mascot; although still text-based, Gopher delivered a hierarchical, menu-based method for providing and locating information on the Internet. Gopher made using the Internet much easier. Over the next few years, the Internet became more commercialized. This was partially due to the lifting of restrictions by NSFNET on the commercial use of the Net. Some of the events that made significant differences in the usability of the Net are listed in the next few paragraphs.

Improvements were made in the system's infrastructure: in both the software ease-of-use and a spreading awareness of the potential of the Internet. Commercial Internet eXchange (CIX) Association, Inc. was formed by General Atomics (CERFnet), Performance Systems International, Inc. (PSInet), and UUNET Technologies, Inc. (AlterNet). **Wide Area Information Servers (WAIS,** www.wais.com/) was invented by Brewster Kahle and released by Thinking Machines Corporation. WAIS servers provided the technology to effectively search the Internet for information. In 1991, the European Laboratory for Particle Physics in Switzerland **(CERN,** www.cern.ch/) released the **World Wide Web (WWW,** www.w3.org/), developed by Tim Berners-Lee, now in residence at the Massachusetts Institute of Technology (wwwmit.edu). The Web uses hypertext transfer protocol (HTTP) and hypertext links—the ability to transmit and receive several types of media such as text, photos, sound, motion, and color; these attractive additions caused more interest in the Internet because of the Web component—thus changing the way information can be organized, presented, and accessed on the Internet. As an analogy, the difference between the Internet and the Web is similar to the distinction between a computer and a multiuser program that runs on the computer. (Internet Introduction 1998, 2) To ensure privacy on the newly formed Web, Pretty Good Privacy (PGP), a security program, was released by Philip Zimmerman. The U.S. High Performance Computing Act then established the National Research and Education Network (NREN), and NSFNET traffic passed one trillion bytes per month, ten billion packets per month. The Web is a major step for the Internet, technology, and the world.

In 1992, the **Internet Society (ISOC,** www.isoc.org/) was chartered; this organization is a voluntary membership whose purpose is to promote global information exchange through Internet technology. The First Multicast BackBone (MBONE) audio multicast (March 1992) and video multicast (November 1992) were seen and heard on the Internet. A new Gopher space search tool, Veronica, (several search tools are whimsically named after comic book characters, for instance, Archie, Jughead, and Betty), was released by University of Nevada, while the popular term Surfing the

EXHIBIT 5.6 WORLD WIDE WEB GROWTH AS PORTRAYED IN HOBBES' TIMELINE

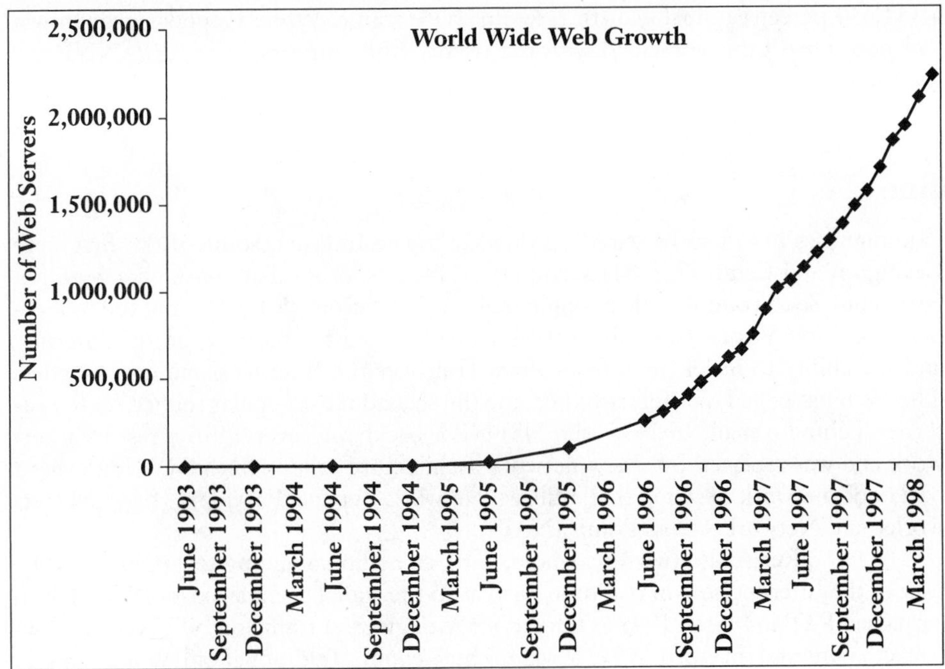

(www.isoc.org/zakon/Internet/History/HIT.html) Source: Internet Society

Internet was coined by Jean Armour Polly (www.well.com/user/polly/about/surfing.htm). In 1993, the NSFNET backbone network was upgraded to **T3,** meaning it is able to transmit data at speeds of 45 million bits of data per second, or about 1400 pages of text per second. Not only could the user begin to speed on the Internet, she could enlist sound and color to look good while surfing. This was a major breakthrough in the way the world would begin to communicate. A user could now communicate faster and with more style using graphics and sound to portray his concepts. Speed of communication would soon become one of the most important factors in the use of the Internet.

The World Goes Graphical

Now that the Web had been released, a need arose for better technology and an easier interface. Thus, during the period of 1993 through 1994, the graphical Web **browsers Mosaic** and **Netscape Navigator** were introduced and spread through the Internet community. Due to their intuitive nature and graphical interface, these browsers made the Web and the Internet more appealing to the general public. **InterNIC** (www.internic.net/) was then created by NSF to provide specific Internet services, such as directory and database services (AT&T), registration services (Network Solutions, Inc.), and information services (General Atomics/CERFnet).

Worms of a new kind were finding their way around the Net; WWW Worms (W4) are joined by **Spiders, Wanderers, Crawlers,** and **Snakes.** Unlike the original Worm, these programs made it easier to find information on the Internet. In 1994, Internet Talk Radio began broadcasting, the United Nations (UN) came online, and the

U.S. National Information Infrastructure Act was passed. Now, businesses and media really began to take notice of the Internet, and Mosaic, an application that simplifies accessing the World Wide Web, took the Internet by storm. The Web propagated at a 341,634 percent annual growth rate of service traffic. While Gopher's growth was 997 percent. All this coincided with the twenty-fifth anniversary of ARPANET and the Internet.

Consumers Go Online

Communities began to be wired up directly to the Internet, some of the first were Lexington and Cambridge, Massachusetts. This was a sign that consumers were not far behind; soon commercial shopping malls, cyberstations (RT-FM), and the first cyberbank, First Virtual (www.firstvirtual.com/), opened for business on the Internet, and the ability to order pizza from Pizza Hut over the Internet came into practice. The Web has edged out Telnet to become the second most popular service on the Internet, behind e-mail. In 1995, the NSFNET backbone reverted to a research network and was replaced by a new network architecture called vBNS (very high speed backbone network system) that utilizes Network Service Providers, regional networks, and Network Access Points (NAPs).

In 1995, RealAudio (www.realaudio.com), an audio-streaming technology, let the user of the Internet hear in real time, as near to the actual event as possible. The Web surpassed FTP in March 1995 as the service with greatest traffic on NSFNet based on packet count and, in April 1995, based on byte count. Traditional online dial-up systems such as CompuServe (www.compuserve.com/), America Online, and Prodigy (www.prodigy.excite.com/) began to provide Internet access. A number of Net-related companies went public, with Netscape leading the pack with the third largest ever NASDAQ IPO share value (August 9, 1995). Registration of **domain names** was no longer free. Beginning September 14, 1995, a $50 annual fee was imposed, which up until then was subsidized by NSF; NSF continued to pay for .edu registration, and on an interim basis for .gov domain.

In 1996 the Internet allowed phone companies to sign up users allowing the user access to the Internet; various **ISPs** suffered extended service outages, bringing into question whether they would be able to handle the growing number of users: AOL (nineteen hours), Netcom (thirteen hours), AT&T WorldNet (twenty-eight hours, e-mail only). MCI upgraded its Internet backbone adding approximately 13,000 ports. This brought its effective speed from 155 Mbps to 622 Mbps. The Web browser war began, fought primarily between Netscape and Microsoft. The Internet had rushed in a new age in software development, whereby new releases were made quarterly with the help of Internet users eager to test upcoming (beta) versions. In 1997, the American Registry for Internet Numbers (ARIN, www.arin.net/) was established to handle administration and registration of IP numbers to the geographical areas currently handled by Network Solutions three (InterNIC). There were 101,803 Name Servers in the WhoIs database at the end of 1997.

In 1998, Robert H Zakon released a Web-based version of the Hobbes Internet Timeline (www.isoc.org/zakon/Internet/History/HIT.html). Hobbes' timeline existed for many years, but until 1998, it resided on a Gopher server and not a Web server. This is a great source for information about the history of the Internet, and much of the history portrayed in this chapter has been adapted from Hobbes. Also in 1998, the government made things a little easier by creating electronic stamps. Through the U.S. Postal Service (www.usps.gov/), stamps can be purchased online.

The Internet has evolved through a series of advancements in networking and computer technologies. From its beginning in 1969, the ARPANET provided a testbed for networking research and development. An important emergence that grew out of ARPANET developments was TCP/IP protocols, which provided standard rules for networked computers to communicate with each other. Other significant events included the introduction of the desktop computer, the development of networking tools such as Telnet, FTP, Gopher, World Wide Web, and the release of graphical browsers. Advancements in networking enabled the NSFNET to upgrade its speed several times, allowing more and more connections.

Current Internet Usage Trends

Now that a clear picture of how the Internet got started has been formed, it is time to take a look at the current usage trends of the Internet. A wise marketer should investigate and ascertain what consumers are using: processor speed, modem speed, version of software, color versus black-and-white monitors, or the type and version of browser. Where should the marketing efforts be directed to reach the greatest audience? Where are the target markets hanging out on the Web? A good place to start looking at the statistical data on Internet trends and usage is at Yahoo (www.yahoo.com/Computers_and_Internet/Internet/Statistics_and_Demographics/), where many useful sites are listed under the topic Computers and Internet/Internet/Statistics, Or at Stat Market (www.statmarket.com/), a global site that keeps statistics on most used browsers, operating systems, busiest times of the day, and other useful Internet usage research. These sites cover statistics derived from published estimates or backed up by public surveys. It is not always the most current statistical collection, but these sites contain a lot of pertinent information for marketing program usage. You should take a look at how you might go about finding the demographic information on the Internet's audience using Yahoo.

What Can a World Wide Web Address Report?

Through a Web address additional information on Web travelers can be obtained; different sources supply different insights into the Web regulars. Many different types of people and businesses use the Web. Often you can glean some information about the person or organization that created a Web page by the address or **Uniform Resource Locator (URL)** of the page you are viewing. A URL has the following format, scheme://host.domain[:port]/path/data, using numbers and letters, but no spaces. The scheme, host, and **domain** can give information about the page's authors, such as their names; the organization to which they belong; if the organization is educational, commercial, governmental, or a network; or perhaps the country of the messages origin. A close review of the URL might help you decide whether or not to respond to the communications. Web page traffic statistical packages can be installed on the Web page to count the total hits, unique visitors, domain origins, and time parameters, such as hour of the day or day of the week or month, to summarize pertinent user personalities. Understanding and knowing the logic of the address assists both the consumer and the marketer in judging whether to respond and how to structure the address creatively and intriguingly.

Current Internet Operation and Tools

The architecture of the Internet is simple. Based on the concept of a client–server relationship between computers and a line of transmission, some computers act as servers, or information providers, while other computers act as clients, or information receivers. The client–server architecture is not a one-to-one relationship: A single client computer may access many different servers, and a single server may be accessed

EXHIBIT 5.7 EXAMPLES OF DOMAINS USED IN UNIFORM RESOURCE LOCATORS (URLs)

Domain	Explanation
edu	Educational
com	Commercial entities
org	Nonprofit
net	Network providers
mil	Military organizations
gov	Government
ca	Canada
uk	United Kingdom
jp	Japan

by a number of different client computers. A client computer is often a PC, whether it be a palmtop, laptop, desktop, or mainframe. The connection link to be network is also flexible; the computer might be linked through telephone modems or cable, fiber optic, microwave, or satellite transmissions; because of these varieties of connections, the Internet allows easy access to many communications tools. Users will find it easy to employ electronic mail, bulletin boards, Internet news groups, and chat rooms to discuss and explore everything from movie reviews to PC technical issues to hiring robotic shopping agents. Information on any subject is only an Internet connection away. Each day the world gathers information on the latest headline news, sports, weather, reference information, and much more through their computers. Here is a short description of some of the tools that make this gathering of information possible.

E-mail

E-mail stands for electronic mail. It was designed for personal and business communications through the Internet. To use e-mail, a user must have an electronic post office or e-mail address. This address is comprised of a user name, a machine or host name, and a domain. For example, if you sent an e-mail to jdoe@ritchie.acomp.uoa. edu, this address would direct e-mail to Jane Doe at a server named "ritchie" in the department of Academic Computing at the University of America. Along with e-mail come List Servers or listservs. List Servers are programs that allow one e-mail message to go to many people on a list. The lists for these programs are created by people subscribing to them or being subscribed to them. Lists are usually made up of people with similar interests. Listservs can be very powerful tools for the marketer. They can be used in many ways such as monitoring customer opinion, keeping up with competitors, and building goodwill among your target audience. A list of lists can be found at www.liszt.com or www. Egroups.com. Other types of lists that may also be useful to marketers and many users of the Internet are directory assistance lists such as Four 11 (www.four11.com) and the Yellow pages (www.yellowpages.com). These lists are much like their published counterparts and can be used in the same manner.

Telnet

One step beyond electronic mail is the ability to control a remote computer using Telnet. Telnet allows users to virtually teleport anywhere on the Internet and use resources located physically at that host. Some **hosts** have gateways to other hosts, which have still more gateways, allowing you to go on forever. To use Telnet, you need a Telnet program; an example of Telnet is Microsoft's HyperTerminal that comes with the Windows 95 and NT operating systems. It is a program you can use to easily connect to a remote computer, a bulletin board, or an online service, and replaces Terminal from Windows version 3.1. Telnet can be used to access remote computers for **Multiuser Dimensions (MUDs)** or **Multiuser Simulation Environments (MUSEs),** which are virtual realities used for role playing in games, collaboration, and exploratory discovery.

File Transfer Protocol (FTP)

File Transfer Protocol (FTP) is the program used to retrieve a text document, software, or other item from a remote (as in long distance) host. Normal practice is to FTP to the host you want and logon as "anonymous." Some sites use the password "guest," while others require that you enter your network address as "password." Uploading a file refers to the process of sending information to a remote computer, while downloading implies accessing information from another computer and copying it to a hard drive or disk. Some popular FTP sites are ftp.netscape.com and ftp.microsoft.com.

The World Wide Web (WWW)

In March 1989, Tim Berners-Lee, a British physicist working at the European Lab for Particle Physics (called CERN), proposed the beginnings of the World Wide Web as a protocol for an Internet distribution system to be used among high-energy physics research groups. It was later adopted by others who formed a consortium. This consortium is now referred to as W3; W3 (www.w3.org/) pooled its resources to develop Web standards, and it continues to create standards still today. The Web is officially described as a wide-area hypermedia information retrieval initiative information system that links data from many Internet services under one set of protocols. The Web uses browsers or Web clients to interpret hypertext markup language (HTML) documents delivered from what are called Web servers. Servers and viewers communicate via hypertext transfer protocol (HTTP). HTTP is an equalizer, allowing users to create HTML documents on any platform (PC, Mac, UNIX, OS/2) and deliver them to any other platform in a consistent manner. The Web is capable of providing access to the many resources available on the Internet.

In the last few years, a new phase of commercialization has surfaced. Originally, commercial efforts mainly comprised of vendors providing the basic networking products and Internet service providers (ISP) offering the connectivity and basic Internet services. The Internet has now become almost a commodity service, and much of the latest attention has been on the use of this global information infrastructure for support of other commercial services. This has been tremendously accelerated by the widespread and rapid adoption of browsers and the World Wide Web technology, allowing users easy access to information linked throughout the globe. Products are available to facilitate the provisioning of that information, and many of the latest developments in technology have been aimed at providing increasingly sophisticated information services on top of the basic Internet data communications.

Search Tools You can find information on the Web in a variety of ways. One way is to use one of the many search tools that are available. When you click the Search button on your browser toolbar, it provides access to a number of search services that offer different kinds of searching capabilities. Try out the different search services to see what kinds of information they provide. You can search for terms, people, or businesses by choosing a different search tool. Then, after going to a Web page, you can search for specific text on that page by using the find tool, which is usually found under the Edit menu option on your browser.

Summary

The Internet has changed much in the three decades since it came into existence. It was created in the era of time-sharing, but has survived into the era of personal computers, client–server relationships, peer-to-peer computing, and the network computer. It was designed before local area networks existed but has accommodated that new network technology. It was envisioned as supporting a range of functions from file sharing and remote logon to resource sharing and collaboration, yet it has also spawned electronic mail and more recently the World Wide Web. Most important, however, it started as the creation of a small band of dedicated researchers and has grown to be a commercial success with billions of dollars of annual investment.

However, the Internet has not finished changing. Although a network in name and geography, it is a beast of the computer. It will continue to change, evolving at the speed of the computer industry in order to stay in the game. It is now changing to provide such new services as real time transport to support, for example, audio and video streams. The availability of the Internet along with powerful affordable computing and communications in portable form (laptop computers, two-way pagers, PDAs, cellular phones) is making possible a new paradigm of mobile computing and communications.

This development will bring new applications—Internet telephone and, slightly further out, Internet television. The Internet is evolving, permitting more sophisticated forms of pricing and cost recovery. It is changing to accommodate yet another generation of network technologies with different characteristics and requirements, from broadband residential access to satellites. New methods of access and new forms of service will breed new applications, which in turn will continue to drive the Internet revolution.

Key Terms

ARAPNET

Backbone

Browser

CERN (European Laboratory for Particle Physics)

CERT (Computer Emergency Response Team)

Crawlers

DARPA (Department of Defense Advanced Research Projects Agency)

Domain

Domain names

Freenet

Gopher

Hosts

InterNIC

IRC (Internet Relay Chat)

ISOC (Internet Society)

ISP

Microsoft Internet Explorer

Mosaic

MUDs (Multiuser Dimensions)

MUSEs (Multiuser Simulation Environments)

Netscape Navigator

Networking

NSF (National Science Foundation)

NSFNET

Packet switching

Packets

Snakes

Spiders

T1/T3

TCP/IP Protocol Suite (Transmission Control Protocol and Internet Protocol)

Telnet

UNIX

URL (Uniform Resource Locators)

WAIS (Wide Area Information Servers)

Wanderers

Worm

WWW (World Wide Web)

QUESTIONS AND EXERCISES

1. The Internet has become one of the buzz words of the marketing world. Write a two-page paper describing what Internet is and what impact it is expected to have on marketing in the future. Will the Web expand its residents beyond the direct marketing element? Why?

2. From what you have learned in this and previous chapters, list five business activities that you can accomplish by putting your company on the Internet. Give specific examples of electronic research, communications, or transactions and what their purpose is. Be prepared to discuss examples of how this is currently being done by others, or explain original ideas as appropriate in your next class.

3. The Internet has not always been as widely-known or popular as it is today. Certain events in the history of the Internet have increased this phenomenon. What was the major invention that stimulated popularity for the Internet, and why did it take this piece of the Internet for the business world to determine it was beneficial for their organizations?

4. Listservs are useful for communicating with a large number of people with like interests. How would you as a marketer use this to your advantage? Find at least two lists (preferably very active ones) that are of interest to you and subscribe to them. After three weeks of observing the list traffic and participating in the discussions, write a short paper on the content and tone of the discussions and the positives and negatives of e-mail lists for marketing intelligence gathering.

5. In a very short time, the Web has been transformed from a plain-looking, black-and-white visual text to a full-color, sound and motion communications vehicle. Using your imagination, describe three visions of how you see the Web's marketing or commerce capabilities in the year 2020. Remember that marketing serves customer interests and satisfaction; how will your visions support these objectives? Write a one-page outline describing the marketing opportunities, the technology needed, and company benefits and consumer benefits of each of your three ideas; address your comments to the director of strategic planning in your company.

6. Search tools are very important to the marketer for many reasons. List some examples of advertising or promoting on a search engine home page and how they would be useful for providing exposure for your company. These examples might be advertising banners available with the click of the mouse, listings high on the search hierarchy, or sponsorships of news such as headlines or weather. Conduct these searches on the Internet and print samples of five promotional elements. Be prepared to share your examples and explain how different promotions might reach different targets contained within your marketing program.

7. The proper domain name and URL can be important in a marketing strategy. Does your company need its own unique domain name? How do you decide? Explain why this is important, then find two examples of companies that have a perceived image advantage due to their domain name and two who missed out because someone else got there first.

8. Marketers use demographics and trend studies to determine the best way to approach their target market. In this context, why is it important to know who uses the Web? Discuss in five paragraphs how you would go about determining the information you need to know about Web users. Be sure to cite any Web sites that you would use to find your information.

9. It is always important to know where consumer trends are going, and the good marketer knows that he can learn from the past. Take a look at the Web sites containing Internet usage trends discussed in this and previous chapters. What are the most important trends, such as Web access, and computer usage growth of concern to the marketer? Write an e-mail to the European manager of your company listing ten trends to watch for or research from your Internet marketing experience in the United States.

10. Now that you have a general understanding of how the Internet was developed and what tools are available, you should be aware of how you might use it to support your marketing efforts. Besides supporting sales or creating a corporate presence, what are some other ways within the promotional mix that the Internet can support marketing efforts? E-mail a short response to your professor.

Bibliography

Internet introduction. 1998. Microsoft Corporation, 1, 2.
Kupfer, Andrew. 1998. Four forces that will shape the Internet. *Fortune*, 6 July, 93.

CHAPTER 6

Concept of the Virtual Store for Marketing Products and Services

"Visa in coming weeks plans newspaper ads promoting the use of its cards on the Internet in general, and at online service Yahoo! and online music retailer Music Boulevard. Visa is betting that e-commerce will soar. Over the next twelve months, Visa plans to spend about $25 million on e-commerce promotion including online and garden-variety advertisements and sponsorship. That's more than 10 percent of Visa's estimated annual advertising budget of $230 million. Yet, e-commerce transactions now account for less than .5 percent of all Visa payments in the U.S., which in 1997 totaled $525 billion. Says Alan Brew, partner with branding consultancy Addison, 'Clearly they've got to be investigating the potential of e-commerce, but the problem with e-commerce is that it's yet to be proven. Visa believes that potential is huge.' In 2003, Visa estimates e-commerce transactions with its cards will hit $100 billion, or 10 percent of all U.S. payments. Visa estimates its current share of e-commerce transactions at around 50 percent, in line with its overall credit and debit-card market share of 51 percent."

(Beckett 1998)

LEARNING OBJECTIVES

- To differentiate between the practices of virtual retailing and traditional retailing and relate each to e-commerce
- To present the advantages and disadvantages of operating the virtual store
- To discuss strategies in building an awareness for the virtual store

Introduction

Established retailing and wholesaling companies are reinventing themselves to keep up with consumer tastes, distribution efficiencies, streamlined selling systems, and promotional innovations. Those that do not modernize their operations, finances and payment systems, and marketing are usually doomed, such as the defunct Zayre's, Woolco, W. T. Grant, and struggling Montgomery Ward and Sears. Technology has been the competitive advantage for such retailers as generalist Wal-Mart and specialist Foot Locker (www.footlocker.com), the world's largest seller of athletic footwear and apparel through its 2,000 stores in North America, Europe, Australia, and Japan. Over the last twenty-five years, the trend in detailing has been toward experimentation, from narrow specialty formats such as Banana Republic safari wear, to direct marketers establishing standing stores such as Sharper Image, and to membership warehouse clubs like Sam's Club (www.samsclub.com). Much of this experimentation includes communications technology; some extremely successful examples include Wal-Mart's sales and inventory control satellite reform system, and some embarrassingly unsuccessful examples include Victoria's Secret's (www.victoriassecret.com) **streaming video** fashion show in February 1999. E-commerce workings began as an experiment, and as Iconocast newsletter notes:

> Another area where the Internet has made significant strides is e-commerce. In early 1997, Amazon announced 1996 sales of $15.7 million. Last year, it was $610 million. In March 1997, Nielsen Media Research reported that 15 percent of Internet users had purchased something online in the past year. An **Arbitron** survey of 1,350 fall 1998 diary keepers found that 26 percent 'use the Internet for shopping' [Pew Research's more rigid, albeit lower, yardstick, '11 percent have bought something online in the past thirty days,' is preferable]. (Tchong 1999)

In the previous issue, Iconocast made its observation on e-commerce growth for the entire 1998 year:

> Forecast-Forrester Research began 1998 with a business-to-business forecast of $17 billion. By November 1998, the company had raised its forecast to $109 billion. The consumer e-commerce forecast of $4.8 billion was similarly upped to $7.8 billion. But that figure pales in comparison to the Boston Consulting Group's $13 billion estimate in a study commissioned by Shop.org. And most of these commerce forecasts will be transacted online through virtual merchants and stores on the Web. (Tchong 1999)

Much of these commercial transactions will be enacted by merchants and virtual stores on the World Wide Web. How the virtual stores or storefronts enable these consumer and business-to-business transactions to occur will be discussed later.

Retailing Approaches: Virtual versus Tangible

In creating and supporting the traditional tangible store, management has always balanced three primary functions of the business entity, particularly in retailing: the financial aspect, the operations aspect, and the marketing aspect. While building and maintaining the virtual store are novel, electronic retailing and wholesaling still follow these principles but do so in a **back office** manner, hidden from physical contact to the public. This invisible management is inevitable since the nature of the business is comprised of invisible electronic data (Web site merchandise or offerings), housed and promoted on an electronic medium (Web sites, e-mail, listservs, discussion groups), and delivered by an electronic distribution system (often the World Wide Web). While this may seem to describe television, the biggest difference is the capability of interactivity that none of the traditional mass media can match. For this interaction capacity, most of the nation's leading department and specialty stores have created a companion Web site to complement their traditional tangible outlets of stand-alone or mall stores. Recently, Macy's (www.macys.com) joined the retailers on parade via a Web presence as well as the Gap, Limited, Dillard's (www.dillards.com), and JCPenney. Different retailers have different Web strategies that are featured prominently on their home pages. Macy's for example, encourages the shopper to click on the standard Customer Information, Community Relations, and Store Locations, but Macy's offers a distinctive service, MBA, Macy's By Appointment, which is personal shopping by appointment, www.macys.com/mba. (Macy's boasts they can update your wardrobe, help with special requests, and take care of the details.) This ultimate convenience is available toll-free for anyone east and west of the Mississippi and for international customers, as well. Macy's is providing convenience for the time-pressed customers through this program; an alternative method of shopping is to "shop ē-ssentials, online shopping for life's little necessities." Besides Macy's bridal and gift registry and gift links, the ē-ssentials page attractively presents selections such as wardrobe basics and necessities for men, fashion essentials for women, or wardrobe necessities for women. In addition, the Macy's site offers merchandise gift certificates, which are featured at the bottom of the hyperlinks. While Web page design will be discussed, the Macy's home page and subsequent pages are well balanced between design elements and just the right amount of copy that can be described as terse headlines and sparse explanation copy as subheads.

What was the major factor in Macy's move to the Web? Was it purely a marketing and sales decision? Was it an operational motive? Was it a financial decision? It appears to be somewhat related to all of these issues. From a marketing standpoint, the decision to embrace a Web presence suddenly gave Macy's a global exposure. From an operational view, the Web could help with the distribution, as well as make better use of the company's resources with a twenty-four-hour shopping service. From a financial perspective, as well, usually when a superb marketing performance is coupled with a streamlined operational effort, the financial results generally take care of itself. So it seems that as these three forces are balanced, equilibrium is in place as the enterprise moves forward; when one is misaligned, the other two suffer, incapable of recovering to the way business was conducted before. The marketer who is an excellent analyst of the symptoms can sniff out the business entity that is not performing and make the proper corrective moves. Notice also that factors within the Web can be both a positive or negative effect, all within one medium. Therefore, the marketer's business efforts should be intertwined, not tangled within the strategic and tactical focus of the company.

The JCPenney Monster Web Site

JCPenney's (www.jcpenney.com) presents a most ambitious home page that is directed to shoppers, the community in general, and stockholders or investors. This home page produces a three-page printout that appears to have something for everyone. JCPenney (JCP) takes an expansive tact with its Web site, which presents many different JCP programs such as links to coupons, special net savings to say thanks for visiting the JCP site; the JCP Grandparents club, savings for frequent customers; the JCP Insurance Group, offering insurance basics, health tips, and financial tidbits; Dress Code 101, class favorites that can fit your school, students, and budget; as well as Secure Shopping Online, an electronic order blank to shop the online store via the

JCPenney®
secure online shopping

home | gift registry | shopping bag/checkout | customer service | request a catalog

Welcome to the JCPenney Internet store

To shop from a catalog, enter the item number (A123-4578) GO

SUBSCRIBE to e-mail promotions & updates!

your e-mail here

subscribe

JCPenney® stores.catalog.internet.

SEARCH the store!

store departments

men's
women's
children's
toys
home & leisure
jewelry

specialty shops

what's new!
arizona jean co.
casual collection
gift shop
star wars

other sites brought to you by JCPenney®

services

fresh flowers
gift cards
catalogs
custom decorating
about jcpenney

secure online ordering

store departments: [men's women's children's toys home & leisure jewelry]

specialty shops: [what's new! arizona jean co. casual collection gift shop star wars]

services: [fresh flowers gift cards catalogs custom decorating about jcpenney]

navigation: [home gift registry shopping bag/checkout customer service request a catalog]

Copyright/Legal Notice and Privacy Statement

© JCP Media L.P., 1999. All Rights Reserved.

JCPenney (www.jcpenney.com)
This Web site is full of retail content as a general merchant's site should be. The design resembles a printed newsletter featuring "Cybershopping & services," "Summer Fun," and "What's in Store."

JCPenney catalog. There are also links to James Cash Penney's founding principles, JCPenney privacy statement, and stockholder information that includes first quarter earnings, past month's sales results, and FAQs. The information contained on this site is overwhelming. This site is more than a menu; it is more of a newsletter with shopping, fashion, investor, and historical information, as well as year 2000 solutions, community relations, and career opportunities. This site is almost completely text without photography or illustrations; the JCPenney site represents the extreme commitment to content over graphical advertisement style.

On the minimalist side, compared to the JCPenney's site newsletter, is the representation of Dillard's coast-to-coast service area. The Web site opens with a map of the United States, broken into regions by color scheme, to demonstrate the sales coverage of Dillard's. This timid application of a Web site is typical of the new or test user of the Web in that the entire site has full information resembling a magazine or newspaper advertisement but no interactivity for shopper gratification. The Dillard's site presents the geographical map and a standard list of menu buttons, but the consumer cannot view or buy online any of the merchandise. The site offers to search for a particular item the consumer may find out of stock locally, and then send an e-mail if the garment or item becomes available. The site also has an e-mail address/hyperlink and a toll-free number that allows the customer to correspond with the company. This site is not a bad approach for integrating the Web capacity because many retailers have jumped headfirst onto the Web rather than test this distribution concept, slowly adding elements as the medium continues to prove worthwhile. Many marketers expect instant results from a new media vehicle test or from a new promotional opportunity. As the Web proves its value in attracting consumers, expect Dillard's to maintain a slow rollout and low profile in its Web presence. Tiffany & Co. (www.tiffany.com) has taken a middle ground, offering information on diamonds, care of jewelry, distribution of catalogues and brochures (by U.S. mail), and store locations. This site represents good content wrapped around the famous Tiffany robin's egg blue box, which is used on each Web page. Which is the correct execution for retail business? It depends on the corporate objectives, the marketing objectives, the clientele preferences, the current methods of retailing and distribution, the promotional sensitivities, and the current retail geography, in other words, the *who, what, when, where,* and *why* of a transition to e-commerce. This is an impossible question to answer without knowing the retailer and customer's interactions; intelligent marketers will probably ask *why* a hundred times before venturing any opinions or conclusions. As many issues of industry are circular, the proper decision making is a blend of art of concept and the science of numbers. It takes a special mindset to be able to switch between hard data and soft flows that Web commerce demands. Flexibility is a virtue.

The Advantages of a Virtual Store

As with almost all marketing programs there are advantages and disadvantages associated with every strategy and decision. No marketing strategy is risk free, but there are ways to minimize financial exposure. If the strategy of the retailer is to expand her distribution to a wider geography, the Internet may be a wise move. The retailer, however, should not give up the physical retail location if and when the Web site supports sufficient e-commerce. This might be considered a belt-and-suspenders approach toward business because of this double security strategy. Many things can go wrong as a Web virtual store is being developed. You may have received messages that the banking system is temporarily down and you should try again later, and you then worry if any records of your finances remain. Likewise, with government agencies, airlines, universities, libraries, and other centers of high volume calling, encouraging the caller to try again at a later time is unacceptable. If the company's computer system crashes and should the caller want immediate service, he is unable to access his assets and credit card balances, to use e-mail, or to access the Web site. The marketer, therefore, should give the new electronic system a sufficient enough time to prove its reliability. Further, until the universe of potential Web customers buys a computer and gains connection with an ISP, there probably is not enough Web transactions to generate break-even finances—another reason to maintain a dual sales basis.

Generally, the benefits of operating a virtual storefront fall into several areas of business strategy.

- A company's distribution channels can become expanded with the presence of a virtual storefront, which in turn can transfer more power to direct marketing, which is the most targeted communications vehicle. This capability allows the company to choose what is to be the purpose of the Web site: online sales, online advertising, online customer service, or other sales or communications activities. Using the Web as a new distribution channel will require a strategic review of the company's other distribution channels to streamline the direct marketing function. Many times the type of merchandise, such as dry goods or services, will influence the integration of the Web into the promotional and distribution strategy.
- With a virtual presence, capital expenditure is much less in starting consumer- or business-to-business–directed marketing programs. The capital expenditure to open an electronic storefront is much less than opening a tangible store (real estate and structures); this factor should reduce the amount to borrow, which is probably earmarked for electronic equipment, ISP server, and necessary software to support the virtual storefront.
- There is much more flexibility in providing a base for operations to support the virtual store. The flexibility is such that an entrepreneur could maintain sales and service from any location.The Web site can operate twenty-four hours every day, and this capability is valuable for those firms that market overseas. The barrier of time zones is removed, erased by the capability of fax-back or e-mail confirmations. Whether the staff is actual people or an automated system, the customer is relieved in having her order acknowledged.
- To expand the firm's credentials and qualifications, the retail Web site can dispense marketing or sales materials automatically on request. Sales brochures can be obtained by prospects (as well as competitors) through a Web presence, and with the proliferation of color printers, sales brochures retrieved from the Web are as attractive as the printed sales piece. As stated before, these sales materials are available to download and print twenty-four hours a day.
- Because of the general business uncertainty, whether it is in chaotic Southeast Asia or the struggling countries of Eastern Europe or Russia, volatile business environments should be tempered by some measure of market controls. Whether the company operates in a highly competitive business or faces rampant hyperinflation, there are electronic systems to update prices, specifications, or other product or service data hourly if necessary. This control of product pricing is of some relief to the marketer and allows the product to keep up with the market as it might swing up or down. Because of the computer-based pricing system, competitors may not be able to match the computer-driven price adjustments.
- Producing a first-class Web site will enhance the virtual presence of the company using the promotional mix elements. Company-sponsored promotions

that are translated into the company's Web site (for instance, Pizza Hut's use of a hot button, or link, on its Web site to connect to its long-running Book It campaign encouraging childrens' interests in reading) follows the paradigm of integrated marketing communications. With the advent of the color, sound, movement, and selectivity of the Web, other promotional tools can be incorporated to the page design or as a banner on a search engine home page; this will be discussed more extensively in Chapter 9.

- Rather than having customers wait for an answer from the order tracking department, inquiries can be investigated more quickly on an organization's Web site. In many instances, the company will give the customer a tracking number so that he may follow the package through its delivery. The Web allows the company to render fast and responsive customer services. The virtual store is well suited to perform solid customer service because many virtual firms are no more than personnel staffing a telephone call center. When a call comes in from a customer, the call center personnel merely pulls up a customer record and addresses the caller cordially confirming the customer's name and past purchase habits. Order status can be ascertained immediately. The order confirmation is your record that Pizza Hut (www.pizzahut.com) or Domino's (www.dominos.com) keeps and tracks your patronage; database collection will be addressed in detail in Chapter 12.
- The opportunity to test new products or services may be one of the biggest advantages of the Web. This interactive ability can also be employed into sampling new product or service concepts among existing customer bases. It is a great way to get feedback on customer opinions for future use. According to *The Wall Street Journal:*

> Some advertisers are quietly experimenting with direct marketing of niche products on their Web sites. Last month [July, 1998], Nabisco Holdings, of Parsippany, New Jersey, began selling its Knox NutraJoint gelatin drink mix direct to consumers (www.knox.com) at a 20 percent discount. The nutritional supplement isn't carried by many grocers. "Not only can you continue to enjoy the benefits of flexible joints, but also the convenience of having Knox NutraJoint delivered directly to your door," the Web ad reads. (O'Connell 1998)

Experimentation with new technology is also possible using Web-based testing. New tools are available almost daily and integrated into Web sites for customer evaluation and convenience. Another report by *The Wall Street Journal* observed:

> Lands' End Inc. is adding a feature to its Web site that will allow shoppers to see what clothes will look like on their bodies. The feature, called Your Personal Model, enables a user to select hair color, height, shoulder width, waist and hip size to match her body. The technology then combines those features to form a three-dimensional virtual body. The site (www.landsend.com) then selects clothes to suit that body type, and a shopper can click on items to see them on the model. The technology allows for fifteen different feature combinations.
>
> The catalog retailer is the first U.S. company to offer this online feature. The technology behind the concept was developed by Public Technologies Multimedia Inc., Quebec. Canadian retailer Boutique San

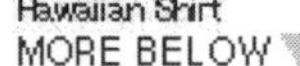
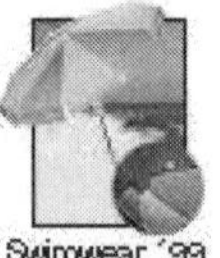

Lands' End (www.landsend.com)
The traditional direct mail marketer goes online with innovative of electronic tools such as "Your Personal Model," the "Intelligent Order Blank," and the "Oxford Express" to provide new services for the e-shopper.

Francisco has offered the virtual model on its Web site for a year. (Lands' End site will let users "model" clothes on body type 1998)

- Many marketers are eager to sell internationally with minimal electronic sales support. There are many marketing issues to be considered in addition to the operational and financial issues in selling and delivering the product or service abroad. A good place to ask these business questions is in a discussion/listserv environment. Discussion groups' members range all over the globe, so with the proper no borders product, an effective marketing program could tap selected test markets. The reach of the Web is international, so with language-correct packaging and close scrutiny to accommodate the countries' legal restrictions, usage patterns, and consumers' values, the marketer can sell throughout the world at an amazingly low communications cost.

The Disadvantages of a Virtual Store

The preceding list of benefits is hard to deny, but as an objective participant, the marketer will investigate the disadvantages and potential pitfalls of opening a **cyberstore.** The prospect of a virtual store is both enticing and intimidating; as the marketer considers launching a probe into cyberspace, he should evaluate the disadvantages of hosting a virtual storefront.

- Not every product or service is appropriate to Web sales exposure. Many consumer goods like perishable or dated goods are not being sold on the Web as of yet. The obvious examples of these kinds of goods might be alcoholic beverages or pornographic materials. The not-so-obvious might include packaged goods of nominal value (for instance, few if any boxes of saltine crackers or bars of soap are sold via direct mail) or items of clothing. Many companies just are not prepared for Web selling. The major retailers are not going to approach this possibility without careful planning of access, merchandise mix, pricing, logistics, and customer service to the standards that currently position the company today. As *The Wall Street Journal* observed:

  Everyone agrees that ads offering online shopping options are the most effective. Though P&G [Procter & Gamble] and Unilever (www.unilever.com) say they are gearing up for direct Web sales, they aren't doing it yet. Distribution snags have so far limited growth of online grocers like Peapod (www.peapod) and NetGrocer (www.netgrocer.com). And traditional retailers like Wal-Mart are only now moving onto the Net. Online sales of food and beverages will total $168 million this year estimates Forrester Research, while sales of drugs and health and beauty aide products will be a puny $16 million. (O'Connell 1998)

- While capital expenses may be reduced, site offerings, communications, and maintenance require many hours, days, or weeks of a Web master's attention. It might even require the work of multiple Web masters. Web marketing is a time-intensive activity; the good Web master should be surfing the competition at least an afternoon during the week and double checking the position of her Web page ranking on all the major search engines. If the marketer has engaged a World Wide Web consultant, the marketer must oversee that company's work and contributions to the Web strategy.
- The twenty-four-hour service pledge is a double-edged sword; the pitfalls can produce severe repercussions if the service activities falter. Few marketers

Peapod (www.peapod.com)
Billed as the #1 Internet grocery and drug store, Peapod delivers right to the user's door. Peapod now serves eight metropolitan markets and has filled over one million orders.

realize the time and money commitments to customer service, distribution, and communications associated with a twenty-four-hour, seven-day operation. The necessary training is a responsibility in assuring the night shift is dispensing the same quality of information as the morning and the afternoon shifts do. Here operational talents will be needed for a quick and slow transition into three, eight-hour shifts or two, twelve-hour shifts. Which associates are interested in working the night shift needs to be determined, and paying shift differentials to encourage workers needs to be decided upon. Many large and petty quarrels will surface as this operations' change goes into effect.

- Besides the people portion of a twenty-four-hour work day, the marketer's organization is dependent on its equipment, communications software, and its ISP connections. The marketer owes his customers continuity of service by ensuring the computer systems are operational, possibly with a **redundant system** such as a backup system that takes over when outages unexpectedly happen. This point is particularly sobering for the company or corporation to maintain its customer records, which would probably be impossible to recover if the entire network crashed. The marketer's motivation is directly proportional to the importance or value of the customer records she plans to retrieve. Both motivation and retrieval interests should be high.
- Another double-edged sword is the anonymity of identity inherent to the Web. The consumer is not certain who the company is or what it stands for. Likewise, the company is unsure who the buyer is and what the buyer's intentions are. The risk, therefore, is borne by both the buyer and seller. In the near future, a system of commerce is expected to be established to eradicate this uncertainty; the program deals with certification that introduces a third party to the exchange. This certificate status will be discussed in Chapter 15.
- As the fact that the reach of the Web is worldwide is being recognized, the reality today is that of limited penetration and exposure to the general public at

present. A marketing target on the Internet within China, for example, consists of 1.175 million people of the estimated 1.2 billion population. That is less than one percent of the Chinese people. No one knows for certain what the Internet accessibility will be for this huge and attractive market.

- As another double-edged sword, the virtual storefront continues to present merchandise or services as long as the server is running or the Internet provider is being paid. Much as the cows on the dairy farm must be milked daily to preserve their health, the Web merchant also gets few days off if she is intent on filling and shipping merchandise orders or communicating daily to customer inquiries. The good news is that the store is open, and the bad news is that the store is open. For business continuity, it is not wise to occasionally pull the site off the Web because if the site has been bookmarked by a customer or prospect, the customer expects to find the site again without difficulty. If the site is missing, the customer or prospect will dismiss the address entirely, and it will be most difficult if not impossible to attract that client again. If the enterprise is small, it still requires daily hands-on attention; plans for vacations or even illnesses should be developed to prevent a customer outage.

The Value of the Virtual Storefront and the Cybermall

As in the game contract bridge, start your strategic plan by playing from your strengths. What are the attributes the Web can deliver almost flawlessly? The answer includes reliability, consistency, privacy, accessibility, accuracy, and responsiveness. These are the strategic potencies for building long-term relationships with customers along with the tactical energies of selecting, offering, and satisfying the customer segments. Retailing power builds on the fundamental usage nature of the Internet: the demographics of connectivity, content, and customer motivation. The demographics of connectivity are simple. What is the match between Web-user demographics to the product or service the marketer is offering? The demand for inline skates may founder if marketing was directed toward senior citizens. Research would tell the marketer not to market aluminum bats to professional baseball players because the Major League has banned the use of such implements. Again, some product/market matches are obvious; others will take more digging before ill-fated deal breakers arise. Words of caution as Web marketing strategies are developed: Astute marketing professionals and researchers will remember that the users' skew is approximately 60 percent male, with ages predominantly ranging from 25 to 45 years, well educated, and sporting an average income of more than $50,000. These prospects are geographically disbursed yet may be clustered in educational employment. These consumers, as well, are elusive as they access their connections from work, libraries, community centers, schools, universities, or even cybercafes. Consider the other uses of the Web: locating information, idling in the chat rooms, or playing games or other such entertainment.

The virtual store usually has a specialty draw of interest to the technological shopper—usually products with narrow breadth but considerable depth within the product category. A good example might be a cyberstore that stocks only movie posters, vintage to current releases. Search engines help prospects find the address of the cyberstore, and with attractive graphics, deep inventory, and careful handling and shipping, the prospect becomes a customer. Individuals are surfing and shopping all day and all night long, and the marketer or merchant has developed an order system to collect and sort the orders in a timely fashion, usually forty-eight hours. The marketer will recognize that many surfers are only shopping to gather information on alternatives before making a purchase decision; many shoppers will end up buying off the Internet, frequently using a toll-free number that serves the virtual storefront sales activities. Again, the habit of many cybershoppers is to cull the Web sites for a selection and then purchase that selection using the perceived security of a telephone land line.

When several cyberstores band together, thus giving the customer more selection of merchandise in one location or address, this gathering of Web sites is considered to be a **cybermall.** Like the concrete shopping malls, the marketer with assistance from her associates will investigate cybermalls, which feature an anchor cyberstore with a large traffic count and possibly the capabilities of furnishing an overflow of traffic, to produce a good match to the marketer's merchandise, information, or similar offerings. The operators of cybermalls charge the individual storefront owner a fee (which can be a flat monthly rental or a sliding scale of rent depending on the number of visitors or hits to the storefront) for residing at the cybermall. An alternative to banding with a cybermall is to be a **linked storefront,** in which the storefront address is hyperlinked within a popular general interest site. Examples of these linked e-commerce sites are the Stuff/Merchandise link offering paraphernalia associated with the entertainment industry and the banner ad advertising for sale a videotape of the *Titanic* movie priced at $9.99 on the E!online (www.eonline.com) site. The banner ad links Reel.com (www.reel.com), which sells discounted movies with banner headlines such as "Hanks Happens!" On the *X-Files* site, merchandise is also offered by clicking on an embedded link for miniature sculptures of alien figures or books with titles such as *Whirlwind*, *Goblins*, or *Antibodies*. These sites may be owned as a merchandise property, such as FoxWorld, as in the case of the *X-Files* site, or the advertising banner may be leased from the site owner. Which arrangement is best? It depends on the match of the site to the complementary products or services being sold. The better the match, the better the sales opportunity. As in the advertising media industry, the higher the circulation or the bigger the audience, the higher the cost of the space or time.

An enlightening study by the professor of marketing, Sunil Gupta, of the University of Michigan Business School and a member of the Hermes Project (a system for semantically integrating current and possibly heterogeneous information sources and reasoning systems, www.cs.umd.edu/projects/hermes/overview/), in association with Jim Pitkow of Georgia Tech's GVU Center, brought forth information on the Web user and his online information and buying patterns for a six-month period ending on May 10, 1995. The Survey 3, published June 10, 1995, comprised of over 13,000 interviews (10,482 persons from the United States, 1,276 from Europe, 718 from Canada and Mexico, and 530 from Asia, Australia, and New Zealand) inquiring about online shopping habits. "The sources of shopping-related information were reported as noncommercial, Internet-based sources such as newsgroups, Web sites, and other Internet sources continue to be used more than traditional direct mail. There is a clear lag compared to the use of print media. Blurring the picture may be the popularity of E-zines or E-papers." (Colleen Kehoe 1995) These observations will be expanded in Chapter 9. The study notes that consumer activities included online information-seeking and buying within the last six months; the primary use of the Web was to gain information and shop. The researchers attribute the lack of specific purchases to the deficient security and reliability of online shopping. As to the security concerns, respondents attitudes on online transaction-related information include the following reasons for not purchasing online.

- Providing credit information online is just plain foolish, as 60 percent replied they agree somewhat or strongly.
- Security concerns are a primary reason for not buying [online], as was voiced by 56 percent who agree somewhat or strongly.

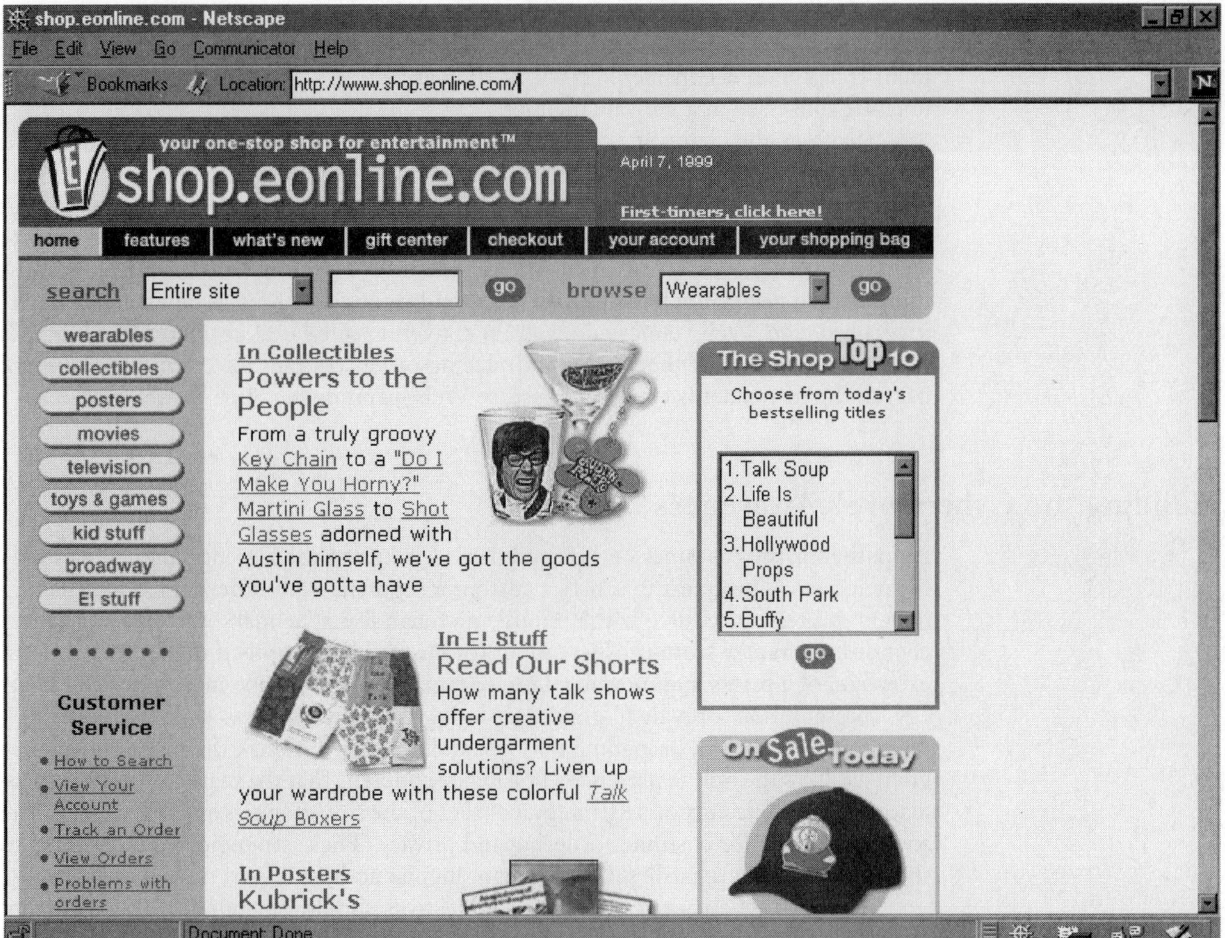

E! Online (www.eonline.com)
Entertainment news and merchandise populates this popular Hollywood-focused site. Celebrity news, an online boutique selling merchandise such as "Hanks Happens" or Seinfeld's "The Kramer" tee-shirts, and the "Celebrity Courthouse."

- Providing credit/purchase information online to a far away merchant or to an unknown merchant when away from home is more risky than providing that information over the phone or through fax.
- Given each of several payment options, sending credit card information through e-mail is liked least.
- Toll-free call/fax is tied with secure transmission. There seems to be some residual reservations about electronic transactions.
- The respondents expressed a clear preference for the involvement of a third party in the transaction. The scenario stated that the user would set up an account with a third party who would then complete the transaction with participating vendors. Shipments would be made directly from the vendor to the buyer. There is a clear preference for involvement by a credit card company or a bank. (1995)

What are online information seekers seeking? Men are more frequent purchasers than women, and men make purchases exceeding $50. Common items of interest are software, hardware, and electronics, and if a purchase is consummated, it represents price shopping for less expensive products. Respondents stated they have bought music and books online. What the online consumer is *not* buying is apparel or legal services, and of little interest are investments or travel services. From Professor Gupta's research, consumers are actively on the Web, and they appear to navigate through the commercial sites for information. Further, a cybermerchant must recognize the payment transaction is considered risky, so the perception and reality of secure payment must be addressed in a fail-safe manner.

What are the characteristics of a cybermerchant that would give reassurance to the cybershoppers? The e-commerce site must offer *quality information* regarding the purchase options or categories for choosing a Web vendor. Respondents noted that having the lowest price is least important. Respondents are risk adverse. They rate vendor *reliability* and security of their financial information quite highly. Importantly, these are the two characteristics that Web vendors are perceived as being at a competitive advantage. Web vendors do well on convenience related characteristics, such as the ease of contacting the vendor and placing orders. With these attributes in mind, overall the respondents expect to increase Web spending by 70 percent.

Building the Cyberstore's Awareness

Empathy for the customer's wants and desires is one of the key ingredients for storefront success. This quest to satisfy a customer segment is no different from attracting buyers to a real store filled with desirable merchandise. The marketer develops a merchandising strategy from prospect input (or customer reactions if the storefront is an extension of a bricks and mortar selling organization). From the merchandising strategy (presentation of which goods, ordering systems such as online/credit card, telephone/credit card, or mailing options, and delivery options), the marketer will begin to address the online presence. The major concerns that the marketer must manipulate are matching corporate strategy, content of the site, graphics and text appearance, and site security for customer ordering and privacy. These strategic and tactical issues should be constant regardless if the site is a singular address or part of a cybermall.

Minding the corporate or division objectives should be stated in the corporate marketing plan; these objectives might be dictated as generating 60 percent sales and profits from the young adult novels division, developing new distribution channels to serve European markets, or extending current customers' interests in health and exercise videos. Specific objectives, which are usually expressed numerically as a sales volume or percentage return on investment or asset, will depend on the environmental or competitive forces facing the company as a whole or the division in particular. With these corporate directives, the true measure of a skilled marketer is decided by the orchestration of the art and science of marketing activities.

Deciding the Online Marketing Objectives

In achieving the marketing missions, the marketer will decide what objectives will be appropriate for the new (or existing) Web marketing activities, and these marketing decisions require a full knowledge of product or service history, retailer or distributor relations, and customer expectations, in other words, a full familiarity of the offering's strengths, weaknesses, opportunities, and threats. The marketing possibilities can be sundry, but an experienced marketer will boil myriad directions down to two or three feats that are attainable. As a promotional element, the Web presence and its mechanisms cannot sell as many clients as corporate officers expect. The Web presence, likewise for print or broadcast advertising, can only inform and create interest or curiosity; with this interest established, the job of selling is transferred to a real salesperson, the staff of a call center, or to the ordering apparatus on the Web site. It is wise to keep the abilities of various promotional elements in mind in order to have realistic expectations of the marketing programs.

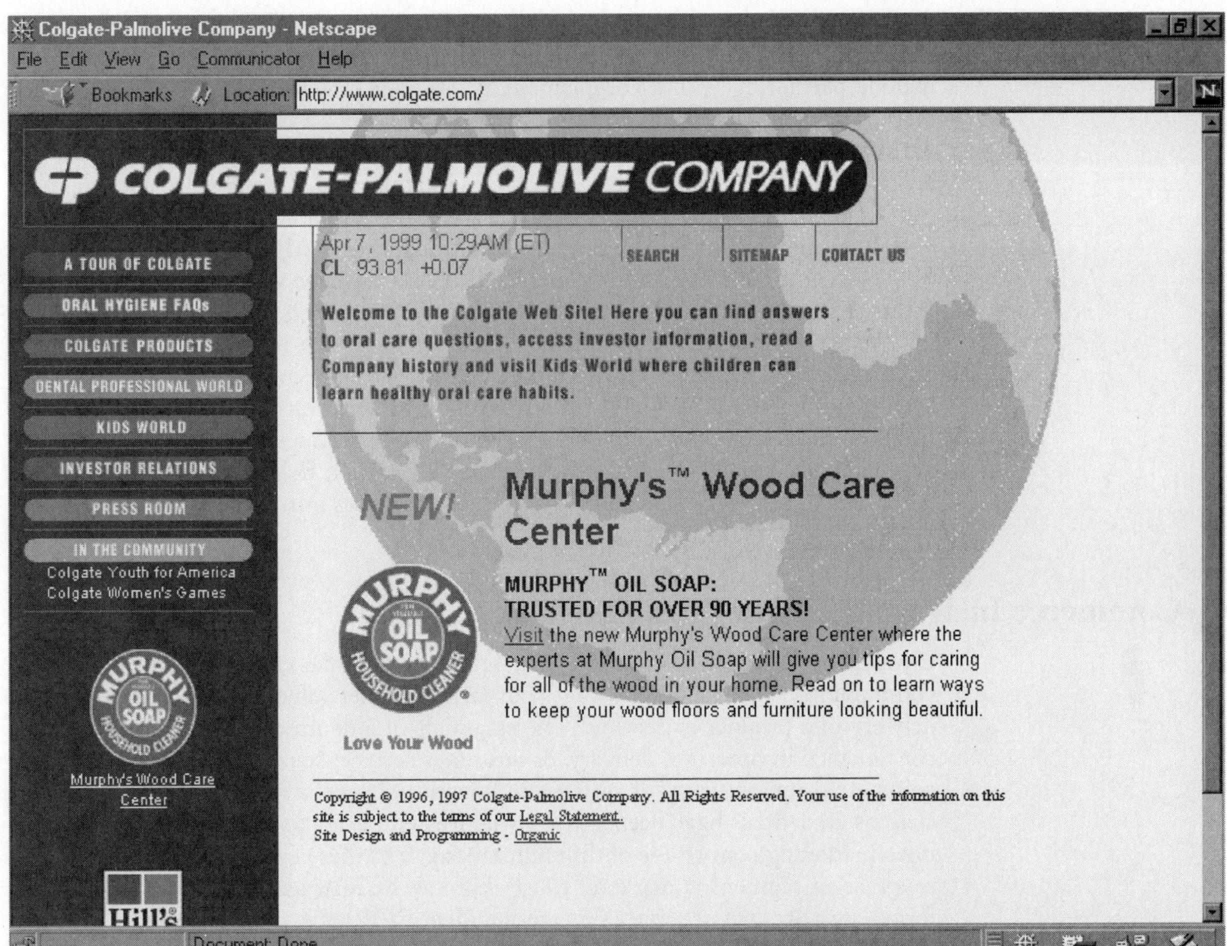

Colgate-Palmolive (www.colgate.com)
Oral care is highlighted on the Colgate site with an FAQ on oral hygiene and a page, "Kids World," where children can learn healthy oral care habits.

What are the appropriate goals for online marketing? As in traditional marketing, new products can be launched from a unique site or from a company offering. Perhaps the objective is to extend the brand franchise awareness for Colgate Total toothpaste, toothbrushes, and floss (www.colgate.com/products) with being blessed by the trusted Colgate name. As has been discussed, the online objective might constitute a new distribution channel to consumers or trade segments, or honing in on promotional element usage such as publicity effort. Another possible objective might be the enhancement of customer service among already satisfied account holders.

The competitive difference of this online vehicle compared to the traditional media is the online opportunity for interactivity. Not only can a marketer produce a persuasive commercial on the Web, he can also process a direct request from a customer inquiry. Direct marketing has succeeded for more than a hundred years, but in purchasing directly from the manufacturer, a significant time lag, frequently disclaimed as a four to six week delivery, was part of the purchase experience. The online marketer should plan for responsiveness since the Web vehicle brings interactive orders with little time delay. Why should customers have to wait?

Since online commerce has been deemed an extension of direct marketing, the marketer can learn from the playbook of direct response marketing. In studying the effectiveness of direct marketing, the success is usually based on some type of sampling or couponing. Sampling might include free inducements, such as an online demonstration of a free e-quotation for auto or life insurance, free minutes as

PrimeCo (www.primeco.com) has promised for digital telephone services, or free movie tickets for test-driving an Oldsmobile (www.oldsmobile.com); sampling might include partnering with a complementary product or service to appeal to a similar market, such as McDonald's promoting the new Disney World Animal Kingdom, or partnering with disparate companies, such as the AltaVista search engine (www.altavista.digital.com) publishing a Johns Hopkins and Intelihealth Health Care (www.intelihealth.com) general interest Web site as public service information; or sampling might include an internal promotion, such as MCI long-distance services (www.mci.com) offering a $5 per month discount for those who also sign up for MCI Internet service. Couponing can also take many forms such as cents or dollars off for savings at checkout, rebates for dollars after purchase, two-for-one offers, or coupons to be exchanged for a different product made by the same company. The objective for both sampling and couponing is the marketing expectation that once a customer has tried the product or service, these discounts will be recouped over a long-term relationship with the buyer. With an outstanding product, this discount strategy is not harebrained; new Web sites may have to buy their ways into consumers' preferences.

E-Commerce Image and Identity Development

If you, the marketer, could build a virtual presence for an e-commerce site, how would you build it? What qualities would your target market value in online awareness and delivery of a product or service? The essentials of a depth of merchandise selection; convenience in ordering, delivery, or customer service; speed and accessibility of the commerce site; accuracy of order fulfillment; and security and privacy of the purchaser's credentials have been generally addressed in this textbook, thus far. In creating a marketing plan recipe of different measures of these qualities that are presented to a market segment, a marketer must examine the interaction of these attributes to formulate a product or service's image and identity. What is the difference? The image is the bundling of what the marketer wants the market to think of when the prospect or customer considers the product category. Hopefully, the marketing Ps have elevated the product or service into the buyer's evoked set, or list of brands for purchase consideration. Image is the what, the impression of the good for consumption. In the watch category, a consumer might summons up an impression for Rolex as expensive and prestigious, or for Swatch, young and faddish, or for Timex (www.timex.com), utilitarian and affordable. Each brand image has carefully been cultivated through consistent and concentrated marketing of the brand to its targeted market category. It may take years of marketing consistency to create a brand and its franchise among consumers. Longtime brand associations that come to mind are Nabisco or Campbell's products (www.campbellsoup.com) or NBC's or CBS's services that generations have grown up with. Brand image, the *what* associations, can on occasion be developed more quickly, such as the Microsoft software applications, the Apple Macintosh products (www.apple.com), or the Southwest Airlines' service. Each of these brands is less than twenty-five years old but readily creates brand impressions within its category users and supporters.

Identity can be described as graphic, music, or sound elements used to convey the image. In e-commerce terms, the appearance and performance of the Web site; product packaging; traditional advertising or sales promotion; signage's, invoices', or videocassette covers' design; or the manner in which telephones are answered is part of the identity execution, and thorough marketers give attention to every identity element that comes into contact with the target market. Image is the *what*, and identity is the *how*. Bernd Schmitt, a professor of marketing at Columbia Business School, and Alex Simonson, a professor of marketing at Georgetown University, both experts on the process of product branding, succinctly sum the process as, "Identity creates image." (1997, 36) Careful construction of image through identity workings creates brand value that in e-commerce is a difficult quality to capture and nurture. Otherwise, the product or service becomes a commodity usually left to price competition or outright warfare. As in traditional marketing, the key to product or service value is deliberate differentiation.

Recently, though, there has been a trend, particularly in the high tech industries, to link company images to the magic of Internet highfliers by adding the suffix .com to the company name. Spurred by the success of Amazon.com, the market welcomed new, sometimes repackaged firm names such as Beyond.com, Tman Global.com (easily recognized as a martial arts company), ImaginOn.com, Siti-Sites.com, Financial-web.com, and Software.com among others. Branding consultants are not sold on the practice of adding .com as a glamor tactic.

> Not everyone thinks the cattle rush of companies branding a .com on the end of their corporate monikers to take advantage of the current mania for all things related to the marketing aesthetics by Internet is a good idea. "A big part of a brand name is as a differentiator, and you can't be different if everyone has your name, as .com becomes more and more commonplace," says Allen Adamson of Landor Associates, the corporate-identity firm. "Branding based on distribution is never a long-term play." Instead he urges businesses to think further ahead. "A company name is something that a business has to live with for fifteen years or more, so I ask clients what business they want to be in then," says Mr. Adamson, who notes there are a lot of tactical ways to indicate your business is Internet related, such as direct marketing and public relations. (Swisher 1998)

Searching for the Product or Service Differentiation

As part of the initial marketing plan, the marketer should consider the trait or traits, perceived or real, for differentiation that no other product or service can easily match. After all, what makes a American Express card better than a Visa card? Or Levi's better than Lee jeans? Or a choice between Swedish automobiles Volvo (www.volvo.com) or Saab (www.saab.com)? From a utility viewpoint, each product or service seems equally functional. From a positioning strategy, however, different features or benefits are emphasized in the communications objectives. For instance, taking the Swedish automobile products, Volvo has stressed its commitment to safety, to protect the passengers. Saab's advertising heralds its performance and engineering skills acquired from Saab fighter-jet technology. In segmentation terms, this strategy of selecting different features valued by different people is called a niche marketing strategy, which carves out a specific group of consumers that the product or service is carefully tailored to the group's wants or expectations. The goal is to own that segment by creating a point of real or perceived differentiation, which is built by brand image, from other products within this category. Surveys, observation, usage, focus groups, or other methods of research can be helpful in defining the uniqueness and in conveying this image through identity materials. The British journal, *Director*, states this view on creating differentiation online:

> Customisation and particularly personalisation are critical factors in creating and sustaining competitive advantage on the Internet. Companies that can achieve this with their Web sites will build "switching costs" for customers and gain the information they need to further differentiate their offerings. Without this, many innovations on the Internet are easy to copy. An established brand can help, as can a vast archive of difficult-to-replicate

1999 School
Foodservice Program

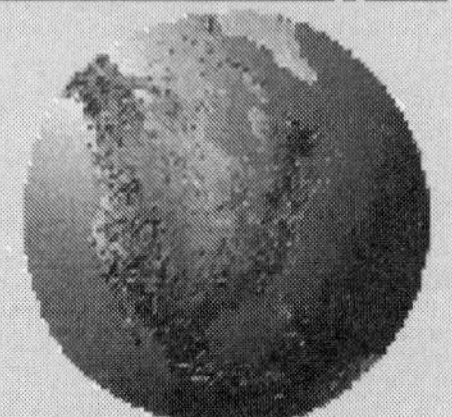

SELLING FOOD IN THE NEW MILLENNIUM
January 10 and 11, 2000

Florida Department of Citrus:

- About Us
- Notice of Meetings
- Job Opportunities

Contact Us:

- FL Citrus Commission
- FDOC Staff
- Brokers
- Cooperatives
- Fund Raisers
- Gift Fruit Shippers
- Grove Management
- Growers
- Handlers
- Order Takers
- Processors
- Roadside Stands
- Sales Agents
- Sections/Salads/Juice
- Shippers
- Wholesalers

Find It Fast:

- Citrus Forecast
- Citrus Fruit Laws
- Crop & Weather Report
- Economic Information

Time For An Oil Change... Replace oils and refined sugars in your cooking with healthy citrus concentrates and juices.
More than 100 new citrus recipes to choose from ....

The World's Largest Orange Juice Glass . . . In honor of National Minority Cancer Awareness Week, the Florida Department of Citrus and the American Cancer Society have teamed up to help heighten minorities' awareness of cancer prevention. More...

"Florida Cuisine" Emerges ... Inspired by Florida's wealth of citrus culture and year-round sunshine. This great tasting new cuisine is emerging that is naturally healthful and a culinary delight (great for diets, too)! To Read More....
Get the recipes....

Florida Citrus (www.floridajuice.com)
The message on the Florida Citrus Commission is that "orange juice is for more than just treating." Information on "Florida Cuisine" recipes, gift fruit, healthy grapefruit dieting, and sections/salads/juice can extend behavior habits for increased consumption and strengthened product loyalty.

> information. Otherwise, competitors can quickly imitate what you are doing.
>
> The important issues for companies considering a Web presence are to work out how to move from simply replicate existing services in electronic form, to the personalisation of services and the development of new services such as online help facilities based on the experiences of multiple users. Companies also need to decide whether they want to capture more of the "value chain" for their product—for example, by eliminating distributors or suppliers—and how this can be achieved. This is a classic management problem in using channels. The key issue is whether or not someone else is going to make the move anyway and hence undermine your competitive position. (Pearson 1998)

Some differentiation strategies have been developed from countries of origin (Dutch cheese, French wines, German beer), from ethnic groups (Italian hoagies, Greek gyros, Cuban bread), from geographic locations (San Francisco sourdough bread, Buffalo wings, Boston baked beans, Florida oranges [www.floridajuice.com]), with usage patterns (drinking Corona beer [www.corona.com] with a lime wedge, giving Godiva chocolates [www.godiva.com] on special occasions, or turning the Hallmark card [www.hallmark.com] over to check for the logo), and from other examples of celebrations or time: season, day, or even hour (New Year's stroke of midnight and Korbel champagne [www.korbel.com]). What could be your point of differentiation? Preferably, just about any aspect that no other product in your category embraces could be your point of differentiation; the marketer is wise to avoid price competition because price is not a long-term sustainable advantage. The cyberstorefront must be attractive or intriguing at first glance with some product or service benefit to keep the shopper clicking through product selection. Possible ideas to utilize this cyberstorefront need might include collectibles of various types, information or club memberships, corporate gifts, colorful posters or prints, or warranty or replacement information. Differentiation championed on the Web site experience and benefits can lead to customer loyalty.

> If various merchants can't separate themselves from the pack, they are likely to transform most online markets into low-margin commodities businesses. Price cuts will become the main weapon in a chaotic battle for market share. Hoping to avoid this profit squeeze, online companies are spending heavily to try to create brand loyalty in cyberspace. They are pumping up ad budgets, developing online communities of what they hope will be loyal customers, and trying to make it hard for customers to go anywhere except their site. (Anders 1998)

E-commerce can reward a creative outlook or fresh interpretation of the segment's interests, the establishment of a product or service niche, and a solid and sustainable differentiation strategy. An active imagination supplemented with lots of surfing can produce great communications ideas, site presentation, advertising, sales promotion, and logistics strategies.

Summary

Given an interest in exploring e-commerce, the marketer will discover there are many methods to achieve this mission. Customers can be served by a hyperlink from a frequently visited Web page that sells advertising space, from a virtual storefront, or from a virtual storefront housed within a cybermall. The marketer should weigh the advantages and disadvantages of the various methods of cyberselling before engaging in online marketing programs. Several retailers' sites were discussed to point out different ways and different commitments to online selling or providing information.

As with any retailing venture, consumer awareness of image and identity of the retailer's products or services is critical to success. Awareness is crafted with several marketing strategies, and the marketer must balance realistic online marketing objectives, segmentation and differentiation strategies, as well as brand image development. These processes can take many years to formulate a well-recognized brand, and this brand franchise can provide marketing success and resulting profits for many decades if carefully managed.

Key Terms

Arbitron

Back office

Cybermall

Cyberstore

Linked storefront

Redundant system

Sampling

Streaming video

QUESTIONS AND EXERCISES

1. What are the factors that could encourage a traditional retailer to invest time and money in developing a Web presence and site? Write your answer as a memo to the merchandising executive of your company, either supporting or rejecting an online sales tool for your company.

2. Create an outline of the steps you would take in adopting a virtual store strategy and prepare a proposal to present to your management on the benefits to the operations, finance, and marketing functions. Write the proposal as a pros and cons view of the effort, telling management what results to expect after the virtual store goes online.

3. If you were charged with opening a Web site directed to the consumers on mainland China offering current music videos with choices of either Szechwan or Cantonese-dialect subtitles, create a list of steps you would perform in establishing a Chinese language Web site. Write a memo to the director of Asian operations for your music reselling chain. Think about the payment, shipping, and distribution systems, and incorporate these functions into your plan.

4. From the text discussion, investigate a successful story of a traditional retailer moving to the Web as an alternative sales channel. Isolate four reasons why the opening of this sales and communications function was successful and present your views as substantiation. Pick an industry you are familiar with and treat this exercise as a competitive intelligence report prepared for the president of your company.

5. As in the exercise above, report on unsuccessful Web experiment by a traditional retailer that closed its online sales operation or converted it to another purpose such as technical support or customer service. Isolate four reasons why the opening of the Web function was

unsuccessful and present your views as substantiation. You may have difficulty locating a terminated Web activity, so you might ask your friends for leads or check a local Web address directory for retailers. Input the addresses and see if they are still in operation. Treat this exercise as a competitive intelligence report prepared for opening a company of your own.

6. Prepare a three-minute speech on how a disadvantage of using the Web for commerce can also be an advantage of the medium. An example might be that stringent security protocols may add time in processing each order; the advantage is that the merchant is more likely to be paid for each transaction. Select your topic, discuss it with your Instructor, and support your topic with two to three examples of the advantage/disadvantage proposition.

7. In your opinion, what would be the top two attributes of competitive advantage for the following businesses that are establishing a Web awareness?

   a. a chain of flower shops

   b. a manufacturer of sticky labels

   c. a hospital bill reviewing consulting service

   d. a nationwide chain of shoes for infants

   e. a regional group of insurance agencies

   Write a paragraph on each attribute, two for each scenario, to hand in the next class.

8. How should a company decide on a differentiation strategy for execution on the Web? What steps should it consider in establishing a unique differentiation from others in its category? Assume the company is in the technical/trade educational business. Write a strategy selecting points of differentiation to present on its Web site. Also assume the company has a twenty-five-year track record in graduating successful technical people from its eighteen-month programs.

9. Your company is a manufacturer of asphalt roofing shingles and has long enjoyed a premier position in the home building business because of the unusually long twenty-year warranty of your shingles. In the last two years, a boom of new home construction has brought new competitors into the marketplace, and you recently learned that a newcomer to the shingle business is now offering a thirty-year warranty. The differentiation of your shingles being known as the "Two-Score Shingle, the Nation's Longest Warranty," is no longer true. What Web message strategy should you adopt? Do you change your differentiation/message strategy, ignore the competitor, wait and see what evolves, lengthen your warranty to match or exceed the competitor's, or take other actions? This message will be used beyond Web messages to be incorporated into an integrated marketing communications program. Be prepared to form a three or four person marketing committee to present your strategy to the class.

10. Of the possible competitive advantage online attributes of speed, accuracy, accessibility, or convenience, which one do you as an e-merchant consider most important? Write an e-mail justifying your selection to your college marketing professor when she asks about the marketing direction that you set for your photo finishing company.

Bibliography

Anders, George. 1998. Comparison shopping is the Web's virtue—unless you're a seller. *The Wall Street Journal*, 23 July, A1.

Beckett, Paul. 1998. Visa touts ease of shopping on Internet. *The Wall Street Journal*, 30 October, B12.

Gupta, Sunil, and Jim Pitkow. 1995. Survey 3. Report taken from the following Web address: www-personal.umic.edu/~sgupta/hermes/survey3 [cited 10 June].

Lands' End site will let users "model" clothes on body type. 1998. *The Wall Street Journal*, 16 November, A12.

O'Connell, Vanessa. 1998. Soap and diaper makers pitch to masses of Web women. *The Wall Street Journal,* 20 July, B1, B4.

Pearson, Michael. 1998. Attractors: Building mountains in the flat landscape of the World Wide Web. *Director,* July, 81.

Schmitt, Bernd and Alex Simonson. 1997. *Marketing aesthetics.* New York: The Free Press.

Swisher, Kara. 1998. Companies rush to add ".com" to names. *The Wall Street Journal,* 31 December, B5.

Tchong, Michael. 1999. The Internet is under-hyped. Iconocast newsletter, 27 February, 2, 3.

PART TWO

Integrating Electronic Marketing Resources

In Part One, The Concepts of Electronic Marketing, the foundation was laid using the traditional marketing process of situation analysis, marketing planning, and marketing implementation. With the corporate, division's, service's, or product lines' objectives delineated, the marketer then creates the strategies to achieve the objectives. The marketing program, which is a mix of product, pricing, promotion, distribution, and performance goals, is formulated to satisfy a market segment that shares similar characteristics, needs, and desires. With this framework, the marketer can now introduce and streamline the marketing process by engaging the tactical resources of electronic marketing.

CHAPTER 7

The Tools of Electronic Marketing Resources

"In addition to the convergence of media and customer change and information delivery level, we are seeing a fundamental change in the average consumer's lifestyle delivered by the acceptance of technology. This change has been driven first by the technologically enabled, then the early adapters and gradually the consuming public. Cellular phones are a great example. Ten years ago, most cellular phones were limited to CEOs or super sales reps. Today, most are not sold to businesspeople, but to family members. Proliferation of cellular phones has become so great that many areas are being forced to add additional area codes to handle the volume of numbers and activity. Fax machines are another example. As little as five years ago, fax machines were primarily found in offices. Now the fastest growing segment is for home use. PC sales have now overtaken TVs in dollars sold each year. We, as a society, are gradually becoming more technically enabled and less phobic of new technology." (Brady, Forrest, and Mizerski 1997, 304–305)

LEARNING OBJECTIVES

- To introduce and explain the tools and software applications of electronic marketing
- To present the advantages and disadvantages of electronic marketing tools in implementing an online marketing program
- To anticipate the problems associated with maintaining a marketing Web site

Introduction

Electronic commerce cannot function without electronic equipment, networks, or transaction systems. As was discussed previously, though, consumers and businesspeople do not purchase tools or systems of commerce. Who wants to buy a scanner or upgrade megabytes for their computer's memory? These devices are expensive and sometimes of limited utility. However, the consumer or business does wish to purchase technology that will improve the efficiency or effectiveness of the designated activity. In most cases, information interactivity delivers an overarching sense of customer gratification. What defines gratification? The customer defines gratification, perhaps in appreciation of speed, convenience, accuracy, and even accessibility such as actually logging on without getting a busy signal or a server malfunction. Over the last twenty years, great strides have been made in communications and database capabilities so that the technology is available to most persons and businesses, even in many diverse commercial situations. The purposes and operations of popular electronic marketing resources will be reviewed and discussed here so that you will have a foundation in personal and business electronic communications.

With any technological advance there are advantages and disadvantages with its diffusion in the marketplace. The tools of electronic marketing are no different; the purposes and situations that justify the largest disadvantage, that of cost of the devices and systems, will be reviewed as well. Usually the justification of spending money and time on electronic resources is a betterment in terms of efficiency and effectiveness; however, cost/benefit analysis studies are wise practices to confirm the marketer's premises. As more time passes in technology maturation, the best is yet to come in the development of speedier, more accurate, and more convenient marketing tools.

The Electronics of E-Commerce

Electronic marketing resources have proliferated over the last ten years, and most notably, the reach for most marketers has been inward from communications to mass markets to markets of one, as in individual purchasers or prospects. If this textbook were written in the fifties, sixties, seventies, eighties, or even in the early nineties, electronic marketing resources would have been defined and utilized in media messages using television, radio, telephone, and **facsimile** delivery. For this discussion, though, the focus on electronic marketing resources will be broadened (or perhaps narrowed to markets of one) to include other essential electronic tools that marketers can use for communications, segmentation, or memory enhancements of customer preferences. Besides the previously mentioned tools, e-commerce resources now encompass **videography, CD-ROM, interactive kiosks,** pagers, **optical scanners** at checkout, low-powered frequency modulation (FM) transmitters for in-store transmissions, and **smart cards** for recording transactions. However, in facilitating e-commerce activities, this review will be limited to computer and computer-based technologies. The power of the communications spectrum runs throughout electronic marketing tools, and interactivity is the capability that provides the strongest link between the vendor and its customer because of the gratification factor of speed, accuracy, or convenience. Much of the electronic tools combine computing abilities with telecommunications' reach. More than message delivery to a targeted audience, these resources allow direct, interactive communications in a manner increasingly comfortable and convenient to the customer or prospect. The hallmark of today's interactive electronic marketing tools is the combination of direct, targeted communications with instantaneous response. If you want to dig deeper into interactive marketing tools, you might wish to read a comprehensive book by William Martin, *Interactive Marketing.* (1994) When today's electronic marketing tools are spoken of, exactly which resources have become so valuable to the marketer?

The Data Warehouse

When you look at the Web, most of you probably see a transient medium of communication, where the usefulness of the site seems to be embodied in its graphical interface. This, for the first few years, was the driving force of good Web site development. That is, how can a site engage the viewer most effectively? The Web was viewed as the next paradigm for distribution of marketing communications, akin to television, radio, and other electronic distribution methods. The astute marketer has now come to view the Web in an entirely different way. Specifically, traditional media have become viewed as read-only or push mechanisms in that the information is pushed one way—toward the user. The Web is a truly interactive way of captivating the audience. The viewer or listener has now become the participant in the two-way dialogue. As the dialogue has intensified, it has become incumbent upon you as marketer to find new ways of harnessing in real time. Enter a corporate database. This is actually the traditional medium of the Information Systems (IS) departments of average to large firms. However, the methods of capture and delivery of information have changed dramatically. The Web introduced a new component of the otherwise familiar frame of data processing: instantaneous, massive volumes of incoming and outgoing data. Rather than having a Web site contain stagnant marketing information, the brilliant, successful multipurpose sites today combine effective marketing messages with truly impressive data-gathering systems. In many cases, the participants are unaware they are part of an intensive fight for useful information. How many of you have visited sites like Pepsi (www.pepsi.com), which boasts impressive graphics, and have not been impressed? More subtly, how many of you have visited this site and are aware that even as you navigate the site, statistics are being collected about you to add to Pepsi's electronic warehouse of consumer information? Your browsers are transmitting unique information about you, including e-mail addresses, your machine or computer, length of time on the site, or mouse clicks, and your most recent session is then paired up to other information already known from other visits on the Web.

Thus, a new technology has arisen in recent years to address the disparities between the marketer's effort to maintain a business (operation) and the marketer's effort in forecasting the future direction of the business (corporate strategy that includes the marketing strategy). This technology leverages the vast quantities of information gleaned over many years and many transactions to be placed in a massive repository, with the express purpose of garnering this data for current and historical trend and analysis. The technology is called **data warehousing** and **enterprise reporting,** and with this, the database of the past has been put into new service. From a marketing strategy, this makes great sense because past consumer behavior generally predicts future consumer behavior particularly in attitudes of brand preferences and shopping purchases. These predictors are not solely to the merchant's benefit. Equally important has become the exchange of the vital statistics of the transaction with the participant. Many of you have probably been to sites such as Amazon.com. Here you not only find your book of interest at a reasonable price, but as consumers, you enhance your shopping experience and decision processes. For the designers of this site, the site yields another important piece of information: What segment or segments of people, profiled from demographic, psychographic, or behavioristic characteristics, selected the same book for purchase. It is a direct result of new database technology, the data warehouse? An example is Oracle Corporation's new product, Oracle 8*i*; it is geared specifically toward Internet-based data warehouses. This technology has enabled Amazon.com, Yahoo!, and other Internet-based merchants to provide sites capable of sifting through endless quantities of information and to then return participant data that bear directly on his online experiences. This forthright effort by the vendors to engage their customers in a shopping conversation has helped to create a new era of soaring stock market capitalizations, where net worth is valued not by profit or near-term potential but by the exorbitant potential value of the Internet itself.

E-mail, a Hardworking Messenger

E-mail has become the most prevalent communications tool for exchanging messages at the local, national, or international scope. Fueling its growth has been the growing popularity of the general audience Internet services such as America Online, Prodigy, CompuServe, MCI, GTE, and other national and local IP services; AOL has expanded to serve more than fourteen million members, and new entrants appear every year. Recently low-to-no cost e-mail providers have included Yahoo!, Hotmail (now a Microsoft property), AltaVista e-mail, and freenets in all sizes and regions. E-mail software packages might include educational-issued products such as Pine or Eudora or commercial products such as MS Mail, cc:Mail, Notes Mail, or Vines Mail. E-mail is becoming a standard feature for most IP services and search engines since once the connections are established, communications software is not a problem. E-mail emerged from the research and educational communities, and some educational facilities still use a version called **PINE** that is text based (no graphics and a one-color display). While not very pretty when compared to the **graphical user interfaces (GUI)** of many browsers, e-mail is a virtual workhorse, much as a rotary telephone served its public for decades. Companies have embraced e-mail systems because e-mail is a low-cost messaging system that is very flexible for reaching internal individuals, groups, or company-wide audiences. It is also well suited for external communications such as links to customers, business partners, and prospects. E-mail provides efficient communications in building mailing lists; thus, a single e-mail message can be sent to many addresses at one time. These lists can be private, monitored by a list administrator, or public, allowing individuals to add their addresses by inquiring to the list administrator. List administrators, also called moderators, monitor the submissions to the list (often called listservs or discussion groups) and decide if messages are appropriate and of interest to the list members. Some lists are not moderated, which means messages are posted to the list without supervision. Lists that are both moderated and not moderated can contain excellent information, but the marketer should take caution in investigating the source of the transmission to be sure that the information is authentic and accurate. E-mail can be anonymous, leaving the receiver unsure of the origin of the information. The receiver should therefore develop a rapport with the sender before any great decisions or transactions are initiated. You never know who is on the other end of the line.

E-mail is a quick response vehicle particularly suited for acknowledging the receipt of the sales order or for responding to an information request. For example, the consumer might access a commercial site such as CDnow (www.cdnow.com) to purchase several compact discs. The order would activate an automatic reply, possibly thanking the customer for the purchase and giving an estimated delivery date. Perhaps a prospect would have a question about the method of payment, and an automated message would list the credit cards accepted, terms governing personal checks, or the acceptance of money orders. Many customers ask about the same information, so a predetermined list of automated responses, those FAQs discussed earlier, can save the call center and the customer time and energy.

Where does e-mail work? The largest category of the GVU User Survey respondents report having one e-mail account that they access from home (25 percent). Overall, 42 percent of interviewees report having one e-mail account, while 56 percent report having more than one. Europeans are more likely than U.S. users to have multiple accounts and to access them from multiple places (30 percent Europe versus 20 percent U.S.). Europeans are also more likely to access their accounts only from work, regardless of how many they have; this might be a powerful fact for business-to-business marketers selling overseas. Older respondents are more likely to access accounts from home (65 percent). They are also more likely to have only a single account (74 percent). (GVU Eighth WWW User Survey 1997)

E-MAIL A CALVIN KLEIN MODEL

Calvin Klein is Finally Going Digital. Kind Of.

The designer does not have a Web site yet, but print, television, radio, and billboard ads for the cK one fragrance will feature e-mail addresses for the three models who appear in these ads. Consumers who send an e-mail to the ad-stars will receive written replies in the fictional voices of each of the models, complete with emotions. "The next cK one generation has different values and communicates in a very modern way," said Calvin Klein. "What you have is a new intimacy that's really a paradox—people all over the world are more in touch than ever, but they're doing it one-to-one on e-mail and the Internet. When we take this campaign to e-mail, it makes it very personal."

"A copywriter will supply the steady stream of e-mail responses that will be mailed to the consumers in irregular intervals to mimic the real, random nature of e-mail communication. The three new characters span cK one's target audience: Anna, a sophisticated 13 year old; Tia, a 20-something professional; and Robert, a hip, middle-aged city dweller."

E-mail a Calvin Klein model. 1998. *Wired News* [cited 25 November online].

What a difference a single year makes. An enlightening comparison is outlined in the following table from the 1997 to the 1998 GVU survey on what respondents considered indispensable technology. The top six categories of indispensable technology are:

Technology	GVU 9 survey	GVU 8 survey	Percent change
E-mail	93.3	84.3	+ 9.0
WWW	90.6	88.7	+ 1.9
Java/Java Script	29.7	21.6	+ 8.1
Chat	23.9	22.3	+ 1.6
Audio	20.9	17.1	+ 3.8
Video	7.9	6.0	+ 1.9

E-mail is expected to continue to grow as more and more people gain access to the Internet. As was discussed in Chapter 1, it has been speculated that e-mail is helping to revive the lost art of correspondence. Conversations on the telephone take little effort and little thought; once said, the communication is forgotten. However, with e-mail, conscious thought is required to express the message, so writing rather than speaking produces a more succinct statement. As well, the writer's message is more tangible because it remains paper and ink or in the in box of your e-mail program, rather than a fleeting voice transmission instantly lost. While e-mail messages may seem somewhat cybermall, emotions can be expressed through the use of **emoticons,** which will be discussed in Chapter 10.

The Internet's Interconnections

Most people in the business world are familiar with the Internet's origins. As we discussed in Chapter 5, historically the Internet began as a government defense project in the late sixties, and its purpose during these Cold War years was to create a network of interconnected computer networks, a redundant system that could route communications through and around computer nodes. The government's goal was to prevent interruption of telephone or satellite communications' links in case of nuclear war or natural disasters. This interconnection of computers was supervised by the government agency, DARPA, the Defense Advanced Research Projects Agency, and eventually was turned over to the National Science Foundation (NSF) for use by the research and education constituencies. From its simple beginnings of joining together telephone lines to four universities, the Internet has grown to the powerful and virtually ubiquitous network as it is known today. The public breakthrough that made the Web more user-friendly to navigate was the development and affordability of graphical browsers, the first of which was the **Mosaic** browser developed at the University of Illinois, and now represented by the various versions of Netscape Navigator and Internet Explorer. Since the commercialization of the Web component of the Internet, more people are signing on to the rich graphics and well composed text for their information and enjoyment. Various departments besides marketing are using the Web for public relations, recruitment, investor and stockholder information, keeping track of dealers or suppliers' inventories or deliveries, or for research and developments. People are using the Internet at work and at home, usually via a personal computer. What is considered full access to the Internet? To be fully functional online, most experts recommend having access to the World Wide Web, Usenets and newsgroups, e-mail, as well as FTP (File Transfer Protocol) and Telnet connections. Probably the best software and communications access are those that the marketer's customers, associates, and suppliers use. Access has little use if the sender and receiver are not compatible, and the marketer should investigate the compatibilities of his audiences.

The Wonders of the World Wide Web

Some people wonder how they survived without the assistance and companionship of the World Wide Web. The Web is a relatively new marketing and communications resource that was introduced to the public in 1991. Since that year, much intensity, innovation, and imagination have been directed toward creating entertaining and persuasive virtual presentations for companies, organizations, networks, and individuals. Some Web sites are all business, some are irreverent, some are informative, and some are humorous. The coming of color monitors, faster modems, sound cards with speakers, along with the sharpened expertise of Web designers and technicians has produced lists of new "cool" Web sites trumpeted by search engines on a daily or weekly basis. The leaps in technology have produced a marvelous communications vehicle unmatched by the traditional media vehicles. The features and innovations will continue to fascinate consumers and challenge marketers and designers for decades to come.

Within the last several years, commercial Web sites have come alive with the addition of motion and sound as well as the manipulation of colors and graphics. Earlier, these embellishments were virtually impossible to accomplish because of the limited capabilities of the average individual user's hardware. Modems were unable to load the huge amounts of data required for recreating photographs or intricate illustrations; sound bites also demanded great amounts of RAM to reproduce the music, voices, or sound effects that add to the ambiance of the site. With faster modems, improved resolution of color monitors, and faster workstations with expanded memories, some Web sites now bear resemblance to mini motion pictures. In fact, movie marketing frequently employs video clips of the coming attractions, typically only a few seconds in length and somewhat rough in video detail. With the recent refinements in video reproduction, Web sites have become more intriguing, persuasive, and motivating as a premier marketing vehicle. As everyone now knows, full trailers have become more common on Web sites, frequently combined with archival scenes and movie animatics;

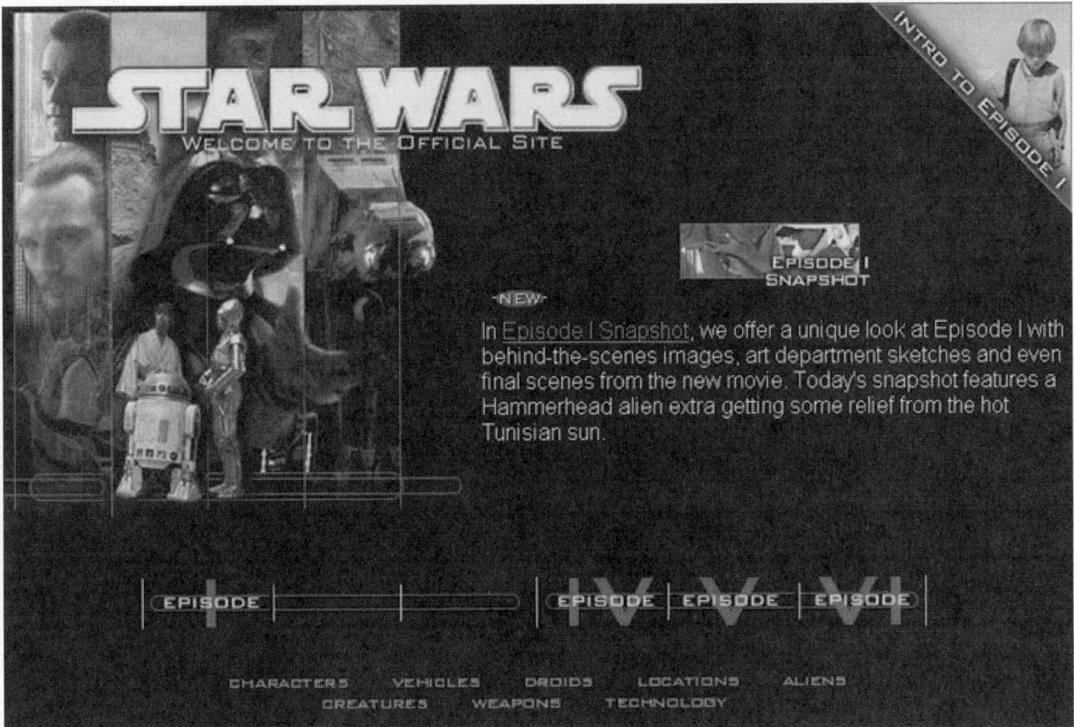

Star Wars (www.starwars.com)
Episode I The Phantom Menace, a prequel film 16 years in the making, has courted the online audience with extensive information on the film production, the actors', lives, and a fantasy expansion of the Star Wars' mythology and trivia, what fans were thirsting for.

see the twenty-year graphic improvements of the *Star Wars* movies re-released in 1997 (www.starwars.com).

With these embellishments, the Web has become considered a killer application among marketing circles because of the visual, sound, and interaction capabilities. Web designers enjoy working on Web sites; the developers often view their craft as fun and games. The combination of elements is endless, and creativity is highly valued. Web sites are playing a larger role in marketing communications programs, particularly in support of advertising and public relations efforts. Its persuasion abilities, the dispersal of its wealth of information, and interactive ordering efficiency are just now being deployed correctly by these Web designers in appropriate scenarios. Perhaps you are interested in Web page design; there are many Web page design guides and books available today. You can take classes or teach a class yourself on this subject. Check with your local university or public library for instructional classes, or consult Web references such as the Library of Congress (http://lcweb.loc.gov) HTML guides found at the address http://lcweb.loc.gov/global/ for the hyperlinks, Explore the Internet.

Another example of Web site enhancement that has improved information retrieval is integrating a site search engine. Rather than click through every page on the site, the viewer can use this consumer-friendly tool to speed up the information search, just as the viewer would type in key words (now the viewer can enter entire questions in hopes of retrieving an answer) on the Yahoo!, Lycos.Excite, Infoseek, or Excite search boxes. Ease of use is a motivating, possibly differentiating feature that sets one site apart from the others within the category, and as has been discussed, satisfying the individual is a constant effort for the electronic marketer.

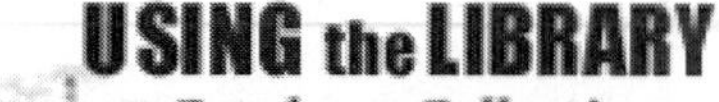

The Library of Congress (http://lcweb2.loc.gov)
The many services and collections of the Library of Congress are now online and available to schoolchildren throughout the nation.

The Advantages and Disadvantages of a Web Presence

From a marketing viewpoint, flexibility is a key feature of a product or company Web site. Production costs for the site can range in cost from a few hundred dollars to several million dollars, depending on the intricacies of the site, such as integrating a database of inventory, reporting performance, customer names, and purchasing habits; a fax-back or automated e-mail response system; or supporting international operations. Furthermore, the site can be updated as often as the marketer wishes in order to make such changes to prices, to current merchandise selections, to dealers, or for special promotions. Graphics can be replaced or enlarged in a matter of minutes; maps, menus, and **mouse overs** (those small text boxes containing descriptions or explanations that pop up as the mouse is moved over a **hot spot**) can be added or corrected equally fast. These maintenance activities can be performed by in-house staff, the position often titled the **Web master,** or by a communications supplier, such as an interactive advertising agency or specialty boutique. There also is flexibility in this maintenance issue since the time frame to update the site is a matter of an afternoon, perhaps no more than a forty-eight-hour wait. Traditional advertising vehicles can require weeks or months of production time, as in filming and post-production of television commercials or in designing, producing, or printing elaborate sales brochures. Web revisions are completed almost instantaneously, which no other advertising tool can match except perhaps radio copy changes. Even changing the message on the fast-paced radio medium typically requires twenty-four hours to complete.

There is flexibility, as well, in how the customer or prospect can interact with the Web vehicle. The session can be entirely for information gathering, for retailer or dealer locations, for creating a cost estimate as with automobile or watercraft pricing, for e-mail communications with the company's customer service staff, or for downloading site databases. The marketer can devise a Web site for prospects, current users, lapsed customers, suppliers, or sales outlets. Each of these user situations might require specialized information, and the marketer can cater to these audiences' information needs. All the more reason for the marketer to know his audiences well.

You have most likely been subjected to the current technological advances in customer service via telephone. While these technologies have a definite impact on the ability of many businesses to stay competitive in the face of mounting challenges, nevertheless, it is questionable whether this technology has created a positive consumer experience. Some examples of this technology include **transfer technology** and **hold statistics technology.** Transfer technology is the method of employing touch-tone, or voice-recognition, menus to route calls to the appropriate department. While this is cost-efficient compared to the traditional receptionist position, it places the burden on the customer in listening to, and responding to, lengthy prompts. Likewise, hold statistics technology allows the customer to know fairly precisely how much patience she will be required to exhibit in order to get the attention she is requesting.

Flexibility runs neck and neck with the potential for an almost instantaneous response. Instantaneous response is the requirement for the shopper who chooses to help himself to a catalog of information. A Web site enables a user an almost guaranteed instantaneous collection of information from the FAQ site—the time it takes the user to print the desired information off of the site. These time and convenience features outdistance the typical telephone inquiry of being forced to use the audiotext menu of contacts and of being shuffled around by telephone transfers from department to department. With this annoying transfer technology, one would wonder if the marketing or customer service managers had ever tried to call into their own automated systems. Early in the textbook, the time pressures facing today's consumers were discussed. The Web helps remedy these time pressures with such time savers as menu selections, FAQs, site search engines, and text e-mail boxes.

To many marketers, the global commerce potential is most attractive particularly with the emergence of free market economies throughout the world. Standards of living are moving upward, and middle class means, especially in South America and in Indochina, are growing for durable and packaged goods. Consumer expectations are flourishing in the former Soviet Bloc countries as technological entrepreneurs develop computer-based industries, notably in former Czechoslovakia and Hungary. The Russian and Chinese markets should be booming in the first decade of the twenty-first century. A good measure for the speed of Internet adoption is the number of Internet servers or host computers. In its latest survey, MIDS estimates there were sixteen million Internet hosts worldwide in 1997, up from 12.8 million in 1996 (MIDS Study 1997). In the same breath as tapping into the international sales activity, the Web site is operational twenty-four hours, seven days a week. Customer or prospect interaction is most attractive for companies serving many consumer markets throughout various continents; the more universal the product or service, the better a twenty-four-hour operation schedule becomes.

Internet Culture Blossoms

As the Internet emerged and was nurtured by the academic and research sectors, the Internet was perhaps taken advantage of, maybe in concept only, with the expectation that using the Internet would always be a free commodity. The infrastructure was free, the transmissions were free, domain names were free, and registration of these names was also free. Factions considered the Internet a precious and fragile thing that should be protected. The federal government footed the bill, and that was fine with most Internet constituencies. There was an expectation that commercial interests had no place on the Internet, and if they were allowed to join, exploitation was certain. This was the stance through the seventies and eighties until the mid-nineties when commercial use of the Internet began showing up frequently. This did not set well with the academics or special interest groups whose charter was to protect the Web from mismanagement. Should the Web be public or private, commercial or nonprofit, educational and research use only versus commercial usage? These are questions that were raised frequently, but for now it seems the market has relegated this argument to the sidelines of academic thought.

The Spread of Interface Culture

Steven Johnson, the editor-in-chief of FEED magazine, (www.feedmag.com) has documented an interesting phenomenon that is pervasive in our society today—the spread of interface culture. In his recent book, *Interface Culture: How New Technology Transforms the Way We Create and Communicate*, Johnson tackles the bringing together of technology and culture to demonstrate how the pervasive interfaces have earned a rightful place in our homes and workplaces. Certainly, these interfaces are descendant from the early Apple Macintosh and the following Windows graphical interfaces that were designed to use a symbol rather than confusing technical jargon or misunderstood international languages; these graphics might be compared to the much earlier international traffic symbols of Don't Walk and Walk—the flat mannequins' illustrations or open/closed palms with circles and slashes as appropriate. These graphic symbols were accompanied by color to be more attention-grabbing. Johnson demonstrates how interfaces—those buttons, graphics, and words on the screen through which information is controlled—influence not only our daily lives, but how these interfaces also track their roots to Victorian novels, early cinema, and even medieval urban planning.

> As our machines are increasingly jacked into global networks of information, it becomes more and more difficult to imagine the dataspace at our fingertips, to picture all that complexity in our mind's eye . . . representing all that information is going to require a new visual language, as complex and meaningful as the great metropolitan narratives of the nineteenth-century novel.
>
> Aids such as Microsoft Bob, flying toasters, and the landscapes of video games tell our digital society how to imagine self and how to get around in cyberspace's unfamiliar realm. Interfaces have spilled over, beyond computers and keyboards. Automobile dashes sport icons for headlights, windshield wipers, and cigarette lighters; more icons are sure to be used as products are marketed internationally. Production costs should be reduced by the use of graphical icons, and confusion by the user should also be reduced. You see this trend already with copier buttons, coffee maker buttons, VCR buttons, and any other electrical and nonelectrical products. Companies would be wise to consider GIS in simplifying their products' operation. (Johnson 1997)

Robot Shopping Agents

Many of the same products are sold by different e-merchants throughout the Web; who is to say that the shopper is receiving the fairest price when making a purchase?

Certainly comparing prices from site to site could ensure the lowest expenditure for the consumer, but the cost in time and effort might not be worthwhile, especially for inexpensive products, for instance priced at around $20. As popular products like movies, compact discs, and books fall under this price, they also fall into the purchaser's shopping cart. These automatic shoppers are becoming a great convenience to the consumer, possibly an inconvenience or a sale-robbing threat to the e-merchant. How does this price sleuth work? Perhaps you are interested in purchasing a Parker Posey movie, *Party Girl.* You could visit the Web sites of Blockbuster, Columbia House, Amazon.com, Borders, Webmarket, or Reel.com. How many sites do you wish to shop before your time is worth less and less? There are search tools, however, that do the work for you. For example, if you visited the site Jango, and typed in your request, Excite's Jango product finder will commonly list up to the twelve lowest prices among several categories (laser/DVD or VHS, new or used) and the retailers' online ordering systems that facilitate the purchase. Simply hitting the Buy button will complete the purchase, and the merchandise will be shipped to your credit card address.

Beware that not all sites will participate with **shopping robots (bots).** Some Web sites simply slam the door on shopping bots and refuse to answer requests for Web pages that come from known bot sites. Therefore, some of the most popular retailers' prices do not appear on the price comparison list, giving the appearance that Amazon.com or Borders is not competitive. Some of these popular retailers might try and confuse the robots by changing the Web site's format or appearance, so the bot does not know where to look for the pricing information. Jason Olim, (founder of CDNow, one of the hottest music retailers on the Web) does not like the invasive bots; he routinely blocks them from the CDNow Web site to prevent them from taking his prices and stacking them up against his competitors. Why are merchants afraid? Some fear shopping agents will turn the Internet into a bargain basement or flea market where bottom dollar wins, and added value customer services built into retail Web sites will be less attractive to traffic. These sites wish to compete on factors other than price. "You don't buy based on price alone. There are multiple aspects, like the convenience of having everything in one place," says Vieky Harinarayan, a vice president of Junglee (www.junglee.com). Amazon.com has acquired this bargain-seeking site but has promised Junglee will not play favorites to its listings over book sellers and other merchants' information. Therefore, another decision that you the marketer must entertain is whether or not to participate with the shopping agent technology. The answer should come from your knowing your market and its shopping preferences for low prices, for convenience, for the social experience of visiting a physical location, or for the ultimate purchase. Customer marketing information should reign. (Quick 1998)

The Extended Memory of CD-ROMs

Marketers are finding more applications for these plastic, aluminum-coated discs than just for playing music. The CD-ROM, an acronym for compact disk read-only memory, has the ability to store huge amounts of data through the use of laser optics technology. Because they warehouse data optically, CD-ROMs have a much higher capacity than a three-and-a-half-inch or a five-and-a-quarter-inch computer disk that stores data magnetically. However, common CD-ROM drives, the devices used to access data information from CD-ROMs, are less flexible in storage and can only read information from the disk and not write to it. As a comparison, CD-ROMs can hold large amounts of data and are therefore popular for storing databases and multimedia materials. The most standard CD-ROM holds approximately 630 megabytes while a regular floppy disk holds approximately 1.44 megabytes. Quite a difference in capacity.

CD-ROMs and audio compact discs are almost identical in structure and data format. The difference between the two lies in the device used to read the data, either a CD-ROM player or a compact disc (CD) player. CD-ROM players are used almost exclusively as components or peripherals and access data much faster than the typical computer hard drive. While speed is important to the marketer, the multimedia capabilities offer even greater benefits. Persuasive and entertaining marketing presentations are often placed on CD-ROMs to be played during field sales calls by company representatives; the graphics and sound quality are excellent. The equipment is compact and can be demonstrated in many settings. CD-ROMs have also become a transfer medium for software; data placed on a CD-ROM downloads more quickly than floppy disks or Internet retrieval. Marketing applications for CD-ROMs will become more popular as technology advances disks that can record, erase, update, or save data a number of times.

The Benefits of Database and Other Software Marketing Tools

Improving corporate memory has been the goal of database management applications for many years. Only now can small and large companies benefit from database management. Small firms might use Microsoft Access as their database application to keep a customer roster or to keep minimal inventory records, whereas, large companies have the opportunity to use several powerful database packages, such as Oracle Developer 2000 or Oracle Data Warehouse. The operative words are "It depends," and it does. What are the company's objectives or operations scope, the geography to be covered, the staff, or the budget for inventory or customer records management? Keeping extensive personnel records, maintaining national service records on fleet automobiles, and carrying detailed finance records is required for a successful usage of database management. There is a database management tool to fit the situation. Most times database applications are complex and dictate a level of expertise in assessing and integrating the application. Sometimes clients choose to hire an in-house software developer or engage an outside software development company. Again, it depends on the situation of the client and sometimes on the length of the project. According to Oracle Corporation, a recent study by a top preeminent IT industry market research firm reported that enterprise data warehouse implementations tend to be multi-year projects. A data mart, on the other hand, is a scaled-down version of an enterprise data warehouse with implementation cycles of three to six months. Different database applications enable organizations to not only respond rapidly to changing business conditions, but also to help perfect emerging business opportunities for potential exploitation. Imagine a field representative, two thousand miles from the pharmaceutical headquarters, dialing with surgical accuracy into a pharmaceutical's database from a physician's office to check side effects and dangerous reactions of new drugs she recommends and to find answers to this physician's questions. On real time. This certainly is an assistance to the doctor and demonstrates a competitive advantage over other pharmaceuticals companies. Creation of a simple database situation using Microsoft Access in a marketing application will be investigated further.

Front-End or Back-End Application?

You may hear the descriptions **front-end** or **back-end** devices. This refers to the arrangement of multiple software applications used in conjunction to build a certain system. Many developers use Lotus Notes as the front-end of a system, one that provides the client software and the client then inputs data, probably in marketing or IT/IS/MIS departments. The back-end might be composed of an Oracle system

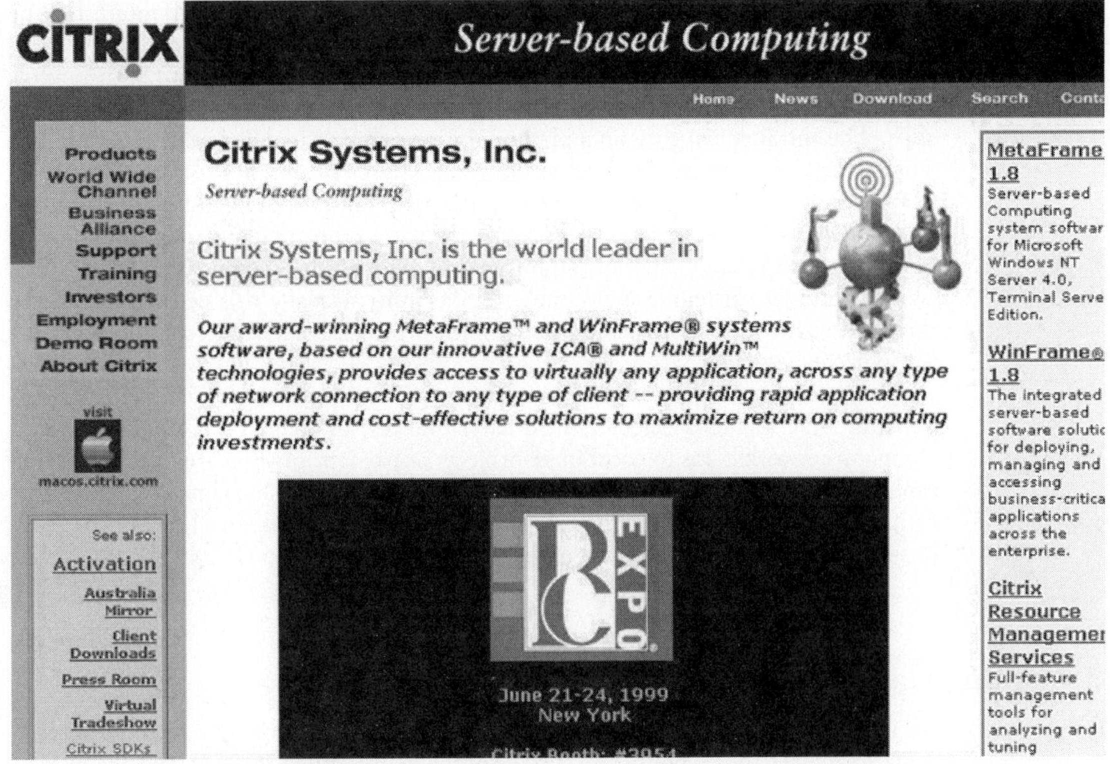

Citrix Systems, Inc. (www.citrix.com)
Leasing server capabilities to companies that do not require heavy-duty server operations is a flexible alternative Citrix makes available to information technology companies.

database located wherever the server is located—within the company or routed to an outside supplier that might have superior, more flexible servers or other hardware systems. Many computer service companies, Citrix (www.citrix.com), for example, lease server usage to companies that do not require heavy-duty server operations. The databases created in the back-end application in a basic database, which probably would not require a sophisticated platform such as Oracle, can be combined to transactional or relationship databases, which would necessitate a more complex and powerful system. A simple example of a front-end–back-end combination is your own computer system and the server of your university or business. The front-end of your PC is your browser, probably either Netscape or Explorer; you input your information requests through the keyboard. The browser then contacts the university server who acts as the back-end to send the message or retrieve the information. To make matters more interesting, some applications can be used on the front-end or the back-end such as Lotus Notes; this too adds flexibility so that the software developer can choose the best applications for the system.

Communications Networks

Marketing communications are gravitating to service specialized audiences, no longer addressing mass audiences. It is more effective to create networks designed for employees, vendors, clients, the press, or other special interests as beneficial to the company. One network might be a company **Intranet,** a private access communications network designed most frequently for the employees within an organization. Think of the Intranet as an electronic in-house newsletter that addresses issues of interest to the company's constituencies. The Intranet can also be known as a repository for work-in-progress so that project files can be accessed in meetings on-site and other distant offices or by employees working at home, which is a convenience for clients and staff alike. The Intranet can contain a plethora of information including company notices, work schedules, or even classified ads offering kittens or puppies for sale. The company Intranet can be a source of pride for the staff, but it does need frequent gardening to keep the site fresh and timely. Someone within the company must volunteer or be assigned the job of keeper of the Intranet because without someone taking responsibility, Intranet gardening is no one's responsibility. Usually this person assigned to the maintenance of the Intranet chooses a password and can access the Intranet only through the password.

A second type of network is a company **extranet,** a private access communications network that includes selected external suppliers and clients. This outside-the-company network helps to coordinate projects or participants that are distant in geography or those who infrequently are involved in the project. One company takes ownership of the project and assigns passwords that can be activated to learn of the latest progress or problems on the assignment.

Software Working Hand in Hand

Businesses often engage in national or international commerce, so rapid communications are vital to the response and success of the management. E-mail now occupies an important place in corporate communications as a basic electronic tool for messaging between individuals, groups, or offices. However, more complex data management that provides a competitive advantage can be derived from more powerful and reliable tools such as Lotus Notes or Lotus Domino. These applications can establish Web-enabled information repositories and complete service request tracking systems. As a simplistic description, Lotus Notes is a large proprietary networking system, for diverse industries in manufacturing, dairy, personnel services, retailing, fast food, and entertainment.

Some software tools work in conjunction with one another. Communications systems might wed Lotus Notes or Domino server software to an on-demand, automated fax-back system, which are capable of handling an extremely heavy volume of fax requests and responses. The automated fax-back system is capable of capturing fax images and can create records in a Lotus Notes database. There is great flexibility and complexity as these communications and database tools are combined. Great care should be given to analyzing the needs of the company, selecting the hardware and software necessary, and interviewing competent and innovative software systems developers.

Reporting and Planning Systems

Business requires clear and concise decision making and frequent reporting on project status to management and to peers; reports have become more visual in the last five years as graphics packages have grown more sophisticated. Software systems must be able to access, analyze, and develop accurate assessments for making strategic decisions. The resulting data must be easy to read and understand, as well. No marketing presentation is delivered without pages of plans, charts, graphs, and tables that represent the performance of the current marketing program in force. Marketing also means planning, and within the last few years, planning competencies have expanded and gained much more accuracy. In particular, large projects with horizons of many years benefit from planning applications, such as Business Objects (www.businessobjects.com), which helps to set direction and timelines, milestone points, and overlap and down times. The better information can be controlled and manipulated, the better all business processes, including marketing, will perform.

Optical Scanners

The old grocery counter scanner has been pressed into new and varied services in manufacturing, in the medical industry, in the aircraft industry, in lumbering, in measurements of all kinds, and by the U.S. Postal Service. Officially called **Optical Character Mark Reader (OCMR),** or more simply optical mark scanners and readers, this equipment usually by passing a wand over a preprinted bar code eliminates manual data entry. This electronic tool saves many hours in pricing and counting inventory, coupons, or contest entries. Scanners are compound photoelectric sensors that use multiple surfaces to provide additional information and can cover a larger area than typical photoelectric sensors. An object passing between the transmitter array and the receiver array will block several beams of a linear bar code. The number of beams blocked, the spacing between each bars, or each bars' width, length, height, or diameter can identify this object. Optical scanners often dispense coupons or discounts at checkout on store, sale, or competitor brands similar or equivalent to items purchased in this transaction. The scanner reads the code, locates the equivalent product and size, and then prints a coupon on the back of the receipt. The sale coupon is intended for use at the next shopping opportunity, and the procedure is quick and easy, both for the consumer and for the attendant. More uses in different sectors that will involve the cash register are expected, and retailing creativity will enhance the potential for the optical scanner.

Data from optical scanners assist marketers in increasing performance by tracking results of sales promotions, by counting units sold, by checking prices, by verifying identities, or by hundreds of other marketing and operations considerations. Wal-Mart has used optical scanning and satellite data transmissions as a powerful marketing weapon. This system constantly records unit sales to update inventories, check product sales movement, and revise pricing as needed; these data are then transmitted by rooftop satellite dishes, and inventory replenishment begins. Financial data are recorded, and adjustments to pricing, product mix, and selection are made. While optical scanner systems serve all functions of the retail or wholesale activity (financial, operations, and marketing), it is difficult to argue that the marketing and sales functions are aided the greatest.

Fax-Back Systems

An older reproduction system, the facsimile, has been reborn to serve the distributed information systems, more so than on a one-on-one transmission. Although slower and probably not as neat as an e-mail message or an e-mail attachment, faxing systems can be less costly when the marketing situation requires a high volume of repetitious information. If the marketer must support a number of salespersons, particularly nationwide, a fax-back system makes much sense. Again, the salesperson needs to access an information repository that contains parts inventory, units available, or as in the previous pharmaceutical example, drug interactions or side-effects on which perhaps only the pharmaceutical company has accurate records.

In each case, the salesperson dials into a bank of fax machines that then query the database to return a hard copy fax to the field salesperson. Several dedicated fax systems can be introduced into the communications infrastructure; two of these faxing networks are FAXback and RIGHTfax. As with any application or system, there are

ELECTRONIC MARKETING CASE HISTORY

On-line Knowledge Management—Bayer's Information Gateway

Bayer Pharmaceutical. A world-class drug manufacturer with a reputation for first-class support. In order for Bayer to maintain a high profile in a competitive industry, they must constantly strive to be innovative, and caring. And to do this, they have to be right on the front lines of support for their products, many of which are used in life and death situations by healthcare professionals.

Enter Bayer's Clinical Communications Department. This area of the Sales and Marketing division employs a number of Drug Information Specialists whose job is to provide support to Bayer's customers. For example, physicians frequently require critical information about a Bayer drug while a patient is in the operating room. The problem is that a seemingly simple request can require a great deal of effort to fulfill.

In order to complete a call, a specialist gathers supporting information by combing through Bayer's extensive library of information. Legal and regulatory concerns play an important role, since multiple individuals are required to carefully review the accuracy of each letter to be sent, and a record for each sent letter must be created. In addition, all of Bayer's scientific data used in the process must undergo rigorous scrutiny before it can be provided to the public. When this was largely a manual process, meeting and exceeding the expectations of the caller was a monumental task, since a typical response often took hours, or even days, to complete.

There had to be a better way. And so, Bayer decided that an electronic solution was required, and called on a cadre of trained computer specialists to build the Information Gateway. The system's primary objectives would be:

To quickly identify the information the specialist needed to complete the call;

To package that information into a single electronic document; and

To retain a complete record of the request and the response for regulatory and marketing follow-up.

But there was a problem. According to Sherlyn Celone, Bayer's Manager of Marketing Communications, "we knew we had a major problem since the information was everywhere, and it took too long to find it. With Bayer hiring people left and right, it was only a matter of time before it snowballed. We had to do something." As it turned out, some information was contained in massive medical tomes, some in cabinets filled with documents, and some on hand-written sheets of paper. Other information was on proprietary computer systems within Bayer's information domain. And just in its inchoate stages were masses of disparate information accessible only via the Internet. All this information had to be available from a single resource, and easily packaged for Bayer's customer, quickly, easily and securely. The only viable solution could be an Intranet knowledge management system.

Why? Because, Intranets help Bayer's specialists by providing a consistent browser-based interface, and, unlike the Internet, are completed isolated from, but allow access to, the Internet (a requirement of the U.S. FDA). Knowledge management systems logically organize information resources. In the case of the Bayer's Information Gateway, the Bayer specialists can scan for items of interest, identify important details, and even navigate to non-Bayer sites. Links to valuable medical data sources on the Internet help the specialist to find relevant information instantaneously. They can also search for information by keyword, using a powerful search engine. Linking to multiple data sources from one interface allows the specialists to traverse their world of information faster than ever before.

So how does the information get packaged and delivered in an age of technological heterogeneity? Well, the Information Gateway sports a slick packaging interface called the Information Gateway Assistant that sits on each specialist's desktop. This "shopping cart" style document repository allows them to select documents anywhere (even from their word processor, not just in their browser!) to create a single digital package (an Adobe PDF document, for the technically inclined). In this way they continue their thought process while simultaneously preparing an information package for the recipient. Compare this to manually compiling a stack of information, and it's easy to see the benefit.

The Assistant, in turn, is directly connected to Bayer's E-mail system, fax server, and high-end printers (for those recipients who are electronically challenged). Additionally, as the document wends its way along the information highway, the Assistant creates a complete record in a powerful Oracle reporting database. Bayer uses this data warehouse not only to keep track of these transactions but also to monitor areas of concern in the health care community on behalf of government agencies as well as Bayer's own Sales and Marketing department.

According to Ms. Celone, "the process of responding to calls has been greatly enhanced. And the predictive analysis that the team can conduct also has been improved, allowing the group to better direct resources based on customer need." While the outside customer does not see the system, the business impact has been equivalent to many market-facing systems. The business process has become more closely integrated with customer demands, and the system delivers its product with increased speed and reduced associated costs.

The overall result? Bayer can provide potentially life-saving information in a timely manner to the people who need it most. And this is how Bayer Pharmaceutical lives up to its credo, "Changing the world with great care."

(Personal interview with Sherlyn Celone, Bayer's Manager of Marketing Communications)

Bayer (http://bayer.com)
A worldwide corporation with interests in biotechnology, polymers, and specialty chemicals, the Bayer site finds time for fun with a downloadable "Run or Repel" game featuring its insect repellent Autan warding off swarms of mosquitoes.

pros and cons in selecting the appropriate software. Marketers work closely with the vendor representative to understand these factors and then develop plans to minimize the disadvantages and maximize the advantages of the correct system. Again, diligent preplanning will eliminate major surprises that confront the marketer.

Web Portal Sites

The online services businesses have discovered a new feature to develop and promote in their efforts to expand their audiences. The new offering is called a portal, or **metasite,** which has been described as an all-in-one Web super site; the portal is the entry point that offers a broad array of resources and services, such as e-mail from the Web site, forums, a variety of search engines, news broadcasts, personal Web pages, and online shopping malls. As CNNfn online news service reported:

> **Web portals** are becoming more important as companies strive to become the "first stop" for people online. As the Web grows, users are faced with a baffling array of new Web page offerings. Internet companies believe users will welcome a jump-off point with links, both old and new, to sites related to their individual tastes. In addition, many portals hope to become centers for Internet commerce, a potentially lucrative enterprise as more people begin to shop online.

Make the RightFAX Decision.

Products | Support | Training | Partners | Channel | Company

- RightFAX v6.0 fax servers and Symantec's WinFax PRO 9.0 team up to offer an integrated network-based fax solution. (North America only)
- **Introducing the** RightFAX Connector for SAP™ R/3® - adding full fax functionality to your SAP R/3 system.
- Use our **Fax Cost Savings Calculator** to see how much your company can save with a RightFAX fax server.
- RightFAX **Year 2000** Information

| Home | Products | Support | Training | Partners | Channel | Corporate |
| Sales | Contact | Site Map | Privacy | Y2K |

RightFAX (www.rightfax.com)
Fax-based communications to support salespeople in the field with information-intensive data or quickly-changing situations is the RightFAX competency in online skills.

> Portal services are very attractive to online retailers and other marketing-oriented companies. Most portals require you to register and, in doing so, provide demographic information. Portal firms can then use that specific information by selling targeted advertising geared to each individual user. (Shultz 1999)

American Online (AOL) is still the largest and most successful portal in history. Consumers may view a Web portal as a one-stop service to access the best on the Web. A marketer might look at advertising exposure on several portal sites as he would analyze programming on a television network. If the portal programs to a younger, middle-aged, or mature adults markets, this format might match well to the marketer's product or service promotional plan. Portal development is being formulated even as this book is being written, so many innovative features will satisfy market needs and desires that cannot be forecasted at this time.

As noted, AOL is creating a two-tier portal—one with fewer features and one more heavily laden perhaps with resources such as personalized news, choices of e-mail options, free Web pages to users, and smarter search engines. There is much speculation as to what features are being considered or being beta-tested. The

MOUSE AND PEACOCK

If there's money to be made in portals, it's a safe bet that the major media companies will try to get a piece of the action. In June, 1998, the Walt Disney Company and NBC—two of the biggest behemoths—made investments in existing sites. Disney (which, according to its chief executive officer Michael Eisner, will be "aggressively competing on the Internet, and . . . aggressively competing as you enter the Internet") agreed to purchase 43 percent of Infoseek. The Web gateway [or portal] could end up as a home of Disney's formidable portfolio of media properties—from ABC News and ESPN cable channel to *The Lion King* and *The Little Mermaid.*

NBC, meanwhile, bought a stake in Snap, CNet's portal. Details of the deal are sketchy, but NBC intends to heavily promote the site to TV viewers. "Must-See Web," anyone?

(Li-Ron, Yael. (1998, August). Portals into the Future: What's up Next? *PC World Online.* [Online]).

well-known search engines, Infoseek, Excite, Lycos, and Yahoo!, already are offering e-mail and personal home page at the following addresses:

America Online, www.aol.com

ChickClick, www.chickclick.com

ESPN, http://ESPN.SportsZone.com

Excite, www.excite.com

HotBot, www.hotbot.com

Infoseek, www.infoseek.com

iVillage, www.ivillage.com

NetCenter, www.netcenter.com

Snap!, www.snap.com

Yahoo!, www.yahoo.com

(Petersen 1998)

New portals/metasites include:

Everything-but-the-Kitchen Sink

Where Everybody Knows Your Name

AOL Lives!

Build Your Own Portal (a portal of the future)

The Limitations of Electronic Marketing Resources

With every improved business practice or convenience, there is a tradeoff, usually price. Because of the tradeoff, the improvement must be proven superior, faster, less risky, or of some significant betterment than the old way of doing things. Marketing technology is no different. Cost-benefit analyses are usually conducted as a starting point in determining whether the cost of the proposed new marketing system can save money over the current system or systems involved. Much as mergers and consolidations are affecting the media, banking, and airline businesses, hardware consolidation fortifies cost-savings and staff-economies by central or regional media centers. In previous times, connections were slow, servers were slow, and hard drives were small. Technology is expensive, but the rewards are now greater than ever.

The marketer can lay off some of the risk by investigating her options in scalable software and hardware or other high tech equipment for future growth. Careful choice of electronic tools and vendors that are knowledgeable in marketing, inventory, and fulfillment systems will be worth the effort in improved practices. Scalability has become an important, even critical, issue in systems' specifications because businesses have found that prior equipment purchases cannot be expanded and, therefore, are seemingly worthless. Wise questions to ask in systems' negotiations should include the expansion capabilities as a business grows and interchangeability of hardware components should different manufacturers or vendors recast in the future. The marketer should be aware of which systems can operate which software applications, as well. While no one has the future firmly in grasp, partial success is derived from asking the right questions and recognizing the right answers.

As recognized from the early days of computing during the late forties and throughout the fifties, managers and programmers recognized the value of quality data. A familiar saying, Garbage in, garbage out, articulates the point that poor or inaccurate data are processed into poor decisions. As marketing plans are guardedly developed and executed, marketers are equally cautious in formulating the program's data with an eye on accuracy and timeliness in retrieval. Marketers further recognize that systems' successes do not happen magically. As systems can perform more functions, communicate with more offices and people, and work twenty-four hours each day, these systems are becoming more and more complex. To achieve maximum productivity, marketing-savvy companies stress training and retaining qualified, competent people. Training is to your staff and associates as maintenance is to your machinery. Without training people can become stale and unchallenged; without scheduled maintenance of parts replacement and lubrication, machines will fail. Some resourceful companies spend handsomely on training to retain their best employees. Given the sophistication of the software packages (and even the video games), serious instruction in optimal operation is beneficial to the entire company, including marketing and MIS/IS/IT departments.

Another significant problem in electronic marketing resources, at least in the short term, is the low penetration of the World Wide Web into American households (and businesses), and presumably the households of the world. Connectivity costs money, usually a monthly fee varying from $15.00 to $60.00, depending on the level of services, the type of connection (for example, a fiber optic connection is more expensive), and the type of promotional program the user signed up for. Currently a PC and modem are also required for Internet access although **WebTV** and other set-top units have been introduced and are less expensive than the PC equipment. At present, less than one home in four (actually 23 percent in 1998 and expected to top 40 percent by 2000) has access to the Internet. While that might be discouraging compared to 98 percent penetration of broadcast television and 69 percent penetration of cable television in the United States, in 1996 only five percent of the homes were connected. Therefore, the growth of Web access and its features has been extraordinary and is expected to escalate and then level off through the year 2010, as the members of Generation X begin to mature comfortably in their mid-thirties. Another short-term obstacle is the general lack of faith in financial transactions over the Web; business groups are concentrating on secure commerce activity spearheaded by Visa and MasterCard. For marketers and retailers, this Secure Electronic Transactions (SET) protocol had been promised for introduction for the past two Christmas seasons, and late deliveries in SET standards for the new online sales channel were blamed for soft holiday sales in 1996 and 1997, at least in the retailers' minds. Acceptance of electronic commerce is proving varied according to industry. Computer equipment and accessories are popular among computer technicians and aficionados. However, clothing and other dry goods are lagging in sales. Marketers are learning that products or services purchased on price decisions as in commodities sell well; products bought for color, texture, or style are more difficult to merchandise. For international marketers, stumbling blocks could be the limitations on language laws and currency, possible cultural differences in the exchange process. The marketer must, therefore, be willing to take on the roles of financier, fashion buff, linguist, world traveler, and pop culture watcher.

The biggest problem, however, in understanding and balancing your electronic marketing requirements is communicating your real needs to your suppliers so that the proper trilogy—software system, hardware, and budget—is attained. This positive relationship begins with a marketer who honestly knows her business and the areas in which this business can be improved, and finishes with knowledgeable suppliers that become consultants and teachers to their clients, recommending the appropriate, not necessarily high commission, software and hardware products to solve the client's problem or situation. It is a rare but gratifying exchange that might last for decades, as long as each party performs as promised. This situation is the basis for relationship marketing, the most mutually beneficial and profitable association for both the client and supplier. Marvelous accomplishments can be attained when the chemistry between both is positive and respectful.

The Problems with the Web Site

As a practical, everyday communications tool, there are several significant obstacles to be aware of as a marketer integrates Web site activities into the marketing plan. The most commonly experienced Web-access problem, construed by the GVU Ninth WWW User Survey, is that of taking too long to download pages; this complaint was voiced by 64.8 percent of the study group. (1998) As modems are upgraded for speed or faster modems are purchased, Web pages are becoming more heavily laden with images, animations, scripts, programs, and plug-ins, all of which take extra time to download. In particular, retailers should know that 53 percent of respondents reported they left a Web site while searching for product information simply because the site was loading too slow.

Another complaint among consumers was the growing problem of broken links or dead Web pages. Although solutions for dealing with broken links or receiving a "File Not Found" are well known to Web designers (such as redirecting bad URLs to a search page), most sites do not seem to employ any technique for correcting these problems. Besides these operational issues, the content on the Web, such as the misuse of the Internet for business and the blatant postings of pornography and other sexually explicit activities, is most controversial to many supporters of free Internet dialog and traffic.

What equipment does the user own to access various Web sites? As for modem speed, most Web users connect at 33.6 K, but more people are upgrading to 56.6 K. Almost a third (31 percent) plan to upgrade their speed in the next six months, and 17 percent plan to upgrade after already having upgraded over the last 12 months. In researching equipment used by the consumer, the most common piece of hardware owned is a printer, either black-and-white (44.4 percent) or color (62.8 percent). Following the printer is fax machines (27.9 percent) and scanners (34.4 percent).

The World Wide Web has also caused an impact in the customer service capabilities. Of course, the basic change is in the hypertext appearance, which presents a more attractive, fully graphical representation of whatever the marketer or advertiser wishes to display. The entire site atmosphere can be enhanced with color, motion, or sound clips that might reduce the level of dissatisfaction should a disgruntled customer be the viewer. It is better, though, to head off potential problems before they happen, and orders or inquiries to Web purchases can be acknowledged automatically via e-mail or via a fax-back system. In fact, a friendly Web site, full of content, might be the only factor separating a commodity-type product such as office supplies or agricultural items. Electronic marketing may be the only supporting service that sets the marketer's organization or product apart from the competition.

Summary

Marketing programs are only as good as the performance of its tools and components. While marketers have at hand the most powerful, interactive communications vehicle presently available, excellent planning and execution of the best electronic resources will not mitigate poor marketing planning. The marketer must know what the proper roles are for various types of communications systems, such as e-mail and Lotus Notes; for database software, such as Oracle and Microsoft Access; and for dedicated networks, such as company intranets and extranets; the marketer must also know the functions of the multipurpose Internet. Technology changes quickly as evidenced by Netscape Navigator 2.0, 3.0, 4.0, and now the 5.0 releases and by Netscape Communicator, as well. Some industry observers say the race is on between Netscape and Microsoft to produce new models or issues mirroring the automobile industry.

You as a wise marketer will stay on top of new electronic marketing tools development by reading industry publications, visiting industry trade shows, and touring facilities where the tools are already in place. Marketers are an odd bunch; when a program works well, marketers are hesitant in sharing a program's success. Therefore, you the marketer must seek out these magic programs through inquiring among suppliers and associates in noncompetitive firms. Marketing intelligence works, no matter whether you, your assistant, or a research firm performs the activities. As has been discussed, some competitor always has a better execution or better tool than you. It is up to you to level the playing field by being more persistent or more innovative than the industry.

Key Terms

Back-end system

Balloon

CD-ROM

Data warehousing

Extranet

Emoticons

Enterprise reporting

Facsimile (Fax)

Front-end system

Graphical User Interface (GUI)

Hold statistics technology

Hot spots

Interactive kiosk

Intranet

Metasite

Mosaic

Mouse over

Optical Character Mark Reader (OCMR)

Optical scanner

PINE

Robot shopping agents (bots)

Smart cards

Transfer technology

Videography

Web portal

Web master

WebTV

QUESTIONS AND EXERCISES

1. As a written exercise, define the following terms:
   a. software
   b. hardware
   c. Intranet
   d. extranet
   e. data warehouse
   f. data mining
   g. front-end application
   h. back-end application
   i. enterprise reporting
   j. PINE

2. As an inventory manager of a medium-sized hospital supply company, you are approaching an important date, the annual inventory of merchandise. In the past, you have used an outside supplier to perform this task, but the supplier's charges have grown rapidly over the last four years. You wish to investigate buying or leasing your own database resources. Outline the steps you would take in developing a cost/benefit analysis to compare the costs of using a supplier, leasing equipment, and buying your own hardware and developing software systems. Input your projections into an Excel spreadsheet for the financial officer to review.

3. After reading this chapter, what would be the three and only three electronic marketing resources you would choose for operating your bicycle manufacturing company? Assume you are in a startup situation and the company can afford only three resources. Justify each resource in a one-page memo to your stockholders.

4. If you operated a virtual storefront selling wildlife and scenic photography calendars and prints of various sizes, would you allow robot shopping agents to enter your site? Consider

your products to be medium priced. Write an e-mail explaining to your brother-in-law and partner what the advantages and disadvantages of your decision may be. Would you change any of the marketing mix elements (raise or lower your prices or cut or increase promotional elements, for instance) depending on your decision? Fully justify your marketing decision.

5. You are thinking about opening a virtual storefront to sell pop culture T-shirts internationally. These T-shirts will be colorful to be displayed on a Web site and will feature timely slogans or headlines in English. This will be a part-time venture, so the site must operate almost autonomously. What topics should you be investigating to provide excellent service to your purchasers? List and explain these topics as to how you will operate the twenty-four-hour site.

6. In the Bayer Pharmaceuticals case history, what other means of communications could the field sales staff have considered in gathering accurate information to supply to physicians? Make a list of alternative communications channels and technology to accomplish this same goal. For each alternative, list the advantages and disadvantages to either the physician, the salesperson or the Bayer Corporation. Submit this list to your instructor acting as your sales manager.

7. In the Introduction to this chapter, a statement was made that, "Interactivity produces gratification for the user." Interpret this statement from the marketer's and consumer's viewpoints. Cite examples as you write a one-page explanation of the concept for the sales staff.

8. One of the problems of Web operations is maintenance of the existing site. The Web site should be continually evolving, updated frequently with fresh content and product or service offerings, and consistently accessible by the server. The tasks and skills of a Web master were discussed in detail in the text. Should this Web master be a staff employee (subject to using his singular style and subject to stagnation of new ideas and promotions) or should the Web master be an outside supplier (subject to longer service or repair times or subject to higher charges because of only occasional service)? Consider the advantages and disadvantages of both situations and be prepared to discuss the Web master scenario in a class discussion.

Bibliography

Brady, Regina, Edward Forrest, and Richard Mizerski. 1997. *Cybermarketing*. Lincolnwood, Ill.: NTC Publishing Group.

GVU Eighth WWW User Survey. 1997. [Online] Atlanta, GA.

GVU Ninth WWW User Survey. 1998. [Online] Atlanta, GA.

Johnson, Steven. 1997. *Interface culture.* New York: HarperCollins.

Martin, William. 1994. *Interactive Marketing*. Erskineville, NSW, Australia: Sear Printery/Prentice-Hall of Australia.

MIDS Study. January 1997. [Online} Austin, Tex.

Petersen, Andrea. 1998. What is a portal—and why are there so many of them? *The Wall Street Journal*, 10 December, 12.

Quick, Rebecca. 1998. Web's robot shoppers don't roam free. *The Wall Street Journal*, 3 September, B1, B8.

Shultz, Randall J. 1999. The battle for the portals. *CNNfn Interactive Network* [cited online 19 January].

CHAPTER 8

Segmenting and Analyzing the Target Market

"Successful Singles ranks among the top five segments for ages 25 to 39 and among the lowest five for all adults under age 22. [This] ranks first in the number of nonfamily households and has one of the highest concentrations of single adults (47 percent). The number of single-person housing units is over twice the national average (55 percent). Median household income is 50 percent above the national average; per capita income for [this segment] is nearly three times the national average. Over 17 percent of these households earn over $100,000 a year. Over 50 percent of the working population takes advantage of public transportation, ranking Successful Singles second in this category. Nearly six in ten adults possess a graduate or undergraduate degree. These individuals rank second in total white-collar employment and first in the number of professional specialists such as doctors and lawyers. (National Decision Systems Psychographic Handbook, 1995)

LEARNING OBJECTIVES

- To understand the concepts involved in using geographic, demographic, and psychographic research
- To understand the value of electronic resources in identifying demographic and psychographic prospects in the marketing segmentation process
- To be able to analyze geographic, demographic, and psychographic data in making informed marketing decisions

Introduction

Marketers are demanding more performance for their promotional expenditures, and who can blame them? Media advertising and national sales promotions are expensive; one thirty-second television commercial broadcast during the Super Bowl XXXIII championship football game cost more than $1.5 million. While Super Bowl telecasts are not targeted, arguably perhaps to men, electronic marketing resources can assist in the delivery of messages to markets with specific characteristics. Traditional demographic research coupled with lifestyle and behavioral analysis can now be enhanced with electronic market tracking to increase the probability of promotional messages being exposed to the e-merchant's prospects. As the Web breaks new ground daily, so does tracking technology. Smart e-marketers ask questions beyond the number of impressions, hits to a particular Web site, or visits to the advertiser's home page. These marketers inquire about specific views on the page, unique visitors, origins of domain, competitors' sites visited, and bottom-line, products' sales revenue. If a higher capability of targeting communications and creating custom product offerings attractive to individual or group tastes have been reached, as partners in the exchange process, the marketer should pursue these information-gathering technologies to furnish the customer or prospect with the best choices to match his needs or wants. This chapter will pursue the happenings in customer identification and segmentation in both electronic and traditional research methods.

Searching through 130 Million Households

As database retrieval has been married with large scale databases, in particular the data collected and stored by the Census Bureau, marketers have become quite proficient in locating the most productive areas in which to promote their products and services. This geographic targeting is available for profiling states, counties, zip codes, and Census tracts for approximately four hundred households as well as the locations of eight to ten households from the expanded zip code with the four additional numbers. Marketers can pinpoint the target areas using geo-demographic software modeled and prepared by companies such as National Decision Systems (NDS, www.natdecsys.com) in San Diego and then engage marketing fulfillment companies such as Val-Pak (www.valpak.com) to deliver direct marketing messages to each household in the area of interest. The services of these database-enabled, geo-demographic companies are broad and thorough; they offer many reporting, **mapping,** and other consumer and business-related identification services. As the name geo-demography implies, the two elements of identification are geography, stretching from urban to suburban to rural areas of residence, and demographic characteristics of fifty **household clusters.** Using National Decision Systems' **geo-demographic** analysis, American households are distinguished by different attributes, and the company has divided and named the clusters to give each a personality. This aspect of **psychographic** segmentation, the self-described lifestyle patterns, will be discussed shortly, and the identification and descriptors as detailed in a NDS data report will be used, as well.

The Value of Marketing Databases

Databases are simply collections of things, usually similar things; by classifying like items into smaller groups, the marketer finds communication and service easier tasks. Marketers jealously guard their databases because ultimately the customer becomes involved and purchases from someone. Sometimes years of data collection form a database. An example of a longitudinal database is Disney's release of videos by generation;

Val-Pak Coupons (www.val-pak.com)
Geographical couponing and proprietary databases throughout the nation help local retailers target their markets' with effective incentives. The "light blue envelope" is recognized for delivering value among consumer markets.

every twenty to twenty-five years *Lady and the Tramp* or *Bambi* will appear on video retailers' shelves to delight new viewers. Likewise, Procter & Gamble (P&G) could keep careful records of female births knowing that baby girls will grow into women who in turn will have children of their own. Baby products such as diapers, wet wipes, lotions, toys, and clothing can have memories for the moms, so a coupon offer of discounted products might keep a lapsed user (through childhood and teen years) a recovered user when a baby comes along. How could P&G compile a baby database? One way is by reporting the announcements of live births in hometown newspapers. Taking this database situation further, perhaps the marketer was based in Sherman Oaks, California, and the company he worked for operated a chain of music stores. His manager instructed him to investigate the research triangle area of North Carolina, a state and area he had never visited. By ordering market information reports on the area, the marketer could begin to familiarize himself with the market dynamics before he toured the Tar Heel State. Afterwards, he could use the data as decision-support information to determine whether opening stores on the East Coast was a wise decision for his company.

Properly maintained, databases provide marketers with accurate, up-to-date information regarding population, households, and businesses nationwide. Clients are able to look at a geographical area, whether it is a neighborhood, county, region of a state, state, region of the nation, or the nation as a whole, to define the population within the chosen area in terms of **demographics,** socioeconomics, housing characteristics, lifestyles, and consumer purchasing behavior. Databases also assist marketers in analyzing businesses within an area in terms of specific **SIC code (Standard Industrial Classification),** employee size, occupational mix, annual sales, and type of business, as well as even more detailed characteristics. Using these databases, marketers can obtain specific information on the supply and demand dynamics, such as whether a city or region is growing in population or losing businesses in certain commercial categories. Depending on the population trends, a marketer might decide to open stores or to not open new stores, place sales representatives in new territories, or introduce new products or services in these trade areas. Market data companies can also supply marketers with comprehensive lists of consumers for direct marketing. These lists are accessed through the company's affiliate network of outside direct marketing companies that specialize in compiling and maintaining consumer databases. These lists help marketers to select and target consumers by comparing the MicroVision, the lifestyle profile, to the demographic profile. (National Decision Systems 1998)

Why Are the Concept and Practice of Segmentation so Important?

Demographers have found that people of similar demographic, economic, and social characteristics tend to live among other similar persons, and for marketing purposes, these clusters of people with similar means, aspirations, and motivations can be matched to products and services related to their life circumstances. This clustering of like consumers is built upon segmentation, the separating of consumers into smaller groups of like characteristics. Once the marketer has decided upon the consumer or business segment or segments, the matching clusters are defined and selected from the descriptive characteristics for marketing purposes. Perhaps the marketer's product is fine jewelry, and the list of clusters contains several upscale, fashion-oriented segments to which the marketer could use a service such as Val-Pak to either mail or offer electronic inducements to these consumers. Likewise, the marketer could use this same strategy of demographics, economics, purchasing habits, and self-concept to assist in determining an appropriate retail store location. The consumer data can produce several reports that estimate retail spending within a geographical area, and depending on the target segments, the marketer can better decide where best to locate his or her discount, midline, or exclusive retail outlet. The basic formula for geo-demographic segmentation is place of residence compared to level of income.

By the use of a segmentation decision as to whom and where the intended prospect is—young, middle aged, or elderly; affluent, middle income, or lower income; graduate, college, or high school degrees; married with children or without children, single, or divorced; owning or renting their homes (the demographic information in an NDS report is extensive)—the marketer has plenty of profiling information to locate and identify her target of residential consumers from the universe of all residential consumers. Once the marketer has identified who the consumer is, she will need to identify where the consumer is—living in an urban, suburban, or rural environment, residing in a home in a residential neighborhood or on a five-acre spread or residing in an apartment in a small complex or possibly in a high-rise apartment. Matching these two profiling situations give the marketer considerable direction in the promotional program. Successful segmentation strategies are borne by the marketer in knowing well the market based on demography, the numerical portion of the grouping, and the corresponding psychographical profile of those areas of highest marketing potentials. If demographics deal with the harder side of numeric characteristics, why are psychographical profiles considered the softer side of segmentation?

Investigating the Typical Demographic Report

What is to be found in demographical and psychographical reports produced by companies such as National Decisions Systems? Generally, the data presented are fashioned to assist decision support, to demonstrate the logic used by the manager. It is often said that a manager cannot have too much information. While that might be true, it helps if the information is well organized. In NDS's case, it typically organizes and sells information divided into five categories:

- Demographics—NDS provides over eight hundred demographic, socioeconomic, and housing characteristics from the 1990 U.S. Census. (The Census will conduct its next research in 2000.) Some of the most important selections, or choices, are population, sex, age, household types, property values, education, occupation, household income, and residence types. Almost all demographic information is derived from the ten-year census, and as time passes between each Census report, the demographics company begins to model its data to adjust for changes or corrections that could not have been anticipated early in the decade. Like a moon shot, a small error at launch can become a huge error in trajectory millions of miles out. The first U.S. Census was taken in 1790; cows and outhouses were among important things counted. The United States has conducted a census every ten years since 1790, and the information and the techniques in the gathering of this information have become more and more complex and complete.
- Demographic updates and projections—It is good to know how the market is comprised today, but what will be the population composition in five or ten years from now? Business infrastructures are expensive to construct; if the market turns soft or booming, will a marketer have time to make adjustments? Most demographic companies will provide corrected updates yearly and five-year projections for population, households, income, and wealth.
- Age by income—The more detailed the age categories, the better. This data provides a detailed breakdown of total current households within a defined geographical area according to fifteen categories of ages and nine household income ranges. It is helpful to have a breakdown in terms of number and percentage of households. By combining age and income percentages, the marketer can get a rough estimate of whether the selected populace is young, middle-aged, or older and whether the selected populace falls into the upper, middle, or lower income groups.
- Business facts—This report supplies summary counts of businesses for easy analysis of the quantity and composition of businesses within an area. Counts can be obtained for total businesses by major predetermined categories or by any single or combination of user-defined selections, including SIC codes, employee size, annual sales, and business type. Summary counts can be obtained by zip code, county, or tract.
- Retail facts—Depending on the market data company, marketers can acquire valuable reports on shopping centers and tenants, financial information for individual bank and S&L office locations, restaurant information, insurance information, consumer expenditure potential for several major retail categories, and reports of many other types. These data can be critical in determining the success or failure of commercial establishments, and you the marketer are wise to investigate the proposed market area *before* any financial commitments are made.

Q & A: MARKETER REACHES BLACKS ONLINE

With millions of people using the Web on a daily basis, online advertisers are beginning to segment their advertising to segment ethnic groups, particularly black consumers. Larry Tuckett, the CEO of Tuckett/Parshall Interactive, has pioneered online marketing to the black community since 1990. Tuckett's company designed the *Essence* magazine Web site and counts among its clients Motown Records, Home Box Office (HBO), and Morgan Stanley. When Tuckett/Parshall was acquired last summer [1997] by InterActive8, Tuckett became director of ethnic marketing. He recently spoke with Tech Web's Mo Krochmal about the rising importance of black consumers.

Q. Why should the black community be important to online marketers?

A. A Nielsen study this summer said 24 percent of blacks, or 6 million people, are now connected to the Internet. That's a 53 percent increase in the past nine months.

Q. But 6 million isn't a huge market. Why is this online group attractive demographically?

A. As you get to the higher income, more educated people online, blacks are as connected as whites. Black people have $500 billion. That's what we purchased last year.

Q. Is it unfair to ask you to speak for the entire black community?

A. No, I can't speak for the entire black community, but I'm a member of the NAACP, I live in the Bronx, [and] I have a wife and an eight-year-old girl with her own Web site and a pen pal in China.

Q. Is your daughter typical of black children her age?

A. Among my colleagues who are professionals, yes, she's typical. She has a lot of friends who don't have computers in the home that love to hang out at our house. They love to get on the Internet so they can play CD-ROM games.

Q. What are the barriers the black community faces in going online?

A. It is about price and it's about parents understanding what a computer is. A lot of times the parents are afraid. They don't know what to buy. I had a lot of hopes about WebTV being very pervasive in the black community but it hasn't happened.

Q. What do the technology companies looking to do business with this community need to do?

A. I think it is education and giving key information that is going to help make a right decision with the purchase. Like when you buy, what software are you going to need? How do you connect to the Internet? What is the difference between AOL and AT&T WorldNet? I get a lot of questions about what it costs to be online.

Q. Where do you go online?

A. There is one site I frequent a lot, *The Black World Today*. Whenever they talk about black Web sites, they always mention two sites, Black Voices and Netnoir. Black Voices is owned by the Tribune. Netnoir is partially owned by America Online. Their content is very light and very sparse, more about chat and community. *Black World Today* is the only serious news site on the Internet for Black Americans.

Krochmal, Mo. 1998. Q & A: Marketer reaches blacks online. Tech Web [cited online 17 November].

Psychographics, the Clustering of Households with Similar Lifestyles

The demographics report can tell a marketer only so much. Primarily it states what the numbers are but not how the population's lifestyles and egos are sorted. For example, a demographic report can indicate a cluster of individuals earning an annual income of $100,000, but is this income from old, inherited money; from investments; earned as a wage; or for the sake of discussion, illegally earned? It might be important to know that the money was earned as a sales representative rather than as the owner of a profitable machine shop. A $35,000 salary might be spent differently by a long-haul truck driver than by a Manhattan junior auditor or a cowboy riding herd on a picturesque Montana range. The point is that the amount of salary is the same, but is it spent on golf courses or in bowling alleys? If differences such as these are important to the marketer, how can these data be obtained?

The alternative method, or supporting method, to demographics is psychographic research. Psychographics is about lifestyles, and marketing information companies believe that there are multiple and distinct household compositions in the United States. This is an alternative method of segmentation to demographic composition; psychographics is a customer segmentation and target marketing that identifies the number and concentration of households of each segment located within a trade area. The National Decision Systems' psychographic information product is called MicroVision, which provides a link between consumer households and their unique purchase behavior, media and financial habits, consumption, and lifestyles. With psychographic data, marketers can segment, locate, quantify, and target their best prospects within any defined demographic area. The demand potential can be determined for the product, marketing communications to consumer needs can be tailored, and prime consumer households within this geographic area can be targeted. The consumer data identifies the number, percent, and concentration of households in each MicroVision segment located within a trade area.

The NDS report details a lifestyle description of a neighborhood; for example, NDS dubs the young up-and-comers market as "successful singles" and describes this segment as "young, single renters, older housing, ethnic mix, high education, medium income, managers/professionals, very high bank card accounts, very high installment activity, very low retail activities." To further expand the marketer's knowledge of the area, MicroVision describes fifty segments from "upper crust" to "stars and stripes" to "late-life laborers." All is not jolly in each segment; some of the segments reflect life's realities. One segment, "hanging on," is described as: "black, large families, low income, low education, laborers; high retail activity, low installment activity." While some descriptors may seem humorous, substantial research has been conducted to substantiate these fifty segments. There is even a college category, "university USA," described as: "students, singles, dorm/group quarters, very high income, medium-high education, technical/sales, low financial activity, high retail activity." Does this sound like an accurate description of you and your friends?

Since each market segment represents consumers with a unique pattern of purchasing, consumption, media usage, and financial behavior, the marketer can more easily identify, quantify, and locate the best customers and prospects. These market segments are defined using more than two hundred variables provided from U.S. Census information and consumer demand data. As was stated previously, no marketer can sell to everyone, so this segmentation method is one more strategy to select the best mix of product and prospect.

While demographic analysis generally deals in aggregate numbers, psychographics identifies the number and percent of households and population in each market segment to give the marketer an index of measurement. An index of over a hundred means there is a greater than average concentration of this segment or group in the marketer's trade area as compared to the base area as a whole. Conversely, an index of less than a hundred means that there is a lower than average concentration of that segment or group present in the marketer's area. This rationale is founded on the premise that the average is one hundred. A measurement of 110 in a geographic area such as a zip code means that the segment has a 10 percent higher propensity to purchase a product in a category that has been targeted by the marketer. A measurement of 87 in a product category means that the residents of a certain geographical area are 13 percent less likely to purchase. This methodology is similar to the product and service research conducted by Simmons Market Research Bureau (SMRB); sample research reports of SMRB can be found in most university libraries. Again, knowing your market is the key to marketing the right product in the right place at the right price. Geodemographic and psychographics are aids in helping the marketer make the wisest marketing decisions for her product or service.

EXHIBIT 8.1

A Description of a Sample Cluster of Lifestyle Data

Profile Behavior	Percent Penetration	MicroVision Index	Rank
Listens to classical radio	21.5	750	1
Has a Gold American Express card	36.6	710	2
Has made at least three foreign trips in the last three years	22.9	483	1
Uses a dry cleaner (at least $100 in the last six months)	26.5	481	2
A member of a frequent flyer club	39.7	430	1
Uses an ATM card	33.8	397	1
Reads travel magazines	19.6	394	1
Traveled at least fifteen nights to foreign designations	19.0	383	2
Listens to "all news" radio	29.1	381	1
Invests in U.S. bonds, notes, and bills	8.6	376	1
Maintains a mutual bond fund	12.3	371	1
Bought or traded public stock last year	16.9	363	2
Drinks imported wine	29.6	350	1
Attended a live theater performance last year	47.2	345	1
Has a passport	57.2	340	1
Visited a museum last year	45.8	334	1
Exercises at a health club	28.2	319	1
Went snow skiing last year	15.6	316	1
Reads *Epicurean* magazine	17.6	310	1

Microvision Marketing Guide, Lifestyle Data, July 1995.

A Description of a Sample Cluster of Lifestyle Data (www.siterreports.com)
A MicroVision report on the activities of a lifestyle cluster as reported by National Decision Systems. Note that the report contains a MicroVision index column comparing the cluster against the national average index of 100.

Researching the habits and the lifestyles of your chosen markets can improve your effectiveness in all of the promotional tools including media vehicle selections, appeals, advertising scheduling, and sales promotions. The research is available through demographic data companies and can be bought as a one-time purchase or on a subscription basis. Again, the more you know about your customer, the better you can serve them.

Finding Clusters of Similar-Minded Consumers

Individuals see themselves in certain ways—wise, sporty, conservative, technologically enthusiastic. There are many psychographic niches in which an individual can occupy. It is the marketer's assignment to locate these possibly scattered prospects and deliver a compelling message to them. This is particularly important for the product or service that is a discretionary good, one that the consumer does not absolutely require.

While demographic analysis might point the marketer to areas of numerical significance to sell the necessities of life, the consumer with an inflated ego might want something better. Hence, the study and application of group psychographics becomes an important key to marketing. The affluent consumer is chased by many marketing programs; the marketer finds that marketing costs are greatly reduced when groups of consumers are courted as opposed to the costs of marketing to one. Using the MicroVision groups manual, several segments are combined into groups of similar but not identical characteristics. MicroVision bundles the fifty segments into eleven groups for the marketing economy; these eleven distinctive market groups will vary in composition depending on the geographical area selected. The marketer will see a recurring emphasis on money, age, marital status, and risk-tolerance states of mind, all timeless values upon which marketing programs can be built and adjusted. The following is a list of the eleven groups as categorized by MicroVision. The first column of the list stands for MicroVision group 1, etc.

MVG01	Accumulated Wealth
MVG02	Mainstream Families
MVG03	Young Accumulators
MVG04	Mainstream Singles
MVG05	Asset-Building Families
MVG06	Conservative Classics
MVG07	Cautious Couples
MVG08	Sustaining Families
MVG09	Sustaining Singles
MVG10	Anomalies
MVG11	Unclassified

These MicroVision groups might have an index substantially greater or lower than one hundred, depending on the market composition. For example, a retirement community might house more Cautious Couples with behavior affected by the Depression or the two world wars. Likewise, downtown Detroit might be home to more Sustaining Families because of the low socioeconomic conditions found there. Many of these segment descriptions have been present in America for generations, but several, particularly in the suburbs, have developed within the last fifty years. Marketers realize that a substantial number of households are situated in the suburbs, and these are areas of sizable discretionary spending.

The marketer must, therefore, define his best profiles—one or more that will be most receptive to purchasing his product or service—and then categorize these profiles from the fifty lifestyle segments. (There are actually forty-eight definable lifestyle segments since the last two are catchalls that may or may not exist in each geographical area.) This selection process should be ranked by number of households or percentage of households. This number should be totaled enabling the marketer to determine acceptable market penetration levels. If the potential market totals to be a small number—not a large enough number of consumers to generate enough profit to be worth marketing to—the marketer may need to expand his market by adding two or more segments to reach an acceptable market level. What is an acceptable level? It depends. For example, geography may play a part in determining an acceptable market level for athletic equipment. This equipment would be consumed differently by urban dwellers than by rural residents. Computers and online services purchases might be viewed differently by those with higher education than those with lower education. Wines may be held in appreciation for different reasons by different market segments (fine wine collectors versus street people). The same argument must be reviewed for each of the psychographic (or the effects of demographics) characteristics that define a consumer, such as occupation, social status, income, and residence. Marketers must be intuitive and sensitive in fitting products to prospects since product usage is a reflection of who the marketer is as individuals within communities.

Some characteristics are definitely more important than others in certain types of durable purchases. High to medium income earners tend to use low amounts of installment credit; they instead keep large balances of revolving credit with low retail accounts. These consumers have the money to pay off debt quickly thus avoiding interest charges. It would be foolish for the marketer selling a mid-priced automobile to develop elaborate long-term financing programs to the consumer likely to pay cash for the automobile. Many companies have been very successful servicing the low-income earners by understanding their consumption preferences and habits. An insurance company developed many loyal customers by devising a sales plan in which salespeople visited Hispanic communities door-to-door, collecting premiums on a weekly basis. This sales strategy was built on the habit of using medium- to high-installment purchasing. The insurance customers looked upon the insurance company as a partner that was helping them achieve some financial security. In both cases, marketers investigated the preferences of its prospects and produced sales programs tailored to their needs and desires.

The iVALS Internet Psychographics Methodology

Marketers can explore psychographic segmentation online through the Internet Values and Lifestyles Web site (http://future.sri.com), a repository of psychological and motivational research originally developed in 1978 by Stanford Research Institute of California (SRI, www.sri.com/val/iVALS/). Its hypothesis is that all Americans can self-identify themselves into clusters of lifestyles—eight segments in the VALS2 categorizations in earlier methodology and ten segments in the **iVALS** profiles that pertain to recent Internet research. In fact, the iVALS survey can be taken online with lifestyle typology results generated within minutes to the individual. According to SRI's Web page, SRI created "iVALS to enhance the usefulness and quality of online environment for end-users, content providers, and intermediaries. IVALS is for *affinity-mapping* software that makes smart connections—connecting people with contents of interest and businesses with customers of interest and vice versa. The point is to create an environment with more signal and less spam for everyone."

Individuals are segmented into the following ten segment profiles.

- Wizards
- Pioneers
- Upstreamers
- Socialites
- Workers
- Surfers
- Mainstreamers
- Sociables
- Seekers
- Immigrants

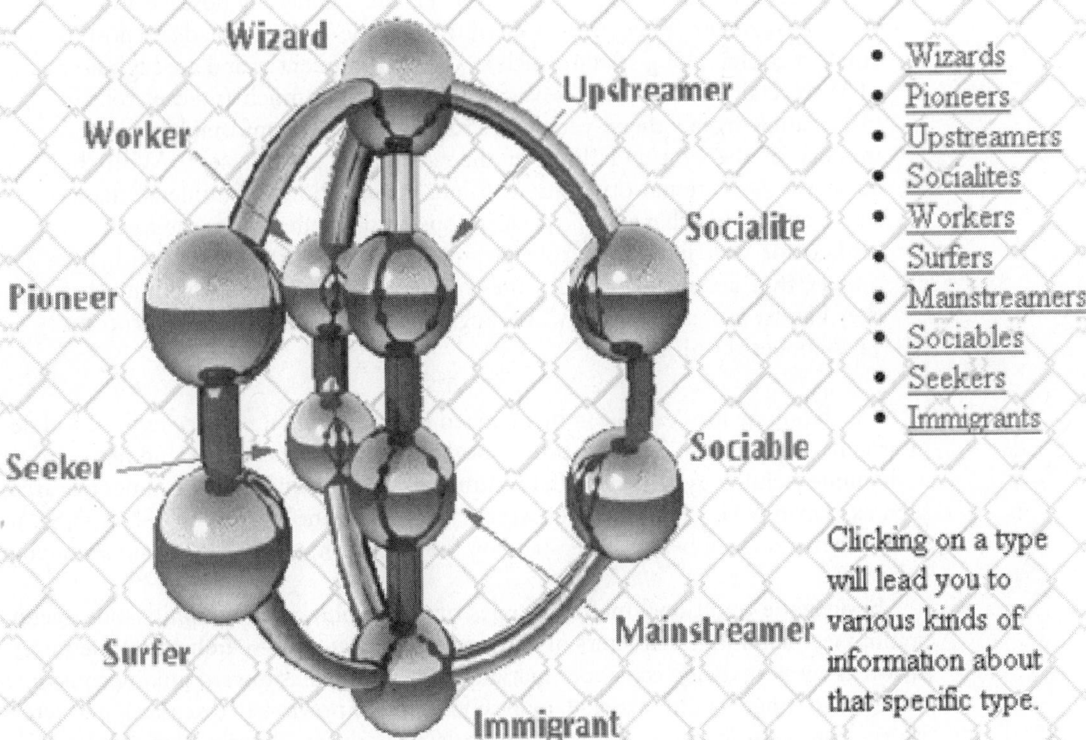

iVALS Segment Profiles (http://future.sri.com)
Stanford Research Institute developed the Values and Lifestyles typology for Internet and computer users. Take the online iVALS survey to evaluate your own segment's characteristics.

Different lifestyles bear different descriptions of values in work, information usage, and computer usage.

> *Seekers* are a very work-focused group. Productivity is their principal reason for using computers. Becoming power users or wide-ranging Net explorers are not priorities. Accordingly, Seekers focus their time online to specific work tasks—information searches, communications, document sharing among them. They see the Internet as one of many tools in their day-to-day activities, but they often wonder if its usefulness outweighs its various difficulties. Because Seekers' activities are often based on accomplishing specific tasks, they can get very frustrated by obstacles. They generally do not have the patience for learning via trial and error, but they sometimes end up doing so to get things done. Yet when they have a task accomplished or it's the end of the work day, most Seekers would rather leave the computer behind than use the Internet recreation.
>
> One of the oldest Web segments age, Seekers are a prime segment for information filtering and meta information applications and services. They see the current Internet as an information hierarchy, and they resent the

> amount of effort necessary to separate the wheat from the chaff. [The description continues several paragraphs.] (iVALS Segment Profiles, http://future.sri.com/vals/seekers.html, 1999)

Another segment is *Pioneers.* They are described as the following.

> At 10 percent of our Web sample, Pioneers are a generally positive and active user segment. They spend a lot of time on the Internet, read and post to comfort conferencing systems such as Usenets frequently, and are high user of Web retail sites. Solitary voyages, they don't get much Internet-related information from others, yet most Pioneers have a comfortable technical mastery of the Net and think of themselves as 'power users.' With the strongest recreational orientation of any group, Pioneers immerse themselves heavily in cyberspace. An exception to this immersion is their general disdain for chat-like social role playing or sexual flirtation. As with the *Surfers,* they are enamored with the Internet as a medium—a medium that they handle professionally. (iVALS Segment Profiles, http://future.sri.com/vals/pioneers.html, 1999)

The typology for iVALS can be matched with traditional psychographics and demographics to produce a clearer profile of the prospect or customer and her comfort with online technology. SRI also offers online information on other consumer research, such as "Japan-VALS," "Consumer Acceptance of Technology," and "GeoVALS," to assist the marketer in better understanding the factors that motivate consumer buying behavior.

Besides the traditional methodologies of geographic, demographic, and psychographic segmentation, marketers of consumer products also use **behavioral segmentation** as a way to divide consumer markets. The rationale is toward linking consumer behavior to usage—light, average, or heavy users. As previously discussed, marketers are eager to identify the heavy users comprising perhaps 20 percent of customers in number but consuming 80 percent of product or service sales. The difficulty in labeling consumers as light or heavy users is that the identification is not constant through the product categories; consumer usage varies according to products. Female groups may be heavy consumers of cosmetics and hair products but may be light consumers of alcoholic beverages or sporting publications. Psychographic segmentation also lacks a general consistency; some persons consider themselves active in appreciating fine arts, such as symphonic music, but disdain modern art. Therefore, the marketer must conduct various types of consumer research to cross-tabulate the real profiles of his market segments.

Electronic Marketing Tracking Tools

As electronic commerce develops, more and more technology resource will be directed toward identifying and tracking the behavior of online purchasers. Wholesalers and retailers are eager to gather information on demographics and usage of Web participants so that the best marketing mix of products and services can be presented to potential shoppers. Electronic tracking and reporting methods are controversial among consumers and Internet privacy advocacy groups, and the marketer should investigate this targeting tactic fully before incorporating this technology into her marketing activities. Tracking and profiling software, called "cookies," are easily installed and easily turned off in the individual computer owned by a Web user. Some view cookies as beneficial in building long-term relationships with customers by getting to know the consumer's preferences. The software technologies company, Engage (www.engage.com), discusses the concept of cookies on its home page with the following description: "to see the world through each visitor's eyes and to market to each individual's realities." The technology of I-frontier (www.ifrontier.com), an interactive advertising agency, has developed tracking systems that promise to tie users' site behavior and purchases back to specific ads and campaigns. (Wang 1998)

On the other hand, many persons view these electronic tools as marketing surveillance akin to a breach of privacy. "They're an invasion of my privacy." "Every time you get one, it reads your whole hard drive." "It's like getting a virus, and it can even read all of your private accounting documents!" What are these nefarious cookies, and what is their purposes? Simply described, cookies are packets of information. Netscape defines a cookie as "a general mechanism which server-site connections (such as CGI scripts) can use to both store and retrieve information on the client side of the connection." (Persistent Client State HTTP Cookies, http://www.netscapte.com/newsref/std/cookie_spec.html, 1999) When your browser contacts a Web server, the server may send a piece of data called "state of information" that will be stored in your machine. This information includes a range of URLs that may access the information. If you once again request a document from any server within that range, the "state of information" object is sent to the server as part of the request. What information does a cookie retrieve? The following list comprises the different information a cookie can retrieve.

- the domain from which the cookie originates if the cookie requires a secure transmission or not
- specific URLs that may access the cookie
- the cookie's expiration date
- the name of the cookie item
- the actual data for the cookie item

Marketers use the information from cookies to track a user's visits to a page and track which advertising banner that user has been seeing so that the site can present a new banner when the user visits next. The marketer is also able to study site navigation from cookies to determine, for instance, what pages are most popular. A page that is visited infrequently could be revised to offer more attractive products or more useful information. Consumers can choose to participate in this tracking process. If you, as a user, want to know each time you are being sent a cookie, both the latest Navigator and Internet Explorer can be configured to notify you when a cookie is sent. Once you have done that, you will see just how many sites are using cookies. You may wish, however, to provide information on shopping habits and preferences. (Clark 1997)

Insightful information might be gained using other measurement technology such as Alexa (www.alexa.com) or a new model of advertising viewership called **clickstream analysis,** developed by Thomas Novak and Donna Hoffman of Vanderbilt University and Patrali Chatterjee of Rutgers University. Alexa technology involves tracking Web site visits to offer the consumer a pop-up screen advertising a competitive brand, thus, supplying the viewer an alternative product to compare. Clickstream analysis is a study of consumer response data detailing the content and advertising banners that consumers click on during the online navigation process. Previous studies by newspaper and magazine publishers employed *eye tracking* analysis to determine what draws the reader's eye first—the headline, the illustration or photography, or other elements such as the logotype or white space. In other words, eye tracking studies can be likened to clickstream analysis as ways of better understanding how the viewer navigates through advertising materials, either print or electronic and both

Alexa (www.alexa.com)
Alexa is of the many new technologies being introduced to the Web that permits consumer navigational tracking. As the viewer moves from site to site, a pop-up box presents a competitive advertising message to allow the consumer an alternative item.

graphical in content. The concept of clickstream analysis is young; it would be best for the marketer to monitor its development by consulting documents such as Project 2000's "Modeling the Clickstream: Implications for Web-based Advertising Efforts" written by Chatterjee, Hoffman, and Novak. You can keep up with clickstream developments by accessing the address http://www2000.ogsm.vanderbilt.edu/papers/clickstream/clickstream.html.

Art and Science

There are two important areas of judgment in marketing. One area is in the judgment of the creative marketing process in determining whether new sales programs or creative campaigns will work. The other area is in market or segment selections in determining who is the appropriate consumer of a product or service? In this context, there are no hard and fast rules for success, only experience and the results of trial and error. The practice of investigating demographics and psychographics hopefully will eliminate some of the error, but not every marketer will interpret the numbers and the nuances properly. In fact, two marketers might take the same information, arrive at different conclusions, and both be correct in their marketing strategies. In a marketing strategy, it is possible to take different paths and arrive at a successful destination. In assembling marketing facts and opinions, the demographics are the numbers from the past. These numbers do not necessarily represent the present or the future. Some, however, may argue this point, psychographics are more future-leaning since few persons change their habits unless under dire circumstances. Employing psychographics is an art that not every marketer has patience for, but it is a longer-lasting strategy for ultimate success. Manufacturers and marketers can match product, price, promotion, and place, but few can occupy or replace the positive ego enhancement a customer receives from consumption of a desirable and satisfying product.

An Exercise in Demographic and Psychographic Analysis

As an exercise to familiarize yourself with demographic and psychographic data reports, you will find in Appendix B a printout of comparable geographic areas and consumers. These printouts are typical of the information that a marketing director would ask in making a marketing decision; it is your assignment to analyze the data and answer the questions on the assignment sheet. The demographic data included in the appendix projects the important factors as population and household growth, owner versus renter occupied units, and income figures. The psychographic questions included in the appendix basically concern the level of education, types of occupations, and marital status of the consumer. Given the marketing scenario, it is your job to review the data and make an informed decision that could, if wrong, cost your company millions of dollars. Conversely, a correct decision could earn your company millions of dollars over a ten-year period. You have all the necessary information in Appendix B; since this is a hypothetical situation, no outside research is necessary.

The Segmentation Technique of Geographical Mapping

Utilizing geographical database technology is fast becoming a popular tool for marketers. Databases can be very complex to work with due to the type and amount of information they may contain. Databases can contain thousands of variables. Each variable may contain the key information required to make a decision. When it comes time to analyze the database and the results that are pulled from a database query, there are many approaches that may be taken. If geography is a variable in the marketing plan, one of the best ways to analyze data is by displaying it on a map. Specialized mapping software can act as a front-end of a database by displaying data in graduated shapes, colors, pictures, or patterns.

For example, if you were assembling a direct marketing plan and were analyzing fifty zip codes in a designated market area (DMA), given the fact that your database contains all of the following variables, there are numerous ways that you could display your data. One of the most analyzed variables is income distribution. A marketer could pull from their database the median incomes for all fifty zip codes in the target DMA. There are at least two other ways to analyze this data. The marketer could have a traditional spreadsheet with two columns—zip code and median income. You could, of course, sort the zip codes by your target income, but there is not indication of the geographical locations of the zip codes. If your advertising budget is allowing you to use saturation mail to the top fifteen zip codes by income, you would know the top fifteen zip codes, but you would not know their geographical location without consulting a second source. The marketer that is using a mapping application can pull the same information from the database and apply it to a map. This mapping application could then highlight the top fifteen zip codes on the map, label the zip code and median income, and identify hot zip codes by highlighting them in red and indexing them separately. This is an extremely simplistic example as there are most often many variables that are considered simultaneously when making decisions.

There are so many aspects to mapping. Naturally, one of the components is geography. A marketer can analyze data at many different levels of geography. There are carrier routes (the route of one mail carrier), zip codes, census tracks, DMAs, states, and custom created sales territories, just to name a few. Before any information is gathered, the marketer must know the type of research that is desired and at what level of geography the results should be displayed.

Benefits of Mapping

A key benefit to utilizing mapping software in marketing analysis is organization. When determining how to display information so that it may be interpreted, organization is critical. Due to the amount of data that is processed in databases, properly organized results displayed in mapping or traditional database format will allow for better decisions to be made. Because data that has been mapped is easier to read and follow, much time can be saved and utilized in other areas of marketing. Another benefit to mapping is ease of analysis. Mapping may use colors and patterns to demonstrate a physical number of variables present in a given area, percentages, frequency of use, or simply the location of each variable. Mapping results allow for time-saving analysis that is always supported behind the scenes by traditional database facts.

As was mentioned earlier, mapping is a front-end display that tells the story of data that is in the background. That story is the relationship of the variables that reside in a database or that are pulled from multiple databases by a series of queries. The map and database must always correlate. The data always dictates what is displayed on the map.

The information that is displayed on a map does not directly come from a database as the pieces that one would think of in a traditional map. That information is often the geography or topography information. Mapping software users have literally become map makers as they have their choice of layers to use when building their maps. Those layers may consist of streets of all types, railroads, landmarks, buildings, zip codes, and state lines, to name a few. This gives complete freedom to the marketer to create a customized map for each analysis. Key layers may be included or excluded to aid in the analysis. Surely if you were doing an income analysis of the state of Texas and were shading each county by its median income, it would not be necessary to see every residential street that exists. Possibly the interstates would be shown with the county and state lines for a clean map, making it easy to see county boundary designations.

It is also critical to have your layers on your map up to date. For example, it would be necessary to have current zip code boundaries when conducting research at that level. Streets and carrier routes are just two more layers that constantly need to be updated as they change quite often. As the mapping layers change, the database information must also be updated and congruent. If a database has the income information for three newly created zip codes that are represented by one original zip code on the map, there will be errors because the map and database do not speak the same language. Most often those errors will appear as missing information on the map.

EXHIBIT 8.2 **MEDIAN HOUSEHOLD INCOME FOR ZIP CODES IN HILLSBOROUGH COUNTY, FLORIDA**

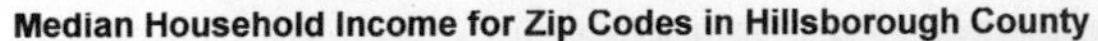

Courtesy of Val-Pak, Inc., www.valpak.com.

Database Mapping and the Electronic Marketer

There are three types of database mapping that will be discussed including site analysis, territory management, and database plots. Each function has its benefits to the e-marketer. Would you ever open up a store only knowing that it was in zip code 33618 or that it was located at the corner of Highway 1 and Main Street in Fort Lauderdale? As a marketer, the answer would be never. The site analysis will give marketers key information about their site selection and surrounding area. For example, if Firestone were looking at several locations in the Tampa, Florida market, it would be extremely important to know the raw number of homes in the area. From that number, ratios could be built such as the percentage of households in a five-mile radius that had one, two, or three cars. It may be equally important to know what the median incomes of those households are as well. The type of information required varies by the type of business.

The site analysis is also a key when deciding on traditional direct marketing. Direct mail, for example, can be distributed at many different levels, as previously discussed. If zip code saturation was to be used, the client would be wise to determine what type of household demographics and psychographics make up the areas that are to be targeted. Should a small day care open up in a neighborhood when the day care's budget allowed them to saturate ten zip codes? Demographics such as percent of households married with children and single parents with children would be crucial when making that zip code media purchase.

EXHIBIT 8.3 **MEDIAN AGE FOR ZIP CODES IN HILLSBOROUGH COUNTY, FLORIDA**

Courtesy of Val-Pak, Inc., www.valpak.com.

Another way of making a direct marketing purchase using geo-demographics would be by the number of households closest to the business doing the marketing. If a business wanted to mail to the closest ten thousand households, the households would be selected by distance from the business. Mapping can play a key role in the closest household purchase. It is quite possible, however, for the closest households to not be the most likely to visit a business location. For example, the map may show that two thousand of the closest households would need to travel over a toll bridge to reach your location. Chances are that if you are a convenience store, those customers are going to visit another location. It would be wiser to select houses that have no geographical obstacle in reaching your location.

Another benefit to mapping is the aid to managers when creating or maintaining sales territories. It is critical to businesses to follow the areas infrastructure and geographical changes over time. As these changes take place, the territory can weaken, no longer performing its function as it did when it was designed.

Where would a manager start when building a sales territory? A map would be a good start, but a computerized mapping system would be a great start. The computerized mapping system can utilize functions and databases to help create optimized territories. Where does the salesperson need to go to make her calls? The computer can create a matrix based on distances between locations while including city factors and while balancing territories based on drive time. Mapping systems utilizing database information can also see the number of potential customers and then balance by workload. The computer can also utilize database information by demographic and psychograpic information to create optimized sales territories based on the nature of the business. One key to building a sales territory is being very familiar with the sales force. Every sales force has its stronger members. A sales force could be ranked according to their strengths and placed into the computer as a variable to consider when building territories. This information would prove invaluable when creating territories. Experienced sales staff may require a workload that is higher than that of a salesperson with less experience. This additional information will help create territories that will maximize sales.

A third type of mapping that can benefit the marketer is a database plot. Do you know where your customers live? It is nice to have a list of addresses, but viewing a map with dots placed at each customer's household location is even better. Furthermore, the marking of the customer's location can tell you added information without consulting the data itself. You could color code each customer marked by the number of purchases they have made or the number of days or months since their last purchase. Database plots can help determine what areas are performing well and what areas are not. Database plots can also aid in other marketing decisions. The marketer can create a customer loyalty program based on customer location and spending. Database plots could also assist in determining the location of billboard advertising or where to hold a radio remote promotion. Mapping applications are only as good as the information contained in the marketer's database, as it is only another way to display results. The electronic marketer can never know too much about their current and potential customers. More information in the database allows for more ways the information can be queried. Results displayed in a map are well organized and visually appealing, and for the number-hungry managers, the information displayed by the map is always supported by raw data that can also be presented.

Summary

As computers have been able to capture and organize marketing data, marketers are expected to make more correct decisions than incorrect ones. Much of the decision-support resources are derived from demographic and psychographic information about the prospect, the local market area, the general economy, and projections for the economic future. In this chapter, what and how demographic and psychographic data are collected and how the marketer uses this information to make better informed decisions are examined. Different data retrieval companies offer different versions of marketing reports; those data reports supplied by National Decision Systems are reviewed in this chapter.

Demographics are the numbers side of marketing analysis—the number of new citizens, new households, and new automobiles bought or introduced to a market over a period of time. Knowing the increase or decrease in sales within a certain industry can cause an adjustment in the marketer's future programs. The direction of sales movement can be ascertained from market data; the type of prospect or buyer can also be ascertained by studying the psychographics for a given geo-demographic area. In either case, better, more solid marketing direction decisions can be produced. While there are many answers or solutions to the same marketing question, analysis of demographic and psychographic data can help set a more efficient, effective program. These are contemporary electronic marketing resources that supply more than an aggregate quantity; engaging research from an online data source such as iVALS can provide insights into to the consumer and the Internet. Demographic and psychographic research add a rich understanding as to the how and why of dynamic consumer motivations.

Lastly, visualization is important in translating numbers into concrete strategies. Mapping, whether defining market areas or establishing target populations, is a valuable tool in recognizing the dynamics of a marketplace's dynamics. With the sophistication of database information and reporting, a picture is worth a thousand words.

Key Terms

Behavioral segmentation

Clickstream analysis

Demographics

Geo-demographics

Household clusters

iVALS

Mapping

Psychographics

SIC codes (Standard Industrial Classification)

QUESTIONS AND EXERCISES

1. You are the owner of an antique phonographs store specializing in collectible 45s and 78 rpm records. To identify your best zip codes for promotional mailings, which segmentation strategy would best suit your merchandise? Who do you think would be collectors of vintage phonographs? Develop a profile of the collector and match it to a segmentation strategy. Write it as a memo to your marketing data representative.

2. Research the definitions of undifferentiated marketing and differentiated marketing. Which strategy do you think would be best served by segmentation methods? Write an e-mail to your instructor explaining the differences of the two marketing terms and how segmentation would benefit either one, if any.

3. There are inherent advantages and disadvantages using any method of market segmentation. From your readings and experience, make a list of advantages and disadvantages for geographical, demographic, geo-demographic, psychographic, iVALS, and behavioral segmentation. Be prepared to discuss these concepts in class.

4. Access the iVALS site (http://future.sri.com) to take the Internet psychographics test. Print out the cluster matrix, research your projected personality cluster or clusters, and write a memo to your personnel manager stating whether or not you agree with the assessment. Turn the assessment in to your instructor for his analysis.

5. Electronic tracking of consumer usage of the Internet is controversial among various public interests. Privacy interests say there is an invasion of privacy using tools such as cookies. E-merchants counter with an argument that tracking software helps them to become acquainted better with their customers' preferences for online shopping. Some consumers object to devices such as cookies while others are noncommittal about merchants gathering data on their shopping habits. The government seems to take no stand. Write a letter to the editor of your local newspaper stating an opinion of support for two of these four interest groups. Why are privacy arguments possibly correct? Or why are e-merchants' arguments possibly correct? Follow the same logic if you wish to support or deny e-shoppers. Keep in mind the interests of the government.

6. Access the site Alexa (www.alexa.com) to report on its methodology of displaying competitive advertising on a selected site. How are competitors' ads displayed on the site? Is this method of profiling a sound business strategy or unfair competition? Write a report on the Alexa process.

7. Consider geographic mapping as a segmentation method. What are the advantages and disadvantages of this market segmenting process? Write a memo to your advertising manager outlining these points.

8. In Appendix B, you will find data reports that pertain to designated market areas in Florida—the Tampa Bay region and the Orlando metro region. There is an exercise for your analysis of market data information referencing the demographic and psychographic profiles plus retail expenditures for each area. You are the eastern manager of a rental furniture company, Rooms to Rent, and it is your responsibility to conduct a market analysis to select the next location for a store for Rooms to Rent. You can only choose one location between the two; information contained in these data reports from National Decisions Systems will help you make an informed decision.

Bibliography

Clark, Scott. 1997. HTML tips and trips: The Web master's bakery. *Web Developer*, archived [cited online March/April].

National Decision Systems. 1998. Excerpt from brochure. July. Microvision Marketing Guide, San Diego, CA.

National Decision Systems Psychographic Handbook. Excerpt from description of successful singles.

"Persistent Client State HTTP Cookies." [http://www.netscape.com/newsref/std/cookie_spec.html]. April 1999.

"Pioneers." iVALS Segment Profiles. [http://future.sri.com/vals/pioneers.html]. April 1999.

"Seekers." iVALS Segment Profiles. [http://future.sri.com/vals/pioneers.html]. April 1999.

Wang, Nelson. 1998. Custom ad tracking winning out over site analysis tools. *Internet World* [cited online 29 June].

CHAPTER 9

Integrating the Promotional Mix

"If advertisers have their way, online ads are poised to get a whole lot bigger and more complicated. That's because a new study of online ad effectiveness suggests that the bigger and more complex the ad, the more memorable it is. Trouble is, many online media sellers are likely to balk at souped-up cyberspace commercials. In fact, they are already rejecting some complex ads. Even Procter & Gamble has been turned down. The cyberspace people say ultra-complex ads clog up the pipes and pose the risk of turning the World Wide Web into the World Wide Wait. They wish advertisers would just stick to the box-like "banners" while awaiting better technology. 'The last thing they want to do is turn away money,' says Rich LeFugy of the Internet Advertising Bureau, which represents media sellers. 'But you don't want to kill the goose that lays the golden egg by eliminating the consumer.' He says he understands advertisers' desire to run bigger ads, but says: 'The question is, when is the right time to accept them?'

". . . A study [conducted by Ipsos-ASI Inc., a Stamford, CT unit of a French research company] probed how consumers reacted to more than eighty different Internet ads. . . . Among the findings: Larger, more-complicated ads are more memorable, communicate more information and are more likely to engage customers. Average recall of complicated ads was 46 percent to 63 percent higher than average recall for standard banner ads. 'Now that we have hard data that larger, more-complex ads are generally more effective than basic banners and can be consumer-acceptable in a real-world environment,' says Mike Wege, associate director of advertising at P&G. 'In order to be really effective, you have to have a measure of interactivity,' says Marianne Caponnetto, director of IBM world-wide media strategy and operations."

(Beatty 1998)

LEARNING OBJECTIVES

- To explain what the value of an online awareness is and its importance to relationship marketing

- To introduce the elements of the promotional mix as applied to online marketing
- To differentiate the advantages and disadvantages of the promotional mix elements
- To develop a promotional strategy geared toward online marketing

Introduction

Target information to targeted audiences. That is the promise and practice of the World Wide Web to e-marketers and e-merchants, and larger advertisement are only one of these electronic promotional mechanisms. Another new technology, Web-use tracking, brings desired product or service data to interested consumers and observes their purchases to form a profile of their shopping habits. How does this happen without invading the customer's privacy?

> "Talk about targeted advertising. Internet retailers now have a way to advertise right in their competitors' virtual storefronts—without being accused of trespassing. The unusual service comes from Alexa Internet [a tool that is discussed in Chapter 8], a free Web navigation business that has attracted more than one hundred advertising heavyweights like Amazon.com and CDNow since it began selling ad space last year. Alexa is a service that tracks users' surfing patterns to deliver them "smart links" to relevant sites and in-depth statistics on the pages they visit. People who go to Alexa's Web site to download the service get a second toolbar on their computer screen.
>
> The toolbar delivers statistics on different Web sites, like a company's address, the number of online hits it receives, and financial data. It also delivers ads, and Alexa can target the ads so they only appear when the user is visiting designated Web sites. Amazon.com, for instance, bought ads to appear by a list of other both-related sites like barnesandnoble.com, the U.S. Library of Congress, and various campus bookstores. So when an Alexa logs onto barnesandnoble.com, a small ad for Amazon appears at the bottom of the screen. Click that ad and it becomes quite big, superimposed on top of the barnesandnoble page. Cutting-edge interactive solutions combined with industry-leading high technology public relations and marketing communications ensure that messages are conveyed to customers clearly and powerfully. (Targeted advertising takes on new meaning online 1999)

In addition to the capability of interactivity, global awareness can be achieved by use of online communications. Both these facilities, interactivity and online communications, are new and unfamiliar to traditional marketing strategies. Marketers must learn to use different tools in different situations, such as recognizing the conditions in which the use of radio, broadcast television, or cable television might perform best. Likewise, given budget limitations, a marketer must know when to use local newspapers rather than national magazines to cost-effectively deliver advertising messages. Marketers must now know how to reach targeted audiences using electronic newspapers or e-zines, new and transformed editions of the traditional printed vehicles. New technology for promotional vehicles will lead to new strategies and new tactics; these new capabilities should be defined in an appropriate, cost-conscious, and realistic marketing and promotional program. The elements are incorporated into the programs, and the electronic marketing resources attract and service the consumer. Because the marketing cycle begins again and again, this process of marketing is thus the end and beginning of electronic commerce.

As e-commerce benefits from online speed, accuracy, and accessibility, the promotional elements of direct marketing, **advertising,** sales promotion, **public relations,** and surprisingly personal selling benefit as well. The first four elements are mass media-based, so electronic delivery plays a tested role in their performance. New communications and messaging technology assist the salesperson in the field as if she were sitting behind a desk in her office. Before the online strategies of electronic marketing are discussed, the functions of promotions management in pointing out the difference between the traditional promotional mix and the electronic promotional mix should be reviewed. In some cases, traditional promotional elements such as broadcast may be more appropriate for creating brand image and may be more cost efficient. In these cases, online advertising would take a support role in backing up the primary media. To understand and formulate effective and efficient strategic promotional thrusts, therefore, the marketer must ask *who*, *what*, *when*, *where*, and *how* of his tactical weapons in his promotions arsenal to determine which weapons would be best to deploy. You will learn in this chapter how to logically build an electronic promotional effort, with attention both to strategic and tactical issues.

Developing the Online Awareness

The World Wide Web is exceptionally well suited for the presentation and persuasion aspects of the marketing mix. This textbook has studied thus far how the Web can be employed to conduct consumer research as well as competitive research, and how it provides an e-mail platform for internal and external communications. These tasks are important in laying the marketing substructure and in supporting links of hands-on, internal communications. It is now time to explore the uses of the Web in determining its ability to present products and services, convey prospect or consumer information, and establish an external sales and continuing service connection. The capabilities of the Web have matured greatly during the last few years, and marketers are introducing new service applications, such as the abilities to personalize the user's site and comparison search engines, improving the site's navigation, and partnering with complementary products and services. These evolutions are in sync with keeping with the Web's major benefit—saving the viewer time and effort, which translates as added convenience. How does the Web fit into the grand promotional plan? An excellent and comprehensive review of the Internet advertising environment from the potential of buzz words to advertising successes has been written in *The Internet Advertising Report* by Mary Meeker on behalf of Morgan Stanley Dean Witter (www.ms.com). The report can be found by clicking on the "Technology News" hyperlink and then clicking on "Internet Quarterly Report." The report is divided into four sections that can be downloaded by Adobe Reader; the fourteen-chapter report covers Internet advertising and operations through 1996. As the specifics become dated, this promotional overview is broad and fundamental and can be used to set subject points for monitoring and updating in the future. Before the tactical issue of Web actions is entertained, the strategic promotional value of online promotion needs to be discussed.

In 1997, online household penetration was less than one in four homes, and at the time of this writing, that penetration level was projected to top 40 percent by 1999. Therefore, for consumer persuasion, the Web should be considered a support media vehicle for most all consumer goods and services with maybe the exception of computer hardware and software marketing. As a support vehicle to print or broadcast, online marketing's function should build on the awareness process because of the

EXHIBIT 9.1 WEB BRAND LEADERS

Companies that help set the computer industry's standards—Intel, Microsoft, and Netscape Communications—have the strongest brands as far as Internet issues go, according to a consumer survey by Ziff-Davis' Infobeads.

Percent of home PC buyers who rate brands as "very strong" on the Web:

Microsoft	73 percent
Netscape	69 percent
Intel	66 percent
Gateway	62 percent
IBM	55 percent
Dell	53 percent

SOURCE: Infobeads, www.infobeads.com.

unique capability of viewer interaction. As a simple concept for interactive online strategy, the marketer should focus her attention on thinking dialog rather than monolog since this vehicle provides two-way communication with interested audiences. Further, the marketer must produce appropriate content guided by information rather than exaggeration. The two-way dialog sets the Web apart from traditional media since the majority of mass vehicles—advertising, sales promotion, direct marketing, and public relations—direct their messages through one-way dialog. Basically, the process is all-telling with no mechanism for response. Direct marketing does allow the recipient to order by mail, telephone, or possibly with a Web address, but the response time is lagged perhaps by days or weeks before the company receives the order. The fifth element of the promotional mix is personal selling, which does allow instant response through **dyadic communications;** however, the physical reach of personal selling is limited since a salesperson can contact few customers or prospects each day. Network applications for remote information retrieval is helping to extend the reach of salespeople in the field, though, with fax-back and palm computer technology. Given these limitations to the promotional elements, the Web becomes the ideal marketing medium because of its global reach and accessibility, as well as its interactive potential. This is true for both communicating with the consumer and the business-to-business market.

Creating the online awareness is a balance of setting the proper communications objectives for recognition purposes: The marketer must cultivate *the sequential stages of online visibility, online believability, then online longevity.* As Web sites proliferate because the number of which will continue to grow, it is becoming more difficult to gain site visibility. It is not sufficient for a company to produce a Web site and expect viewers or search engines to seek out their page. The site will require its own marketing to *establish visibility;* a planned and concerted effort using classified ads, participation in online forums such as Usenets, publishing the address on all company materials, placing announcements in directories, and sponsoring discussion groups must be organized for exposure to the selected audiences. It may seem odd that the marketing vehicle must be marketed; however, until the household penetration of PCs and the reach of the Web broadens, the Web as a marketing and sales alternative must be constantly nurtured. As a comparison, a metropolitan newspaper has a reach averaging 70 percent on a daily basis with the Sunday edition slightly higher.

The next stage of building awareness is that of *building believability.* This too is a long-term endeavor and is one of the most difficult tasks for the electronic marketer, especially if the enterprise is a startup company or a small, aspiring-to-be-bigger firm. Online credibility is part of the equation to turn prospects into customers. The Web is a very anonymous marketplace, and no seal of approval thus far has been established to separate the genuine merchants from the scam artists. The Web's cloaked commerce channel, the veil of vendor invisibility, the uncertainty of online ordering, and the question of product quality are all issues that the marketer must address and allay. The way to assuage is to present a content-filled, graphically attractive, easy-to-navigate, and responsive site that offers benefits to the viewer. The marketer must demonstrate how the merchandise or services will prove worthwhile to the consumer and may later become invaluable to the consumer. (Letters from satisfied customers will help to support this contention.) A Web site will eventually earn its stripes as the qualities of expertise, reliability, functionality, professionalism, and uniqueness are transformed by performance. The higher the quality and more accurate the information, the more valuable the site resource is to the consumer; the more useful the content, the better the believability in the company's offerings. Developing excellent content is difficult and will require many revisions as the target markets provide feedback, criticism, or encouragement. Through trial and improvement, the consumer will recognize quality service, and consumer trust will follow. Trust will perhaps not develop tomorrow, but within a manageable time frame.

The third step of establishing an online awareness is that of *fostering online longevity*, as the benefits of long-term relationship marketing have been reviewed previously. As the customer would like to know whom he is buying from, the marketer should also be concerned with to whom he is selling. Creating an atmosphere of mutual regard gives the impression that the merchant appreciates the customer's business. One step toward expressing appreciation is to personalize the customer's name on e-correspondence or to acknowledge the length of time that the two have been doing business. There is a certain sense of recognition if a company remembers (by collecting the information on data entry) the buyer's birthday or a five-year anniversary of service. A single line of a personalized greeting, even a mention of children's or pets' names, can bring some individuality to routine paperwork. If you have ever ordered from Amazon.com, the home page acknowledges your first and last names on the "Ship to" box confirmation. Everyone believes, rightfully so, that she is special, and the reinforcement of this opinion can become the basis for a beneficial marketing relationship.

To be perceived as an excellent, valued resource, much time and effort are required by the marketer. These demands should not surprise the marketer since any aspirations of excellence take hard work. Successful online marketing is like any other marketing or sales activities; success exacts planning, dedication, and persistence. Realistic expectations are also necessary since electronic marketing is not the end-all. Electronic marketing will require integration and support from the traditional promotional mix elements.

Commerce and Communications

In each step of this awareness strategy, the importance of communications in the electronic exchange process escalates. The marketer should eventually balance commerce with electronic communications. If the message or mechanics of the Web are not working or are out of sync with the market, no merchandise orders can be fulfilled. The marketing process must have some method of communications, for instance, online communications, to succeed in satisfying customer demands. Enduring marketing relationships leads to repurchase opportunities, repurchase leads to reviving interest among customers, revived interest leads to restocking the merchandise, and fresh merchandise leads to new messages and graphics exposed to your customers. This process is ongoing to produce inventories of fresh and worthwhile items. What are the various promotional strategies in which the Web can facilitate the relationships of customers with the company? An insightful model depicts four approaches that the marketer can enlist to achieve marketing relationships with consumer segments. In an enlightening discussion, the GartnerGroup (www.occ.com), a highly regarded information technology consulting firm in Connecticut, developed a paradigm of the importance of relationship marketing and customer service. The model calls for enterprises to differentiate themselves by constantly providing superior service at every point of contact with the customer.

Relationship marketing, in this book's application to electronic commerce, can be influenced by the World Wide Web's contact with the various customer segments. These points of contact may be the first or last communication with the prospect or customer, and the marketer should take great care in anticipating the customer interaction at each point of contact. This anticipation might include sales or telephone personnel training, creating appropriate sales materials, or concentrating Web content to satisfy the needs of current customers. Relationship marketing can encompass or influence four opportunities of customer and prospect interaction as formulated by the GartnerGroup:

- *Customer acquisition.* An informative and innovative Web presence may help to attract new customers. This execution answers the question, "How can we acquire this customer in the most efficient and effective way?"
- *Customer retention.* Reorders from satisfied customers are the most efficient manner for conducting business and are the best way to measure service performance in pursuit of a mutually beneficial relationship. Continuing excellent customer service answers the question, "How can we keep this customer for as long as possible?"
- *Customer extension.* Introducing new products or services to an existing customer is also cost efficient. As the marketer strengthens the relationship, there is a good possibility that complementary goods might appeal to the current customer's interests or tastes. Book of the Month does an excellent job of cross-selling videos, calendars, compact discs, and companion clubs such as the History Book Club. Mindful analysis of database collection can answer the question, "How can we increase the loyalty and the profitability of the customer?"
- *Customer selection.* During the commerce relationship with existing customers, some people purchase more frequently or in greater amounts, and these customers should be identified as preferred customers. This pattern relates to be consumer behavior observation called the "80/20 rule"—20 percent of a firm's customers purchase 80 percent of the merchandise. These heavy users should be pinpointed, again through database management, and special promotions should be directed to this segment. Many marketers develop frequent purchaser programs in which discount points (Book of the Month awards "dividend" points) can be accumulated and used for price reductions on future orders; Pepsi has created "Pepsi Points" to be redeemed for merchandise and prizes. E-mail offers are effective messages to those loyal customers. This database mining activity is very productive, and it answers the question, "What criteria determines who will be our most profitable customers?" (GartnerGroup 1996)

Different promotional strategies need to be developed depending on the target market, customers, prospects, or even idle shoppers. With this realization in mind, the marketer can enlist electronic resources such as customer segmentation, database management, Web-enabled communications, and one-on-one customer service to effectively bring together markets of one or markets of many.

The Unique *Push* Property of the Web

An interesting application has developed around the direction of information flow transmitted by the Internet. In conventional terms, client/server applications send data to a client's machine without the client requesting any information. The Web was first based on **pull** technology (as were and are traditional advertising media) where the client browser must request a Web page before it is sent. As a direct marketing vehicle, the Web was thought to be evolving into a **push** medium delivering customized news and advertising to individuals in the workplace. *Push* advertising messages along with desired news, weather, and sports information would make a conducive atmosphere for commercial messages, or so it was thought by early marketing users of the Web. Technology problems, specifically band width, have cropped up and have slowed the growth of *push* advertising, perhaps even stalling it. The dilemma arose as advertisers and their advertising agencies began packing the small advertisements with complex motion, dissolves, and other graphical effects that consume many megabytes. Longer and longer download times turned viewers off, and progression through many layers of a Web site diminished. Until the band width hitches have been resolved in Web transmissions, this technology should be carefully considered among a variety of potential Web-medium solutions, rather than *the* solution, for online advertising. One successful example of remedying the band width problem has been a PC channel called PointCast (www.pointcast.com); this software integrates news wires, newspapers, magazines, and other business resources (sports information and Internet portal, as well, if the viewer chooses) into a screen saver that displays a frequently changing menu of stories, stock market information, weather, or whatever the viewer selects from the startup menu for the program. PointCast sells this advertising and information sponsorships to the business community to pay for the news and information content. The information can be updated any hour of the day, and depending on the number of news channels chosen, the download takes about fifteen to thirty minutes to complete. The viewer must click on the ad to request information from the advertising site; the viewer can choose not to click through the ad or even load the channel software altogether. This voluntary participation would seem to fit well within the Internet-user culture. How can the marketer, however, integrate the *push* interactivity into the promotional program when appropriate technology allows?

Marketers can combine the *push* interactivity and the promotional program into a push and pull strategy at the same time. On the Web, an excellent example of this push and pull strategy is a playful Nabisco site called "Candystand" (www.candystand.com). This site is an advertising message that utilizes an interactive game featuring Nabisco candies and gums with a chance to win merchandise by achieving the highest scores. Some of the names of the games are LifeSavers Field Goal Challenge, Fruit Stripe Coloring Book, Bubble Yum Major League Baseball Home Run Derby (win a Mark McGwire Bamm Beano), Gummi Savers Big Air (win a Limited Snowboard), and Creme Savers Bowling. The arcade format appeals to younger and older customers as does the competitive format of winning prizes. This site demonstrates an outstanding use of interactivity, flow, and the building of brand relationship. Would you consider the promotional strategy as advertising, sales promotion, or public relations? Would you consider it as push or pull? Or a combination of all of these strategies?

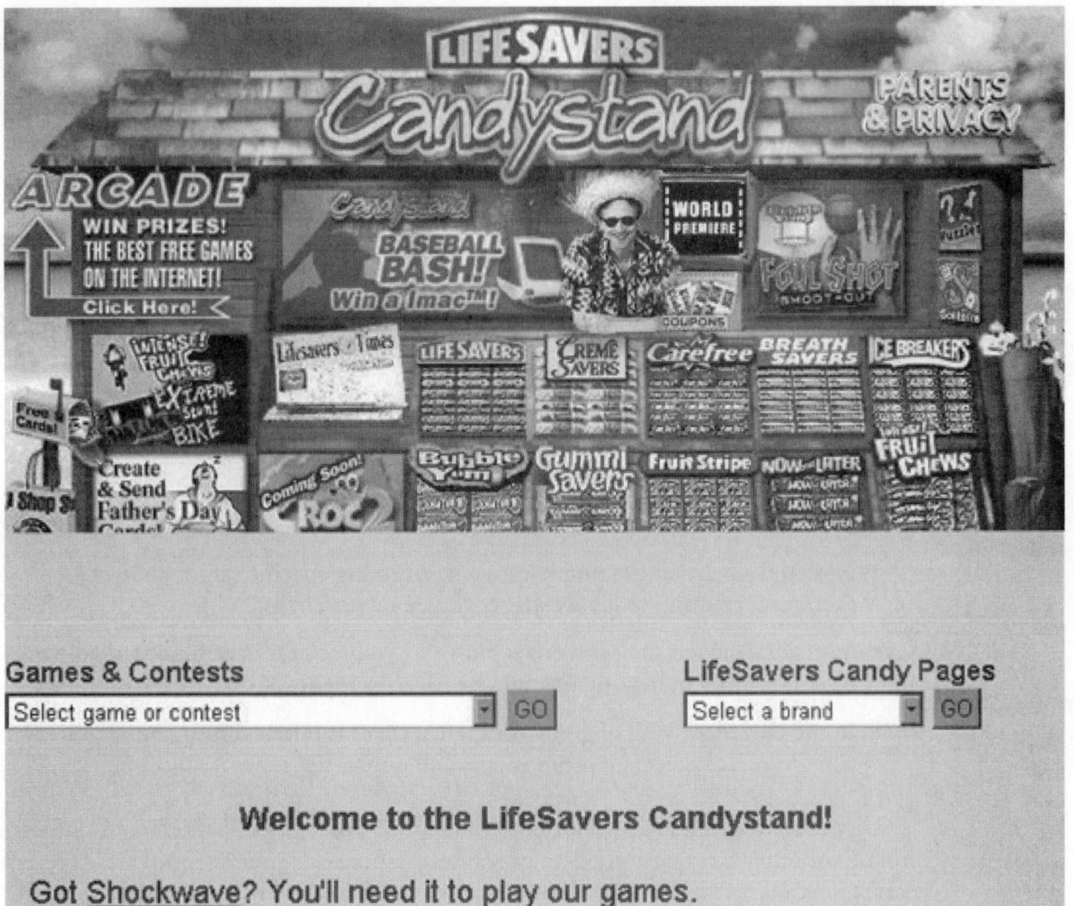

Lifesavers Candystand (www.candystand.com)
This is an excellent and creative example of a Web site that combines interactivity and memorability while building brand loyalty. Using an arcade theme, the high scorers of the week can win candy, gum, Nintendo, gift certificates, and other prizes, depending on the arcade game. Nabisco is careful to advise those under 18 to obtain parents' permission.

Formulating the Promotional Strategy

This book has gone to extensive lengths to segment and characterize the market segment or segments to which a promotional program will be directed. The product or service component of the marketing process as well as the distribution considerations and performance elements have all been examined in this textbook. The final marketing mix P, the promotions function, now will be addressed. The promotional mix consists of advertising, sales promotion, public relations, direct marketing, and personal selling. Each element has its strengths and weaknesses, and electronic communications can mitigate some of these weaknesses that have hampered the promotional mix for decades. These promotional tools can complement one another, such as television advertising to support a special offer like the $.10-a-minute, long-distance calling sales promotion by AT&T. Promotional programs can breathe life into established products and services, such as Bart Simpson of the Fox network greedily protects his Butterfinger (www.butterfinger.com). Some elements are more effective at launching a new product or introducing a new brand extension, while some are better at creating credibility for the corporate image. With experience, the marketer knows which promotional tactic or combination of tactics to employ for marketing augmentation.

Advertising is any paid form of nonpersonal message about an organization, product, services, or idea by an identified sponsor directed to a mass audience. Some of the advantages of advertising include the following.

- In relative costs, advertising is an efficient method to communicate with large audiences, especially for national marketers.
- Advertising can also be used to create images and symbolic appeals for a company or brand that is important for establishing goods appealing to differentiated or functional attributes.
- Advertising is a high profile, image-oriented promotional element well suited for brand awareness.

Some of the disadvantages of advertising include the following.

- The cost of national advertising coverage is expensive as are the production costs for creating the advertisement or commercial.
- National advertising is not selective in targeting specific target audiences, therefore, creating much wasted coverage or readership.
- In general, advertising materials must be produced far in advance and allow little flexibility in making changes to advertisements or commercials quickly.
- In the current advertising environments, there is much clutter among advertising messages, vehicle promotions, and public service announcements.

Direct marketing is a promotional element in which organizations communicate directly with the target customers to generate a response or transaction. Within recent years, direct marketing has expanded past the customary use of direct mail to encompass direct response advertising using television, newspapers, magazines, **telemarketing,** and the World Wide Web, especially because of the Web's direct interactions with consumers or businesses. Following is a list of some of the advantages of direct marketing.

- The ability to target customers via database collection provides high selectivity.
- Direct marketing pieces can contain large amounts of product or service information.
- Direct marketing allows for the capability to personalize direct mail, magazine, and Web messages by adding the recipient's name to envelopes, cover letters, e-mails, and Web sites.
- Direct marketing has the ability to send product samples to prospects or target users of a competing brand.
- With the introduction of direct marketing to the Web, e-mail campaigns can be cost-efficient.
- There is opportunity for repeated exposure according to the marketer's plan.

Some of the disadvantages of direct marketing may include the following.

- The costs of direct marketing using traditional media are high since the message is presented to target groups usually small in number.

- There are image problems that are traced to junk mail, to annoying telemarketing calls, or to "spamming" e-mail; all three are examples of unsolicited advertising messages.
- As with advertising, direct marketing fights the clutter problem.

Sales promotion are those marketing activities that provide extra value or incentives to the sales force, distributors, or to the ultimate consumer. Often presented through mass media, sales promotion is usually considered a discounting tactic, whereas, advertising is regarded to be an investment in brand equity. Consumer-oriented sales promotion is targeted to the end user; familiar sales promotion items are coupons, sampling, premiums, rebates, contests, sweepstakes, and programs such as frequent flyer mileage or frequent shopper bonuses. Trade-oriented sales promotion is targeted toward retail or wholesale intermediaries within the distribution channel; trade sales promotion might include merchandising allowances, price deals, sales contests, and trade shows to encourage the trade to stock and promote a product. The advantages of sales promotion may include the following.

- Sales promotion can cause a rapid increase in sales activity and volume.
- The various techniques of sales promotion can attract new buyers to trial purchases.
- Sales promotion activities can defend an established brand against new competition.
- Sales promotion can reward loyal customers as they continue to be product users.
- Sponsoring sales promotion activities can provide retailers with additional marketing support.

Some of the disadvantages of sales promotion include the following.

- Marketers and retailers can become dependent on sales promotion by training their customers to buy only when the product is featured as a special offer.
- Matching competitors' sales promotions can lead to a **sales promotion spiral** in which no competitor can afford to not participate, as in double or triple frequent flyer mileage rewards.
- Extensive sales promotion can erode brand perception because of the discount nature of sales promotion.
- There is substantial opportunity for sales promotion abuse such as fraudulent coupon redemption or sweepstakes and contests misrepresentation.

Public relations and publicity are associated with nonpersonal communications regarding an organization, product, service, or idea not directly paid for or run under identified sponsorship. Public relations is a management and planning function that evaluates public opinion and executes actions to earn public understanding and acceptance. Publicity, though extremely powerful, is only one of several tools that are specified by the public relations program. In the last decade, public relations has emerged as a primary promotional strategy moving from a support or secondary function in an integrated marketing communications program. An important part of public relations is the recognition of various publics, much like segmentation, which the organization should reach with information of interest to these audiences. Publicity has also joined

TRAVELOCITY.COM BRINGS BACK POPULAR BONUS MILES PROMOTION FOR FREQUENT FLYER BOOKERS TO RECEIVE 1,500 BONUS MILES

Travelocity.com, the online travel expert, is getting travelers 1,500 bonus miles, a repeat of the popular promotion held last fall. From February 26 through March 31, Travelocity.com members who purchase an airline ticket on select airlines, in addition to a hotel stay or car rental, can claim 1,500 extra frequent flyer miles on top of the travel provider's standard mileage awards. "The bonus miles promotion Travelocity.com conducted last September was so well received that we wanted to offer it again to our five million members," said Terry Jones, chief information officer of the SABRE Group (NYSE: TSG). "This promotion is just one example of the many ways Travelocity.com members received added value booking their travel through our site."

The SABRE Group is a world leader in the electronic distribution of travel and travel-related technology solutions for the travel and transportation industries, including customized software development and software products, transactions processing, consulting and total information technology consulting.

SOURCE: Travelocity.com brings back popular bonus miles promotion for frequent flyer bookers to receive 1,500 bonus miles. 1999. *Industries Channel.* PointCast Channel [cited online 26 February].

the other electronic resources by offering online distribution of news releases; major disseminators of electronic news are PR Newswire (www.prnewswire.com) and Business Wire (www.businesswire.com). The advantages of public relations may include the following.

- Because of its attitude surveys, public relations can act as an early warning system to protect the organization's franchise within the community and with its audiences.
- Positive publicity efforts produce an aura of credibility as the media becomes unbiased, third-party endorsers.
- A thorough public relations program can earn the company's recognition as a solid community citizen.
- Public relations is a low-cost promotional strategy.

Following is a list of possible disadvantages of public relations.

- Publicity can be positive or negative; negative publicity can do irreparable harm to the organization's reputation and its relationships with its public.
- Public relations programs are not always under the control of the marketer; many programs take months or years to cultivate into positive results.
- Public relations plans are extremely time consuming since PR programs should be developed for each of an organization's constituents; these audiences could number ten or more.

Personal selling is the last element of the promotional mix and is quite different from the others. Personal selling is defined as a form of person-to-person communication in which a seller attempts to persuade a second party to buy, rent, or lease. This persuasion is not based in mass media, and unlike the other four elements, a customer or prospect response can be gained immediately, achieving a level of interactivity. Also, the message can be tailored according to the individual's or segment's specific needs. The advantages of personal selling may include the following.

- Because of the nature of personal selling, beneficial relationships can be formed and can last for many years.

PR Newswire (www.prnewswire.com)
Publicity dissemination is extremely efficient using online news services such as PR Newswire and Business Wire. News releases can be targeted by news networks throughout the country.

- Depending on the reaction of the prospect, dyadic communication allows the sender to alter or tailor the message according to the prospect's inquiries; with electronic communications, this would be considered interactivity.
- As in the term, personal selling is a face-to-face experience, disregarding mass media.
- Personal selling yields more immediate and precise marketing results.

The following is a list of possible disadvantages of personal selling.

- The cost of a personal sales call is quite high, an expense estimated in excess of $300 per appointment.
- The reach of personal selling is extremely limited since an individual can meet with so few clients, customers, or prospects each day or month.
- There often is concern among management that the field sales representative is not presenting the product or service with the same and consistent information that the home office intended.
- Many times the purchase cycle can be quite long, perhaps several years in the purchase or repurchase of durable goods. (Belch and Belch 1998, 14–20)

Using Different Tools in Different Situations

With these five building blocks, marketers create new promotional strategies year in and year out. These elements can be applied to consumer and trade promotional programs; local, regional, national, or international agendas; campaigns for products and services; and promotional efforts for business services or farm products. They are used for startup companies or firms hundreds of years old. Certain promotional mix elements perform better than others in different categories or in different stages of the **product life cycle,** and to maximize the promotional benefits, the marketer soon recognizes the situation and its appropriate solution. For startup companies and those in their growth stage, advertising and public relations can build awareness for the enterprise, and during this stage, marketing and communications expenses are disproportionately large. In fact, recent Internet properties have been reporting that spending is up to 70 percent on marketing activities of a startup company's initial public offering's funds. During this period, a new company is attracting customers from existing competitors or possibly attracting new users into the market because of a unique product benefit. As the product matures, its potential for attracting new customers as well matures, and growth peaks. Many competitors emerge, and frequently price wars flare. Advertising is reduced substantially since the prospect of capturing new customers is substantially reduced. Promotional dollars are spent in large amounts (shifted from the media advertising budget) on consumer sales promotions that are designed to encourage current customers to continue buying the product. Public relations activity is also reduced since the product is possibly well known and of diminished news value.

As the product reaches the declining stage of the cycle, to entice retailers and wholesalers to stock the product, allotted budgeting money is again shifted from consumer sales promotion to trade sales promotion. These monetary incentives, such as promotional allowances, price deals, or sales contests, are probably the last of the push strategies by the manufacturer until demand and sales volume diminishes into an unprofitable national or regional brand. An interesting phenomenon has appeared in the last ten years—that of entrepreneurs buying a discontinued brand from a manufacturer, one that was valued and popular years ago, to reintroduce the brand to a new generation of purchasers and to nostalgically remind past consumers of their usage years ago. One brand that has been refurbished is the Westinghouse light bulb, which was discontinued in 1983 when purchased by Philips Electronics; Angelo Brothers Company, a maker of specialty light bulbs, licensed the name, the circle W logo, and the positioning theme, "You can be sure if it's Westinghouse." Angelo Brothers found an interested buyer of the Westinghouse light bulbs, who considered the brand still viable, in the shopper of the large home-improvement retailer, Lowe's. Another example of this form of marketing is the Volkswagen Beetle, absent from U.S. showrooms since 1979. The automaker reintroduced the new Beetle, which led the way for the best U.S. monthly sales in thirty years for the company. (Barmash 1998) Most companies, though, stick with and support their brands that are in established distribution channels serving their current customers.

In the declining stage of the product cycle, personal selling complements the trade sales promotions in pushing sales of the product as long as possible. Personal selling is used heavily in contacts with trade since many retail buyers and purchasing agents make decisions for potentially hundreds or thousands of retail outlets on distribution and stocking. Traditionally, marketers used direct marketing in the declining stage directed to the trade channel members and in the growth stage to sample and extend awareness to prospect groups. These trade offers are mainly to push monetary or additional merchandise to the outlets. The direct marketing element strengthened by the Web's new interactive capabilities is the promotional tool that shows the most promise during all stages of the product life cycle. Web communications can support product information and awareness through Web address publications in traditional media vehicles as television, newspapers, or magazines; it can enhance a blossoming franchise development during the growth stage; and it can be effective in trade communications with the onset of the maturity and declining stages. As the Web is currently a support medium, its greatest contributions may be in the growth and maturity periods as consumers cultivate relationships with the product. Such mature products that have utilized the Web are Kool-aid (http://www.kraftfoods.com/kool-aid/ka_index.html), and Land O'Lakes butter (www.landolakes.com). These brands have existed for decades, and an emotional attachment from past usage and positive product performance keep these brands on the shelves. While the Web might not be the proper channel to sell drink mixes or butter, the Web is an excellent vehicle to keep the mystique or the friendliness of many products or services. The Web communications abilities will fold into the integrated strategy. The discussion will now address how this image or performance message is developed and delivered.

Developing a Unique Creative Strategy

The strength of interactivity of the Web can enhance the performance of each of the promotional elements. The technological strengths of sight, motion, color, and sound and the user-friendliness of the Web put it into a unique category of marketing communications. The Web is able to tell the story of the product, and it can react to the impressions or questions that the viewer might have after the online session. Before the Web's tactical role in the communications delivery is investigated in this textbook, the process of isolating the unique benefits, sometimes called the **unique selling proposition,** needs a critical analysis because once the product feature is selected, the foundation for the communications plan is underway. Certainty or at least soùnd intuition is a required skill for marketers undertaking promotional programs costing in the millions of dollars. The creative process begins with translating the product features into consumer benefits that may be either rational features (the information-oriented facts such as affordability, investment, medical services, or functionality), or emotional or psychological needs (desires to be thin, to be macho, to buy a car that protects the children, or to dress professionally). There are countless benefits that can be demonstrated in countless communications executions; in fact, the challenge to create a ingenious and original solution to a communications problem is the motivating factor in the writer's or artist's mind.

Creativity has been defined as the "ability to generate fresh, unique, and appropriate ideas that can be used as solutions to communications problems." (Belch and Belch 1998, 244) This ability to visualize new combinations, novel situations that present a product in a familiar yet unconnected relationship to the product, is a highly prized talent in the marketing and advertising industries. An example of a creative marketing association is the 1984 Super Bowl introduction of the Apple Macintosh (www.apple.com). In this instance, Apple used a parody of IBM as the big brother in the context of George Orwell's futuristic novel *1984.* Microsoft, as well, rolled out the Windows 95 version using the Rolling Stones' song, "Start It Up." The combination of Nissan's 300ZX with toys that helped GI Joe court Barbie to the dismay of her boyfriend Ken helped Nissan market this line of automobile to the consumer. Another example of creative marketing associations is the ad for Pizza Hut that uses Elvis dancing while muttering his appreciation, "Thank you, thank you very much." Each of these commercials started with a creative platform that delineated the benefits of the product; this creative platform is transformed into the creative strategy. The creative platform is a summary of all the significant research, consumer attitudes, competitors' stances, and client input and directives. For the online service, PointCast, its creative platform might have included a summary line such as, "PointCast is an online news service that is accessible to the businessperson at work." Not very exciting in describing the service, but the description contains the unique talking points to start the creative people, the copywriters, and the art directors toward producing a novel creative strategy for the awareness campaign. The creative people now have a direction to knead and massage, and their result becomes the creative theme for the elements of the creative campaign. The resulting campaign theme for PointCast was a succinct

Value America (www.valueamerica.com)
This new online retailer offers more than a dozen categories of "merchandise for the new millennium," presumably electronics, appliances and consumer items. The site is easy to navigate with product photography leading the way.

and meaningful summary, "PointCast. The desktop newscast." The positioning for the performance of the 3Com equipment was a simple statement, "More connected." A virtual computer retailer, Value America (www.valueamerica.com), has positioned itself as "The marketplace for the new millennium." From these positioning lines, the balance of the campaign can be rendered into the necessary communications tools, such as Web site and screen design, brochures, advertising rate kits, messages for business newspapers and magazines, and other collateral materials necessary for extending the campaign strategy and communications appeals. Used long and consistently enough, the brand name is instantly associated with its theme line. Certainly Nike is synonymous with "Just do it," Prudential with "Solid as the rock of Gibraltar," or Microsoft with "Where do you want to go today?" Many vices such as cigarettes, beer, or alcohol have enforced and reinforced memorable campaign lines through heavy advertising and sales promotion. Some long-running themes have been "Winston tastes good like a cigarette should," "The king of beers," "Tennessee sipping whiskey," or "Absolut, Absolute (you fill in the blank)." Repetition of a constant phrase is a powerful method to create a mental association with a product or service.

In creating Web site appeal, the rational or informational approach, as supported in the opening quote in this chapter, appears to be the most common since many Web viewers are searching for product specifications influenced by price or selection. A site can be scrolled down, up, right, or left indefinitely, and the links can point to link after link. The marketer should remember why the viewer is using the Web—in search of convenience, quality, efficiency, delivery availability, and performance. The text or copy of the home page and subsequent product or service pages should appeal to these influences. This is true for both business-to-business and consumer Web messages and graphics. The writer's knowledge of product performance or efficiency of operation will assist in creating buyer-friendly messages. This textbook has stated before that Web advertising cannot sell, but it can inform. The marketer must realize that in Web communications, content is king, and the fuller and richer the description, the more powerful and positive the Web visit will be. Web messages are evolving from a static representation of the company, product, or service into more emotional graphics, such as pictures of grandparents with their grandchildren while the copy describes the benefit of life insurance or photos of trim, energetic shoppers representing a lifestyle with Healthy Choice foods. In developing the creative direction, the marketer should judge the creative solutions as objective as possible. While the creative process is an exciting and entertaining activity, the marketer should overlook the creative progression so that the marketing strategy parameters are observed. Not every Web product can or should be presented in a humorous fashion. The entire process is focused toward selling merchandise and servicing customers. Producing excellent online communications is a serious business and should be approached with that mindset. An excellent caution on creativity for creativity's sake was flagged by Bob Plishka, a PR executive, in *Fortune* magazine as he lamented: "At the heart of the problem is a failure to distinguish between artistry that makes a selling message memorable and artistry that overwhelms your selling message. In other words, marketers should temper their creative impulses with straightforward communication." (Lukas 1998)

Like any specialty industries, certain requirements should be mandated in communications materials. It seems mandatory these days to include a Web site or e-mail address in all advertising and activity materials. Another emerging must appears to be the substantial and creative thought to domain names that are immediately recognized as the company label. Consistency also should be in resemblance of the Web address to a similar e-mail address. The smartest way to establish a company's online recognition is to first investigate the proposed domain name through the interNIC registration site, check the availability of the name, and then proceed with the basic identity items. The InterNIC is a cooperative activity between the U.S. Government and Network Solutions, Inc. Another suggestion is that a company needs no more than one domain name, such as a second level domain name like company.com. A third level domain might be smith.company.com. Having more than one domain name confuses people and might suggest there is some disorganization within the marketing and communications departments. To avoid this impression, centralize the naming process so that everyone in the company has an address with the same domain. Lastly, the marketer should inquire with the company's ISP to ensure the firm's address can accept a non-www subdomain. This would allow a user to type http://www.company.com or http://company.com and arrive at the same address. This is recommended for a company and is an easy task to do. Just ask the ISP for an alias to the site's DNS entry point. Usually there is no charge for this service. (Synder 1998)

Still Appealing to the Senses

Long before television, copywriters found that descriptions that appealed to the senses or the stimuli that trigger sensory reactions, such as smell, taste, touch, sight, and sound, could conjure up an association with certain product features. For decades, products have been described as promoting "a fresh minty taste," "a lemony smell," "a silky touch," "laundry that looks newer than new," or "speakers that produce a symphony hall environment." Services as well as products can also appeal to the senses or a state of mind. The American Express card for years advised the traveler to not leave home without it, and in recent years has expanded its usage to more than travelers by encouraging the cardholders to "do more," such as purchase groceries or gasoline with Jerry Seinfeld practicing his "perfect squeeze." As an appeal to security, Allstate Insurance has comforted policyholders by the knowledge that they are "in good hands with Allstate." To soften a harsh and uncertain issue, Metropolitan Life (www.metlife. com) hired Snoopy and friends to make the pledge, "Get Met. It Pays." The marketing and communications strategy should build upon these senses or psychological influences to then introduce the inherent qualities of interactivity. This approach is absolutely necessary in delivering premium pricing value. Differentiated marketing is also the most profitable strategy and with caring and careful attention can be sustained for many years.

Assistance from an Interactive Advertising Agency

As the Web has generated many industries and companies within the advertising industry, so has it conceived a new type of advertising agency and new capabilities that enhance the World Wide Web's communications talents. This resource is called an **interactive advertising agency,** an advertising company that conceives and produces new media campaigns and materials based on electronic vehicles. Some interactive agencies have spawned from traditional advertising agencies, and some are independent startups founded by principals familiar with communications and computer potentials. In either case, these agencies have short histories but very promising futures. As in the traditional agencies, the interactive agency assists clients with the investigation and implementation of marketing and communications processes; many agencies have developed unique insights in employing online media. For this reason, these agencies are developing valuable specialty services that are being integrated into traditional marketing strategies. Recently, an association of interactive agencies was formed to advance the new media agenda; the affiliation, Real Agencies Affiliates Program (www5.real.com), has adopted a platform to "serve as an ad agency resource program designed to facilitate and promote the use of streaming video, video and animation technology in online advertising. The primary beneficiaries will be agencies' clients who will have access to more effective creative tools for online advertising, enabling them to heighten the users' experiences." (RealNetworks introduces real agencies affiliates program 1998) The help of an experienced interactive agency is available, and the services these agencies provide will now be addressed.

The services of an interactive agency will be examined by reviewing the credentials of a successful shop, CKS Group (www.cks.com). According to the firm's own Web site, CKS is a marketing communications company for the digital age. Well situated among technology suppliers, the company is located in Silicon Valley, and it combines state-of-the-art technology with a unique, multidisciplinary approach to business and marketing that effectively helps companies communicate, inform, and sell. Many of the services are derived from traditional marketing, while some are the offspring of electronic entrepreneurs.

> CKS Group is a provider of communications and business programs that integrate strategic counsel with traditional marketing disciplines, such as product branding and advertising, as well as advanced technology solutions and new media, including Internet and Extranet development, database architecture, and enterprise systems integration. CKS clients include Audi (www.audi.com), Citibank, Computer Associates, Fujitsu PC (www.fujitsu.com), General Motors (www.gm.com), Levi Strauss & Co., MCI, Royal

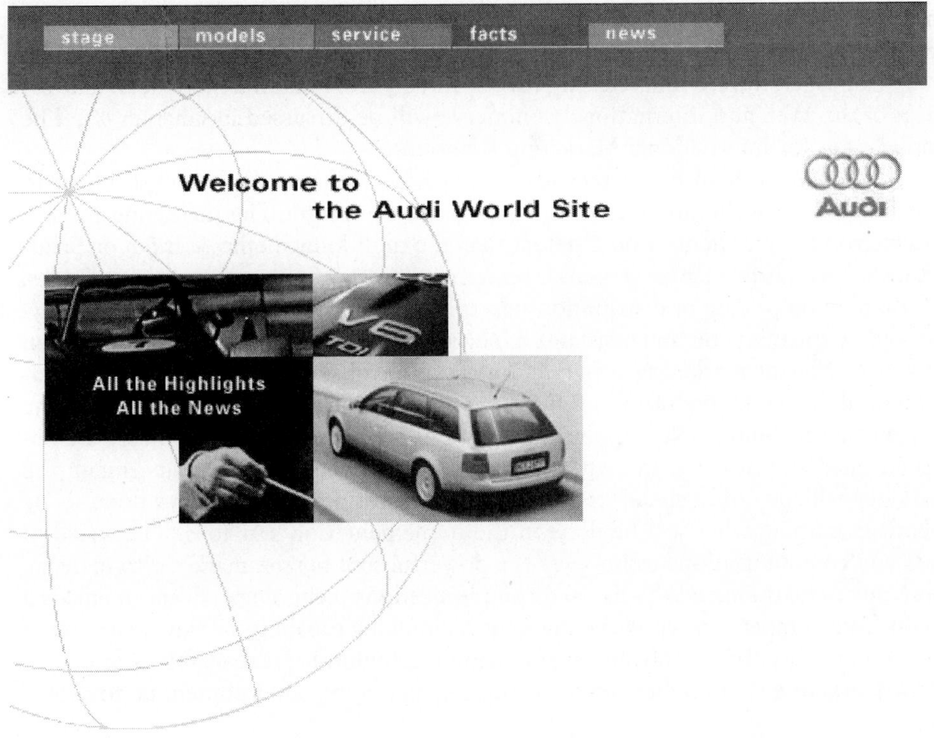

Audi (www.audi.com)
Sports car enthusiasts, along with luxury car owners will enjoy Audi's site. Not only can the viewer peruse information about new models and service, but they also can get information about recent advances in automotive technology.

> Caribbean Cruise Lines, Visa, and 3Com (www.3com.com). CKS Enterprise provides unparalleled sophistication to your Web site needs. The Enterprise group can add dynamic page creation capability to your sites with a relational database. We can enable your sites to perform secure electronic commerce and integrate personalized technology for user customization. Our streaming media expertise allows our clients to exploit the benefits of Web casting and high performance Web serving. CKS offers services for the development and production of Interactive Kiosks for Retail and Trade Show applications, Laptop Sales Presentations, and Hybrid CD-ROMs. These programs help our clients build their brands and sell products with engaging product demonstrations and simulations, video, audio, animated graphics, and music. (November 20, 1998)

This venue is probably similar to other interactive agencies that are serving similar high profile clients throughout the United States. It is interesting as well that CKS has several domestic offices and two offices in France and Germany. The European potential for online marketing services is great but somewhat complex because of the many languages, different purchasing habits, and different cultural influences. The aspects of the Web and international commerce will be discussed in Chapter 17, The Implications for International Marketing Programs.

In working with an interactive advertising agency, the marketer will still have to direct and oversee the progress of the interactive campaign. The marketing process for electronic components is no different than the traditional methods. Input on product or service performances, research on user or prospect preferences and attitudes, information on pricing or distribution strategies, and competitive data all must be organized by the marketer and assistants to share with the interactive agency to craft an effective, efficient marketing program. Nothing changes from the traditional paradigm until the marketing planning and marketing implementation stages integrate the new media capabilities. New applications for electronic media and commerce are being unveiled almost daily, and with this fast pace of technological enhancement, the marketer will probably spend as much time monitoring what is being done as he spends examining what will be done in the implementation activities. The speed of sales and communications technology is a powerful tool for the marketer to manage, but conversely, the speed of sales and communications technology advancements is a threat from competitors who have the same technology capabilities. Staying on top of technology is a full-time job, and again giving the **technological-watch** assignments to the marketing staff might keep the company's marketing environment up to date.

The Components of the Promotional Plan

The interactive or traditional advertising agency should be charged with developing a creative platform and theme that details in a road map style the direction and destination of the communications objectives. This promotional plan is composed of many process elements, each a small but important link that on completion should result in meeting corporate objectives. In using the process strategy, each element must be identified and scheduled and then given consideration as to its role in the promotional mix, the message, and the media. Creative themes start the advertising ball rolling, and the careful planning and execution steps shape and extend the creative direction throughout the campaign. This road map may have stops in it, specifically when specific campaign elements must be defined. Much like a child's board game (remember Candyland, www.candyland.com, which can be found at www.hasbrotoys.com), the process pieces move forward and unfortunately sometimes backwards along a prescribed path to an expected destination. These points of consideration may vary from product to service to industry idiosyncrasies, but in general a plan for creative development might include:

- *Source selection*—Who or what is going to deliver the message. Will it be a spokesperson, a character or symbol (like the Energizer Bunny or Playstation's Crash Bandicoot), a corporate entity, a celebrity, or perhaps an unidentified source? The source does not have to be written words per se; instead of speaking, the source can be a musical signature, such as Intel's four notes, or a totally visual signature, such as Marlboro cigarettes or Chevis Regal scotch.
- *Message(s) selection*—What are the messages that can be unique to the company, product, or service? Research should have brought to light the motivations by which the market is moved and the benefits the market receives by using the product. Marketing managers should give input regarding the message selection, and then the advertising agency or creative boutique translates

the benefits (message selection) into memorable creative themes or advertising executions.

- *Media channels*—What media channels (assuming there is more than one) are being selected? The creative people must be advised on the nature of the creative materials they are conceiving so that these materials will fit the media plan and production schedule. It is difficult to refit the elements of a television commercial into a magazine ad at the last moment. What will be primary and support media? Are there special media requirements, such as painting transit buses with a convenience appeal to the benefits of working at home, a special request to produce an advertising blimp to fly over football stadiums, or flying a mini-blimp over a crowd in a hockey arena to distribute coupons? There are many media applications available that can be advantageous and innovative, and it is up to the marketing and creative staff to make a competitive marketing manager say, "I wish I had thought of that."

Now that the creative theme and the framework of the media strategy are decided, the objectives for the promotional mix are to be considered in an effort to balance all of the situation's influences and market factors. As the inputs to the traditional marketing plan have been tracked, it is now close to setting objectives for each of the promotional functions. Again, objective setting is important in measuring the final results of the marketing program. Each promotional mix element should be evaluated before and after the campaign. Some marketing programs use all five of the promotional tools, while some engage only two or three depending on the breadth and depth of the campaign. Objective setting is broken into the following specific promotional actions.

- The marketer should define what the online communications objective(s) is planned to be. Will the electronic resources support an introductory mass media product merchandising? Should the electronic marketing resources focus on improving database collection and output analysis? Will the Web site be static or will it be a Web-enabled one that can filter and link several databases for relational information? An example of how to make a Web site Web-enabled might be through an analysis of the average customer expenditure and then cross-referencing this information to sporting goods inventory activities during the holiday season, November 25 to December 25. Is the objective creating awareness, accelerating repurchase frequency, selling gift certificates, introducing a new product, or generating publicity about the company training systems? With no objective in mind, the marketing program is rudderless; direction is critical to effectively and efficiently maximize the corporate assets.
- Advertising objectives have to be set for the master marketing plan. What is the situation that advertising is to face? Will national, regional, or local television or newspapers be the primary vehicles? What market segments are to be targeted, and are there advertising vehicles that can reach these markets? Perhaps the advertising campaign by a major food manufacturer will be directed toward a trade group such as grocers, and the objective is to expand distribution of the food product by entering new geographical areas. The primary media probably would be direct marketing and trade magazines such as *Progressive Grocer* (www.progressivegrocer.com), while support media could be a functional Web site displaying information important to the grocer trade such as number of SKUs the product offers, incentives and promotional allowances, details on slotting allowances, or the consumer advertising schedules for commercials' clips of consumer advertising with media calendars displaying the newspaper and television schedules. The Web site can contain extensive

amounts of information, much more than a brochure or personal letter, and can deliver information and receive responses much, much quicker.

- The marketer should extend the marketing plan through online media. Take for example on the consumer front, perhaps there is a new sports card shop that is planning for extensive mail order business. This product or service might appeal to a narrow market, so the advertising objectives should be to create awareness among a rather limited market size. Television would probably be an expensive venture because of the wasted viewership, but specialized magazines and newspapers are read by ardent collectors of baseball, basketball, and football cards. Newspapers such as *Sports Collectors Digest* (www.krause.com) or magazines such as the Beckett family of sports cards and memorabilia magazines (www.beckett.com) are excellent media in advertising to a targeted market. In both types of print vehicles, the Web site of the card shop could be supported by including the Web address in each ad or publicity release. Someone has said that a Web site is something someone does, not something someone reads. The Web site could do more than inform the viewer of the inventory in text; it could showcase pictures of the premium cards. The site could link to the various Beckett services and products such as the Beckett Online Auction, Beckett Price Guides, the card show calendar by states, or other timely promotions. It could link to the Baseball Hall of Fame (www.baseballhalloffame.org) in Cooperstown, New York or to the Web pages of major league teams (www.yankees.com), (www.atlantabraves.com), which of course offer team merchandise for sale. Publicity articles could be placed on the PR Newswire or the Business Newswire, which deliver electronically news releases to targeted publications. The business owner of the card shop, as well, could develop a bulletin board of customers' want lists of cards or an e-mail discussion of current or controversial topics, such as the continuing use of the designated hitter or the controversy surrounding Pete Rose's desire to be inducted into the Hall of Fame. The owner could compile an e-mail list of her customers in order to contact them when new baseball, football, basketball, or hockey issues are received; she could organize a special promotion, possibly a swap night, and use e-mail to advise and invite customers to the special event.

  In each of these examples, the media plan was extended by online media, first for the national food manufacturer and secondly for the corner shopkeeper. In each case, electronic media is able to target customers, communicate with them in a convenient manner, enrich the merchandise presentation, and integrate into traditional advertising, sales promotion, public relations, and direct marketing.

- The online capabilities need to support the advertising objectives. What awareness or action is the advertising materials stressing? Is it the opening of a new store? Is it an announcement of the receipt of a new line of fashionable women's clothes, such as Nicole Miller (www.nicolemiller.com)? Is it the acquisition of another company that will fit with both companies' business strategies, customer leverage, and merchandising lines? Is it a new financing program that is most attractive to consumers? All of these situations are worthy of integrating online consumer communications with business communications since so many magazines have narrow, absorbed readership as well as the enthusiastic supporters of various television programs. The Web's average audience is educated and intense about many interests, which are funneled through the narrow portals of the Internet.

- Sales promotion is a solid method of introducing new products, and while less precise in its targeting capability, the combination of a special event with a compatible location can draw the user profiles the marketer wishes to attract. When Biore (www.biore.com) was introducing its Pore Perfect Strips, the company engaged a huge sampling program to put the product in the hands (or faces) of its target market, teenage girls. To help accomplish this goal, Biore staged its sampling program in urban shopping malls throughout the country. Sampling strategies are very important in matching the product to the prospect in the right place. Frequently, products appealing to the young adult will be distributed on college campuses; new food products are often sampled in grocery stores or at special community events. Samples of suntan lotions are liberally distributed at the beach, particularly if a beach volleyball tournament is being held. Golf carts are test-driven as transportation in retirement communities; even the Apple Macintosh was available for a weekend of test driving when it was introduced in 1984. Can services be supported by sales promotion? Yes, remember the free calling minutes from Sprint (www.sprint.com) or MCI or free usage hours by AOL. People can have their carpets shampooed on a trial basis by Sears. An airline promotion might offer a half-price ticket to anyone who buys a full-fare ticket. A movie theater might give away free popcorn to anyone who has seen five movies in one month at that particular movie theater. In all cases, there is a reward for the consumer for trying the product or service.

The marketer should define the sales promotion objective(s) before initiating the sales promotion—that special incentive to use the product or service—to be able to judge whether the goals were met. Was the objective to accelerate sales of new or existing products? Was the sales promotion directed at consumers, but the higher (and probably unspoken) goal was to placate retailers by increasing the sales traffic to the stores? Was the sales promotion a special toy or ornament in a children's meal, which of course was an inducement to create higher sales by attracting children or coercing the parents to patronize the fast food restaurant. Sales promotion has proven quite effective in the last ten years with cosponsorship of sales promotions such as McDonald's vying with Burger King to be the cosponsor of a children's movie, usually a Disney production. Special promotions bring kids and adults to the restaurant with bonus items, such as characters from the *Lion King*, *Aladdin*, or *Rugrats* movies. Sometimes the sales promotion is more popular than the service or product. A recent example of how offering a very popular product or service as a bonus was the Beanie Baby promotion sponsored by McDonald's. Not only did this promotion take away from the marketing plan's real goal of attracting customers, but it resulted in bad publicity for McDonald's due to the not-so-uncommon fistfights over the last item, sidewalk camping in order to be first in line, or black markets taking advantage of consumer demand. An overpowering sales promotion can be as bad as one that flopped. Projecting the rate of usage or redemption is very difficult because the marketer is uncertain how popular or unpopular the special promotion will be. If a marketing promotion is too successful, the lack of the toys or discounts might disappoint the customer and provoke anger at the company that could lead to accusations of false or misleading advertising. If the promotion was aimed at children, a raincheck is a disheartening substitute for the toy or game promised.

An unsuccessful sales promotion could lead to promotional merchandise that could not sell. The company might have difficulty in discarding the remaining items, especially if the merchandise has a company logo printed on it. Sales promotion events can be very entertaining, such as an automobile dealership sponsoring a circus or carnival on the car lot to bring sales traffic to the dealership or a new shopping mall or children's medical center bringing in a celebrity to help open the doors. The right sales promotion targeted and appreciated by the marketer's segments can be a strong incentive to bring traffic into the store or to boost direct marketing sales from customers and prospects who might live far away. From the early part of the twentieth century until today, cereal manufacturers have always produced some incentive for buying their cereal products—inserting toys into the cereal box, printing puzzles on the box, or merchandising products through points collected from each box or from the proofs of purchase. Everyone has found a toy in a box of Cracker Jacks. As sales promotion has remained a viable promotional tool through the entire century, this promotional element must have produced excellent returns, or the manufacturer would have discontinued sales promotions many years ago.

Individuals working within the sales promotion department must possess the same type of creative mind as those in advertising or product development departments. The marketer must know his market well in order to postulate the likes and dislikes of the market and then develop the complementary special event or promotion to motivate consumers to participate. Creativity in sales promotion concepts and production is always helpful to set the product or service apart. Cadillac engages its sales promotions strategies in supporting and being highly visible among the senior market by sponsoring golf tournaments on the Senior PGA tour. Nike and Adidas (www.adidas.com) continually battle to sign celebrity athletes as authoritative figures to wear and promote their brands of athletic shoes and apparel. Different products and different markets demand different sales promotion communications. A sales promotion for elementary schoolchildren might be a free backpack with a $30 total purchase of pens, pencils, and other grade school necessities. A sales promotion for the college student, on the other hand, might be a pack of ten floppy disks with a $100 purchase of textbooks, case books, study guides, or other required course materials. Sales promotions can be staged all year long, depending on the store's revenue needs and inventory positions. The marketer should keep in mind the possibility of sales promotion wars, offering too steep a discount on the product, staging too often an annual sale, or creating a sales promotion event that far exceeds the price of the merchandise. Businesses also can engage in internal sales promotions aimed at either their sales and support staff or their important channel members, such as distributors, wholesalers, retailers, and the staff of the retailers. The objectives for these trade sales promotions are usually to support and push the products to the retailers' shelves by offering cash or merchandise deals to the retailer and by offering cash bonuses or prizes to the retailers' sales staffs. Retailers have experimented on the various ways to energize their sales staffs by designing sales contests in which winners would receive elegant vacations to Europe or Hawaii, sets of golf clubs and bags, jewelry, or wrist watches. Survey results, however, confirm what managers already believe—the best motivator of all is cash because the salesperson can spend the money on whatever she wishes.

Sales promotions seem to be the fastest way to increase sales over the short term. After the sales promotion period is over, however, the sales levels drop back to the previous level before the promotion started, and sometimes the levels are below the prior period. Why? The consumer may have loaded up his pantry with extra products purchased at lower prices. Like publicity, sales promotion can produce commanding results, but when used incorrectly or blindly, it can lead to many uncontrollable consequences, mostly on the negative side. The marketer should learn what sales promotion to use, what the expected positive returns can be, and what the possible adverse side effects or consequences might be. Many marketers have been blindsided by a weak promotion as well as an overly popular one. Pepsi recently initiated a sales contest called "Pepsi Points," in which consumers could collect product points to be redeemed for merchandise featuring a Pepsi logo. Unfortunately, the program was too successful because Pepsi ran out of the most popular merchandise only to disappoint its loyal drinkers. Therefore, too much success can be as damaging as too little success.

The products or services to be marketed may be perfect for developing a public relations program. In describing it as perfect, the product might be one of great public benefit, such as new applications to improve public health, to improve public education, to reduce air pollution, or to make foods more nutritional and possibly less fattening. Most public relations programs are built around excellent products or services that improve some general or specific consumer problem. As other promotional mix elements have been described, public relations objectives should be set for the program. As was noted in the general explanation of public relations capabilities, PR depends heavily on publicity, and publicity can be the greatest friend or the greatest enemy to an organization. Therefore, the public relations efforts should be carefully examined and cautiously pursued in generating positive press relations. What could be appropriate objectives? Probably ambitious, but greatly beneficial, would be in setting goals of having the product story appear on the two strongest television stations, generating two feature stories in the largest local (better yet national) newspaper and magazine, and staging product demonstrations among the five most influential business or community groups. The public relations program will proceed at a steady pace, deliberate and patient at each turn. Of course, the company or product must be noteworthy, and it must be credible and serviceable as promised. The marketer should go through the same process of segmentation to decide which benefits match which segments best; this is the same segmentation process that was discussed as part of the traditional marketing process.

- This process of segmentation, more frequently termed as designating the audiences in PR language, is a fundamental and critical part of the public relations program. Audience selection requires that a marketer recognize that the product, along with the construction of new production facilities, will interact differently for different audiences, and communications aimed at each audience will require different PR programs. Think of the public relations programs that a major university should maintain. Public relations works best at proactively influencing rather than quickly rushing in a reactive fashion. Public relations are proactive when action plans and remedies are recognized with solutions to put into place before a situation arises; reactive programs are exactly the opposite of that. No one has anticipated the problem, and impromptu solutions are engaged with little thought given to the possible results and consequences. A public relations programs for a major university would be comprised of smaller programs directed toward important external and internal audiences. Who would have a stake in the operation or the future of the university? Students would first come to mind, and an ongoing plan should be devised to maintain an ongoing relationship with undergraduate and graduate students. The overriding purpose of a public relations plan is to keep in touch with attitudes and opinions of the various constituencies; from these attitudes, pertinent programs can help to fulfill the expectations of the audiences. Another group who might have a stake in the future of the university might be the parents of the students; parents might like to know what the university is doing for their daughter or son. Another important group could be the alumni of the university; as they make donations to the school, they might be interested in knowing what resources, laboratories, buildings, and athletic resources are being created from their donations. Faculty and staff of the university deserve to know what is happening to their departments. These are all internal audiences since each is a **stakeholder** in the operation of the university; usually when good things happen at the school, good things happen to them. There are also external stakeholders or audiences to consider. Future students such as high school seniors or transfer students might like to know about the university's ranking of educational performance or what the campus life is like. Depending on the state's organization, positive relations must be maintained with the state government or assemblies to justify how the universities' budgets are being spent and what results are being achieved. Local government is likely to want to know what growth is expected at the university since local government has to produce supportive services such as fire and police departments, roads and other infrastructure, and emergency medical facilities. One last external audience might be the general public including retailers that serve the annual college influx; this group would also like to know about the size of the student population, expected growth, and the start and finish dates of the academic year, the homecoming date, or the finals or orientations schedules because many companies increase or decrease sales or support staff as the student population ebbs and flows.

A communications program might be needed, after studying the environment, for each of these constituencies; some programs may be as simple as preparing a calendar for the public at large and local businesses in specific. Some communications programs such as those for students registering for classes term after term might be very complex since many new services are added every semester, from the number of computer labs to prerequisite course title and content changes. A comprehensive tool used to communicate with faculty and staff usually is a printed newsletter, which is now migrating toward an e-mail document since so many universities' faculty and staff have personal computers. To communicate with external audiences such as local businesses, the university Web page can have a link to the names, addresses, and merchandise or service specialties that students can patronize. (Should the educational institution wish to raise some money, advertisements could be sold on the university's or college's Web site.) To keep the legislators and local governments in the loop, an intranet accessible by a special address can be created, much like a newsletter directed solely with disseminating information of interest to government officials. This information might include enrollment figures, awards won by different academic departments, profiles of outstanding students, or the number or dollar value of new buildings and facilities constructed on the campus within the last year. The intranet has been previously discussed in Chapter 7, The Tools of Electronic Marketing Resources, as an excellent information-laden method for carrying privileged communications. The intranet could be a competent carrier of confidential documents. So in applying public relations activities, the capabilities of the Web seem to allow something for everyone; this is good because it keeps the public informed as to what the company, product, or service is doing to satisfy each special interest publics.

- It seems redundant or perhaps circular to revisit direct marketing since online tools have been addressed quite extensively. Rather than looking at the situation in a micro perspective, the marketer must decide the objective(s) in a macro sense. While online marketing falls within the umbrella of direct marketing, other vehicles such as television, newspapers, magazines, telemarketing, and direct mail are also contained within this promotional category. Each is an alternative method of direct marketing, and each performs differently depending on the product. Some products require considerable explanation, and telemarketing can provide this information with persuasion. Some products like the Chia Pets (www.chia.com) allow viewers to exercise their green thumbs, or CD clubs offer the viewer a chance to buy the sounds of the seventies or other decades by using television very effectively to appeal to mass markets. Some products can be enticing to narrow markets such as collectors of Hummel figures, and these prospects are probably reading lifestyle or collectors magazines. Advertising to Hummel enthusiasts via magazines is a good idea. An even better and more direct way to advertise to this market is for the marketer to join Hummel listservs, sponsor a Hummel discussion group, and register the Hummel collectors site with every major search engine. Magazines produce selected profiles of readers as search engines do of their users of the Web. Magazine readers will respond to advertisements, buying items as they choose; these are only a few types of direct marketing. Using the selectivity of the World Wide Web will reduce the waste coverage of the major mass media of television, magazine, and newspapers. Perhaps these mass vehicles can be used less frequently, though not entirely eliminated, as the Web promotional elements are integrated into the direct response channel.

Engaging in online explorations for unique merchandise, the shopper can find a one-of-a-kind product such as dragonwood-carved sword, walking canes handcrafted by Graceworld (www.graceworld.com). Searching for the matchless Meerschaum pipes (Tinsky/Hayes Tobacconist, www.cybersun.com/scripts/webcatalog); chasing an antique $1000 paper bill from 1840 (Sammler, http://sammler.com/coins/banknotes); seeking antique Lalique glass decorative arts from 1860 to 1940, perhaps a "Eau de Lubin" frosted-scent bottle and stopper, after 1920 (Bonhams, www.bonhams.com)? These are not items the affluent shopper can find in her neighborhood mall. The affluent shopper, however, probably has access to an Internet-connected home personal computer.

- You might be asking how personal selling objectives can be woven into the global reach of a computer-based communications system. As other people have the capability to tap into vast databases worldwide, so does the salesperson. For example, the salesperson could be working with a client that has offices throughout the world, and this client, therefore, asks the salesperson if a particular product, say replacement bearings for heavy equipment or a special type of lubricant, is available to European-based construction operations. The salesperson using his laptop computer queries the Paris office's inventory database and is able to answer the construction client in a matter of seconds. These capabilities build long-term relationships because of the speed, accuracy, and accessibility of information between the client and the supplier. Besides using Web-enabled sites connected to inventory databases, the field salesperson can use e-mail to report the results of critical meetings to his superiors or can engage automated fax-back systems that query and receive standard questions without human assistance. These tools increase enterprise organization without even considering the impact of wireless communications, such as cellular telephones, cellular faxes, and wireless pagers with alpha/numeric readouts; these electronic communications tools combined with electronic marketing resources create a virtual environment in which the user engaged in personal selling is never out of touch with individuals, offices, or international managers. The salesperson wields a competitive weapon of instant information to the benefit of her customers by offering this informationin hard copy, transferred to a hard floppy, modemed to the purchasing department, or posted to an intranet site to be retrieved. This convenience of

Graceworld (www.graceworld.com)
Specialty products are easily found with the Web's search capabilities. Finding unique products such as dragonwood-carved sword canes or model train accessories are in the departments of the online store, Graceworld.

information manipulation is extremely powerful and should be contained by security layers, which will be discussed in Chapter 15, on the E-Commerce site.

This information advantage is commanding, but since technology continues to grow more pervasive and less costly, the marketer should embrace strongly a technological watch on new technology that could be applied to the marketing effort and on new developments among competitors. A company cannot survive unless it keeps its eyes on competitors' marketing and communications initiatives. Technology is fast in coming, and it is a much better management technique to seek out before the technology is adopted by the competition. Nowhere is there more beneficial advances in the last few years than in personal communications, and these personal digital assistants (PDAs), such as the Palm Pilot (www.3com.com), enable the tasks of the sales professional to be better organized and better documented for reporting purposes. Personal selling is both harder and easier than ever before. It is harder because the competition can utilize the same technology, perhaps drawing upon better electronic resources that makes the personal seller work harder. Personal selling, on the other hand, is easier than ever before because of electronic links to all of the company's functions—marketing, operations, and financial departments. Efficient and secure information transfer can differentiate the company and produce a better-armed sales representative, but this differentiation must continue to undergo improvement. A corps of well-trained personal sales professionals can be the best weapon of a company if the salespeople are great listeners who pass client and competitor information along to the company's management. Good listeners produce great products and services.

- As the other promotional mix elements are being decided, the media strategy should be decided as well concurrently, starting with the media objective, which leads to the appropriate media strategy, and then to the media tactic. Here is a list of the major media available within most markets, the strategic usage of the media, and the short-term or tactical actions afforded by each vehicle. This listing is by no means comprehensive because new applications of traditional media and new media are being introduced every day.

Medium	**Strategy**	**Tactic**
Business newspaper	Product launch	Toll-free number; Web address
Local newspaper	General awareness; local sales support	New product introductions; dealer support locations
In-flight magazine	Product launch	Toll-free number; Web address
General interest magazine	Image launch/ongoing awareness	Offering general product information; toll-free number
Industry magazine	Image launch/ongoing awareness	Specific technical data and dealer locations
Television	Product launch; image support	Regional support as co-op with manufacturer
Radio	Image support/sales	Co-op with manufacturer
Outdoor	Image support	Dealer locations
Transit	Image support	Dealer locations
Interactive kiosks	Transactional	Transactional
Airport displays	Image support	General product information
Stadium/scoreboard	Image support	Dealer locations
Miscellaneous collateral	Image support	Toll-free number; Web address

- This media strategy must work within the budget established by the marketing manager. Many of the marketer's associates, subordinates, and suppliers may groan that the budget is inadequate to complete their parts of the marketing program. However, as individual portions of the marketing program are assigned to different individuals, bringing all of these disciplines together will create the whole of the quarterly or yearly marketing effort. Portioning out various assignments demands more attention by the marketing manager to confirm that all jobs are progressing to be finished at the designated time. One indispensable responsibility of the manager is seeing that the media planning and placement are proceeding toward closing dates because even the most compelling advertisement is lost if the ad is not seen by the target market due to some missed connection between the agency and the media. Missing a primary advertising vehicle can reduce, if not totally derail, the marketing campaign. Because each vehicle has an important media function, the various mediums will be assigned individual goals for the campaign. Perhaps televisions or magazines are expected to provide introductory or reinforcing awareness of the brand and product. Media suppliers must work closely with the marketing manager or the company's advertising agency to establish the objectives for the current campaign, such as awareness of new advertising campaigns, support of primary vehicles, reinforcement of advertising themes, support of sales promotion activities, or dissemination of corporate views on business or social issues. The better the media supplier is briefed, the better the individual mediums perform well.

With the objectives of major media determined, the purposes of the secondary media, such as outdoor, mall or terminal advertising, and online advertising, can be specified as well as setting budget levels. As informational or persuasive as media advertising can be, there often is at work an even more powerful and credible factor—word-of-mouth referrals.

Consumers Are Actively Searching for Helpful Sites

In addition to the marketer's promotional outreach, the customer or prospect is not sitting idly by. Web users are surfing for sites that satisfy their needs. The online consumers pursue their search for information from the Gupta and Pitkow Study 3 (a research project on the commercial uses of the World Wide Web), word-of-mouth contacts with friends, and others' Web pages. "Magazines and news groups seem like a possible way to initiate (and reinforce) this process. Users may have developed hotlists, also called bookmarks, which are the most common method of navigating to a Web site. So, understanding how these hotlists get formed, and then evolve, is important. While these methods take some diligence, the marketer should note the relatively large role of serendipity in finding sites. Being listed on as many related sites, [which is done with search engine registration, which is] more word-of-mouth exposure as possible is clearly very important." (Gupta 1995)

Summary

There is logic when it comes to integrating online communications with the traditional media mix, and one of the biggest decisions is what traditional vehicles should be isolated to include the capabilities of interactive channels. Some traditional vehicles can provide substantial reach in introducing new products and services but lack the ability to respond instantaneously. These widely read or viewed vehicles can direct the consumer to Web site addresses that can produce a two-step response mechanism in which the prospect reads the ad and then either calls a telephone number or dials into the Web address for more information. These mechanisms give the prospect alternatives for company contact and also allow the interested party to read copious amounts of product information if he desires to do so.

Different vehicles should be used in different situations; however, the Web is an excellent response tool regardless if an audience is an individual shopping for information on various mutual funds or investment houses' services. The marketer will learn when and how to engage the Web to be either a primary vehicle for awareness or a secondary vehicle for providing a depth of information. The Web has proven to be a primary shopping and ordering channel for computer hardware and software, and it is expected to serve consumer industries such as consumer electronics, entertainment, and information content.

More and more companies are bringing expertise and imagination into the electronic tools of the promotional mix. The marketer along with the interactive advertising agency builds a product awareness and brand personality from the promotional mix elements of advertising (both traditional and online)—sales promotion, public relations, direct marketing (where online communications brightly outshine the traditional direct response vehicles because of instant interactivity), and personal selling (in which the traditional methods are enhanced by online resources). In each category, the online promotional resources will never replace the traditional vehicles because of staunch media and shopping habits. The Web, however, adds to better purchase decision making because of its depth and variety of information resources. After examining how the interactive Web capability can enhance each of the five promotional elements, the marketer can create a much improved, consumer-friendly promotional program. This chapter closes with the realization that, despite all the electronic marketing persuasion, the strongest endorser of all is that of word-of-mouth referrals. Trusted relatives and friends are the primary source to start the consumer decision making process, and good experiences make for good referrals. Customer service is an important after-sale factor in positive product experiences. This issue of customer service will be investigated further in Chapter 13, Considerations for Ongoing Customer Communications.

Key Terms

Advertising

Creativity

Direct marketing

Dyadic communications

Interactive advertising agency

Personal selling

Product life cycle

Public relations

Publicity

Push versus pull media

Sales promotion

Sales promotion spiral

Stakeholder

Technology-watch

Telemarketing

Unique selling proposition

QUESTIONS AND EXERCISES

1. Some advertisers use different messages in different media at the same time. Their justification is that they are advertising different products to different markets that have different media habits. How do you counter this statement or do you agree with the advertising strategy? Give some thought to consistency, knowing well the customer, segmentation strategy, and trying to be all things to all people. Write a memo to your advertising manager expressing your opinion on the correct strategy.

2. In the opening quote of this chapter that forecasts larger Web ads, do you think this occurrence will assist the shopper or alienate the viewer? Is there any happy compromise that would serve both parties? Write a letter to the editor supporting the shopper, or the viewer, or develop a give-and-take proposal for Internet users.

3. The interactive tracking technology evidenced by Alexa.com seems acceptable to many Americans. If you are a multinational or global marketer, however, how would this technology fit with more private cultures? Would you have to develop several privacy policies? Would your e-marketing policy be global or local? Develop a privacy policy for those cultures or governments that might be offended or that might be considered illegal interactive tracking technology.

4. In your opinion, which of the traditional media mix elements has online communications most affected in the negative sense? Which has online communications strengthened the most? How has interactivity affected each of the five elements? Be prepared to discuss your answers in class.

5. In your opinion, will any of the five promotional mix elements become less effective or even obsolete in the next fifty years because of advances in electronic communications? Radio suffered as television advertising became more popular, and afternoon and evening editions of daily newspapers folded because of television news programs. If you think any of the promotional elements might become obsolete, which promotional elements or medium (media) do you think this might happen to? If you do not think any will become obsolete, why not? Write a memo to the head of strategic planning.

6. Under what circumstances do you feel is it appropriate to mass e-mail various groups of e-mail users, such as Usenet groups as DejaNews? Or a listserv, such as Online Ads? Or a proprietary e-mail address list, such as the entire employee group of a private company? Or a government organization? Or the entire faculty of a university? Write an unsolicited e-mail policy paragraph for each group mentioned.

7. Concerning the design of your company's domain name, surf the Web to locate ten domain names that you consider memorable or creative or both. After each name, write a paragraph explaining why you think it is special—humorous, double entendre, a unique meaning, or a unique initial?

8. You are the media liaison for a large public utility. You are new in your position, but you have experience as an assistant public relations director. The first task you decide upon is to organize your customer constituencies according to special interests. You begin to develop e-mail lists for news releases; what would be the e-mail lists that should be directed to each of your market interests? Different groups may require different news releases or announcement slants; what information would you need directed to each customer constituency? Write an outline listing each group and type of information you would release to them.

9. Many times (almost always) sales promotions that award prizes ask for the contestant's e-mail address. Why? E-newsletters also request e-mail addresses for the obvious reason of delivering the newsletter online. Why? Why is sales promotion so popular among marketers dealing with consumers and businesses alike? Write an e-mail to your marketing manager suggesting a sales promotion for your class project's product or service citing these reasons.

10. From the list of strategic and tactical promotional media tools on page 207, collect samples of each and place them on pages in a portfolio. The items you might find are magazine or newspaper ads, signs or billboards (photograph any that will apply), brochures or flyers, publicity articles, packaging from products, and, of course, printed Web pages.

Bibliography

Barmash, Isadore. 1998. Faded brands are finding new life. *Industries Channel.* Reuters and PointCast Network [cited online 24 July].

Beatty, Sally. 1998, Companies push for bigger online ads. *The Wall Street Journal,* 20 August, B5.

Belch, George, and Michael Belch. 1998. *Advertising and promotion.* 4th ed. Chicago: Irwin/McGraw-Hill.

CKS Group, www.cks.com [cited online 20 November, 1998].

GartnerGroup. Block, J., Weksel, J., Nelson, S., & Hopkins, W. August 6, 1996. "Database Marketing: Using Information Technology to Manage Customer Relations." Gartner Analytics.

Gupta, Sunil. 1995, June 10. *Survey 3, Purchases and Perceptions* [cited online].

Lukas, Paul. 1998. Creativity glut cripples admen. *Fortune,* 8 June, 48.

RealNetworks introduces real agencies affiliates program. 1998. *Industries Channel.* PointCast Network [cited online 13 January].

Synder, Joel. 1998. Improving your image. *Internet World,* February, 30–32.

Targeted advertising takes on new meaning online. 1999. Reuters [cited online 9 February].

CHAPTER 10

Using the Internet

". . . [T]his miracle [of the Internet] owed its existence to the confluence of four forces: the ongoing evolution of interconnected networks, the presence of large numbers of personal computers on local area networks next could be connected to the bigger via a 'universal gauge,' the spread of multimedia to personal computers, and the Berners-Lee search method. Just as a mixture of chemicals consisting of just the right ingredients can undergo spontaneous combustion, this confluence brought about an explosion of public interest in the Internet. But is that explosion a flash in the pan or does it signal the start of a more lasting change? It so happens that as I was writing this book, Intel's semiannual strategy gathering was coming up. My role at these occasions is to describe our business environment as I see it, and to call attention to any significant changes. I felt that the Internet was the biggest change in our environment over the last year." (Grove 1996, 171–172)

LEARNING OBJECTIVES

- To understand what sources of marketing information are available on the Internet and discuss the applications in various examples
- To differentiate between the personal and commercial use of the World Wide Web
- To introduce the special culture of the Internet and its code of conduct

Introduction

The capabilities and the appearance of the Web have grown tremendously since its introduction in 1991 and its addition of the multimedia capability in 1993. Back in 1991, messaging was only textual, described by the technical people as character-based and only in black and white. Most information was available by dialing in remotely to academic resources; you then issued unforgiving and arcane commands to puzzling menus in programs such as PINE (Program for Internet News and E-mail), a textual e-mail that replaced an older e-mail program called Elm; Veronica, a textual search engine for Gopher retrievals; or Archie, a textual search engine that searched for files anywhere on the Internet by file names. Marketers were somewhat limited to scarce e-mail partners and academic research studies at sites throughout the world. Use of the Internet was awkward and required a long and frustrating learning curve for the layperson. These events and electronic systems are now ancient history in the timeline of Internet and Web user-friendliness and information retrieval for marketers, both students and professionals.

Now we have more information than we can ever need or use. One key ability for the marketer to master is how to find the *right* information, not *all* the information. Developing this skill takes judgment and practice. The marketer must learn to use search engines and search techniques, understand electronic advertising and sales promotion development, comprehend electronic media, be adept at organizing and disseminating electronic public relations, participate in Usenets that might apply to his products or customers, and be willing to invest time on the Internet surfing and reading about marketing and industry trends in his off hours. These are subjects of exhaustive scope and require commitment from the marketing enthusiast. One mindset for the marketer to accept is the notion that a marketing or advertising person should have an intellect like the Mississippi River—six miles wide and one inch deep. This is not a criticism of the marketer's mind, but an observation of all there is to know about all environments and factors of the marketplace and how she must deal with both the broader and narrower pictures. With the assistance of tools like the Internet, perhaps the marketer can become more of a specialist in areas of interest. Likewise, with the assistance of the Internet, perhaps the marketer can be more of a generalist. These extremes and points in between allow for a satisfying career in the marketing, communications, and e-commerce industries.

Just What Can You Get from the World Wide Web?

The marketer should be aware of the content available via the Web and be able to judge whether information is appropriate for his industry and of use to his customers. Much of this decision will revolve around how well he knows and understands the information his market needs and demands. He can retrieve industry data such as economic indicators, sales histories, and sales forecasts; read Web pages of competitors for product pricing and specifications; perform marketing intelligence by monitoring news groups and Usenets and by receiving feedback from real customers; answer e-mails from prospect inquiries; collaborate with experts from around the world; and access the latest opinions in consumer trends and perceptions' information. Assume the marketer is in touch with the market and is proactive in looking for new marketing and communications opportunities. There are two major considerations: Is the company selling to the consumer or is the company selling to business-to-business organizations? Different purposes require different approaches and different content. This textbook will now explore the various ways in which retailers present content to the consumer and the ways in which manufacturers or resellers place content on their Web sites in order to attract business customers. First consumer content will be considered.

A View of the Page Menu

One of the best marketing tools in examining the different retailer offerings to customers is to look at a competitor's Web page. Hopefully the page has been in use for some time, and you can compare several retailers' content to one another. Take a look at Wal-Mart's home page, to see what elements have been designed into the "Wal-Mart online" site. At the top of the page is a topical or seasonal message, a worthwhile rotation of items or promotions, to keep the page fresh and timely. The feature here is "Star Wars' Phantom Menace" with an invitation to "click here" to retrieve information related to the movie merchandise. Back on the home page, there also is an illustration of a helpful Wal-Mart employee with arms open wide, mirroring the friendly gesture depicted in the Wal-Mart television commercials. The Web communications strategy appears to offer a variety of information from which the reader can pick and choose specific content. The page is divided into three columns, much like a newsletter or small newspaper. At the top of column one, is a hyperlink list of product categories linked to the product. An internal search engine allows the viewer to search for specific products, such as "baseball bats" rather than the general "sporting goods." More sites are adding internal search engines to encourage the viewer to find the desired element within the pages.

The next section after "Search Products," is "Customer Service," which Wal-Mart has pledged a strong stand in other media. Hyperlinks include a selection for an optional $3 shipping fee for parcel delivery, a "Security Guarantee" that promises the utmost in online security to protect your credit card numbers and a voucher for monetary replacement should anything go wrong. The next hyperlink under "Customer Service" is "Review Shopping Cart," an invitation to register to maintain a "**virtual shopping cart.**" This feature allows the shopper to have a record of her shopping information, a useful tool when she is buying for a long list. The information is carried over from year to year, also a valuable customer retention tactic.

The next column showcases several color photographs of popular merchandise with their current prices such as a Midland Speakeasy 14 Channel Family Radio 2 pack, $169.96 or a new song by Jan Karon, $13.72, it then lists hyperlinks without photos of merchandise, like Leapfrog Odyssey Atmosphere, $279.97 or the Mark McGwire Combo Pack, at $24.95. You can be sure that customer research has been conducted to select merchandise that will pull customers into its stores; in analyzing this merchandisers column, all items are geared to children or teenagers which are super shoppers. And they can badger their parents into visiting the retailer of their choice. At the bottom of the column, one last hyperlink, "More Featured Items . . . ," is a last grasp should the consumer wish to check more special items if they have time.

The last column, "Company," is a formal, corporate presentation of the Wal-Mart Stores, Inc., information. The hyperlinks list includes "Newsroom," for press resources and articles for interested party, "Career Opportunities," the employment page, a "Store Locator," ending at the Wal-Mart philanthropy programs such as "Scholarship Fund", and "Wal-Mart Foundation." After the corporate pages, another search engine, "Go To Location," permits the viewer to search the site for other than merchandise. This search might be for the advertising department, or for the location of the purchasing department. The last item in the "Company" column is a hyperlink to the special events "in a store near you!" and a hotspot which highlights the in-store "Toyland," again attractive to the younger shopper.

At the bottom of the home page is an offer to apply for a Wal-Mart MasterCard from Chase, a large bank that deals with retailers around the nation. The MasterCard is embellished with the Wal-Mart logo and its slogan, "Lower prices. Always." Last but not least in the communications chain is a message to "Click here to send us your comments, or call 1-800-966-6546 to speak with a Customer Service representative." Comments and criticisms can be delivered by e-mail, or a secondary line is the 800

Wal-Mart (www.wal-mart.com)
Not only does Wal-Mart supply almost every dry good, you can obtain a Wal-Mart credit card from Chase. Wal-Mart works hard to provide convenience with online credit approval.

number. The marketer is doubly sure she or he has a listening post at ground level, the customer. This Web page is most comprehensive and informational; its page design is easily read for navigation. Wal-Mart has reported increasing site traffic and sales traced to the Web presence. This is a good format for prospective merchants to consider as they research site design and continuity of incorporating current marketing messages and themes.

A Home Page for Commercial Content

Suppose you are not selling to the general public but to other businesses. Does the home page design change drastically? This depends on the industries in which your firm is engaged. Among high-tech companies, the content is very informational, stressing technical support and downloading capabilities. If the firm is involved in services, customer service and testimonials are prominently featured. If the firm sells commodities such as finished hardware (nails, bolts, and building materials), the content of the site is informational reassurance toward the inventory availability, delivery, quality, and price. Take a look at the Oracle Corporation home page (www.oracle.com), representing a more complex content structuring, that of high technology and services sales. Oracle Corporation is a leading manufacturer of software and a heavy

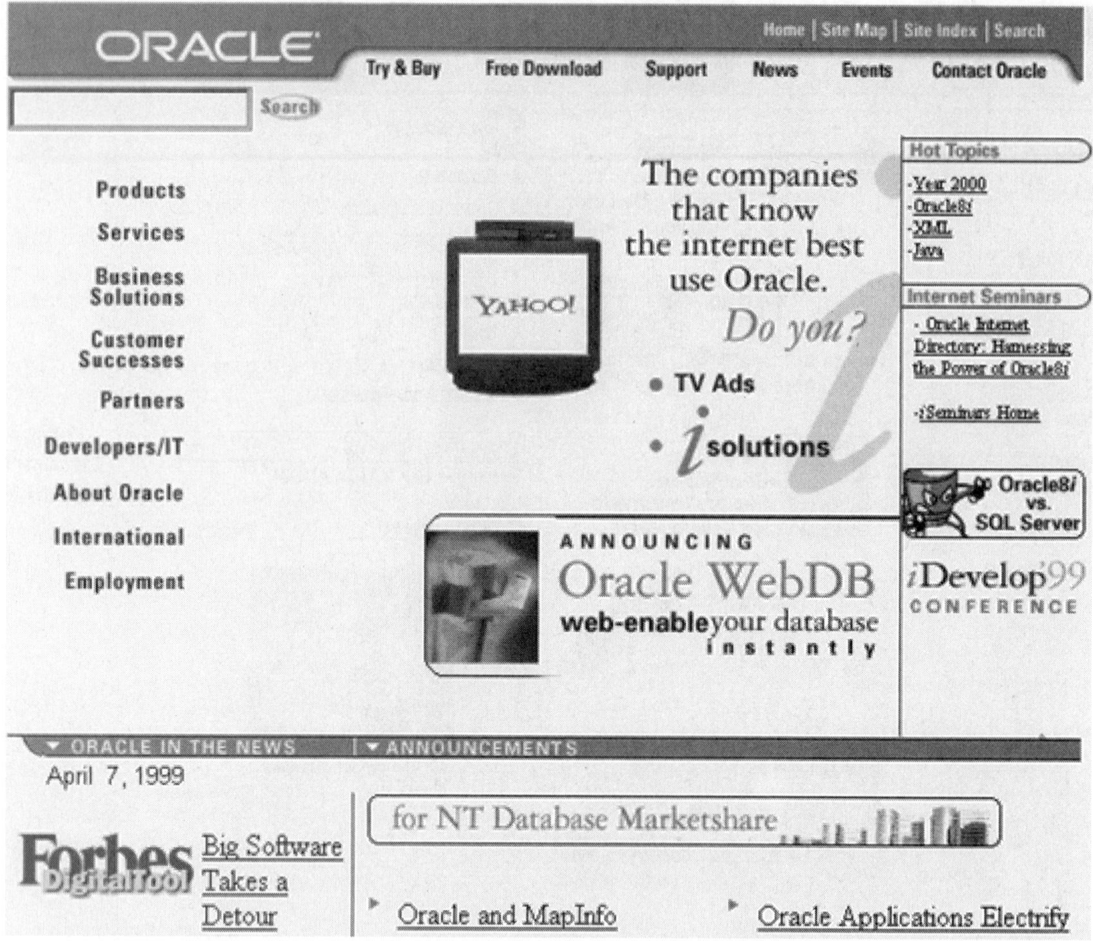

Oracle (www.oracle.com)
The Oracle home page carries many customer benefits. A testimonial from Yahoo!, publicity from Forbes Digital Tool, sample television ads, announcements of new products and conference sponsorships all add to the perception of software leadership for the Oracle company.

seller to businesses and government. Again, the Oracle home page possesses a clean, legible design on a white background; dark or busy backgrounds reduce legibility and take much longer to load. Printing is more difficult on complex backgrounds since the printer codes also load longer and print longer. The Oracle page contains much information so that it requires two menu bars—one along the top red Oracle border and a second vertical bar along the left margin. Sales features, photographs, and a sales promotion, "Million Dollar Challenge," are positioned in the center of the page while timely information forms the right margin. Which of these menu bars is most important? It depends on the interests of the viewer. Is the viewer already an Oracle product user? If so, technical support and free downloads are of particular advantage. Is the viewer shopping for database software? The left menu featuring products might be well visited. Is the viewer an Oracle business partner looking for support materials as he represented Oracle in business systems? Is the viewer a software developer needing information about the Oracle application she is working with? All user situations are quite common, and none are more common than others.

On a day following the printing of the Web page featuring the "Oracle Million Dollar Challenge," Oracle had introduced new graphics, "Oracle's Internet Billing Solution," which is a prominent feature of another Oracle solution. Above the centered graphics is a red menu that presents different hyperlinks to Oracle sales and public relations programs. The first hyperlink, "Try & Buy," is an encouragement to test Oracle products on a $4.95 demonstration CD-ROM before buying the software product. The demo CD-ROMSs are an excellent sampling technique; with good, established products, this is a low risk (as in low amount of returns) sales tactic. The next hyperlink is "Download free and trial products."

For a thirty-day trial license period, the user can decide if the software is right for her business. Next is the "Support" button, extensive choices of how Oracle support can be a specific rather than a general support function. The page is titled "Support Web Center" led by a hyperlink, "OracleLifecycle," that delivers customized, industry-focused, full life-cycle support solutions to Oracle technology. This hyperlink is followed by "ExpertOnline," offering answers to the DBA skills shortage. These are intriguing approaches to making the hyperlink more valuable.

Personal Use of the Web

As retailers divine ways to satisfy the consumers' purchases on the Web, partners are wise to understand the reasons for the purchasers personally using the Web. The most mentioned reason for using the Web for personal shopping was convenience (65 percent), followed by the availability of vendor information (60 percent), the no pressure from salespeople (55 percent), and aspect of saving time (53 percent). Personalized shopping services were not the reason for using the Web for most people (14 percent), which could be explained as the result of unfamiliarity with shopping services. It is still unclear whether attitudes will change on this point as more personalized services become available. Males and females both ranked convenience first, but female users valued the notion of no pressure from salespeople (54 percent) slightly over vendor information (51 percent). Experts and respondents aged 19 to 50 years old were more enthusiastic about Web shopping in all categories.

In general, consumers mention convenience, discounts and sales, and special promotions as the prime motivators that bring shoppers to the Web. Convenience reigns whether the shopper wishes to avoid crowds or considers himself too busy to spend time in the store reviewing the merchandise. A harried Christmas shopper noted:

> A growing number of shoppers agree [that the Web is a viable alternative to traffic at the malls.] "Are you kidding? There's no way I'm going near [the stores] on Black Friday; there's way too many people," said Carol Letter, a homemaker in Kent, Washington. Instead, she fired up the computer and headed to eToys, an online toy store, where she bought a pair of toy binoculars for her three-year-old. Her only complaint: She wishes more retailers had Web sites. "If they get more stuff online, I'll stop shopping in the stores all together." (In the malls, on the Web, a Christmas crush 1998)

Of course the holiday seasons propel more traffic on the Web, and the increase in hits and purchases have been substantial from year to year. The numbers are telling from the day after Thanksgiving and the ensuing weekend. *The Wall Street Journal* observed during the 1998 Thanksgiving shopping spree:

> Many customers ventured into cyberspace to do their Christmas shopping. Though still just a fraction of overall retail sales, commerce on the Web is widely expected to double from last year [1997], to $2.3 billion this season. Some Web retailers reported even sharper gains. Amazon.com Inc. said its orders on Friday were four times higher than a year earlier. CDNow, an online music store, said traffic at its Web site tripled. And iQVC, the Internet

> site of television shopping giant QVC Inc., had record sales Friday and Saturday as customers ordered nearly $800,000 in merchandise, up from about $350,000 a year earlier. (ibid.)

There is another personal side for an individual to use the Web, that of being able to personalize the browser's home page to retrieve information from specific Web resources. Most major search engines allow the user to program site information retrieval by using the "My" page option; the viewer then selects those addresses to load first. For instance, from associated news services, the browser presents to the viewer the latest news, weather, supports scores, stock quotes, or whatever data the viewer likes to monitor. The selectivity of information is available on Yahoo!, Excite, Infoseek, Lycos, and other user-friendly search engines. The viewer tends to visit personal favorites, usually daily, so it is a matter of convenience to preprogram the sites. Of all information retrieved, the weather sites are the most popular and frequently accessed; this is logical since many travelers are business users of the Web. Sports, stock market updates, and online daily newspapers are also very popular. As this trend toward personalized information grows, search engines will continue to court the viewer because higher page traffic equates to greater advertising revenues. Yahoo!, Excite, and other search engines are most eager to become habit forming to Web users.

Consumer Habits Are Being Formed

Realizing that the hypertext component of the Web is yet in its genesis, consumers are welcoming the power and variety of the Web's treasury of information, and users are adapting their daily activities to accommodate their online practices. From the GVU Eighth User Survey (1997), consumers are willingly altering their everyday behaviors to accommodate quality online time. The frequency with which respondents characterize their interface with the Web is reported as 85 percent accessing the Web daily. The largest category of respondents uses the Web one to four times per day (45 percent), with 41 percent using it more often than four times daily. Males employ the Internet slightly more often than females. Those persons aged 19 to 50 years old use it more frequently than other age groups. Expert users are much more likely to log on to the Web daily (94 percent) than novice users (74 percent).

Being appraised of the search engine of choice is an important factor for the marketer to know for two reasons. First is on the consumer side; the software developer can create sites designed to the lowest common denominator—the most persons have the ability to access the site and its appearance is attractive without losing any copy or graphics because of inconsistencies among browsers. The second critical decision concerns **search engine popularity;** the marketer should register the Web site with the most popular search engines. The registration procedures are largely uniform, but some engines charge for the listing while others do not. For navigation services, the GVU Eighth User Survey published these observations:

> Yahoo! is frequently visited by 84 percent of our respondents. However, since the survey is advertised on the Yahoo! site (among others), this number may be artificially high. On the other hand, other sources have established Yahoo! as one of the most visited sites on the Web so it is not surprising that a high percentage have visited it in the past six months. Next most popular are the major search engines: AltaVista (67 percent), Excite (66 percent), Infoseek (60 percent), and Lycos (59 percent). European respondents favor AltaVista over the other search engines more strongly than their U.S. categories. Older users are more likely to use specialized e-mail/address search services such as Four11 (a unit of Yahoo!), Bigfoot, or WhoWhere

than younger users. All three levels of experience report using Yahoo! more than any other navigation service, but novices are most likely to use Yahoo! and Excite; intermediates use Infoseek, Lycos, and AltaVista; while experts mainly use AltaVista. (GVU Eighth User Survey 1997)

Knowing the Expectations of the Clientele

Can the marketer know too much about her market's wants, needs, expectations, or preferences? Can a company be too successful? Possibly, but most marketing managers would jump at the prospect of having too many successful products or too much sales volume. One of the most determining factors in marketing prowess is the ability to anticipate consumer trends as well as listening to customers' expectations in the level of purchase satisfaction. This book will discuss the most minimal marketing mechanisms that the marketer must offer among online resources and the means in which these mechanisms assist in the customer's capability to access information or place merchandise orders. Knowing customers' constraints (as well as the customers' plateau of patience or frustration) is most valuable in giving the customer what he wants, another bromide of the retail trade. An example of customer involvement parameters is the amount of time a user will spend searching for relevant information, with the largest category of users devoting between five and fifteen minutes searching before finding useful data (40 percent). The next largest group spends less than five minutes (24 percent). Experts tend to find things a bit faster (less than five minutes, 30 percent experts; 22 percent novices) but not much faster. Knowing these searching habits is essential to building a responsive, content-laden, and interactive Web site that draws the surfer into the merchandise or material without obfuscating the e-commerce experience. Consider the **hit ratio,** the number of searches that produce successful results. Survey respondents report that most of the time they find what they are looking for (49 percent). The next largest group only find what they are searching for about half of the time (22 percent). Only 16 percent of experts always find what they are looking for, and 13 percent of novices do as well. Facts like these make a strong argument for designing a user-friendly, intuitive-to-navigate Web site. This conscientious design guide will simplify the customer's purchase abilities, and friendly sites bring the customer back for repeat purchases. This is just another example of relationship marketing where both parties benefit.

Taking Polls of Your Customers' Opinions

Besides understanding how your markets gather information, it is necessary to try to learn what they do with this information. There are many sources of information for marketers' intelligence purposes; two of the best resources revolve around consumers expressing their opinions about product experiences, both positive and negative usage and voicing what products or product features are missing in the marketplace. One comprehensive Usenet site is **Deja News** (www.deja.com), the home of hundreds of discussions about various topics of interest to their participants. The Deja News service allows Web users to create their own discussion forums or "Deja Communities" for public or private conversations among businesses, clubs, teams, work groups, alumni associations, friends, families, or any other collection of interests. The home page suggests starting communities for holding ongoing discussions, meeting in chat rooms, recommending favorite Web sites, promoting group events, creating and taking polls, collaborating on projects, or making announcements. The marketer can start her own discussion group, monitor consumer comments or attitudes expressed in the discussion, and interject or counter written opinions concerning her product or service. The contributions are dated and threaded, meaning the reader can view the sequence of comments to understand the train of communications that brought about a specific criticism or praise. The marketer could then e-mail the contributor to learn more about the problem.

In mid March 1999, the most popular, talked-about discussion groups, "Top Forums," were:

Can Lucci finally win one?	rec.arts.tv.soaps.abc
Dow heads for 10,000	misc.invest.stocks
In praise of Joe DiMaggio	alt.sports.baseball.ny-yankees
What will he think of next?	alt.politics.Clinton
A passengers bill of rights?	rec.travel.air

If you were a marketing or public relations manager or associate for an airlines, it would be wise to consult the last discussion group to watch the opinions of air travelers, regulators, or other contributors to the list. You may have input that you would like to post. The discussion groups are organized by topic with some catch-all categories:

newusers, for beginners

comp, computers—examples, computer apps and computer software

rec, recreation—examples, rec.animals and rec.antiques

sci, science—examples, sci.archeology and sci.chem

alt, alternative—examples, alt.sports and alt.politics

soc, society—examples, soc.college and soc.feminism

talk, examples, talk.origins

new, examples, news.announce and news.software

biz, business—examples, biz.jobs and biz.marketplace

misc, miscellaneous—examples, misc.entrepreneurs and misc.consumers

bionet, examples, bionet.microbiology and bionet.immunology

bit, lists—examples, bit.listserv.stockphoto and bit.listserv.blues-1

k–12, education—examples, k-12.lang; k-12.chat

After you learn the abbreviations system (for example, the post "uk.rec.cars. classic" or "rec.autos.makers.honda" will be "classic cars in the United Kingdom under the recreation" or "Honda-make automobiles under the recreation category), you will recognize helpful and intriguing discussions immediately. Deja News also maintains regional lists for all the states plus the District of Columbia and thirty-two foreign countries. The marketer can, therefore, easily tap into local, national, or international opinions with minimal effort and without traveling. Another discussion metalist resource previously discussed is Liszt, www.liszt.com, another extensive compilation of listservs. Again, the marketer can gain valuable input, ask questions, and monitor a wide variety of topics by logging onto one site. With the Deja News and Liszt resources, the cost is free to the user.

Specialty among Equals

While browser manufacturers promise equal performance in retrieving information, some browsers handle different search engines differently. It is well to plan your search before you start because this will save you time. In fact, Walter S. Mossberg in his "Personal Technology" column in *The Wall Street Journal* stated that studies show people who use the World Wide Web spend much of their time just trying to locate useful information by employing so-called search engines. "It's a sign of both the vastness of the Web and its confusing lack of organization." (Mossberg 1998) He notes that search logic is organized differently on the various search engines; for simple searches, he uses Yahoo! because "it isn't an automated, machine-driven engine but a directory written by humans who have applied some intelligence in their selections." For more complicated or narrower terms, he employs AltaVista since this search engine "uses computers to index individual words." There are newer search engines too besides these old standbys. A new entry Goto.com (www.goto.com) is a "clean, simple site [that] charges other sites a fee to promote them in search results list, and then lets the user know what each site has paid for, a prominent place in the results list. The result is full disclosure, but it also may be a useless and distorted set of hits." (ibid.)

More search engines have caught Mossberg's eye.

> At HotBot (www.hotbot.com), you'll find a first-rate search engine that makes it easier than most to qualify your search terms, by specifying whether they are a phrase or a name or by looking only for materials within certain dates. Direct Hits is a 'popularity engine,' which presents the top ten sites other people have visited for any search term. You can also try Direct Hit at www.directhit.com. It's the brainchild of a company of the same name in Wellesley Hills, Mass. (ibid.)

Mossberg touches on a search engine called Dogpile. "More and more Web surfers are turning to **Meta search sites,** which blast your request to numerous search engines then create one huge list of hits. A good example is Dogpile, www.dogpile.com." This textbook will discuss the concept of meta, or comprehensive tools later. Mossberg ends his column noting that these are a few of the new search engines available, and that the Web user should experiment with many that populate the Net. Find the one that serves your needs best and apply it.

> A fresh light has been shed on the browser wars. We now know that a) the dominant method people acquire browsers is via bundling with hardware, software, and Internet Service Providers (ISP), and b) the majority of users never switch browsers, even among users who have been on the Internet for over three years. Given these new findings, it is not surprising to see the slow, but steady emergence of Internet Explorer in market share is being gained primarily from new users who receive the browser bundled as part of other computer-related purchases. (GVU Eighth Users Survey 1997)

In the ninth GVU survey, even more was learned about concerning the usage of search engines and browsers. The survey queried the use of navigation tools such as search engines (like AltaVista), Web indices (like Yahoo!), and people-finding services (such as Four11), all of which are important navigation services. On the home pages of these popular navigation elements are also prime locations for advertisers to place banners or information sponsorships, and from these advertising revenues, these sites have been expanding their consumer awareness. In addition to performing regular searches, users can check local, national, and international news, check the latest sports scores, translate a page from one language to another, chat with friends or celebrities, apply for a credit card, or download free software. New services are being added daily. Even traditional consulting firms are developing e-commerce tools such as Andersen Consulting's Bargain Hunter, which performs similar shopping services. Many sites offer personalization of the content as well as free e-mail accounts. The following table compares the eighth and ninth survey responses:

Electronic Tool	Ninth GVU Survey	Eighth GVU Survey	Percent Change
Yahoo!*	93.4	84.1	+9.3
AltaVista	81.4	67.3	+14.1
Infoseek	70.2	60.3	+9.9
Excite	69.9	66.1	+3.8
Lycos	68.2	58.5	+9.7
HotBot	46.2	34.3	+11.9
WebCrawler	45.6	46.1	−0.5
Four11	32.9	37.4	−4.5
Bigfoot	25.2	22.2	+3.0
WhoWhere	24.8	23.1	+1.7
AOL NetFind	20.8	12.3	+8.5
Other	17.5	17.7	−0.2

*The GVU study notes that the survey was advertised on Yahoo!, which may inflate these figures.

Techniques for More Efficient Web Searches

Searching on the Web can be quite sophisticated if you use the proper search strategy. To do this, you will require little knowledge on how to use a Boolean search string. Boolean searches (named after English mathematician George Boole) are created using operators that tell the search engine what terms *must* be on the page or what terms *must not* be on the page. You can also search for full phrases such as "electronic marketing" by using double quotation marks.

Here are some examples of the instructions you can find for doing advanced searches on some of the more popular search engine sites. The table below contains the syntax for most search engines. These are good for at least Yahoo!, Excite, InfoSeek, and Lycos but will probably work for the others as well.

Operator	What It Does	Example Search
+ or AND	Attaching a plus sign to a word requires the word be found in all of the search results.	*police* versus *police + sting*
− or NOT	Attaching a minus sign in front of a word requires the word not be found in any of the search results.	*python* versus *python − monty*
t: or title:	This will restrict searches to document titles only.	*joe boxer* versus *t:joe boxer*
u: or url:	This will restrict searches to document URLs only.	*intel* versus *u:intel*
""	Phrase matching is done by putting quotes around a set of words. This will only find results that match the words in that exact sequence.	*great barrier reef* versus *"great barrier reef"*

*	Wildcard matching is done by attaching an asterisk to the right-hand side of the word. This will return anything that matches the left side.	*cap* versus *cap**
Combinations of the above	You may combine any of the above as long as the syntax is combined in the proper order. The proper order for using the syntax is the same order of the operators listed on this table	+, −, t:, u:, "", and *.

The Culture of the Internet

It is odd that the Internet is considered for its commercial purposes because its origin was far from that. As the Internet was born, of academic research and communications, a culture of sharing and noncommercial usage flourished among the gatekeepers of the Internet. The resources of the Internet were free, not to be abused by any contingency of Internet users. One of the tenets of the Internet was its academic, not commercial, foundation, and most academic users were determined to keep this wonderful asset untainted. This intention became to be viewed differently with the introduction of color, graphics, and augmented text in 1993 to the Internet; this enhanced research vehicle became an attractive and persuasive commercial medium as the elements matured, and more people, other than researchers and educators, discovered the boundless holdings. In some respects the emergence of the Web, the graphical band of the Internet, as a commercial entity resembles the loosening of the noncommercial requirements of National Public Radio (NPR), which now allows a broader interpretation of sponsor announcements. NPR has had funding cutbacks and has turned to more commercial sponsorships to supplement the cost of its operations. The government agency the National Science Foundation had upgraded the ARPANET, the older Department of Defense network, to its own NSFnet with a high-speed backbone starting in 1982. In 1995, the National Science Foundation relinquished its oversight and dismantled the NSFnet; it was replaced with a commercial Internet backbone. Is anyone in charge of the Internet? Not really. While several organizations have been created to administer domain names and other clerical work, the Internet seems self-sustaining and available to people around the world.

In following the traditions of the Internet, the marketer should try to extend this cultural style and perceptiveness of his site. Consumers will appreciate this Internet sensitivity and will be more receptive to forming marketing relationships with businesses that respect the Internet spirit. Internet expert and writer Richard Seltzer, a Compaq alumni, has written extensively on the formation of Internet communities as a marketing strategy. In his book, *The Way of the Web*, Seltzer makes these suggestions for encouraging communities to enhance commercial sites:

> The ideal business on the Internet would build a loyal audience by providing an attractive environment in which users could discuss matters of common interest with one another and with experts. In addition, this site would provide lots of related information for free. Searching and abstracting capabilities as well as information that has time-sensitive value could be available for a fee or by subscription. Then on top of such an infrastructure, a publisher and its sponsors could offer all manner of content, goods, and services for sale—backed by graphics, audio, and video—all the glitz that technology can provide—and an easy-to-use online payment system.

Imagine a Web site that not only provides information but also acts as a "user group"—a place for readers to talk to one another, share their thoughts, express their opinions, and help one another. This could be in the form of online Letters to the Editor, welcoming readers to react to articles in your magazine or newspaper and to one another's comments. It also could be part of a product support system, where users can post their questions as well as their insights and innovations and for responses from company experts as well as one another. Remember the experience of talk radio and talk television—the candid comments of ordinary people can be compelling, especially when the audience knows they too can participate in the dialogue if they wish. And remember too that some of your customers may know more about your products than your best support people and may be proud and pleased to share what they know with their peers. Also remember that positive word of mouth is the best marketing tool. So if you have products that are worth talking about, then you could provide a virtual meeting place and empower your customers to talk to one another and to other others, becoming sales people for you.

Depending on your business model, you could aim to build a global virtual community of people with common interests—staking out your subject-matter niche—or you could use this medium to forge closer ties with your local, physical community. For instance, an online bookstore or book publisher could include virtual "rooms" and "events" where customers could talk to one about the books that they have read and for-a-fee forums where they could interact with authors, editors, reviewers, and other experts and celebrities. Or a small newspaper could use these capabilities to allow citizens to discuss matters of common interest with one another and with figures from local government and the education and business communities. (Seltzer 1995))

Learning Proper Netiquette

Quite simply, **netiquette** is Internet etiquette, the informal rules of behavior for the Internet. These Internet customs have evolved over time and have helped make the Internet a pleasant place. In addition, many organizations develop their own **Acceptable Use Policies (AUPs),** a set of rules specifically for an organization's network. There are Netiquette guidelines for most Internet resources including e-mail, mailing lists, news groups, Telnet, and FTPs. Some Internet resources share Netiquette rules; for example, the accepted guidelines for e-mail and mailing lists are also used in news groups. A long-time user of electronic communications, Arlene Rinaldi of Florida Atlantic University has written an excellent guideline for new users to follow in practicing proper Netiquette.

E-mail, Mailing List, and Usenet Newsgroup Netiquette

Following Rinaldi's sensible guidelines, here are some of the more frequently committed oversights of widely accepted Netiquette standards that are used for e-mail, mailing lists, and Usenet newsgroups. When participating in these forums on the Internet, you should be aware of these guidelines.

- Use normal upper- and lower-case letters. Avoid using all capital letters in a message; this is known as SHOUTING and is generally frowned upon.
- Do not assume that your intentions will be understood; remember there is no body language or facial expression to indicate your intentions. Careful

use of emoticons can help get your point across clearly. Here are three examples:

:-) smile (humor, happy, encouragement)

:-(frown (sad, disapproval)

;-) wink (kidding, joking)

WHAT IS NETIQUETTE?

The Internet is rapidly developing its own unique culture formed by a diverse group of people of various religions, nationalities, genders, and experiences. The Internet, commonly referred to as "Cyberspace," is a worldwide melting pot of opinions and ideas. The people using the resources on the Internet have been known to call themselves "netizens" (network citizens), which qualifies them into a whole different social and cultural evolution of a new community of people. They are adventurers on an electronic frontier, where their individual voice can change and shape the future of electronic communications as we know it.

Terms used frequently in exploring and discovering Cyberspace are "mining," "surfing" and "driving the information superhighway." The Internet is a place where worldwide information and communication is constantly expanding and evolving. Just as with any culture, there are customs that provide guidelines and cohesiveness to the people involved.

When I first started working on the Internet in 1990, there were fewer people interfacing with the Internet, and of course, fewer resources. Originally, there was an unspoken "agreement" among users to act and respond in a certain way while working on the Internet. If this agreement was broken, the user could expect to be "flamed" (a Net term meaning to receive an argumentative or belligerent response via e-mail) or possibly even lose Internet access depending upon how flagrantly the "rules" had been abused. The rules have not changed even though resources are greater now and the people coming online (onto the Net) are more diverse and understandably unfamiliar with nebulous "agreements."

When I first started working with e-mail and Usenet several years ago, I made simple but honest "mistakes" and was thoroughly chastised for them either in the form of teasing or irate e-mail messages. Just a few of my "simple" mistakes were:

- Typing mail messages all in upper case (Typically considered SHOUTING!)
- Sending a subscription notice for an online discussion group directly to the list instead of to the listserv handling electronic addition/deletion of members. Over one thousand people received my personal e-mail message that stated I wanted to subscribe to the discussion group. I received a great deal of irate mail on that mistake. (Subscription details are sent to the listserv. Only messages meant to be read by the entire group should go to the list.)
- Sending a personal mail message to a Usenet group that I thought would only go to the original poster of the message who lived locally. It was in the form of "let's meet for lunch and talk about this." Well, I received quite a few teasing mail messages as to whether I would "buy" for everyone reading that particular Usenet newsgroup. (Same issue involved as above: Personal messages should go to the individual's e-mail address, not the entire list.)

I began to investigate whether there were any online guides that would assist in putting an end to my "newbie" approach towards working with electronic communication. At that same time several people on the Internet began to define guidelines by which to assist users in communicating via an electronic medium, which did not allow for a great deal of personal or graphical creativity. The method for creating electronic mail messages does not allow any of the "bells and whistles" that standard word processing software packages make available in formal letter writing. The universal format for an electronic mail message is ASCII, or as it is commonly known now as, "Plain Vanilla ASCII." If a user of the Internet wanted to highlight text when sending electronic mail, they could not use underline, bold, or italics to make a specific point. Other punctuation mark standards needed to be invented to globally symbolize a point. Most of the guidelines uncovered online were specific to Usenet or e-mail, but none answered questions on the multiple resources available on the Internet. When I provided Internet training to the faculty and staff at Florida Atlantic University (FAU), I decided to help those taking my courses by creating guidelines using my own experiences and using other online documents geared towards network etiquette. I also created guidelines for the different resources available on the Internet, i.e., FTP, Telnet, LISTSERV. I wanted the document to be simple, to the point, and not overly excessive in "do's and don'ts." Moreover, because of the ever changing face of the Internet, I also wanted the document to be easy to change as Cyberspace itself changed and grew.

- Avoid **flaming** (inflammatory or antagonistic criticism), or sending insulting, abusive, or threatening remarks. A flame war is the back-and-forth volley of insulting e-mail and is considered a waste of network resources.
- Remember that e-mail is not necessarily private. Your messages can be forwarded to many people without your knowledge. In addition, most e-mail servers have programs that archive the e-mail messages that they handle. Before sending a message, read it over, make sure it is what you want to say, and double check the recipient(s).
- When replying to a news group posting, be sure to include the portion of the original message (or provide a summary of the message) that you are responding to. It is usually unnecessary to include the *entire* contents of the original message.
- Always identify yourself and keep messages as brief and to the point as possible.
- Avoid **spamming,** the practice of sending unsolicited commercial e-mail messages in bulk, or making similar postings to news groups. Spamming also refers to the unkind act of purposely overloading someone's mailbox or server with messages.
- When sending or posting to multiple mailing lists or news groups, indicate that you have done so as follows: "This message cross-posted to [names of mailing lists or news groups]."

Telnet Netiquette

Telnet also has a set of unwritten rules that need to followed when you use it. Here are a couple that you should be aware of.

- Do not stay logged in to a terminal longer than necessary. Be sure to log off properly when the Telnet session is over.
- If Help pages are provided at a Telnet site, download them to your local terminal and read them after logging off.

FTP Netiquette

File Transfer Protocol (FTP) Netiquette is important to understand; much of the problems it can cause have the effect of slowing down the network. You can find yourself in trouble if caught not paying for the software that you use or if caught copying someone else's work. Be conscious of these guidelines and considerate of your fellow Net travelers.

- Try not to download large files (larger than one megabyte) until after normal business hours. Use the time zone that applies for the FTP server that you are accessing, not your local time.
- Users are responsible for checking copyright or licensing agreements for the files that they download.
- If downloading shareware, be sure to pay the appropriate fees.

Adding Body Language to Netiquette

Messages are so sterile in black-and-white text displayed on a flat and unemotional monitor. To add some animation, and perhaps some unspoken depth to messages and conversations, emoticons or smileys found their way into online dialog. These graphics clarify the tone and intent of the sender, reducing misunderstandings. Following is a table of common emoticons, or smileys, used in online communications.

Smiley	Explanation
;-)	A smiley used as a wink to give the impression of kidding or joking.
:-(	A smiley used as a frown to show sadness or disapproval.
:-O	A smiley used to represent surprise.
8-)	A smiley used by someone who wears glasses.
:-)	Your basic smiley. This smiley is used to inflect a sarcastic or joking statement as well as add humor, happiness, or encouragement.
:-I	An indifferent smiley.
:->	A sarcastic smiley is used to make a really biting sarcastic remark.
>:->	A devil smiley is used to create the atmosphere for a really mischievous remark.

Summary

This chapter began by asking, What can you get from the Internet? Now after this chapter's discussion, the answer seems to be, Almost anything. So with this expanse of information, the marketer should give thought to what facts or opinions she needs before blindly undertaking an information search. The knowledge needs differ from the consumer and the business entity, and the marketer must recognize this before the information search is outlined and conducted. Familiarity with the strengths of the leading search engines will speed accurate information retrieval; likewise, keeping up with the technology improvements of these engines may cultivate even better specificity, accuracy, or timeliness as the search applications mature.

Netiquette refers to the generally accepted rules of behavior for using the Internet. By following Netiquette guidelines, users help to make the Internet a civil place to communicate and share ideas. Netiquette rules apply chiefly to electronic mail, mailing lists, and Usenet news groups; however, there are also Netiquette guidelines for use with Telnet and FTPs. Netiquette is not taught per se, but it can be learned. To investigate proper Netiquette more throughly, you can visit Emily Postnews, ftp.ra.msstate.edu/pub/docs/words-1/funnies. Basically, if you are a considerate person and use common sense, you will practice proper Netiquette.

Key Terms

Acceptable Use Policies (AUPs)

Building Internet communities

Deja News

Search engine popularity

Flaming

Intuitive navigation

Hit ratio

Meta search sites

Netiquette

Personalized home pages

Spamming

Virtual shopping cart

QUESTIONS AND EXERCISES

1. In this chapter, methods to retrieve marketing information on the Web was discussed. Make a list and define those electronic tools that assist in locating and narrowing information searches.

2. Through this chapter's discussion, you observed that much competitive information can be gathered by studying a rival company's Web site. Pick a retailer's Web site home page of your choice and explain the elements. What are the elements displayed? What information can you gain from the products or services listed on the site? Print out the Web pages you are commenting on and include them with your written report.

3. Probably more specific information can be obtained from a business's Web site. Pick a business-to-business Web site home page of your choice and again explain the elements. What are the elements displayed? What do you know about the businesses? What information can you gain from the products or services listed on the site? Print out the Web pages you are commenting on and include them with your written report.

4. Why does the design and content of a business-to-business Web site differ from a consumer retailer's site? What elements might appear on the business site absent from the consumer site? Write a four-paragraph memo to the Web master in your company. Print out examples to demonstrate your points.

5. What is the leading reason for consumers to use the World Wide Web when personal shopping is the objective? Give three examples of your choice and write an e-mail to your marketing manager suggesting that a Web site would be appreciated by your customers.

6. Web sites should be designed to the lowest common denominator for browser display. What does this statement mean? There are so many attention-getting applications for sound, movement, and other surprises, why should a Web site be limited in its memorability and appeal? Be prepared to discuss this concept with your Web designer.

7. Using a search resource such as Deja News, produce three posts each on the following subjects:

   a) sports injuries such as tendonitis or a shoulder separation

   b) the occult such as where practitioners buy their ingredients for spells or potions

   c) creative writing tips for writing Gothic novels

   d) blues music concerts reviews for the artist Roxy Perry, New York Blues Queen

8. If you were building Internet communities, how would you start? Most marketers build a hierarchy of constituencies such as current customers, past customers, so forth. How would you rank eight groups of special interest? Describe these groups and what content you would place on your Web site.

Bibliography

Grove, Andrew S. 1996. *Only the paranoid survive.* New York: Currency-Doubleday, 171–172.

GVU Eighth User Survey. 1997. [Online] Atlanta, GA.

In the malls, on the Web, a Christmas Crush. 1998. News Roundup. *The Wall Street Journal,* 30 November, B1.

Mossberg, Walter S. 1998. Some search engines can cut the time you waste on the Web. *The Wall Street Journal,* 12 November, B1.

Seltzer, Richard. 1995. *The way of the Web.* Excerpt from chapter 5, Building communities on the Internet [cited online, www.samizdat.com] Marlboro, MA.

CHAPTER 11

Web Page Design

"So you're thinking about launching a Web site? Before you dive in, it's a good idea to step back, take a deep breath, and try to see the big picture. If you ask most companies why they have a Web site, they'll tell you 'because the competition does.' Here's a radical thought: Forget about the Web for a minute. Think about what communications needs you and your customers have now and might have in the future. Are you able to fulfill them using more traditional technology, be it phone, fax, or e-mail? If you can, you just saved yourself a lot of time, trouble, and expense because you don't need a Web site. If, however, you can identify some room for improvement, then perhaps establishing a presence on the World Wide Web is the right move."

(Sweetman 1997)

LEARNING OBJECTIVES

- To establish the groundwork for developing Web-based communications
- To provide the knowledge necessary for the marketing student to create a business or personal Web site
- To define what elements should be included on every Web page

Introduction

At this point, this book has discussed the concepts and processes that the marketer should employ to develop diligent, thorough, and consistent online marketing programs for products and services. The promotional element has been stressed as a potentially powerful awareness and information tool, which marketers are learning by trial and error. Many of the errors are resulting from misused or ill-designed Web sites and pages. In this chapter, the issue of presenting appealingly and efficiently the products' benefits and satisfaction will be delved into. To create these wonderful sights and sounds of the World Wide Web, the marketer or graphic designer must learn the alphabet and language of the Web, Hypertext Markup Language or HTML. HTML is the backbone of interactivity, whisking viewers from one site to another, one graphic to another, and one document to another. HTML is presented in up to 16 million colors, for display on all sizes of color monitors, is used to create fascinating video games and amusing greeting cards and is used to enable the educational sites to help children learn, to touch up on just of few of its functions

It is also the language of other Web instruments for gathering information with surveys and order and search forms. HTML forms assist the marketer in collecting and organizing data that set the performance parameters for marketing contact, customer response, and transaction requests. By designing effective Web sites and pages, electronic marketing resources can be fully utilized in the marketing plan, ensuring speed, attractiveness, accuracy, and convenience for the consumer.

Web Site Design: Both Simple and Complex

Just what is a Web site and what is the relationship to the individual Web pages? A Web site is a file of information residing on a server connected by an address to the World Wide Web, and a Web site may include text, photographs, illustrations, music, or other computer programs. On the Web site are smaller files called Web pages that are accessed by clicking on hyperlinks, usually colored text or icons of instructions directing the computer to other pages on the Web site or to other sites on the World Wide Web. As you know, the address is called a URL, and every URL is unique to one certain site. If the consumer, therefore, knows the URL address of the Web site, he can access information found on individual Web pages that collectively make up the Web site. (Microsoft Corporation)

Designing a Web site can be both a complex and rewarding activity. In light of this, there are many issues that need to be planned and well thought out before actually designing a Web site. The planning stage is often more important than learning how to use the programming language required to create Web pages. The marketer must be prepared to answer questions such as: What is the purpose of the Web site? Is it a primary or supporting vehicle? Should it provide exposure, house publicity articles, or support retailers or field sales representatives? Who will be reading your pages? Should the graphics be fast-paced for a younger market or more conservatively paced for a middle-aged viewer? Should you include sound or motion, or will that be a distraction to your market? What types of computers will the typical user be using? What browser software will they have access to and how fast are their connections to the Internet? What search engines does your market prefer? Will they be viewing your site with a color or black-and-white monitor, and, generally, what size of monitor will they be using? Answering all of these questions before you begin designing your Web site will help you determine exactly how your site should look and operate.

Once these types of questions have been answered, or at least been answered with an educated guess, a design should be created for a working plan. This plan should be configured with the limitations and restrictions of the Web in mind. It is also important to understand how Web pages are created and what is actually possible. This chapter will begin by providing some parameters and suggestions for good Web-site design. Once you have set the objectives for the page, a concept for the appearance of a good site should begin to form in your mind. This chapter will lead you into actually learning the code behind Web pages. Web pages are created with a very simple, text-based scripting language called Hypertext Markup Language (HTML). You may ask, Why would I need to learn the code when there are so many editors available to do the coding for me?

Much like the argument of elementary school children concerning why they should learn math when calculators are available, learning the code is just as important in designing a Web page as is understanding the fundamental concepts of addition, subtraction, division, and multiplication. While calculators are much like HTML editors, it is easier to use the editor. These feelings are somewhat justified; there are many good editors available with more appearing every day. Like inputting numbers in an expensive calculator, however, even the best editor can make mistakes or inhibit your creativity and ideas concerning your Web site. If you are familiar with the HTML code, you may be able to get the exact effect you are looking for in a much shorter amount of time. Learning HTML can also allow you the freedom to create Web pages with very limited resources. All you need is a computer and a basic text editor such as Notepad or SimpleText and you are on your way to great Web pages.

Issues of Web Site Design

There are basically three stages to the design of a Web site: the analysis phase, the design phase, and the building phase. Exhibit 11.1 depicts the process of putting your Web site together. Each stage has an important role in developing a useful site, which your audience will want to explore and revisit. The next few sections of this chapter will expound on the three phases and walk you through the planning stages of your first Web site design.

Analysis Phase

The analysis phase is important in the development process because it provides the designer with the proper background in setting the site up correctly for the audience, without forgetting the purpose of the site itself. The setting of objectives and goals gives direction to the remaining portions of the process. First, you must identify the audience for which the site is being designed. Who are you trying to reach? Will it be a site for children or parents? Is the site meant to appeal to the single, working, middle-aged group, or the rambunctious, impatient teenager? What is the educational level—high, medium, or low? Male or female? The research the marketer performed in the situation analysis of the marketing process should provide sufficient direction to answer these questions. As with the marketing process, a Web site cannot be designed to appeal to all markets. By the findings of the segmentation analysis, markets that hold the greatest potential for success should be identified.

In the next aspect of the analysis phase, the types of technology this audience is most likely to have should be determined. Is the market going to have access to fast connections, or will they be dialing into a slow modem pool? Will the audience be familiar with the workings of the Web, or will they need assistance in navigating around sights with interfaces, such as numerous help screens or tips? Will specific browsers be used by the audience, or should more than one option be offered to them? A good way to approach this task is to create a survey for the intended audience on the Web and to ask them what types of technology (modem speed, size of hard drive, monitor size, and so forth) they are using. (The creation and usage of surveys will be discussed further in

EXHIBIT 11.1

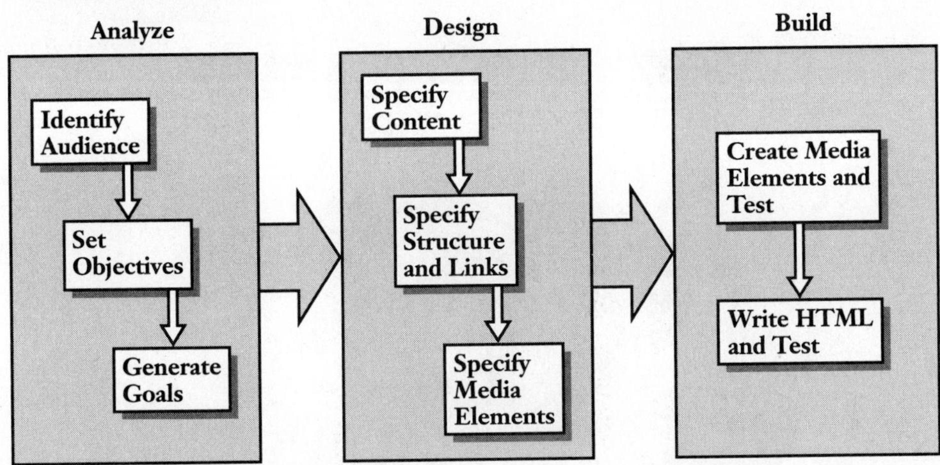

This flowchart depicts the general planning strategy of creating a Web site for any purpose. Keep in mind this is just a guideline and your Web site may require additional stages of planning.

Chapter 12.) After answering questions like these, you should be able to settle on the media elements that can or should be included in the Web site. There should also be some understanding of how to add navigation and what type of structure you might want to use in your site.

Now that you have some understanding of your audience and equipment, you should determine what you want to accomplish with your Web site. Do you want to provide information? Do you want to collect information? Do you want to communicate with your audience in other ways, such as issuing press releases for online wires or distribute e-mail newsletters to your customers? What marketing purpose is this Web site going to serve? The answer to questions such as these should provide the basis for objectives and goals for the site. Once again, a survey of your intended audience may be the best way in determining how to serve this audience and interact with them using your Web site. Another possible way to create a successful Web site that serves and interacts with your audience is to monitor the sites of close competitors. What is their strategy and how did they accomplish their aims? How are you going to accomplish these objectives and goals? The design phase now begins to play a role in the Web site strategy.

The Actions of the Design Phase

By now you should know your audience and have some Web site direction in mind. Once you have reached this point, you should collect any textual information that you will need to include in your site. On paper, make an outline of the topics that you might like to include and determine what information you need to gather and the order in which it is to be presented. Decide what items or information are most important to your market and present that information first or display it prominently. If you are including a catalog, you need product numbers, prices, and ordering information. If you want to include a survey, you will need to write the questions (but not the

EXHIBIT 11.2 AT&T's Universal Card Services

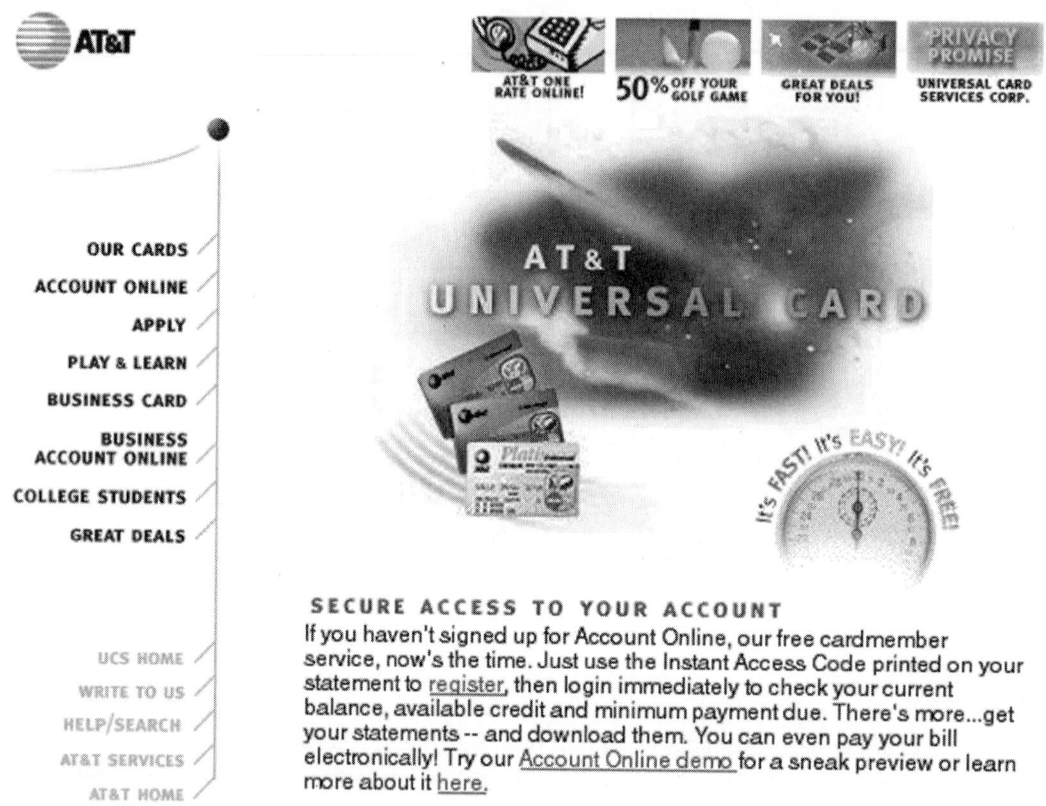

AT&T's Web site (www.att.com/ucs) shows a good example of how to use navigation to assist users in viewing what they want to see on their Web site.

answers). You might want to provide product information; this information must be coherently written and ready to transfer to your Web site.

The next aspect of the design is planning your intended structure of the Web site. Think efficiency. A good rule of thumb is to not require the user to click too many times in order to obtain desired information. Reward the user's work (clicking, navigating, filling in a form) with a result or answer each time. This requires either a fairly flat structure, rather than a deep site requiring many clicks or selections, or a clear system of navigation. Decide if you want to keep your site simple with only a few textual links to important information or if you would like to create a graphical interface that uses buttons and icons to navigate throughout. Flow is a critical concept in Web design. The flow of your Web site will be crucial in keeping your audience interested and connected to your site. The concept of flow and rhythm will be discussed in further detail later this chapter.

A solid design tip is to limit graphical elements on the opening Web page to one screen. The marketing information should be contained on this one page with hyperlinks; this tactic is called "designing above the fold." The concept comes from newspaper days when advertisers requested their ads run above the fold, the crease that divides the top and bottom of the newspaper. Advertisers believed that people quickly scanned the top of each page only, and readership of their ads was better with this placement. Using a single screen, the designer can assist the viewer by more convenient placement of elements without having to scroll the screen down or sideways.

Plan carefully and remember that extra media elements such as graphics, movies, sounds, and animations will make your site larger, more unwieldy, and harder for someone with a slow connection to use. Think of two empty swimming pools of similar size. One is filling with water via a one-inch garden hose; the other is filling with a six-inch PVC pipe. Speed and modem connections can be likened to this example. The bigger (more capacity), the faster the site will load. Choose graphics, sounds, and motions only if they are appropriate to your market and make the site stronger. A mature marketer will know when these embellishments are needed. In other words, choose wisely among these frills. Before implementing any decision regarding the design of your Web page, it may be useful for you to draw a flowchart or a map of your site. This preplanning layout will give you a structure to follow when creating your pages and will allow you to see if you have forgotten anything. Look at the Avon, Kraft Foods, Saturn, and Nabisco Web pages on the following pages for good sites and good site maps that incorporate successful design techniques. Each site map is available to the user as a navigational tool as well as an overall picture of each site's products.

Develop the Look and Feel (Building Phase)

When you begin to develop the actual appearance and feel of your site, there are many things that you need to consider. What skill do you need the consumer to learn or possess in order to navigate your site? How will your site grab the attention of the consumer? How will your site involve the consumer in order to keep her interest? Finally, how will your site intrigue the consumer to see, do, or buy what your site is offering? How does your site encourage interaction? There are many names for this process, but one that describes it quite well is **Flow.** Flow is a function of control, content, and motivational characteristics. As described by Thomas Novak and Donna Hoffman of Vanderbilt University, "[F]low is the holistic sensation that people feel when they act with total involvement." (1994) The consumer is hooked and wants to continue investigating the site that has caught his attention. The consumer may be actively learning or playing or may just be fascinated, but he needs to be involved. Therefore, how do you get this intense, rhythmic involvement from a Web site? Interactivity is the key. Intimacy with your consumer grows through interactivity. The more you know about your customer, the better you can program the flow interaction and satisfaction.

First, you must attract the consumers attention by creating a site that is easy to use, fun, and fast. It should be personalized, comprehensive, highly visual, and easy to navigate. Keeping your site consistent and aesthetically pleasing will help the consumer navigate easier and will keep her logged on to your site longer. The site should control the consumer by focusing her attention, curiosity, and intrinsic interest on your product and the benefits she will derive, all while making her feel she is in control. To grab the consumer's attention, you can use media elements such as graphics (colorful pictures or photographs that can be related to), motion (a video or animation), and sound (music, singing, even harsh or discordant sounds). You can also catch the consumer's attention with content that is well structured and enticing or by value-added offers. Flowerlinks's (www.flowerlink.com) Reminders, Avon's (www.avon.com) Tips and Ideas, and Kraft's (www.kraftfoods.com) Recipes by E-Mail are all examples of how these companies utilized value-added offers to entice the consumers. Once you have the consumer's attention, it is imperative that you keep this attention by involving the user in your site. Your consumers' attention may next be piqued when they find a Web site with information of personal interest that they can delve into and interact with. After the initial attention grabber, you can stimulate this curiosity or interest using proper navigation and flow control. As an example of interactivity, the

click here for ANEW Day Force Vertical Lifting Lotion

- **Shop Online:** Buy now! The easiest online shopping is at your fingertips- just point and click for select Avon products! Join the A-List for e-mail updates on new products, specials and sweepstakes. We also offer direct mail shopping, order the Beauty and Fashion by Mail catalog today.

- **All About Avon:** There's more to us than meets the eye! Learn about how Avon is Celebrating Women with special programs like Avon's Breast Cancer Awareness Crusade, Avon Running and The Avon Women of Enterprise Awards (Click Here for 1999 Application). Are you interested in learning about becoming a Representative, click here for your Path to Opportunity. Are you interested in pursuing a career at Avon? We want to hear from you at AvonCareers. Interested in investing? Visit Investor Relations, or sift through the Newsroom.

Avon's site (www.avon.com) is quick loading yet very visually effective. Their good navigation control, consistency, interactivity, and search capabilities make the site easy to use. The value-added customer service areas provide consumers a gift reminder, a catalog request, an online catalog, and tips and ideas.

curiosity-seeker could log onto the new Volkswagen Beetle's Web site to experiment with exterior and interior colors and packages to custom design the Beetle of his choice. Many automobile sites feature this type of involvement as well as pricing and financing details; the consumer can become well educated in the area of car pricing by obtaining the manufacturer's suggested retail price off of the Web for the car of his dreams.

Flow involves the merging of actions and awareness with concentration so intense there is little attention left over to consider anything else. Proper flow design will provide the consumer with a sense that she is controlling her interactions on the Web site. A Web site should allow the consumer to focus her attention on the interactions while finding the site mentally stimulating. When designed properly, irrelevant thoughts and perceptions are filtered out and the consumer's attention is focused entirely on interacting with your Web site. Now, they are in the right frame of mind. This interaction is a form of relevant stimulus that allows the consumer to learn at a proper speed

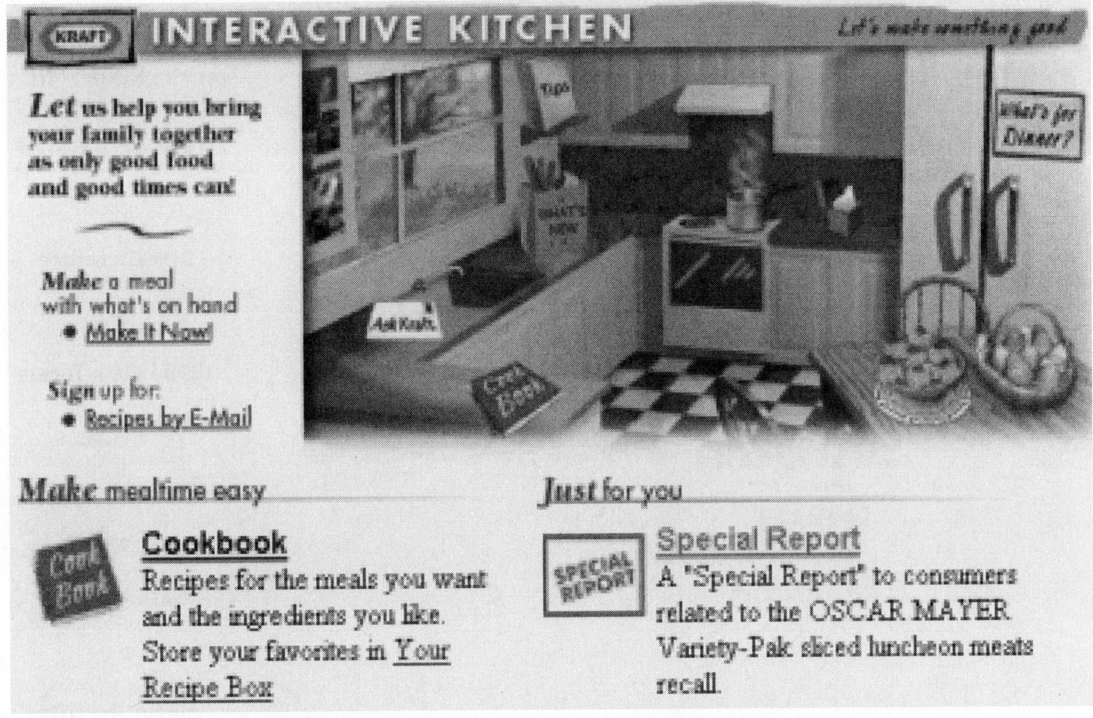

The Kraft Foods' site (www.kraftfoods.com) has an interesting interactive kitchen design. There are plenty of value-added items. The site is very visual and has good graphic appeal, yet it loads fairly quickly. The "Ask Kraft" area and the "Simple-Meal Planner" bring consumers back to the site over and over. You can also become a regular Kraft product user with the Kraft recipes by e-mail feature.

for your product, ensuring the consumer feels he is getting the information he wants. It engages consumers in the activity of learning about your products, making them actively participate rather than be passive viewers. Flow design at its best should be a process of seeing a selection, clicking a selection, seeing another selection, clicking another selection, with the process repeated over and over with no hesitations. The viewer doesn't notice the time speed by. Total concentration. Hyperlinks are the main tools that marketers use to create this interactivity on a Web site. The culmination, the flow process using interactivity, is a sense of gratification—the user accomplished his Web objective.

Hyperlinks, either in the form of navigational buttons, tool bars, or textual links, make the process of interacting with a Web site easy. Your Web site should use this rhythm to your advantage. It should give the consumer control but not too much control. Determine what level of interactivity is appropriate for your prospect and your product. Then guide the consumer through your content in the direction you want them to go. Remember, there are no time limits to customer interaction. The idea is to keep them on your site, doing what you want them to do. As is noted earlier, the following Web sites have successfully utilized the concepts of proper Web page design. As you look at each, good characteristics you may want to adopt in your designs will be pointed out for each Web page.

Creating HTML Documents: The Language of the Web

Hypertext Markup Language (HTML) is the scripting language in which documents seen on the Web are written. It is a simple text-based language that can be read by

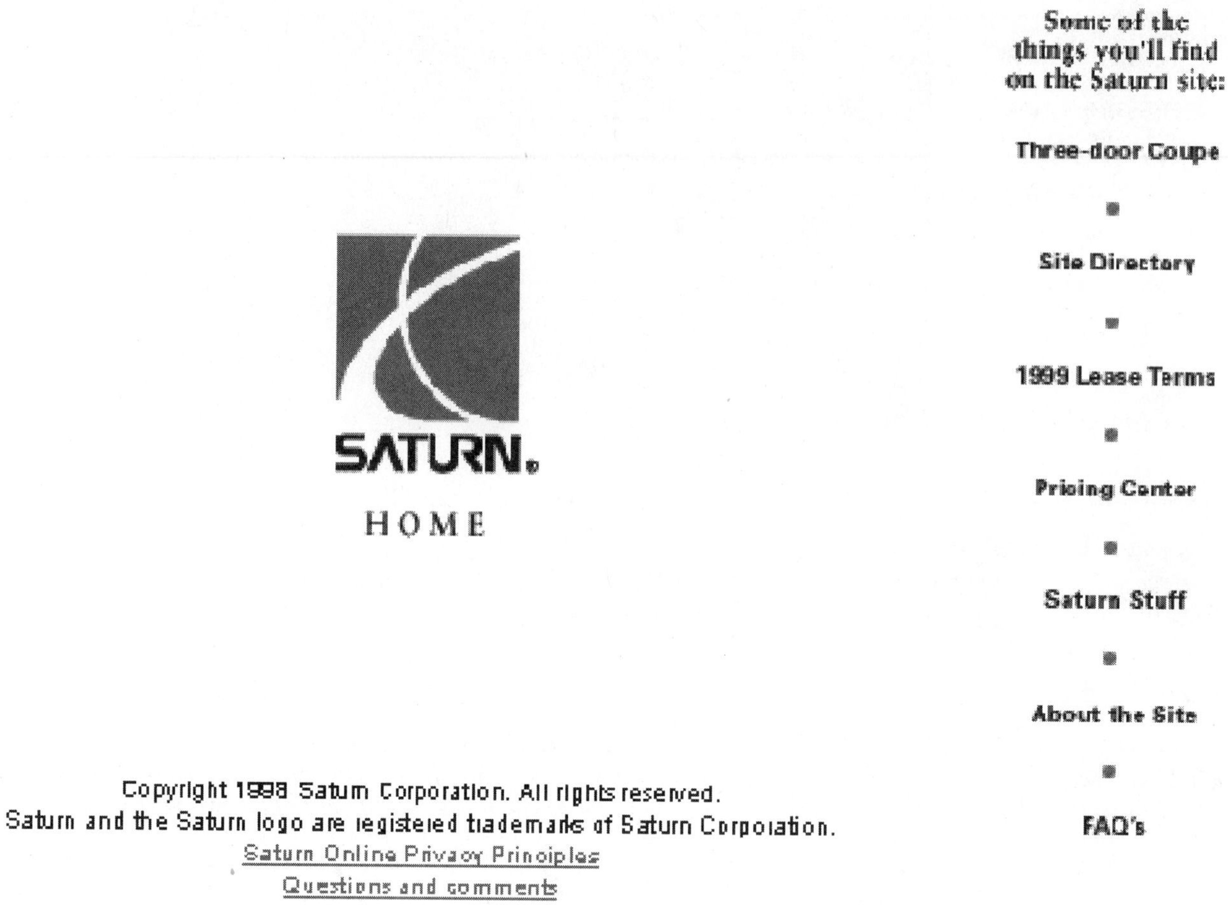

Some of the things you'll find on the Saturn site:

Three-door Coupe

Site Directory

1999 Lease Terms

Pricing Center

Saturn Stuff

About the Site

FAQ's

SATURN.

HOME

Saturn Online Privacy Principles

Questions and comments

Saturn (www.saturn.com) has a very clean look with an interest-grabbing animation on their Web site. A consumer can interact with the site using the interactive pricing center. Saturn's site will be discussed in more detail when the discussion delves into forms and surveys in chapter 13.

both machine and human. Web documents contain content that is then interpreted by Web browsers such as Netscape Navigator (www.netscape.com) and Internet Explorer (www.microsoft.com). The content consists of codes called **tags** or elements with attributes that tell the computer what to show on the screen. This section discusses HTML codes in order to lay a foundation for understanding how designing a Web page is restricted to the limitation of the current HTML standard codes and the browsers of the marketer's audience. However, as you learned in Chapter 5, there are now many HTML editors available to make the job of creating a Web page much easier. HTML editors provide a familiar document interface with menu options and button bars inserting HTML tags at your command. They are useful tools for creating HTML documents with little or no knowledge of HTML tags or elements. There are many places on the Web where you can download full or trial versions of these programs to assist you in developing a Web presence, such as at the TUCOWS software center site, www.tucows.com.

In addition to full HTML editing programs, many word processors and other software programs now have the ability to Save As HTML. This allows for the creation of documents in a familiar environment, such as Microsoft Word or Corel WordPerfect, and then the document conversion to HTML for use on the Web. Existing documents can also be converted, saving time and money in the development of your Web presence. The only problem with converting existing paper-based docu-

Nabisco's Web site (www.nabisco.com) is a bit slow loading but worth the wait. It has an interactive image map that lets the consumer choose places to go. The location at which you arrive is shown in the task bar at the bottom of the window as you run your pointer over a hot spot. This is an interesting way to create navigation. Nabisco also uses frames and a navigation bar in this site, providing more options for the consumer and keeping the look consistent. The added value items such as recipe collections, the health club, collectibles, screen savers, and games will bring many repeat visits. Try a trip uptown and downtown to see just how much Nabisco has created for the consumer to do at this site.

ments to Web-based documents is that Web documents should be designed for the screen, not for paper. On that note, it is time for a discussion of good and bad Web page designs.

HTML Standards and Practices

When creating HTML pages, it is important to note that there are standards and practices that are generally accepted in the world of HTML. If these standards and practices are followed, the Web pages will work with most of the current Web browsers. The look and feel of the pages will of course depend on your tastes and the needs of your company. Here are just a few suggestions to make your pages look and run better.

Good and Bad HTML

Good HTML follows the current version of HTML, as specified in the HTML DTD (Document Type Definition). A current version of this document can be found at http://nyst.uio.no/nyst/kurs/Webprod/styles.html. The code or HTML used in a Web page should be clean and should follow these standards to the best of the author's abilities. In order to get off on the right foot, a Web page should begin with the ⟨HTML⟩ tag. This tag is part of what is called an HTML container, meaning it contains information between two tags. The ending or matching tag is ⟨/HTML⟩ and must be present at the end of the document in order to close the document. The slash (/) preceding the tag ⟨HTML⟩ is to close most elements. Remember when designing for the Web, your audience is most likely looking at your pages from a computer and modem at their home or through a connection at their office. These connections tend to be slow, and using too many fancy graphics, sounds, animations, and movies can cause a real bottleneck. Choose wisely and only use what is necessary to convey your ideas and generate the emotions you are looking for.

Bad HTML is considered to be documents that ignore these standard practices. Usually this means nonstandard browser specific extensions, loading up on headers, poor choices of backgrounds, and using large graphic files. Following these suggestions will make your pages compatible with the widest range of Web browsers.

What Are Tags and How Are They Structured?

When reading about the creation of Web pages on the Internet, you will often run into terms that you may not understand. Things like tags, elements, and URLs may tend to confuse you. Do not worry; these are just words used to describe the parts of code used in HTML. Tags are the instructions that the computer is looking for in order to decipher what the code is telling it. An example is the ⟨HTML⟩ tag that was discussed earlier. There are different types of tags or elements, but they all have one of two basic structures. They can either be container tags or tags that stand on their own. Container tags need an ending tag to inform the computer to turn off what was turned on. A good example of this would be a tag to make text boldfaced (⟨B⟩). If you only wanted a few words boldfaced for emphasis, you would need to turn off the boldfaced tag (⟨/B⟩) when you were ready to type regular text again. Therefore, the text you want to have boldfaced is contained within the two parts of the container tag. Other tags, such as one to create a line feed or line break (⟨BR⟩), would not need an ending because the computer needs only one command, go to the next line.

What Should Be Included on Every Web Page?

Now that you are getting the idea of how things work, you need to be aware of what should be included in every Web page. The following items need to be included on every Web page: a head section, a page title, and a signature or contact information. These are all important tags with important attributes that will need to be included so your pages will be found by consumers on the Internet. The most important of these is the signature, which allows a user to contact you. Another important piece of the puzzle comes from our programmer friends. All good programmers comment their codes (i.e., ⟨!—Last revised by SJS on 1-3-99—⟩, which tells another programmer that Shauna Schullo made changes to the document on 1-3-99). This will allow you and others to update the code easier because you can leave yourself notes and hints to work with in a few months when you may have forgotten what you had in mind. A comment that you do not want the browser to show but that you would like to have in the source code for clarification can be placed between these codes ⟨!—*text goes here*—⟩. The head section will be discussed in greater detail in the next section, but for now, the discussion will progress towards giving your page a title.

The title tag names your document by identifying a string of text, which is the name or title of your document. This title is the universal resource locator that is the address

EXHIBIT 11.3

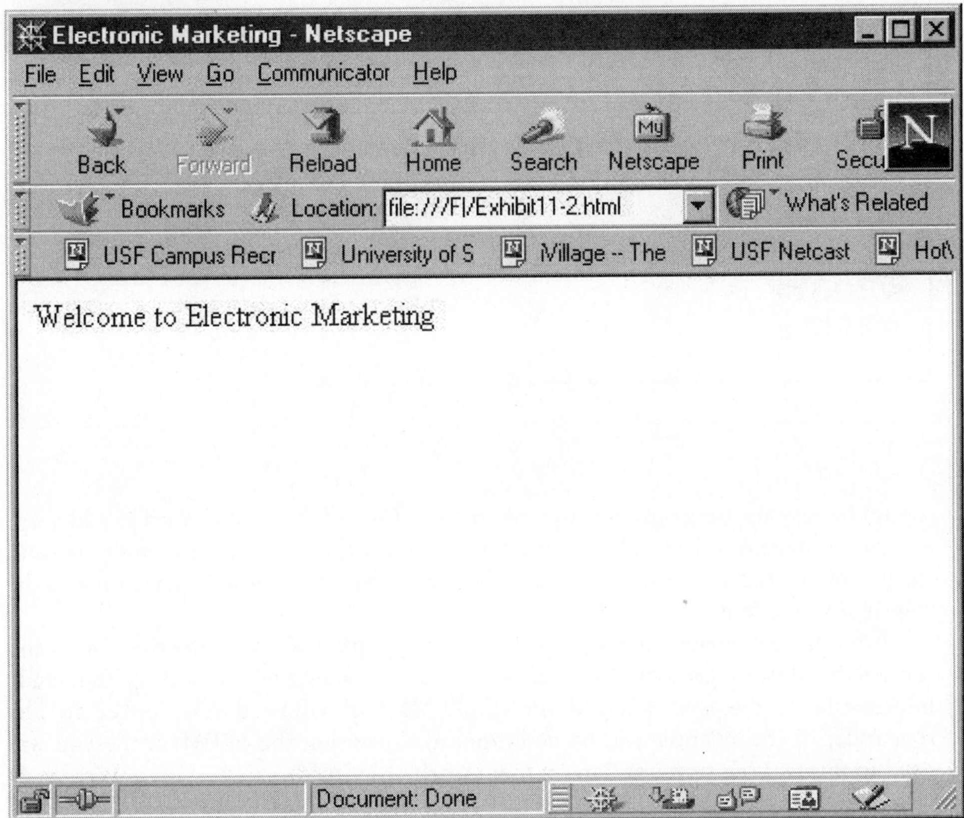

Example of the most basic of Web pages. The code you see in the box is all that it took to get this information in a form a Web browser could interpret. However, the title is only seen in the bar at the top of the window, so it is important to put words and images in the body to act as titles and headings on a Web page.

of your page on the Web. The title must start with ⟨TITLE⟩ and end with ⟨/TITLE⟩; therefore, it is a container tag. This tag is interpreted differently by different platform browsers. Usually it is only seen in the title (usually the dark blue bar) at the top of the window, so keep it brief. Use meaningful titles that will be easily discernable by your user; this title will be what your user sees in her bookmark list if she saves your page URL. Concise, memorable titles serve three major purposes:

- Titles are used by applications such as searches and indexes to identify your pages.
- Titles act as indicators of what to expect.
- Titles are at the top of the HTML document giving you an easy visual clue to identify the source files quickly when you need to make changes or corrections.

A signature, usually at the end of the document but before the ⟨/HTML⟩ tag, can be handled in many different ways. Your Web page can list the contact information for your company, the contact information for the Web master, and the contact information for the page author. Keep in mind, though, that whatever information is supplied

EXHIBIT 11.4 EXAMPLE OF MINIMAL WEB PAGE CODE

```
<HTML>
<HEAD>
<TITLE>Electronic Marketing</TITLE>
</HEAD>
<BODY>
Welcome to Electonic Marketing
</BODY>
</HTML>
```

should be easy for the consumer to find and use. One of the easiest ways to add a signature to a page is to have a hyperlink that will allow the consumer to send e-mails to the person in your organization responsible for answering questions pertaining to the page and its content.

From the following basic Web page example, you can see how the title works and can see that it is not present in the actual page the consumer will be seeing. To include information on the page, some additional HTML tags will need to be looked at. The remainder of this chapter will be dedicated to explaining the HTML code you will need to format your pages and make them work properly.

The 〈HEAD〉 Section: Making It Searchable

Most good HTML documents contain a header that provides additional information to the browser. The Head section defines the function of the document and adds a quick reference for Web browsers. Although information contained in the Head section is not visible to the consumer looking at your page, it supplies the document title and establishes a relationship between HTML documents and directories. It can also signal Web browsers to index the document since these are the words for which the browser searches. This section is also called the meta tag area of the page. The head section can be complicated, but it is an important piece in making sure your Web page is retrievable. The head element encloses the head section. It is a container and, therefore, requires two tags: one at the beginning (〈HEAD〉) and one at the end (〈/HEAD〉).

There are many related tags that can be placed between the two head tags that warrant some discussion. These are listed in the table below, but for the purposes of this brief tutorial, only those that will be immediately useful will be described. (Explanations of the others can be found on the Web in many places.) One important tag that has already been mentioned is the Title tag. Beside the search capability, this tag allows you to name your page and provides a name for the consumer to see in a bookmark list or a search list. The 〈META〉 tag contains information about the document, such as keywords, expiration date, author, page generation software used, and many other document-specific items. It also supports the refresh option that allows a document to load after a specific delay. The meta tag is important when you want your document to be found in a search of certain keywords, such as electronic marketing; the name of your company; or the product that you sell.

The HEAD Tag

Example	⟨HEAD⟩ ⟨TITLE⟩Electronic Marketing⟨/TITLE⟩ ⟨META NAME="Keywords" CONTENT="Marketing, Consumers, Electronic Commerce"⟩ ⟨/HEAD⟩
Function	Encloses the tags that comprise the Head section
Attributes	None
Related Tags	⟨TITLE⟩—Used to place a title in the top bar of the window ⟨BASE⟩—Used as a base reference for all the pages ⟨LINK⟩—Defines the relationship between two files within a Web site ⟨IS INDEX⟩—Used to provide a single line input field to collect query information ⟨META⟩—Important for adding additional information for searching and indexing ⟨SCRIPT⟩—Used when scripting languages, such as JavaScript and VB script, are used ⟨STYLE⟩—Used with cascading style sheets to provide consistent style

The ⟨BODY⟩ Section: Holding It All Together

The body of the HTML document contains the majority of your information. It is here that you will want to do the most formatting and, therefore, will need to know something about HTML formatting tags. This section will discuss how to start the body and how to use tags to format the text within the body.

The BODY Tag

Example	⟨BODY BGCOLOR="white" TEXT="#ff0088" LINK="#DD0FF00" VLINK="#00FF9A"⟩ . . . All document content and HTML code will go here . . . ⟨/BODY⟩
Function	Contains all content and tags that comprise the document body
Attributes	ALINK—Used to set active link color BACKGROUND—Can be set equal to the URL for an image to be used as a background for the Web page BGCOLOR—Used to set background color LINK—Used to set link color TEXT—Used to set text color VLINK—Used to set visited link color
Related Tags	More than can be listed here. All the remaining tags that will be discussed are related to the body tag.

The body tags form a container that encloses the content of your HTML document. Everything between these two tags is interpreted as HTML formatting or object codes. The body tag should follow your ending heading tag and close before your ending HTML tag. The above example of basic code demonstrates that creating a Web page is really not as hard as you may have first thought. Even though a basic Web page is easy to construct, you will want to expand on this process to create a site that is more visually appealing.

Formatting the Page: Making It Look Good

HTML provides many tags that can be used to format text to allow for uniqueness and creativity in your textual design. Text level formatting can occur in two ways: Using HTML, you can format the actual font properties, or you can describe how the text is being used. These are called physical styles and logical styles, respectively. Physical styles will include font-specific tags, such as font, bold, italic, and underline. Logical styles will include phrase-specific tags, such as address, code, definition, and emphasis. Additional formatting of text can be accomplished in a block-level format. This would include tags such as blockquote, break, center, and headings. To get even more fancy in your text layout, you could use formatting styles for lists and tables, but that will be discussed a little later. For now, the discussion will center around how to use some of the tags previously discussed to format the text on your pages.

The FONT Tag

Example	⟨FONT SIZE=5 COLOR="navy" FACE="Arial, Helvetica, Times"⟩Text goes here . . . ⟨/FONT⟩
Function	Sets the size, color, and typeface properties for the text. BASEFONT can also be used to set the font properties for the entire document. FONT would then be used to change these properties for certain portions of the text and would need to be a container tag.
Attributes	SIZE—Used to specify the size of the font
	COLOR—Used to specify the color of the font if different from the page default
	FACE—Used to specify a font face
Related Tags	⟨BASEFONT⟩—Used to set the base font for a page

The BOLD Tag

Example	⟨B⟩Text goes here . . . ⟨/B⟩
Function	Contains text to be made boldfaced
Attributes	None
Other Similar Tags	⟨I⟩—italic
	⟨U⟩—underline
	⟨TT⟩—Fixed-width font, usually courier or a typewritten-like font
	⟨SUB⟩—subscript
	⟨SUP⟩—superscript
	⟨SMALL⟩—smaller than the default size
	⟨BIG⟩—bigger than the default size
	⟨STRIKE⟩—strike through

When using phrase formatting tags, how the browser will display the text is dependent on the browser because you are only giving it a description of what type of text you are intending. The text will still be set off from regular text, but it may look a bit different on different browsers. Therefore, if you are trying to get a certain effect, you will need to test your pages on multiple browsers; this is a good way to double check the functionality of your Web site anyway. Some useful logical style tags are discussed below.

The ADDRESS Tag

Example	⟨ADDRESS⟩shauna@usf.edu⟨/ADDRESS⟩
Function	Contains either a postal or electronic mailing address. Text that is marked with this tag is usually seen in italics.
Attributes	None
Other Similar Tags	⟨ACRONYM⟩ ⟨CITE⟩ ⟨CODE⟩ ⟨DEL⟩ ⟨DFN⟩ ⟨EM⟩ ⟨INS⟩ ⟨KBD⟩ ⟨Q⟩ ⟨SAMP⟩ ⟨STRONG⟩ ⟨VAR⟩

Using HTML, it can sometimes be difficult to get the look you desire. HTML does not recognize extra spaces and tabs. For those who are accustomed to creating paper-based media, this can pose quite a problem. One solution to this is using the block-level formatting tags. Following are some examples of what can be done.

The blockquote container (⟨BLOCKQUOTE⟩ and ⟨/BLOCKQUOTE⟩) is used to provide a uniform indent for text. It is often used for citations or quotes or used to set off text. Blockquote is a container that requires an ending tag. It can contain other HTML codes and does not retain line feeds.

The BLOCK QUOTE Tag

Example	⟨BLOCKQUOTE⟩Text goes here . . . ⟨/BLOCKQUOTE⟩
Function	Contains quoted text that is to be displayed indented from the regular body. Can also be used when you merely want to indent a paragraph in your document.
Attributes	CITE
Related Tags	⟨Q⟩

As you have seen, HTML uses normal text. However, it does not recognize extra spaces and carriage returns as line breaks. Therefore, special tags are needed to create paragraphs and add vertical spaces. The paragraph tag ⟨P⟩ is used to separate text for easy reading. Although this tag is technically a container tag, it does not require an ending tag (⟨/P⟩). You can use other tags within the paragraph tag. The paragraph tag will allow text to wrap so that it will fit into the browser's window. This means when the user adjusts the width of the window, the text will also adjust.

The PARAGRAPH Tag

Example	⟨P ALIGN="CENTER"⟩Text goes here⟨/P⟩
Function	Denotes a paragraph. The paragraph tag adds one extra line of vertical space after the original line feed. Most browsers ignore the use of multiple paragraph tags to increase the amount of vertical space in a document.
Attributes	ALIGN
Related Tags	⟨BR⟩, ⟨HR⟩

If you specifically want to break the text at a certain point, you must use the forced line break tag ⟨BR⟩. This signals the browser to enter a line feed creating a single spaced output unlike the paragraph tag, which puts a blank line after the text. The ⟨HR⟩ tag will use a horizontal line to separate paragraphs of text. This tag places a fixed-weight, shaded line across the width of the area being viewed. It does not require an ending tag, and it places a paragraph break before and after the line.

The BREAK Tag

Example	⟨BR CLEAR="LEFT"⟩
Function	Inserts a break in the document. It is similar to a line break or carriage return in a word processor. Carriage returns are not recognized as line breaks on the screen in HTML unless the break tag is used. The break tag adds additional vertical space after the break.

Heading tags allow you to format the text and add extra vertical spacing in one tag. This is useful when creating a leveled structure in your page similar to an outline or a chapter structure. Headings are container tags and require endings. If you do not remember to end your heading tag, it will not take you long to figure out what you did wrong.

The HEADING Tag

Example	⟨H1 ALIGN="CENTER"⟩Text goes here . . . ⟨/H1⟩
Function	Establishes a hierarchy of document heading levels. Level 1 has the largest font size, while level 6 has the smallest font size. All headings are in bold and have a little extra line spacing above and below them.
Attributes	ALIGN
Related Tags	None

Preformatted text tags contain information that already looks like you want it to. There is no need for paragraph or line break tags. The tag ⟨PRE⟩ requires a closing

⟨/PRE⟩ tag because it is a container. Other tags can be used within this container, but it is not considered good HTML to use them extensively.

The PREFORMATTED Tag

Example	⟨PRE WIDTH="43⟩		
	Name	Address	Phone
	Kathy	kathy@usf.edu	974-1234
	Mark	mark@GTE.com	982-9955
	⟨/PRE⟩		
Function	Denotes text to be treated as preformatted. Browsers display performatted text in a fixed width font that are browser and machine dependent. White space characters, such as spaces, tabs, and carriage returns, are not ignored. This makes preformatted text a useable option for presenting tables of information. However, the text will not be as appealing as it would be if a real HTML table were to be used.		
Attributes	WIDTH		
Related Tags	None		

Now you have the basics to begin your Web site. From here, elements that will add style and usefulness will be introduced. This will allow you to use bullets and tables to highlight your important points, add links to provide navigation through your site, and most importantly, add graphical elements for visual appeal.

Lists are another form of block-level formatting that can be very useful when organizing and presenting information through HTML. This section will discuss what types of lists are available and how to use them. HTML tags provide different types of lists for different types of information. Here are a few that will be looked at.

numbered lists

bulleted lists

definition lists

Both the numbered and the bulleted lists use the ⟨LI⟩ tag to mark the individual items in the list. This tag must precede each item in the list. By using the START attribute with a numbered list, you can set the starting value of the numbering sequence from the default value of 1 to any other value you choose. You can modify the numbering scheme in a numbered list or the bullet character in the bulleted list by setting TYPE to one of the different list types available. These types are listed below.

The LIST ITEM Tag

Example	⟨LI⟩First Item⟨/LI⟩	
	⟨LI⟩Second Item⟨/LI⟩	
Function	Denotes items in a list	
Attributes	**START**	**TYPE**
	1	Arabic numerals
	A	Uppercase alphabet
	a	Lowercase alphabet
	I	Uppercase Roman numerals

continued

The LIST ITEM Tag *(continued)*

Attributes	START	TYPE
	i	Lowercase Roman numerals
	Disc	Solid circular bullet
	Square	Solid square bullet
	Circle	Open circular bullet
Related Tags	⟨OL⟩	
	⟨UL⟩	

EXHIBIT 11.5 EXAMPLE RESULT FOR AN ORDERED LIST ON A WEB PAGE

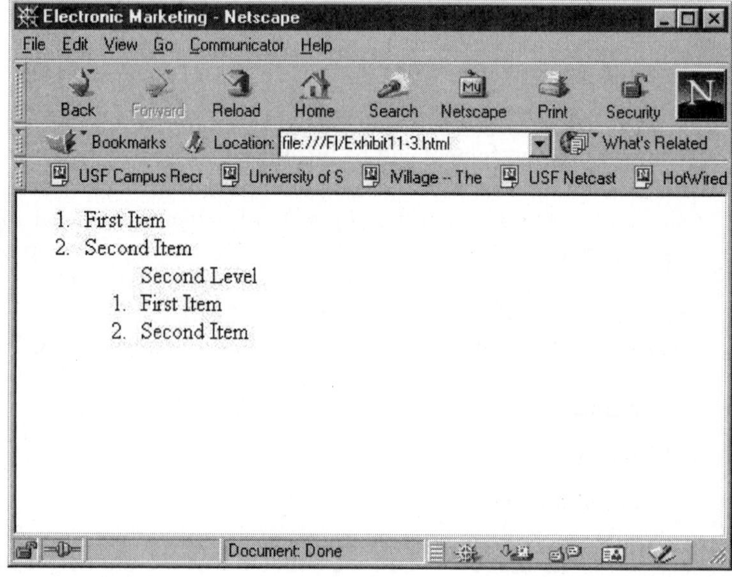

EXHIBIT 11.6 EXAMPLE OF HTML CODES FOR AN ORDERED LIST

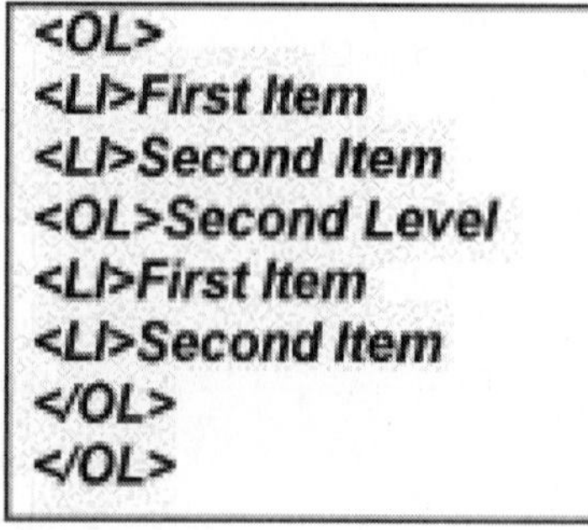

```
<OL>
<LI>First Item
<LI>Second Item
<OL>Second Level
<LI>First Item
<LI>Second Item
</OL>
</OL>
```

Numbered or Ordered Lists

Numbered or ordered lists are created using the ⟨OL⟩ and ⟨/OL⟩ container tags. This list must begin with the ⟨OL⟩ tag, and each item must be preceded by the ⟨LI⟩ tag. The list is then finished with the ⟨/OL⟩ tag. An example is shown in Exhibits 11.5 and 11.6.

Bulleted or Unordered Lists

Bulleted or unordered lists are similar to ordered lists, but they use the ⟨UL⟩ and ⟨/UL⟩ container tags. The ⟨LI⟩ tag must still precede each item. Exhibits 11.7 and 11.8 show an example.

EXHIBIT 11.7 EXAMPLE RESULT FOR AN UNORDERED LIST ON A WEB PAGE

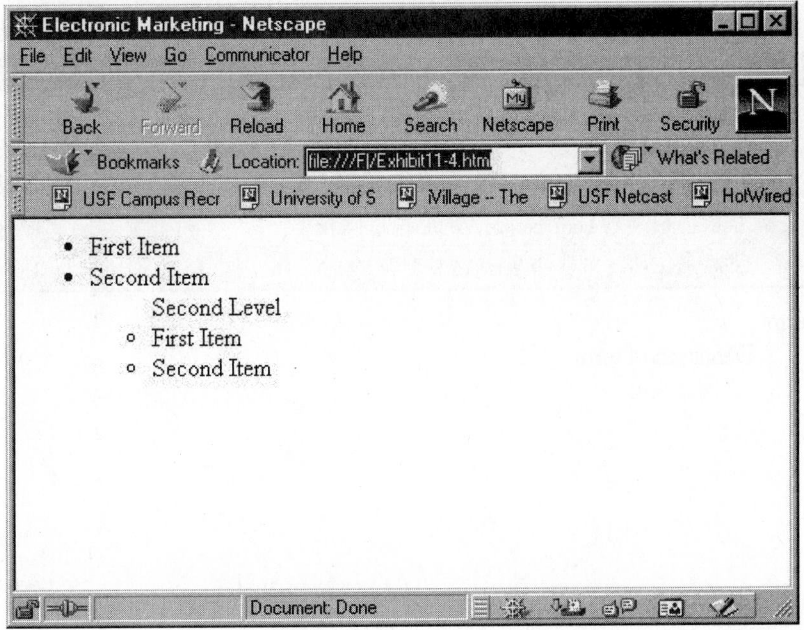

EXHIBIT 11.8 EXAMPLE OF HTML CODES FOR AN UNORDERED LIST

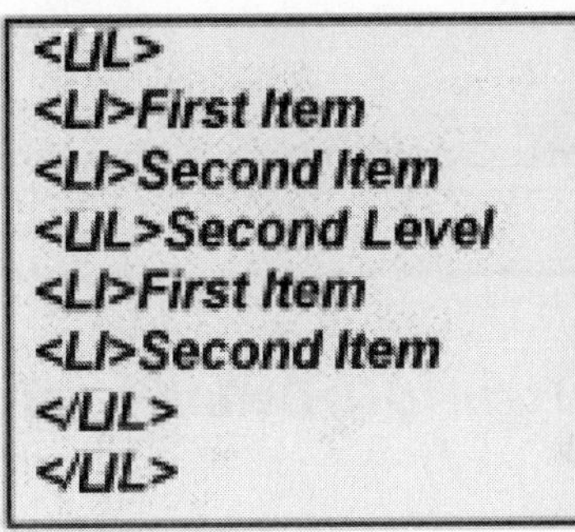

```
<UL>
<LI>First Item
<LI>Second Item
<UL>Second Level
<LI>First Item
<LI>Second Item
</UL>
</UL>
```

Definiton and Glossary Lists

Definition lists or glossary lists provide for a dictionary entry-like format. It requires a ⟨DL⟩ and ⟨/DL⟩ container. Inside the container, the ⟨DT⟩ tag marks the term and the ⟨DD⟩ tag marks the paragraph. See Exhibits 11.9 and 11.10.

As you can see, HTML has severe limitations when it comes to layout of page design. One way in which you can work around the layout problems you may encounter is to use tables as a means of formatting the way your page looks. Tables are not only a great way to present information neatly but also act as a useful layout tool. The HTML 4.0 standards have expanded the use of tables in several ways, allowing for better control of your layout.

Tables start with an optional caption followed by one or more rows. Each row is formed by one or more cells, which are differentiated into header and data cells. Cells

EXHIBIT 11.9 EXAMPLE OF A DEFINITION LIST ON A WEB PAGE

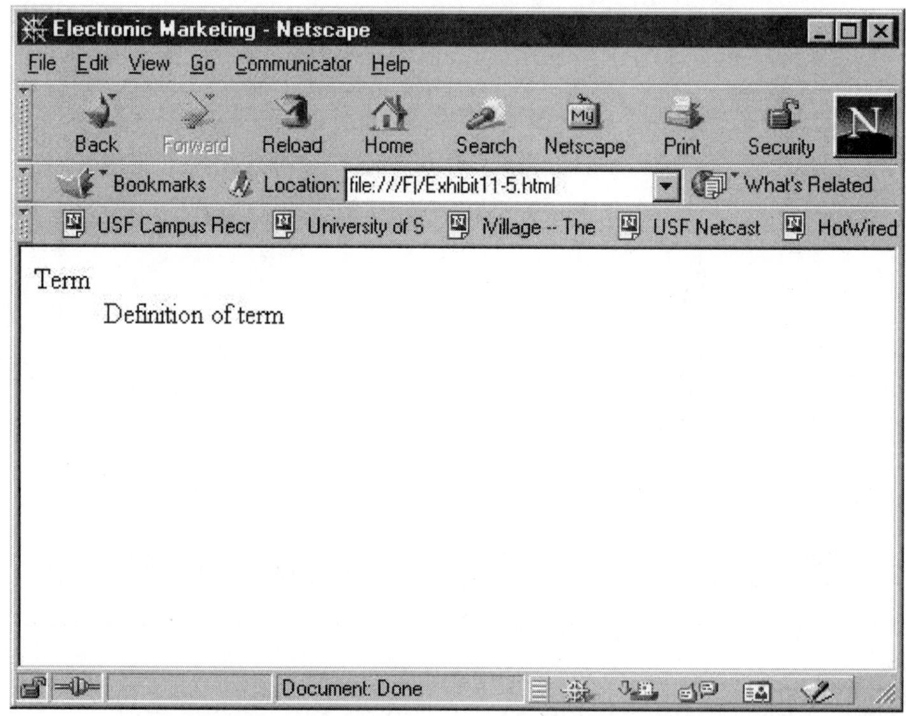

EXHIBIT 11.10 EXAMPLE HTML CODES FOR A DEFINITION LIST

```
<DL>
<DT>Term<DD>Definition of term
</DL>
```

can be merged across rows and columns. Special attributes are included to assist in rendering to speech and Braille, or for exporting table data into databases. The model provides limited support for control over appearance, for example, horizontal and vertical alignment of cell contents, border styles, and cell margins. You can further affect this by grouping rows and columns together. Tables can contain a wide range of content, such as headers, lists, paragraphs, forms, figures, preformatted text, and even nested tables. Here are some of the codes that you will find useful when creating tables.

The TABLE Tag

Example	⟨TABLE BORDER⟩
	⟨CAPTION ALIGN=TOP⟩Caption for the table⟨/CAPTION⟩
	⟨TR⟩
	⟨TD⟩Content of cell 1A⟨/TD⟩
	⟨TD⟩Content of cell 1B⟨/TD⟩
	⟨TD⟩Content of cell 1C⟨/TD⟩
	⟨/TR⟩
	⟨TR⟩
	⟨TD⟩Content of cell 2A⟨/TD⟩
	⟨TD⟩Content of cell 2B⟨/TD⟩
	⟨TD⟩Content of cell 2C⟨/TD⟩
	⟨/TR⟩
	⟨/TABLE⟩
Function	Contains all HTML tags that comprise a table
Attributes	ALIGN
	BORDER
	BGCOLOR
	CELLPADDING
	CELLSPACING
	COLS
	FRAME
Related Tags	⟨CAPTION⟩
	⟨THEAD⟩
	⟨TFOOT⟩
	⟨TBODY⟩
	⟨COLGROUP⟩
	⟨COL⟩
	⟨TR⟩
	⟨TD⟩
	⟨TH⟩

Many of the attributes and related tags you see in the table above warrant some additional discussion in order to understand how useful tables can be. Following is an example of how the table is constructed using the ⟨TR⟩ and ⟨TD⟩ tags.

Example of HTML Codes for Table

```
⟨TABLE BORDER=1⟩
⟨CAPTION ALIGN=top⟩Caption for the table⟨/CAPTION⟩
⟨TR⟩
⟨TH⟩⟨/TH⟩
⟨TH⟩⟨/TH⟩
⟨TH ROWSPAN=2 COLSPAN=2⟩⟨/TH⟩
⟨TH COLSPAN=2⟩Head A-B⟨/TH⟩
⟨TH COLSPAN=2⟩Head C-D⟨/TH⟩
⟨/TR⟩
⟨TR⟩
⟨TH⟩⟨/TH⟩
⟨TH⟩⟨/TH⟩
⟨TH⟩Head A⟨/TH⟩
⟨TH⟩Head B⟨/TH⟩
⟨TH⟩Head C⟨/TH⟩
⟨TH⟩Head D⟨/TH⟩
⟨/TR⟩
⟨TR⟩
⟨TH ROWSPAN=2⟩Head 1-2⟨/TH⟩
⟨TH⟩Head 1⟨/TH⟩
⟨TD⟩Cell 1A⟨/TD⟩
⟨TD⟩Cell 1B⟨/TD⟩
⟨TD⟩Cell 1C⟨/TD⟩
⟨TD⟩Cell 1D⟨/TD⟩
⟨/TR⟩
⟨TR⟩
⟨TH⟩Head 2⟨/TH⟩
⟨TD⟩Cell 2A⟨/TD⟩
⟨TD⟩Cell 2B⟨/TD⟩
⟨TD⟩Cell 2C⟨/TD⟩
⟨TD⟩Cell 2D⟨/TD⟩
⟨/TR⟩
⟨TR⟩
⟨TH ROWSPAN=2⟩Head 3-4⟨/TH⟩
⟨TH⟩Head 3⟨/TH⟩
⟨TD⟩Cell 3A⟨/TD⟩
⟨TD⟩Cell 3B⟨/TD⟩
⟨TD⟩Cell 3C⟨/TD⟩
⟨TD⟩Cell 3D⟨/TD⟩
⟨/TR⟩
⟨TR⟩
```

```
⟨TH⟩Head 4⟨/TH⟩
⟨TD⟩Cell 4A⟨/TD⟩
⟨TD⟩Cell 4B⟨/TD⟩
⟨TD⟩Cell 4C⟨/TD⟩
⟨TD⟩Cell 4D⟨/TD⟩
⟨/TR⟩
⟨/TABLE⟩
```

The caption tag is a container tag that specifies a caption for the table. It can be used to place a caption on the top, the bottom, or to the left or to the right of the table using the ALIGN attribute inside the caption tag (⟨CAPTION ALIGN="TOP"⟩). The table head (⟨THEAD⟩) and table foot tags (⟨TFOOT⟩) define the header and footer sections of a table, respectively. Because the header can be defined separately from the table elements, the browser can duplicate it when the table is split across more than one page.

The main definition of the table is accomplished using the table row (⟨TR⟩) and table data (⟨TD⟩) tags. Each time a new row is needed in the table, the ⟨TR⟩ tag should be used. To separate cells, the ⟨TD⟩ tag should be used. The table header (⟨TH⟩) is a form of the ⟨TD⟩ tag that formats the text in that cell as boldfaced and horizontally centered. Each of these tags has a number of attributes that help with the format of how they look.

The following is a discussion on a few attributes that can be partnered with the above tags in order to format the table, making it easier to use for layout design. BORDER is an identifier that can be added to the table tag to specify the thickness of the table border in pixels. The code BORDER=0 would produce a table with no border. The ALIGN attribute identifies the placement of the table on the page. To center the table, you would use ALIGN=CENTER in the table tag. Tables with align values of right or left will float on the margin and allow text to wrap around them. The background color attribute (BGCOLOR) sets the background color to use in the cells of the table. CELLPADDING and CELLSPACING control the amount of white space around the text and the cells of the table.

The formatting of the rows and cells can be enhanced using the ROWSPAN and COLSPAN attributes, respectively. Using these attributes allows you to specify the number of rows or columns that a row or cell will span. This adds great depth to

EXHIBIT 11.11 EXAMPLE OF HTML TABLE CODE RESULTS

Caption for the table

		Head A-B		**Head C-D**	
		Head A	**Head B**	**HEAD C**	**HEAD D**
Head 1-2	**Head 1**	Cell 1A	Cell 1B	Cell 1C	Cell 1D
	Head 2	Cell 2A	Cell 2B	Cell 2C	Cell 2D
Head 3-4	**Head 3**	Cell 3A	Cell 3B	Cell 3C	Cell 3D

layout creativity. An ALIGN attribute can also be used with the row and cell tags. The values for ALIGN are right, left, and center. Additionally, the VALIGN attribute aligns the text vertically with choices of top, bottom, and center. Exhibit 10 shows an example of a table using some of what has been discussed.

Your Web site should now consist of pages that look the way you planned textually. There are still two very important areas of HTML code that are required to make the pages work together: being interactive and having visual appeal. This entails using hyperlinks and images. Hyperlinks let you move from one place to another on the Internet or within a Web site by maneuvering the mouse. This allows for navigation from a table of contents or a menu. Hyperlinks are created with the ⟨A⟩ tag.

The Hyperlink Tag ⟨A⟩

Example	⟨A HREF="URL of linked document"⟩ What the user sees and clicks on ⟨/A⟩ OR ⟨A NAME="name of anchor in document"⟩ The text that will be used as a bookmark or anchor in the document ⟨/A⟩
Function	Used with the HREF attribute; ⟨A⟩ sets up a hyperlink from whatever content is found within the container. Used with the NAME attribute, you establish a named anchor within a document that can be targeted by other hyperlinks, for example, a table of contents.
Attributes	ACCESSKEY HREF NAME REL REV TABINDEX TARGET
Related Tags	None

Hyperlinks are probably the most important part of a Web site. The hyperlink is what makes the Web easy to explore by linking Web resources from one place to another. With hyperlinks, you can have your audience looking at your product information and then immediately able to place an order from your order form without having to find where the order form is on your site.

Adding Visual Appeal with Images

To add the visual appeal necessary to make your site attractive to your audience, you can use images and image maps. Without images, the Web would just be another textual browser, and it would not be as popular. However, be cautious when using graphics that you do not use too many or ones that have large file sizes. These will slow down the access of your page and may discourage your intended audience from exploring your site. Placing images on your pages is accomplished with the ⟨IMG⟩ tag. It is a standalone tag and is simple to use. However, it does also have many attributes that can be used to modify how the image is presented.

The Image Tag ⟨IMG⟩

Example	⟨IMG SRC="URL of image file"⟩
Function	Places an inline image into a document
Attributes	SRC
	WIDTH
	HEIGHT
	ALT
	BORDER
	ALIGN
	HSPACE
	VSPACE
	ISMAP
	USEMAP
Related Tags	⟨MAP⟩

When using images, it is also possible to add a hyperlink to them by adding a button or an icon. Here is an example of how to combine the two tags of ⟨IMG⟩ and ⟨A⟩ to make a button or graphic that can be clicked on in order to access another section of your Web site: ⟨A HREF="Destination URL"⟩⟨IMG SRC="URL of Image"⟩⟨/A⟩. Another way to create an image that can be clicked on is to use an image map.

Image maps are interactive graphical maps. They allow the user to click on a specific area or hot spot to access another HTML document or to activate a script of one kind or another. Image maps use a mapping process to define specific shapes in the image that correspond to a defined action. The graphic itself is the same as other graphics in your documents, except the areas that can be clicked on have been programmed for a certain response.

This process is accomplished by determining the pixel coordinates of the hot spot's boundaries in the graphic. This can be done using a graphics program such as Photoshop or Paint Shop Pro, but there are many programs available on the Web that will automate this procedure. Here are a few you could try.

- *Advanced Imagemap Designer*—Advanced Imagemap Designer (www.altersoft.com) is a tool that helps you create dynamic, Java-based image maps for your Web pages. All you have to do is design an image map visually by defining the hot spots on an image. The image maps you create can display pop-up images and play sounds when the user passes the mouse over a hot spot, clicks on the image, or selects it. Since Advanced Imagemap Designer is a visual tool, you do not need any Java or HTML programming knowledge to use it.
- *Coffee Cup Image Mapper++*—There is very little this program cannot do for you when you are building a map for your Web site or home page. It guides you right through on how to make "mouseover text" on link areas. Plus, you can save your map as a separate HTML file or copy the map to an existing page. (www.coffeecup.com/mapper/)
- *LiveImage*—Client-side Image Mapping Program for Windows 95 and Windows NT 4.0. LiveImage is a user-friendly, "don't know much about all this image mapping stuff" program. LiveImage supports GIFs, JPGs, Progressive JPGs, and the new PNG graphic files.(www.mediatec.com)

- *Map Edit*—A graphical editor for World Wide Web image maps. It is simple, fully functional, and easy to use. (www.boutell.com/mapedit/)
- *Splash! Image Mapper*—The Splash! Image Mapper (www.gosplash.com/) is a standalone image mapper with the smooth interface of the Splash! Web Authoring program. It is a new tool for users who want to quickly generate the laborious code needed for client side image maps.

An image map consists of four basic components that are required for your image map to work.

- An image map program that resides on the server in the cgi-bin directory (see information on Client-side Imagemaps)
- A graphic image file saved in a gif format for the user to click on
- A map file to give information that will convert points on the image into URLs
- An HTML file to link the image and the map file

Image maps come in two flavors: server-side and client-side. When a user clicks on a server-side image map, the server interprets the coordinates that the browser sends using a program on the server. This program determines the URL the browser should load. To accomplish this, the server must have access to a file containing information about the areas on the image map that can be clicked on and the URL that those areas are linked to.

With client-side image maps, the browser processes the information from the user's click instead of sending it to the server for interpretation. This is a much more efficient process. In order for the browser to interpret the information from the users click, it must also have access to the same information about the areas that can be clicked on and their partnered URLs. This information can be stored in the HTML file with the image map, but it does not have to be. The tag that is used to store this information is the ⟨MAP⟩ tag.

The Imagemap Tag ·MAPÒ

Example	⟨MAP NAME="navigation"⟩ ⟨AREA SHAPE="RECT" COORDS="23,47,58,68" HREF="search.html"⟩ ⟨AREA SHAPE="CIRCLE" COORDS="130,246,150,246" HREF="about.html"⟩ . . . ⟨/MAP⟩
Function	Contains HTML tags that define the clickable areas of an imagemap.
Attributes	NAME
Related Tags	⟨AREA⟩
AREA Attributes	ALT COORDS HREF NOHREF SHAPE TABINDEX TARGET

This chapter has covered the basics of HTML that are needed to create a workable and appealing Web site. There are still many elements that can be added that have not been discussed. As this is written, the current HTML standard is 4.0. In HTML 4.0, multimedia elements such as sound, video, and animation can be added to enhance the Web site. Frames and forms are useful elements in creating easier ways to navigate and in collecting customer data. Although these frames will not be discussed in this book, forms will be discussed in Chapter 13. There are also elements such as style sheets that can make creating a large site easier. If you have the ability to program or have a programmer available to you, Java or Active-X can be used to make the site more interactive and appealing. As you can see, in the fast-paced world of the Internet, the limits of what can be done keep moving. To keep up, you must also keep learning and moving toward the future.

One last lighthearted comment on design: You have all seen good and bad Web page design, and one site keeps its eye open for the best and the worst in eye appeal. For lessons in what not to do in Web page design, this site with an attitude is the iconoclastic Web Pages That Suck (www.Webpagesthatsuck.com, Flaunders Enterprises, 1999). The author, Vincent Flanders, believes that the viewer can "learn good design by looking at bad design," and he presents examples of good and bad design and his reasoning for coming to that conclusion. The site has pictorial examples with intriguing copy such as "Really demand bad computer store," "Naked and dead bodies," and "Fixing and preventing Web pages that suck." The site does have many helpful strategies and tips to improve Web site design.

Test the Site

Your site is ready to be made public, or so you think. It is very important that you test the work you have done in different environments and for different browsers. Your HTML code may not be perfect, or you may have a link that has changed since you began your work. The code you have written for Netscape may not work in Internet Explorer or on an AOL browser. These are very important issues to deal with before you plaster your new URL all over your printed material or send your new address to the services that help consumers find you on the Web. The first step to testing your Web pages are to view them yourself in all browsers that you have available and in all platforms that your consumers will be using. Your site may look very different on a Macintosh using Internet Explorer than it did on a Windows 95 machine using Netscape. You may find you need to make adjustments to consistently get the effect you were looking for.

There are also tests to be done on the HTML code that you have written. Fortunately, there are some easy ways to check this. One way is to send your URL to a testing site like DR HTML (www2.imagiware.com/RxHTML/), the W3C validation service (validator.w3.org/), or Dr. Watson (watson.addy.com/). These sites run your Web pages through a program to see if they are standardized and are working correctly. They then give you feedback on what is wrong, and some even tell you how to fix it. Investigate to see how your pages rate, or do an Internet search for even more useful validation tools.

Your pages are working, and now you want to let people know where they are. How do you get your site in all those neat search engines to make sure it will be found when consumers search for related information? This deals with two separate issues. One is the proper use of the meta tag that was discussed earlier. The other is notifying the world that you are online. Here are some ideas for both of these tasks.

Be Sure to Register Your Site

Now that you have a working Web site, how is the consumer going to find your site? By word-of-mouth, advertisements or brochures, or news releases? The surest way of gaining exposure for your site is by registering with the appropriate search engines. Again, the marketer has choices in this vital exercise of site registration. He can hire a service to register the site, since there are more than two hundred search engines to consider. However, you will get more than adequate awareness registering with the top ten search engines. You might consider a sample service like Did-it.com, (www.did-it.com), which will also check your site for bugs in the HTML programming. You can also pick and choose the search engines by doing the registration yourself with InterNIC. If you do it yourself, you may receive a better understanding of the differentiation between search engines. For example, Altavista is considered to reach a more professional viewer, while Yahoo! is a general-audience search engine.

Summary

After reading this chapter, you should now have a good understanding of where to start in creating a marketing Web site. The major emphasis should always be on communicating with your audience during all stages of designing your site. First and foremost, you should get to know your audience and the needs that this Web site will serve. Each page should be designed from the beginning with a good understanding of the look and feel you wish to accomplish. From there, the basic concepts provided in this chapter on using the HTML language to create Web sites should be helpful in producing the product that you have designed. Each Web site should take into account the current standards and practices of HTML. Be sure to review the site looking for good and bad elements of design, including how friendly it will be to your target audience. Does it accomplish the goals that you set out or do you need to rethink your ideas? A general knowledge of the basic tags used in HTML should have been obtained from this chapter but will need to be reinforced by actually creating a few pages. Please do not stop with the basics of this chapter, but investigate the many resources available on the Web to make your site all that you have envisioned. Once your site has been completed and you are satisfied with the way it looks, be sure to test it in different browsers, at different connection speeds, and in different computing environments to be sure your audience will be satisfied and not frustrated. Finally, do not forget to register your site so that it will be found by all those who are interested and are searching for information that you are providing. Good luck in your attempts to create user-friendly and effective marketing Web sites.

Key Terms

Block level formatting

Body

Clickable icon

Code

Comment

Deep

Elements

Flat structure

Flow

Head section

Hyperlinks

Image maps

Logical styles

Meta data

Physical styles

Search engines

Tables

Tag

Text based language

Text level formatting

Textual links

QUESTIONS AND EXERCISES

1. The Web can be a powerful form of communication between the consumer and the marketer. It can be used to gather vast amounts of useful and useless information. In order to develop good Web-based communication, the tools of the trade must be studied and understood. Both the limitations and the reach of these tools must be considered to effectively communicate with the consumer. How can a marketer better ensure effective Web-based communications? List methods or actions that should improve your company's Web design performance. Write an e-mail to your interactive advertising agency to explore these areas.

2. Why is HTML called "platform independent," and how is this important in marketing on the Internet? Be prepared to explain this concept in a class discussion.

3. Over the years, browser manufacturers have declined in number. Today, the browser battle seems to be dwindling to two major players: Microsoft Internet Explorer and Netscape Navigator/Communicator. From a consumer standpoint, is this lack of competition healthy or unhealthy in the marketplace? Write an opinion in a proposed letter to the Federal Trade Commission on the subject justifying your stand.

4. The Web is a picture window for consumers to compare one company to another and one offering to another. Go to the Web and find other companies that are similar to your company, supposing you own a company or work for one. How do their sites compare to your ideas? If you were a potential customer, what would be the content elements (such as price or store location convenience) that you would be looking for? Make a list of decision elements to compare and contrast two different companies in the same industry.

5. In learning HTML, the marketer encounters many new terms that she should be familiar with; define in writing the following words or concepts:

   a) Meta tag

   b) Stand alone tag

   c) Container tag

   d) Site map

   e) An anchor tag, ⟨A⟩

   f) A .gif extension

6. Address in writing each of the following:
   a) The difference between ⟨P⟩ and ⟨BR⟩ tags
   b) Define a ⟨HR⟩ tag
   c) The purpose of the tag ⟨/HTML⟩
   d) The difference between ⟨TR⟩ and ⟨TD⟩ tags
   e) Define a ⟨IMG⟩ tag
   f) The function of the tag ⟨HEAD⟩

7. As more and more people access the Web, users of different physical capabilities are part of the population. How can a marketer's Web site accommodate persons with visual impairments or speech impairments? Write an e-mail to your human resources director suggesting how these accommodations will be beneficial to your company and its constituencies.

8. According to the text, every Web page should contain four elements. What are these four elements, and why is each important from either an information or a marketing standpoint? Write a four-paragraph explanation to turn in to your instructor.

9. As with most marketing materials, the more experienced Web designer will have accumulated more skills and tools in providing solutions to Web site or page designs. A more advanced designer might use tables and frames. What is the difference between the two elements, and what does each do for the appearance of a Web page? Prepare an outline to be orally delivered to a high school electronic graphics class.

10. This chapter has discussed learning the basics of HTML editing and compared this knowledge to learning an alphabet to create words and sentences for communications. HTML editors that automatically format typed sentences into HTML code has also been described. Why is it advised for the marketer, designer, or even the viewer to learn the basic tags, attributes, functions, or other conventions of HTML rather than rely solely on an HTML editor? What are the benefits of understanding HTML code? Be prepared to discuss this question in class.

Bibliography

Hoffman, Donna and Thomas Novak. 1994.
Microsoft Corporation. "Web Site." Copyright 1993–1998, 1.
Sweetman, Bill. 1997. Web site strategies. *Internet World,* March, 63.

CHAPTER 12

Capturing Customers Profiles and Data Management

"The decade of the nineties [was] the decade of the massive consumer marketing database. General Motors reportedly has 14 million GM credit card holders being contacted, questioned, tabulated, tracked, and romanced each month when the credit card statement is delivered. Marriott has over 5 million members in its Honored Guest database; Waldenbooks Preferred Reader Program has over 4 million members; MCI keeps tabs on 12 million Friends & Family long-distance callers; there are 34 million-plus travelers in frequent-flyer-club databases; and millions upon millions more are in the relational databases of hotels, department stores, financial service companies, HMOs, and all the rest. Getting customers is still important, but information-driven strategies keeping them *have become vitally important to marketers everywhere in the world. The first step in the process of retaining customer loyalty is to go out and learn everything worthwhile you can about the bookmarked individual. Keeping track of the customer's personal characteristics, preferences, and purchases in a relational database, and pushing a customer-focused marketing strategy, together represent the single most significant development of modern-day marketing."*

(Rapp and Collins 1996, 11–12)

LEARNING OBJECTIVES

- To introduce the marketing database and its importance in organizing the characteristics of market segments
- To demonstrate how a database can be constructed using Microsoft Access software
- To plan and build a sample marketing-oriented database using Access

Introduction

With all the raw information floating around, what is a marketer to do? The best strategic move is to collect and categorize as much information as possible pertaining to the market—names, e-mail and street addresses; ages; gender; and preferences in literature, music, entertainment, food, and fashion; the characteristics for data capture can be extensive. The best tactical decision is to create customer **databases** to record these almost endless facts and profiles to which your marketing programs are targeted. Yesterday's mass mailings have been transformed into customized, geographically delivered, personalized advertising messages that speak to tens of like households, not tens of thousands. With database management, the marketer can keep track of items purchased, dollar volume purchased, patterns of purchasing, infrequent purchasing, zip codes, census tracts, areas of concentrated purchasing; creativity in database design and management can be a highly prized quality of top-flight marketers. This has not always been the case. Highly effective database programming and performance have evolved in the last twenty-five years, paralleling the expanded capabilities of business and personal computers. Software applications have multiplied as the cost of database computing has dropped, and marketers in almost every industry or service have embraced building databases as one manner of getting to know their customers better. Better knowledge of customer histories suggest better service in future needs. Accurate marketing database programs assist in forming long-term customer relationships and brand loyalty. Database creation and implementation are another electronic marketing tool that intelligent and diligent marketers should possess as a competitive skill to best serve her customer segments, company performance, and customer satisfaction.

Keeping the House in Order

Good marketing programs are built around good information, and good information is collected, categorized, and saved for future analysis and usage. While data collection is not considered a glamorous activity, the most highly regarded companies have extensive databases that contain records of its customers' likes and dislikes; this familiarity of their customers' preferences set the a company apart and above their competition. Again, in thinking about the future, the idea of a one-to-one relationship between the customer and the vendor is most attractive. This relationship will not be formed overnight; it may take months or years to build a sufficient database formed from purchase **transactions** and, possibly, customer surveys. However, given a long enough and beneficial relationship, the association by each party will develop its own expectations of the other. These expectations are not guesses; they are constructed upon past performances that are generally good indicators of future action. These preferences and purchase activities are recorded in a database—any collection of searchable information. This database can be searched by people or computers; the collection of information can be contained in a large computer file or system. In its simplest form, the database could be a list. In its most complex form, it could be millions of records that are interconnected, or in database terms, that are relational. Databases are good ways to provide information and customer support, and if the marketer's databases are exceptionally helpful, this tool can be used to draw visitors back to his site for repeat visits. (Brady, Forrest, and Mizerski 1997, 196) As for the marketer's requirements, databases can hold a variety of information about a customer, and this information can be searched and utilized in the company's direct marketing program. From the start, the marketer should be involved with the specifications of the company's database capabilities. The marketer should never underestimate the **value** of data collection. Recently, a major airline purchased the South

EXHIBIT 12.1 **THREE POINTS OF ENTRY FOR INFORMATION GATHERING OVER THE INTERNET**

- Gathering data—A marketing database is only as powerful as the data it houses. To accomplish effective database marketing applications, the marketer must develop a source data strategy to maximize the collection of the right data for his applications.
- Utilizing technology—Technology represents the ability to manage consumer data and access that data for decision-making capabilities. The marketer should harness technology in order to provide a platform to access the information he has collected about customers and prospects.
- Research techniques—Segmentation and modeling techniques complete the final building block. Via research, marketers unlock the power of data they capture and more.

American routes from another airline, not to create a presence in South America (it already had extensive coverage to the major cities) but to acquire the selling airlines' customer databases to develop a more loyal customer roster.

Businesses began to formulate their database systems in the late sixties and early seventies, and what was very complex at the time has in the nineties become much more manageable, quicker to sort and retrieve, and more powerful. First delegated to assist accounting, customer records, and inventory functions, database design and management is now a primary tool for the marketing function. For the marketer, database usage can be linked to internal memory systems, or it can be linked to external resources already existing on the Internet that are appropriate to the marketer's business. These external sites can be linked as well to the marketer's Web page.

A good example of a large database might be a university library with its cataloging of its various resources, such as books, periodicals, government publications, reserve materials, microfiche, video stock, and checkout status. Every item has a **record** within the database, and each record is usually accounted for in the collection system. The marketer's responsibility regarding database usage is similar to a library's database usage. For a marketing database, the raw information will need to be divided into logical groups and subcategories—an unsorted pile of numbers is meaningless. From the database design, these data are then linked in a hierarchical manner to the top of the **table,** which is the main **entity** within a database that holds the **fields** and records of the database. The records, the entities within the table that hold the fields for a database entry, are then divided into fields, the entities within the table and records that hold the individual portions of the records, such as the name or date. The data entry person inputs the name or other information into cells; this approach can provide a very efficient database. The entire page of cells is considered to be a record, a unique representation of someone's personal data. Each marketing application will most likely be different; if, however, the marketer understands the conceptual aspects of database design, each marketing data **project** will be similar in construction just different in specific application. The conceptual elements of database design are the data, the technology, and the research technique. These building blocks for linking the database marketing applications to the information systems are well described in *Cybermarketing* by Brady, Forrest, and Mizerski. (1997, 310–311)

These three elements described in Exhibit 12.1 should be present in all database designs to create a consistency of analysis. As for the elements, the data collection will only be as good as the source strategy—the data collected, be it garbage or gold, are the right data for the marketing analysis. The second element, technology, is present in the ability to manage customer data and to access the necessary information for decision making. The last element, the research technique, which entails the segmentation and modeling approaches, will help the marketer understand the analysis of the data collected and stored.

Once the database application is developed, the ongoing communications program to query current customers or prospective ones can be initiated. Anyone running a personal, low-traffic Web page probably does not need anything more complex than a Web counter that keeps a tally of how many surfers have accidentally or intentionally stumbled across their site to date. However, corporate and commercial Web sites will require a more complex system for keeping track of visitors: Bandwidth costs money, and the personnel costs for keeping a dynamic, healthy Web site operating is even more expensive. The *who, what, when, where*, or *why* questions evoke the basic information needs and traffic reports of Web sites. Essential information could be simply knowing who is visiting a Web page to discern whether a site is pulling in its desired target audience. (*Internet World* Labs Report 1997, 75–76) With computer-aided data collection, such as smart cards or devices with magnetic strips, information retrieval has never been as easy and as accurate to compile. Optical scanners in retail stores, for instance, produce accurate data for sales movement, inventory balancing, and price determination.

Measuring the Values of the Database

Accountability can be derived by giving specific attention to the data within any database. Significant changes to the company's offerings may result from decisions supported by the data analysis. Customized products, new distribution and communications channels, and multiple pricing options will drive 70 percent of enterprises to reengineer and automate their marketing process. Historically, marketing has been managed by focusing on products and their associated metrics, for example, market share, product performance, and penetration. Today, increasingly, customized products and services, new distribution and communications channels, and multiple pricing options are making the marketing process dramatically more complex and difficult to manage. Traditional product-oriented marketing management will not be able to scale up to handle this vastly more complex and information-intensive environment. Already traditional metrics are proving inadequate in measuring marketing activities across multiple-product categories, diverse placement channels, and constantly changing retailer discounts and consumer sale price points. New fact-based metrics will let enterprises dynamically allocate marketing resources to the activities with the best return on investment (ROI) or the best lifetime customer value (LCV), the aggregated dollar value of total repeat purchases over the average number years of a customer relationship.

> [With the measurement of LCV, companies are] able and eager to pour millions of dollars into the development of sophisticated systems for cultivating the relationship with their best customers. There were new models to follow when it came to identifying the 20 percent of the market who were the "heavy users" and 80 percent of the revenue, giving them the special attention they warranted. (Rapp and Collins 1996, 250)

Technology and automation will be the key in managing these new marketing processes. However, the vast amount of detailed data that must be collected and analyzed to make effective decisions in this environment will task information systems.

Building a Transactional Database

Probably the best database for e-commerce is the transactional database, which is assembled by ongoing transactions with customers. With a transactional database that has an enabled or linked data capture system, a marketer's company is able to keep track of customers' transactions or purchases. Such transactions could include the type of condiments that the patron of Pizza Hut orders on his pizza, which location he buys from, and the time or day of the week he transacted with Pizza Hut. Likewise, this consumer might be purchasing sporting goods, and the marketing manager for the sporting goods company may be preparing a profile of persons that buy scuba and other water sports equipment. The transactional database is considered superior to public databases because the customer is already buying from the marketer's company.

If you have visited Walt Disney World in central Florida with an annual pass, your visitation habits have been recorded by Disney's marketing analysts. The card is swiped at the gate documenting the time, date, and which park is being entered, for example, the Magic Kingdom, EPCOT Center, or the Animal Kingdom. The information gathered by the marketing department might define the visitor's behavioral patterns and move Disney's marketers into several promotional programs. If the visitor has not frequented a certain park in recent years, coupons or vouchers might be sent to the absent cardholder to encourage a visit. Perhaps the guest has not toured MGM Studios; an incentive for that attraction could be dispatched to the cardholder. Depending on the use of the card, purchases are recorded from shop to shop, again defining the merchandise interests. From documentation of behavior as the Walt Disney World example, marketing programs such as bonus points, discounts, or special invitations during the holidays could be established. Even particular attractions or shops never visited by a season pass holder could create opportunities to encourage more frequent patronage. Tracking past visitations and purchases can predict possible future behavior.

The marketer should be aware that predicting future behavior by examining past behavior is not a perfect science. An example of this concept is that of the very successful venture by Disney in building Disney World-Tokyo (officially Walt Disney Enterprises of Japan, www.disney.co.jp); the Japanese visited frequently and spent handsomely. Taking the same formula to France to be at the front door of Europe, Euro Disney (officially Disneyland-Paris, www.disney.fr) was not met with the same positive and instant embrace. Database management could not have predicted that the Japanese enjoyed Disney's reflection of the American style of entertainment, while the French and other European nationalities were put off by Disney's blatant, Americanized approach to entertainment. Other factors contributed to the success and failure of Disney's ventures. Disney-Tokyo opened in the early eighties when economic indicators were very positive; Euro Disney opened in 1992 amidst hard economic times. The Japanese chose to spend freely at Disney-Tokyo, while many Europeans were frugal at the park. Also, most Japanese guests to the park chose to stay in one of the Disney hotels within the park, while the European visitors made a day trip to Euro Disney, causing Disney to miss out on substantial lodging and food service revenues. With changes to the cultural elements, food service, and a revised pricing schedule, Euro Disney began to realize a profitable operation in the winter of 1994.

The Compiled Database as an Alternative

The marketer may opt to use a compiled database, which is a collection of public records, such as drivers' licenses, birth records, hunting and fishing licenses, automobile registrations, or marriage licenses. Marketers using these compiled databases may have promotional programs that use these compiled databases. An example of public records that trigger promotions is the birth of a child in which the parents are often deluged with offers of photography, diaper services, nanny services, or even offers for enrollment in daycare centers, four years hence. Another public record that triggers promotions is a marriage announcement; this type of compiled list may be of interest to home builders, decorators, automobile dealers, or home appliance dealers. How to use public database—National Decision Systems or its competitors, Claritas, Cluster Plus, and Acorn, all of which approach database interpretation by geography—was discussed in Chapter 8. These geo-demographic services help the marketer to better focus on the correct geographic and psychographic market areas. The marketer should decide how the company's database is to be assembled: 1) compiling customers' profiles by demographic and geographic information; 2) compiling customer preferences by psychographic profiles; or 3) creating a proprietary database from the data of the company's activities with either consumer or business-to-business customers. This proprietary database would consist of the return of warranty cards, e-mail inquiries, or perhaps customer service data input. These are excellent sources in maintaining a database because the end user has provided accurate information for future dealings with the company. As a plan for data management, the design of the tracking system must be considered as well. The intended system should be in place before the data comes streaming in.

Designing a Proprietary Marketing Database

The marketer is wise to have a system input from other departments, which might be integrated into the customer or prospect databases. The inventory management group might have special needs that the marketing flow system can incorporate. A product or service design group might gain from having customer service e-mail forwarded to them for review. Certainly input on the performance of the advertising or other promotional mix elements would be valued by the in-house advertising department or by the interactive or traditional advertising agency. This input can be accommodated by the information system, but the input should be received *before* the information system is developed. The importance of integrating special data collection features in the planning stages will make the system development a much smoother, no-surprises production. Many marketers have not given the planning of the database system sufficient attention, and they have attempted to add an application at the end of software development. This last minute oversight can be compared to replacing a brick on the bottom row of a wall. Literally, the wall would have to be dismantled to add the brick, and this effort is unproductive considering the delay to other home building activities. The questions a marketer should be asking are the standard *who, what, when, where,* and *why* questions. These questions form the basis for all database ventures. The marketer might ask parallel questions such as price, warranty length, or return policies, for example. Most company managers know what information they require to produce the end product or to deliver the service experience. Often the most difficult aspect of planning for data collection is getting everyone from the various departments together to create a plan.

At the planning stage, thought should be given to the report formats that are derived from the data collection. Giving proper attention to the formatting of the report is imperative, otherwise, various managers could be looking through a twenty-page printout without finding the information that is needed. What are the important figures that drive the marketer's department? Sales in units, volume, regions, or by category? Or in service delivery, what is the measurement of consequence, hours spent in design or in execution, profit margins, or hours billed? Every industry and every company have different expectations when it comes to efficiency. Through industry associations' memberships, the marketer can ask the reference or library service of the association for the reasonable margins, hours billed, operating costs, or salaries by position, for examples, of a firm of a certain size in a certain region. Before any comparison can be made, however, a collection and reporting system must be in place. In fact, sufficient attention should be given to each report so that salient information is presented for each manner in a reader-friendly way. The report format can be readily changed if a new manager is promoted or hired to fit the manager's information expectations. Green bar sheets can be adjusted by interested parties; no report format is totally unchangeable.

Software Systems for Traffic Measurement to Web Sites

As other components of the marketing process are measured, so should the performance of a Web site for attracting viewers and encouraging longer visits to the site. While measuring the total number of **hits** can be misleading, there are several areas of accountability that bring objectives and results into better focus. Some software packages can be readily integrated into the Web site and can accomplish a number of tasks, like counting unique visits (one person one visit) and the number of hyperlinks visited recording the **domain** extension of the **visitor** (com, edu, gov, so forth), and keeping track of hourly, daily, and monthly visits. These visits can then be compared to and judged against other advertising, sales promotion, direct marketing, or public relations efforts in determining whether these promotions might also be connected to the Web traffic. For clarity's sake, the term hit means that there has been a successful file transfer from a Web server to a Web browser. However, in marketing terms, a hit is a request for a **file,** which can result in a successful file transfer, an unsuccessful file transfer thus an error, or a null transfer in which the person making the request stops the transfer; to the marketer, only the successful file transfer counts in communications. Further, what is the definition of a file? A file can refer to either a page of text in HTML conventions or an object such as a graphic, sound, or motion. Critics note that each graphic on a page counts as a file, so accessing a page with many graphical elements registers many hits or many page views.

Other terms should be similarly defined and understood by the marketer. Besides a proper definition for hits or page views, the cybermarketer should be comfortable with measurement terms such as visitors and sessions. Visitors are the number of unique persons accessing a site. This is a difficult number to ascertain because one address could serve hundreds of people all working at the same business or organization. A session is a series of uninterrupted mouse clicks from a visitor; any period of inactivity constitutes an interruption. As writer Paul Chen postulates, "If a user is visiting the site and takes a forty-minute lunch break, then resuming where she left off, a **session** is recorded on the Web server." (Chen 1997, 22) The distinction between the two is that a visitor can account for more than one session. The point is, like frequent customers, a repeat visitor is probably more valuable to the site. Chen advises that the best way to estimate visitors is to issue cookies, the bits of information generated at a Web server but stored in browsers. (Cookies were discussed in Chapter 7.) Requiring session identifications or registrations is the best way to estimate sessions. There are shortcomings to issuing cookies. One objection is that some users consider the cookie record an invasion of computer privacy. Another objection is that three people using the same PC could be counted as three visits by one user. Lastly, cookies are not always reliable because a computer user and Web surfer can turn off the cookie option on the browser.

Statistical software packages try to **filter** the true numbers of page views that may result in inaccurate reports. An example of this issue could be a software package measuring traffic that includes the miscounted total number of requests to the server for information. This information counted might include elements of text

EXHIBIT 12.2 THE BIG 8 BY INTERNET WORLD

Accounting for traffic to your Web site is imperative. These tips can improve your understanding of customer profiles, Web site or page performance, or viewer behavior in accessing your site.

What log-file analyzers (or site traffic records) tell you:

1. How to increase the number of visits to your site. Once you determine which links lead Web site visitors to your Web pages, you can do things to promote even more visits, such as purchasing an advertising banner on the sites that generate the most traffic to yours.
2. Which pages are being read the most. The raw number of hits to a page is not as important as how many visitors are sticking around to read the whole thing. You may find that important messages are being ignored or that, perhaps, all those juicy graphics tax your visitors' patience, causing them to hit the Back button too soon or too often.
3. Visitor demographics. Are you attracting the kinds of visitors who will do you some good, or are your pages a haven for teenagers looking for free software to download? Log-file analysis tools can tell you what kind of organizations are visiting your site or even what country they come from.
4. Which files are being downloaded. Are visitors grabbing your products' demos? Is most of the interest concentrated on press releases? Do your graphics seem to offer the most allure? Considering the cost of bandwidth, not knowing what the graphics allure can be, and having the information available can help you offer more of what visitors want.
5. Validate traffic for BPA Interactive Audit Reports. If you have advertisers, this is crucial information for justifying your rates. A log-file analyzer that generates BPA-approved reports can pay for itself in days.
6. Is everybody using older browsers? Your site may intentionally attract academic types or other kinds of visitors using older browsers. If so, you may want to curtail all that effort put into HTML 4 features that only a small number of visitors can benefit from. Or, it might make sense to offer pages in dual versions.
7. Do you have missing files? You may not know that many visitors are having trouble accessing a page until you scan the error reports produced by your analyzer. A fix can be as simple as replacing a damaged graphics image.
8. When is your page the most popular? If you receive the most hits (or visits) on a certain time of the day of the week, or at certain times, there may be a reason for that which you can exploit.

Busch, David D. 1997. The big 8. IW Labs. *Internet World*, June, 79.

(which counts as one), four graphical elements, such as photographs or illustrations, and five hyperlinks or hot buttons; the total number of registered hits would be ten hits, which of course is an exaggeration. What precisely should be measured is an HTML page transfer. A package such as Microsoft's Market Focus 3 (www.interse.com) filters extraneous access information to register the correct number as one page view. Similar packages and measurement services to review and try are Internet Profiles Corp. (www.ipro.com), NetCount (www.netcount), SoftwareWebTrends (www.egsoft.com), Aqua Inc.'s Bazaar Analyzer Pro (www.bazaar-suite.com), net.Genesis (www.netgen.com), Open Market (www.openmarket.com), and MK Stats 2.2 (www.mkstats.com/download).

The best information for clickstream analysis would be to have the numbers on session IDs and on cookies; this would enable the analyst to detail the sequence of page requests made by any group of visitors. Analyzing the clickstream would help designers structure sites more effectively to allow visitors to obtain desired information as quickly as possible. For effective analysis, the marketer should start with counting sessions and page transfers. Chen notes that these are fundamental measures for overall traffic and help justify (or deny) the site's continued existence. The marketer should next track the referring URLs since this would require the use of an extended log format to follow the path of the referrals. Lastly, the marketer should analyze the page transfers by individual pages. Hopefully this will tell the marketer what the visitors find interesting. The understanding gained from these activities can help the marketer decide where to allocate creative resources, what pages need frequent updating, and where to overhaul or eliminate content. Having measurement numbers in hand adds a bit more science to the art of marketing. (ibid.)

A Quick Overview of Database Definitions

As has been discussed previously, a database is a collection of information related to a particular subject or purpose, such as tracking customer orders, maintaining an inventory, or basically gathering any related information in one place. This data can be stored, manipulated, and used in many ways. If information like this is not stored or only partially stored on a computer, you may be tracking information from a variety of sources that you are having to coordinate and organize yourself. This is a very tedious and inefficient way to manipulate data. By using a database program, you can manage all of your information from a single database file. A database file is simply a container for your data with many small partitions dividing it into logical parts. Within a database file, it is easy to divide your data into these separate storage containers, which are called tables. You can then view, add, and update table data using online forms; find and retrieve specific data using queries; and analyze or print data in a specific layout by creating reports.

In order to store your data logically, one table for each type of information you wish to track should be created. After you have set up different tables for each subject in your database, you need a way of telling your database how to bring that information back together again to be compiled for different purposes. The first step in this process is to define relationships between your tables. After you have done that, you can create queries, forms, and reports to display information from several tables at once. As was mentioned before, this is why most databases are called **relational databases.** A **form, report,** or **query** may include information from any number of tables. For instance, say your report, formatted for printing, contains information about customers, orders, categories, products, and shippers. Each of these topics would be in a different table, but they would all be linked together by common information, and elements of each can be viewed in one place. Additionally, to find and retrieve only the data that meets your needs, including data from multiple tables, the marketer can create a query. A query can also update or delete multiple records easily, and perform built-in or custom calculations on your data.

To easily view, enter, and change data directly from a table, you can create a form. This provides you an effective and appealing interface to manipulate your data. When you open a form, your database retrieves the data from one or more tables and then displays this data on the screen. This form will display using the layout you chose for your form, allowing you the freedom to design for your needs. To analyze your data or present it in a certain way, you can create a report. You might print a report that groups data in categories such as region, age, or purchase type. You can also use reports to calculate totals or provide statistics. Different reports with different data formats can be used for print jobs such as mailing labels or catalogs.

What Exactly Does "Relational" Mean and How Does It Work?

You will first need to understand relationships from the perspective of a customer order in order to understand how these relationships work. In a relationship, the fields in multiple tables must be coordinated so that they show information about the same customer order. This coordination is accomplished with relationships between tables. A relationship works by matching data in **key** fields, which is usually a field in both tables, with the same name. In most cases, these matching fields are the **primary key** from one table, which provides a unique identifier for each record, and a **foreign key** in the other table. For example, an order number can be associated with a customer number, creating a relationship between the customers table and the orders table using a customer number field.

For this discussion's purposes, the type of **relationship** that will most often be used is a one-to-many relationship; therefore, this one type of relationship will be discussed here. However, be aware that there are **many-to-many relationships** and one-to-one relationships as well. In a one-to-many relationship, a record in table A can have many matching records in table B, but a record in table B has only one matching record in table A. A good example of this is the product and the supplier table. Each supplier can supply multiple products, but the supplier's information is only listed once in the supplier table; therefore, a **one-to-many relationship** is established between each product in the product table and the one supplier in the supplier table. This alleviates redundant information.

Understanding the Database Elements

Tables

A table is a collection of data about a specific topic, such as products or suppliers. It contains all product or customer records and any related specific information regarding these records. Using a separate table for each topic means that the data is stored only once, which makes for a more efficient database with fewer data-entry errors. Tables organize data into columns, which are called fields and **rows** that are known as records. Most databases can be added to, edited, and reviewed in a configuration that resembles a table. A table can be checked for spelling and then printed, it can filter or sort records, and its appearance and structure can be altered by adding or deleting columns. An entire table can be created from scratch, or an existing table can be customized by adding or deleting fields.

When customizing a table using Microsoft Access, you can add or rename a field, open the table in design view, set a field's data type, choose a primary key, or set field properties. Data in data sheets can be viewed differently by inserting, deleting, or renaming a column; checked for spelling and printed; sorted; and filtered. Individual records in data sheets can be added or deleted as well. Tables will be discussed in more detail later when this book's discussion delves into creating tables.

Forms

You can use forms for a variety of purposes. For example, you can create a switchboard or starting form to open other forms or reports, create a data entry form to enter data

EXHIBIT 12.3

Example of a customer table taken from the sample files provided with Microsoft Access, the Northwinds example.

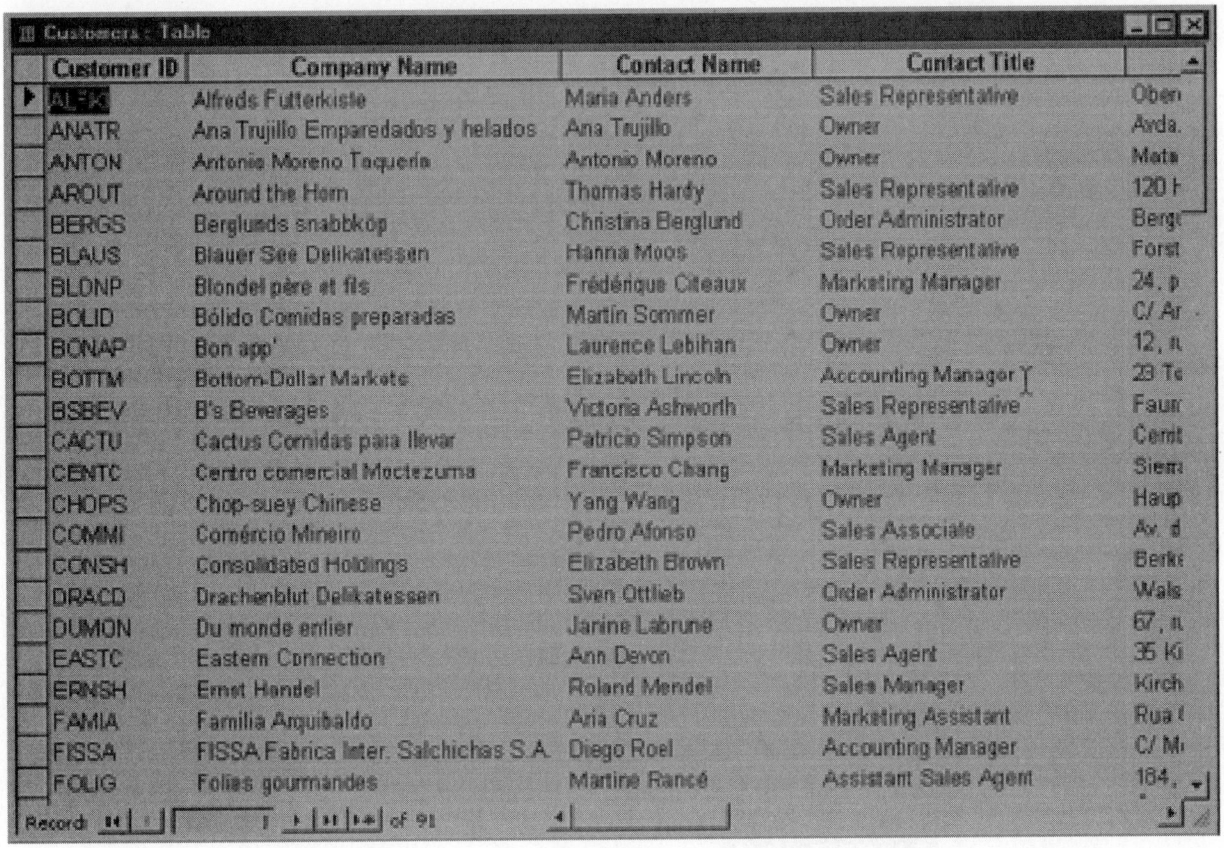

Customers : Table

Customer ID	Company Name	Contact Name	Contact Title	
ALFKI	Alfreds Futterkiste	Maria Anders	Sales Representative	Obere
ANATR	Ana Trujillo Emparedados y helados	Ana Trujillo	Owner	Avda.
ANTON	Antonio Moreno Taquería	Antonio Moreno	Owner	Mata
AROUT	Around the Horn	Thomas Hardy	Sales Representative	120 H
BERGS	Berglunds snabbköp	Christina Berglund	Order Administrator	Berg
BLAUS	Blauer See Delikatessen	Hanna Moos	Sales Representative	Forst
BLONP	Blondel père et fils	Frédérique Citeaux	Marketing Manager	24, p
BOLID	Bólido Comidas preparadas	Martín Sommer	Owner	C/ Ar
BONAP	Bon app'	Laurence Lebihan	Owner	12, r
BOTTM	Bottom-Dollar Markets	Elizabeth Lincoln	Accounting Manager	23 Ts
BSBEV	B's Beverages	Victoria Ashworth	Sales Representative	Faun
CACTU	Cactus Comidas para llevar	Patricio Simpson	Sales Agent	Cerrit
CENTC	Centro comercial Moctezuma	Francisco Chang	Marketing Manager	Sierra
CHOPS	Chop-suey Chinese	Yang Wang	Owner	Haup
COMMI	Comércio Mineiro	Pedro Afonso	Sales Associate	Av. d
CONSH	Consolidated Holdings	Elizabeth Brown	Sales Representative	Berke
DRACD	Drachenblut Delikatessen	Sven Ottlieb	Order Administrator	Wals
DUMON	Du monde entier	Janine Labrune	Owner	67, r
EASTC	Eastern Connection	Ann Devon	Sales Agent	35 Ki
ERNSH	Ernst Handel	Roland Mendel	Sales Manager	Kirch
FAMIA	Familia Arquibaldo	Aria Cruz	Marketing Assistant	Rua (
FISSA	FISSA Fabrica Inter. Salchichas S.A.	Diego Roel	Accounting Manager	C/ M
FOLIG	Folies gourmandes	Martine Rancé	Assistant Sales Agent	184,

Record: 1 of 91

into a table, or create a custom dialog box to accept user input then carry out an action based on that input. Most of the information seen and used in a form comes from an underlying record source that is located in the tables. Other information in the form is stored in the form's design. Parameters that will be stored in the form's design rather than a table can be such items as descriptive text, graphic elements, and expressions for calculations. The items stored in an underlying record source are your data. To create the link between a form and its record source, graphical objects called controls can be used. The most common type of control used to display and enter data is a text box. You can affect the look of the form by moving, sizing, or aligning controls; changing label text or a control source; adding a field or control; or changing a control to another type.

Forms can be divided into sections to increase their effectiveness. Most forms have just a detail section, but a form can also include a form header, a page header, a page footer, and a form footer section. You can also use sections in a sub-forms, or forms within forms. For example, a sub-form can use a form header and form footer in addition to the detail section. The form header can display labels for each column of data, while the detail section can display the records. The form footer can then display the controls that calculate the totals for each column. There are many ways to work with forms. You can switch views; edit, check spelling, or print; sort, filter or find records; add or delete records; and navigate through the records in your database. Forms will be discussed in more detail later when this book's discussion delves into creating forms.

EXHIBIT 12.4

Example order form taken from the sample files provided with Microsoft Access, the Northwinds example.

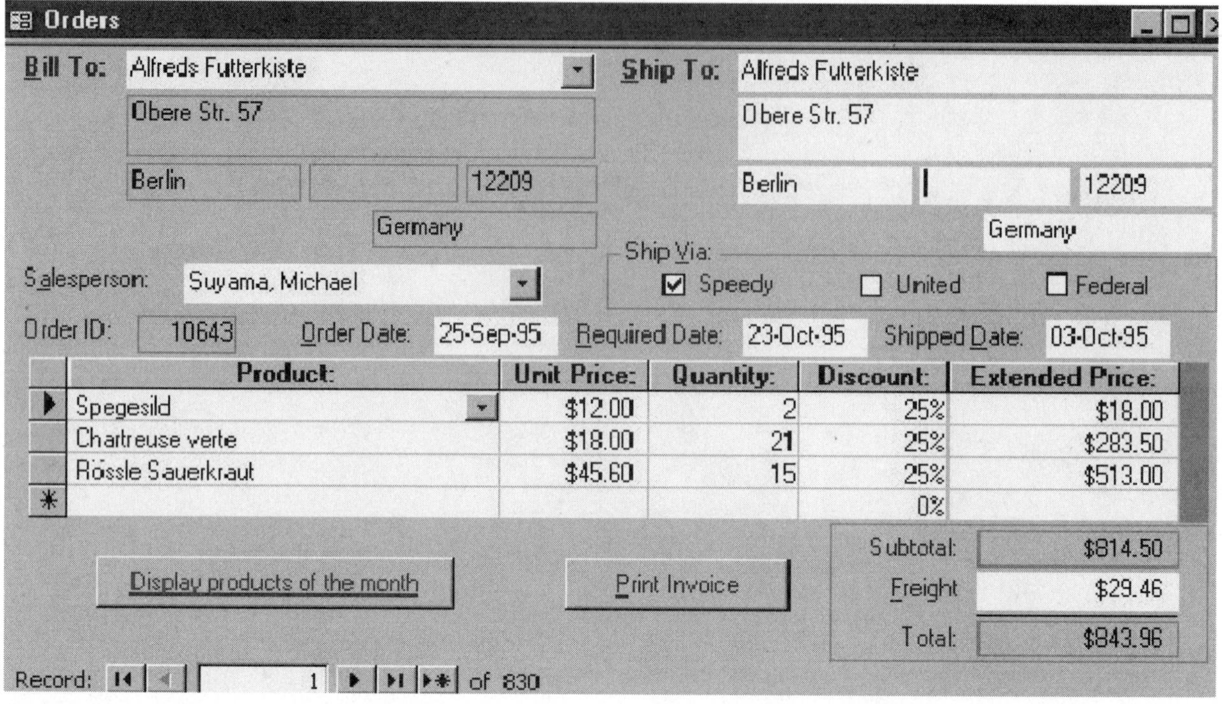

EXHIBIT 12.5

TIPS ON GATHERING INFORMATION OVER THE INTERNET

- Limit information requests to a form that can be completed in three to five minutes. It is too easy to exit a site if the site's involvement is too complex.
- Do not ask for information that requires the user to leave her workstation; she probably will not come back to your site. Exceptions to this are the registration of serial numbers or some other transaction that will benefit the user in some way.
- Limit response options per question. This will enable you to analyze the results better.
- Use open-ended questions when quantitative response measurements are not necessary.
- Build in questions that separate surfers from customers and prospects.

Brady, Forrest, and Mizerski 1997, 100

EXHIBIT 12.6

Example of a query of customers and suppliers by city. This example is taken from the sample files provided with Microsoft Access, the Northwinds example.

Customers and Suppliers by City : Union Query

City	CompanyName	ContactName	Relationship
Aachen	Drachenblut Delikatessen	Sven Ottlieb	Customers
Albuquerque	Rattlesnake Canyon Grocery	Paula Wilson	Customers
Anchorage	Old World Delicatessen	Rene Phillips	Customers
Ann Arbor	Grandma Kelly's Homestead	Regina Murphy	Suppliers
Annecy	Gai pâturage	Eliane Noz	Suppliers
Århus	Vaffeljernet	Palle Ibsen	Customers
Barcelona	Galería del gastrónomo	Eduardo Saavedra	Customers
Barquisimeto	LILA-Supermercado	Carlos González	Customers
Bend	Bigfoot Breweries	Cheryl Saylor	Suppliers
Bergamo	Magazzini Alimentari Riuniti	Giovanni Rovelli	Customers
Berlin	Alfreds Futterkiste	Maria Anders	Customers
Berlin	Heli Süßwaren GmbH & Co. KG	Petra Winkler	Suppliers
Bern	Chop-suey Chinese	Yang Wang	Customers

Record: 1 of 120

Queries

Queries are the most mysterious of the database elements. You can use queries to view, change, and analyze data in many different ways. They can also be the source of records for forms and reports. For example, if you wish to calculate a sum, a count, or another type of total and then group the results, this would be done with a query. Bringing together data from multiple tables, sorting it in a particular order, and performing calculations on groups of records is a query's specialty. The most common type of query is a **select query.** A select query retrieves data from one or more tables using criteria you specify and then displays it in the order you want. When you run the query, your database retrieves the records that you specified then displays the combined data in an order that you want.

Queries are created using a wizard or are created from scratch in a query design view. In design view, you specify the data you want to work with by adding the tables or queries that contain the data and then by filling in the design grid. The fields, sort order, and criteria you add to the design grid determine what you will see in the query's results. Field lists show the fields in the tables or the queries you add to your query. A **join** line tells your database program how data in one table or query relates to data in another query or table. You can add fields to the design grids by dragging them from the field lists. There are many ways to customize your queries. You can specify criteria, add tables or queries, add or remove fields, choose calculations, and specify a sort order. It is possible to select more than one field as criteria in your query, By using Boolean operators, such as OR, AND, and AND/OR, you can easily select one, two, or three fields.

Another type of query is a crosstab query. Crosstab queries are used to calculate a sum, average, count, or other type of total for data that are grouped by two types of information—one type that is down the left side of your data sheet and the other type that is across the top. You can create a crosstab query using a wizard or from scratch in your query design grid. In the design grid, you specify which field's values become column headings, which field's values become row headings, and which field's values to

EXHIBIT 12.7

Example of a sales report taken from the sample files provided with Microsoft Access, the Northwinds example.

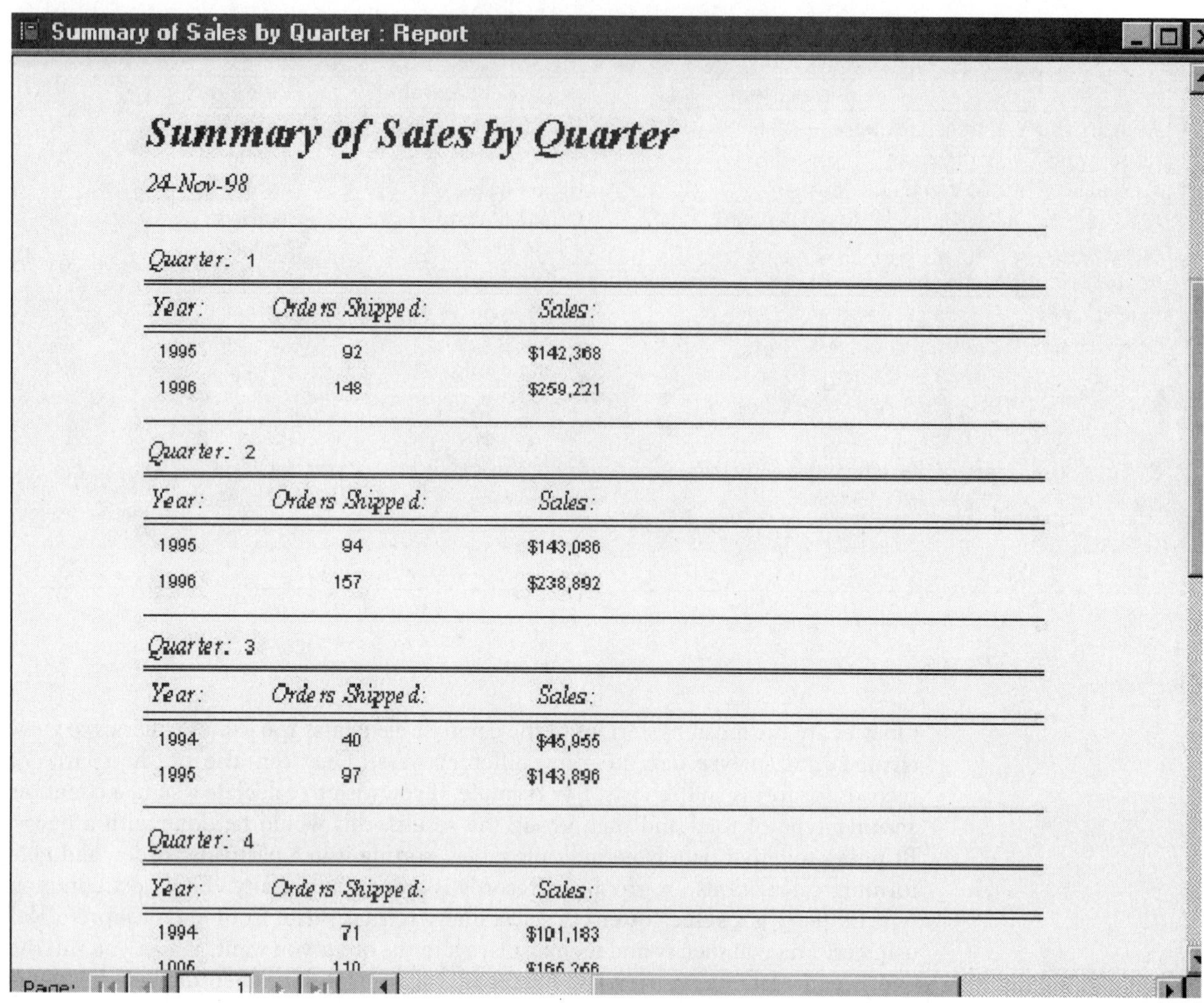

Summary of Sales by Quarter : Report

Summary of Sales by Quarter

24-Nov-98

Quarter: 1

Year:	*Orders Shipped:*	*Sales:*
1995	92	$142,368
1996	148	$259,221

Quarter: 2

Year:	*Orders Shipped:*	*Sales:*
1995	94	$143,086
1996	157	$238,892

Quarter: 3

Year:	*Orders Shipped:*	*Sales:*
1994	40	$45,955
1995	97	$143,896

Quarter: 4

Year:	*Orders Shipped:*	*Sales:*
1994	71	$101,183

Page: 1

sum, average, count, or otherwise calculate. Join types are used in queries to show the database program how the data is related. The type of join indicates on which records the query selects or performs an action.

Reports

A report is an effective way to present your data in a printed format. Because you have control over the size and appearance of everything on a report, you can display the information the way you want to see it. The following are examples of what reports might accomplish: creating mailing labels, showing totals in charts, grouping records in categories, adding a logo or picture, or calculating totals. Most of the information in a report comes from an underlying table, query, or **SQL (Sequential Query Language)** statement, which is the source of the report's data. Other information in the report is stored in the report's design. The design stores information such as column headings, an automatic date, or totals calculated from underlying resources. You create the link between a report and its source by using graphical objects called controls.

Controls can be text boxes that display names and numbers, labels that display titles, and decorative lines that graphically organize the data and make the report more attractive.

Reports can be customized in the same manner as forms. Like forms, reports can be divided into sections. Each section has a specific purpose and prints in a predictable order on the page in the report. These sections include a report header, a page header, the detail (data) section, a page footer, and a report footer. In the report design view, these sections are represented as bands, and each section that the report contains is represented once. In the printed report, some sections may be repeated many times. You determine where information appears in every section by placing controls, such as labels and text boxes. By grouping records that share a common value, you can calculate subtotals and make a report easier to read.

Database Design

Now that you are familiar with the elements that are required in a database, it is important to take time to design your database correctly before you actually create it. A good design is the foundation for creating a database that accomplishes your goals effectively, accurately, and efficiently. Following is a discussion of the seven basic steps you should go through in designing your database.

1. Establish the purpose of your database, as discussed previously.
2. Decide what tables you need in the database to accomplish this task.
3. Determine what data will be collected and placed as fields in your tables.
4. Identify these fields with unique values.
5. Determine how the tables will relate to each other. Review and refine your design to be sure it accomplishes the goals in step 1.
6. Enter a sampling of data and create any other database objects that are needed.
7. Design and implement your interfaces using forms, reports, and queries to make the database easy to use and productive.

The first step in designing your database is to determine the purpose of the database and how it is to be used. You need to know what information you want from the database. From there, you can determine what subjects you need to store facts about (the tables) and what facts you need to store about each subject (the fields in the tables). To facilitate this task, look at examples of databases that work in a similar fashion to yours. Talk to people that will be using the database regularly and to those who are currently collecting and reviewing this type of data for your company. On paper, think about the tables and how they will be related to one another. Brainstorm about the questions you would like the database to answer. Gather any forms or surveys that you currently use to collect or record data. Determine how you want the final reports to look and sketch them out on paper. Is the design of your tables adequate to create the reports that you have determined will be necessary? If not, now is a good time to make adjustments to the design.

Determining what tables you need in the database can be the trickiest step in the database design process. That is because the results you want from your database, the reports you want to print, the forms you want to use, and the questions you want answered, do not necessarily provide clues about the structure of the tables that produce them. It is not necessary, or wise, to design your tables using a database program first.

EXHIBIT 12.8

Example of relationships between tables in Microsoft Access. This example is taken from the sample files provided with Microsoft Access, the Northwinds example. The boldfaced field in each table is the unique ID for that table, and there should not be duplicates of this information in the table. For example, each supplier should have an individual ID in the Suppliers table.

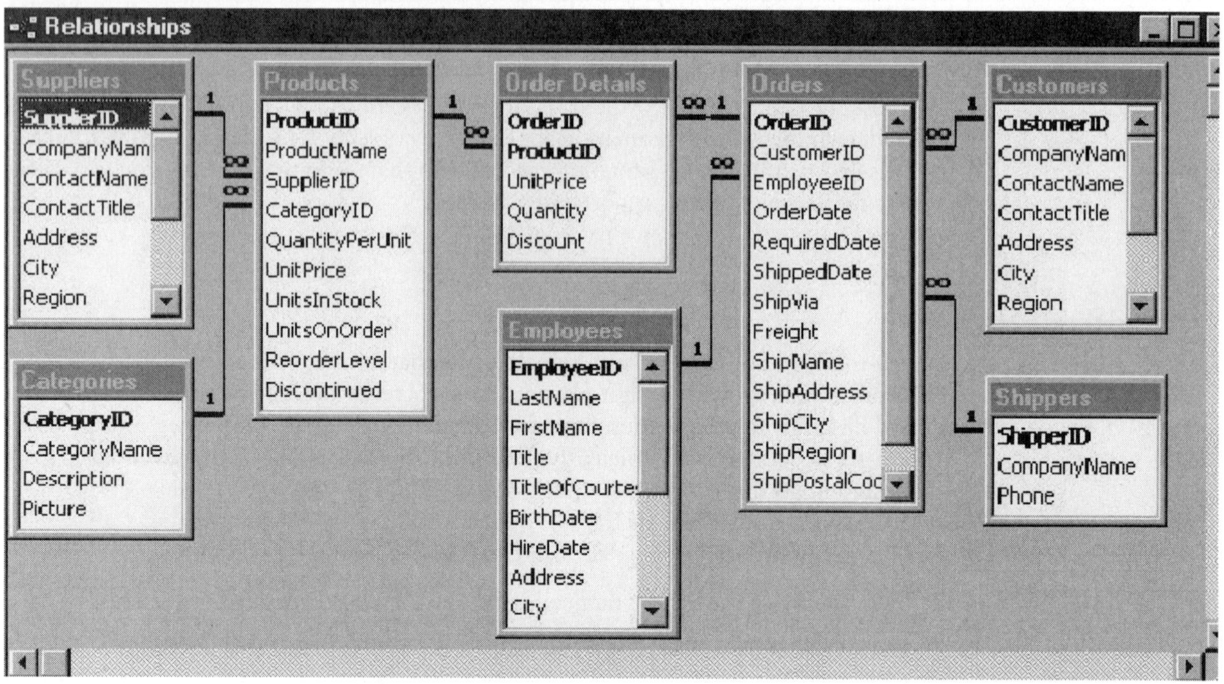

In fact, it is best to sketch out and rework your design on paper first. When designing your tables, divide up pieces of information and keep the following in mind: A table should not contain duplicate information, and information should not be duplicated between tables. When each piece of information is stored in only one table, you update it in only one place. This is more efficient and eliminates the possibility of duplicate entries that contain different information. For example, you would want to store each customer address and phone number once, in one table, and their orders in another related table. This would allow you to delete an order without deleting the customer information.

Each table contains information about the same subject, and each field in a table contains individual facts about the table's subject. For example, a customer table may include first and last name, address, city, state, and phone number fields. When sketching out the fields for each table, keep these tips in mind:

- Relate each field directly to the subject of the table.
- Do not include data that can be calculated by the computer using other collected data.
- Include all the information you think you will need.
- Store information in its smallest logical parts (for example, first name and last name, rather than name.)

To relate information stored in separate tables, for example, to connect a customer with all the customer's orders, each table in your database must include a unique field or set of fields that identifies each individual record in the table. This is called a primary key. Having divided your information into separate tables and set primary keys, you now need to relate the table to each other so the database can bring the information back together in meaningful ways. To do this, relationships must be defined between tables. To understand how this works, it may be useful to view the relationships in an existing well-designed database similar to yours. If you are using Microsoft Access to create your database, there is a good sample database that you can look at to understand how things work. You should find it in the Samples directory in your Microsoft Office files. To see the relationships in the Northwinds sample database, open Northwind.mdb and click on Relationships in the Tools menu.

After you have designed the tables, fields, and relationships needed, it is time to study the design and detect any flaws that might remain. It is easier to change your database design now rather than after you have filled the tables with data. Use your database program to create your tables, specify relationships between the tables, and enter a few records of data in each table. Work with the database to see if you get the answers you want. Create rough drafts of your forms and reports to see if they show the data you expect. Look for redundant data and eliminate any you find. When you are satisfied that the table structures meet your design goals, then it is time to add all your existing data to the tables. You can then create any queries, forms, reports, macros, and modules that you may want. For additional ideas on designing a database, you may want to look at example databases and the database **schemas** for the built-in wizards in your database program.

Creating a Database in Microsoft Access

Because of the fact that there are so many database programs available in the software market today, how each one physically works cannot possibly be fully covered in this textbook; this book will merely generalize. However, in order to discuss the actual creation of a database, Microsoft Access will be used as the example program. The topics that are discussed in the next few sections are specifically directed at using Access but should translate to other database programs as well. The buttons and labels may be a bit different, but the process should remain fairly consistent across the board.

Microsoft Access provides two methods in creating a database: the wizard and the old fashion way, by scratch. The way that is going to describe here is not the easiest, but gives you a better understanding of your database and allows you to be more creative. However, you do need to be aware that a database wizard is available in helping you create in one operation the required tables, forms, and reports for the type of database you choose. This book's approach will be to create a blank database and then add the tables, forms, reports, and other objects later. This is the most flexible method, but it requires you to define each database element separately. Either way, you can modify and extend your database at any time after it has been created.

To really learn the ins and outs of database design, follow these simple instructions to get you started.

1. When Microsoft Access first starts up, a dialog box is automatically displayed with options to create a new database or open an existing one. If this dialog box is displayed, click Blank Database, and then click OK.
2. Specify a name and drive location for the database and click Create.

After you create a blank database, you must perform additional steps to define the objects that will make up your database. Following are the steps on how this is done.

If you want to make it easier, you can follow these simple instructions to use with the database wizard.

1. When Microsoft Access first starts up, a dialog box is automatically displayed with options to create a new database or open an existing one. If this dialog box is displayed, click Database Wizard, and then click OK.
2. In the Databases tab, double click the icon for the kind of database you want to create.
3. Specify a name and location for the database.
4. Click Create to start defining your new database.

Creating Tables

Microsoft Access provides four ways to create a blank (empty) table. As mentioned before, you can use the Database Wizard to create all the tables, forms, and reports required for an entire database, but you cannot use it to add tables or the like to an existing database. Second, you can use the Table Wizard to choose the fields for your table from a variety of predefined tables, such as business contacts, household inventory, or medical records. The more flexible, but not quite as easy approach would be to enter data directly into a blank data sheet. When you save the new data sheet, Microsoft Access will analyze your data and automatically assign the appropriate data type and a format for each field. Lastly, you can use Design view to specify all of your table details from scratch by yourself. Regardless of what method you choose to create a table, you can always use the table Design View at any time to customize your table further with options such as adding new fields, setting default values, or creating input masks.

To create your table from scratch using the Design View, entails a lengthy process. However, when you are finished, you will have a better understanding of how your table works. The advantage of the Design View is that Access will help you. Access assigns data types to each field (column) based on the kind of data you entered. If you want to customize a field's definition further, for example, to change its data type or define a validation rule, you need to use the Design View. In addition to renaming and inserting columns, you can delete or reorder columns at any time before or after saving your new data sheet. Here are some simple step-by-step directions to get you started.

1. If you have not already done so, switch to the Database window. You can press F11 to switch to the Database window from any other window.
2. Click the Tables tab, and then click New.
3. Double click Design View.
4. Define each of the fields in your table.
5. Define a primary key field before saving your table. You do not have to define a primary key, but it is usually a good idea. If you do not define a primary key, Microsoft Access asks if you want it to create one for you when you save the table.
6. When you are ready to save your table, click the Save button on the toolbar, and then type a name for the table following the Microsoft Access object-naming rules.

Another option for designing your database tables is by using the DataSheet View. It is a bit harder but not too terribly harder. Here you are required to determine what type of data you are going to enter and how it is to be formatted. To do so, follow these directions.

1. If you have not already done so, switch to the Database window. You can press F11 to switch to the Database window from any other window.
2. Click the Tables tab, and then click New.
3. Double click DataSheet View. A blank data sheet with twenty columns and thrity rows is displayed. The default column names are Field1, Field2, and so on.
4. Rename each column you will use by double clicking the column name and then typing in a name for the column following Microsoft Access object-naming rules. Press ENTER.
5. If you need more than twenty columns, you can insert additional columns at any time by clicking in the column to the right of where you want to insert a new column. Go to the Insert menu and click Column. Rename the column as described in step 4
6. Enter your data in the data sheet.
7. Enter each kind of data in its own column (each column is called a field in Microsoft Access). For example, if you are entering names, enter the first name in its own column and the last name in a separate column. If you are entering dates, times, or numbers, enter them in a consistent format so that Microsoft Access can create an appropriate data type and display format for the column. Any columns you leave empty will be deleted when you save the data sheet.
8. When you have added data to all the columns you want to use, click Save on the toolbar to save your data sheet.
9. Microsoft Access asks you if you want to create a primary key. If you have not entered data that can be used to uniquely identify each row in your table, such as part numbers or ID numbers, it is recommended that you click Yes. If you have entered data that can uniquely identify each row, you can specify this field as your primary key.

An easier way you can try creating a table is by using the Table Wizard. To get started, follow these directions then follow the directions that the Table Wizard prompts you with on the screen.

1. If you have not already done so, switch to the Database window. You can do this by pressing F11. Pressing F11 will always switch to the Database window from any other window.
2. Click the Tables tab, and then click New.
3. Double click Table Wizard.
4. Now as like above, follow the directions in the Table Wizard dialog boxes.

If you have already collected your data and do not want to have to retype it all, you can create a table with existing data by importing the information from the program it is already in. There are several options available.

- You can import or link data from another Microsoft Access database or data in a variety of file formats from other programs.

- You can perform a make-table query to create a table based on data in a current table. For example, you can use make-table queries to archive old records, to make backup copies of your tables, to select a group of records to export to another database, or to use as a basis for reports that display data from a specific time.

This book will not go into the process of importing existing data, but if you would like to learn more about how it is done, you can use the help feature in Access.

Creating Forms

Once again, creating forms can be done in multiple ways. There is a Form Wizard that will help you create a form, or you can create a form on your own. The Form Wizard speeds up the process of creating a form because it does all the basic work for you. When you use a Form Wizard, Microsoft Access prompts you for information and creates a form based on your answers. Even if you have created many forms, you may want to use a Form Wizard to quickly lay out all the controls on your form. You can then switch to the Design View to customize your form.

To create a form with a wizard, start with these beginning steps then follow along with the wizard's prompts.

1. In the Database window, click the Forms tab.
2. Click New.
3. In the New Form dialog box, click the wizard that you want to use. A description of the wizard appears to the left side of the dialog box.
4. Click the name of the table or query that includes the data you want to base your form on. You do not need to do this step if you click the Form Wizard option; you can specify the record source for the form in the wizard.
5. Click OK.
6. If you clicked Form Wizard, Chart Wizard, or PivotTable Wizard in step 3, follow the directions in the wizard dialog boxes. If you clicked AutoForm: Columnar, AutoForm: Tabular, or AutoForm: DataSheet, Microsoft Access automatically creates your form.
7. If the resulting form does not look the way you want, you can change it in Design view. If you click one of the AutoForm options, Microsoft Access uses the auto format you last specified, either in the Form Wizard or by using the AutoFormat command on the Format menu in Design view.

If you are feeling adventurous and would like to try creating your form on your own, the process is more tedious, but not difficult. Here are some steps to get you started.

1. In the Database window, click the Forms tab.
2. Click New.
3. In the New Form dialogue box, click Design View.
4. Click the name of the table or query that includes the data you want to base your form on. If the form you are creating will not contain data (for example, if you want to create a form to use as a switchboard to open other forms

or reports or you want to create a custom dialogue box), do not select anything from this list. If you want to create a form that uses data from more than one table, base your form on a query that includes the tables you want to include.

5. Click OK. Microsoft Access displays the Form window in the Design View. It is here that you can add additional controls if you would like.

Inserting Customer Data

Now that you have your database created and forms to use, it is time to do your data entry. This process, although somewhat tiresome, is a very real part of using a database. The database is useless without data. Often this process is automated by pulling the information from existing resources as mentioned before. It can also be automated by extracting the data from forms that are filled out by the customers. A good example of this is the Web-based forms that you probably see all the time. These are very useful for gathering information as long as they are properly done and targeted at the proper audience. If your audience does not surf the Web or visit your Web site, a Web-based form of data collection is useless.

Additional Database Resources

If you are interested in more material on databases and marketing, there are many good resources that will give additional information. You can also do a search on the Web to see how others are using databases and how they are combining database, Web, and marketing concepts.

Summary

Marketing has come full circle—from the person-to-person selling of the village baker and tailor and shoemaker of centuries ago to the impersonal world of mass media and mass merchandising, and back once again to highly personalized customer accommodation and cultivation (one customer relationship at a time) now made possible by new information technology and the new interactive media on a vast scale. (Rapp and Collins 1996, 251) It is to the advantage of the marketer to learn about customer data collection, database storage, and customer data retrieval to out-service the competition, as Rapp and Collins describe as "personalized customer accommodation and cultivation." As the chapter opening quote emphasized, companies are collecting millions of customer names and characteristics, and it is most difficult to deal with this enormous amount of data. Companies such as Oracle Corporation have built back-end software systems to organize and sort extensive information to the benefit of consumer and business marketers nationwide. With this information, the marketer that wants to survive into the twenty-first century must embrace many new marketing technologies including database management. "Unless you are selling a single low-price, low-usage product with very limited LCV, your company can and should make [full use of the database] a vital of your sales strategy." (ibid.) Reviewing the profitable companies serving the consumer and business markets, it more often than not is the added-value products that are bought with discretionary income, as opposed to necessities such as food, electrical or gas power, or potable water. These added-value products, therefore, become enhanced by strategic and tactical marketing programs driven by information from databases.

Key Terms

Database

Database management

Domain

Entity

Field

File

Filter

Foreign key

Form

Hit

Join

Key

Many-to-many relationship

One-to-many relationship

Primary key

Project

Report

Query

Record

Relationship

Relational database

Row

Schema

Select query

Sequential Query Language (SQL)

Session

Table

Transactions

Value

Visitor

QUESTIONS AND EXERCISES

1. Perhaps your company is very small with few but very active customers. You have analyzed the electronic database method, but you feel that it will be too costly and time-consuming to track your customers via an Access database. What would be your alternative for keeping accurate records on your customers' purchase history and preferences? Make a list of the

types of data that you feel is important for ongoing customer knowledge and how you would record this information. Direct your list to your purchasing or inventory staff in a memo form.

2. Different businesses use the database function for different purposes. Make a list of twenty businesses or industries and speculate what each would use database management for. Compare your list to other members of your group.

3. What is the difference between transactional and relational databases? Define the two and give examples of the usage of each one. What types of businesses would use one or the other, or both? Prepare a memo on the concept for submission to a retail client you are servicing.

4. What is the difference between many-to-many database relationships and one-to-many database relationships? What types of businesses or suppliers would use one or the other? Write an e-mail to your instructor defining the concepts.

5. Define in writing the following words or concepts:
   a) query
   b) record
   c) table
   d) field
   e) row
   f) value

6. Define in writing the following words or concepts:
   a) search
   b) filter
   c) join
   d) schema

7. What is the definition of a primary key? The definition of a foreign key? Write an explanation of the two and how each would be used in database activities.

8. Microsoft Access is very flexible in the implementation of database design; there are several ways to perform the same function, such as designing a table. What are the four ways to create a blank (empty) table in using Access. List and explain the four methods.

9. The text discussed two major ways for designing and executing a database table, either using a Design Wizard or creating it from scratch. Explain the differences between these two methods. In what situations is the marketer better served from one or the other method? Give examples of business situations that apply to each. Be prepared to discuss this design concept in class.

10. Using the suggestions developed by the text and help screens in Microsoft Access, prepare a simple marketing database for a video rental store. What would you as a marketing manager wish to know about your customers' characteristics. Make a table of twelve to fifteen personal items (first name, last name, street address, so forth) that would be unique to each customer. Create the table and enter six real or fictitious persons. Print the database and turn it in to your instructor. If you need assistance, call the computing department at your university or perhaps the help lab at your business school for more information on Microsoft Access.

Bibliography

Brady, Regina, Edward Forrest, and Richard Mizerski. 1997. *Cybermarketing.* Lincolnwood, Ill.: NTC Publishing Group.

Chen, Paul. 1997. Hit-or-miss measurement. *Marketing Tools,* March, 22.

Internet World Labs Report. 1997. *Internet World,* June, 75–76.

Rapp, Stan and Thomas L. Collins. 1996. *The new MaxiMarketing.* New York City: McGraw-Hill.

CHAPTER 13

Considerations for Ongoing Customer Communications

"It would be a crime to ignore an ideal way to communicate with your customers. Even so, most companies are building World Wide Web sites in order to communicate to *their customers instead of* with *them. The majority of Web sites are created to provide an electronic brochure, essentially the Internet version of a sales pitch, a sort of online television ad. Yes, people can get the specific information they're interested in, but there is little thought given to two-way communication. The Internet offers a whole new way to establish rapport with customers. Answering customer questions, solving their problems, selling them additional products can now be computerized. It took a healthy bit of prodding to push banks into the twenty-first century with automated teller machines. Now, all companies can provide their customers push-button service without installing networks of cash machines. They can do it all through the World Wide Web.*

The Web offers means of creating the all-important bond of trust and loyalty between buyer and seller. Different companies are using the Web to sell different products and services, and give their customers another means of conducting business. The rewards have been lower customer service costs and higher customer satisfaction. These are clearly goals to be envied."

(Sterne 1996, 1–2)

LEARNING OBJECTIVES

- To demonstrate how the Web can be used to facilitate customer service
- To present techniques to encourage customer response, the two-way communications benefit of the Web
- To show how HTML can be used to construct customer and prospect survey instruments

Introduction

Chances are that if your company is a successful online marketer, it will be receiving great amounts of customer and supplier communications. These might come in the form of letters, postcards, telephone calls, faxes, and e-mails; the subjects of these might be inquiries, orders, compliments, or complaints. Many customers judge a company on its responsiveness to their communications, and the communications that become lost in the cracks is equivalent to a slap in the face for either praising or protesting customers. As a proactive measure in dealing with thousands of calls or e-mails daily, responsive companies are installing e-mail software systems to acknowledge that the company has at least received your message. A recent article written by Richard Schaefer in *Fortune* magazine adds to the above point about Web use: "Consumers are using e-mail much more frequently because there is no per-minute charge and no holding for the customer service rep." (1999) Customer service is being **automated** by electronic resources as a method for achieving competitive advantage.

Customer service may be added as an ongoing function to the *P*s of the promotional mix, especially for companies that are serious about relationship marketing. The other *P*s transpire (and expire) as the purchase is consummated. Savvy direct marketing companies like Lands' End and L. L. Bean have long been recognized for having the stance that customer needs may extend past a singular purchase, and these organizations have built pliable customer service programs and personnel to react to customers' input. After-purchase, strong customer service as a competitive advantage can bring the purchaser back full circle to become a shopper among the company's products. If word-of-mouth referrals are the largest source of online sales, attentive customer service should be the largest online listening post.

The Value of Repeat Customers

Retailers and wholesalers along with their suppliers are forever running around looking for new customers and trying to determine what these new customers like. The retailers chant, New business, new customers, where can I get more? Many suppliers such as advertising agencies and public relations firms have actually conducted new business programs for some clients, misguidedly assuming they should be doing this for their clients when in reality it is not necessary. It is the retailer's or service's responsibility to produce products and services attractive to a niche market, and then retain these customers through product satisfaction and customer service. In this textbook and in other classes, you have heard that it is six to twenty times (depending on the study and the industry) less expensive to sell to existing customers than to attract new ones. Why? Just think of the monies expended on production of new lines of goods and on media advertising, particularly the television expenses of air time and production; the expense of beefing up the servers' and modems' capacities; the price of designing and printing vast amounts of brochures and other collateral material; the cost of establishing new locations and exterior signage; the expense of hiring new staff to maximize the media coverage; the fees of sundry consultants from financial to legal to design to public relations counsel; and the possible cost of licenses or franchise agreements to expand to serve this new business. These are significant figures when combined, all for the sake of new customers.

Marketers should instead consider spending a fraction of this amount to satisfy and enhance the goods' performance and services' delivery to past customers who are satisfied with the product or service. The proof of a product is not in the initial purchase, which could have been influenced by a steep discount, two-for-one incentives, compelling advertising, or even the recommendation of a trusted friend or relative. The proof of a good product is in the customer's *repurchase* of a good or service. This

IS THIS REALLY CUSTOMER SERVICE?

Companies are bombarded with hundreds of messages per day, each from a valued customer who expects a rapid response. Now computer technology is trying to solve the problem it helped create. Chances are, next time you send a note to Corporate.com, the personalized answer you get will come from software that has guessed what you're after—the Internet's equivalent of the form letter. This may or may not result in better service, but one thing is clear: On the Web, the robots aren't coming; they're here.

Robots is the term given to software that can scan the text of an incoming e-mail and respond intelligently—without human intervention. **Natural language understanding**—or the ability of computers to understand and respond appropriately to written sentences of the kind that people use every day—hasn't advanced nearly as far as speech recognition, which is passing into the mainstream. Despite limitations, customer service without human intervention is the wave of the future.

Sterne, Jim. 1996. *Customer service on the Internet.* New York City: John Wiley & Sons, 1–2.

is mindful of the old saying, Fool me once, it's your fault; fool me two times, it's my fault. The merchant could concentrate his marketing resources on good customers that have chosen to shop at the site or store. Electronic marketing provides excellent tools for focusing efforts on fewer persons, attempting to achieve a mutually beneficial relationship; on one side is customer satisfaction and on the other, profitable operations. The Web's capabilities can be programmed to deliver gratitude, congratulations, or confirmations to existing clients; provide technical support for new product users; conduct surveys inquiring what changes the customer would like to see; expand communications to outside suppliers and the general community, and supply associates with the latest company news first. Previously, several different vehicles were needed to deliver information to these diverse constituencies, and now the Web serves as a singular news carrier, be it good or bad tidings.

Where Do You Stand?

Like the steps of the marketing process, it is best to learn what customers think about a product or service before the marketer launches new, ambitious customer service programs. Therefore, in a customer relations effort, the marketer should establish a benchmark as to what customers and potential customers think of your site and its offerings. The Web is well suited for conducting prospect and customer, supplier, and ex-customer opinions. Why are customer attitudes and opinions important? Many companies today strive for a value-added customer service strategy, much as the company has anticipated the needs, inconveniences, and problems of their customers and have put into place programs and policies to supply the needs or alleviate the inconveniences and problems before they happen. One software resource that can be installed on a company home page is a program developed by "Ask Jeeves" (http://askjeeves.com); it produces instant responses to customer inquiries on the corporate Web site—another demonstration of acknowledgment. Marketers want the consumer to have a positive impression of the company and its products, to be thought of as a good neighbor to the community, and to be considered the employer of choice. These perceptions are even more important for the e-marketer because of the anonymity of cyberspace and the lack of physical presence. It is doubtful that an electronic shopper or surfer would return to a site that does not provide honest information, answers to e-mails, or the option to repair or exchange an unsatisfied product or refund money for this product. Customers and e-customers expect better treatment. While many of these thoughts are common public relations activities, the marketer should make effective customer service a high primary within her marketing plan.

Electronic marketing tools allow the customer extensive knowledge about a product or about a company through information on a company's Web site or through hyperlinks on the Web site, both which can share enormous amounts of communications about the company's activities or the product's benefits or performance records. As was discussed previously, the Web site can be an extensive repository of business information at the prospect's or customer's fingertips. Automobile sites are examples of giving the customer a broad range of product information about various models; each hyperlink connecting to more specific data. Looking at the Ford Motor Company (www.ford.com) Web site, for instance, the first page is a choice of two hyperlinks: one for company information and one for product information. The product link furnishes ample information for "Models," "Customer Service," "Find a Dealer," "Warranty," or "Car Care." As you click on more links, you navigate to the information you desire. This site is an example of self-service customer service. Another example of self-service information is the American Express site (www.americanexpress.com); a comprehensive form guides the viewer through choices of information that will be sent immediately. After all, the purpose of marketing and customer service is to facilitate the consumer in doing business with you, and hopefully only you.

As business speeds along, people send or ship time-sensitive material and merchandise via specialized couriers, such as UPS and FedEx, both having the capabilities of tracking a package's entire route. A shipper can then pull this information regarding his package from the appropriate Web site. The Web is an enabler in instant situation knowledge, whether it be world news, sports scores, or product inventory. Answers to customer service questions can be obtained by accessing hyperlinks, and many people are the self-service type who want to do it themselves, probably to avoid busy signals or even speaking to an uninformed representative. The marketer should develop a full customer service plan and test it before putting it on the company's Web page. Why? As a caller is disappointed when a telephone number is nonworking, the viewer is equally annoyed when she cannot find an answer regarding an organization among the standard FAQs on this organization's Web site. Customer response or opinion polls can be conducted on Web sites or by e-mail to determine advantages or disadvantages of the performance of an existing product's Web site or to gain feedback on proposed new product concepts, as was the strategy of Volkswagen in designing the new Beetle. This kind of research can also be conducted through lapsed buyers, people who are past customers. An e-mail survey might be appropriate to receive honest answers. People are less hesitant in expressing their opinions electronically or by mail than they are face to face to an interviewer.

Companies are finding substantial cost savings in information transfer between offices that have heavy paperwork involving high sales volume tied to customer service records. Dell Computer would be a good example of this tactic with its Web site and telephone sales of its products. Customers expect Dell to know the intricacies of the systems they have purchased; with questions, the user telephones or e-mails the customer service department, which maintains extensive customer equipment records. With either a name and zip code, serial numbers, or purchase order numbers, customer support can be dispensed with minimal time both to the Dell user and to the Dell customer representative. Companies with extensive human resources records also benefit from electronic tools, this case EDI (electronic data interchange). These information transfers can travel across the street, across the nation, or across the continents; faster and faster interchange technology will provide new and more convenient applications for the e-customers and the e-marketer.

Should It Be Called Customer Communications?

The value of positive customer communications is glaringly apparent from this consumer research finding. In a study of customers' dissatisfactions, it was found that two-thirds of the reasons for the customer displeasure were breakdowns in communications, and only one-third were attributable to actual product failure or poor service. Customer relationships are vital for long-term benefits of both parties, and never before has customer communications been as expedited and rich as with today's electronic vehicles. Of course, this dialogue does require initiative by the marketer for establishing and maintaining the lines. Hopefully, the dialogue presents an imbalance, that of little effort on the part of the customer or prospect, and more effort on the part of the company. Marketers are computing the value of ongoing relationships, whether it be longtime customers, light or heavy users, or consumer or business prospects; communication is the issue, not the category. (Whiteley 1991, 55) Further, studies have shown that dissatisfied customers will tell at least ten other people about their bad experience (which, of course, is bad advertising for the company). However, with the Internet, that figure could potentially be multiplied by thousands. There are several news groups on the Net (like the Deja News site) where consumers trade information about the treatment they have gotten from companies. Now a consumer who feels ripped off or mistreated does not have to settle for telling a handful of people—she can broadcast her story to thousands. It is something companies should take into consideration. "After all, a company's reputation is the most powerful advertising around." (McDonnell 1998) Following are addresses of two news groups that contain interesting stories about customer service: alt.consumers.experiences and misc.consumers.

Given this awesome reach and speed of communication, who reaps greater benefit in maintaining a positive dialogue? Is the customer more interested in having his questions answered, or is the marketer more interested in servicing this potential business? Ranking the value of quick responses to interested prospects and customers, you would expect an inquiry entering the customer service or marketing departments to be given high priority. Take the act of replying to a customer e-mail, Jupiter Research found there were gaps in service performance:

> Forty-two percent of the top-ranked Web sites either took longer than five days to reply to customer e-mail inquiries, never replied, or were not accessible by e-mail. [The Jupiter report] illustrates that Web sites are ignoring the opportunity to communicate with existing or potential customers, discouraging brand loyalty, and opting out of a user-initiated, one-to-one relationship by not offering, delaying, or eliminating responses to e-mail. Jupiter found that of the 125 sites examined, most retail shopping sites performed the best, with 54 percent responding in less than one day. However, in some segments there is ample room for improvement. For example, 19 percent of the travel sites tested took at least three days or never responded to Jupiter's inquiries.
>
> "This effort that many Web sites have been unable or unprepared to respond to the flood of user questions that come in via e-mail from their sites, [is a big problem]." says Ken Allard, group director of Jupiter's Site Operation Strategies practice. "Answering thousands of questions per month is an enormous challenge for sites offering complex products and services, especially if they never had a traditional call center. Yet, companies that delay responses to user questions instantly lose a significant degree of credibility and user loyalty, and not responding perpetuates the consumer notion that using the Web site is not a reliable method of doing business with that company."
>
> Jupiter recommends that sites develop or utilize some form of **"auto-knowledge"** features that responds to all incoming reports stating that the question was received and estimates a time frame for how long it will take to respond to the question. (Jupiter Communications 1998, 2)

It is the marketer's job, therefore, to initiate, nurture, and improve the customer service process. Is customer service a process? Surely you will notice that "ongoing" is included in this chapter's title. No merchant should go forward with e-commerce without the mindset that there is no finish line. Are managers satisfied with the company's customer service activities?

> A Jupiter Research survey of thirty executives across online travel, financial services, and retail sectors indicates that most believe their current customer service solutions are inadequate. Ninety percent of these managers indicated that they plan to change their customer service offerings within the next twelve months. "Online retailers are now waking up to the growing customer command for support and are beginning to recognize the opportunity to convert shoppers into purchasers, via more proactive customer service," said Fiona S. Swerdlow, analyst, Digital Commerce. "However, online merchants must reserve costly human intervention for activities directly related to customer conversion and automate functions such as order tracking and suggestive selling." (ibid., 1)

Success revolves around relationships, and relationships revolve around longevity. There is nothing worse than dialing an address that you enjoyed only to find that a "File not found" message returned or dialing a telephone number again to find that the number you have dialed is no longer in service. With longevity in mind, how should an e-marketer structure her ongoing customer service program?

Establishing the Electronic Customer Service Program

You might begin establishing your electronic customer service program by asking yourself, How would I like to be treated if I were the customer? You might then investigate competitors' customer service pages and programs, particularly the successful competitors. What can you learn from the response process to e-mail inquiries or the schedules for promised delivery? From this situation and competitive analysis, the marketer is suited to make better judgments for the customer service standards. Remember as well that one standard cannot serve all the audiences that deal with the company. Should these standards vary between companies and industries? It depends. Some industries are fast-paced, while others move slower. You would expect the computer and advertising industries to want everything yesterday, while some commodities firms dealing in ores and other raw materials might have less stringent time requirements. The decision on customer service standards should come from the marketer's customers. They should dictate what their expectations on timing or accuracy should be.

Evaluating the Sources of Feedback

Linda Silverman Goldzimer, in writing *I'm First: Your Customers Message to You*, developed a solid hierarchy the marketer can follow in gathering feedback from the many customer and noncustomer segments that a business encounters and interacts with. The marketer would be surprised how many audiences he deals with on a weekly basis, and the feelings of these audiences produce the aggregate image of the company either online or in their place in business society. In any plan for commerce, online or traditional, these **listening posts** must be identified and ranked so that appropriate communications mechanisms can be set to gather opinions—positive and negative. What are some of the sources that should be monitored? Goldzimer produces a comprehensive list of valuable sources, arranged in a descending order of importance (not that any are unimportant).

Source 1: Customer Complaints

Customer complaints are most pointed and immediate. People want their orders fixed here and now. An important part of conflict resolution is not start by trying to affix blame but rather to solve the problem. In fact, good e-merchants should shoulder the blame (It is all our fault, and how can we make it right?), accept responsibility, and move forward toward solving the problem. If there is a weak link in your fulfillment system, be it a person or a policy, investigate this issue later. Be sure to instruct the customer service manager to keep a list of complaints, and entering the data into a program probably is the most efficient and accurate way to keep these records. After a while, the most common customer complaints will become evident. Take initiative to prepare a FAQ page on the company Web site to answer simple customer questions. (Preview Travel (www.previewtravel.com) displays a simple but relevant FAQ section to travelers on its "Customer Service" Web page.) Then, in a more studied fashion, the customer service activities can be reviewed with changes made as necessary. Perhaps customers are complaining about breakage problems that would lead the manager to inspect the packing materials, the handling procedures, or the procedures by the delivery supplier. There may be a constant complainer among your customer base, but be patient. For each constant complainer, you may have one hundred solid, loyal purchasers who are pleased.

Source 2: Direct Customer Contact

Within the realm of cybermarketing, feedback from direct customer contact may be rare, but whenever the marketer comes face to face with a customer—present or past—the marketer should take the initiative to ask question after question about the customer's online experiences. These encounters might occur in business-to-business settings such as meetings at industry trade shows or perhaps appointments with key accounts that order large amounts of the company's products. These are excellent opportunities to find out, as New York City ex-mayor Ed Koch used to ask, "How am I doing?" or what the competition is doing better than the marketer's company is doing. Usually with direct questions, you will receive direct answers. After these valuable interviews, the marketer should write up the exchange and circulate it among his associates, customer service included.

Source 3: Your Own E-mail

Goldzimer originally wrote her third source as mail, but to update and make this source more relevant to this book's discussion, both e-mail and U.S. Postal Service mail will be considered. Some disgruntled customers might pick up the telephone to complain, while others are less confrontational and would therefore choose to write the customer service department a complaint. E-mail seems more immediate and possibly threatening, but letters carry equal weight of complaint and should be remedied with similar dispatch. Not everyone has access to the Internet, so the proportion of opinion letter writers to e-mail writers might be equal even though the purchaser bought online. Successful executives make practice of reading their correspondence daily and answering all e-mails by the end of the day. This involvement is a sound communications and public relations action that both solves short-term problems with customers and creates goodwill among customers and associates.

Source 4: The Formal Customer Survey

This activity should be considered carefully, or customers might consider this to be a spamming or an unsolicited e-mail. E-mail and HTML lend themselves well to surveys, and the responses should be analyzed carefully. Again, over time great suggestions might come from your customer base. It has been said that the best ideas come from your customers; all the marketer has to do is listen. For surveys, it might be wise to engage a marketing research firm to develop the questionnaire and then have the research firm administer the first two surveys for answers' compilation and analysis. Thereafter, the manager of marketing or customer service can apply the procedure to future surveys. The survey should ask simple questions to generate direct answers. After the survey is completed, the marketer should act on the results and suggestions. Too many surveys and too much money have been wasted if the survey results went unheeded. While the Internet is a less costly way to survey the company's marketing segments, the results are no less credible or valuable.

Source 5: Suppliers and Manufacturers

These sources are additional listening posts within the marketplace, and the prudent marketer should take advantage of suppliers' and manufacturers' opinions and observations. These businesspeople work with many different organizations, and see and hear what interests or trends are forming or what is going out of style. Most suppliers are dedicated to seeing their customers succeed because success means more business for them. This holds true for the manufacturer as well. This point assumes that the e-marketer is doing just that—marketing the goods and services made by other companies or assembled from suppliers' materials—and, therefore, there is little competition between the distribution chain. With a spirit of cooperation, suppliers and manufacturers tend to look out for their customers.

Source 6: Employee and Associates Sessions

Many successful executives take it upon themselves to visit far-flung facilities to gather input on the customer opinions of that region. It is easy to sit in your office and cut yourself off from the real world—associates, customers, market conditions. This marketer, however, does not last long in a position of authority. While electronic commerce is organized differently from traditional businesses in that the Web brings distant customers to the site, the marketing manager of the Web site can sample employee opinions within the organization. This requires an eighties management technique of management by walking around to learn who is doing what and how well. The marketer must remember that employees are an important segment of customers that the company must entertain. Agitated employees will deliver agitated and possibly negative customer communications, and it takes very little empathy for the customer to read an unhappy customer service representative's feelings, even over the telephone. You should keep close to the employees' feedback as an important gauge of overall company self-satisfaction.

Source 7: Your Neighborhood

In this case, the marketer should participate in the business organizations to gain better insight into the workings of the local business community. Intimate knowledge of the local Chamber of Commerce, business round tables, government officials, or business task forces can be helpful in establishing positive company credentials, and the business sector could be a helpful customer group. You can volunteer to create a news group for the organization and become the monitor and expediter of group ideas and online activities. Feedback from these groups can be valuable in the long-term standing of the company. The marketer should budget her time to attend meetings and follow through on committee assignments because the performance of the individual representing the firm will be reflective of the expected performance of the company. If the individual's work is poor or sloppy, the perception of the company will be the same.

Source 8: Community Involvement

As in working the business community, the marketer should participate in projects for community benefit. Again, as marketer you could organize a neighborhood news group to share ideas or publish news. This might also entail organizing food or clothing drives during the holidays, joining United Way and encouraging the staff to join, or supporting a local children's home; there are dozens of worthwhile causes and charities to assist. Within the community news group, these projects are news. These activities build both the employees' self-esteem and the firm's image as well as add to the betterment of another important opinion group. Hopefully the firm's activities can be related to retailing interests that would reinforce the e-commerce purpose of the company.

Source 9: The Online Community Involvement

If the firm should sponsor a special online conference that concerns the entire online community, something such as privacy or secure electronic transactions, the e-commerce company could gain enormous feedback for their initiatives. At this point, what is good for the cybermarketer is good for the industry. The promotional efforts to expand the image and services of e-commerce should occupy the minds of e-marketers and take a place in e-marketing plans. Speaking frequently with online merchants and storefront developers will provide firsthand feedback on the state of the business and probably generate new ideas for the e-marketer. This business communications is another example of staying close to the customer and in determining what programs are working. E-commerce is young, so the marketer should seek feedback from all corners. Promotional efforts will be discussed in greater detail in Chapter 14. (Goldzimer 1989, 68–96)

Delivering Service as the Number One Priority

Sometimes the only concrete proof of an e-commerce firm is its performance in customer service. Yes, the merchandise was delivered or downloaded to the purchaser, but the e-commerce site did not manufacture the goods. Therefore, the importance of solid, consistent customer service is the discerning factor that sets one company above the others. In organizing a customer service program, two ingredients create a winning program: First, the marketer must insist on hiring excellent representatives; secondly, superior training of these representatives must be undertaken. These two steps can be followed up with the other portions of the customer service program, such as setting standards for customer service, time-lapse elements, and activities schedule to solve problems. Common sense treatment emerges: Do not let the phones ring more than three times; call in on your lines to see how you are treated; and consider designating a person to check the e-mail bin every two hours. People do not like to wait. Act rationally on this input because problems rarely go away, and consumers are typically well-informed merchants. Now that you should have a good basis for information-gathering methods, the making of electronic forms and surveys should be discussed.

Making Web Forms

Forms are one of the most popular features on the Web for conducting business. They can add a flexible dimension of interactivity to your Web documents by allowing you to conduct surveys, take orders, sign up users, gather feedback, even administer tests. Forms can be very simple or highly complex. However, forms by themselves do nothing but collect the data entered by the user and archive the data until you decipher what to do with the information. This is done with a small program or **script** that is usually placed in a directory on the Web server called the **cgi-bin.** In many places, these directories are only accessible by the **system administrator,** due to security risks that programs such as these can cause. The following table outlines some sites that have good examples of using forms on the Web.

Description of Web Form	URL of Web Form
Wal-Mart' customer survey	http://w3a.wal-mart.com/survey
Nabisco's Guest Book Form	http://www.nabisco.com/
Buick's Talk With Us	http://www.buick.com/buickhome/project/talk_with_us/talk/ta_index.htm

Nabisco (www.nabisco.com)
The Nabisco Neighborhood invites visitors to sign its "Guestbook" page on the Web site for recipes, e-mails, and other special offers. This registration also builds an e-mailing list as well as consumer and product data.

Although you can create a form, and even have the script to run it, you alone will probably not be able to make it work. If you have questions, your system administrator can review your script for security loop holes and place your script into the cgi-bin so that you can use your form. HTML 4.0 has made it possible to run the scripting necessary from the client side of the Web browser, if the Web server you are using has been set up that way. If this is the case, you can create and use forms without the help of the system administrator. For security reasons this will probably not be available in most cases just yet. However, your service provider may offer some general CGI (Common Gateway Interface) scripts in a library that could be utilized for many purposes. CGI is a set of standards by which servers communicate with external programs. This will be discussed in greater detail later in this chapter. A couple of general script examples that may be offered by a service provider are a hit counter and a guest book feature. (See Nabisco's Guest Book site for a good example of this feature.)

What Is a Form?

A form is a graphical user interface that uses text entry fields and areas, buttons, **check boxes,** pull-down menus, scrolling lists, and other specialized graphics. A form can be simple or intricate. It can fill the whole Web page, or it can be part of a document. However, the form will need to consist of at least a few elements or tags in order to work properly. The most important tags are ⟨FORM⟩, ⟨/FORM⟩, and some type of input tag. A form can also contain additional tags to make them more attractive, and these tags can even be placed in a table to create a more stylized look. Here is a table showing the tags that can be used in a form.

The FORM Tag

Example	⟨FORM ACTION="URL of processing script" Method="GET or POST"⟩ . . . ⟨/FORM⟩
Function	Contains the text and tags that comprise an HTML form
Attributes	ACCEPT-CHARSET, ACTION, ENCTYPE, METHOD, TARGET
Related Tags	⟨INPUT⟩, ⟨SELECT⟩, ⟨OPTIONS⟩, ⟨TEXTAREA⟩, ⟨BUTTON⟩, ⟨LABEL⟩, ⟨FIELDSET⟩, ⟨LEGEND⟩

Some of the attributes of the form tag are very important. The **ACTION attribute** points the form to a URL that will accept the form's information and do something with it. If you do not specify an ACTION, the server sends the information back to the original URL. A little explanation about how the Web form works could be useful in understanding how important this attribute is. Web servers are programs that know how to distribute Web pages. It would not be feasible for them to be programmed to process data from every possible form as well, so they hand off the information gathered from the form to another program that is designed in conjunction with the form and knows how to process the information. This hand off occurs with the help of the Common Gateway Interface (CGI).

Therefore, in order for the forms that you create to work, they must have an accompanying script or small program that deals with the information to and from the form. Forms by themselves do nothing but collect the data entered by the user and wait for instructions by the user in determining what to do with the data. This script is typically called a **CGI script** or a CGI program. The CGI script performs some manipulations of the data and composes a response that is typically sent back to the user's browser as an HTML page.

The **METHOD attribute** tells the form how to send its information back to the script. The most common type of method is **POST,** which sends all the information from the form separately from the URL. The other option for METHOD is **GET.** GET tracks the information from the form to the end of the URL. POST is usually the best method to use, however. The data passed by the METHOD is the information that the script reads and processes. The outcome of the data depends on how the script is written. CGI scripts will be discussed in a bit more detail later.

In order to actually collect data from your form, there must be a way for the user to input information and a way for the browser to collect it. The tags related to the form tag are used to accomplish this. The most versatile is the **INPUT** attribute. INPUT is a single tag option for gathering information, which contains other options for gathering information. It is the most versatile HTML tag because it has many different options and many attributes. The input options are listed in the following table.

The INPUT Tag

Example	⟨INPUT TYPE="CHECKBOX" NAME="field_name" VALUE="field_value" CHECKED DISABLED⟩
Function	Places one of the following form controls on the form: Text, password, or hidden fields Check boxes Radio buttons File upload fields Image-based buttons Scripted buttons Submit and reset buttons
Attributes	Each type of input tag can have different attributes. They will be discussed separately, but here is a list of possible attributes: ACCEPT, ALIGN, CHECKED, DISABLED, LENGTH, MAXLENGTH, NAME, ONCLICK, USEMAP, VALUE, READONLY, SIZE, SRC
Related Tags	None

Since the different input types can vary so much and are so important to creating the perfect form, the following discussion will summarize each of them. Most input types require a **NAME attribute** that sets a unique name for the information being passed to the server. An example is a text box for entering a last name, which might have a NAME of "last." This name must be the same in the form and in the script that will process the information. Most input tags also use the **VALUE** attribute to assign an original or default value to the input. For example, the **TEXT** type displays a simple line of text. The NAME option is required so that the script will know what is being input by the user. TEXT can use the **LENGTH** attribute to specify how many characters will show in the input box. It can also use MAXLENGTH to limit the number of characters that can be entered by the user. The VALUE option would be used to provide text present in the field initially (in other words, a hint to the user or a default input). The **PASSWORD** type is a modified text field displaying bullets instead of the characters actually typed. This is used to protect the user's password from watching eyes, but it does not encrypt the password when it is sent to the server. The same options are used here as with TEXT. Hidden fields are used when you want to send a value to the server, but do not necessarily want the user to see it. The **HIDDEN** type attribute uses NAME and VALUE. As the user will not actually see this input, you must pass the value you wish it to contain to the server in the form code.

The CHECKBOX type is a valuable resource for surveys and order forms. It displays a simple check box that can be either checked (preset to a value) or empty to start. It should be used when there can be more than one choice. The options available with the check box are NAME (required), VALUE, CHECKED, and DISABLED. The RADIO type is a more complex version of check box that allows only one of a set to be chosen. They are good for items that require a yes/no or either/or answer. **Radio buttons** are grouped together using the NAME option The remaining options are the same as CHECKBOX.

In order to provide a file upload feature, you must use the FILE type. This provides the user with a file manager-like window, allowing them to look for and insert the path of a file to upload. The FILE type uses the NAME, VALUE, ACCEPT, and DISABLED attributes. The IMAGE type is used to create an image-based button. The SRC attribute tells the browser where it can find the source image file for the button similar to the SRC attribute in the IMG tag presented earlier. The ALT attribute provides a textual alternative to the image in case the user does not have a graphical browser. **ALIGN** can be used to control how the image is aligned on the page, and USEMAP can be used as it is in a regular image map. DISABLED will disable the button. A scripted button can also be used to execute a script when the button is clicked. This type uses the VALUE attribute to specify the text that will be on the button face. The ONCLICK attribute is set equal to the name of the script to be executed. The script for these types of buttons is not the same as for the CGI script that processes the form data. The button scripts are usually written in a programming language like Javascript or VBScript. This button can be deactivated using the DISABLED attribute.

The **SUBMIT** type displays a push button with the preset function of sending data from the form to the server. VALUE can be used to change the text on the button. The RESET type displays a push button with the preset function of clearing data from the form to the original values. VALUE can be used to change the text on the button. If DISABLED is used, the buttons will be turned off.

Other tags that can be used in a form provide different ways for the user to input information on your form. For example, the TEXTAREA tag allows you to provide an area for multiple-line text entry. A TEXTAREA shows a blank field with four rows of information, forty characters wide by default. It can be made any size by setting the ROWS and COLS in the tag. Text can also be entered by placing it between the TEXTAREA tags. The following table lists the options for the TEXTAREA tags.

The TEXT AREA Tag

Example	⟨TEXTAREA NAME="Addresses" ROWS="2" COLS="60"⟩Please delete this test and enter your address here . . . ⟨/TEXTAREA⟩
Function	Sets up a multiline text input box on the form
Attributes	COLS, DISABLED, NAME READONLY, ROWS
Related Tags	None

The **SELECT** tag shows a list of choices in either a pop-up menu or a scrollable list. It contains an opening and closing tag with a number of choices listed in between. The SELECT tag requires a NAME attribute to define the name for the data in the script. You can specify how many choices to show at once using the SIZE option. If you omit size or set it to 1, choices are shown as a pop-up menu. If you set it to 2 or higher, it shows choices in a scrollable box. If you set the SIZE larger than the number of choices you have within SELECT, a nothing choice will be added. When the user chooses this, it is returned as an empty field. MULTIPLE is used to allow multiple selections when using a scrollable list. The choices are presented to the user by placing them within the SELECT tag inside of the OPTION tag. A VALUE can be assigned to a choice. This value is what is sent back to the script and does not have to be the same as what the user sees. Use SELECTED on the OPTION tag if you want one of the choices to be set as a default. The following table is an example of the use of a SELECT tag.

The SELECT Tag

Example	⟨SELECT NAME="Color" SIZE=5⟩ ⟨OPTION⟩Red⟨/OPTION⟩ ⟨OPTION⟩Navy⟨/OPTION⟩ ⟨OPTION⟩Black⟨/OPTION⟩ ⟨OPTION⟩Beige⟨/OPTION⟩ . . . ⟨/SELECT⟩
Function	Creates a list of choices from which a user can make a selection of one item or many items.
Attributes	DISABLED, MULTIPLE, NAME, SIZE, VALUE
Related Tags	⟨OPTION⟩

How to Make CGI Scripts Work

As was discussed previously, for the forms that you create to work, they must have an accompanying script or small program that deals with the information to and from the form. Forms by themselves do nothing but collect the data entered by the user and store it until you to tell the forms what to do with the. This script is placed in a **cgi-bin** directory on the Web server. Usually, these directories are only accessible by the system administrator. Although you may be able to create your forms fairly easily, scripting is a little harder and often requires some programming ability. A script for forms like those that have been considered here are usually created in a programming language. How to create scripts will not be discussed in this book; that may be a subject for a more-advanced course on Web site design. Exhibit 13.1 however, shows a form like the ones discussed above.

Your script and your form must match up in order for the script to handle the information the form is passing. This means that the name of the variables (for example, First, for first name) must be the same in both places. This is why it is important to communicate with whoever is creating your scripts so your forms and their scripts can work together. It is not highly probable that you will actually have to create your own scripts, unless you have programming skills, but you must understand how they are created and work so you can communicate to complete the task.

An exemplary place to look at scripts is **Matt Wright's Archives** at the World Wide Mart. A large collection of CGI scripts reside on this site and are available for downloading and editing. You can download them and explore how they are setup and how the forms that go with them work. This is a good way to get started understanding how forms really work. These scripts will need to be edited to fit your purposes,

EXHIBIT 13.1

```
##############################################################################
#Basic Random Image Displayer    Version 1.2                                  #
#Copyright 1996 Matt Wright      mattw@worldwidemart.com                      #
#Created 7/1/95                  Last Modified 7/20/95                        #
#Scripts Archive at:             http//www.worldwidemart.com/scripts/         #
##############################################################################
#COPYRIGHT NOTICE                                                             #
#Copyright 1996 Matthew M. Wright All Rights Reserved.                        #
#                                                                             #
#Basic Random Image may be used and modified free of charge by anyone so      #
#long as this copyright notice and the comments above remain intact. By       #
#using this code you agree to indemnify Matthew M. Wright from any            #
#liability that might arise from it's use.                                    #
#                                                                             #
#Selling the code for this program without prior written consent is           #
#expressly forbidden. In other words, please ask first before you try and     #
#make money off of my program.                                                #
#                                                                             #
#Obtain permission before redistributing this software over the Internet or   #
#in any other medium. In all cases copyright and header must remain intact.   #
##############################################################################
#Necessary Variables
 $basedir = "http://your.host.xxx/images/":
 @files = ("first_image.gif","test.gif:","random.gif","neat.jpg");

#Options
 $uselog = 0; # 1 = YES; 0 = NO
     $logfile = "/home/mattw/public_html/image/pics/piclog";

#Done
##############################################################################

 srand(time^$$);
 $num = rand(@files); # Pick a Random Number

#Print Out Header With Random Filename and Base Directory
 print "location: $basedir$files[$num]\n\n";

#Log Image
 if ($uselog eq '1' {
 open (LOG, ">>$logfile");
 print LOG "$files[$num]\n;
 close (LOG);
 }
```

but often instructions are included to help you figure out what to change. However, if you do use one of these scripts for profit, you must first notify the author. For non-profit educational purposes, they allow special privileges. Be sure you read all documentation provided on this or any other site to be sure you are not infringing on any copyrighted material.

Summary

The Web is an excellent vehicle for practicing random acts of kindness with the customer as the recipient. This activity—customer service—aims to assist the customer in receiving the ultimate product utility and satisfaction. The marketer must know how and when to act by improving service delivery, by introducing new products or services, and by monitoring customer communications. Several methods can be employed to stay in touch with the customer, and electronic marketing tools are well suited to provide timely and accurate opinions and information to the marketer. In this chapter, the basic premises of monitoring customer service as well as Web-enabled instruments and their construction using an HTML editor have been discussed. Surveys, forms, polls, and similar reporting devices can be built into Web sites, and this information is provided directly by the consumer of the services or products without filters to modify the meaning or urgency of reform. Excellent customer service programs enhance repeat purchasing, and recurring revenues are the most profitable of all commerce, electronic or otherwise.

Key Terms

ACTION attribute

ALIGN attribute

Auto-knowledge

Automated response

Checkbox

cgi-bin

CGI (Common Gateway Interface) script

GET attribute

HIDDEN attribute

INPUT attribute

LENGTH attribute

Listening posts

Matt Wright's Archives

METHOD attribute

NAME attribute

Natural language understanding

PASSWORD attribute

POST attribute

Radio button

Robots

Scripts

SELECT attribute

SUBMIT attribute

System administrator

TEXT attribute

VALUE attribute

QUESTIONS AND EXERCISES

1. In your opinion, what is the most effective way to deliver responsive customer service? What is the most inefficient way? Compare the advantages and disadvantages of each method. Write an outline of your thoughts to your customer service manager.

2. Describe the various benefits of a strong, consumer-oriented customer service program as a strategy to build competitive advantage. What would be the five most important policies with which to build a program of relationship marketing? Write an e-mail of suggestion to your customer service manager in London.

3. Does automated response and robot e-mail systems constitute a workable customer service program? Do they represent a responsive customer service program? Do they deliver a gratifying customer service program? Write a memo justifying the aspects of each system consequence, workable versus responsive versus gratifying customer experience.

4. As electronic customer service becomes more widespread, the capabilities of this electronic marketing resource is also becoming more flexible. Its benefits are primarily speed, accuracy, and convenience. Which of these three benefits do you consider most important in serving your customer groups? Be prepared to justify your opinion in a class discussion.

5. Define in writing the following words or concepts:
   a) natural language understanding
   b) robots
   c) CGI-bin
   d) CGI scripts
   e) listening posts
   f) Matt Wright's Archives

6. Define in writing the following words or concepts:
   a) the purpose of the METHOD attribute
   b) the purpose of the POST attribute
   c) the purpose of the ALIGN attribute
   d) the purpose of the SUBMIT attribute
   e) the purpose of the ACTION attribute
   f) the purpose of the INPUT attribute

7. In developing surveys and other types of forms, the respondent might not wish to have her responses easily read by some parties. How would the form-maker solve this problem? What parts do the attributes PASSWORD and HIDDEN play in this situation? Write an e-mail to your director of security explaining this issue of privacy and cite some examples of this scenario.

8. Access a consumer survey form on any Web site and click on the View option on the browser. Then locate the View Source button to see the HTML code displayed. Select a half-page section and explain the various tags and attributes of the form. Prepare a written explanation and include the section of the code you selected. Turn the report in to your instructor at the next class.

Bibliography

Goldzimer, Linda Silverman. 1989. *I'm first: Your customers' message to you.* New York City: Rawson Associates.

Jupiter Communications. 1998. Customer service, site operation strategies. *Digital Digest* [cited online 20 November, www.jup.com/reseach/so/], 2.

McDonnell, John. 1998. *The Internet's complaint desk* [cited online 10 December, wyslwyg://32/http://www.geocities.com/WallStreet/6100/cs.hml].

Schaefer, Richard A. 1999. Handling customer service on the Web. *Fortune,* 1 March, 204, 208.

Sterne, Jim. 1996. *Customer service on the Internet.* New York City: John Wiley & Sons.

Whiteley, Richard C. 1991. *The customer driven company.* Reading, MA: Addison-Wesley.

PART THREE

Implementing the Commerce Concept

The investigation and planning have now been completed, and the e-marketer is ready to transform concepts into reality. It is wise at this point to recognize that commerce is more than buying and reselling; it is much broader, including various aspects of human interaction. The e-merchant is building trust and respect for and among consumers. Steps the marketer or merchant must take involves selection of goods and services, customer service, payment systems and their authentication, and the subjective issue of value. E-commerce adds new responsibilities for the marketer in privacy protection, encryption/decryption systems, public and private keys, certificate authority, and many concerns that merchants of twenty years ago could not have possibly anticipated. However, as consumers clamor for convenience, speed, and selection, purveyors in e-commerce appear determined to make electronic systems work for everyone. The best solutions will still be a vending system of goods worth the prices paid.

CHAPTER 14

Establishing and Promoting a Virtual Store

"The further that commerce departs from a simple cash-and-carry transaction, however, the greater the need for trust [between merchant and customer] and the higher the risk that trust may be misplaced. The buyer might have exceeded the credit limit on the card or might be using a stolen credit card. The merchant selling over the telephone might be selling defective goods or might simply take the customer's money and deliver nothing. To be sure, the merchant or bank can easily validate a credit card number and the credit limit, and check that other forms of ID match those that the buyer gave when he or she applied for the card. Credit card companies also afford buyers a certain measure of protection, by allowing them to "charge back," or refuse to pay for defective goods or for purchases charged by someone not authorized to use the card. Thus, when commerce is conducted between parties at a distance who have had no prior business relations with each other, assumptions must be bolstered by mechanisms that offer protection to both the buyer and the seller."

(Grant 1996, 213)

LEARNING OBJECTIVES

- To explain the online responsibilities in opening a virtual store
- To identify the suppliers and resources necessary in opening a virtual store
- To introduce promotional strategies and explain how these strategies work to gain awareness for the virtual store

Introduction

All of your research and planning thus far now provide the basis for building an efficient and responsive Web site and in creating a unique presence for it. You will have many decisions to make, from developing the site yourself using HTML or taking your market research and your ideas to a Web storefront developer to have that company or individual build and place your Web site on the suitable search engines to selecting images you have deemed appropriate to achieve the objectives for your site. Another decision will be in determining whether to station your Web site as a standalone address or to join a cybermall to increase exposure. This decision will probably be made only if you locate a cybermall that matches your demographic and psychographic profiles; the management of the cybermall should have traffic profiles and purchasing research to help you select the right cybermall. An important part of your decision will be affected by budget allocation. Can you afford the rent and the associated services until your Web site generates a profit? Will you perhaps choose to establish your site as a unique address and promote and register the site yourself? After the site goes live, there will be even more decisions. Who will be your Webmaster for ongoing maintenance—you or someone in your organization or an outside Web company? You have, however, developed a marketing and implementation plan, so you should have anticipated many of these contingencies.

As your site becomes operational, you will have decisions to make about the site promotional plan. Which elements of the promotional mix—online or traditional advertising, sales promotion, public relations, direct marketing, and personal selling activities—will you employ to create an awareness for your site? You will weigh the advantages and disadvantages of each element. Will your strategy include a site branding technique? Will you partner with a portal? These marketing and communications decisions can create exciting and satisfying results for your e-commerce project. It is important to explore the ways your Web site concept can be executed in cyberspace.

The Best Advice is "Go Slow"

The marketer as the merchant should investigate the pitfalls before he begins to extol the potentials of e-commerce and become blinded by its advantages. The suspicious marketer will perform much better than the casual or misinformed one because there are many details to address that unorganized, sloppy managers may skip. These sloppy managers spend most of their time lining their pockets with receivables, never to be collected. To avoid commerce overconfidence, the general strategy of setting up commercial units by function should not be any different for e-commerce activities. Traditional organizational responsibilities for establishing financial affairs, production concerns, and marketing actions should be determined in the same manner for virtual commerce companies. After all, the same series of steps should be undertaken as running a real business. Which of these responsibilities is most important? The only answer is, they all are. The only variance might be in the order in which a manager addresses these functions. As has been stated before in this book, an imbalance in one of the triad causes imbalance in the other two.

To extend this discussion, balancing the commercial functions is critical. For example, if the marketing department over-prices the merchandise, sales will slow and may affect cash flow, which in turn destabilizes finances. With slowing sales, the operations/manufacturing function also slows, and maximum utilization of resources is lost. Another scenario is that finance agrees on too high an interest rate for funds earmarked for plant expansion. Finance also presses for higher prices to repay the loan, forcing marketing to reduce its budget for research and development thus making the products less competitive in design and pricing. Slower sales again result in marketing and operations inefficiencies, not to mention a new production facility running at one-third capacity because of lack of orders. The last but equally problematic situation is for an unstable production department that misses deadlines, mishandles deliveries, and operates over budget. The missed deadlines cost the marketing department its customers and sales, which in turn results in lower sales revenue and upsets in the financial function. An important axiom to follow, regardless of electronic or tangible commerce operations, is that the business should perform on time, on spec (specification), and on budget. Relationships are cemented when the merchant delivers these qualities to a customer or when a supplier produces the same to a commercial enterprise.

The Triad in Action

The virtual marketer must arrange for financing (or perhaps pay for staff, products, and services with his personal funds as the entrepreneur) to purchase hardware and software materials, establish an office (or not), and arrange for personnel and business necessities, such as telephone lines, stationery, and other office commodities. Necessities are stressed because few bankers wish to loan money for opulent offices, past due debts, expensive automobiles, and marketing and advertising expenditures. The banker's logic is that advertising success is a gamble, and the bank would rather pay for equipment and materials used in the expansion of an existing business, not for a business that does not yet exist. Therefore, all of the financial details, such as budgets, sales forecasts, cash flow projections, and profit or loss expectations (if a loss is expected, for how long?), must be researched and reported in a thorough and professional manner. An operations/production plan that describes the product or service to be produced and delineates the work processes to be initiated in order to produce the proposed goods should also be created. More and more often the operations function elevates a great company from the pack of average ones. Among hotels, the Ritz-Carlton (www.marriott.com) organization is known for its service excellence and execution; the Ritz-Carlton's reputation is based on experience to have become a standard by which other hotel organizations are judged. The secret? Extensive detail is paid to the operations criteria, particularly the quality of its staff and training; the maintenance of the buildings, amenities, and grounds; and the exquisite and consistent food service. While the Ritz serves an affluent and business market and is grounded in tangible offerings of intangible service, e-commerce offerings regardless of the market should consist of well-trained customer and technical service personnel, first-rate communications systems including adequate servers for timely page response, sufficient and well-maintained modem banks for quick connections, and ample telephone lines for those who might not use or have access to the Web. Every business has its standard processes, such as how orders are received, how inquiries are handled, and how shipping is best managed, but it is the online merchant through the close inspection of each step of the production process who can improve upon these standard operations by making them more accessible, quicker, accurate, and convenient; less costly; and easier to understand. Enough minor improvements can win the marketer customers for life and can confound competitors as to how the operation was performed.

Rounding out the triangle of finance and operations is the marketing function working to investigate customer wants and the proper, highly-exposed delivery process for these bundles of benefits. Marketing many times is synonymous with promotion, and two companies that give high priority to the promotional effort are Microsoft and Outback Steakhouses (www.outback.com)—Microsoft because of its ubiquitous advertising exposure and Outback because of its low advertising profile that still has people standing in line outside to eat every night. Late in 1995, Microsoft introduced Windows 95 to the world. In an around the world rollout starting in

THE DILEMMA OF QUIET ADS

How Do You Launch an Ad Campaign That Will Get Noticed, But Not Too Much?

That was the dilemma facing Estée Lauder when it decided to launch the advertising for its new Clinique online shopping service. The famous makeup brand wanted to attract cyberspace shoppers but was worried about enraging bricks-and-mortar retailers such as Macy's and Bloomingdales that fear losing customers on the Web. The result is a surprisingly low-key campaign that uses the Internet and an electronic mall to plug the surplus overtly while slipping the Clinique Web address more discreetly into traditional magazine and television ads. "We're very sensitive to our department-store partners," says Angela Knapp, vice president, special markets and new media for Estée Lauder. "You're not going to be seeing big posters that say 'Buy Clinique online' in the middle of Macy's." You won't be seeing discounts, either: Clinique's Dramatically Different Moisturizing Lotion still costs $19.50 for four ounces on the Web, for example. Clinique says it is convinced the online effort will help it grab consumers who don't shop in department stores, without stealing customers who do.

Parker-Pope, Tara. 1998. Clinique solves Web dilemma with quiet ads. *The Wall Street Journal*, 12 November, B1.

Australia, country after country lined up to buy a disk of Windows 95—Microsoft's most significant consumer software improvement in five years. Television advertising encouraged users to Start it up, and the Rolling Stones song by the same name accompanied the visuals. Sales promotions featured celebrities turning the Windows 95 introduction into a street party in many countries. Bill Gates broadcast a vision statement for Windows 95 throughout the globe; at the time, the press could not run enough stories on Windows 95.

Outback promotes its eateries too but in a lower-key manner. Outback has produced television commercials featuring the likes of model Rachel Hunter in its early days of development; however, because of its strong word-of-mouth reputation, the media advertising has turned to low-cost radio and special occasion advertising in the newspapers. Strict server training is still stressed, and advertising monies seem to be directed toward food quality and employing excellent staff. Outback bought the rights for a college bowl game, featuring SEC and Big Ten football teams. The Outback Bowl is nationally televised every year, bringing attention to Outback and the Tampa Bay area. Restaurant locations, franchise availabilities, and investor news dot the Outback Web site; there is nothing outlandish. Quiet efforts by Outback Steakhouse and the glitzy feats by Microsoft can be effective promotional strategies for online companies; what method to use depends on the marketing strategy set by the marketer.

Do It Yourself or Hire a Developer?

One of the biggest decisions, particularly for the small company or individual, is how to set up its online storefront, and this decision may hound the enterprise for years to come. The decision usually revolves around the answers to the following two questions: How experienced in business is the person responsible for setting up the online storefront, and how technology-savvy is this individual? The greater business acumen and the more familiar with the Internet technology, the more likely the individual will put the virtual storefront together himself—this can be a great learning experience as well as a time-consuming experience. Many people, however, have the entrepreneurial spirit. Take, for instance, Jeff Bezos. He left his Wall Street job in 1994, jumped on Interstate 90, and arrived in Seattle, Washington and founded Amazon.com. His first distribution center was his garage; his first customers were his book-buying friends. He developed his business plan while driving his Chevrolet to Seattle, and now

Amazon.com is one of the world leaders in e-commerce. What fueled his e-commerce vision? As a financial analyst on Wall Street, he was watching Web usage grow by 2,300 percent each year, and he knew that the Internet would be everywhere soon. He wanted to offer a great variety of books on the Internet. Today, Amazon.com offers millions of books, compact discs, and DVD titles to millions of customers through world-class customer service. (History of Amazon.com 1998)

Certainly Jeff Bezos and his associates have made mistakes, but their philosophy of working hard, having fun, and making history has brought similar people with a similar vision together. "Our company mission is to leverage technology and expertise to provide the best buying experience on the Internet. Put another way, we want people to come to Amazon.com, find whatever they want, discover things they didn't know they wanted, and leave feeling they have a new favorable place to shop." (Philosophy of Amazon.com 1998) Establishing a **virtual store** is part finding a niche to fill, attracting and training good people, and creating an attractive company culture. These are some of the intangible qualities (plus a little bit of luck) it takes to shape a successful e-business. To establish an electronic presence, it will also require some tangible equipment to access the Web. While bigger is always thought better, higher capacity and faster machines do have merit in the infrastructure of e-commerce. If the virtual store were to be undertaken by the individual, the following list of items should be considered minimal to adequately service the store's clientele: Faster speed or larger capacity would be nice, but careful scrutiny of the added expense to the added speed or features should be considered; cost versus benefit should be a question to analyze for any size business; and the marketer should remember that never is a good time to buy a computer or other equipment because in six months, faster computers will be introduced at lower and lower prices. Another good reason to avoid purchasing a computer and to pay to use a hosting service's equipment is that as upgrades and repairs are needed, the Internet service provider (ISP) bears the expenses.

Whether or not the e-marketer employs a developer or does it herself, the storefront must have reliable access to the Web as well as these elements:

- *Virtual store-building software.* The marketer must do his homework on this item. Different storefronts have different needs, and different software packages have different features. Developer software is becoming more available and is often tailored to the e-merchant's needs. Examples of such software include "Store," billed as e-commerce in one box and "Cat@log," a joint venture of Pandesic and the Vision Factory, boasts to be a tool for the design, development, and operation of Web-based storefronts.
- *Virtual online information sources.* There are many sources of information the e-marketer can access and use to develop a virtual storefront. One major and excellent source of information is the Web site, Web Developer News (www.internetnews.com), an online newsletter chronicling the latest in various types of site developer software. Other sites for storefront development/ e-commerce strategies are C|NET's E-Commerce site (www.news.com) or the ZD Journals' e-commerce @lert (www.zdjournals.com), both of which are rich in e-commerce topics such as the cost of scalability or server performance on e-commerce sites. Both online newsletters are must-reads for the novice as well as the seasoned e-merchants. Still important sources include some of the Internet magazines, such as *e-Commerce News*, and the more mainstream computer magazines, such as *PC World*, *Byte*, and *Wired*. One last source of information is in speaking with established storefront operators; these merchants are usually happy to share their triumphs and are also quick to share their missteps. The marketer should select the category of goods or services, write down a few addresses, and again attempt to begin an e-mail dialogue with

merchants willing to participate. Certainly everyone enjoys retelling her successes and possibly her mistakes. The beginning e-marketer can learn practical tips of what to do—and what not to do—during these conversations.

- *A 300MHz or faster PC.* Speed is a prime commodity on the Web, and recently 400 and 450MHz PCs have been introduced to the consumer, adding additional speed for a marginal increase in cost. These computers perform best with the Pentium II processor. No brand is recommended over another; most PC clones and mail order computers such as Dell perform to the highest standards. Again, price and features comparisons should be undertaken by the marketer to obtain the appropriate equipment.
- *A large hard disk, perhaps 4 gigabytes of memory or larger.* In 1997, 2 gigabytes of memory were standard, and in 1998, 4 gigs were affordable. Perhaps 6 or 8 will be standard in the next few years.
- *Sixteen or more megs of ROM memory.* The more memory you have, the better, particularly with the heavy drain on memory that graphics, sound, and other plug-in programs pull.
- *A large color monitor.* This is really a necessary commodity. A seventeen-inch screen offers a dot pitch of 26mm, a maximum resolution of 1280 × 1024 at 75Hz, use of 256-colors, and an allowance for a 4-meg video card. For larger startups with multiple work stations, a smaller fifteen-inch monitor offers a 28mm pitch, use 256 colors, and a one meg of memory on the video card. The larger the monitor, the more comfortable with which to work for long periods.
- *A 56.6 baud modem if possible, 28.8 at minimum.* Modems continually gain speed, so 100 baud plus modems are around the corner for availability and affordability. For customer convenience, the faster the better.
- *A browser.* There are several options for browsers that accommodate the modem. Some enthusiasts prefer Netscape Navigator or Netscape Communicator, while some fancy Internet Explorer for Internet access. Both brands of browsers are beta-testing their 5.0 versions, and the contest for features and popularity will continue, at least for the near future. At present, there are uncertainties about the Web mergers of Netscape/AOL and Microsoft, but these general guidelines for equipment should serve for the next several years.
- *Printers.* For printers, you might consider having several. Color laser printers are very affordable now and make the enterprise look impressive printing color materials. Black-and-white laser printers may also be needed for invoices and general office tasks. Printer resolution is generally 600 DPI for either a black-and-white or color printer.
- *Scanners.* For marketing purposes, a scanner may be required to manipulate photographs and other graphics in your Web site and printed materials. You can achieve a substantial cost savings in reproducing small quantities of brochure or collateral items using an in-house scanner, rather than going to an outside supplier.
- *Telephone service and Internet service provider.* Not the last but at a minimum, the e-business will require telephone service and an Internet service provider. Shortly in this chapter, there will be a full discussion on choosing an ISP. Talk to several providers to establish the level of need and to find out the ISP's services and fees. A reliable supplier with Web design and production capabilites is GTE, which serves most regions of the United States.

Certainly these specifications will change as services and technology improve and equipment matures. The marketer must keep technology advances in sight as he continues with e-commerce.

Engaging a Storefront Developer

Service companies have evolved to produce the entire virtual storefront in a turnkey fashion. The marketer supplies the developer with a marketing plan, and he directs the company according to his understanding of the target market. This direction might include the operational capabilities, such as an e-mail ordering system, the appearance of the site, software for reporting visits or for measuring traffic, or production in the HTML editor with Java scripts as appropriate. The **storefront developer** would design the site for the most popular browsers and specify the necessary equipment to implement the design on the Web. The developer will work from the marketer's direction and will look to the marketer for input and feedback as well as decisions for approval of design phases as the project continues. The site is not to ultimately benefit the storefront developer; the design and function are to benefit the marketer and the company's marketing foundation. Therefore, the marketer cannot turn over the entire process, saying to the developer, "Build me a Web site." It takes great involvement and imagination on the marketer's part to integrate online marketing into the other traditional marketing elements. For online experience, you might consider the storefront developers Yahoo! Store, iCO, or Netscape to explore **turnkey services.** Cost estimates for the site production are, of course, important and should be sealed before the Web developer begins work. The marketer can get a rough estimate, though, enlisting an automated site pricing service such as Webshowplace.com (www.webshowplace.com); these sites ask what features are to be included with a resulting cost estimate. These sites are handy since you might wish to add or subtract features on your shopping list, particularly if you have a tight budget.

Generally, the marketer supplies the developer with input, and the developer returns with a storyboard (sketches of how the various screens will look) or perhaps has already developed the pages to be viewed on a monitor. The marketer must use objective judgment in reviewing these layouts to determine if these conceptual Web pages follow the objectives of the marketing plan. It is easy to be dazzled by graphics; however, the marketer must ask himself the following questions:

- Does the design and copy fit the objectives for the online marketing?
- Is the design attractive, memorable, and motivating?
- Does the design ask or require the viewer to do something, such as click through the site, register for a promotion, visit a dealership or retail store?
- Is the site reflective of other company marketing materials? Would it be recognized as a Ford, Microsoft, or FedEx graphics continuity?
- Can the site be produced for the budget allotted and within the time frame allowed?
- Do the site strategies match the corporate strategies of the company?

As so many marketing encounters evolve, good personal chemistry between the marketer and the storefront developer is crucial. When one party respects the other and vice versa, powerful things can be accomplished. The marketer's major functions are to provide input and supervise the project; the storefront developers major

A CHECKLIST FOR DEVELOPING A VIRTUAL STOREFRONT

1. Has a thorough study of the online prospect segment and proposed product niche been completed? Did the study indicate a profitable and sustainable business for the site?
2. From this information, have you developed an electronic marketing plan that delineates the elements of the promotional mix, mainly product, price, alternative distribution, alternative promotion, and performance goals?
3. How will the Web site be organized; which departments will manage which portions of the activities (think of the marketing, finance, and operations balance).
4. What do you intend to call the Web site, what will be your URL address, and have you contacted InterNIC to learn if the address is available? The developer will follow through on the registration details.
5. What specific products or services do you intend to sell, rent, or lease on the Web?
6. What image do you wish to portray on the Web site using the textual message, graphics, interactive features, depth of information, multiple languages, so forth?
7. Have you decided on the Web site features such as the domain name or a canonical domain name, for example, http://reedy.wwz.com?
8. What management details do you plan for your Web site such as traffic counter, guest book, feedback form, local search engine, so forth?
9. What store details do you plan for your storefront such as secure order forms, page formats, shopping cart system, secure credit card systems, products for sale, so forth?
10. Are you considering any artificial intelligence features for your storefront such as automatic tech support, answer-man, so forth?

 Last modified November 28, 1998. From the Delaware CyberMall Web site, www.delmall.com.

functions are to create an imaginative and error-free marketing site that follows the objectives of the project. When the project is finished, there may be an occasional need for maintenance or updates to the site. The marketer should ask the developer what the process is to make changes to the site, the developer's availability on a timely manner, and what costs might be entailed in site alternatives. The experienced storefront developer will be able to answer these questions with some degree of accuracy.

There are many more decisions to be made during the design and production process, and each decision must be reflective of the objectives and goals agreed upon at the onset. Deviation of direction is a trap that leads to unsuitable Web sites, overspending of the budget, and blown deadlines. Web site management is like any other responsibility; it does not run by itself. Someone must be assigned the task of minding the details.

Joining a Cybermall?

After the site is created and the metatags are tested, the next decision for the marketer is how to maintain an optimal awareness for the site. Step one in this process is to register with the variety of search engines so that the consumer can locate your offerings. Step two might be an assessment in maintaining a stand-alone site as opposed to participating in the bundling of cybermall retailers. The cybermall is a virtual collection of sites, usually bringing financial, insurance, or automobile sites together, that offer the shopper many hyperlinked addresses to follow from one page. The major benefits of signing on with a cybermall are expanded exposure over and above the efforts of a single site (disregarding the natural pulling power of a Metropolitan Life or a Sears site that serves national audiences), the selection to be found at the cybermall's address, and the site maintenance services by the cybermall operator. The major disadvantages are of course the cost of joining and renting space monthly, although the monthly charge is often between $50 to $75, and the heavy competition on say an auto

THE DELAWARE CYBERMALL'S OFFERINGS

Currently there are approximately 40 million users (customers) online all over the world and what's more, approximately 250,000 new users (customers) are coming online each week. That's 1500 new users (customers) every hour. This is where Delaware CyberMall (DCM) can help your business. The Delaware CyberMall is a Delaware-based, Delaware-oriented (but not exclusive) family mall on the Internet. Here is your chance to advertise *and* receive responses over the Internet! With our help any business, whether merchandise or service, can set up a store front in our CyberMall on the Internet. We will actively advertise the CyberMall everywhere on the World Wide Web to bring the customers into your store!

Once someone enters your store, this is your chance to describe your business in full! Your store front contains two to four times as much information as a full page ad in the yellow pages at a fraction of the cost! Plus there are *no* territory boundaries on who can visit your store front. This type of advertising will open new avenues for you and will probably change the way you think about advertising your products or services!

Millions of people from around the world are on the Internet everyday. This is your chance to transform your business from a local business to an international business!! We will help you describe your business effectively, get your home page (store front) set up, and help take customer orders and inquiries if you need help. DCM also offers information on and links to software, games, noncommercial classifieds, career and education, and Delaware points of interest to entice people to visit our mall and shop in your store.

Advertising with us requires no equipment and no technical skill on your part. Simply fill out a two-page form describing your business and one of our Web masters will transform your text into a colorful home page (store front) for your business. We can even help with content if needed. After your store front is set up, we will give you your specific World Wide Web (WWW) address (URL) that gets people directly into your store. Your WWW address can be used in any other form of advertising you currently use!

Sell your products or services in your area or around the world. Offer your catalogue, get peoples names and addresses for your mailing list, and get inquiries through your store front. Describe your products in detail, including up to two color graphic images at no additional charge. Run specials once a quarter at no additional charge. Take orders right over the Internet. If you are in a service business, tell people what territory you cover. Tell people what your specialties are. List your experience and credentials. Share testimonials from your satisfied customers. Two-typed pages of information is an enormous opportunity for you to convey exactly what you do and is all covered in one flat monthly cost. We have methods for you to sell your products and services that *do not* require customers to give their credit card or other sensitive information over the Internet. This type of information is not secure on the Internet right now, but the technology is evolving. DCM projects that secure transfers will be available within the next two years. Wouldn't you like to have a matured, well-established site on the World Wide Web when that happens?!?

We have structured pricing so the small business owner can advertise as effectively as a large company. The cost for a standard store front is a flat $75.00 per month. This includes a total of two type written pages that will be transformed into a colorful home page (store front). Your store front can include two graphical images and methods for your potential customer to communicate to, and buy from, you through your store front at no additional charge. That's it, no hidden costs, no costs per sale. You will be given a chance to modify your home page (store front) four times a year.

 Last modified November 28, 1998. From the Delaware CyberMall Web site, www.delmall.com.

insurance cybermall. Like many other forms of promotion, the more popular the site, the more the competition chooses to join. The more competition, the harder it becomes for the smaller business to differentiate itself from the rest.

A recent formulation has been added for online retailers to create their own Web shopping networks as was announced by nine leading specialty retailers just before the 1998 holiday shopping season. The network will link each online store, giving the network a capability of reaching an audience of 7 to 8 million viewers. The purpose of this network, the ShopperConnection, is to guard against the expansion of the shopping giant Amazon.com and to take some of the spotlight and dollars spent on the Internet away from Amazon. This particular network is comprised of a toy store, eToys; consumer-products retailer, Cyberian Outpost; travel-services provider, Preview Travel; music retailer, CDNow; brokerage, Datek Online; garden-equipment, Garden.com; florist, PC Flowers & Gifts; movie seller, Reel.com (www.reel.com); and wine and gift shop, Virtual Vineyards. Different from shopping mall image with its difficult-to-navagate shopping sites, the ShopperConnection network is not, in itself, an online destination. Instead, the shopper will first log onto a favorite retail Web site, such as CDNow, and then be given a chance to link to others only after making an initial purchase. Only after the confirmation will the ShopperConnection link be presented, and it becomes the shopper's choice to click onto links of the other members' sites. This is a new type of preemptive collaboration by retailers and it will be interesting to see if these proprietary networks offer perceived and real benefits to the online shopper. (Online retailers form Web shopping network 1998)

The Marketing Duties of a Web Site Master

The company or the marketer has decided to embrace the Web by setting up an online presence. What are the necessary elements to begin the project correctly? A detailed study of the Internet and the Web as well as the peripheral promotions and communications capabilities nested on the company desktop are required. Proficiency at a word processing program such as Microsoft Word or Corel WordPerfect is most desirable, without mentioning the ability to type. An understanding of advertising procedures, graphics, and copy is also helpful in achieving your goals, as well as communicating effectively with advertising suppliers. In managing the electronic elements, you must be cognizant of technology changes, in hardware and software, and be able to judge if new equipment or applications would improve the site's performance. As a benefit, your marketing skills will be enhanced by knowledge of Web communications conventions such as familiarity of HTML editing and linking hyperlinks and an acquaintance with frames and tables page construction; as your knowledge increases so will your expectations for your electronic marketing tools. An appreciation of customer service and conflict resolution are pluses as well as a general proficiency in basic communications. The marketer must show good judgment in deciding what features are to be exhibited on the Web site.

- Will you have drop-down menus within your navigation plan or perhaps a site map for clearer navigation?
- Should the site have a page that builds confidence, such as quotations from clients or comments from customers?
- Will you have a search engine on your site to provide linking convenience?
- Are the Help features and FAQ lists included and easy to find and use?
- Will you utilize an e-mail alert to notify customers of new merchandise or services available?
- Do you want customers or prospects to learn more about your company, creating an "about the company" link?
- Is customer service important to your business process? Should there be a link to customer service representatives?
- Can customers contact you if your computers are down? Should a telephone and fax number as well as a street address or post office number be prominent?
- Should an e-mail directory be displayed, along with the company audiotext directory, for contacting different departments?
- Would an employment page be of benefit to the company's recruitment efforts?
- If the company has employee events, should a monthly calendar be posted to the site?

- If publicity and press coverage are important to your industry, should one hyperlink direct the viewer to a menu of press stories that carry news of products, company accomplishments, or employee profiles?
- Should there be a page explaining the company's work process?
- Will staff résumés help build confidence with the company, and will these résumés be posted to a page within the site?

The **Webmaster** has many duties in maintaining the e-commerce site, and a sense of organization is absolutely necessary. The Web site is your lifeline to the customer; if this channel is neglected or placed in low priority, the e-commerce venture will surely fail.

Choosing an Internet Service Provider

There is much talk regarding usage of the Internet, but no one explains how you accomplish using the Internet or how you find a place to host your Web site. It is time to consider how you want to access the Internet and for what purposes you will be needing the access. In the next few paragraphs, common questions and misgivings about choosing an Internet Service Provider (ISP) for personal or business purposes will be addressed and answered.

An ISP is a company that can provide you with a connection to the Internet as well as other Internet-based services. This connection can be through different means and have many different parameters depending on the ISP that you decide to use. There are also many types and levels of ISPs available. ISPs can be part-time hobbyists who are inexpensive but also not well equipped to handle a business Web site. These types of providers can be good for personal access or family Web pages but should probably not be depended on for electronic commerce sites. Some ISPs are small businesses that are quite successful and can be well equipped to handle a business Web site that gets moderate traffic. Those that are good usually have excellent customer service and competitive prices. Large providers deal in volume. If you are expecting your site to have heavy traffic, this might be a better option. Large ISPs often provide many services to businesses and have in-house technical support. The downfall to using a large ISP is that they may not be as flexible. They are well established and not as eager, which is often reflected in their customer service. However, large providers will most likely have the best equipment and fastest connections to the Internet. You can also use a commercial provider such as AOL, CompuServe, MSN, and Prodigy. These are national services that offer a convenient sign-up procedure and get you started right away. Problems often arise with these servers when you look at the pricing structures, the access numbers, and the connection speeds available. These services may not be flexible enough to run your business the way you want and within your budget. However, they are a good way to get your feet wet and see what the Internet is all about. To find an ISP, you can search on the Web, ask others in your area, look in the yellow pages, or even check an ISP reference service similar to those used by physicians. Here are some sites that provide lists of ISPs and other resources to help you find one that is right for you.

- Advice on choosing an ISP—http://gea.nm.sik.si/silicon_graphics/ISP.choose.html
- Boardwatch Magazine—http://www.boardwatch.com/
- The List—http://thelist.iworld.com

Now that you understand what an ISP is and where to find them, what should you consider when investigating which one to use? This will depend primarily on why you want an ISP. If you want one for personal use, a local small business might be better as they may be more helpful. If you want one for business purposes, reliable service is going to be a major issue. Here are some questions that you might ask when looking at ISPs for either case.

> First, are you able to communicate with the service representatives of the ISP? Are your personal and business goals understood, in other words, does the ISP speak your language?
>
> If you are able to communicate with the ISP, can you check their references? (If they are unwilling to provide references, this is a bad sign.)
>
> What type of reputation do they have? (Talk, e-mail, even survey their current customers to be sure their reputation and references are in line with your goals.)
>
> How reliable is the ISP? Are your customers going to be able to access your site, or are they going to get frustrated? (Try accessing different sites provided by the ISP at different times of the day to see how the systems react. Next, check what level of service they provide.)
>
> Are you able to do everything that you want with this ISP? Do they provide e-mail access wherever you might need it at a reasonable cost? Do they host Web sites and what limitations do they set on them?
>
> If you need news groups, does this ISP provide access?
>
> If your site will need scripting, how does this ISP handle that situation?
>
> What is the pricing structure? How much does the service they provide cost and what are you getting for your money? (Often you can get unlimited service and space for a Web site for a reasonable fee.)

You should determine what type of connection the ISP provides (modem, T1, T3, ISDN, or cable modem) and which is best for your purposes. If you are concerned with speed, you should investigate what type of connection you can get from the provider you are considering. You should also be aware of any limitations that may be placed on the modem banks and what the ratio of modems to users is. A low modem-to-user ratio can help alleviate busy signals and frustration.

Next you should consider what software is provided by the ISP. Although most software that will be provided is usually shareware and easily accessible on the Internet, it is less of a hassle if the software to be used is provided and more importantly supported by your ISP. You should now consider the following technical support issues. Who will service your account? What type of technical support is available? If they are only available by e-mail and you cannot get a connection, you will never receive help. Make sure support is available when and how you need it. If you will be using a local provider, check to see if they offer on-site support. On-site support can come in handy if you are having trouble getting connected and properly set up. The Internet is technology, and technology is not failure proof. For this reason, it is important to determine if the ISP you choose has redundant equipment. Backups are also quite important. If they do have some failure, how often are your files backed up and what is the procedure for restoring your information?

Once you have chosen an ISP to host your Web pages, there are still a few things you need to be aware of. First thing to consider is regarding space. What are the limitations set by the ISP on the size of the Web site? More important than size limitations are limitations on access. If you plan to have a site that is accessed often, you need to check for limitations and additional fees for excess hits on your pages. A couple of minor questions, but worth asking, are how your files will be transferred to the ISP and what type of access will you have for editing those pages once they are in place? Due to security issues, many providers also have limitations on scripts. These scripts may be necessary for your forms in making your site interactive. Check to see if scripts are allowed or if they are provided by the ISP themselves. If your site is to be an electronic commerce site, security issues will play a large role in the ISP you choose. Is the provider you are looking to capable of handling the security necessary for your type of site? Once your site is up and working, you will need to be aware of how effective it is. This is accomplished through the statistics collected about your site. What statistics are available from your ISP, how easy are they to obtain, and in what form will they be provided? Good answers to these questions will make your marketing analysis much easier to manage.

One last concern you should address regarding ISPs is the issue of **ownership.** This is especially important if your provider also designs your Web site. Make sure that you have ownership of the design and content of your pages and that you have thoroughly read the contract your ISP should happily provide you. You should make sure that your domain name is registered to you and not to the ISP. It is possible for the ISP to register the domain name for you, and it be in your name. If you wanted to change providers, these issues would become very important. No matter how well you investigate the ISP you choose, it is always possible that you may at sometime and for some reason need to change providers. For this reason, you should prepare for the worst by keeping up to date on your next few ISP choices. If you are aware of the competitive nature of supplying Internet services, you can be sure you are getting what you are paying for.

Promoting the Web Site

Many marketing decisions have been discussed to this point. The central proposition of product or service research led to the formulation of a niche product that fills a void in the marketplace. To enhance the product's acceptance, competitive research was conducted on competitive entrants in the category according to product offerings, pricing, and distribution. This situation analysis provided the solid foundation for setting the marketer's strategic and tactical thinking on the product's features, such as length of warranties; depth of product selection; usage training if necessary; customer service ramifications; pricing strategy, such as value-added versus economy pricing, pricing with and without service warranty plans, and lump-sum payment versus installment payment; the distribution strategy of exclusive versus mass outlets, online, mail, or delivery services; and the impact to the wholesale-retail-purchaser value chain. All of these decision factors affect and influence one additional aspect of the marketing process, that of the promotional effort to attract interest to the product. The twist in online promotion is that no one has a long history doing it right and doing it well, so much experimentation in promotion is ongoing. The marketer must cut through the vast arena of overnight experts. The confusion in promotions is that the Web reads like a newspaper, but it is not. The reader cannot hold it in his hands nor can he clip coupons in the traditional sense. The Web is like television, but where are the programs? It has sound like the radio, but where is the music? Promoters of Web advertising speak of billboards, but try to find one of the huge, ubiquitous structures along the information highway. Therefore, imbalanced by these uncertain metaphors, the marketer must approach online promotion carefully, probably more so than in planning the traditional promotions for her industry.

In perspective, some certainties have turned upside down with the advent of the World Wide Web. Two-thirds of Internet users would give up their phone or television

THE UNKNOWNS

"There are so few rules here," says Anil Singh, a principal in an Internet directory service. "Creativity is crucial," he says. Still, whether online advertising can live up to its champions' hopes is unclear. Rates are steep enough that some marketers wonder whether they can get enough response to justify the cost. Most advertisers pay at least as much to reach an Internet audience—typically $10 to $40 per 1000 viewers—as they would for TV or magazine ads. And while audiences often greet ads with a yawn, as measured by "clickthrough rates" of sometimes 1 percent or less. The rates show how often computer users point their mouse at an ad and ask more information. "A lot of Internet banner ads are like billboards on the side of the highway," says Martha Deevy, a senior vice president at Charles Schwab & Co., a brokerage firm. "People drive right past them and don't bother to look."

Anders, George. 1998. Internet advertising, just like its medium, is pushing boundaries. *The Wall Street Journal, 30 November, A1.*

before their Web connection, reported in the Roper Starch Worldwide and America Online study of 1001 people. In this study, 77 percent of the respondents said the Internet has enriched their lives, and nearly half said it is a necessity. (Internet more important than TV and phone 1998)

Planning and Organization

With so much happening on the Web, it is easy to become distracted. Therefore, with a product concept in mind, you will need to prepare a solid marketing plan, focusing on the promotional elements to expose the product and display the discipline to follow it. This is your only defense against these distractions. Your plan takes into account your resources and goals, your competition, and your customers. It is a road map to your destination. From Atlanta, you can set a marketing plan to arrive at San Francisco traveling through St. Louis, or you can blindly set a plan to travel through Miami and Roanoke with the end destination of the City by the Bay. What are the elements of the online communications marketing plan (your road map to marketing on the Web)?

- *Online marketing plan.* The plan usually begins with a statement reflecting the corporate mission, it then focuses on specific resources, the strategic weapons you will use to meet your goal. The online marketing plan should be integrated with the traditional marketing plan to take advantage of the synergies of Internet marketing communications.
- *Online promotional program.* This promotional program is dovetailed with other promotional vehicles as television, magazine, newspaper and the support media. As you have learned, online exposure is simply inadequate at this time to carry a media program except for certain computer and entertainment products and services. The marketer should, therefore, consider planning and integrating primary and secondary activities.

There is little divergence between traditional marketing efforts and online marketing activities; both require people, tools, and time. With a realistic marketing plan in hand, much confusion and aggravation are eliminated. As you come closer to communicating with your prospects and customers, you should now have a clearer idea of how to use the electronic tools to attract attention to your product or services.

All marketing requires resources, and the marketing document identifies what time, personnel, and money will be needed to implement your plan. Considered a trivial or mundane effort, budgeting is a crucial step to be submitted to the financial department. Without a budget allocation for these efforts, there is no marketing.

INTERNET COMPANIES EXPAND ADVERTISING TO OFFLINE

"Branding value is clearly very important in determining who's going to win on the Internet, and its hard to reel a real brand without getting it through TV and friends," said Darryl Peck, chief executive of Cyberian Outpost, an online computer store. The Connecticut-based company launched the first of a two-part television and print last week. The current ninety-day campaign includes a humorous but daring TV spot that aims to gain brand awareness simply by catching the viewer's attention. Peck said he is planning a follow-up campaign that would be more informative with specifics about the Web site's offerings. "There's no question that TV is a good way to get people talking. It's part of the risk we're taking here, but we think it's worth it," he said.

Evan Neufeld, an analyst at Internet research firm Jupiter communications, said "it's a definite trend, and it's new, but it's also Marketing 101. The media is fragmented, so you can't advertise in just one place. We've always said not to put all your eggs in one basket." According to Neufeld, the Internet business has evolved into a more sophisticated industry in which companies can no longer rely on banner ads and word-of-mouth to establish themselves, especially if they want to become a major player. "It used to be guerrilla marketing—and it still is for people who don't have money—but the general thing we've seen is that the price of admission has gone up if you want to become an e-commerce brand," said Neufeld.

Iwatani, Yukari. 1998. Internet companies expand advertising to offline. *Industries Channel.* PointCast Network [cited online 23 November].

Though nonmonetary, a most important resource you will devote to online marketing is time. Time to design, implement, monitor, and respond and to participate in discussions. If you budget time for marketing duties (perhaps in the morning 10 a.m. until noon) for each day or week, you will learn to stick to it. This is another example of the trait of a marketing organization and a way to approach it. If you have a staff, you can probably divide up the online marketing duties among several people.

After you have decided on your consumer or business-to-business targets, begin to formulate how to reach and establish a dialog among your target markets. Each target requires a specific time commitment, so the number of targets you will choose will be determined by your time budget. More importantly then fitting these targets into your time budget, however, is choosing these targets by marketing potential; those with the highest interest will produce for your company the best communications resources. Each of these target segments has its own requirements and tactics; learn these requirements well before you move on. Depending on the target market, the contact vehicles might be one of the following tools.

Tactical Online Targeting

The means by which you will use to communicate with your primary targets are established online vehicles such as e-mail and discussion groups. The marketer should learn which of these vehicles are appropriate to which markets, at what time are they appropriate, and when are they appropriate. For example, DoubleClick, Inc., an ad-sales network based in New York that represents more than seventy sites, offers suggestions to clients and prospects on advertising delivery. If their clients want to reach women, the DoubleClick client site such as foodtv.com, an off-shoot of cable television's Food Network, is suggested. If they want small-business owners, the Web site for Fast Company might be discussed. (Anders 1998) Your marketing strategy should specify which targets are most appropriate; here is a list of online tactics to consider:

- *Mail servers and e-mail.* Many businesses have an automated mail reply feature called a mailbot or mail server that can automatically respond to an inquiry from someone requesting information. Because the e-mail message is being requested, you are free to respond with less subtle advertising, such as one or more signatures, an electronic brochure, an announcement, or perhaps a special offer.

- *Electronic or virtual storefronts.* One of the first elements to greet the customer should be a coordinated design for the image and identity of the elements, such as a storefront, logo, and positioning themes; complementary page graphics and text; coordinated stationery; packaging; internal and external business forms; a domain name; and plans for how the store's contents and collateral will be used today and how they will evolve over time. From this Web site, the merchant establishes her e-commerce business; the marketer should, therefore, think before he executes.
- *Advertising.* Advertising is a growing area of expertise for online response. This might include a banner with ad headlines or messages with ad body copy, sponsorship of stock market quotes, or national weather information; a static billboard design or hot billboards that drop down after you access a site; ad locations such as on the Yahoo! home page; a confirmation of order message; regional advertising using the PointCast network; and an ad monitoring and response tracking system that provides a printout of traffic to the site. More and more innovative advertising techniques are surely on the way.
- ***Electronic publishing.*** There needs to be a plan for publishing a series of documents, sometimes called a white paper, that includes a particular address (that the viewer can access), the electronic document itself, a signature or introductory paragraph that identifies you and how to get further information, and a system to track what you published and who referenced the work in consequent writings. The writing can be on any topic related to the virtual storefront business, the storefront's product, or even the merchant's particular interests. Within the storefront address can be placed a file containing an archive of these writings; some topics can become resources for other e-merchants. If content is used in another site, acknowledgments are generally requested and received, which results in additional exposure.
- *Hard copy publishing.* Another exposure opportunity is to publish within the industry, and, once written, the marketer becomes an expert. A major publishing house imprint becomes a seal of approval or credentials for the product; electronic news releases can start this process.
- ***Conferences venues.*** A conference sponsorship or cosponsorship is a high profile special promotion in which a sponsor, usually a company, brings together the experts or interested parties to discuss a topic or pressing issue, such as privacy on the Internet or the Y2K threat. As a sponsor, the company can publish a pre-conference information sheet that outlines why the topic is important, lists suggested questions, lists scheduled panelists, and describes the sponsors. Conferences are other opportunities to build the company's stature among its e-commerce peers.
- ***Cookies.*** This tactic is very controversial because of its effect on privacy issues but results in a story-telling path of site visitors. Many Web sites tag visitors' computers with small files known as cookies, which help identify users on return visits. If the user never comes back, though, the cookies vanish. However, with frequent visits, the cookie files grow accumulating buyer preferences; the marketer can then spot returning visitors, and the people can be greeted with more ads for the original merchant. Privacy advocates deplore these tracking devices as an invasion into personal rights and would like to see them banned.

- ***Sig Files.*** Text signature blocks at the end of e-mail, list, or news group postings are called signature (.sig) files or sigs. Usually these are short, five to six lines maximum, that give your name, your company name, e-mail address, phone and fax numbers, and, most importantly, your home page URL. Sometimes quotations are included as well as illustrations formed from keyboard characters. Your sig is a small, discrete ad for your Web site and business.

- *FAQs.* These Frequently Asked Questions are developed so that regular readers of the postings do not have to see the same questions and same answers month after month. Take any look at several FAQs to understand the Q&A usual style, and read the postings of a group for a short while to gauge the type and level of the questions. Then select a subject area that is appropriate to your business and create a FAQ. This can help establish your businesses expertise, build confidence in your business, and give your business a sense of increased approachability. The FAQ is definitely not an advertisement, though you can mention your company, if appropriate, and include your URL.

- ***Usenet Newsgroups.*** There are an estimated ten thousand Usenet news groups covering almost every topic. The best approach to targeting your message is to locate groups to investigate their FAQs and to read their charters. The FAQ "How to find the right place to post" is invaluable for hunting down elusive groups. You can find it at http://www.cis.ohio-state.edu/hypertext/faq/usenet/finding-groups/faq.html

The above techniques to exposure can easily be carried out by one or two people, is very inexpensive to start and maintain, and can be later expanded with a storefront or electronic catalog as business and the number of target markets grow.

Lastly, to promote your site, consider a cross-fertilization between your Web site and your traditional marketing media to increase the success of your Web presence. Your URL and e-mail address should be placed somewhere in every print media ad and printed collateral materials, such as letterhead, business cards, brochures, fax cover sheets, press kits, press releases, newsletters, and promotional items. Also, the presence of Internet addresses on your printed matter projects a modern, up-to-date image for your company, even to those who do not use the Internet.

Because a critical task in Web marketing is to get people to visit your home page, you as marketer can increase visibility through the following actions:

- Register your site with Web search engines, listings, and catalogs.

- Participate in discussion lists and Usenet newsgroups and the use of informative .sig files; not only will you gain exposure, but you will also become an active participant in formulating the topics of the day within the discussion group's direction.

- Make online announcement and use news releases; make sure the announcements are newsworthy and appropriate for the news group's charter.

- Study FAQs; this saves you and the list moderator time and effort. "Newbies," new users of the Web frequently overlook this manual to the site, news group, or organization.

- Use cross-linking of your page to other relevant pages. Not only does this provide an expansion of knowledge to usage of your products, but it also adds credentials, for example, a link to Underwriters Laboratory on standards for flame-retardant children's clothing, sleepwear, or perhaps Halloween costumes.

KEYS TO BUILDING A SUCCESSFUL COMMERCIAL WEB SITE

There are no invisible Web sites. Register your site with all online search engines.

There are no Dead Web sites; some sites look like a ghost town because no one has been tending to them. On a good site, the content is always fresh. New pages are added and old pages are updated.

Successful pages are information-rich. A successful site offers good and thorough content.

The pages have clear navigation. Users can move around and through the site consistently. The user can see where she is going and can return to previous pages easily.

The pages do not funnel the user out too quickly. Some pages have links at every stop. Do not send the viewer away with too many links to other sites.

The site has true value added. Services, content, products, or other resources are evident. A successful site is not just a place to market and sell; users can get real information and services for free.

The site maintainers are responsive. Questions are answered quickly, and the maintainers troubleshoot problem links. The documentation is correct.

The site has organizational or institutional support. The whole organization knows about the site; there is a budget and personnel support.

The site is capable of gathering information. Information about users is routinely gathered through contests, newsletters, or surveys, so that maintainers know who has been visiting and know these users' preferences and reactions.

The Web site is a marketing channel integrated with other channels. The Web and the Internet are integrated with print media, television, and radio.

The Web site is supported through other Internet tools. A good Web site has related Gopher and FTP sites and is supported by e-mail.

The site has good design. The following is a general list of guidelines to follow regarding design. (This is discussed in greater detail in Chapter 11.)

- There is text and small image alternatives, called thumbnails, to represent large images without having to load large graphic files initially.
- Interactivity with people is available, such as speaking with customer service representatives.
- The site is sensible versus hot; the graphics, design, and colors are in sync with the corporate image.
- The site has relatively consistent imagery and content from page to page—providing a sense of visiting one site, not just a collection of pages.
- The URL is not a funny-looking URL with lots of mixed cases and tildes.

The marketer should remember that this is your customer's site, not yours. Companies love to talk about themselves. Make your Web site a mirror of the interests of the individual users—your customers. Tell and show them what they want to hear and see. Great examples of sites that are entertaining yet serve the customers' needs are some of the following. Check them out to determine what benefits each offers its viewer. Site examples:

- Mama's Cucina, www.eat.com (fun and food)
- Crayola, www.crayola.com (educational kits)
- CBSdirect, www.cbsdirect.com (online ordering of computer buying services to business members)
- LEGO Online, www.lego.com/ (the joys of plastic blocks)
- *The X-Files*, www.thex-files.com (imaginative site with stars' bios, episode guide, merchandise offers, fan feedback, and more goodies)
- *Time* magazine, www.timeinc.com (online access to magazine materials and back issues)

How Can You Get Web Surfers Hooked?

In order to hook a Web surfer you first have to get someone to visit your home page. It is important to then keep the Web site visible on the Internet and in your print media as well. After the initial visit, activity and interactivity will encourage your visitor to return to your site.

- *Curiosity.* If you have a large site, and there is too much information to see in one online session, visitors will come back. If your content is intriguing, the site is valuable—worth returning to for more exploration.

- *Item turnover.* Provide at least some items that change frequently or even every time someone visits. This may be a "What is new" feature, but often it can be something as simple as a new daily saying or a listing of the birthdays of people (or customers) born on that day or a mention of a current event or a new audio file.
- *Indispensable tool or resource.* Your page can offer links to existing databases, collections of Internet and Web guides, search tools, or a repository of images and files. Your site is more likely to bring people back if the collection of links is unusually complete or high in quality. While the links can be on any subject, it makes sense to have them relate in some way to your business.
- *Unique event or resource.* The page can provide contests or giveaways. Depending on the business purpose, some sites have given away gold coins, cars, or computer equipment for retailers. For professional services, online conferences around tax preparations time can increase interest in your business activities and image. The marketer can offer an "Ask the Expert" feature—users can leave messages or e-mail questions, and answers could be placed on the page. There are lots of possibilities for making your page unique and worth returning to.

Sources for Professional Net Advertising Information

The University of Houston's College of Business maintains a large listing of all kinds of World Wide Web information called WWW Yellow Pages. The Advertising and Marketing entry currently contains experienced advertising agencies such as Advantage Solutions, Dataquest, NetMarket Group, and Modem Media Poppe Tyson Advertising among others. This site is very dynamic, so check it frequently. The address is http://www.cba.uh.edu/ylowpges/yabc.html.

The Present State of Online Commerce

What are the dynamics of consumers actually buying online? Contrary to the doom and gloom media reports of credit card number packet snatching, just over three-quarters (76.2 percent) of the GVU Ninth WWW User Survey respondents reported that they have "ordered a product or service by filling out a form on the Web." From gender and experience standpoints, respondents were usually U.S. males familiar with the Internet activities. In reviewing responses, only 1.9 percent actually had a bad experience with online purchasing. Only 4.5 percent found the process too complicated or thought the process would be too complicated.

The buying populations of the most popular products and services were discussed in Chapter 3. You should have learned from this discussion that almost 40 percent of online purchases were of software. Technological consumers are most comfortable in the online environment, and they are probably very familiar with the qualities of the product they are purchasing. Iconocast newsletter notes that as the Internet population homogenizes, purchase patterns are certain to change. In fact, America Online reported a different mix of popular purchases during the holidays. With a larger population of users, AOL disclosed that its top-selling items were flower arrangements, Starbucks coffee, and Omaha steaks. Within the concept of virtual storefronts, here is a sampling of successful e-commerce sites, as estimated by Iconocast.

Site ranking	1998 Run Rate (in millions) *
1. Cisco	$4,100
2. Dell	$1,016
3. Amazon	$160
4. Microsoft Expedia	$150
5. Preview Travel	$150
6. Onsale	$75
7. Barnes and Noble	$40
8. NECX	$35
9. 1-800-FLOWERS	$32
10. CDNow	$32

Sources include Cowles/Simba and Iconocast, April 1998
*Run rate is the annualized revenue based on the most recent period.

Review of Future Estimates by Consumer Product/Service Categories

What are the trends in consumer purchases that e-businesses selling online should be aware of for the immediate future? Computer and accessories; entertainment such as books, compact discs, and videos; and securities trading services presently are the categories of leading sales, but sales of auction services, toys, and apparel are gaining popularity. Besides specific products, e-commerce markets with the best growth potential are those closely tied to shifting demographics such as financial instruments, health, travel, and gardening for aging Boomers and apparel, music and other entertainment for Gen-Xers. Here are estimates for the U.S. and global markets in eleven product categories; figures are broken out for online and offline purchasing.

ONLINE PURCHASING BY PRODUCT CATEGORY, ESTIMATES FOR 1999

Rank Product Category	Offline U.S. (in billions)	Offline World (in millions)	Online '99 (in billions)
1. Leisure travel	N.A.	$3,000*	$7,798
2. Computer hardware	$53.4	N.A.	2,404
3. Apparel	14.3	N.A.	1,340
4. Books	N.A.	82.0	1,166
5. Software	5.3	N.A.	1,147
6. Gifts and flowers	15.0†	N.A.	563
7. Health and beauty	120.0	N.A.	50
8. Consumer electronics	76.0	N.A.	411
9. Music	12.5	38.1	374
10. Videos	7.9	16.0	301
11. Toys	22.6	N.A.	158

SOURCE: November 1998. Forrester Research; January,1999. *Forbes;* December 1998. *Business Week.*
*Entire travel industry; † Flowers only

Summary

There are as many ways to open and sustain a virtual storefront as there are types of retail and business-to-business enterprises. While the hardware, software, and operations tools are surprisingly similar, the successful e-commerce storefront requires an added element to be successful and memorable. It demands from the e-merchant and marketer imagination—imagination to bring something fresh to the Web, imagination to anticipate customer fancies and necessities. Imagination to have the confidence to try and try again. There are many decisions to be made, such as a imploring a do-it-yourself execution of the storefront as opposed to engaging a storefront developer or joining a cybermall to sell to excess traffic from adjacent sites. Each decision takes research, and from this research, better decisions are made.

As the virtual storefront is taking shape, marketing decisions concerning the promotional mix become imminent. Image and positioning judgments are weighed, identity materials are designed, and customer communications programs are developed—all to create a memorable virtual experience for shoppers and prospects alike. The experience is heightened by imagination, creativity, and curiosity. There are rules evolving about storefront site design, and these are good measures to consider. First, however, introduce imagination and creativity, and keep in mind that rules are made to be broken. Keep the content factual, solid, and changing, but interject intrigue and humor into the site, particularly if it is a consumer/retail storefront. Customers return to those sites that offer the most to them. Develop and design the site as if you were going to meet the shopper only once. Make the experience count, and the shoppers will return.

Key Terms

Canonical domain names

Clickthrough rates

Conference venues

Cookies

Dead webs

Electronic publishing

Mailbot

Preemptive collaboration

.sig files

Site ownership

Storefront developer

"Thumbnails"

Turnkey development

Usenet discussion groups

Virtual stores

Webmaster

QUESTIONS AND EXERCISES

1. Describe the tasks and responsibilities of the e-marketer concerning establishing and promoting the newly established e-commerce Web site. In one sentence, explain the tasks in order and give an example of each. Prepare a written outline to give to your Web designer.

2. You are developing a Web site for your own business, and you are concerned about selecting the right ISP for your business. Make a list of the services and equipment you want to rent from the ISP you choose. Compile the list of items and write a letter to your partner, who is supplying the money for your venture. Explain why you need each item.

3. There are advantages and disadvantages in preparing the Web site yourself and in hiring a storefront developer for the assignment. Suppose you are planning to open an online store that is a full-service iguana shop. You will carry a complete line of iguana supplies. Prepare a list of the top five advantages and the top five disadvantages of creating the site yourself; then prepare a list of the top five advantages and the top five disadvantages of hiring an outside source to create the site. The list is for your own planning purposes.

4. Contact a storefront developer and interview the company to understand what services they provide to the online merchant. Give the representative a product or service scenario, and write a one-page report on your interview.

5. In your opinion, what are the advantages and disadvantages of operating both a traditional retailing location and an online store? Prepare a list of advantages and disadvantages of operating each at the same time. Be prepared to discuss your opinions in the next class meeting.

6. Write an e-mail to a storefront developer requesting a proposal for the design and implementation of a virtual store. In the e-mail list what services you are looking for and what specifications there are for the hardware to operate your site. Be detailed in your instructions.

7. Of the promotional tactics listed in the text, which three do you feel will be most effective for building initial awareness of a consumer-oriented virtual store? Of a business-to-business virtual store? Justify your thinking in support of these three awareness elements and prepare your thoughts as a speech outline to be delivered before a college business fraternity.

8. .Sig files can create a personalized signature for your correspondence. Write your own .sig file for your e-mails and use characters, numbers, letters, or designs that you think are distinctive to your personality. E-mail your instructor with an e-mail displaying the .sig file.

9. What catches your attention on commercial Web sites as you surf? Select six Web sites you believe are creative or memorable and write a paragraph on each stating reasons each caught your eye. Print each Web site out to accompany your report. Assume this is research to assist your Web designer in developing a site for your company.

10. You are planning a Web site to support your virtual storefront that specializes in sports pins commemorating sporting events. They were originally made to be worn, but a collectors' hobby has emerged. In planning your site, you are considering incorporating the following items; make a list of the advantages and disadvantages of each element.

    a) color photography of each pin for sale or trade

    b) sound bites of sports music

    c) sound effects to match the category of sports pins

    d) video clips of famous moments in sports

e) Java scripts of sports teams' logos in motion

f) site search engine

g) trivia test page

h) offer to subscribe to Sports Pins Collectors' Newsletter, a text-based online newsletter you write and e-mail each month

What other ideas do you think might be effective in gaining attention and site loyalty?

Bibliography

Anders, George. 1998. Comparison shopping is the Web's virtue—Unless you're a seller. *The Wall Street Journal,* 23 July, A4.

Grant, Gail. 1996. Emerging platforms for commerce over the Internet. *The Internet Strategy Handbook.* Edited by Mary J. Cronin. Boston: Harvard Business School Press.

History of Amazon.com.1998 [cited online 16 December].

Internet more important than TV and phone. 1998. *TechWeb.* CMP Net [cited online 3 December].

Online retailers form web shopping network. 1998. Reuters Wire on the CMP Net [cited online 23 November].

Philosophy of Amazon.com. 1998 [cited online 16 December].

CHAPTER 15

Security on the E-Commerce Site

The basic idea behind Access Certificates for Electronic Services (ACES) is to provide a third-party certificate authority for verifying the identities of computer users who want to access private information or transact business with government agencies electronically. The ACES guidelines say the authentication will take place online, primarily by cross-referencing the applicant's stated identity with information that exists in a variety of different databases across the Internet. By "cross-vetting" the applicant's data, the certificate authority could verify the user's identity without requiring the individual to appear at an office and present a photo ID. Once the individual's identity is verified, the certificate authority would send a "certificate"—a piece of software or the means to access the software over the Web—via postal mail. The process would take three to five days.

"There are several flaws in the plan, but one of the biggest questions is who will pay for the service," [said] Patricia Edfors, president of PNE Associates, a security consultant. "They're talking about charging a fee for each transaction, but they haven't even defined what constitutes a transaction," she said. "And if the money from this program comes out of [Federal Telecommunications System] funds, and then the agencies have to pay a certificate authority for the service, aren't they paying twice?"

(Wilson 1998)

LEARNING OBJECTIVES

- To explore the basics of cryptography and its role in e-commerce
- To investigate the digital certificate, the foundation for payment systems
- To discuss methods of security, Secure Sockets Layer versus Secure Electronic Transaction protocols

Introduction

During the rise of e-commerce on the Internet, security had been the primary source of trepidation among would-be customers of many online sites. In appearance, the Internet may have started as a noncommercial network of computers, was not designed with security as a paramount objective. Quite the contrary, it was designed as a means of allowing research scientists in geographically disparate regions to share information among their colleagues. Sharing, not privacy, and documents, not transactions, were the prime objectives.

The primary goal of online shopping and other retail sites has been to provide the same level of quality and convenience as that experienced by a consumer in a real-world setting. In many cases, the methods and practices, as well as the law and governing rules, have been modeled after a combination of fair trade practices and mail-order commerce. For example, the rules governing the handling of money is instructive. When a **merchant** receives credit card information from a consumer, the law does not allow the merchant to actually charge the customer until the purchased goods have actually left the merchant's premises. This may seem like a trivial matter, but in fact it is not. When a consumer purchases an item in a store, the transaction is completed simultaneously—the consumer pays for the merchandise and walks out of the store with it. In the virtual store, however, this is not the case. In fact, the consumer probably will not ever speak or communicate directly with another person before, during, or after the purchase.

The objectives of this chapter are to describe security from two vantage points: that of the consumer's information and that of the merchant's transactions. Specifically, the basics of cryptography (the key to security on the Internet), digital certificates, and the inner workings of the SSL (Secure Sockets Layer) and SET (Secure Electronic Transaction) protocols will be outlined. The preceding two protocols leverage the power of cryptography and digital certificates to solve the inherent problem of reliable authentication, thereby providing the basis of security and transactions on the Internet.

A Survey of Cryptography

In order to understand the concept of encryption within the confines of SSL and SET, it is necessary to delve into the world of cryptography, which is as ancient as mankind's desire for **privacy** in communications. Cryptography in the last century has risen to a high art and has been in a large measure the key to critical events in the last world war. (For a fascinating journey through the rise of cryptography as it relates to World War II, read *The Code Breakers*, by David Kahn, which details how the United States employed the language of the Navajos in an effort to establish completely secure verbal communications.)

Cryptography results in the creation of cryptographic methods, also known as cryptosystems. There are two kinds of cryptosystems: symmetric and asymmetric. **Symmetric cryptosystems** use the same key, or the secret key, to encrypt or scramble and decrypt or unscramble a message. **Asymmetric cryptosystems,** on the other hand, use one key to encrypt a message and a different key to decrypt it.

Asymmetric cryptosystems are also called **public key** cryptosystems and rely on technology in which two keys, the *public key* and the *private key*, are used to encrypt or decrypt data (either key can be used to encrypt, but the other is required to decrypt). Typically, a user gives his public key to other users, keeping the private key to himself. Data encrypted with a public key can be decrypted only with the corresponding private key, and vice versa. This technology was first identified by Whitfield Diffie and Martin Hellman in their 1976 publication *New Directions in Cryptography*. However,

RSA Data Security (www.rsa.com)
To keep clients and prospects abreast of security developments, RSA has taken a newsletter-like design for its home page. Many timely hyperlinks connected viewers to important security news such as SSL and S/MIME protocols.

when Public Key Partners' patent on the Diffie-Hellman algorithm expired on April 29, 1997, cryptologists were able to freely incorporate the standard, along with extensions by cryptographers like Taher ElGamal, into their programs.

RSA is a public-key algorithm invented by Rivest, Shamir, and Adleman and involves the product of two large prime numbers. The difficulty of breaking RSA is generally considered to be equal to the difficulty of factoring integers that are the product of two large prime numbers of approximately equal size. As computers become more computationally advanced, the ability to factor large prime numbers, likewise, becomes easier. However, that just means that the prime numbers, likewise, must become larger. This large prime number is represented as the number of bits, or binary integers, needed to create it. Therefore, for example, 40-bit algorithms yield smaller integers than 128-bit algorithms. The sizes of the integers in the algorithms are what the U.S. government carefully controls with respect to domestic versus international use.

In order for electronic commerce, or any other secret traffic over the Internet, to proceed, a method must be employed that allows two parties, without prior arrangements, to exchange messages in such a way that they agree upon a secret key that is known only to them. This is known as a *key-agreement algorithm.*

Symmetric cryptosystems are the easier of the two to implement, since only one key is required. They do have a problem, though: How do you transport the secret key from the sender to the recipient securely and in a tamper-proof fashion? If you could send the secret key securely, you would not need asymmetric cryptosystems since you would simply use that same secure channel to send your message. In the case where symmetric cryptosystems must be employed, trusted couriers are employed as the deliverers of the secret key. However, where trusted couriers are not available, public key cryptosystems are the answer, and the most widely used asymmetric cryptographic standard is that developed and published by RSA Laboratories (www.rsa.com) and known as Public-Key Cryptography Standards (PKCS). RSA Laboratories developed PKCS in 1991 with representatives from Apple, Digital, Lotus, Microsoft, MIT, Northern Telecom, Novell, and Sun Microsystems. Since its publication in June 1991, PKCS has become the de facto standard of Internet security mechanisms. RSA Laboratories' role with regard to the PKCS standards is in the standards-making process, specifically in the following:

- Publishing carefully written documents describing the standards
- Retaining sole decision-making authority on what each standard is
- Soliciting opinions and advice from developers on useful or necessary changes and extensions
- Publishing revised standards when appropriate
- Providing implementation guides and/or reference implementations

Digital Certificates

Beyond privacy and confidentiality with respect to digital communication, cryptography has been extended to the area of authentication. **Authentication** is the process of verifying that people or entities are who or what they claim to be. In the real world, people recognize people at the bank by their faces or at a crime scene by their fingerprints. Authentication is the digital equivalent. It is the most essential of all the security services because it is the basis of access control, permissions and authorizations, enforcing accountability, and achieving non-repudiation. One of the key applications of cryptography for authentication is the digital certificate.

Digital certificates are in effect virtual fingerprints, or retinal scans, that authenticate the identity of a person or thing in a concrete, verifiable way. The certificate itself is simply a collection of information to which a digital signature is attached by the issuer, also known as a Certificate Authority (CA). A CA is a third-party organization that is trusted by the community of certificate users and whose role is analogous to that of the Department of Motor Vehicles (DMV), which issues drivers' licenses and is broadly acknowledged and accepted as a trustworthy means of personal identification. CAs typically offer a combination of cryptography technology, an infrastructure of highly secure facilities, and a specification of practices and liability that establishes its ability to operate as a trusted third party. Customers may contract with the CA to handle routine certificate administration tasks, or they may elect to assume responsibility for certificate issuance and revocation themselves, thereby maintaining a higher level of control. You can get such certificates from companies like VeriSign, a leading provider of Public Key Infrastructure (PKI) and digital certificate solutions (www.verisign.com).

A typical digital certificate is a data file of information, digitally signed and sealed by the CA and encrypted using RSA encryption techniques that can be verified by anyone. This certificate includes:

- The name of the holder and other identification information, such as email address
- A public key, which can be used to verify the digital signature of a message sender previously signed with the matching mathematically unique private key

- The name of the issuer, or Certificate Authority
- The certificate's validity period

Every time someone sends an electronic message, they attach their digital certificate to sign and encrypt that message. The recipient of the message first uses her own digital certificate to verify that the author's public key is authentic. She then uses that public key to verify the message itself. In order to create a digital certificate for an individual, the CA must confirm the identity of the person, device, or entity that requests a certificate. This is typically accomplished through a combination of the following, depending on the level of security required:

- Personal presence; the person may physically appear before a trusted entity.
- Identification documents; a Certificate Authority can make use of identification documents such as a passport, a driver's license, or an employee badge.

Digital certificates may be distributed online—even through unsecured networks—because the certificates are self-protecting. Typical means of distributing certificates include:

- Certificate accompanying signature; the signer has a copy of his own certificate and can attach a copy of that certificate to the digital signature. If this is done, anyone who wants to verify a signature will have the certificate in hand.
- Directory service; when using public-key technology, the message originators must first obtain the certificates of the intended recipients. When multiple parties are involved, this can be a complex task. Directories provide an easy way to search for and find certificates on the Web.

Under some circumstances, digital certificate revocation may be required (for example, an employee terminates employment with the organization). The decision to revoke a certificate is the responsibility of the issuing company, generally in response to a request from an authorized person. For added security, the CA typically will authenticate the source of any revocation request. Verisign is the world's largest CA. Visit them at www.verisign.com for more information.

Secure Sockets Layer (SSL)

Also known as the *s* in https://, SSL was introduced in 1995 by Netscape as a component of its popular Navigator browser and as a means of providing privacy with respect to information being transmitted between a user's browser and the target **server,** typically that of a merchant. Soon that introduction enabled broad public access to online information security. SSL uses public key cryptography and its protocol can be used to secure the communications between users **(merchant servers)** and non-merchant servers as well. For example, a corporate sales report residing on a server at a company's headquarters and accessed via the browser of an employee on the road would be a logical choice in initiating the deployment of SSL.

SSL establishes a secure session between a browser and a server. Authentication between the browser and the server is thus taking place while the browser is logged onto an SSL server, but SSL does not authenticate the parties who are using that software. Rather, the nature and mechanism of SSL protocol were created to provide channel security. A channel is the two-way communication stream established between the browser and the server, and the definition of channel security indicates three basic requirements:

- The channel is reliable.
- The channel is private.
- The channel is authenticated.

By virtue of SSL's requirement of Transmission Control Protocol (TCP) as the transport mechanism, channel reliability is inherent. What about privacy and authentication, the ability of one entity to determine the identity of another entity? Identity is the binding between a public key and a name and the implicit ownership of the corresponding private key. In order to establish privacy between the browser and the server, encryption using PKCS standards and RSA algorithms is employed for all messages. As described previously, this encryption is preceded by a data handshake and has two major phases, as described in the following paragraphs.

The first phase is used to establish private communications and uses the *key-agreement algorithm.* This is where both parties communicate their hello messages. The **client** initiates the conversation by sending the CLIENT-HELLO message. The server receives the CLIENT-HELLO message and processes it responding with the SERVER-HELLO message. At this point, both the client and server have enough information to know whether or not a new master key is needed. When a new master key is needed, the SERVER-HELLO message will contain enough information for the client to generate the message. This includes the server's *signed certificate,* a list of **bulk cipher** specifications, and a connection-id (a large, randomly generated value generated by the server that is used by the client and server during a single session or connection). The client generates the master key and responds with a CLIENT-MASTER-KEY message or an error message if the server information indicates that the client and server cannot agree on a bulk cipher. This master key is the *public key* tied to a user's *private key.* When a new master key is not needed, both the client and the server proceed immediately to the second phase.

It should be noted here that each SSL endpoint uses a pair of ciphers per connection (for a total of four ciphers). At each endpoint, one cipher is used for outgoing communications, and one is used for incoming communications. When the client or server generates a **session key,** he actually generates two keys, the SERVER-READ-KEY (also known as the CLIENT-WRITE-KEY) and the SERVER-WRITE-KEY (also known as the CLIENT-READ-KEY). The master key is used by both the client and server to generate the various session keys.

Finally, the server sends a SERVER-VERIFY message to the client after the master key has been determined. This final step authenticates the server because only a server that has the appropriate public key can know the master key.

The second phase is used for client authentication. The server has already been authenticated by the client in the first phase, so this phase is primarily used to authenticate the client. In a typical scenario, the server will require something from the client and will send a request for that information. The client will answer in the positive if it has the needed information, or send an ERROR message if it does not. When a party has completed authenticating the other party, it sends its finished message. For the client, the CLIENT-FINISHED message contains the encrypted form of the CONNECTION-ID for the server to verify. If the verification fails, the server sends an ERROR message.

Once a party has sent its finished message, it must continue to listen to its peer's messages until it too receives a finished message. Once a party has both sent a finished

GOT A HACKER POLICY?

Almost two-thirds of companies, government agencies, and universities had security breaches in 1997, resulting in a loss of at least $137 million. This was a 16 percent increase over 1996 figures. Cigna Corp. of Philadelphia is using these figures as an opportunity to sell the world's first hacker insurance called Cigna's Secure Systems Insurance. "There are three ways hackers can cause losses to a company," says Nicholas Economidis, director of Cigna's Information and Asset Protection unit. The three ways include loss of data confidentiality, loss of data integrity, and loss of system availability. In order to be eligible for the insurance, a company is required to install surveillance and intrusion detection software. Cigna also requires companies to keep records of log-ons, changes in passwords, and computer backups. Economidis estimates that a coverage of $12 million will cost around $20,000 to $25,000 a year and will only cover losses caused by an external hacker.

Got a hacker policy? 1998. *Forbes*. Industries Channel. [cited online 16 November].

message and received its peers finished message, the SSL handshake protocol is done. At this point the **application protocol** (for instance, HTTP or FTP) begins to operate (as a layer on top of the existing SSL protocol). You can go to http://developer.netscape.com/docs/manuals/index.html for the index of Netscape's documentation, which includes large sections devoted to Internet security. Even if SSL is on the server, it will only work with browsers that support SSL. Although most browsers currently support SSL, some older versions of AOL's browsers do not. Therefore, the merchant enabling SSL should be sure to provide software that coheres with the version of the visitors' browsers. The merchant should alert the users to this possible problem.

Limits of SSL

SSL depends on several cryptographic technologies. As mentioned previously, **RSA public key encryption** is used for the exchange of the session key and client/server authentication, while various cryptographic algorithms are used for the **session cipher.** While the possibility is very slight, successful cryptographic attacks made against these technologies can render SSL insecure. This possibility is primarily dependent on computer processing power. It is, therefore, reasonable to assume that as successful attacks occur, the length—40-bit, 64-bit, 128-bit—of the keys will concomitantly increase.

In addition, attacks against a specific communications session can be made by recording the session and then spending some large number of compute cycles to crack either the session key or the RSA public key until the communication can be seen in the clear. While this approach is easier than cracking the cryptographic technologies for all possible messages, SSL tries to make the cost of such of an attack greater than the benefits gained from a successful attack, thus making it a waste of money and time to perform such an attack. It has been noted that the consequence of the SSL defense is that a brute force attack becomes the cheapest way to attack the private key. Brute force attacks have well-known space/time tradeoffs, and so it becomes possible to define the cost of the attack. For the 128-bit private key (which is only allowed inside the United States), the known cost is essentially infinite. For the 40-bit private key (which the U.S. government allows anywhere in the world), the cost is much smaller but still beyond the cost and time resources of the random hacker. However, it is clearly possible, even probable, that large amounts of resources (for example, governments and extremely wealthy corporations) can in fact penetrate SSL communications.

Secure Electronic Transaction (SET)

On February 1, 1996, MasterCard International and Visa International announced the development of a single technical standard for safeguarding payment card purchases made over open networks. The protocol, called Secure Electronic Transaction (SET), was to be developed by Visa and MasterCard, in conjunction with leading technology companies, including Microsoft, IBM, Netscape, Verifone, SAIC, GTE, RSA, Terisa Systems, and VeriSign. Then, on December 19, 1997, SET Secure Electronic Transaction LLC, also known as SETCo, was formed by Visa and MasterCard (currently the sole owners and decision makers of SETCo) to implement the recently published SET 1.0 specifications. In addition, a memorandum of understanding, awaiting final agreement, was signed that provided for the addition of American Express and JCB Credit Card Company as co-owners of SETCo. Visit www.setco.org for more information regarding the transaction.

Through the use of digital certificates (X509 version 3), SET seeks to bolster confidence in the payment process by ensuring that merchants are authorized to accept credit card payments, thus reducing risks associated with merchant fraud and ensuring that the purchaser is an authorized user of the payment card. In support of this objective, SETCo has been charged to support the SET specification and infrastructure by focusing initially on the following two electronic commerce initiatives:

- The creation, management, and maintenance of an Industry Root Key Certificate Authority, which will manage the Industry Root Key—a component of all software that complies with the SET protocol.

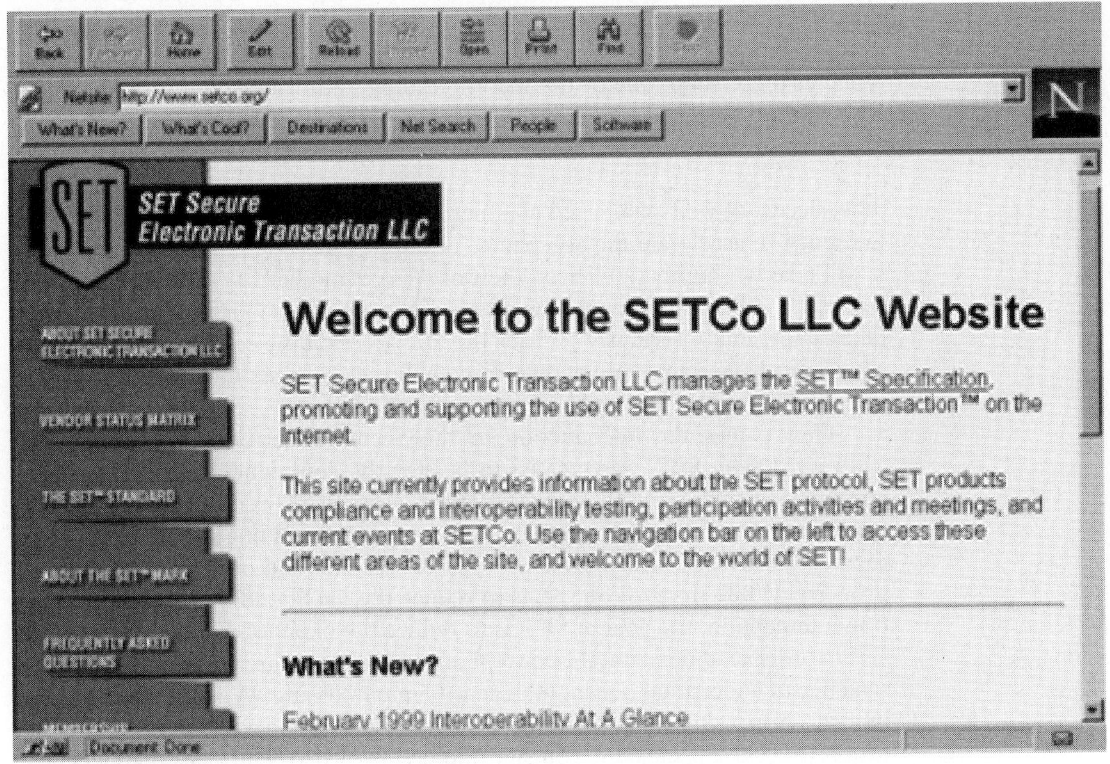

Secure Electronic Transactions LLC (www.setco.com)
The objective of SETCo is to provide a protocol for online payment card purchases. Developed by Visa and MasterCard, SETCo seeks to bolster consumer confidence in online payment and e-commerce.

- The coordination of SET Software Testing and Compliance Services, with Tenth Mountain Systems, Inc., to ensure that the software used by consumers, merchants, and payment card companies is fully compliant with the published SET protocol. Only software that passes all aspects of this testing program will be eligible to display the SET trademarks.

As previously discussed, the SSL protocol provides for channel security, and in that role, SSL is a powerful tool for the secure distribution of information, particularly with regard to intracompany communications. The communications are highly secure, similar to that of a secured phone conversation. As with a secured phone conversation, during which two people are both assured that the conversation is safe from prying ears, further steps must be taken to ensure secure distribution of information and proper identification of senders and receivers of this information. SSL does not address every aspect of security. Thus, while **cardholders** using SSL can submit payment information securely over the Internet, there is still no way of verifying the identity of the online storefront that they are visiting. SSL makes no guarantee that the source and target of the conversation are trustworthy. Specifically, with e-commerce transaction based solely on SSL, risks associated with sending and accepting transactions over the Internet are still prevalent. Among these risks are the following:

- The purchaser must trust the merchant's ability to guard very personal and confidential data, including but not limited to credit card information.
- The purchaser must trust that the merchant is authorized to accept credit card payments.
- The merchant must trust that the purchaser is authorized to use the credit card.

The GartnerGroup, one of the world's leading authorities on information technology, had this to say about purchasing online and the lack of measures to ensure security of these transactions.

> The success of well-publicized commerce sites such as Amazon.com is doing much to accelerate the acceptance of online purchasing. [However, all] it will take is a highly publicized theft of a large number of credit cards, or worse, a small number over a long period of time, for public confidence to take a dent, and to seriously set back the growth of online commerce. Given the relatively insecure state of many e-commerce processes today, we regard this scenario as highly possible.

Thus comes the introduction to the Secure Electronic Transaction (SET) protocol. SET was created to bolster the confidence of the online consumer by mitigating these security risks, particularly as e-commerce becomes a means not only for consumers to pay for goods but also to receive them, as is the case with online delivery of software and other intellectual property. While the goal of SSL is to reduce the likelihood of communication interception, the goal of SET is to reduce the likelihood of fraud.

In order to understand the concept of purchasing security, it becomes instructive to understand non-digital security in purchasing. When you buy an item in a store using a credit card, you are often confronted with the authentication process. Specifically, you sign the credit card receipt, and the clerk probably asks to see two forms of identification, preferably with pictures. This is authentication. The clerk has attempted to verify the authenticity of the credit card purchaser, first by signature, then by formal identification.

The process of purchasing a product electronically is conceptually very similar. The difference is that the communication is subject to interception (whereas in the store the communication is face-to-face), and the validation process with respect to both the purchaser and the merchant must be devoid of personal interaction but no less secure. By incorporating both encryption technology as well as digital certificates, the SET protocol represents an improvement over other Internet security technologies, particularly with respect to Internet-based credit card transactions. Just like the signature on a credit card receipt, SET uses client-side authentication to help protect the merchant from possible fraud by preventing the purchaser from denying that they entered into the transaction. Within SET, only the sensitive information in the transaction (name, address, credit card, etc.) is encrypted. Unlike SSL, communication encryption is not employed. This may at first appear to be a limitation, but due to the use of digital certificates and other encryption, security is established. Because the Web pages are not encrypted as they travel to the consumer, Web site designers are free to use graphics more liberally than would otherwise be necessitated by SSL's inherent channel encryption performance hit.

Workings of SET

SET is an open standard. This means that the specifications are publicly available, and can be used pursuant to ownership acknowledgment and trademark restrictions. In addition, SET is a multi-party protocol, which designates that it uses several protocols, such as digital certificates, working together to provide a secure transaction framework. With SET, merchants do not have access to credit card numbers. This information remains encrypted throughout the purchasing process, revealed only to the credit card processor, who is a holder of a private key required to decrypt the Internet message containing the purchaser's credit card information. According to Steve Mott, senior vice president of Electronic Commerce/New Ventures at MasterCard, "SET technology makes an online credit or debit card purchase at least as safe as handing the plastic card to someone in person."

Interoperability is ensured by the design of specific protocols and message formats that are published and shared with participating software development organizations, whose software becomes certified by SETCo (www.setco.org). SET provides message integrity, authentication of all financial data, and encryption of sensitive data. In addition, SET is designed to permit additional encryption where it is permitted, such as the 128-bit encryption allowed for U.S. domestic applications. SET provides the special security needs of electronic commerce with the following:

- Privacy of payment data and confidentiality of order information transmission. Merchants accepting SET transactions are protected from liability of credit card numbers in their database since they do not receive credit card information. Furthermore, a consumer can make a purchase and trust that no fraudulent activity will take place with his credit card number once the card number has been transmitted.
- Authentication of a cardholder for a branded bank card account. Cardholder account authentication is ensured by the use of digital signatures and cardholder certificates.
- Authentication of the merchant to accept credit card payments. Merchant authentication is ensured by the use of digital signatures and merchant certificates.

The three ways include loss of data confidentiality, loss of data integrity, and loss of system availability.

- Payment information integrity is ensured by the use of digital signatures.
- Special purpose digital certificates.
- Non-repudiation for dispute resolution. The process of digital certificate distribution that takes place during SET transactions also holds the consumer and merchant accountable for information contained in the transaction. Therefore, if a consumer places an order for a product using SET and then receives the product, she cannot deny that the order has been placed. Similarly, merchants cannot later claim that they did not receive the product order.

The Purchasing Process

In order to understand how SET works, the process behind SET needs to be discussed with critical components identified along the way.

The Setup

A merchant applies for, and receives, an account with an issuing bank, just as he would apply for a normal credit card merchant account. In order to be accepted, the merchant must supply the bank with information that the bank will use to verify the identity and credit-worthiness of the merchant. Once the merchant has been approved, an account will be set up with the bank, and the bank will send to the merchant SET payment software (if the merchant does not already have it) and a digital certificate that uniquely identifies the merchant. The merchant then integrates this software into his existing Web site.

A consumer makes an application to an issuing bank for a digital credit card, which is a digital certificate that has been personalized for the credit cardholder. In order to be accepted, the consumer must supply the bank with information that the bank will use to verify the identity and credit-worthiness of the consumer. Once the consumer has been approved, an account will be set up with the bank, and the bank will send to the consumer a digital certificate that uniquely identifies the credit card (and the consumer). After the consumer receives her digital credit card, she adds it to her **browser wallet.**

The Shopping Experience

The consumer browses the Web at a particular site, for instance, an online bookstore. During the browsing event, the shopper initiates an Internet order, filling up an online shopping cart with items and eventually compiling a virtual stack of books and compact discs. At checkout time, the Web site asks for the shopper's credit card. Instead of typing in the credit card number, the browser wallet is queried by the Web site SET software and, following selection of the appropriate credit card and entry of its password by the consumer, the bank-issued digital credit card is submitted to the merchant.

The merchant receives the digital credit card in a digital envelope (this method prevents the merchant from viewing the card number), and from this, the merchant software creates a SET transaction that has the merchant's own digital identity attached. The merchant software then sends the SET transaction to a credit card processor (also known as a **payment gateway** application or **acquirer**) for verification. The credit card processor opens the envelope, decrypting, translating, and verifying the information contained within, and then routes the transaction to the merchant's financial institution, which is set up with SET software of its own. The financial institution performs functions including authorization, credit, and capture (voiding and refund) reversals on the transaction, and following successful processing, the merchant, cardholder, and credit card processor are all advised electronically that the purchase has been approved. Following this notification, the cardholder is debited and the merchant is paid through subsequent payment capture transactions. The merchant can then ship the merchandise, knowing that the customer transaction is approved. The buyer is also protected because the merchant has been verified. The credit card number was hidden from everyone through the entire process but the bank.

IBM offers what is called "End-to-End Service," which is a complete suite of applications serving everyone from the consumer to the merchant to the financial institutions. The applications support IBM's SET Browser Application, Web sites, Internet access, and payment gateway. In addition, as part of this suite, IBM offers its merchant-targeted Net.Commerce application, which features the following:

- Browser recognition, classification, and statistics logging
- A virtual storefront for customized merchandising
- Dynamically populated templates for order entry, search, and shopping basket
- Instant Web page updates and product information
- Tracked statistics for shopping analysis and buyer profiles
- The AVP TAXWARE system for calculating and supplying accurate U.S. and Canadian tax rates.

In addition, Net.Commerce supports the following standards:

- Secure Electronic Transaction (SET)
- Secure Sockets Layer (SSL)
- HyperText Markup Language (HTML)
- HyperText Transfer Protocol (HTTP)
- Common Gateway Interface (CGI)
- Java
- Netscape Server Application Programming Interface (NSAPI), allowing use with the Netscape's Commerce server
- Internet Server Application Programming Interface (ISAPI), allowing use with Microsoft's Internet Information Server
- Electronic Data Interchange (EDI)
- Joint Electronic Payment Initiative (JEPI)

You can visit www.bankamerica.com/spare_change/set_pilot.html for a tour of Bank of America's SET pilot program. VeriFone (www.verifone.com) has a nice site that covers information on SET and other e-commerce initiatives. In addition, CyberSource (www.cybersource.com/html/solutions/geo.html), OpenMarket (www.openmarket.com/business), and CyberCash (www.cybercash.com/cybercash/merchants) have sites full of good SET information.

EXPRESS LANE FOR E-SHOPPERS

Idealab (www.idealab.com) has something new in its back pocket. It hopes that its eWallet software will make online shopping as easy as pulling out your credit card. "If you want to do something fast with impulse on the Internet, it should be as fast like buying something with impulse in the store," send Bill Gross, CEO of Idealab, an Internet business development company based in Pasadena, California. When eWallet software is added to the bottom of a Windows desktop, a single click will propel shoppers through e-commerce checkout lines by Web masters filling in name, credit card, shipping, and other information needed to complete a transaction. Shoppers simply drag icons of their credit cards over an e-commerce page and enter a PIN number, so other users can't shop with the same wallet.

"Filling out fields manually is too cumbersome," Gross said, "and frequent abandonment of online 'shopping carts,' the lists of items at Web stores that visitors have selected for purchase." Gross acknowledged that eWallet can do nothing to attract shoppers unwilling to provide personal data online. But it removes some of the hurdles for shoppers discouraged by the slow speed or inconvenience of the checkout process. "It's a way around the problems that digital-cash faced," said Dick Shaffer of Technology Partners, a technology consulting company. "It's clever technology. But nobody—from the retailer to the customer—has to pay attention to the technology."

Oakes, Chris. 1998. Express lane for e-shoppers. *Wired News* [cited online 25 November].

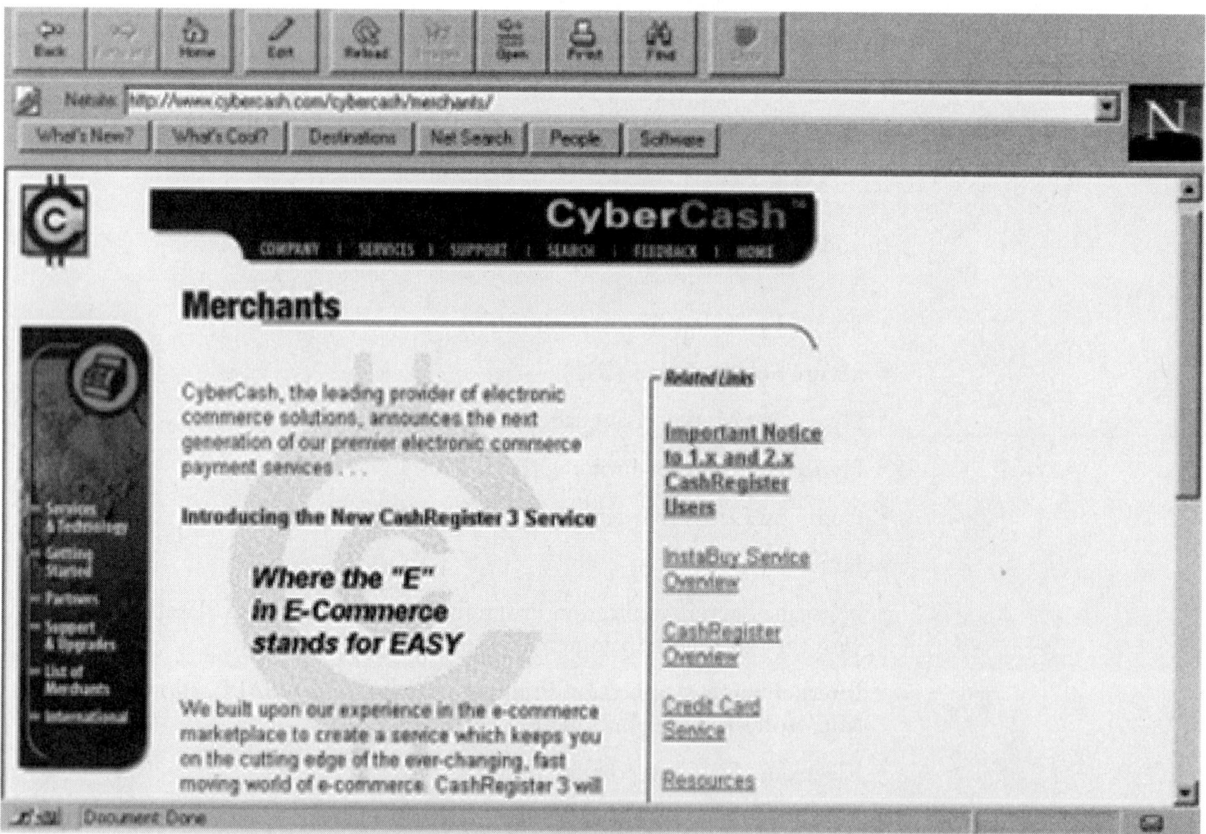

CyberCash (www.cybercash.com)
The online shopper can purchase domestically and internationally with the CyberCash system. There are conveniences and benefits to the consumer, the merchant, the e-commerce partner, the financial institutions, and the biller.

Limitations of SET and SSL

A downside of both SSL and SET protocols is that they both require the use of cryptographic algorithms that place significant loads on the computer systems involved in the commerce transaction. While SET does not encrypt the communication and, therefore, has a lower impact than SSL on the user experience, SET has a higher server performance impact. SSL has a lower impact on the e-commerce server but does less to eliminate the security risk, while SET has a higher performance hit but allows for a much more secure transaction.

As a result of criticism of SET in the trade press, which was generated from the perception of slow performance, the GartnerGroup performed an examination of the expected performance differences over time between the SSL and SET, based on five typical server application scenarios: low, medium, and large e-commerce servers along with small and large payment gateways. In explaining the results, the analysts attributed the criticism to early technology implementations and did not take into account the substantial improvements in performance as the technology was deployed. The GartnerGroup had the following to say about the reliability of SET and SSL.

> The requirement to invest in additional hardware to support SET has been noticed in some early implementations, and some commentators, aware that some sites are already processing 20,000 secure transactions a day with no sign of growth slowing, have taken a 'sky is falling' view and have predicted that SET will not be able to cope. These commentators have also pointed out that many consumers are willing to take the risks inherent in SSL (which is true) and have not thought through the positive impact that can result if additional consumers are willing to participate when security is demonstrably high, or the risk of consumer confidence dropping when stories of fraud start to emerge.

Following Gartner's analysis, they concluded that on the desktop, even using the electronic wallets to provide user authentication information, processing power was more than adequate to handle the cryptographic load required by both SSL and SET. In fact, they compared the increase in processing ability with regard to cryptography as a direct correlation to the increase in computing power as applied to graphic accelerators and numeric coprocessors. Similarly, on the server side, the addition of cryptographic hardware accelerators and improvements in cryptographic algorithms, along with the dramatic scaling of processing power that has become the norm in the IT industry, fully addressed the need for more processing power. Specifically, Gartner concluded that:

- For the low and medium e-commerce applications, there is no additional server cost to support SET over SSL. The performance of the servers in these price ranges, at the anticipated loading, is more than adequate today and through the forecast period.
- For the large e-commerce server application, support of SET requires additional hardware acceleration in the medium term resulting in a 5 to 6 percent difference in server cost.
- For the small payment gateway application, hardware acceleration is required for both SET and SSL in the short term but can be phased out as servers improve in performance and if other performance improvements such as elliptical-curve cryptography (ECC) become available. It is anticipated that over time secure server systems will include cryptographic hardware as a part of their standard configuration.

- The large payment gateway applications will always be based on clustered systems for reasons of robustness and reliability. In these environments, the difference in cost to support SET over SSL will be covered by the investment in additional clustered systems. In the short term, because it is hypothetically possible with significant hardware acceleration to use a single system to support SSL, the cost of requiring a clustered system to support SET would appear to double the cost compared to a single SSL system. Note that this is not a recommended configuration. In the medium term, this payment gateway application will require additional hardware acceleration to support SET resulting in a 5 percent increase in server cost.

Thus, the conclusion is that SET as an emerging technology has a definitive security component that very clearly represents an advance in technology over SSL, and that any deficits that may be related to performance will quickly be rendered minor as hardware-based processing technology rapidly advances.

Summary

The basic four components of e-commerce, namely cryptography, digital certificates, the Secure Sockets Layer (SSL) protocol, and the Secure Electronic Transaction (SET) protocol have now been covered. Cryptography is the cornerstone of all security, while digital certificates, with a cryptographic basis, allow systems and organizations to uniquely identify, or authenticate, the parties involved in electronic transactions. SSL allows for the secure flow of communications between systems and applications, while SET goes even further, allowing such advanced concepts as nonrepudiation of transactions, where the parties involved cannot deny that they have participated in the transaction. These complex tools allow even more advanced media such as digital money, the very nature of which appears to be a conundrum—namely, a solid, material entity (a coin) transported from the real world into a virtual world whose very nature is ethereal and duplicable.

Key Terms

Acquirer

Application protocol

Asymmetric cryptosystems

Authentication

Browser wallet

Bulk cipher

Cardholder

Client

Merchant server

Merchant

Payment gateway

Privacy

Public key cryptosystems

RSA public key encryption

Server

Session cipher

Session key

Symmetric cryptosystems

QUESTIONS AND EXERCISES

1. You are the marketing department's liaison to the IS department of your company. The company operates in fifteen countries and is setting up an e-commerce site to sell rare Beanie Baby collectibles. You are on the committee evaluating software, and the subject of cryptography has come up. Name three factors regarding cryptography that would guide your recommendations and your caveats, with respect to each one. Write a memo to your marketing director explaining your recommendations and caveats.

2. At your company, where you have worked for the last five years, you have this gnawing feeling that you career is at a standstill. You, therefore, decide it is time to hit the road and go out on your own. You want to start an auction Web site to allow your friends and extended family to auction everything including the kitchen sink. However, you are collecting sensitive information about your customers. How will you assure your customers that their information is safe? Create a document that names three possible security problems and how you intend to allay potential fears about them. Write a planning memo to yourself.

3. You have been notified that you must attend a meeting with the security auditor of your firm. The audit in question concerns the new international e-commerce site that you have helped to steer to implementation. What aspects of site security will you research to prepare for the audit? Write a three-page position paper outlining a strategy to ensure that proper security measures have been taken with respect to your customer's confidential data.

4. As the assistant to the CEO of a small company (twenty employees) that does business in four countries, the CEO has charged you with helping to establish an online presence. The company is implementing an extranet that will allow the company's clients to get product marketing literature. What security controls will you recommend? Defend your decision from a marketing, finance, and IS point of view. Write an email to the CEO outlining your concerns on the controls and what they will do for each department.

5. While preparing for your new entrepreneurial venture, you realize that you will need digital certificates to establish the security of your SSL-based site. Create a memo to your prospective partners that outlines why you need digital certificates and what the requirements will be to obtain them, paying particular attention to the timelines for your company's legal incorporation, plus the implementation and subsequent marketing of your online presence.

6. You are the marketing director of a small company (fifty employees) with offices in the United States and Europe. What factors would you take into account in determining the number of digital certificates you will need for two new mirrored sites in New York and London? Write an e-mail to your CFO explaining your needs for the mirrored sites.

7. As the assistant to the CIO of a Fortune 500 company, the CIO has been given the task of creating a Web site to sell products currently being sold through the direct-marketing catalog business. Furthermore, the decision has been made that the site will take credit card payments. The CIO has asked you for information that would help him make some decisions. What factors would you use to determine whether the site should use SSL or SET?

Prepare a two-page discussion of the merits of each protocol and the factors that would come in to play in making a recommendation.

8. As the assistant director of the marketing department of a medium-sized company (four hundred employees) and responsible for creating a new campaign to promote your new secure online catalog, give three security-related advantages that you would promote. In addition, prepare a one-page strategy memo that you would create to communicate your marketing campaign with the IS department that will implement it, showing them that you are sensitive to their needs while being just as sensitive to the needs of your intended customers.

9. You are a marketing consultant for a research firm. Your client has asked for your opinion about whether they should use SSL or SET as the basic protocol for their online catalog. The reason they want your advice is that they want to make that decision part of their marketing plan. What information would you request from them? Prepare a meeting agenda memo that contains the points you expect to ask.

10. Based on what you have read in this chapter, would you use a digital credit card? Why or why not? Prepare a one-page document explaining your position that you will present to a classmate, your spouse, or a member of your family.

Bibliography

Wilson, Tim. 1998. Feds push digital-certificate scheme. *TechWeb* [cited online 13 July].

PART FOUR

Special Topics

Thus far we have studied the electronic marketing process that facilities electronic commerce, learned how to create a virtual storefront and its supporting customer communications tools, and develop an integrated online and traditional promotional program. We will now turn our addition to broader topics than those concerning the e-shopper. These subjects deal with the tremendous opportunities for business-to-business commerce, nascent international marketing programs, the ethics of electronic marketing, and views on the future of electronic marketing resources

These are concepts of great importance to electronic commerce. Business-to-business transactions constitute a great portion of online commerce, and marketers should learn to use online tools to their maximum benefits. The Internet already has global reach, and marketers should employ this capability if international marketing is appropriate for their product, firm, and audiences. As in advertising, the Web is a high profile medium and any abuse to the user, society or system, is given great scrutiny and exposure. There will be no alternative to ethical dealings for the e-merchant in his or her use of the Web. We have discussed the value and fragility of this wonderful invention, and society will expect business to protect and nurture it. Lastly, the future is bright and what conveniences and benefits the Web will deliver to its consumers can only be estimated in terms of our past experience and future expectations. The World Wide Web is a marvelous network for humanity, including marketing and other business endeavors. E-marketers should carefully and responsibly use electronic marketing resources to their fullest potential in delivering customer satisfaction.

CHAPTER 16

Special Opportunities for Business-to-Business Situations

There is nothing cute or sexy about Gordon Sinkez's Web site. You can't find sports scores or racy photos. You can't order best-selling books or download audio clips from your favorite band. But don't be fooled: This is the future of electronic commerce.

Mr. Sinkez runs a two-year-old Web site for CSX Corp., Jacksonville, Florida,which operates one of the nation's largest freight railroads. About 400,000 times a month, customers click on one of its pages—to book shipments, get price quotes or examine a map of CSX's 18,000-mile network, showing the exact location of their goods at that moment. The site lets CSX save money on clerical tasks, while customers get data so complete it's almost addictive. "We get people who sign on daily and keep refreshing computer screens so they can see where each railcar is," Mr. Sinkez says.

Plenty of other people—in corporate settings and in everyday life as consumers—are turning to the Internet and the World Wide Web when it's time to spend money. A few years ago, the Web had a reputation as a digital attic, crammed full of sites offering bad poetry, vacation photos, and obscure product brochures. Now, though, it's coming into its own as a mainstream part of commerce. Web sites are selling everything from ginseng to jet-engine parts, and new customers keep streaming in. (Anders 1998)

LEARNING OBJECTIVES

- To document the factors why business-to-business marketers are shifting sales efforts to online activities
- To demonstrate how the business-to-business organization integrates online marketing with its traditional sales activities
- To present the trends in business and consumer demographics and product sales projections around which business-to-business enterprises can be directed

Introduction

The World Wide Web gives the appearance that it is dominated by sites with fancy graphics and intricate information to appeal to the coming hordes of consumers. Many think that business-to-business selling is pedestrian and lacks visibility. While trade sectors' activities may lack the profile of consumer promotions, its commercial online sales volume is huge compared to consumer sales. Forrester Research estimates that U.S. consumer sales will comprise only 9.5 percent of business-to-business volume, $52 billion to $551 billion for the year 2001. (Forrester Research 1998) Wholesalers and distributors cite speed and convenience as motivators for implementing more online activities and services; these strategic actions lay foundations for company competitive advantage and differentiation. In fact, many businesses foresee the Web as mission-critical to their success; their clients and customers are declaring that, if the mercantile company is not on the Web, the company is off the client's supplier list. For example, networking giant Cisco Systems will no longer do business with suppliers that cannot fill orders via the Web. (Kupfer 1998) Therefore, the Web is entangling itself in businesses' everyday business. There are several perceptions and realities that need to be addressed regarding twenty-first-century commerce building and the assumption that the Internet is essential to businesses' operations and marketing.

The Brave, New World of the Web

The positioning line of United Parcel Service (UPS) sums the mindset of commerce today, "Moving at the Speed of Business." For competitive pressures, business management is looking inward to evaluate its own strengths and weaknesses, defining the corporate competencies and shoring up or **outsourcing** its deficiencies. Speed and accuracy of information and customer satisfaction delivered by the Internet are the driving urgencies that are forcing businesses to change their practices. Uncertainties face large and small companies, manufacturers and retailers, and product and service producers. The astute marketer will embrace change and recognize that change is a constant state for business. He should embrace change, even initiate it, to uncover irreparable incompetencies and failures before they impact company operations, marketing, or finances. To ramp up their capabilities and performance, many companies are turning to the Web as a partial but ubiquitous solution to better serve their business customers. If the Forrester Research projection is correct, almost 90 percent of the e-commerce over the next few years will be enacted by business-to-business enterprises. Therefore, to prepare your company for a paradigm shift, the marketer should examine the dynamics of the four *P*s of marketing (as well as customer service) as they apply to **e-business.** A definition distinction between e-business and e-commerce needs to be made at this time. Assume that e-business entails the activities of marketing and selling to business-to-business firms. E-commerce would encompass both e-business sales volumes and online consumer sales. With this distinction made, two powerful Web sites will be studied, both presenting e-business and both offering specific advice on entering the online business sector.

Defining the Business User

From the opening quote on CSX Corporation (www.csx.com), can you think of a more outdated, tradition-bound, or inflexible industry? The railroads have been bypassed by trucking and air freight; intractable unions ran the operations for many years; and the rail infrastructure is set in the ground by immutable rights-of-way acquired perhaps 150 years ago. Despite its history, though, the railway industry is changing and integrating electronic resources to better serve its customers. From the behavior of the serious Web user, business profiles for early into the next century can be drawn and projected right now. How should you determine the characteristics of the business user? In order to determine the answer to this question, it might be relevant to ask such questions as these, How many business users use the Web at work? and How often is the Web accessed in the business environment? Much research has already been done to determine the answers to these questions. For example, the Iconocast newsletter placed a minimum of 32 million business users worldwide who account for at least 46 percent of the total traffic volume. Following are additional findings by the Iconocast analysis, broken up by common user categories.

- *The business universe.* According to *RelevantKnowledge*, 34 percent of all Web users fit the definition of an "active business user." Based on Iconocast's current estimate of 93.8 million Internet users worldwide, that would amount to some 32 million business users worldwide. IDC, International Data Corperation, a worldwide information-technology consultancy, put the total number of business users in 1997 at 36 million.
- *Site universe.* Dun & Bradstreet reports that more than 40 million companies are listed on its worldwide database. When D&B matched its U.S. business data list against 1.3 million top-level Internet domains, it found that half of the domains, or 665,000, were nonactive business sites. Of the remainder, only half had active business sites. Bottom line: Roughly 333,000 businesses are on the Web, a minuscule fraction of the 40-million universe. (It should be noted that many businesses are hosted on sites such as GTE's SuperPages.)
- *Web usage.* A recent *Thomas Register* and *Visa USA* online survey of two thousand American and Canadian businesses (out of a possible 155,000 *Register*-listed companies) shows that 40 percent say they used the Web at least once in the past month, primarily for quick research.
- Fortune *500 sites.* In October 1997, IDC showed a chart that estimated that 80 percent of all *Fortune* 500 companies had Web sites in 1996. (It can be presumed that the number today would approach 95 percent.)
- *Small/medium/ large segmentation.* In 1997, IDC estimated that small business users made up 17 percent of "total Net use," while businesses with more than one hundred employees made up 28 percent ("total Net use" is a duplicated user figure, meaning that the majority are also home users). Worldwide, IDC estimates that medium and large businesses will account for 49 million users by 2000.
- *Small business.* According to *Cyber Dialogue's* U.S. Small Business Interview Survey, which was based on interviews with one thousand U.S. businesses with less than one hundred employees, 37 percent are online equivalent to 2.6 million small business employees out of a 7 million universe. Each online business averages 8.3 employees, suggesting that 21.6 million small business employees use some combination of e-mail and Web or commercial online services. Worldwide, IDC estimates that this figure will go to up 33 million by 2000, which is a very conservative 1997 estimate. Like consumers, an equal number of small business users, 53 percent, use the Internet on a daily basis.
- *Volumetrics.* Media Metrix reports that business users devote 65 percent more time on the Web than home users. With current home usage running about

> six hours per week, according to NetReadings, the average time a business user stays on the Internet is about ten hours. Based on this data, it is estimated that business usage constants about 46 percent of Internet traffic volume. (Iconocast 1998)

If the above estimates are accurate, there are businesses and business people using the Web regularly, at home and at work, in small, medium, and large organizations. This is quite sensible since businesses should be searching for better, faster, more complete ways to do things. The capabilities of the Web cover all of these areas.

The Logic of Web Usage by Business-to-Business Organizations

The way commercial enterprises conduct business has changed drastically through the nineties, and few managers, marketing included, could have foretold how technology would entangle itself in the Web of business. Business is now racing itself to improve its operations, marketing skills, and financial capabilities. Since 1982, the stock market has propelled publicly-held companies to previously unheard of financial strengths, called the "wealth factor," and with stock swaps and cash transactions, mergers and acquisitions have created huge business entities spread far across the country and world. Mergers and consolidations have caused scaling back of workforces, and this has led to fewer people performing more types of work. Communications domestically and internationally have become more complex; financial securities trade twenty-four hours each day from New York City to Tokyo to London. Managers have higher expectations of performance, from marketing to technology to profitability. Markets

WHOLESALE SHIFTS TO THE WEB

Robert Rodin, president and CEO of Marshall Industries, views e-commerce as the basis for an entirely new business model. Marshall Industries, a $1.5 billion electronics distributor nearly has doubled its revenue since it began a wholesale shift toward e-commerce four years ago. Marshall,the fourth-largest company of its kind in the United States, skills components on behalf of about 150 suppliers—and a big chunk of those sales are taking place online.

Marshall isn't just stapling Web commerce onto an existing business structure. "We've changed everything," Rodin said. "We've eliminated commissions for our sales staff. We've eliminated bonuses based on [profit and loss] in the business units. Everybody now is on a profit-sharing plan, because it's all one, three-dimensional business built around the electronic model." Marshall also is rebuilding its partner relationships around that model. "We think of Marshall first when we have customers that want to business via e-commerce," said John Simari, director of North American distribution at Dallas-based Texas Instruments, one of Marshall's chief suppliers. "This whole [e-commerce] market is still in its formative stages, but as we think about our own Internet strategy, we're drawing on Marshall for their expertise."

Marshall (www.marshall.com) has developed **Extensible Markup Language (XML)** connection with about one hundred suppliers. If the user requests information on a product in the Marshall catalog, the system will go out to a supplier's site, access a data sheet, and present the information transparently via the Marshall site. But browsing product data is only the beginning. Marshall also lets suppliers give Web-based presentations about their products and technology. The Education, News and Entertainment Network, a service of the Marshall site, lets suppliers give live seminars on their products, then archive those presentations for future viewing by potential customers. Marshall will even link the archived presentations for future viewing to the product information in its component catalogues.

Marshall does a significant portion of its business overseas, so its e-commerce data is in twenty-four languages. "Doing business on the Internet is sort of like doing business in another country," Rodin said. "It has different rules and customs, but we look at it as another marketplace. The key is making it easy to do business there."

Wilson, Tim. 1998. Wholesale shifts to the Web. *Internet Week*. CMPnet [cited online 21 July].

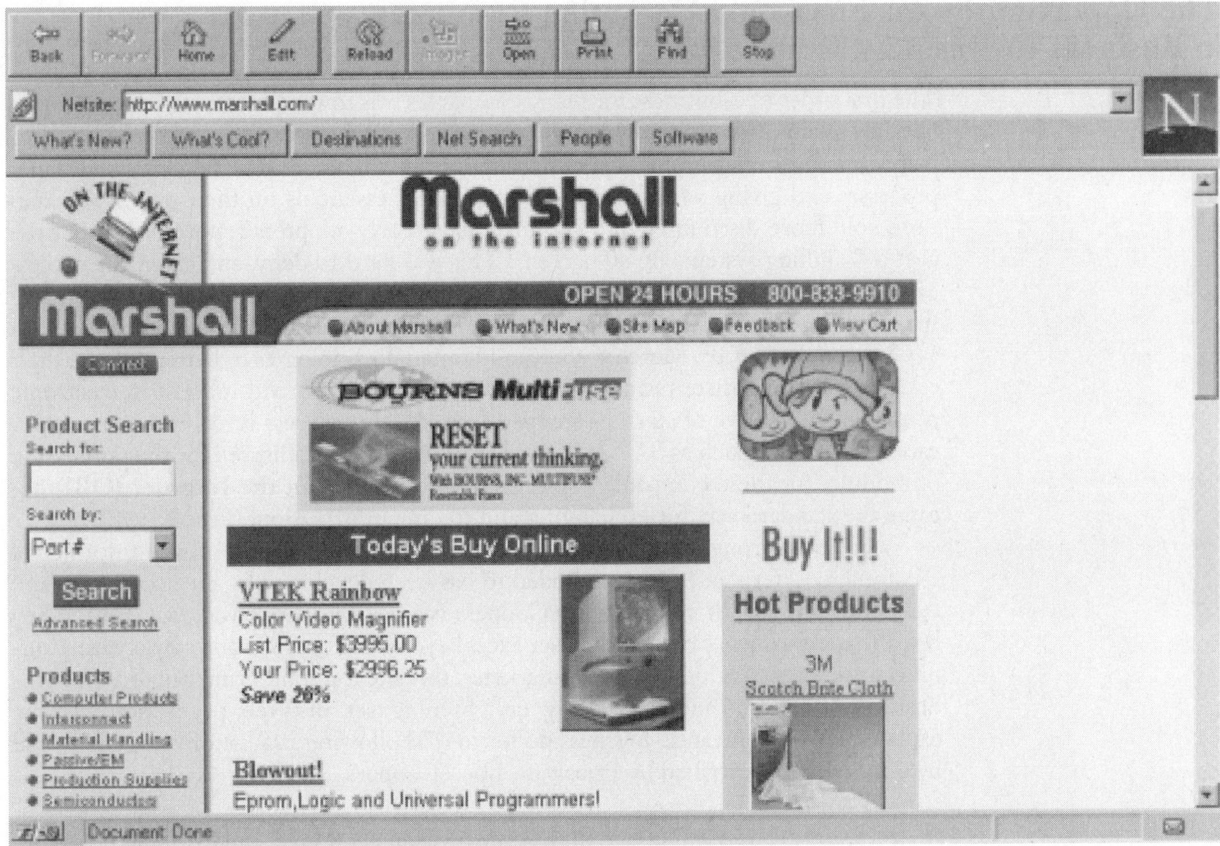

Marshall (www.marshall.com)
One of the largest distributors of industrial electronic components and production supplies in North America, Marshall offers many convenient services to the manufacturing trade. One is QuoteCart, allowing you to get a quick quote for your parts.

are now global-producing, greater competitive threats. Innovative electronic resources are being adopted by a generation of computer users who are maturing into management positions. These marketers are not afraid of change, and they understand what technology can do.

These marketers recognize the greatest benefit of the Web to the business sector is its efficiency. Products can be rushed to the market. Production costs can be reduced by computer-aided design and computer-aided manufacturing. Best of all, the marketing process can be made more efficient with electronic resources. Targeting prospects can be enhanced with Web sites, listservs, or Usenet discussion groups, which are directed specifically to electronic commerce support, entrepreneurial, or venture capital funds. Advertising messages can seek out viewers chosen by these viewers' site selections and search engine choices; electronic publicity releases covering business topics find their ways to news wires. Businesses are finding methods to adjust their business practices in the **information economy.**

Not every company is as progressive as Marshall Industries, nor is every marketer as tuned in as the members of the profiles and studies mentioned above. Many companies and individuals seem to be burying their heads in the sand, denying that business is changing. To many managers, change is frightening. However, to the enlightened ones, it is nothing but hard work. What are the advantages of adopting e-marketing and e-commerce practices over the traditional marketing method? These advantages will be discussed over the next few pages.

The Opportunities for Electronic Marketing Resources in Business-to-Business Transactions

The first order of e-business for many companies was toward automated procurement because much of the material handling involved numbers easily recognized by computer interfaces. Procurement systems became networked, eliminating excessive paper processes and giving workers the ability to order essentials on their own. Web auctions sold more discounted and surplus goods. Early adopters reported they cut the cost of handling systems by 80 percent. This was hard to deny, and given the success of database management, many additional operations and marketing applications were spawned to address specific business needs. Web purchasing enabled companies such as Chevron, Ford, GE, Merck & Co., and United Technologies to better enforce their contracts and negotiate terms with suppliers. In light of broad interest in electronic procurement, a wave of startups stepped forward; this success lured enterprise application developers such as SAP and Oracle into the mix that allowed for the purchasing of modules for these companies' systems. **Open buying on the Internet (OBI)** became the standard way for exchanging and trading information. (Frook 1998)

With this strong start, electronic resources blossomed. One of the informative e-commerce sites that has been alluded to has been developed by the accounting and consulting firm of PricewaterhouseCoopers (www.e-business.pwcglobal.com). They boast that e-business can help the user excel beyond their competition by creating significant sources of value. For the e-marketer, this site is a solid primer on business-to-business benefits. One particularly enlightening set of Web pages presents the explanation, "What can E-business do for me?" Following is a list of values delivered by e-business as described by PricewaterhouseCoopers.

- *Achieve market leadership.* In this information economy, leadership involves the critical factors of operational flexibility, foresight, and innovation. Questions to consider when seeking market leadership: Will my traditional brand reputation and position apply in an e-business setting? How can I train and orient my staff so they can perform in the fast-paced world of e-business? Do they have the access to the knowledge they need to make fast, accurate decisions? How do I calculate my return on e-business investments? How do I get my leadership team "on board" for a common e-business strategy?
- *Reach new markets.* A primary catalyst for embracing e-business is the ability to reach markets far beyond traditional ones, whether distant in geography, customer profile, or another definition. Many organizations have been slow to exploit the Internet channel due to fears of channel conflict. Serious concerns include presenting a consistent brand image across the Internet and traditional channels as well as sharing and integrating information about customers, products, and company resources. Questions to consider when reaching new markets: Will independent sales organizations or wholesalers rebel against direct online sales? What relations cover marketing and sales to consumers on different continents? How do I meet the needs of new customers while maintaining a relationship with my existing base? How do I reconfigure old products and services for e-business—how do I develop entirely new ones? Can my supply chain and customer service system keep new markets served to the standards set in existing markets?
- *Create new products and services.* E-businesses can test and tune their products and services and their marketing strategies. You can quickly learn about and match competitive offers since e-business infrastructure favor fast time-to-market and flexibility. Questions of concern when creating new products and services: What

AN EXAMPLE OF DATA MINING AMONG CUSTOMERS

Businesses have the capability to better acquaint themselves with their customers. The intimacy is particularly valuable as companies began to anticipate their customers' actions with remarkable, almost eerie, precision. It's not magic, but rather the results of "data mining," or tracking the purchase patterns or habits of the company's business or consumer customers. An example is that of Amazon.com book sellers concentration toward customer-friendly technology. One popular page in its Web site is the "section for book reviews by customers who sometimes engage in lively debate. Using **collaborative filtering,** Amazon's computers track the likes and dislikes of people with similar buying patterns, so when a customer calls up a title onscreen, the Web site helpfully lists other books that have appealed to like-minded readers."

Kupfer, Andrew. 1998. Four forces that will shape the Internet. *Fortune*, 6 July, 98.

satisfies my customers? How do I implement mass customization and responsive pricing? What methods can quicken my time-to-market once I know my customers' needs? How can my staff think creatively about new products and services, extending our traditional portfolio in profitable new directions?

- *Build customer loyalty.* Building customer loyalty in the information economy means placing the power and potential of e-business in the hands of the customer. To the customer, e-business really means me-business. Whether presenting a completely new face to the customer, establishing proactive one-to-one relationships, or differentiated products and services through personalization, e-business can help to address a company's lingering worries about customer loyalty and the Web. Questions of concern when building customer loyalty: How do I retain my best customers when the competition also wants to reach them? How can I improve the development and then cross-selling of new products and services of my most loyal customers? How can I collect, analyze, and take action on the customer information that's now scattered throughout the organization? Should my marketing organization be changing and what should it look like?
- *Optimize business processes.* The goals of reducing costs, speeding time-to-market, and improving customer satisfaction are at the core of business today. Customers demand more prices, greater options and customization, higher levels of service, and more personalization. To meet those needs, executives are reconsidering all aspects of their enterprise's operations in light of e-business opportunities. Questions of concern when optimizing business processes: How can I improve product development and launch? How can I integrate and streamline business processes? How can partner relationships be strengthened? How can we enhance responsiveness to and interaction with customers? How can we capture and share real-time and comprehensive data?
- *Enhance human capital.* The capabilities of e-business are trying vast organizational change. No longer are structures and cultures bound by geographic, functional, or even time constraints. The movement to virtual organizations that draw on global resources to serve each customer individually prompts a rethinking of exactly how an organization operates. Questions of concern when enhancing capital: What do I need to do to transform my people and organization into an e-business-enabled, customer focused environment? How do I retain existing staff while gaining new skills and capabilities and attracting new talent? What knowledge management tools can help to collect key information and disseminate it throughout the organization? How can this be used to my advantage? How can I measure gains in productivity and effectiveness of my employees?

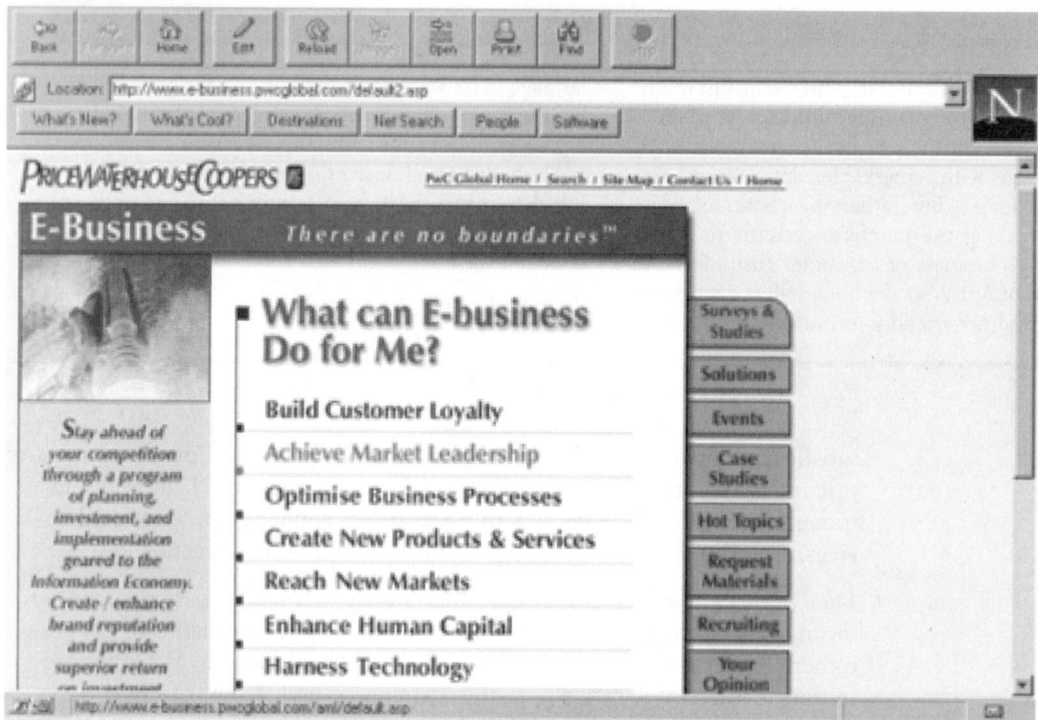

PricewaterhouseCoopers (www.pwcglobal.com)
New virtual businesses sprout up every day, and previously unlikely competitors now vie for market share in spaces never before possible. E-business is a driving force of this phenomenon, and technology provides the backbone and infrastructure behind it. PwC helps its clients gain the e-business edge in this new information economy.

- *Harness technology.* Once an untested set of technologies accessible only to scientists, the Internet has matured and is now open to the world. E-business has broken down both operational and technical boundaries, with flexible and open solutions giving access to anyone—anywhere—with a network connection and Web browser software. An e-business initiative succeeds when it reflects an alignment of all elements. If one part is ignored, the entire project is at risk. Questions to consider when harnessing technology: What makes of technologies will best execute my e-business plan? Will those technologies integrate smoothly with my **legacy systems?** Do I take a go-slow approach with a small technology experiment, or do I dive in with a full-blown investment? Am I poking along while my competition speeds ahead? Does my infrastructure mesh with e-business imperatives? How do I protect my company from security and compliance risks? Is my technical staff trained in new approaches, and can they communicate e-business approaches to nontechnical parts of the organization?
- *Manage risk and compliance.* The issues of risk and compliance are more complex than ever in the information economy as top management faces new challenges in identifying and responding to them. The speed of a paperless infrastructure has benefits, but you must acknowledge the risks. For example, electronic forms of transaction processing and storage may not create a tangible audit trail needed for transaction verification and trouble-shooting. The legal framework regulating digital transactions remains in a state of flux, leaving the legality of certain contracts, signatures, and commitments at question. Questions of

GROUP TO OFFER INSURANCE TARGETING HAZARDS OF DOING BUSINESS OVER WEB

A group of insurers and consulting firms is hoping that the explosion of companies marketing their wares over the Internet will spur demand for a new electronic-commerce insurance product. The coverage known as **"Net Secure"** is the latest in a handful of insurance programs targeted at companies fearful that hackers, viruses, "spammers," or other perils will disrupt their business or expose them to liability lawsuits. "The coverage aims to kick in to pay for property losses if the hacker breaks in and sabotages a vital database or if a virus shuts down a company Web site," said Emily Freeman, a J&H Marsh senior vice president. "It also is designed to protect companies if their network applications pass a virus onto another business, causing losses. Net Secure also will provide a preset amount of loss protection for a company's **'intellectual property'** if it is stored on a network that has been violated. Such coverage may kick in, too, if companies violate copyright laws or libel someone on their Web sites," Ms. Freeman said.

Lohse, Deborah. 1999. Group to offer insurance targeting hazards of doing business over Web. *The Wall Street Journal*, 22 March, B10.

> concern when managing risk and compliance: How do I manage the global policy, regulatory, tax, and legal issues? How can my technical infrastructure guard against electronic fraud and unauthorized access? Can my corporate and customer data be protected? What are the mechanisms I need for auditability and compliance? How do I stay informed of consumer protection laws involving Internet selling in different countries? (PricewaterhouseCoopers 1999)

The above are convincing arguments for businesses to entertain pursuing a portion of their sales from Internet activities. With all opportunities, there are risks. Can these risks be minimized? The box "Group to Offer Insurance Targeting Hazards of Doing Business Over Web" addresses the concern of risk.

What Is the Key Commodity in Business-to-Business Transactions?

For decades, the methods, or even lack of methods, of business-to-business transactions were considered sophomoric and even unprofessional by consumers and marketers. Little attention was given to market research; the style of advertising graphics or tone of copy was hard to sell; and the media options were limited. Business-to-business product campaigns were limited to creating one ad that was then placed in perhaps three trade magazines. Now with the plethora of electronic marketing resources, Web medium included, business-to-business marketing and advertising are greatly matured. This discussion will first explore the issue of the pressing influence on business-to-business commerce—that of fresh, salable information. There has been some controversy on what information—site content and entertainment or customer content and familiarity. *Business Week* recently questioned what type of site information translates into online success:

> Remember "content is king"? That was the rallying cry in the early days of the commercial Internet. America Online, Inc., was the movement's ringleader, while other Web site operators—such as ESPN, iVillage, CNET, and SportsLine—quickly followed suit, cramming their sites with information and entertainment. Content suddenly commanded about as much respect as a court jester. Guess what: Content is in, again. In truth, content never really went away. It was just drowned out by all the hubbub surrounding portals. All the while, iVillages and CNETs continued to create original material on everything from parenting tips to which company was designing the lowest-priced PC.

> Now, those sites are a window to better seeing the true importance of content on the Web. What they've taught us is content is important, it adds value, but it isn't enough. Content by itself won't necessarily translate into profitability or wild success, no matter how unique or deep the information is. To create a true cash machine on the Net, content companies need to layer technology, services, and e-commerce that help them to figure out their audiences' tastes, preferences, and habits. Then they can better tailor the content and more importantly, develop a deep database about their customers that will have advertisers drooling.
>
> CNET (http://home.cnet.com) has latched onto this. The company started out four years ago offering technology news and product news, making money through advertising. But October [1998], after rethinking its strategy, CNET began piling on new revenue streams by playing to the tastes of its audience. CNET furnishes information on 120,000 products on its Computers.com site. That's where it began charging a flat fee to merchant partners for "leads"—customers CNET sends from its site to theirs. That's paying off. CNET says from 8 percent to 10 percent of its 90,000 daily leads actually turn into purchases. Those leads generated $80 million in sales for its merchants in the most recent quarter [winter 1998]. As for CNET, its revenues in the quarter ending December 31 [1998] nearly doubled to $19.2 million versus $10.7 million a year ago. (Green 1999)

E-business Strategies Are Selling Products and Services

The previous CNET story defines a strategy for selling an intangible, abstract quality—information—in a novel and profitable e-business method. There are many other examples and Web sites that are buying and selling tangible products, such as computers, construction machinery, and vehicle assembly parts. At the end of this chapter, e-business categories and sales projections for several years into the future will be presented. Suffice it to say, e-business is conducive for presentation through the catalog medium, and the Web serves the catalog medium well. Listings, color photographs, diagrams, prices, and details subject to quickly change are popular product specifications; Web site selling keeps product information updated.

Management and advisory services are other forms of worthwhile information gaining awareness and sales momentum on the Web. **Consultative selling,** situations where the outside representative becomes a trusted team member of the client's management team and the salesperson's input is highly valued, is a most profitable activity. Most of the big six accounting firms have consulting services; in one case, the consulting arm, Andersen Consulting, outgrew Arthur Andersen CPAs. The practice was split into two firms, largely because each was pursuing separate businesses. An ingenious method for placing financial institutions into a competitive retail frame of mind employs e-business tactics by PricewaterhouseCoopers using its self-evaluating "e-Doctor Questionnaire" (www.pwcglobal.com/frs/edoc_app.htm). In gathering information about a financial organization's electronic channels capabilities, a PricewaterhouseCoopers consultant reviews the questionnaire, looking for service gaps, and then makes e-business recommendations and solutions. The astute marketer will develop ameliorative propositions that include at least a portion of his company's products or services.

IBM has taken another tactic in creating an awareness for e-commerce, initiating the red circle *e* starring in television, magazine, and newspaper ads. The IBM Web site is full of content concerning e-business as is the PricewaterhouseCoopers site. Rather than read pages upon pages, however, IBM has created a "virtual seminar for e-business." On the e-business Web pages in mid-1999, you can participate in the

IBM (www.ibm.com)
IBM presents its net.commerce competencies through the telling of case histories such as that of Lehigh Valley Safety Supply Company (www.safetyshoes.com). This industrial shoe manufacturer expanded its distribution through IBM's e-business strategies, and customer responsiveness, "Year after year, Lehigh Safety Shoes leads the way in the introduction of new products to meet the needs of our customer requests for protective footwear."

virtual seminar by registering. By doing this you will receive welcoming remarks by Peter Rowley, general manager, global/medium/small business, on the potential of e-business and how IBM can become your partner, and then you are presented with several case histories in which IBM plays a starring role with its electronic solutions. The graphics are imaginative and colorful, and while this e-business site uses the case format, the first client, Lehigh Valley Safety and Supply Company of Pennsylvania, is depicted with sound and motion in a fast-moving illustration format resembling a simple motion picture. The announcer describes the graphics as the geographical limits of the Lehigh shoe-mobile traveling to industrial sites, and the announcer then goes on to describe how the IBM e-business contribution to the new distribution strategies of Lehigh Safety Shoes is positive and evident. The virtual seminar is novel, and, while at this time appears simple in implementation, IBM e-business makes the impression that it knows its business, has experience in many industries, and has solid partners to assist in making e-business successful for you.

The Electronic Marketing Resources for E-business

The e-business process is young and full of expectant experimentation. However, some marketing tools are succeeding far beyond expectations, such as the surplus/discounted equipment online auctions and the volume of industrial goods sold over a Web site. The examples of the following electronic marketing resources will be discussed, but keep in mind that few of these resources were available to business-to-business marketers ten years ago. Business-to-business sales activities were being

IBM BROADENS E-COMMERCE THROUGH PARTNERSHIPS

IBM, a pioneer of e-commerce with its payment-server technology, [has] unveiled a slew of partnerships in an aggressive campaign to show e-commerce resellers that it has all of its bases covered. IBM executives extensively discussed how the technology of each of its eleven new business partners enhances IBM's Net.Commerce server product and enables sophisticated order processing and customer support. The company also [has taken] the wraps off its strategy to migrate customers from Secure Sockets Layer (SSL) to the Secure Electronic Transaction (SET) protocol.

The partners basing their technology on Net.Commerce include Business Evolution, CommercialWare, Fisher Technology Group, Garg Data International, IMPAC Technology, Industri-Matematik International, Intelligent Interactions, Narrative Communications, Net Perceptions, NetGravity, and PersonaLogic. Additionally, IBM and DPS (Danish Payment Systems) [are working on] a joint initiative, endorsed by Visa International, to provide certificate-processing and payment hyperlinks-gateways for European financial institutions looking to implement the SET protocol for Internet credit-card payments.

Dunlap, Charlotte. 1998. IBM broadens e-commerce through partnerships. *Computer Reseller News.* CMPnet. [cited online 15 July].

conducted ten years ago, but earlier in this chapter, it was noted that the strongest capability of e-business is efficiency. As you review the list, think about the efficiency, whether it be speed, accuracy, flexibility, or cost-savings; then think about the short histories of each method. Should time and experience help make each resource better? Compare them to the speed, accuracy, and flexibility of traditional marketing activities, such as direct mail or telemarketing. Which would you integrate into your marketing program?

- Commercial auctions to sell surpluses carried with live price boards for common knowledge, either buyer or seller
- Virtual consulting using videoconferencing or virtual reality Web sites
- Speech recognition for routing telephone sales inquiries and security authentications
- Automated kiosks for guard-less entry of lodging facilities after hours, retail order-taking by push key, or printed or graphical information dispensing such as maps or brochures
- **Automatic procurement** and reordering from Web-enabled sites, either automatic reorders or as-needed processing
- Robot shopping for availability of item and best price, for either business or consumer usage
- Delivery tracking, pioneered by the parcel companies such as FedEx
- Customer and prospect profiling for company preferences and buying patterns with analysis using data warehousing and data mining software systems
- Inventory control and balancing, again employing database warehousing and data mining
- Custom communications networks from personal Lotus Notes to company intranets
- Supplier extranets for **partnering** and collaboration
- EDI for fast and efficient passing of large amounts of data such as financial transactions, payroll, and inventory processing

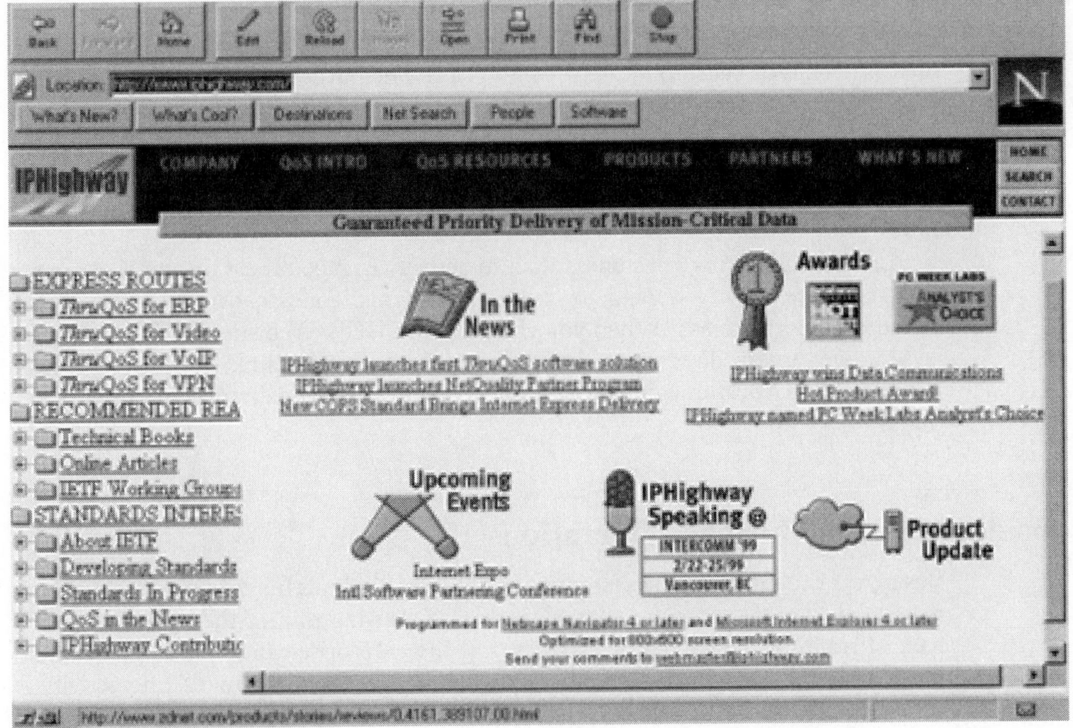

IPHighway (www.iphighway.com)
Important to e-commerce, this company provides priority-driven delivery of time-critical and bandwidth-intensive information, including mission-critical applications, voice and video, through end-to-end policy-based Quality of Service (ThruQoS) network solutions. Notice the use of awards and citations as credibility-building elements.

- Company marketing presence via Web advertising and customer communications and Web-enabled product and service ordering
- Customer service e-mail and call routing systems for customer communications
- **Virtual seminars** and CD-ROM training of personnel for distant company divisions, saving time, lodging, and travel expenses

The marketer should also examine the geographical capabilities of these marketing resources because these marketing programs can be executed on a regional, national, or international focus.

There is also a management strategy that e-businesses are embracing, that of partnering with specialized companies to strengthen all technology and service areas of an e-commerce organization. Outsourcing specialty assignments or hiring technical personnel for short-duration projects is common, almost standard procedure for putting together a state-of-the-art e-commerce endeavor. Bringing in outside suppliers is not an admission of weakness, but rather it is a realistic assessment of the enormity of the project or the awesome depth of technology necessary to produce the desired results.

Several other significant business-to-business applications are being installed Web-ready. On many Web sites the user will find search engines that are time savers in locating information contained within the site. Complementary software embedded on the site and initiated by the click of a mouse speeds up business-to-business commerce not only as a search tool but also as an aid to the seller with identification and authentication verification. This capability eliminates the famous Web invisibility generally equated with online presence. An example cited by *Fortune* pointed out that a business buyer might search the Internet for a year's supply of an office commodity, such as pencils or pads, to locate the best price. The buyer could then place an order. With proper software, the seller could overcome the Internet's fabled anonymity to check that the order was made by a legitimate company, and that the buyer would pay the bill. Companies like Concentric Network and IPHighway (www.iphighway.com) offer technologies for parties in online deals to verify each other's identity. (Kupfer 1998)

Lastly, while many consumers wish to actively engage others on the Web, many companies are eagerly hoping to disengage personal contact, handing off to automated business systems. "When you click 'Yes' on Dell's Web site, the PC maker relays online orders directly to assemblers. That seamless link between user and corporation, hard to imagine [several] years ago, will gradually become the norm." (ibid.)

Internal Considerations for Business Operations

Businesses should always be searching for the best methods for doing business, which may be outside the specific realm of marketing, moving toward the operations or financial realm of the enterprise. However, if the enterprise can function more effectively and efficiently in the operations or finance function, the marketing activity is surely to benefit. In the aspect of organizational execution, a careful deliberation has always been given to the question of whether to make or to buy. Many times this is an exceptional decision because its consequences may positively or negatively impact the company for years. In the Lockheed Martin case history, the make or buy decision was even more confusing and complex because the buy commodity being considered was the technology of the World Wide Web. The ordinary issue is usually whether to dedicate internal resources tying up manufacturing capabilities to possibly gain more control of timing, deliver, or costs or to use a qualified supplier for the same operation thus regaining the internal manufacturing facility for possibly more intricate or profitable operations. A cost versus benefit analysis usually accompanies this decision. The Lockheed Martin (www.lmco.com) case study is an example of internal analysis, decision making, and integration of information resources concerning a business process with a new twist—using Internet technology in a new way.

Competitive forces are pushing many companies to assess the Internet as a competitive tool. Some companies wait until it is too late to recover the distance, expertise, or customer-satisfying services offered by the aggressive, innovative competitor. Electronic marketing resources are a large part of company-specific competitive advantages, both in the near-term and in the long-term. Marketers should be familiar with the electronic tools discussed in this chapter and should be reading marketing technology sites and publications as new applications are introduced on a weekly basis.

Disadvantages of Online Business-to-Business Commerce

While the strength of e-business is streamlined efficiency, companies employing e-business lose contact with their distribution channels and sales personnel. The biggest disadvantage is the threat of alienating distributors and, therefore, loss of physical distribution points. A recent *Wall Street Journal* article stated the following regarding personal business transactions: "For years, [selling business products] has been a people-centered business in which face-to-face meetings, handshakes, and product demonstrations have built customer relations that translated into big money." (Anders 1998, A1) The smart marketer will recognize these relationship bonds and

E-MARKETING CASE HISTORY: LOCKHEED MARTIN CORPORATION

The Decision: Information Management Based on Web Technology?

[Government supported industrial research has] been sharply reduced as the Cold War ended, and as U.S. industry lost its dominance in global business. Deeply affected by severe budget cuts, all aerospace companies have massively downsized. Aerospace companies find that customers have changed from making a "lifetime of the program" commitment to making a commitment by phase, with follow-up work depending on the success of the preceding phase. Both new and [old] systems, processes, and solutions [were examined] in light of the current business drivers. Accordingly, the research and development division (R&DD) reexamined the fundamental assumptions of its business and reshaped those assumptions, where necessary, to ensure the lowest-cost, focused delivery of key information. Using current-day computing technology, the R&DD determined that labor was the key cost driver of the business, accounting for most of the cost of creating, obtaining, using, and storing information. Labor was driving the cost of information delivery in these areas: 1) accessing and using information; 2) creating the systems to acquire, store, and use information; and 3) enabling the "reuse" of information through the management of a "corporate memory" of information already acquired. Moreover trends—stable over the last fifteen preceding years—indicated that labor cost as a portion of the cost of information could be expected to increase, whereas all other information costs would decline rapidly.

The R&DD then looked at various commercially available software programs to determine the potential for reducing the labor content of its information systems. It found that commercially available information applications had several disadvantages, such as requiring users to maintain multiple directories (by grouping information by topic) and "in-baskets" directories (computer locations where incoming information is placed) and offering different user interfaces, commands, and capabilities. It was also extremely difficult if not impossible to use these applications to integrate information such as technical drawings, three-dimensional models, and pictures from multiple sources. The net result was hodgepodge computing rather than a seamless information "system."

The R&DD decided that commercially available applications were not the fundamental reengineering for which it was looking and that the then-available versions incorporated design choices that limited the return on investment to a range far short of the R&DD goals. Further, after assessing the impact of its own near-term vision of the coming technology, the R&DD felt that the life of commercially available systems was too short. What the R&DD required was a common information structure—one that would provide a single computer location where all incriminations and tools would be accessible to the user and easy to use.

The R&DD studied the successes and failures of previous systems implementation efforts, both internal and external to Lockheed, most of which used some form of database technology to centralize information in a single location. Without exception, the implementations that the R&DD examined had ended up with performance, cost, licensing, deployment, or modification problems. The R&DD was determined to avoid, through appropriate design, as many problems as possible.

The Internet provided R&DD with both a source of information and a model for the exchange of information among independent but cooperating organizations. Many of the tools and techniques used on the Internet were transformed into low-cost and highly reliable support tools for gathering, organizing, searching, distributing, and archiving sources. A key strategy was the R&DD's use of the Internet technology known as the World Wide Web (or the Web) to define a standard user access.

The R&DD's new model for information management is based on Web technology, which enables a user to access, search, display, and transfer information from a server to the user's desktop. Specialized information or a specialized method of displaying information is programmed only on the server, leaving the user's desktop software unchanged to provide a "one size fits all" display, no matter what information or application system the user is accessing. This technology, which the R&DD refers to as a "common user interface," is defined as the HTML protocol embodied in the Internet specifications and is implemented in Internet tools such as Mosaic and Netscape Navigator.

Swenson, Steve L. 1996. Integrating information resources. *The Internet strategy book.* Edited by Mary J. Cronin. Boston: Harvard Business School Press, pp. 89–93.

work to maintain offline distribution and online sales potentials. *The Wall Street Journal* in the following passage summarizes the situation facing the marketing and distribution functions.

> With a few mouse clicks, these [medical] customers could buy everything from ultrasound machines to electrodes without ever seeing a salesman. James Cyrier, Hewlett Packard's (www.hp.com) head of medical sales and marketing is intrigued, but if he moves too fast, he risks a mutiny from his traditional sales force and distributors, who don't want to surrender their commissions.
>
> Across the United States, hundreds of manufacturers face the same dilemma. The Internet could prove to be the most effective sales tool since the telephone, letting companies reach millions of potential customers quickly and cheaply. Online commerce is an outright menace, however, to the men and women who do in-person selling or distribution, and who still control 90 percent or more of most companies' order flow. As a result, jittery corporate strategists are trying to capitalize on the Internet's potential without sabotaging traditional sales channels. (ibid., A1)

How are marketers combating defections of distributors? The computer industry and other high-tech fields are feeling the most pressure from traditional PC retailers and are rolling into action to protect their territories. Different companies are trying different strategies to address the distributor or salesperson displeasure. Here are samples of mending or breaking long-term ties in the computer industry.

- In the last six months, Compaq has introduced its own Web commerce site, selling computers at rock-bottom prices directly to small businesses and individuals.
- IBM has tried a gentler approach, using their Internet sites mainly to direct prospects to online ordering sites operated by long-established dealers. This does not take full advantage of the Internet's cost-cutting capabilities.
- In May 1998, Radius, Inc., began online sales of its software for handling digital photos. The company did virtually nothing to publicize the site because it did not want to alienate its traditional distributors. Distributors still provide more than 90 percent of its sales, and the CEO does not want to risk anything that might hurt the profit—and perhaps lead them to stop stocking Radius products.
- Software maker Intuit, Inc., shares an aversion to online discounting. It could market aggressively on the Web, but it hasn't done so in deference to its third-party resellers. Intuit for more than eighteen months has offered best-selling programs such as Quicken and TurboTax on its Web site, but only at list price. (ibid., A14)

Many other industries have been long partnering with distributors or third-party resellers, and e-business marketing strategies should be set with the prospect of gaining or losing key personnel or distribution outlets at any time. Big industries as well as small businesses are wrestling with this puzzle. Automobile manufacturers study and question the future role of individual dealers as they mull selling cars directly to consumers through company Web sites. Airlines are also examining the future value of travel partners such as travel agencies. American Airlines registered 1.6 million people who receive regular e-mails about discount fares available on weekends. According to American's arithmetic, e-mail communications eliminate overhead of $20 each ticket associated with staffing a toll-free telephone bank as well as travel agents' commissions that can be as high as 9 percent.

DISTRIBUTOR USES E-COMMERCE TO BUILD LOYALTY

Ingram Micro, a $16.5 billion computer products distributor, is planning to take its extranet and Internet commerce strategy to a new level by hosting—and at least partially funding—brand transaction sites on behalf of its computer-reseller customers. The effort is aimed at keeping otherwise fickle resellers, who will aggressively shop multiple distributors for the best prize, in the Ingram fold by making it easier to conduct business in a low-cost Internet environment

Key to the strategy is a packaged Internet e-commerce application. Ingram is expected to license Open Market's Transact server and database software for use by **value-added resellers (VARs).** The licensing deal will enable resellers to offer their end-users reel-time inventory, sales tax calculation, transaction processing, shipping, and personalization on their own branded site. The link between Ingram and its customers will be over its existing extranet. Ingram would not dispose all of the specifics of the plan, but its aim is to get as many resellers as possible conducting business electronically for maximum efficiency.

Frook, John Evan. 1998. Distributor uses e-commerce to build loyalty. *Internet Week.* CMPnet [cited online 10 July].

Some companies abhor the prospect of limiting its sales over the Internet. Minnesota Mining and Manufacturing Co. (3M, www.3m.com) lists hundreds of its products on its Web site but generally does not provide a way to order these products directly from the company. This appears deliberate because 3M is protecting its distribution channel structure, taking care not to damage distributor relationships. The marketer must, therefore, consider company objectives, sales and distribution organization, and the value of relationships with various constituencies such as longtime partners and, ultimately, consumers.

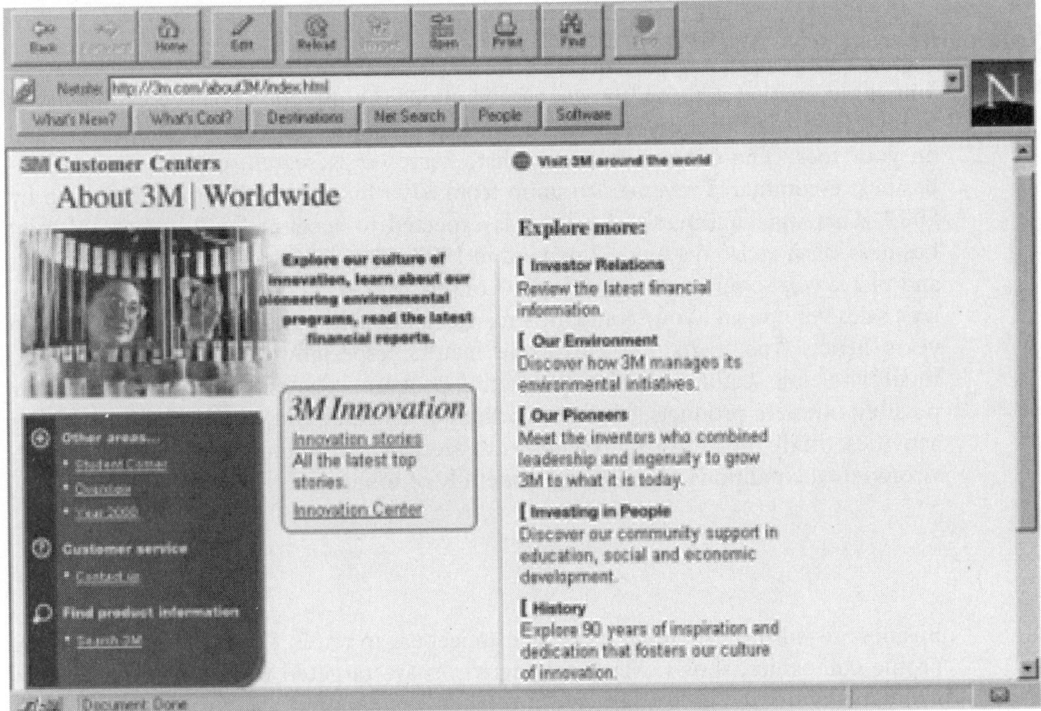

3M (www.3m.com)
While the 3M site offers excellent customer communications and product search capability, the theme in general introduces the many facets of company history, and concern for innovation and for community. Sharing the history of its logotype: "3M has taken nearly 100 years to go through the four phases that led to today's logo and identity system. It is a precious commodity."

EXHIBIT 16.1 REVENUE FORECAST BY INDUSTRY (IN BILLIONS)

Industry	1998	1999	2000	2001	2002	2003
Computing and electronics	$20	$50	$121	$229	$319	$395
Motor vehicles	4	9	23	53	114	213
Petro-chemicals	5	10	23	48	97	178
Utilities	7	15	32	63	110	170
Paper and office products	1	3	6	14	31	65
Shipping and warehousing	1	3	7	15	33	62
Food and agriculture	0.3	3	6	13	27	54
Consumer goods	1	3	6	13	26	52
Pharmaceutical and medical	0.6	1	4	9	20	44
Aerospace and defense	3	7	15	26	34	38
Construction	0.4	2	3	7	14	29
Heavy industries	0.1	1	3	5	29	16
Industrial equipment	0.1	1	2	5	9	16
Total (in billions)	43	109	251	499	842	1,331

SOURCE: Forrester Research Inc., from "A Real Opportunity," Iconocast Newsletter, San Francisco, CA, March 25, 1999.

E-business Sales Forecasts by Industry

You as the marketer should be concerned about the direction that your industry is headed, and for this information, future forecasts will help keep you primed and on your toes. The e-commerce specialist, Forrester Research, expects business-to-business e-commerce revenues to jump from $109 billion in 1999 to $1.3 trillion by 2003. That year, business-to-business is expected to account for 9 percent of total business sales, up from a mere .2 percent in 1997. In making your marketing decisions and plans, you should probably adopt a conservative strategy, projecting your industry's sales volume and your company's market share and volume no further than two years hence. Too many uncontrollable factors, especially in the technology and retail/wholesale sectors, can upset marketing programs planned too far in advance for possibly obsolete products, services, consumer demand, and, most of all, marketing activities. Study the industry projections to see which you find reasonable for the environmental conditions of today and hopefully of tomorrow.

Summary

Business-to-business selling is much like an iceberg in water. Only the tip, the tightest profile companies, shows. Marketing activities are targeted to narrow audiences in many medium-sized industries, yet, in total dollars revenue, the business-to-business sectors are estimated to exceed consumer purchases by nine times. Efficiency in the processes of segmenting, selling, inventory maintenance, distribution, and customer contact and familiarity has been enhanced using electronic marketing tools, such as database and communications software systems, interactive World Wide Web sites, and accurate and fast information transfer, such as EDI. More business can be accomplished because of these tools producing more prospect contacts; wider areas of delivery, locally and globally; and more targeted, satisfy products—all with better corporate memory. E-business is relatively new as is the Web and other electronic resources, and marketers must be aware not only of their companies' competition but also of emerging strategic and tactical capabilities of electronic marketing technology. Companies grow because of competitive advantages, not competitive disadvantages.

Key Terms

Automatic procurement
Collaborative filtering
Consultative selling
E-business
Extensible Markup Language (XML)
Information economy
Intellectual property
Legacy systems
Net Secure
Open buying on the Internet (OBI)
Outsourcing
Partnering
Value-added reseller (VAR)
Virtual seminars

QUESTIONS AND EXERCISES

1. As was discussed in this chapter, the business-to-business environment has changed rapidly in the last twenty years. List five factors in the business-to-business sector that have produced drastic change. What are the advantages and disadvantages affected with each change? Write an e-mail to the company's director of strategic planning naming these changes and their expected consequences.

2. In comparing online versus traditional business-to-business marketing, efficiency has become a highly prized competency. Name five electronic marketing resources that have improved efficiency in e-business activities. Write a letter of inquiry to IBM e-commerce calling out these resources and specifying the benefits of each resource. Ask for a sales representative to make an e-business presentation to you.

3. Access the e-commerce pages of the IBM Web site and critique the services that are offered. If you were starting your own business, which of these services would be of most importance to you. List and rank six of the services and explain why each is important to your business. Write a memo as part of your business plan for interviewing potential marketing consultants.

4. Using the Dejanews Usenet, locate a business-to-business discussion group or groups (probably listed under alt.business or misc.business) that are discussing Web activities in e-business. Find five recent posts, print each out, and summarize the questions and responses, if any. What was the tone of the messages? Are people confident in e-commerce?

5. Review the list of opportunities presented by PricewaterhouseCoopers. From all of these objectives for implementing electronic marketing resources, which four opportunities would be most important to an automobile dealership specializing in fleet sales? A professional basketball team? A regional chain of lumber yards? A national chain of office building maintenance and cleaning services? Explain your logic in an e-mail to your PricewaterhouseCoopers manager, who is also your instructor.

6. You are the marketing manager for a automotive parts supply organization that has recently moved to direct customer sales (such as individuals, service stations, and automotive service centers) via a Web site ordering system. This change in your company's forty-year relationships with exclusive distributors is an uncertain risk. What marketing actions and resources can you implement to placate both long-term independent-contractor sales staff and your automotive parts distributors? Create a list of distributor relations and outside salesperson relations activities designed to support your company's reputation of being a trusted partner. Submit a one-page outline of ideas to your CEO.

7. What are the advantages and disadvantages of an exclusive distribution agreement with a manufacturer? What are the advantages and disadvantages of multiple distribution channels including the Web for the same manufacturer? Select a product to describe these two scenarios. Write a one-page memo to your logistics manager explaining the situations and make a recommendation for future company channel management.

8. Discuss the concept of partnering with other e-businesses. Explain what situations might arise as you serve a large oil company that has charged you with assessing, designing, and implementing a new private e-mail communications system. What would be the steps that you plan for the assignment, and what types of specialized partners would you recommend to the CIO at the oil company? Prepare outlines of the steps to the planning process and of the technology suppliers describing their roles in the construction of the e-mail system.

9. There are parallels between traditional media and online media, such as preparing a publicity program in which news releases on company activities are to be disseminated to the press. Some will be sent through U.S. mail to some news outlets, and some will be posted to electronic news services, such as BusinessWire. Why should you use both traditional and e-marketing vehicles? Would you expect overlap of distribution employing both? What about traditional advertising and Web advertising? Are these duplications of efforts and audience exposures cost effective? Write your opinion on this topic and e-mail your response to a class member who will send you her opinion. Turn the two e-mails in to your instructor.

10. At the end of the chapter, e-business sales projections were presented for several years. Would you expect these projections to be accurate, plus or minus a 10 percent variation? What are five environmental factors that could upset these projections greatly? List the five factors and explain how these conditions could stop or limit the realization of these projections. Which industries do you feel are most vulnerable? Prepare your thoughts for a discussion in class.

Bibliography

Anders, George. 1998. Click and buy: Why and where Internet commerce is succeeding. *The Wall Street Journal,* 7 December, R4.

———. 1998. Some big companies long to embrace Web but settle for flirtation. *The Wall Street Journal,* 4 November, A1, A14.

Forrester Research. November 1998.

Frook, John Evan. 1998. Web proves it's good for business. *Internet Week.* CMPnet [cited online 24 December].

Green, Heather. 1999. Content is prince. *Business Week.* e.biz [cited online 22 March at www.businessweel.com/ebiz].

Iconocast newsletter. 1998. 8 July 2–3.

Kupfer, Andrew. 1998. Four forces that will shape the Internet. *Fortune,* 6 July, 93, 98.

PriceWaterhouseCoopers. 1999 [cited online 21 March at www.e-business.pwcglobal.com].

CHAPTER 17

Implications to the International Marketing Program

The fact that [fellow French billionaires, Francois Pinault and Bernard Arnault], two of Europe's premier dealmakers, are facing off in what could be a bruising battle [for Gucci] only helps confirm that European capitalism is quickly turning into a brass-knuckle fight for survival of the fittest. Consider the rest of the European battlefield: Italy's Olivetti SpA's $58 billion hostile bid for the much larger Telecom Italia SpA, and the unsolicited $37 billion takeover launched by France's Banque Nationale de Paris SA for two other French banks, Societe Generale SA and Paribas SA.

The brewing battle for Gucci is emblematic of the New Europe that is taking shape with the launch of the common currency and the globalization of industry: two Frenchmen squaring off for control of a Dutch-based Italian company run by a U.S.-educated lawyer and an American designer and advised by London-based American investment bankers. "The frontiers have fallen," says Mr. Pinault. "We're at the start of a considerable movement in Europe."

(Kamm 1999)

LEARNING OBJECTIVES

- To examine the similarities and dissimilarities of the international electronic marketing process
- To investigate the demographics and preferences of international Web users
- To explore the potential of e-commerce in various regions of the world

Introduction

This chapter concerns a virtual redundancy. The Internet can be employed for international commerce, but the Internet is already an international medium. Perhaps the intention should be stated as the planning for international commerce rather than for unintentional international commerce. Regardless of the coincidences, Europe is the focus of global e-commerce since the European Union commenced in 1987 and expanded to fifteen member states with the Treaty of Amsterdam in 1997. The euro currency consolidated disparate national currencies at the beginning of 1999. The business world is waiting to judge the political and economic success of the EU. As U.S. companies, many are surprised by the international response to Web postings, and with international inquiries and orders, what are marketers supposed to do with them? In this chapter, the planning for the **international e-commerce** marketing process and the factors pushing the information revolution in different parts of the world will be discussed. What will be the objective of Web communications for the marketer? Ignore or enhance e-commerce opportunities? Sell only to the United States and Canada only? Before any decision on response policy is made, you must fully understand the international marketing landscape.

Analyzing the International Markets by Geography

Is evaluating the international marketing process and potential very much different than the thorough investigation conducted through situation analysis, marketing planning, and marketing implementation in domestic challenges, which you have learned thus far? No, the steps are the same, but the market researcher might be more sensitive to differences in product usage, product perceptions, and cultural diversities. You have learned through the discussions in this book to study the environmental factors of demographic, economic, political, regulatory/legal, and cultural influences that shape markets. Domestic marketers will be wise to carefully scrutinize important practices that might be taken for granted in the United States—stipulations on systems' privacy and distribution of personal data, taxation, and consumer protection laws. (www.europa.eu.int/) International e-commerce is a complex endeavor through such things as monitoring currency fluctuations on the value of digital certificates, varying country regulations on Web site content, allowable types of advertising claims or sales promotions, and even as far as checking levels of literacy among developing countries. Web experts generally agree that companies venturing first into foreign markets and demonstrating a long-term commitment to the citizens' and the country's social and economic benefits are looked upon as valuable partners in the country's development. Public relations and promotional programs can initiate and thereafter foster these perceptions as the company proceeds with its execution of its marketing mix. At what point, however, should you the marketer begin your analysis? For assessing e-commerce potential, a marketer should be alert to several conditions.

- Web user profiles, hopefully on a country to country review
- Web usage profiles and Internet home penetration
- Levels of interest in online shopping and projected purchasing by category and country
- Trends in Web communications appliances

E-COMMERCE AND THE THIRD WORLD?

The next hotbed of e-commerce growth will not be in Europe or even Asia, but the Third World. That's the word from MIT Media Lab founder and digital pundit, Nicholas Negropointe. To those who think it's just not possible for the developing world to embrace e-commerce, he [gives] several examples to back up his contention that in the wired marketplace, the wildly unlikely is rapidly turning into the mundane.

"There's going to be a trillion dollars worth of e-commerce transactions by the end of 2000, guaranteed," Negropointe said. Sources of new growth? Companies giving away computers in exchange for users' demographic data. Such a business model would have seemed "hilarious" a couple of years ago, but now more than one firm has jumped on the free PC bandwagon, he noted. And when the rate of e-commerce adoption among American consumers eventually slows talent, there still will be growth—but not in the places many now expect.

"I was recently in Cambodia, for example, and in Phnom Penh literally everyone uses a cell phone," Negropointe said. "This is because the existing wire-line system works so poorly and is expensive. The same thing is going to happen with e-commerce. The developing world embraces technology in much bigger numbers than is now expected, because it is more desperate for solutions to problems with its telecommunications, business, and educational infrastructure," he said. "They leapfrogged over a whole level of technology because the previous system was so terrible."

In much of the developing world, even citizens of some financial means have little choice of what to buy and few ways to pay for it—right now. But as online payment systems improve, and as the big package shipping companies recognize the market potential that exists in the developing world, an e-commerce boom will follow, bringing goods from around the globe to places such as Africa in unprecedented numbers, he said. "I would also bet on Latin America," Negropointe said Shauna noting that Uruguay is the only country in the Americas with a completely digital telephone system. Such a nation, already having embraced a cutting-edge technology at a faster rate than its rich neighbors, is a natural to embrace e-commerce, he said.

Seminerio, Maria. 1999. E-commerce in the Third World? *ZDNet* [cited online 25 March].

- Costs of access time and computer/appliance equipment
- Products and services usage and online purchase propensity
- Sensitivity to cultural influences that might negatively affect your product's association with the Internet, its content, or its technology in contemporary society

The above information will assist the marketer in segmenting countries into clusters for commonalities. This investigation is by no means comprehensive information, but the marketer can begin a process of comparing apples to apples in the marketing opportunities overseas. As was stressed previously, some of the worst mistakes marketers make are failing to investigate the market's dynamics, such as what consumers are wanting and buying today, the level of category competition, and the differences between each market. (http://australia.internet.com) The marketer should also investigate the country's or region's infrastructure including transportation for distribution, traditional media outlets for primary message delivery, standards of living, the strength of financial systems, the availability of reliable credit sources, the acceptance of credit cards for online shopping, the sophistication and availability of communications networks, and the levels of discretionary income and national and local taxes. The answers to these inquiries will suggest how aggressive host country or region marketing should be, according to your analysis of the online purchasing potential. If the market possesses a more developed infrastructure and economy, chances are the population has more means for general consumption. In countries with a less developed infrastructure and economy, there are still niche opportunities that diligent and perceptive research will uncover.

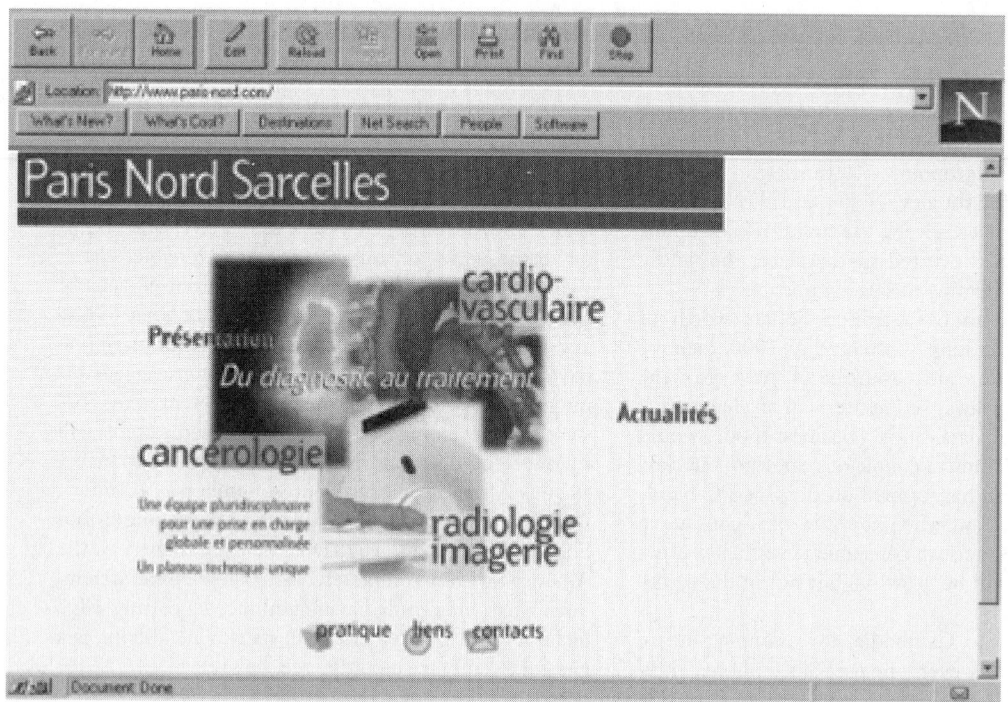

Paris Nord Sarcelles (www.paris-nord.com)
While the majority of Web sites is composed in English, surfers will frequently find sites written in northern European languages. In the 10th GVU WWW User Survey of 369 European users, the languages most frequently encountered on Web other than English are German (11.4%), Dutch (10%), Finnish (4.9%), and French (4.3%). British Isles English comprised 29.5% of the respondents in this survey.

The Geographical Regions of E-commerce Promise

Using the Web's research sites, government transactions and records, even inquiring in Usenet news groups or listservs, the marketer can develop competitive intelligence country by country. (www.paris-nord.com) Watching the multitude of posts about Europe and from European Web addresses will provide you with real insights from real people. From comments on the performance of the communications networks (looking for telecommunications outages or lack of service) to the consumer reactions to online expenses are the types of information requested that add to the reality of the marketing potential. You might gather information on the specifics of European countries as the following Iconocast report did.

- Belgium: According to Brussels-based Initiative Media, 13 percent of the population, or 1.3 million, connected to the Internet in the first six months of 1998 [all population percentages are based on Exhibit 17.1 (on page 375), not on shares reported by the individual firms]. In Belgium, for example, 47 percent of respondents say they surf the Web at least weekly, reports Initiative Media, up significantly from 30 percent in December 1997.
- Germany: In the past six months, the number of people with Internet access in Germany grew by one-third says GfK, a German consumer development firm, bringing the total number of Germans online to 12 million, or 15 percent of the total Internet population.

- Netherlands: Pro-Active estimates that 21 percent of the Dutch population, 3.3 million people, have Net access. Pro-Active expects an additional 1.6 million to go online within the next year.
- Spain: The Spanish Internet Users Association, AUI, reports about 2.2 million, or 5 percent of the Spanish population, have Net access. AUI predicts 8.7 million users will be connected by 2001.
- UK: Which?Online and BMRB International peg the UK's Internet population at about 8 million users, or 14 percent of the total population.
- France: Even the laggard French are getting on ***la toile,*** the potential French word for the Web. While only 2 percent of French households now have a computer and modem, French Telecom and IBM announced a platform that will give 35 million French Minitel subscribers access to the Web.
- Sweden: The emergence of a European market is spurring development of home-grown Internet advertising solutions. Infotizer, credited by Bottnia Internet Provider, gathers information from Swedish surfers even while visiting non-Swedish sites, allowing advertisers to target ads based on surfing habits. It won't be long before we see a host of local inventions. (1998)

The above is rich information that the marketer could use in making informed marketing decision concerning deployment of Web resources. The English have different habits and behaviors from the Germans and the Dutch just as New Yorkers exhibit different lifestyles from Californians or Louisianians. As was discussed early in the text, the better the marketer knows her markets, the more targeted and successful the e-commerce programs will be.

The marketer has to dig deeply for information such as what was provided above from the Iconocast report. You might wish to engage a market research firm as you would in the United States. One international Internet research firm, NUA based in Dublin, Ireland (www.nua.ie), specializes in Internet surveys throughout the world. On a recent home page newsletter, NUA featured studies and news on the following: French e-commerce topped U.S. by 66 million; Survey examines Internet use in Israel; Australia launches anti-spam organization; Americans questioned about attitude to Web; 1.3 million households online in Russia; and Over half of U.S. households now own PCs. NUA and other respected research companies such as Jupiter Communications (www.jup.com) or Forrester Research have assisted many international companies with advice on what *not* to do.

Every Country Has an Address Code

There is an international address code that identifies every country of origin. These letters serve users of the entire country (sometimes islands or territories are grouped together under one identifier) and act as a classification system much like the zip codes in the United States but covering a wider geography. You can determine the Web page's home country by the two or three letters after the domain name, if a domain name, .com, .org, is required. An address that ends as smithind.uk translates as Smith Industries in the United Kingdom. By identifying Web site addresses, you may gather some intelligence on the sponsor and home location of the site. The **Internet Society** has assigned these letter **country codes** to countries as listed in the following table.

Country	A2*	A3*	Number
Afghanistan	AF	A3	004
Albania	AL	ALB	008
Algeria	DZ	DZA	012
American Samoa	AS	ASM	016
Andorra	AD	AND	020
Angola	AO	AGO	024
Anguilla	AI	AIA	660
Antarctica	AQ	ATA	010
Antigua and Barbuda	AG	ATG	027
Argentina	AR	ARG	032
Armenia	AM	ARM	051
Aruba	AW	ABW	533
Australia	AU	AUS	036
Austria	AT	AUT	040
Azerbiajan	AZ	AZE	031
Bahamas	BS	BHS	044
Bahrain	BH	BHR	048
Bangladesh	BD	BGD	050
Barbados	BB	BRB	052
Belarus	BY	BLR	112
Belgium	BE	BEL	056
Belize	BZ	BLZ	084
Benin	BJ	BEN	204
Bermuda	BM	BMU	060
Bhutan	BT	BTN	064
Bolivia	BO	BOL	
Bosnia and Herzegowina	BA	BIH	070
Botswana	BW	BWA	072
Bouvet Island	BV	BVT	074
Brazil	BR	BRA	076
British Indian Ocean Terr.	IO	IOT	086
Brunei Darussalam	BN	BRN	096
Bulgaria	BG	BGR	100
Burkina Faso	BF	BFA	854
Burundi	BI	BDI	108

Country	A2	A3	Number
Cambodia	KH	KHM	116
Cameroon	CM	CMR	120
Canada	CA	CAN	124
Cape Verde	CV	CPV	132
Cayman Islands	KY	CYM	136
Central African Republic	CF	CAF	140
Chad	TD	TCD	148
Chile	CL	CHL	152
China	CN	CHN	156
Christmas Island	CX	CXR	162
Cocos (Keeling) Islands	CC	CCK	166
Colombia	CO	COL	170
Comoros	KM	COM	174
Congo	CG	COG	178
Congo, The Democratic Republic of	CD	COD	180
Cook Island	CK	COK	184
Costa Rica	CR	CRI	188
Cote D'Ivorie	CI	CIV	384
Croatia (local name: Hrvatska)	HR	HRV	191
Cuba	CU	CUB	192
Cyprus	CY	CYP	196
Czech Republic	CZ	CZE	203
Denmark	DK	DNK	208
Djibouti	DJ	DJI	262
Dominica	DM	DMA	212
Dominican Republic	DO	DOM	214
East Timor	TP	TMP	626
Ecuador	EC	ECU	218
Egypt	EG	EGY	818
El Salvador	SV	SLV	222
Equatorial Guinea	GQ	GNQ	226

continued

Country	A2*	A3*	Number
Aritrea	ER	ERI	232
Estonia	EE	EST	233
Ethiopia	ET	ETH	231
Falkland Islands (Malvinas)	FK	FLK	238
Faroe Islands	FO	FRO	234
Fiji	FJ	FJI	242
Finland	FI	FIN	246
France	FR	FRA	250
France, Metropolitan	FX	FXX	249
French Guinea	GF	GUF	254
French Polynesia	PF	PYF	258
French Southern Territories	TF	ATF	260
Gabon	GA	GAB	266
Gambia	GM	GMB	270
Georgia	GE	GEO	268
Germany	DE	DEU	276
Ghana	GH	GHA	288
Gibraltar	GI	GIB	292
Greece	GR	GRC	300
Greenland	GL	GRL	304
Grenada	GD	GRD	308
Guadaloupe	GP	GLP	312
Guam	GU	GUM	320
Guatemala	GT	GTM	320
Guinea	GN	GIN	324
Guinea-Bissau	GW	GNB	624
Guyana	GY	GUY	328
Haiti	HT	HTI	332
Heard and McDonald Islands	HM	HMD	334
Holy See (Vatican City State)	VA	VAT	336
Honduras	HN	HND	340
Hong Kong	HK	HKG	344
Hungary	HU	HUN	348

Country	A2	A3	Number
Iceland	IS	ISL	352
India	IN	IND	356
Indonesia	ID	IDN	360
Iran (Islamic Republic of)	IR	IRN	364
Iraq	IQ	IRQ	368
Ireland	IE	IRL	372
Israel	IL	ISR	376
Italy	IT	ITA	380
Jamaica	JM	JAM	388
Japan	JP	JPN	392
Jordan	JO	JOR	400
Kazakhstan	KZ	KAZ	398
Kenya	KE	KEN	404
Kiribati	KI	KIR	296
Korea, Democratic People's Republic of	KP	PRK	408
Korea, Republic of	KR	KOR	410
Kuwait	KW	KWT	414
Kyrgyzstan	KG	KGZ	417
Lao People's Democratic Republic	LA	LAO	418
Latvia	LV	LVA	428
Lebanon	LB	LBN	422
Lesotho	LS	LSO	426
Liberia	LR	LBR	430
Libyan Arab Jamahiriya	LY	LBY	434
Liechtenstein	LI	LIE	438
Lithuania	LT	LTU	440
Luxembourg	LU	LUX	441
Macau	MO	MAC	446
Macedonia, The Former Yugoslav	MK	MKD	807
Rebublic of Madagascar	MG	MDG	450
Malawi	MW	MWI	454
Malaysia	MY	MYS	458
Maldives	MV	MDV	462

continued

Country	A2*	A3*	Number
Mali	ML	MLI	466
Malta	MT	MLT	470
Marshall Islands	MH	MHL	584
Martinique	MQ	MTQ	474
Mauritania	MR	MRT	478
Mauritius	MU	MUS	480
Mayotte	YT	MYT	175
Mexico	MX	MEX	484
Micronesia, Federated States of	FM	FSM	583
Moldova, Republic of	MD	MDA	498
Monaco	MC	MCO	492
Mongolia	MN	MNG	496
Montserrat	MS	MSR	500
Morocco	MA	MAR	504
Mozambique	MZ	MOZ	508
Myanmar	MM	MMR	104
Namibia	NA	NAM	516
Naura	NR	NRU	520
Nepal	NP	NPL	524
Netherlands	NL	NLD	528
Netherlands Antilles	AN	ANT	530
New Caledonia	NC	NCL	540
New Zealand	NZ	NZL	554
Nicaragua	NI	NIC	558
Niger	NE	NER	562
Nigeria	NG	NGA	566
Niue	NU	NIU	570
Norkolk Island	NF	NFK	574
Northern Mariana Islands	MP	MNP	580
Norway	NO	NOR	578
Oman	OM	OMN	512
Pakistan	PK	PAK	586
Palau	PW	PLW	585
Panama	PA	PAN	591
Papua New Guinea	PG	PNG	598

Country	A2	A3	Number
Paraguay	PY	PRY	600
Peru	PE	PER	604
Phillipines	PH	PHL	608
Pitcairn	PN	PCN	612
Poland	PL	POL	616
Portugal	PT	PRT	620
Puerto Rico	PR	PRI	630
Qatar	QA	QAT	634
Reunion	RE	REU	638
Romania	RO	ROM	642
Russian Federation	RU	RUS	643
Rwanda	RW	RWA	646
Saint Kitts and Nevis	KN	KNA	659
Saint Lucia	LC	LCA	662
Saint Vincent and the Granadines	VC	VCT	670
Samoa	WS	WSM	882
San Marino	SM	SMR	674
Sao Tome and Principe	ST	STP	678
Saudi Arabia	SA	SAU	682
Senegal	SN	SEN	686
Seychelles	SC	SYC	690
Sierra Leone	SL	SLE	694
Singapore	SG	SGP	702
Slovakia (Slovak Republic)	SK	SVK	703
Slovenia	SI	SVN	705
Solomon Islands	SB	SLB	090
Somalia	SO	SOM	706
South Africa	ZA	ZAF	710
South Georgia and the South Sandwich Islands	GS	SGS	239
Spain	ES	ESP	724
Sri Lanka	LK	LKA	144
St. Helene	SH	SHN	654

continued

Country	A2*	A3*	Number	Country	A2	A3	Number
St. Pierre and Miquelon	PM	SPM	666	Tuvalu	TV	TUV	798
Sudan	SD	SDN	736	Uganda	UG	UGA	
Surinam	SR	SUR	740	Ukraine	UA	UKR	804
Svalbard and Jan Mayen Islands	SJ	SJM	744	United Arab Emirates	AE	ARE	784
Swaziland	SZ	SWZ	748	United Kingdon	GB	GBR	826
Sweden	SE	SWE	752	United States	US	USA	840
Switzerland	CH	CHE	756	United States Minor Outllying Islands	UM	UMI	581
Syrian Arab Republic	SY	SYR	760	Uruguay	UY	URY	858
Taiwan, Province of China	TW	TWN	158	Uzbekistan	UZ	UZB	860
Tajikistan	TJ	TJK	762	Vanuatu	VU	VUT	548
Tanzania, United Republic of	TZ	TZA	834	Venezuela	VE	VEN	862
Thailand	TH	THA	764	Viet Nam	VN	VNM	704
Togo	TG	TGO	768	Virgin Islands (British)	VG	VGB	092
Tokelau	TK	TKL	772	Virgin Islands (U.S.)	VI	VIR	850
Tonga	TO	TON	776	Wallis and Futuna Islands	WF	WLF	876
Trinidad and Tobago	TT	TTO	780	Western Sahara	EH	ESH	732
Tunisia	TN	TUN	788	Yemen	YE	YEM	887
Turkey	TR	TRU	792	Yugoslavia	YU	YUG	891
Turkmeni-Stan	TM	TKM	795	Zambia	ZM	ZMB	894
Turks and Caicos Islands	TC	TCA	796	Zimbabwe	ZW	ZWE	716

SOURCE: ISO 3166 Maintenance Agency. Latest change: Thursday Aug 7 17:59:51 MET DST 1997.
*A2 is two-letter country code; A3 is three-letter country code

General Demographics Information on European and World Markets

You may be searching for information on large market groups or you may be investigating small niche groups to which you will tailor your marketing plan. As was stated in the situation analysis in Chapter 2, define the information you think you will need to implement an international marketing plan. Having set information goals, you will have a better direction of the country data you require. From online marketing newsletters; United Nations' resources; the U.S. Department of Commerce's trade records; the International Chamber of Commerce's services; or private sources such as the Internationalist (www.internationalist.com), a Web site for international business information, you can assemble the pieces of information you need for comparison of your target country's or countries' online market. In the GVU Eighth User Survey, it was revealed that respondents from Europe are more likely to have been online one to three years, while respondents from the United States are more likely to have

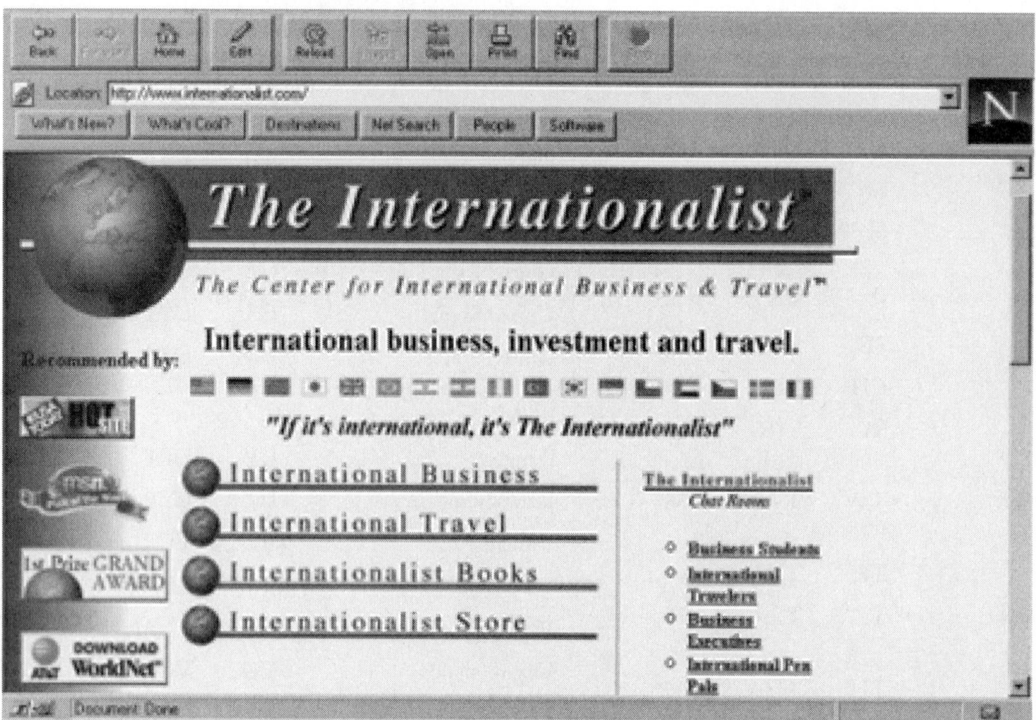

The Internationalist (www.internationalist.com)
International information is valuable, whether you're a businessperson, an international traveler, or an international investor. Intelligence materials for international banks, consultants, law firms, real estate interests, business schools, import/export concerns, and stock markets are wise to learn of business practices, etiquette, and customers before *doing business.*

started on the Internet within the last year. Further, 46 percent of all ten thousand interviewees have created a Web page. Interestingly, European respondents (67 percent) were more likely to have created a Web page than U.S. respondents (43 percent). From various sources, these facts and opinions represented international e-commerce during the summer of 1999. How have the e-commerce conditions changed since then? Which conditions have remained the same? (GVU Eighth WWW User Survey 1997)

The Rate of Change in Internet Acceptance

- Europe [is] a beehive of Internet activity with some countries having as much as 21 percent Internet penetration.
- Market forecast: The number of computers connected to the Internet in Europe will grow from 13 million in 1997 to 69 million by 2002 predicts Dataquest.
- PC growth: In the third quarter of 1998, sales of PCs rose to 5.4 million, a 22 percent increase compared to the same quarter in 1997, says Context, a UK market research firm.
- Internet use: Every country in Europe is online and starting to build a solid block of users. IDC estimates 4.3 percent of all Western Europeans are now Web users. (Iconocast 1998)

Online penetration is important in deciding country selection and segmentation. Here are some estimates of percentage of users by European nations.

EUROPE ONLINE

Rank	Country (in millions)	Users (in millions)	Population*	Percent of Population
1.	Finland	0.9	5.1	17.6
2.	Sweden	1.3	8.9	14.6
3.	Norway	0.6	4.4	13.7
4.	Denmark	0.7	5.3	12.9
5.	Switzerland	0.7	7.2	9.7
6.	United Kingdom	5.5	57.6	9.5
7.	Netherlands	1.4	15.6	8.9
8.	Germany	6.1	82.1	7.4
9.	France	2.9	58.6	4.9
10.	Belgium	0.5	10.2	4.7
11.	Austria	0.4	8.1	4.5
12.	Ireland	0.1	3.6	4.0
13.	Italy	1.4	56.8	2.5
14.	Spain	0.9	39.1	2.2
15.	Portugal	0.2	9.9	1.9

SOURCE: *CIA World Factbook 1997; 1998 IDC.

An international marketer should examine proposed markets for familiarity with Web usage and other online technologies before launching ambitious e-marketing programs. Failure to do this is another example of assuming all markets are equal. This is an example of the unevenness of understanding how the Web operates among European leaders of online activity:

> Despite online access in the UK and Germany moving beyond the 10 percent threshold, consumer understanding of the Internet remains abysmally poor—even among Internet-friendly demographic groups such as the young, the wealthy, and existing users. Jupiter's analyst report surveyed consumer opinion about the Internet in the UK, France, and Germany. Participants were asked to describe their personal understanding of the Internet and the services it offers. In the UK, France, and Germany, only 22 percent, 10 percent, and 19 percent of respondents, respectively, said that they have a "good" or "extremely good" understanding of the Internet. At least 33 percent of all respondents had "nonexistent" understanding. Of those who have Internet access in their households, only 16 percent said they had an "extremely good" understanding and an additional 33 percent rated their understanding as "good." That means that the majority of those with household access to the Internet have a limited, poor, or nonexistent understanding of the Internet. "Although experienced users of the Internet sing its praises, marketers that promote sites and services must try harder to communicate the essence of the network and its services to neophytes," said Nick Jones, analyst, European Internet Strategies. (European Internet Strategies 1999)

What may be familiar and second-nature to most Americans may be complicated and unclear to consumers of other nations. In many foreign communications programs,

CHINA'S INTERNET EXPLOSION

The number of Internet surfers in China jumped to 1.175 million at the end of June, 1998 from 505,000 at the beginning of the year, the *China Economic Times* said. The number of computers wired to the global computer network rose 64 percent from the beginning of this year to 542,000 by the end of June, the newspaper said, quoting a report by the China Internet Network Information Center.

Of the total users, 92.8 percent were male, 83.2 percent were under 35 years old, and 58.9 percent had bachelor's degrees it said. Nearly 41 percent of the surfers spent more than ten hours a week on the Internet, while 26.7 percent spent five to seven hours a week. The report also showed that 88.9 percent of users complained of slow connections and 61.2 percent said online fees were too expensive. Forty-five and a half percent thought that there was not enough Chinese-language information on the Internet.

Only a fraction of China's 1.2 billion people have access to the Internet, but its growth has been explosive, and industry analysts say the number of surfers could reach 7 million by 2001.

China's Internet explosion. 1998. *Wired News Report* [cited online 13 July].

the marketer should remember to sell the game of baseball before selling the Yankees. Uninformed consumers will have no brand preference if they know nothing about the product category. Therefore, in all decision-making situations you should ask yourself if your prospect has sufficient knowledge about what your product does before you began to tell her why your product does it better, both in online and offline communications.

Patience Will Be Required

International marketing is unsettling and uncertain for many persons. These persons may be uncomfortable amid unfamiliar cultures or environments. Still others are looking to different regions for e-commerce potential. If you are among those who like challenges, your boss may hand a situation report like the following to ask for your thoughts and reactions to an international e-commerce opportunity.

> According to Merrill Lynch's economic projections for 2001, the GDP growth of largest LatAm countries (Brazil, Argentina, and Mexico) should decline close to zero next year. In addition, there is significant uncertainty regarding the stability of local currencies. All these factors may slow widespread adoption of the Internet in the region. Another hurdle is the fact that LatAm countries are unable to accommodate the demand for basic telecommunications services. Thousands of customers are still waiting to sign up for basic telephone service. Although the first step towards revamping the telecommunications system has been made since the government-run companies have been recently privatized, the completion of the process is years away. Companies trying to launch Internet services in Latin America are making a long-term investment. The Latin American Internet opportunity is at least four to five years away. The continent's key markets are in the midst of economic turmoil and the visibility for improvement is limited. (Yakirevich 1998)

Negative news like this is often encountered by the marketer, and it will be his choice whether or not to heed the caution. Sound judgment is acquired through experience, and success or failure will be faced in local, national, or international assignments, even with the best research or advisers.

Internet Appliances in Europe

Mention the World Wide Web in North America, and the public generally thinks of personal computers and color monitors. However, in Europe there are many options being developed separate from the PC. Mobile computing promises more flexibility to those on the go; this offer of freedom while still staying in touch is very appealing regardless of your nationality.

> Among the best array of non-PC **Internet appliances** emerging in Europe, Jupiter Communications research projects that smart phones will be the market leader, with over 12.9 million users accessing Internet content in 2002. To compete in this market, content providers must filter and aggregate today's raw Web content for the small size and limited functionality of Internet appliances. Although most new mobile phones will be Internet-enabled (with a microbrowser by 2002), only a small percentage of these phones will be actively used for Internet data services. While Internet appliances will not display Web sites, they will access specially filtered content from existing Web servers. However, Jupiter believes that account management and content management for smart phones and other Internet appliances should be handled from a PC via a Web site. "Companies in this market should think about a Web-centric wireless strategy to gain competitive advantage," said Noah Yasskin, a Jupiter analyst. (Internet Appliances in Europe 1999)

Keeping Web Pages Strong but Neutral

The e-marketer cannot sell to everyone in the world. Therefore, after the situation analysis is completed, the basic marketing questions remain constant—Which markets are being overlooked or which niches can our product fill? These are strategic questions that must be answered fully before any marketing activities or resources are even contemplated. With positive and logical solutions in hand and with management's blessings, tactical programs involving electronic marketing resources can be created with sensitivity and imagination.

As the previous Jupiter Communications report predicted the importance of smart phones, marketers must be careful to develop communications plans and designs that fit the message and the medium. A full-color site with small text will not be legible or even attractive on the monochrome screen of a smart phone. Further, content, both text length and choice of language, must be carefully considered. Today most Web sites are written in English with an occasional second selection button for either French or German. The marketer must know her markets' Web site language preference to be truly effective. Web sites designed for international markets should be sanitized, dropping American jargon, flags, or pop symbols that might only be recognized in the United States A more graphic approach is recommended since photographs or illustrations can be processed visually for consumer or business-to-business information. Asian consumers are less impressed with clever slogans but more interested in what the product will do for them. The less text, the less linguistically confusing the message. Graphical interfaces are easier to follow. Would you prefer to deal with a Web site with more instructions, buttons, pages, or additional navigation? Probably not. Therefore, consider electronic marketing tools with simpler, more evident operation for your customer's convenience, particularly when he might be using an unfamiliar language. This, however, does not imply that international Web sites cannot be creative.

LET YOUR FINGERS DO THE CLICKING

Multimedia companies met in Cannes, France, for the industry's annual Mila awards. While the United States is considered the leader in Web site development, surprisingly the Mila d' Or honors was won by a Scottish reference site, Scoot (http://www.scoot.co.uk), which publishes a British-based yellow pages for UK businesses. Scoot manages to achieve a simplicity that most other directory-type sites lack. Surf to the front page, and you'll see the boxes for you to fill in, "Whatever you need (e.g. plumber, hotel)" and the town where you need it. There are few other options on the page, but Scoot's main screen is appropriately dominated by the basic search capability. If only more Web site designers would mimic that approach.

Weber, Thomas E. 1998. Watching the Web. *The Wall Street Journal*, 19 February, B24.

The Other Problems of International E-commerce

The marketer should be aware that greater obstacles must be overcome that make strategic issues such as the degree of creativity or humor on a Web site trivial. Onlookers of the information age, whether they are business persons, consumers, politicians, regulators, college students, professors—almost everyone living—should be cognizant of the impact that the Internet has on nations and their social and government structures. Different countries view the effects of the Internet with different values in protecting their citizens, their economies, their national security, and their cultures. Because of the seismic nature of the Internet, agreeing on far-reaching issues such as privacy and differences in international law is an extended process, and no country is

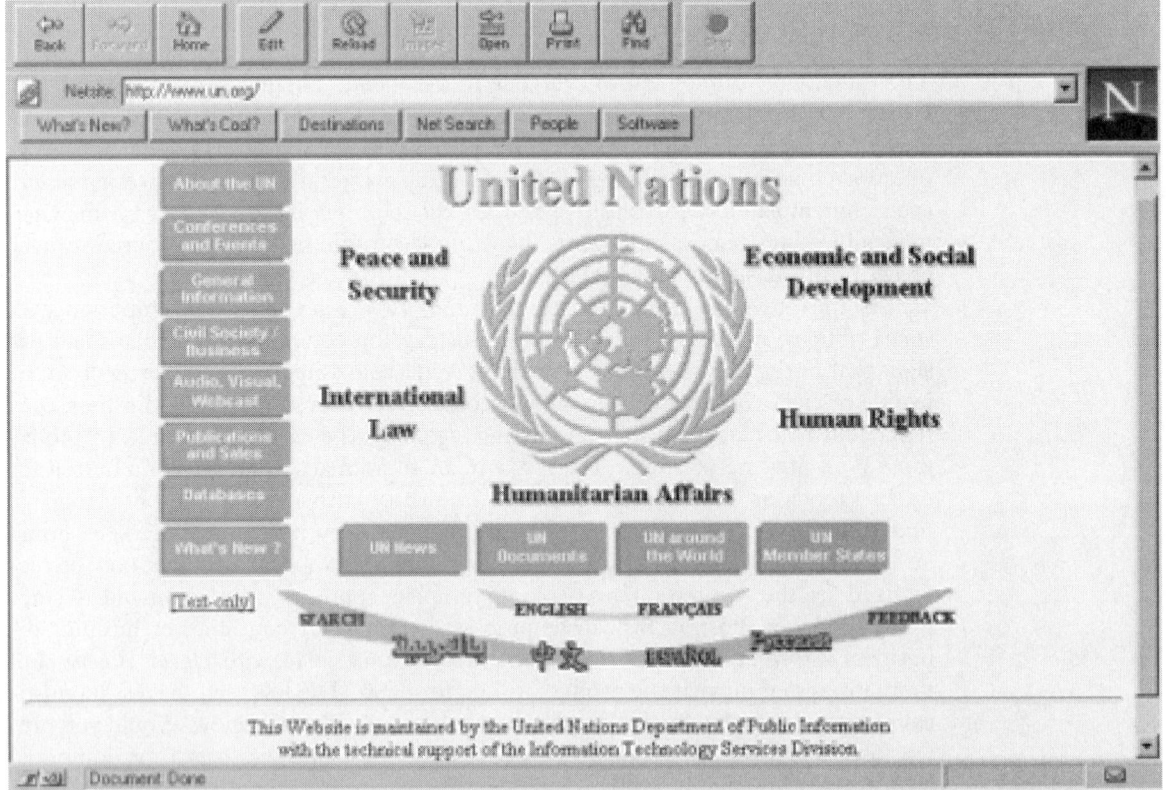

The United Nations (www.un.org)
Given the global activities of the UN, usage of the Web is a practical fact. One of the important hyperlinks on this site, Economic and Social Development, leads to pages on Trade data, Sustainable Development, and Social Development.

EUROPEAN E-COMMERCE

Think That Europeans Are Behind in E-commerce? Think Again.

During the French Open last month, the official tennis site received 3.9 million visits, while hit volume soared 209 percent over 1997. To drive traffic, Ogilvy Interactive in Paris created a real-time banner that displayed short teaser messages about the latest tournament action updated every twelve minutes. On the best-performing site, click-through averaged 11 percent. Ogilvy's interactive brand manager, Julian Mitchell, tells Iconocast that 49 percent of the site's online shop orders came from North America, while 39 percent originated in Europe. The most popular items: players' towels and official T-shirts. (http://www.frenchopen.org)

SOURCE: Iconocast, December 9, 1998.

rushing to create unwise legislation. Laws that restrict gathering and distributing personal information and prohibit sending that data to countries without such laws, or concerns for financial or medical privacy, are troublesome. International e-commerce practices such as taxation, consumer protection, consumer data collection, and fraudulent operations mitigation are all new experiences and will take years to equilibrate. (www.un.org) Marketers want e-business details addressed first, but there is little consensus on the laws for gathering customer data or consumer protection. Marketers are presently assuming a **self-regulating** stance: Companies will adjust their policies on e-commerce and online communication to fit the country's laws that they are doing business with. Some marketers are encouraging a different policy, that of companies following consumer and privacy laws of their home countries and simply disclosing those laws to consumers of other countries. International e-commerce principles will not be easy to create or to enforce.

Top executives of Internet, media, and telecommunications have begun an industry-live campaign called the **Global Business Dialogue** on E-commerce, which is focusing initially on online privacy, taxation, and consumer confidence. The Global Business Dialogue is particularly concerned about the so-called **EU Directive,** a European Union policy that went into effect October 1998. The EU Directive forbids companies from sending personal information out of Europe unless the destination country has certain privacy protections. Many U.S. businesses feel the directive is too restrictive. In partial response to international e-commerce demands and in partial response to privacy critics and regulators, the Global Business Dialogue was established. The GBD goal is to generate industry-led solutions to issues affecting electronic commerce. The nine areas that the group will focus on are:

- taxation
- data security
- online privacy
- liability for online content
- intellectual property-rights protection
- technical concerns about the Internet
- controversial content such as pornography
- who has jurisdiction over Internet transactions
- consumer confidence in e-commerce transactions

If any laws are to be enacted, international businesses want to be a part of the decision-making process. As Gerald Levin of Time Warner, Inc., said, "We feel we have a role to play in the shaping of public policy. We are capable of rising above narrow geographic issues and competitive issues to realize the majesty of this new medium." (Peterson 1999)

Summary

Yes, the Web is global. While continents are moving closer together because of electronic communications, international marketing is becoming more and more similar among nations and among industries. The Internet is becoming the premier, soon-to-be standard tool in marketing to foreign markets. Within twenty years the accessibility to the Internet will skyrocket, giving marketers who use the Web as part of their media and business communications extensive market coverage. Marketers will have to watch carefully as the international community legislates the laws that will govern international e-commerce. Controversial issues such as consumer protection, purchaser privacy, national security, and the practices of international e-commerce will be debated and oftentimes violated in the future. The international e-marketer must develop company policies for engaging in e-commerce, adopting the laws of the host country or following the laws of the company's country of origin. Government and society do not use legal and regulatory precedents governing other means of exchange or communications because the Internet is unlike any other invention, passion, or profession seen in history.

Key Terms

Country code

EU Directive

Global Business Dialogue

International e-commerce

Internet appliance

Internet Society

La toile

Self regulation

QUESTIONS AND EXERCISES

1. Do the customs and assumed behavior actually affect a country's view or usage of the Internet? Surf the Web for three international Web sites that you consider to be uncharacteristic, distasteful, or nontraditional as compared to American values or norms. Print each out and explain why you think these messages, graphics, or offers would not be well received by an average American shopper. Write a letter to each company making suggestions on changes to the site that would be more appealing to the average American consumer.

2. Of the various demographics and economic factors that were discussed in preparing a situation analysis, which two do you consider most important conditions for entering an overseas market? Are they demographic, economic, cultural, or legal/regulatory conditions? Write a memo to your boss explaining your thoughts on the correct indicators for marketing exploration in a host country.

3. What would you do if your boss gave you that LatAm assignment? How would you approach your decision? What would be your deciding factors to take the assignment and what would be your strategy in turning a market around? Say your company is an international chain of radio stations, which country would you select and why? Prepare an outline of your strategic plan for your company's vice president of international marketing.

4. In comparing the international electronic marketing process to the traditional marketing process, what are the similarities and the dissimilarities of each practice? Select the three most similar and the three most dissimilar points and explain your thoughts. Write an e-mail to an associate who is opening a branch office of an internationally-known stock brokerage in Asia. Since this is her first overseas assignment and you have opened branch offices in South America, give her advice on the marketing process' similarities and differences.

5. Why do consumer habits differ from country to country in Europe? If you compare the populations listed in the "Europe Online" table, you will find several countries with populations of less than six million. With common ancestries, small land areas, and small populations, should purchasing and Internet habits be similar? Be prepared for a class discussion on this topic.

6. If you were the owner of a high quality equestrian bridle shop, which two countries would you target in Europe? Why? List four reasons and explain each one. Write your explanation as a letter seeking funds from a domestic bank; the loan proceeds would be used for expanding your Web server and database systems.

7. You are a marketer with a company involved in the EU Directive negotiations. Write a company policy on international e-commerce with regards to the legal liability of the company. Will you operate according to the laws and regulations of the host country or will you operate according to the laws of your home country providing full disclosure of your company's accountability?

8. How would you approach the Chinese population in selling them specialized work apparel? These safety garments are for workers in hazardous jobs such as steel mills, chemical factories, and hydro-electric construction projects. If you used the Internet, why so? What markets would you target and with what messages? If you did not use the Web, why not? What would be your alternative promotional program? Would you consider other forms of online communications? Which ones and why?

Bibliography

European Internet strategies. 1999. *Digital Digest,* 29 January, 1.
GVU Eighth WWW User Survey. 1997. [Online] Atlanta, GA.
Iconocast. 1998. [cited online 2 December], 1.
Iconocast. 1998. [cited online 5 December].
Internet appliances in Europe. 1999. *Digit Digest,* 2 March, 2.
Kamm, Thomas. 1999. Behind the competition for luxury goods firm is a new European ethic. *The Wall Street Journal,* 22 March, A1.
Peterson, Andrea. 1999. Electronic-commerce initiative is set by top executives at 17 companies. *The Wall Street Journal,* 15 January, B6.
Yakirevich, Pat. 1998. Patience required. *Individual Investor Online* [cited online 18 December].

CHAPTER 18

The Ethics of Electronic Marketing

Marketers must accept responsibility for the consequences of their activities and make every effort to ensure that their decisions, recommendations, and actions function to identify, serve, and satisfy all relevant publics: customers, organizations, and society. (American Marketing Association, November 1998)

LEARNING OBJECTIVES

- To discuss the basic ethics of marketing on the Internet
- To reiterate the concept that customer satisfaction leads to long-term marketing relationships
- To establish guidelines along with common sense concepts that can encourage marketers to act responsibly and ethically in the practice of electronic marketing

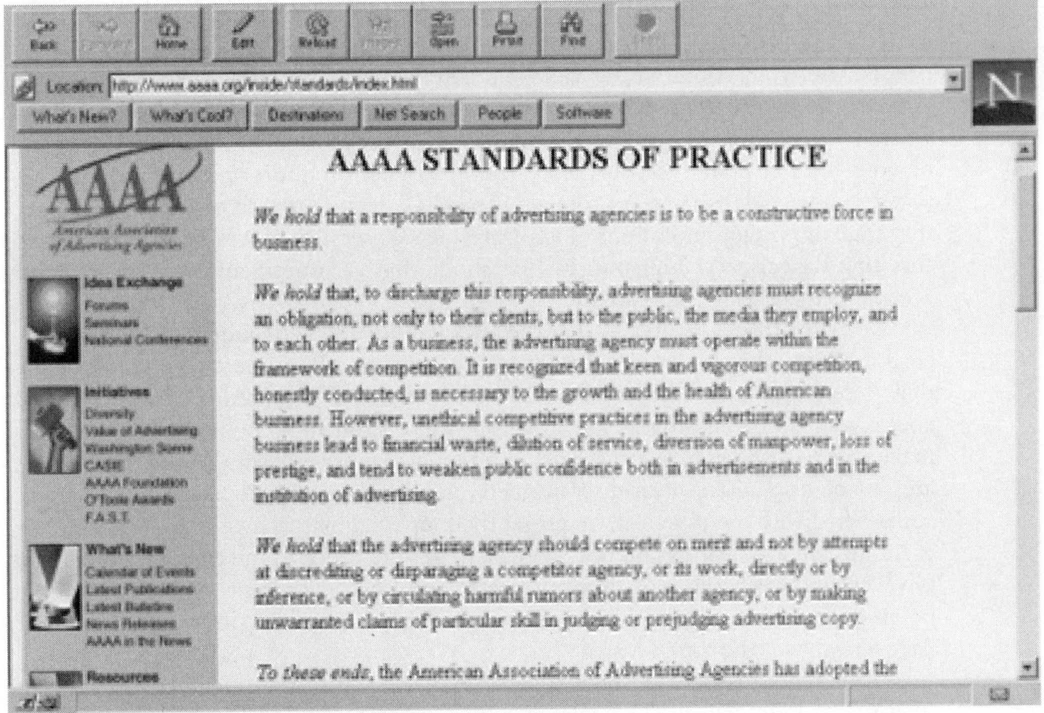

American Association of Advertising Agencies (www.aaaa.org)
Questions arise whether e-commerce will require government regulation in the future. One frequently referenced model of self-regulation is that of the 4As, the prestigious organization of leading advertising agencies. Membership responsibilities include adherence to a "Standards of Practice," adopted in the 1920s to curb abuses and unethical activities which in effect reduced the need for government intervention.

Introduction

Now that the Internet has become a popular medium for communicating and marketing to widespread consumer and business groups, it is important that some time should be taken to consider some of the potential problems faced by marketers in accomplishing their goals. It is imperative in this new era of easy access to information and technology that marketers act responsibly in their usage of the Web. It may require that they self-regulate themselves, to develop a "Standards and Practices Code" as the American Association of Advertising Agencies (www.aaaa.org) did in the early part of the twentieth century. This Web code may facilitate the successful operation of the Internet without creating a need for additional governing. As in any other medium, there are unwritten rules of **ethics** that need to be followed and understood by all who are creating materials for public viewing or commerce. This is a way of helping businesses self-regulate the Internet and make it a better place for all users, businesses, and consumers alike. The following material in this chapter will touch on a few of these issues to begin heightening your awareness.

A Commitment to Customer Service

Treat customers in all communications and transactions as you would like to be treated, putting the needs of the customers first. It is crucial that you provide secure, fast connections and continually improve content in your Web infrastructure. You owe your customers safe delivery and promised satisfaction for the right goods and services they order. The ability to provide twenty-four-hour online response to customers or prospects questions is now at your fingertips. Use it. Keeping the customer pleased with your goods and services and coming back is after all the ultimate goal of your marketing strategy, whether online or otherwise. Be honest with yourself and with the consumer. Do not tempt them with false advertising and then expect them to be your loyal customer. Be sure that when you post Web information or other messages, you provide what you promise. If needed, be sure to add disclosures on pages that state important limitations of your products or services as well as any legal disclosure that is necessary. This information should have a prominent place and be easily accessible to all who visit your site.

Recollect from Chapter 15 that the law does not allow the merchant to charge the customer until the goods have actually left the premises. This means, you must be sure that orders are being filled accurately and on time. If your order process does not check your stock automatically providing the customer with immediate feedback, make sure to respond to the customer in a timely manner regarding items ordered that are out of stock, have been discontinued, or otherwise unavailable. This can be accomplished with a phone call, by postal mail, or even better, by e-mail. If your delivery times tend to be long, do not promise to get the order to the customer overnight. Give accurate estimates of delivery dates, and your customers will not be disappointed. Provide a response to the customers order via e-mail or postal mail so they have a record of the transaction.

If for some reason a mistake occurs, be sure to apologize and accommodate the customer as best you can. This may take some creativity on your part, but think of the four-year-old that did not get her playhouse that was ordered from your site on her birthday. You the marketer should do something special for her. Send her another item of merchandise that might please her and her parents, relatives, and friends. Think of the child as your own. Mistakes are bound to happen; it is what you do to mitigate them that sets the spirit of your Web site apart. You owe your customers a fair and responsive return policy with no hassles when you make mistakes. This may mean not charging them on this transaction, giving them a discount on this or other purchases, as well as a personal note of apology. Use common sense and keep in mind that you too are a consumer in this competitive world. What would make you become a repeat customer? What would make you never want to visit or patronize a company again? If you remain aware of how you are dealing with the consumer, you will be successful.

Personal Privacy

Everyone on the Internet deserves privacy. For this reason, providing assurance of personal privacy is a very important aspect of the ethical and **moral** obligations a marketer has to the consumer and the company. Many of the topics in this section follow the rules of basic common decency and concern and personal consideration for the individual, but some delve deeper into creating a safe personal space for the consumer. After all, would you deal with someone you did not trust?

Electronic mail is one of the wonders of communication, but when abused, it can become as useless as shouting into the wind. Do not annoy potential customers by filling their e-mail boxes with unwanted solicitations and information. **Spam** or spamming has been discussed previously, and it is frowned upon by Internet society.

To contact a large number of people of like interests, you should use a mailing list. For more information on Internet junk mail, try taking a look at the junk mail category on Yahoo, http://dir.yahoo.com/Computers_and_Internet/Communications_and_Networking/Electronic_Mail/Junk_E-mail/.

GUIDELINES TO PROTECTING CUSTOMER PRIVACY

As the marketer begins his relationship with customers, many policies will be put into place. Some are more important than others, but all should be developed with the platform that in transactions the customer is almost always right. In dealing with customers over an electronic medium, the marketer must address the company's privacy issues to give the employees or associates a standard of performance that the customer can rely upon. Marketer Komenar has developed ten points on privacy and customer data collection that is an excellent place to start in a broad sense. These policies fit into the existing culture of Internet usage.

- User information is private and belongs to the user.
- Users should volunteer to reveal their information.
- Users should be made aware of all information collection activity.
- Users should be able to refuse to allow collection of their user data.
- Under no circumstances should the privacy of a user be violated.
- No information about a user should reach a second party without explicit user permission.
- Users should be able to choose the type and timing of information they want to receive.
- Only information that the end user specifically is interested in and wants should be sent.
- No junk mail should ever reach the end user.
- Users should remain in control of there information profile so that at any time they can update that information based on, for example, a recent purchase that no longer entails the user to want specific information.

Komenar, Margo. 1997. *Electronic marketing.* New York: John Wiley & Sons, 396.

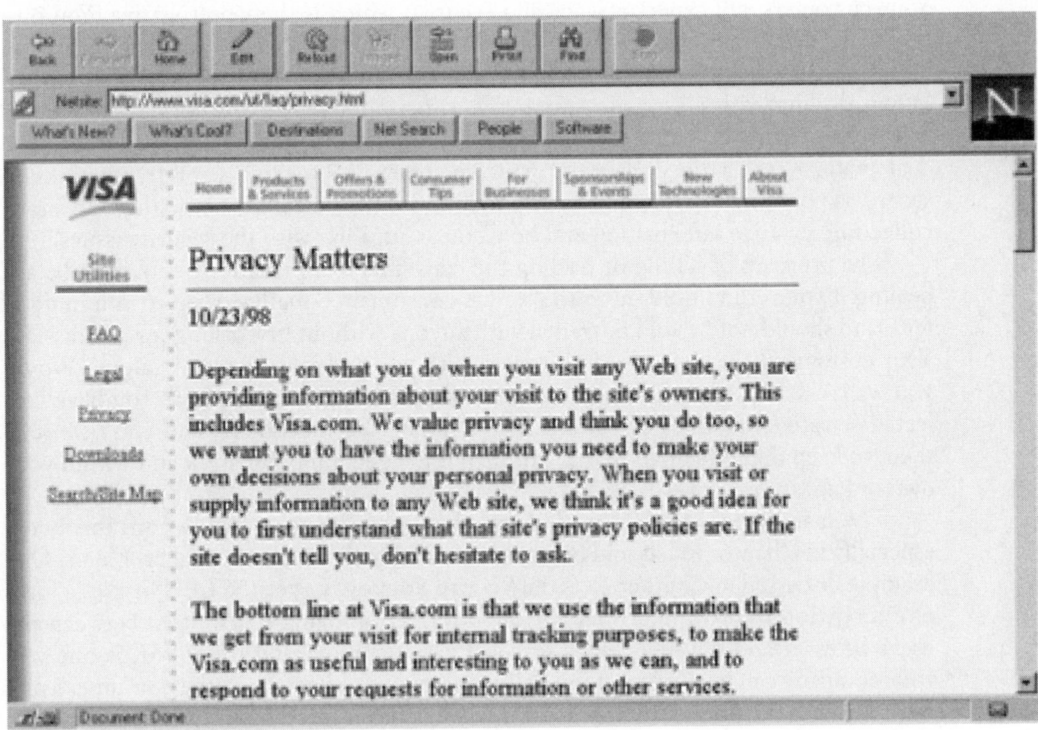

Visa Privacy Matters (www.visa.com/ut/faq/privacy.html)
Privacy is on everyone's mind, and marketers are taking lengths to protect the consumer. The emergence of interactive media presents unprecedented marketing opportunities for marketers and commensurate benefits to consumers. Key to this is the ability of interactive media to accept and respond to input from the consumer; it is important that marketers be guided in their interactive efforts for consumer privacy. The Coalition for Advertising Supported Information and Entertainment, (CASIE), is one such standard, formulating its Goals for Privacy on Interactive Media.

If you are using mailing lists to communicate with your consumers, follow a few basic rules. For each list you create to communicate with your customers, be sure to provide an option for joining the mailing list rather than making it mandatory. If the consumer has taken the time to fill out the information you have requested, do not penalize them by sending them junk mail unless they are interested in receiving it. By receiving an e-mail address from a consumer does not necessarily mean this consumer will want junk mail from you. Regardless of the fact that e-mail is easy and inexpensive to use, there should be no sending of bulk e-mail (spam) to people who are not expecting it or no postings of inappropriate ads to news groups or mailing lists.

To help build your mailing lists with those who are really interested, there are options. It is easy to give the consumer a check box on a consumer information questionnaire that allows them to choose not to be a part of your mailing list. It is allowable to ask your current customers to forward information to others who may be interested or to provide you with a list of people and their e-mail addresses so that you may invite them to join your list. It is also important to provide consumers a way to terminate their subscription to your mailing list. This should be sent to them with the first e-mail they receive from the list. If they delete the e-mail or later need assistance removing themselves from your list, you should accommodate them the best you can.

Security: Validation and Censorship

Your customers will expect privacy and security, which is their prerogative. You owe them a secured transaction as they order products or services or request information online. If the consumer desires, you should have an alternative method of payment. When dealing with electronic commerce, oftentimes sensitive information such as credit card numbers, social security numbers, and phone numbers and addresses are dealt with. Respect the privacy of your customers by making your transactions as secure as possible. Provide a written policy to let the customer know that the site is collecting sensitive information and how you are dealing with the security issues.

The prospect of selling or trading the consumers' information should not be appealing if your ethics hold up to the test. A consumers e-mail is given to you in good faith and should not be sold or traded with anyone without first asking for permission. Your customer has chosen to do business with you and your company alone. Would you want the U.S. Post Office to deliver your mail to a stranger first? You have collected sensitive materials and information about your customers, and you owe it to them to keep that information safe both from the general population and within your own organization.

The many types of security measures that were discussed throughout this book, especially in Chapter 15, should be in place to deal with these potential problems. One example discussed in Chapter 15 is the **Secure Sockets Layer (SSL).** SSL uses a form of **encryption** to provide privacy for the information being transmitted between the user's browser and the merchant's server. Learning about and using SSL is one way your company can help to meet its ethical and moral obligation to the consumer's privacy. Another way to secure transactions when using credit cards is to use the protocol for **Secure Electronic Transactions (SET).** This protocol is proposed to safeguard credit card transactions via open networks. See Chapter 15 for a good discussion on SET. These and other security measures are the obligation of the marketer and the merchant. Make the consumer's environment as safe and friendly as possible, and they will continue to come back to you for service.

Technology Limits Spying on Web Users

Firewalls play an important role in securing the information provided to you by your consumers. An Internet firewall is essentially a system designed to prevent unauthorized access to or from a private network, allowing approved traffic in and out according to a thought-out plan. This lets you select the services appropriate to your business needs while barring others that may have significant security holes. Firewalls can be implemented in both hardware and software, or a combination of both. They are frequently used to prevent unauthorized Internet users from accessing private networks connected to the Internet, especially **intranets.** All messages entering or leaving the intranet pass through the firewall, which examines each message and blocks those that do not meet the specified security criteria. A firewall is considered a first line of defense in protecting private information. For greater security, data can also be encrypted. Firewalls, along with encryption and frequently changed passwords, are ways to help secure your systems against **hackers** or persons with malicious intent. Without thinking about security issues such a these, you leave your company and your consumers open to break ins and the theft of information. For more information on the topics covered in this section, check out these Web sites.

Web Sites and URLs	Description of Site
Yahoo Security Category	Yahoo lists many sites that can be used as starting points for information on security and encryption.
http://dir.yahoo.com/Computers_and_Internet/Security_and_Encryption/	
Yahoos Privacy Category	This site provides information on privacy available through Yahoo as well.
http://dir.yahoo.com/Computers_and_Internet/Internet/Policy/Privacy/	
Better Business Bureau Privacy Program	The Better Business Bureau is one of the contributors of this site, offering some very good tips on how to provide privacy for your users.
http://www.bbbonline.org/businesses/privacy/	
The Online Privacy Alliance	The Online Privacy Alliance also has some good information for businesses and consumers on privacy issues.
http://www.privacyalliance.org/	
Hackers	There is a special category under security and encryption that deals with the topic of hackers.
http://dir.yahoo.com/Computers_and_Internet/Security_and_Encryption/Hacking/	

Other important issues that fall into the broad category of security include such things as validating a person's age or identity before orders are placed or sites are viewed. If your site contains material that should not be viewed by minors, or your products are not to be sold to minors, you need to be sure that they are first aware of this and second will take responsibility by accepting a user or order policy that states they are of age to participate in this site. There is a very heavy debate about censorship of the Internet and how it should affect the way the Internet works. To find out more on this topic, a good place to start would be the **Internet Censorship** category at Yahoo (http://dir.yahoo.com/Society_and_Culture/Issues_and_Causes/Civil_Rights/Censorship/). This location discusses many elements of censorship.

Along with this topic are the legalities of selling across state lines or across international borders. If your site is to provide products that are prohibited in certain states or

CYBERQUEST ATTACKS INTERNET FRAUD WITH S.A.F.E. PROGRAM

CBQ, Inc., is introducing S.A.F.E. (Security Against Fraudulent Exchange) as part of its evolving suite of e-commerce Internet products. Web auction fraud complaints made up almost 70 percent of the complaints on the 1998 roster of Net fraud records compiled by the National Consumers League, up from 26 percent in 1997. The Federal Trade commission and the consumer group Internet Fraud Watch cite online auctions as the cause of more complaints of fraud than any other form of Internet commerce.

Promoters promise to deliver valuable merchandise, from computers to Furbys, then simply fail to deliver the goods, or deliver damaged goods after the buyer has sent a check or money order. "Internet fraud . . . is becoming a significant threat to tens of millions of people who use the Internet regularly," said United States Assistant Attorney General James K. Robinson.

Commenting on Internet fraud, Michael L. Sheriff, chief executive officer of CBQ, stated, "The volume of transactions through our auction site, bid4it, grows daily. It is important to our company that visitors to bid4it are able to purchase goods without fear of being smuggled. We develop S.A.F.E. to protect our customers, and we think our S.A.F.E. program is superior to any other auction fraud prevention systems, putting us a step ahead of other Internet auction sites." Designed to protect both buyers and sellers engaged in Internet commerce on CyberQuest's www.bit4it.com, S.A.F.E. is an in-house escrow system that holds a buyer's funds for thirty days from the date of the order.

The escrow period allows the buyer time to examine the purchased item while providing assurance to the seller that funds will be available for payment. If a buyer is not satisfied with a purchase, the item can be returned and the buyer's money refunded, less a nominal handling fee. "With the S.A.F.E. system," Sheriff said, "we exclude fraudulent operators by requiring sellers to enter into an agreement under which they agree to comply with our escrow system, before they are allowed to list products for sale on bid4it. We protect both sides of the transaction, securing the funds before a seller ships, and holding the funds to ensure buyer satisfaction."

CyberQuest attacks Internet fraud with S.A.F.E. program. 1999. *Industries Channel.* Business Wire [cited online 8 March].

countries, it is important you realize you are globally accessible and must present the limitations and rules clearly. If you clearly state these limitations and ask the consumer to confirm that they understand, there is little else you can do at this time to control this situation electronically. However, consider carefully who will be responsible if these limitations are not made clear to the consumer. You can refuse to ship to locations that are not legally allowed, but you should be sure to notify your customers that you are unable to fulfill their orders. At this time, there are trade embargos between the United States and other countries around the world that have access to the Internet. Chapter 17 discussed in more detail the aspects of international marketing.

Although it is not currently possible for you to check accurately who is on the other end of a transaction, there is a certain responsibility on your part to at least attempt to validate the users identity. Asking questions that will help provide authenticity, such as their mother's maiden name or their birth date, can be useful.

Another approach to validating users is the new **digital certificates** that are becoming quite popular. Digital certificates were discussed in Chapter 15, but to recap, they allow people to authenticate themselves and companies to be authenticated to the consumer. This helps both the e-vendor and the customer ensure operations are legitimate and accurate information is being received every time. The advent of this technology has improved some of the less appealing portions of the virtual transaction. When transactions are completed in person, it is much easier to verify the consumer's identity. In this virtual world, digital certificates are attempting to bring the world closer to an electronic solution to the problems of validation. All this discussion, therefore, about making sure who is using your site brings up a question: Who should be taking responsibility, you or the consumer? It is your responsibility as a marketer to seek out an answer to this question and to not assume that your are in the clear because your Web site had a disclaimer of some sort.

Copyright Issues

With the advent of all this electronic communication comes the temptation to borrow from others on the Internet. Even though it is easier than it used to be, it is still just as illegal to copy someone else's work. Be aware of the current copyright restrictions and follow them. You can get up-to-date information on trademark and copyright laws in many places on the Web, so not knowing is no excuse. If you decide that you would like to link to someone's site or use some material that they have developed, it is best to contact them first. For the most part, Internet users are friendly, and as long as you are not their direct competitor, they are usually amenable to reciprocal relationships. If you see a page that intrigues you and want to make one just like it, copying the code falls under the same category. If you are learning how to write code, you can view it and learn from it. However, when it comes time to put it out on the Web, be sure you have permission or that you have written it yourself. Images and backgrounds are also very tempting. If you need graphics for your Web site, buy them; do not steal them. You might consider even hiring a good graphic artist. It will be worth the investment and is a much better solution than potentially facing a lawsuit. The following are some Web sites that provide good information on the legalities of copyright and how it pertains to cyberspace.

Web Site and URL	Description of Site
CyberLaw http://www.cyberlaw.com	This site offers a periodical that spotlights developments that touch the computer industry.
Cyberspace Law Center http://www.cybersquirrel.com/clc/clcindex.html	This is a useful meta-index of Internet and IP issues that includes the FindLaw search engine.
Cyberspace Law for Non-Lawyers http://www.counsel.com/cyberspace/copyright.html	This site discusses in layman terms how copyrights work online.
Intellectual Property http://www.ipmag.com	This is an online magazine that emphasizes technology concerns and the Internet.
Intellectual Property Mall Pointer Box page http://www.fplc.edu/ipmall/pointbox.htm	This site offers an exhaustive listing of Internet-related sites devoted to IP, technology transfer, and copyright concerns.
KuesterLaw Technology Law Resource http://www.kuesterlaw.com	This is a Web site that includes texts of IP and technology-related cases, as well as bills in the U.S. Congress.
World Intellectual Property Organization http://www.loc.gov/copyright/wipo.html	This is a site containing drafts and agenda of the WIPO Diplomatic Conference, including material relating to copyright issues.

In the academic world, you will often here the term **fair use** when talking about copyright issues. The Fair Use Act provides for the use of small pieces of copyrighted material for the purpose of education. It is an act that is currently causing a great deal of dilemma in the Internet world. Discussions of fair use will continue to advance as long as the Internet continues to grow and technology continues to expand. For good discussions on the limitations of fair use, check out the following Web sites.

Web Site and URL	Description of Site
The Copyright Website http://www.benedict.com/	This is a site that provides real-world, practical, and relevant copyright information to anyone interested.
Copyright Crash Course http://www.utsystem.edu/OGC/IntellectualProperty/cprtindx.htm	This site offers a good crash course on copyright including a thorough explanation of fair use.

Computer Viruses

Computer viruses are nasty annoyances that cause many problems for both the consumer and the marketer. It is important that you take precautions to assure you are not spreading disease to your consumers. Virus protection software is readily available and not exceptionally expensive. It is well worth the money for the piece of mind in knowing you are not adding to the problems by passing unknown viruses to others via the Internet. Viruses can only be passed from one user to another if files are downloaded and opened on the consumers computer, not through your Web site or electronic mail immediately. However, if your site is to have any file downloads, it is important that you keep your virus protection software up to date and provide clean files for your consumers.

Another common problem is the spreading of information on **hoaxes.** The Internet is constantly being flooded with information about computer viruses and Trojans. However, interspersed among real virus notices are computer virus hoaxes. While these hoaxes do not infect systems, they are still time-consuming and costly to handle. Be sure that when you discover a virus, you let your system administrator or Internet Service Provider know about it. Be aware as well that not all you hear via the Internet is always true. There are sites that are dedicated to keeping up with the current hoaxes and urban legends. Take some time to consult these sites before you forward that message about a virus to everyone you know. The following is list of a few sites with information on viruses and hoaxes.

Web Sites and URLs	Site Descriptions
McAffee Virus Software Home Page http://www.mcafee.com/	This site contains one of the best and most popular virus protection software. This software has frequent updates that can be downloaded from the Web.
Yahoo Virus page http://dir.yahoo.com/Computers_and_Internet/Security_and_Encryption/Viruses/	This site provided by Yahoo contains information on viruses.
AVP Virus Encyclopedia http://www.avp.ch/avpve/	This site is an encyclopedia that lists and describes viruses.
The online CIAC Virus Database http://ciac.llnl.gov/ciac/CIACVirusDatabase.html	This online CIAC Virus Database contains the virus descriptions.
Yahoo's Urban legends category	This site is another section of Yahoo's main site that provides information on computer viruses and hoaxes.

http://dir.yahoo.com/Society_and_Culture/Mythology_and_Folklore/Urban_Legends/Computer_Viruses/

The CIAC Internet Hoax page	This page describes only a small number of the hoax warnings that are found on the Internet today and addresses some of the history of hoaxes on the Internet.

http://ciac.llnl.gov/ciac/CIACHoaxes.html

Pirated Software

It is unlawful to copy and use software without purchasing a license. This is called software **piracy.** In the age of new technology, this has become very easy, but it is morally and ethically wrong. It is legal to make a backup copy of software that you have purchased for your purposes only. This archive mechanism is useful for keeping your software in the original condition in case something should happen to your computer. It does, however, offer temptation to borrow the software from someone who has purchased it. There are entities out there that look for companies that are involved in software piracy, and they can drop in at any time. If the ethical issues of this do not keep you from involving yourself in software piracy, the fact that you can go to jail may. For information on software piracy, you can visit the Business Software Alliance Web site at www.bsa.org.

Who Should Be Using the Internet?

This discussion would not be complete without exploring several issues that face the Internet: Who should be using the Internet and who should be deciding what content is appropriate for the medium? The marketer should ask herself questions such as should there be any regulations on usage of the Internet, such as applying to children's usage or extremist militia groups in communications or information retrieval? The balance between the Fifth Amendment Freedom of Speech is often at odds with matters of community morals and decency. Here is an example of the struggle with the issue of freedom of speech as retold by *The Wall Street Journal* after the 1998 Thanksgiving holiday.

> Why should a 14-year-old boy who cannot legally buy a copy of *Hustler* at the corner 7-11 be allowed access to even more hard-core stuff at the local library? Ask the American Civil Liberties Union, which filed suit in Philadelphia against the Child Online Prevention Act, which would impose criminal penalties on anyone knowingly selling or making available adult materials to minors online. Last month U.S. District Judge Lowell A. Reed agreed with the ACLU and slapped a temporary restraining order on the enforcement of the bill. Three days later, another U.S. district judge, Leonie M. Brinkema, told the Library Board of Loudoun County, VA, that it could not use "blocking software" to screen out adult content in its public computers.
>
> But that's no reason to throw in the towel. Our own preference is to let local communities experiment with coming up with their own ways of dealing with Internet porn—as they do with regard to raunchy material on newsstands, in movie theaters and on show at adult clubs—rather than have the federal government impose a one-size-fits-all solution on something that's very much a work in progress. After all, what works in Margaritaville might not fly in Stepford. (Review and Outlook 1998)

RACE IS ON TO FOIL E-MUSIC PIRATES

Record labels were horrified when a small company in San Jose, California, came out with the Rio, a $199.95 Walkman-like player last year. As the first widely available portable player of music downloaded from the Internet, the Rio frees people from having to sit at their computer terminals to listen to free tunes. And that threatens to turn the nagging problem of Internet music piracy into serious financial losses for record companies. Technology heavyweights are racing to develop ways to help deliver music online security. The goal: come up with a way to ensure Time Warner Inc.'s Warner Bros., for example, gets paid each time "Iris" by the Goo Goo Dolls is sent over the Net.

At stake for the technology industry is a lucrative ground-floor position in the next wave of e-commerce: the digital delivery of media products—music, e-books, and movies—via the Internet. The heavy-technology firepower is aimed at an explosion of music available in cyberspace. Currently, there are an estimated ten thousand songs being passed around the Internet ranging from Dave Matthews to vintage Sinatra to new cuts from Public Enemy, many of them pirated from the original CDs. Nathan Myhrvold, Microsoft's chief technology officer, acknowledges that music-industry executives have pleaded with Microsoft to alter its media player [under consideration] so that it can't play the MP3 [compressed files]. Mr. Myhrvold says that you can scrap a popular legitimate feature (not all MP3 files are pirated) just because it is abused by some people. "The software industry loses more money to Iconocast than the record industry makes," says Mr. Myhrvold. He says Microsoft is working with the music industry to find a way to deliver music online securely and easily.

Should technology firms pursue enabling technology to permit the piracy of the entertainment media?

Shapiro, Eren. 1999. Race is on to foil e-music pirates. *The Wall Street Journal*, 22 January, B1.

The following questions are still issues regarding the Internet: Who should be the gatekeeper of Internet content? Is someone's desire to download indecent images and to archive these images protected by free speech? Do content filters, called blocking software in the *Journal* editorial, violate the same principles of freedom of speech by the pornography disseminators? Should the government decide what content is acceptable? Or should the online industry self-regulate itself? In either case, what standards should be set? So far, legislators are hesitant to tackle these issues.

As the user rights are considered, there are other important issues need considering as well. Is access to the Internet a universal right? Should everyone have free access to the network of the Internet as individuals now have free access to television information and entertainment airwaves of the broadcast networks? Should advertisers be allowed to place their messages anywhere on the Internet or should there be safe times or channels free of advertising, such as Saturday morning or commercial-free PBS network television? Should advertising be restricted to promotional channels in which commercial messages are transmitted all day long like the television shopping networks? Much of this depends on your view of advertising as a positive or negative force and whether promotion is a protected form of free speech.

If the twenty-first century will complete the transition of the U.S. economy from an industrial and manufacturing-based economy to an information economy, what kind of workers and jobs will that economic structure demand? Only computer-literate persons? How will computer-illiterate people or those without computers compete within this economy? Will the U.S. become a nation split between the people who have and the people who have not, possibly widening the social and knowledge divides? Can or should community funding pay the costs of the advancement of technology? Or should this technology research fall under the development role of the Federal government? Can economically-disadvantaged school districts or rural school districts distanced from centers of technology prepare their students as well as suburban school administrations for this technology era? Should public buildings such as libraries, post offices, government offices, perhaps even shopping malls be required to be equipped with free public-use computers? How will these technology rights be paid for? Should there be an individual technology grant or an online services tax credit initiated to help students and families keep up-to-date with Internet usage and new applications?

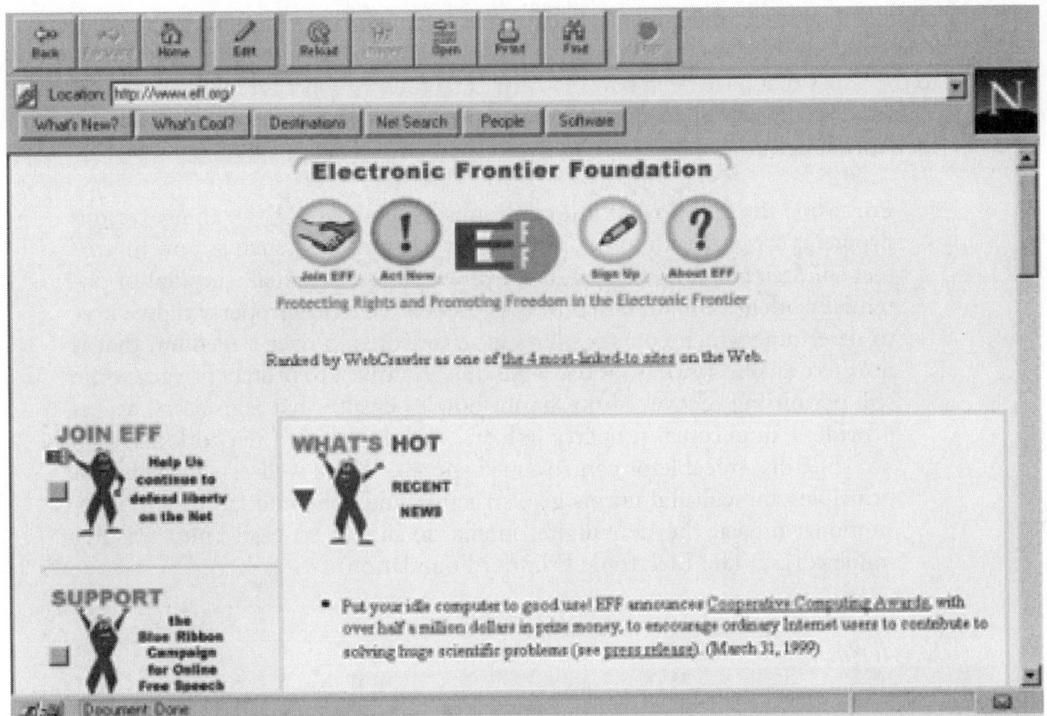

Electronic Frontier Foundation (www.eff.org)
Free online speech is one of many rights that the EFF champions. Liberal, moderate, and conservative interests should be represented on the Web, and the EFF provides protection for each viewpoint as requested.

Pursuing this train of thought, are the demographic profiles leveling out in Internet usage? In the Tenth GVU survey, which ended in December 1998, the answer appears to be uncertain. Of the 5,022 respondents worldwide, American males accounted for just over 64 percent of Internet users (61.3 percent in the Ninth survey); European males figured for almost 82 percent online usage (83.7 percent in the Ninth survey). Average age for all respondents was 35.1 years. Some college-educated plus users comprised over 65 present (80.9 percent in the Ninth survey), with 87 percent being white users (87.4 percent in the Ninth survey). The language most frequently spoken was English by 92 percent (93.1 percent in the Ninth survey) of the respondents, with German being the second-most frequently language preferred at 1.5 percent, and French and Dutch tying at 0.8 percent each.

These people issues deserve observation so that the power and convenience of the Internet serves everyone. There are many unchartered areas of human experience and interaction with the online medium. These ethical and moral considerations should be carefully monitored since the Internet is an anonymous, ubiquitous, and vulnerable entity. Marketers and customers alike must act responsibly, and one behavior will influence another behavior.

Summary

Many of the issues that have been discussed in this chapter are important to the community as a whole, not just the marketer. You as a marketer, however, have the ability to help the Internet become a wonderful place to explore. The **Electronic Frontier Foundation,** a nonprofit, nonpartisan organization funded in 1990, works in the public interest to protect fundamental civil liberties, including privacy and freedom of expression in the arena of computers and the Internet. This group is working toward solutions to the issues that have been covered here. The following paragraph quoted from their Web site is a good way to summarize what has been discussed while leaving you with food for thought.

> For, while the free flow of information is generally a positive thing, serious problems arise when information flows free—problems such as how to protect children and undesiring adults from exposure to sexually explicit or potentially offensive materials; how to protect intellectual property rights; how to determine which country's laws have jurisdiction over a medium that is nowhere and everywhere at the same time; how best to protect privacy while still permitting recovery from harm; how to ensure that legislators, access providers, intellectual property holders, and disgruntled network users do not stifle disagreeable or controversial speech. While well-established legal principles and cultural norms give structure and coherence to uses of conventional media, the new digital media do not fit so easily into existing frameworks. (The Electronic Frontier Foundation)

Key Terms

Computer virus

Digital certificates

Electronic Frontier Foundation

Encryption

Ethics

Fair use

Hackers

Hoaxes

Internet Censorship

Internet firewall

Intranet

Morals

Piracy

Secure Electronic Transactions (SET)

Secure Sockets Layer (SSL)

Spam

QUESTIONS AND EXERCISES

1. Write a one-page paper on how copyright on the Internet affects the marketing process and the current copyright laws. What products or services might have their copyright protection violated by transmission over the Internet? Write an e-mail to your company's legal department asking for verification of your understanding of the Internet and copyright infringement. Include at least two online references besides those listed in this chapter.

2. Do a search on the Internet for digital certificates. Write four or five paragraphs on how to use digital certificates for authenticating users. Do you feel that digital certificates will be successful in aiding e-commerce?

3. Viruses are a dangerous element to computer users. Do a search and find the prominent virus protection software companies. List their Web address and what products they have available.

4. Make a short list of things not to do with electronic mail. Make a short list of ways to make electronic commerce more appealing to consumers who have a fear of losing their privacy. What is the difference between solicited and unsolicited e-mail? Are there situations or organizations that might be appropriate for sending unsolicited e-mail?

5. Access the American Marketing Association (AMA) Web page and read about the standards for ethics they provide. From your experience and dealings with the Web, do you feel that e-marketers are conducting themselves morally and ethically on the Internet? Write an e-mail to the AMA stating your observations and your opinions.

6. Conservatives and liberals disagree on content appropriate for the World Wide Web. Investigate on the Web what measures can be taken to stop minors from viewing sites that are not appropriate. Discuss and support with URLs the different methods available. Do you think they are effective? Write a two-page editorial stating your opinion for your local newspaper.

7. Visit at least three major business sites of interest to you. Find their privacy policy statement and in two-pages, summarize each policy. Do you as a consumer feel comfortable with the protection they say they are providing you? In what areas do these privacy statements compare and in what areas are they contrasting? Which company's privacy statement do you most agree with? Why?

Bibliography

American Marketing Association. Web pages on Ethics. [cited online, http://www.ama.org/about/ama/ethcode.asp].

The Electronic Frontier Foundation. [cited online, www.eff.org/].

CHAPTER 19

The Future of Online Electronic Marketing Resources

"The dawn of the new millennium—which is the greatest measure we have of human time—permits us to think big about history. We can pause to notice what [Andy] Grove [ex-chairman of Intel] calls, somewhat inelegantly, 'strategic infection points,' those moments when new circumstances alter the way the world works. It can happen because of an invention (Gutenberg's printing press in the fifteenth century), or an idea (individual liberty in the eighteenth century), or a technology (electricity in the nineteenth century), or a process (the assembly line early in this century). The microchip has become—like the steam engine, electricity and the assembly line—an advance that propels a new economy." (Isaacson 1997)

LEARNING OBJECTIVES

- To discuss the possibilities of electronic marketing technology in the future
- To speculate on the roles of electronic marketing resources in the future
- To envision the capacities of service delivered by electronic commerce

Introduction

All the cards are now on the table. The marketers must pick them up to shuffle the deck of marketing opportunities. Each marketer will choose cards representing possibilities and capabilities that he can play or fold. Only confident, aggressive people should play, and with a solid understanding of traditional and electronic marketing methods, many constituencies will win—the consumer, the e-merchant, the manufacturers and distributors, the business community, and society in general. Because of a strong foundation in electronic marketing processes, the e-marketer can strengthen and improve the electronic commerce **value chain** to everyone's benefit. This end will involve hard work, some successes, and some failures. However, that is the learning path of all occupations. Schooled in the principles of electronic marketing, the e-marketer should exhibit critical thinking skills of strategic and tactical marketing planning, and she should be able to use the resources of electronic marketing to produce benefits for all marketing communities.

What will be the electronic marketing resources to achieve these goals? There are many electronic tools at hand to work with, but it is the advanced resources that will produce value-added services, not info-junk, and are probably unimaginable in form and in consequence. However, it is laudable to evaluate current conditions to speculate on solutions. To put all the supporting and conflicting information into a semblance of order, the following are four factors or consequences that electronic marketing may influence or may be influenced by: 1) the evolution of technology, 2) the expansion of software, 3) the success of Internet acquisitions and mergers, and 4) the driving desire for marketers to better serve their customers. All electronic marketing resources will impact one of these areas, if not more; e-marketers will have the means to communicate with millions of consumers as easily as minute customer segments. With this spectrum of opportunities available for serving customers, anticipation and preparation will be demanded of the marketer.

What will be the structural areas of importance to the e-marketer of the future? Technical capabilities appear to be the most enabling factor for continued Internet growth, and the one most important project for advancing the Internet is the **Next Generation Internet Initiatives (NGI).** The NGI Initiative is a high-speed version of the traditional Internet that will be capable of transmitting voice, video, and data over the same line. Educational and government institutions as well as large corporations are leading the development. This initiative is expected to revolutionize the way business is conducted through the integration of various means of communications. (Yakirevich, 1999)

The Power of Convergence

So much of the following discussion on electronic marketing's future contains some element of convergence. In the context of marketing technology, convergence is the coming together of two or more disparate disciplines or technologies to provide systems of greater benefit. For example, the so-called fax revolution was produced by a convergence of telecommunications technology, optical scanning technology, and printing technology. As an example of NGI convergence, NGI technology will provide technology for transmission of video components—videoconferencing; video storage; video broadcasting; video delivery of satellite or cable television programming over broadband networks; and video signal switching from **Asynchronous Transfer Mode (ATM)** to other types of networks such as ATM-to-Ethernet, the Internet system wired into many college dormitories throughout the nation. This new infrastructure uses ATM technology and will provide unheard-of flexibility for shifting between networks.

EXECUTIVE SUMMARY OF THE NEXT GENERATION INTERNET INITIATIVES

The U.S. Government's investments in Internet research and development (R&D) have been incredibly successful. The Internet has grown at nearly 100 percent per year since 1988 and Internet traffic has been growing at 400 percent per year. The Internet has created jobs and whole new industries. American business and government organizations are increasingly dependent.

Today's Internet has to meet the demands of users numbering in the millions, and by the year 2000 more than half of the U.S. population is expected to have access to it. In addition, the Internet's current capabilities are strained by the need for higher bandwidth and multimedia applications. In order to meet these needs and allow American industry and the public to benefit from the coming exponential improvements in computing and communications, we must make a few key strategic R&D investments now. The R&D needed to address these requirements is beyond the scope of any single institution, company, or industry. The Next Generation Internet (NGI) initiative, with its broad agenda and ability to involve government, research institutions, and the business sector, is a timely program that will address these challenges. The goal of the NGI initiative is to conduct R&D in advanced networking technologies, to demonstrate those technologies in **test beds** that are a hundred to a thousand times faster than today's Internet, and to develop and demonstration on those test beds revolutionary applications that meet important national needs and that cannot be achieved with today's Internet.

The Federal government has a unique role to play in stimulating technological progress. Through its NGI initiative, the government will help create an environment in which advanced networking R&D breakthroughs are possible. The NGI initiative, together with other investment sectors, will create the foundation for the networks of the twenty-first century, setting the stage for networks that are much more powerful and versatile than the current Internet. The NGI will foster partnerships among academia, industry, and governments (federal, state, local, and foreign) that will keep the U.S. at the cutting edge of information and communications technologies. The NGI will also stimulate the introduction of new multimedia services in our homes, schools, and businesses as the technologies and architectures designed and developed as part of the NGI are incorporated into products and services that are subsequently made available to the general public. The NGI program is essential to sustain U.S. technological leadership in computing and communications and enhance U.S. economic competitiveness.

The NGI initiative is part of a highly successful ongoing multi-agency R&D program. It is a key component of the activities of the **Large Scale Networking (LSN)** Working Group of the Subcommittee on Computing, Information, and Communications (CIC) R&D. This subcommittee reports to the Committee on Technology of the White House National Science and Technology Council.

Overview of ATM in the Context of NGI

Virtually everyone today, whether at home or at work, experiences the Internet using a modem and a telephone line. This is a simple, analog conversation occurring between two digitally minded machines. This may not seem at all odd until one understands the basics of the analog and digital technologies and how they are linked together. Remember that telephones have traditionally used *analog* technology, which refers to electronic transmission accomplished by adding signals of *varying* frequency to carrier waves of a *fixed* frequency of alternating electromagnetic current. This is called *modulation.* In fact, the term is derived from the fact that the modulation of the carrier wave is analogous to the fluctuations of the human voice itself. Now, a modem is used to convert the digital information in the computer to analog phone signals for the phone line and to convert analog phone signals to digital information for the computer. Basically, the modem is the translator of the digital to the analog technology, and herein lies the problem.

Traditionally, telecommunications technology has leveraged the highly predictable nature of voice data and delivered this data efficiently by using dedicated circuits operating at a fixed bandwidth. That is, voice communication is largely constant in the amount of data moving across the line. Therefore, much of the emphasis in telecommunications has been focused on the needs of voice data. The mode of delivery is through what is known as circuit switching technology, which is the foundation of the telephone network. However, this is changing. Telecommunication companies are now embracing networks capable of high-speed transmission of images—broadcast television and cable. While voice communication represents a yearly U.S. expense greater than $200 billion, the data portion of many telecommunication budgets continues to increase significantly.

EXECUTIVE SUMMARY OF THE NEXT GENERATION INTERNET INITIATIVES CONTINUED

The proposed fiscal year (FY) 1998 LSN budget crosscut is $288.3 million, which includes $100 million for the NGI initiative. Congressional FY 1998 NGI appropriations are $85 million, with the Defense Advanced Research Projects Agency (DARPA), National Science Foundation (NSF), National Aeronautics and Space Administration (NASA), National Institute of Standards and Technology (NIST), and National Library of Medicine (NLM) as the participating agencies. The administration plans to propose $109 million for the NGI in each of FY 1999 and FY 2000 with DARPA, NSF, NASA, NIST, NLM, and the Department of Energy (DOE) as the participating agencies. The administration may propose similar amounts for the following two years. This document presents the NGI goals and objectives at these funding levels. NGI activities will be leveraged off of and tightly coupled with the basic network research and infrastructure support conducted by the agencies funded under the LSN budget.

The NGI Initiative Has Three Goals

1. To advance research, development, and experimentation in the next generation of networking technologies to add functionality and improve performance.
2. To develop a Next Generation Internet test bed, emphasizing end-to-end performance, to support networking research and demonstrate new networking technologies. This test bed will connect at least a hundred NGI sites—universities, Federal research institutions, and other research partners—at speeds a hundred times faster than today's Internet, and will connect on the order of ten sites at speeds a thousand times faster than the current Internet.
3. To develop and demonstrate revolutionary applications that meet important national goals and missions and that rely on the advances made in goals one and two. These applications are not possible on today's Internet.

The NGI initiative is closely related to **Internet2,** a collaborative effort by more than a hundred U.S. research universities to create and sustain a leading edge network for developing network engineering and management tools and broadband applications for advanced research and education. The NGI will rely on Internet2 for advanced campus-based, local-area, and select regional network infrastructure. The initiative also will rely on substantial matching funds from its private sector partners.

This document supplements the NGI Concept Paper (available at http://www.ngi.gov/), providing additional details on methods and steps proposed to reach NGI goals.

National Coordination Office for Computing, Information, and Communications. 1998. NGI Implementation Plan, Executive Summary. [Available online at http://www.cclc.gov/ngi/implementation/exe_summary.html.]

However, the networks to support the new technology have remained, at the practical level, in a separate domain.This is because digital communications has quite a different character.

As everyone who has visited an Internet site or downloaded e-mail knows, the traffic is based on images, sounds, text, and even streaming video, which consists of small, irregular streams of data moving with no predictable traffic pattern. The method of transmitting this data uses what are called packet switching techniques, where small parcels of data are transmitted individually across digital communications networks, typically known as **Local Area Networks (LANs)** or **Wide Area Networks (WANs).** While communities using circuit switching and packet switching technologies have remained largely separate in the past, there is now an increasing recognition that technology is required that is capable of meeting both styles of operation. Increasingly, telephone networks have to deal with digital traffic, and this requirement has placed new demands on the underlying network resources (unpredictable data in size and timing) in a way that makes packet switching principles attractive. Meanwhile, the strengths of the telecommunication approach in network management and control have become extremely attractive to the computing community, where network problems even outages result from the use of protocols, or standards of transmitting data, that are not ideally suited to such situations. These are the problems that the Next Generation Internet (NGI) initiative will address.

The recognition has been that no single technology can resolve all internetworking, integration, and other digital communications issues, and as a result, a variety of new standards are being created to address the current deficiencies. One of the standards that will play a central, strategic role in the networks of the future is a new network protocol known as Asynchronous Transfer Mode (ATM). ATM is an open solution based on international and industry standards that combines the best features of the circuit and packet switching approaches. The result is a protocol that is well suited for carrying traffic of widely varying characteristics and bandwidth and has the capability of offering a bandwidth-on-demand service.

In particular, ATM provides for a single network service capable of supporting video, voice, and data transmission needs in a flexible and responsive way and incorporates the following capabilities:

- Much higher transmission capabilities than existing packet or frame-based technologies. From the start, ATM will support LAN speeds ten to twenty times faster than current systems.
- Flexibility and versatility. Voice, data, video, and images can be transmitted simultaneously over a single, integrated corporate network or the Internet.
- Universality and adaptability. ATM technology has the potential to support a wide variety of communications methods, from the ubiquitous corporate network cables to high-capacity optical fiber.
- The ability to meet the needs of each segment of the corporate network, supplementing and eventually supplanting the different networking solutions that now prevail at the work group, Local Area Network (LAN), **Metropolitan Area Network (MAN),** and Wide Area Network (WAN) levels.

ATM implies far-reaching institutional as well as technological changes. While ATM is a nascent technology, standards development continues; standards-making bodies are still resolving some details of ATM specifications, particularly in support of video, voice, and multimedia. In general, the order of implementation of ATM technology will be the Metropolitan Area Network (MAN) level in the institutional/educational campus context, followed by the Wide Area Network (WAN) level, then the corporate Local Area Network (LAN) level, and finally the work group and desktop level implementations.

ATM thus represents a major component of NGI since it brings the internetworking potential of the Internet together with the management capabilities of high-capacity transmission within the traditional telecommunications industry. Many industry analysts expect ATM technology to become a vital component of NGI, and in fact, no less an organization than NATO has had the following to say about ATM technology.

> There are . . . particular problems for ATM exploitation in defense because it has been designed to exploit a near perfect, high bandwidth (fibre optic) transmission medium. In the tactical domain, in particular, where transmission bandwidth are limited and channels are very noisy, ATM is unlikely to be effective and special measures will thus be necessary. Despite these difficulties, however, the importance and the potential of ATM for meeting civil communications requirements suggest that it would be wrong to discount its potential within defense. (The Advanced Information Services Demonstration 1996)

NGI in the Context of Marketing to Consumers

Why is this important from a marketing viewpoint? The consumer drives an organization's marketing, and the explosion of the Internet has placed great strains on the ability of companies to deliver on their marketing promises. Remember that the Internet in its incipient stages became a vehicle allowing companies to create electronic billboards and brochures—in effect, cheap advertising. As consumer confidence has increased through acceptance and vigilance with respect to privacy and security of personal information, the current trend in Internet revenues has been moving increasingly away from straight advertising (double-click revenues) towards the generation of revenue from e-commerce. Several CEOs of major Internet-based corporations have predicted that revenue from online sales will exceed 75 percent of the total revenue of many portal sites (for example, www.yahoo.com, www.netscape.com, and www.excite.com). Examples of online sales and other direct-to-consumer sites include shopping services (www.amazon.com), auctions (www.ebay.com), stock trading (www.etrade.com), banking (www.citibank.com), and even grocery shopping (www.peapod.com). These sites incorporate technologies that were created to exploit the Internet, and they have in their totality been primary contributors to the Internet bottleneck problem. Highlighting this problem was a recent event in which the trading operations of a major online brokerage house were suspended. This was a direct result of network overload at their site caused by a deluge of online traders hoping to expand (and contract) their positions in a small number of Web-based public companies.

Quality of service has thus become the problem with today's Internet. For the consumer transacting a sale, reliability of revenue transactions over the Internet is paramount. For the consumer engaging in Internet telephony, timeliness of data is the prime goal, even when voice quality degrades slightly. There is always a tradeoff between bandwidth, timeliness, and reliability, and improving these areas is the primary goal of NGI with respect to the commercial user. It is what the Next Generation Internet Initiative is meant to address.

As Scott Bradner, senior technical consultant at Harvard University and a member of the Internet2 technical committee, has aptly stated, "If you have an application that's providing real-time, interactive video, and it's competing with 7,000 undergraduates looking at the Playboy page, you've got to make sure the stuff that's making you money is actually going through." (Anthes 1997)

Internet2 Project

Written into the NGI explanation was a mention of **Internet2.** What is Internet2? Officially, Internet2 is a project of the University Corporation for Advanced Internet Development (www.ucaid.edu). Internet2 is a part of the NGI to rededicate a communications network linking research universities as the original Internet was purposed. Its Web page describes the project as follows:

> Building on the tremendous success of the last ten years in generalizing and adapting research Internet technology to academic needs, the university community has joined together with government and industry partners to accelerate the next stage of Internet development in academia. The Internet2 project is bringing focus, energy, and resources to the development of a new family of advanced applications to meet emerging academic requirements in research, teaching, and learning. Internet2 universities, working with industry, government, and other research and education networking organizations, are addressing the major challenges facing the next generation of university networks by:
>
> - First and most importantly, creating and sustaining a leading edge network capability for the national research community;
> - Second, directing network development efforts to enable a new generation of applications to fully exploit the capabilities of broadband networks, and;
> - Third, working to rapidly transfer new network services and applications to all levels of educational use and to the broader Internet community, both nationally and internationally.

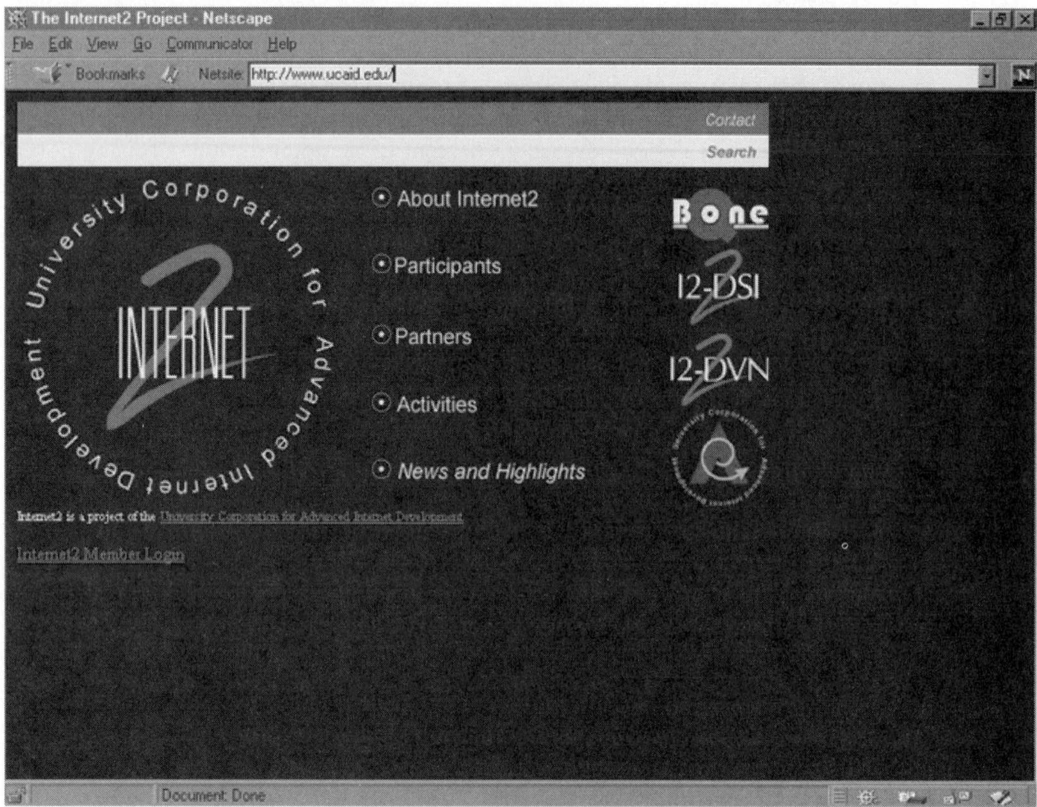

Internet2 (www.ucaid.edu)
An initiative to expand the interests of universities and research facilities is entitled Internet2. The Internet2 project is bringing focus, energy and resources to the development of a new family of advanced applications to meet emerging academic requirements in research, teaching and learning. Internet2 universities, working with industry, government and other research and education networking organizations are addressing the major challenges facing the next generation of university networks.

How specifically will the Internet2 benefit universities' communications on research and development of Internet technology? It is designed to facilitate and coordinate the development, deployment, operation, and technology transfer of advanced, network-based applications and network services to further U.S. leadership in research and higher education and to accelerate the availability of new services and applications on the Internet. The goals of the Internet2 project include the following:

- Enable a new generation of applications
- Recreate a leading edge research and education network capability
- Transfer new capabilities to the global production Internet

Some additional specific objectives include the following:

- Demonstrate new applications that can dramatically enhance researchers' abilities to collaborate and conduct experiments
- Demonstrate enhanced delivery of education and other services (for example, health care and environmental monitoring) by taking advantage of **virtual proximity** created by an advanced communications infrastructure
- Support development and adoption of advanced applications by providing middleware and development tools

- Facilitate development, deployment, and operation of an affordable communications infrastructure capable of supporting differentiated **quality of service (QOS)** based on applications requirements of the research and education community
- Promote experimentation with the next generation of communications technologies
- Coordinate adoption of agreed working standards and common practices among participating institutions to ensure end-to-end quality of service and interoperability
- Catalyze partnerships with governmental and private sector organizations
- Encourage transfer of technology from Internet2 to the rest of the Internet
- Study impact of new infrastructure, services, and applications on higher education and the Internet community in general

The above goals are very ambitious and specific and can establish a bond between the universities and government research. Research dissemination is always a difficult task because of the wide dispersion of academic interests. These objectives can also be beneficial as future network and information needs and applications are anticipated. Over the history of the Internet, technology has always trailed the capabilities of the Internet. Perhaps the Internet2 project will bring the resources of communications technology and networking delivery technology into balance.

The Evolution of Technology

Assume the NGI will provide much relief to the problems of bandwidth thus speeding up data transmission and reducing download time. Given these benefits, what technology would interest the e-marketer? What will be the **appliance** of choice for Internet products and services consumption? The hardware developers are pursuing compact, mobile, hand-held devices containing wireless transmission similar to a cellular telephone in function and a Palm Pilot-like computer in size. An Internet appliance that would serve consumers and businesspeople alike will probably have most of the following features:

- Internet-ready connections
- Color screen for daylight viewing
- Sufficient power for processing
- Voice recognition capabilities with pen-touch stylus
- Memory for storage of text and graphical documents
- Cellular telephone for upload and replication capabilities
- Ear and mouth piece, possibly a headset, to eliminate noise, static, and interference

The above may be an ambitious wish list, but so were the hoped-for specifications of the original personal computer.

Concerning the future, the possible fortunes of business practices and software systems have been discussed at length. Consider a small corner of the hardware outlook. IBM has made a pledge to eliminate the keyboard within five years to facilitate speech-activated technologies, allowing more people to use computers and thus reducing the cost of manufacturing since the keyboard production will be eliminated. Other technologies that will enhance communications by making it as easy as picking up the telephone but with much more impact will use real-time communications, Internet phones, and multimedia e-mail. The marketer will gain the capability of sending information to the consumer as the consumer logs on to his PC or Internet appliance via Internet push technology.

The Expansion in Imaginative Software

E-commerce software of the future will be constructed for one of two purposes: 1) to provide knowledge and convenience to the individual consumer or 2) to provide knowledge and competitive advantage for the company through business systems. To attract the consumer, creative and service-oriented Web sites will render information with several platforms—entertainment, humor, rational information, factual comparisons—as message executions are delivered by advertising techniques. Software applications, the primary building components of Web sites, are expected to be online virtual reality simulations including **Virtual Reality Modeling Language (VRML),** three-dimensional graphic tools technology, and Web browsers that can display these virtual spaces. A mainstay of the virtual reality environment is the **avatar,** an animated figure that represents a person in online virtual realities—a stand-in in cyberspace. Therefore, cyberspace is proving to be a viable place for marketing venues such as industry conferences.

> Contact Consortium, which hosted the last two avatars conferences, put Avatar98 online to "test-drive the medium and measure its readiness for a truly global happening in human contact." The Scotts Valley, California, consortium billed the event as the world's first 3D online convention. "We proved that you could really do a conference, in the traditional sense, with the traditional facility, in cyberspace," said consortium member Bruce Damer, who was in charge of this year's conference. The decision to host the event in cyberspace, rather than in San Francisco, meant that interested parties in far-off countries not only participated but rallied local resources. "People in Helsinki brought in their art museum," Damer said.
>
> The consortium estimated total attendance at over 4,000 with an average 200 to 300 visitors at a time in the main hall and its satellite spaces. Though sometimes slow to render, the virtual world was intuitive, surprisingly convincing, and the conversations and lectures were coherent and interesting. Saturday's default location for the browser was set to the main room of the conference. As soon as one fired it up, the polygons and **texture maps**—the building blocks of all virtual worlds—slowly took form. A hall, not too different from what you'd find at any well-funded convention, appeared. Eventually, sound kicked in and the low rumble of a crowded room, complete with shuffling papers and clinking glasses, added a touch of realism. Whether from Finland or Argentina, most avatars were just alike. The average male figure wore jeans, a T-shirt, and a vest. Females sported skirts of the length and style popular in the original *Star Trek* series. And there were plenty of bearded wizards in long black robes and several dragons.
>
> Much of what happened required some imagination to fully appreciate. Some visitors called the event "glorified IRC chaos." Others complained about download times, which reached 30 minutes or more for many pictures. "Time seems to be distorted," one person wrote. And the banalities inherent in the medium were also in the air, if at a more subdued level than

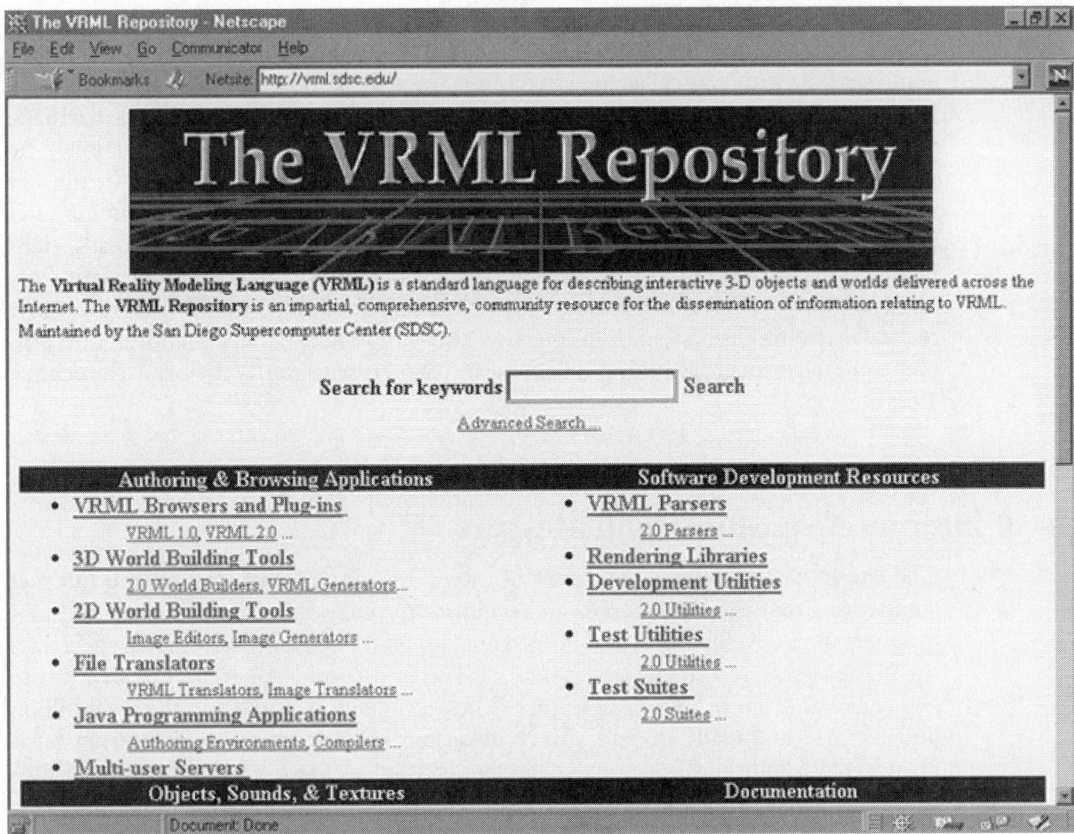

The VRML Repository (http://vrml.sdsc.edu/)
Graphic representations are becoming more sophisticated, approaching "virtual reality," and are being put into imaginative and cost-effective uses such as centralized training sessions though participants may be located countrywide and design and engineering prototype development. The VRML Repository is one of these resources.

> your typical AOL chat room. [Damer] expects Avatar99 to be even bigger. The changing of the millennium, Damer hopes, will drive home the reality of this emerging model of human interaction. (Alderman 1998)

This virtual reality technology will become increasingly important as Internet-based content is available over cable modems and the other inevitable high-speed delivery systems. To learn more about this emerging technology, the VRML Forum houses a collection of technical white papers; one of the best sites to visit, the VRML Repository (http://vrml.sdsc.edu) offers numerous links, bibliographies, user groups, software and hardware vendors, and technical explanations.

Software systems for the business-to-business organization will stress interconnectivity, bringing people and functions together over the Internet. The VRML Web site will be the base for e-commerce, and VRML programs will also assist the company in employee training and product sales demonstrations. Communications systems such as Lotus Notes and Domino are good examples of networking software. Corporate memory will also continue to expand with more sophisticated front-end and back-end data systems. The faster in response and the more intuitive in data manipulation, the better the company can provide customized data requests. These data repositories will be integrated into either the company Internet, intranet, or extranet for information sharing through interconnectivity and interactivity. The speed of business will only continue to accelerate.

Portal sites should continue to mature as elements of competitive advantage for search engine battles and sales collaborations, and concerning e-commerce, portals could set the technological agenda for companies that want to do business on the Web. At present, portals are simply directing shopping traffic to their e-commerce partners; in return, the portal is paid a sales commission on each e-commerce transaction. The process may become more sophisticated in the near future, with each user being sent along with a package of digital information that helps the e-merchant refine a sales pitch. On the horizon are technologies like voice recognition, personalized ads, rich-media banners voice and video streaming, and relationship-management software. Portals are going to have to lead and help their partners deploy and integrate those technologies into its system. Marketers will be wise to keep an eye on portal development and to consider becoming e-commerce partners with the Web portal. (Krochmal 1998)

The Success of Internet Acquisitions and Mergers

The late 1990s saw a flurry of interest in Internet properties by investors and Internet competitors that caused a merger and acquisition frenzy. The large Internet and media companies developed vertical integration strategies amassing new media specialists such as browsers, search engines, e-mail, and other e-commerce entities in an effort to secure beach heads in American homes. These acquisitions totaled in the multibillion dollar range, and many investors were uncertain of the true value of Internet businesses. This doubt did not prevent the culmination of the following business acquisitions.

- Walt Disney Company's partnership with search-engine turned Web portal company Infoseek Corp
- NBC acquiring a minority stake in Snap!, an Internet portal service owned by CNET
- The merger of cable Internet service provider @Home and Web portal Excite
- The $4.2 billion dollar marriage of AOL and Web browser Netscape Communications

If these combinations are successful and profitable, Internet companies will make more and larger investments in Internet technology and systems. Better systems will benefit the consumer, e-marketer, and e-merchant through the qualities of convenience, speed, accuracy, and accessibility. *Wired News* made these observations shortly after the AOL/Netscape combination was announced:

> How will a combined Netscape AOL change the experience of Joe Net User? Don't expect hair-raising changes in Netscape's browser software or AOL's online service, analysts and Net watchers say. Instead, the changes will be more invisible but much more than differences in the Net's look-and-feel.
>
> "In many ways, Steve Case is co-captain with Bill Gates of the ship driving the future of the Internet," said Jeff Chaster, executive director of the Center for Media Education, a national nonprofit seeking an improvement of the quality of electronic media. "AOL is leader in developing innovative e-commerce strategies. Everything becomes an opportunity to market and sell. So, when a company like AOL takes hold of a major portal such as Netcenter, the commercial imperatives will change the nature of

> that service." Chaster mainly sees the buyout as a new accumulation of portal power. The news gives Chaster concern that the Web may meet its greatest destiny as an endless home shopping network.
>
> Hyperbole perhaps, but analysts agree that the alliance would give AOL a new line to a different segment of Net users and therefore wider clients for its e-commerce plans. "In order to reach more Web savvy users—as well as target the 75 percent of U.S. homes that have yet to come online—AOL needs a Web presence, and would likely try to leverage Netcenter [Netscape's portal site] to do that," said Yankee Group analyst Melissa Bane. "What's often missed about the company is they do understand what's important in the consumer online market," added Bane's colleague at the Yankee Group, Joe Bartlett. "It's not really reliable access [that matters], it's primarily user interface and being able to get some usability out of it." (Oakes 1998)

From a business standpoint, these mergers do appear wise. An analyst from the investment firm Brown Brothers Harriman noted, "The network television and cable TV companies, and even the phone telecommunications companies, are all searching for content partners, and eventually portal companies with interactive marketing or a loyal registered user base that can be converted into subscribers." (The Internet: A look ahead 1999)

The Persistence in Serving the Consumer

Competition will drive marketers to search high and low for competitive advantage. Again, they will leverage the strength of the Internet medium—speed, accuracy, accessibility, personalization, and convenience to the consumer—and will serve marketers in ways unimaginable. The marketer will become an information technologist, delving more into information retrieval and information delivery and applying the same framework as he develops creative promotional programs as well as information dissemination. This is an important ability to balance because knowing what should be done is equal to knowing how the program should be implemented. The marketer will need to be schooled in a new science of Internet media habits, a topic dating only from the mid nineties. This developing consumer behavior is crucial in planning for access propensity. How consumers will access the Internet is as important to know as the consumer's print or broadcast media habits. A message is wasted if the target watches only cable television while the marketer has placed all advertising on broadcast television or on the wrong search engine's home page. This circles back to whether or not the Web is to be PC computer-driven, WebTV-accessed, a mobile telephone, or another on-the-drawing boards appliance.

The marketer must give consideration to user-friendly marketing processes. Some sage advice concerning Web publishing was shared among a Jupiter Research Conference audience by Patrick Naughton, senior vice president of technology, Starwave Corporation, Seattle. These suggestions are equally critical to marketers with large and small customers bases.

- Do things in as few ways as possible. (User-friendly systems)
- Design systems for a hundred times your current load. (Capacity)
- Move quickly but cautiously on new technology, and don't jump on the newest and coolest just because it's new and cool. (Investigate technology, but don't forsake your customers' best interests.)

- Put your best people closest to the money even if those aren't typically the highest-paying positions. (An interpretation of "money" could be the customer sales opportunities to which the "best people" should be assigned) In a marketing paradigm, put good systems together with good people, and your customers will benefit. (ClickZ 1998)

Consumer Concerns Will Continue

As potentially powerful as the Internet, there are several crucial issues that the Internet-based industry must face and resolve. These problems were reported in the GVU Eighth User Survey, 1997, and have continued to be voiced in the Ninth and the soon-to-be-published Tenth User Surveys:

Privacy	30.5 percent
Censorship	24.2 percent
Navigation	16.6 percent

As for e-commerce, security remains one of the top reasons Web users report for not purchasing over the Web (cited as "not trusting that my credit card number will be secure," 39.1 percent, and "not being able to judge the quality of the product," 39.3 percent). The opinion of not trusting that personal information will be kept private (26.9 percent) followed, with the opinion of the ability of the respondent being able to find the product faster/easier by shopping locally (22.6 percent) close behind. Supporting the notion that the Web has become an important tool to access information, 84 percent of the users report that they consider access to the Web indispensable, nearly the same percentage as those who feel e-mail is indispensable. That a technology could become so vital in such a short period is truly an awesome statement of the impact of the Web on our society. (GVU Eight and Ninth WWW User Surveys 1997, 1998)

E-Commerce Overconfidence

For all the studies and discussions of electronic marketing and electronic commerce, you should remember that e-marketing is not the easy way out, only an alternative strategy amid the hard work of marketing. E-marketing's efforts must be integrated among traditional promotional and sales programs to enhance the synergy gained by attentive and sensitive marketing activities. Remember the following comment regarding the nature of the Web:

> The Net, by its very nature, is hostile to profit margins. Most investors seem to believe that the Internet will someday produce unusually rich returns because it is a cheaper way to reach customers, without onerous expenses such as paper record keeping, bricks-and-mortar shops, and piled up inventory. Yet the very things that attract users to the Internet—speed, convenience, and unlimited breadth—make it treacherous for profit-hungry merchants. With just a few keystrokes, consumers can play business rivals against each other. That ability is turning the Net into a relentlessly efficient market in which vendors will be hard pressed to win, and defend, any lasting advantage. (Anders 1998)

Bill Gates' Twelve New Rules

In the Microsoft chairman's second book, *Business @the Speed of Thought,* a logical premise is supported throughout the book that only managers who master the digital universe will gain competitive advantage.

> The successful companies of the next decade will be the ones that use digital tools to reinvent the way they work. To make digital information flow an intrinsic part of your company, here are twelve key steps:
>
> 1. **Insist That Communication Flow through E-mail**
> Personal initiative and responsibility are enhanced in an environment that fosters discussion. E-mail, a key component of our digital nervous system, does just that. It helps turn middle managers from information filters into "doers."
> 2. **Study Sales Data Online to Share Insights Easily**
> You need to gather your business' data at every step of the way and in every interaction with your customers. With your partners, too. Then you need to understand what the data means. When figures are in electronic form, knowledge workers can study them, annotate them, look at them in any amount of detail or in any view they want and pass them around for collaboration. Going digital changes your business.
> 3. **Shift Knowledge Workers into High-Level Thinking**
> A company's middle managers and line employees, not just its high-level executives, need to see business data. They're the people who need precise, actionable data because they're the ones who need to act. They need an immediate, constant flow and rich views of the right information. Companies should spend less time protecting financial data from employees and more time teaching them to analyze and act on it.
> 4. **Use Digital Tools to Create Virtual Teams**
> A collaborative culture reinforced by information flow makes it possible for smart people all over a company to stay in touch with each other. When you get a critical mass of high IQ people working in concert, the energy level shoots way up. You're managing data, documents, and people's efforts. Your aim should be to enhance the way people work together, share ideas, sometimes wrangle and build on one another's ideas—and then act in concert for a common purpose.
> 5. **Convert Every Paper Process into a Digital Process**
> Paper consumption [is] only a symptom of a bigger problem: administrative processes that were too complicated and time-intensive. Using our intranet to replace paper forms has produced striking results for us. From more than 1000 [before] to a company-wide total of 60 forms [now]. When employees see a company eliminate bottlenecks and time-draining routine chores from their workdays, they know the company values their time—and wants them to use it properly.
> 6. **Use Digital Tools to Eliminate Single-Task Jobs**
> In the new organization, the worker is no longer a cog in the machine but is an intelligent part of the overall process. Having people focus on whole processes allows them to tackle more interesting, challenging work. A one-dimensional [repetitive] job can be eliminated, automated, or rolled into a bigger process.

7. **Create a Digital Feedback Loop**
   Digital technology makes it possible to develop much better processes instead of being stuck with variations on old paper processes that give you only incremental improvements. You need to be flexible in the face of evolving requirements. You should have a crisp decision process to evaluate change, including a provision for re-evaluating your original project goals.

8. **Use Digital Systems to Route Customer Complaints Immediately**
   Listening to customers means hearing their complaints about current product shortcomings. But getting bad news from customers passed all the way to product design groups is surprisingly hard to do. I recommend the following approach:

   1. Focus on your most unhappy customers.
   2. Use technology to gather rich information on their unhappy experiences with your product and to find out what they want you to put into the product.
   3. Use technology to drive the news to the right people in a hurry.

   If you do these three things, you'll turn those draining bad news experiences into an exhilarating process of improving your product or service. Unhappy customers are always a concern. They're also your greatest opportunity.

9. **Use Digital Communications to Redefine the Boundaries**
   For Microsoft, outsourcing has been a way to temper the expansion of our workforce and reduce management overhead, but it hasn't stopped the growth of our workforce. The Web work style, in which each contributor or company organizes itself optimally, enables us to extend our electronic web of partnerships and—I hope—keeps us from growing big in the wrong areas and becoming ineffective through too much overhead.

10. **Transform Every Business Process into Just-in-Time Delivery**
    Producers of bits can use the Internet to reduce their delivery times to practically zero. Producers of atoms [physical products] still can team the physical objects through space, but they can use bitspeed—digital coordination of all kinds—to bring reaction time dramatically. Unfortunately, the most important "speed" issue for a company is cultural. It's changing the perceptions within a company about the rapidity with which everyone has to move. Everyone must realize that if you don't meet customer demand quickly enough, without sacrificing quality, a competitor will.

11. **Use Digital Delivery to Eliminate the Middle Man**
    If you're a middleman, the Internet's promise of cheaper prices and faster service can **"disintermediate"** you, eliminate your role of assisting the transaction between the producer and the consumer. If the Internet is about to disintermediate you, one tact is to use the Internet to get back into action. For the majority of products, which are available through many outlets, customers will be the greatest beneficiaries [of auction/liquidation-like pricing on weekly e-mailings]. For many products and services, sellers will find more potential customers and may command higher prices. The more consumers adopt the Web lifestyle, the closer the economy will move toward Adam Smith's perfect market in all areas of commerce.

12. **Use Digital Tools to Help Customers Solve Problems for Themselves**
    As electronic commerce booms, it's not just the middlemen who will find

> creative ways to use the Internet to strengthen their relationships and customers. The merchants who treat e-commerce as more than a digital cash register will do the best. Smart companies will combine Internet services and personal contact in programs that give their customers the benefits of both kinds of interaction. You want to move pure transactions to the Internet, use online communications for information sharing and routine communications, and reserve face-to-face interactions for those activities that add the most value. (Gates 1999)

Key Terms

Asynchronous Transfer Mode (ATM)

Avatar

Convergence

"Disintermediate"

Feedback loop

Internet appliance

Internet2

Large Scale Networking (LSN)

Local Area Network (LAN)

Metropolitan Area Network (MAN)

Next Generation Internet Initiatives (NGI)

Quality of service (QOS)

Test bed

Texture maps

Value chain

Virtual proximity

Virtual Reality Modeling Language (VRML)

Wide Area Network (WAN)

QUESTIONS AND EXERCISES

1. In putting all the supporting and conflicting information into a semblance of order, marketers will have to consider the rank importance of four factors or consequences that electronic marketing may influence or may be influenced by: 1) the evolution of technology, 2) the expansion of software, 3) the success of Internet acquisitions and mergers, and 4) the driving desire for marketers to better serve their customers. In terms of electronic commerce, which factor would you consider to be most affected by e-marketing over the next decade? Specify samples to support your contention. Write a one-page memo to your strategic planning manager alerting her of future marketing forces.

2. Assuming the Next Generation Internet Initiatives are successful and achieve the noted goals, what benefits should the small e-merchant expect from the project? What should the large national marketer expect from the project? Make a list of benefits and explain

why these benefits are important to each group. Be prepared to discuss your thoughts in class.

3. The NGI will foster partnerships among academia, industry, and governments (federal, state, local, and foreign) that will keep the United States at the cutting-edge of information and communications technologies. This is a lofty objective for the project. In your opinion, what are the advantages and the disadvantages of these three groups (academia, industry, and government), which have different agendas and expectations from NGI, working together? Prepare your thoughts as a three-minute speech to be given to a MIS department at a state university.

4. Do research on the benefits and disadvantages of analog versus digital data transmission. This research refers to the technology, Asynchronous Transfer Mode. Why is ATM expected to be the technology of choice for the NGI? Summarize the benefits and disadvantages in a one-page memo and e-mail it to your instructor.

5. How are ATM technology, Web portals, and e-commerce tied together? Describe buying products or services by entering a portal. What is the process from entering to exiting the portal? Write a one-page explanation of online portal purchasing.

6. In the text, one vision of a future Internet appliance for accessing the Web was discussed. What would be your description of a consumer-oriented Internet tool that you would like to use? List the features and explain why each might appeal to the average consumer. Develop a one-page memo.

7. Describe how you see programming languages such as VRML and Java enhancing Web designs and graphics of the future. Is there a danger that Web sites may be designed more for entertainment than for commerce purposes? Make a list of five commerce objectives that you would expect your Web designers to follow in preparing company Web sites. Write it as an internal company memo.

8. In the next decade, do you envision consumers becoming more or less concerned with privacy, privileged information selling, or abuses of fraudulent e-merchant transactions? Address each situation and express your thoughts on consumer reactions; write a letter to the editor of your local newspaper describing your support or concerns.

9. You will remember this comment: "The Net, by its very nature, is hostile to profit margins." What is the basis for making this comment? How as an e-marketer would you plan strategically to foil the Net in this context? Write a one-page strategy statement that would deal with a commercial Web site selling autographed photos of celebrities or mounted posters from the classical movie era.

10. Of Bill Gates' twelve new rules, which one do you as an e-marketer agree with most, and how do you plan to integrate it into your e-commerce practices? Which rule do you disagree with most, and why do you object? Write each explanation as a book review for reference by your marketing manager. Make your opinions one page in length.

Bibliography

The Advanced Information Services Demonstration, a cooperative program within NATO. 1996.

Alderman, John. 1998. From earth to avatars. *Wired News* [cited online 23 November].

Anders, George. 1998. Comparison shopping is the Web's virtue—unless you're a seller. *The Wall Street Journal*, 23 July, A1.

Anthes, Gary H. 1997. Strain for 'net gain. *Computer World* [cited online 6 September].

ClickZ. 1998. Jupiter Conference. 13 August.

Gates, William H. 1999. *Business @the speed of thought.* New York: Warner Books.

GVU Eighth WWW User Survey. 1997. [Online] Atlanta, GA.

GVU Ninth WWW User Survey. 1998. [Online]. Atlanta, GA.

The Internet: A look ahead. 1999. *CNN Financial Network* [cited online 19 January].
Isaacson, Walter. 1997. . . . driven by the passion of Intel's Andrew Grove. *Time*, 29 December, 50.
Krochmal, Mo. 1998. Portals could take tech leadership role. *TechWeb* [cited online 17 November].
Oakes, Chris. 1998. For Joe Net, more consumption. *Wired News* [cited online 23 November].
Yakirevich, Alex. 1999. FVC.com: Trailblazing next generation Internet. *Individual Online Investor* [cited online 29 January].

APPENDICES

Marketing Exercises and Other Resources

Appendix A: An outline for an online marketing and promotional program
Appendix B: Geo-demographic data and assignment worksheet
Appendix C: Internet Marketing Resources
Appendix D: Situation Analysis Questionnaire for Business Interview

Appendix A: Electronic Marketing Project Outline

I. Introduction

  A. Summary of proposed project

  B. Objectives of marketing project (What are your objectives and why?)

  C. Team members and project responsibilities

II. Situation Analysis

  A. Relevant market research/input

    1. Define what information you require.

    2. Is that information available?

    3. Where can you obtain this necessary information?

  B. Proposed market description

  C. New product or service explanation

  D. Environmental factors and market trends

  E. Statistics, customer category characteristics, and demographics/psychographics

  F. Company history and/or competencies (if applicable)

  G. Competitive analysis and evaluation

  H. Assessment of niche opportunity

III. Marketing planning

   A. Numeric objectives

   B. Prospect segmentation (all possible segments)

   C. Market targeting (develop measures and profiles of possible market segments to enter)

   D. Benefits analysis and statement of benefits chosen

   E. Product positioning (establish the image or benefits valued by each segment)

   F. Assumptions

   G. Defining the marketing strategy by marketing Ps

      1. Prospect profile (Which segment(s) selected and why?)

      2. Product/service definition

      3. Price strategy

      4. Distribution (What is your sales plan?)

      5. Promotion strategy

         a. creative platform (selecting and translating selling proposition)

         b. creative strategy (rationale for selecting communications appeals)

            1) source selection

            2) message(s) selection

            3) media channel(s) selection (primary and support)

         c. select mix of promotion elements

            1) online communications objective(s)

            2) advertising objective(s)

            3) sales promotion objective(s) and events (consumer and/or trade if applicable)

            4) public relations objective(s)

            5) traditional direct marketing objective(s)

            6) personal selling objective(s)

         d. creative implementation and list of priority

         e. media objective(s)

         f. media strategy

         g. media budget and schedules

   H. Master marketing budget and rationale

IV. Marketing implementation

   A. Customer/prospect tracking strategy and report format

   B. Customer service communications and feedback strategy and report format

C. Setting operations, financial, and marketing priorities for action

D. Definition of online resources, providers, and support needed

E. Assigning staff responsibilities

F. Assessing supplier needs and tasks

G. Setting twelve-month, roll-out calendar

H. Setting measuring sticks for performance

V. Summary

A. What did you learn?

B. What was a waste of time?

Examples of Marketing Planning Objectives

Marketing objectives

Usually numeric such as percent of market share, dollar sales volume, dollar sales quota per sales representative, percent of return on investment or asset, dollar sales volume per territory, so forth

Developing a marketing budget

Communications objectives, more specific and informational

Developing awareness for new products/services

Explaining benefits or usage of products

Encouraging repeat or more frequent usage of product

Reminder messages for reinforcing brand image

Defensive messages for countering new competition

Online communications objectives, still more specific

Reinforce brand or company image

Provide product/service information less expensively

Improve customer service or customer support

Gather customer opinions or survey prospects

Initiate a direct marketing/ordering program

Introduce new product or service offering

Advertising objectives, still more specific

Define product benefit and select strategy of either rational or emotional appeals

Create awareness using highly visible/highly visual media

Promote trial of product/service featuring sampling via coupons or other service trial experience

Develop ongoing customer communications vehicle using quarterly newsletter

Media objectives, usually concentrate on target profile, geographic priorities, and scheduling requirements. Targets or tactics might include some of the following:

Targeted to light, medium, or heavy product users

Women, aged 25 to 54 years

Household size 3 or more persons

Skew media support east of Mississippi

Schedule twelve months support

Set performance goal, accountable level such as GRP/TRP or CPM goals

Set allocation strategy for media expenditures, such as percent for print, percent for broadcast, percent for support media, percent for direct marketing, so forth

Appendix B: Demographic/Psychographic Profile Interpretation

You are the eastern manager of a retail furniture store, Rooms To Rent, and you have the assignment to select a central Florida location for the newest sales facility. You can select only one location and will use the Infomark geo-demographic prospect profiles as the basis for making your decision.

Rooms To Rent has been very successful renting furniture to college students and younger couples that live in apartments. You narrowed the next location either to Tampa at the University of South Florida or in Orlando at the University of Central Florida. The demographic and psychographic information has been sent to you for your traditional market area, a three-mile radius around each university. Be sure to use the three-mile data for your comparisons.

From previous experience, you research market areas looking for specific resident characteristics; from Infomark, you have received profile information modeled to 1998 from the 1990 Census. The pertinent comparisons for store selection are derived from analyzing the following questions:

Demographic Analysis

USF	UCF	Advantage	Question/Requirement
_____	_____	_____	1. Household growth must exceed 40 percent
_____	_____	_____	2. Rental units must exceed 65 percent of occupied units
_____	_____	_____	3. Per capita income must exceed $19,000
_____	_____	_____	4. Population of ages 18 to 34 years must exceed 35 percent
_____	_____	_____	5. Population by educational level (some college plus) must exceed 50 percent
_____	_____	_____	6. Occupied units must exceed 90 percent
_____	_____	_____	7. Furniture/furnishings expenditure per household must exceed 0.02 percent of income per year

Psychographic Analysis

USF	UCF	Advantage	Question/Requirement
_____	_____	_____	8. Combined percentage of clusters that mention rental apartments or housing
_____	_____	_____	9. Combined percentage of clusters that mention singles or young couples
_____	_____	_____	10. Combined percentage of clusters that mention medium to high education
_____	_____	_____	11. Combined percentage of clusters that mention medium income
_____	_____	_____	12. Combined percentage of clusters that mention students

Which geographic area will you choose? What are the major deciding factors?

Wed Mar 17, 1999

Page 1

CUSTOM SUMMARY REPORT
(POP FACTS: FULL DATA REPORT)
BY NATIONAL DECISION SYSTEMS 800-866-6510
PREPARED FOR
Electronic Marketing

3 and 6 Mile Radii of U.S.F.

	COORD: 2806296	8241321
DESCRIPTION	3.00 MILE RADIUS	6.00 MILE RADIUS
POPULATION		
2003 PROJECTION	100,281	255,197
1998 ESTIMATE	95,426	246,004
1990 CENSUS	88,175	234,511
1980 CENSUS	65,916	193,513
GROWTH 1980-1990	33.77%	21.19%
HOUSEHOLDS		
2003 PROJECTION	42,820	104,222
1998 ESTIMATE	40,449	100,032
1990 CENSUS	36,990	95,230
1980 CENSUS	26,060	74,620
GROWTH 1980-1990	41.94%	27.62%
1998 ESTIMATED POPULATION BY RACE	95,426	246,004
WHITE	74.79%	73.14%
BLACK	18.76%	21.75%
ASIAN & PACIFIC ISLANDER	3.13%	2.25%
OTHER RACES	3.32%	2.86%
1998 ESTIMATED POPULATION	95,426	246,004
HISPANIC ORIGIN	14.47%	13.87%
OCCUPIED UNITS	36,990	95,230
OWNER OCCUPIED	36.05%	53.22%
RENTER OCCUPIED	63.95%	46.78%
1990 AVERAGE PERSONS PER HH	2.26	2.40
1998 EST. HOUSEHOLDS BY INCOME	40,449	100,032
$150,000 OR MORE	3.18%	3.03%
$100,000 TO $149,999	3.93%	4.51%
$ 75,000 TO $ 99,999	5.53%	6.54%
$ 50,000 TO $ 74,999	14.83%	16.53%
$ 35,000 TO $ 49,999	15.41%	16.27%
$ 25,000 TO $ 34,999	14.99%	14.68%
$ 15,000 TO $ 24,999	19.81%	18.04%
$ 5,000 TO $ 15,000	16.79%	15.50%
UNDER $ 5,000	5.52%	4.89%
1998 EST. AVERAGE HOUSEHOLD INCOME	$44,186	$46,752
1998 EST. MEDIAN HOUSEHOLD INCOME	$30,254	$32,883
1998 EST. PER CAPITA INCOME	$19,001	$19,130

Wed Mar 17, 1999 Page 2

CUSTOM SUMMARY REPORT
(POP FACTS: FULL DATA REPORT)
BY NATIONAL DECISION SYSTEMS 800-866-6510
PREPARED FOR
Electronic Marketing

3 and 6 Mile Radii of U.S.F.

DESCRIPTION	COORD: 2806296 3.00 MILE RADIUS	8241321 6.00 MILE RADIUS
1998 ESTIMATED POPULATION BY SEX	95,426	246,004
MALE	48.76%	48.12%
FEMALE	51.24%	51.88%
MARITAL STATUS	71,846	187,658
SINGLE MALE	20.36%	16.28%
SINGLE FEMALE	17.70%	14.23%
MARRIED	41.10%	47.24%
PREVIOUSLY MARRIED MALE	7.37%	7.50%
PREVIOUSLY MARRIED FEMALE	13.47%	14.75%
HOUSEHOLDS WITH CHILDREN	10,873	30,809
MARRIED COUPLE FAMILY	59.78%	62.84%
OTHER FAMILY-MALE HEAD	6.66%	6.12%
OTHER FAMILY-FEMALE HEAD	31.37%	29.30%
NON FAMILY	2.19%	1.75%
1998 ESTIMATED POPULATION BY AGE	95,426	246,004
UNDER 5 YEARS	6.96%	7.07%
5 TO 9 YEARS	6.94%	7.18%
10 TO 14 YEARS	6.17%	6.54%
15 TO 17 YEARS	3.05%	3.55%
18 TO 20 YEARS	5.74%	4.34%
21 TO 24 YEARS	8.03%	5.95%
25 TO 29 YEARS	10.01%	8.46%
30 TO 34 YEARS	9.91%	8.53%
35 TO 39 YEARS	9.16%	8.68%
40 TO 49 YEARS	14.00%	15.16%
50 TO 59 YEARS	8.49%	10.00%
60 TO 64 YEARS	2.74%	3.39%
65 TO 69 YEARS	2.27%	2.92%
70 TO 74 YEARS	2.09%	2.79%
75+ YEARS	4.45%	5.43%
MEDIAN AGE	31.56	34.05
AVERAGE AGE	33.48	35.38

Wed Mar 17, 1999

Page 3

CUSTOM SUMMARY REPORT
(POP FACTS: FULL DATA REPORT)
BY NATIONAL DECISION SYSTEMS 800-866-6510
PREPARED FOR
Electronic Marketing

3 and 6 Mile Radii of U.S.F.

DESCRIPTION	COORD: 2806296 3.00 MILE RADIUS	8241321 6.00 MILE RADIUS
1998 ESTIMATED FEMALE POP. BY AGE	48,896	127,617
UNDER 5 YEARS	6.76%	6.77%
5 TO 9 YEARS	6.71%	6.79%
10 TO 14 YEARS	5.89%	6.16%
15 TO 17 YEARS	2.97%	3.35%
18 TO 20 YEARS	6.34%	4.48%
21 TO 24 YEARS	8.00%	5.87%
25 TO 29 YEARS	9.43%	8.16%
30 TO 34 YEARS	9.58%	8.33%
35 TO 39 YEARS	8.87%	8.54%
40 TO 49 YEARS	13.58%	14.95%
50 TO 59 YEARS	8.64%	10.04%
60 TO 64 YEARS	2.76%	3.44%
65 TO 69 YEARS	2.43%	3.09%
70 TO 74 YEARS	2.30%	3.16%
75+ YEARS	5.74%	6.87%
FEMALE MEDIAN AGE	32.04	35.05
FEMALE AVERAGE AGE	34.42	36.62
POPULATION BY HOUSEHOLD TYPE	88,175	234,511
FAMILY HOUSEHOLDS	68.30%	77.04%
NON-FAMILY HOUSEHOLDS	26.52%	20.51%
GROUP QUARTERS	5.17%	2.45%
HOUSEHOLDS BY TYPE	36,990	95,230
SINGLE MALE	16.28%	13.16%
SINGLE FEMALE	15.58%	15.23%
MARRIED COUPLE	37.23%	44.05%
OTHER FAMILY-MALE HEAD	3.90%	3.80%
OTHER FAMILY-FEMALE HEAD	12.93%	13.82%
NON FAMILY-MALE HEAD	8.59%	6.04%
NON FAMILY-FEMALE HEAD	5.48%	3.91%
POPULATION BY URBAN VS. RURAL	88,102	234,651
URBAN	100.00%	98.54%
RURAL	0.00%	1.46%

Wed Mar 17, 1999 Page 4

CUSTOM SUMMARY REPORT
(POP FACTS: FULL DATA REPORT)
BY NATIONAL DECISION SYSTEMS 800-866-6510
PREPARED FOR
Electronic Marketing

3 and 6 Mile Radii of U.S.F.

	COORD: 2806296	8241321
DESCRIPTION	3.00 MILE RADIUS	6.00 MILE RADIUS
FEMALES 16+ WITH CHILDREN 0-17: BASE	36,492	97,322
WORKING WITH CHILD 0-5	5.77%	5.35%
NOT WORKING WITH CHILD 0-5	0.64%	0.51%
NOT IN LABOR FORCE WITH CHILD 0-5	2.37%	3.00%
WORKING WITH CHILD 6-17	9.62%	11.05%
NOT WORKING WITH CHILD 6-17	0.57%	0.54%
NOT IN LAB. FORCE WITH CHILD 6-17	3.03%	3.07%
WORKING WITH CHILD 0-5 & 6-18	3.21%	3.28%
NOT WORKING WITH CHILD 0-5 & 6-18	0.30%	0.24%
NOT IN LAB. FORCE W/CHILD 0-5 & 6-18	1.74%	1.83%
WORKING WITH NO CHILDREN	42.26%	39.37%
NOT WORKING WITH NO CHILDREN	2.57%	2.21%
NOT IN LAB. FORCE WITH NO CHILD.	27.91%	29.54%
HH BY AGE BY POVERTY STATUS	36,893	95,318
ABOVE POVERTY UNDER AGE 65	71.67%	70.66%
ABOVE POVERTY AGE 651	9.73%	13.63%
BELOW POVERTY UNDER AGE 65	16.67%	12.64%
BELOW POVERTY AGE 651	1.93%	3.07%
POPULATION 16+ BY EMPLOYMENT STATUS	71,008	185,027
EMPLOYED IN ARMED FORCES	0.18%	0.19%
EMPLOYED CIVILIANS	66.56%	65.10%
UNEMPLOYED CIVILIANS	4.54%	4.06%
NOT IN LABOR FORCE	28.73%	30.66%
POPULATION 16+ BY OCCUPATION	47,261	120,444
EXECUTIVE AND MANAGERIAL	11.37%	11.94%
PROFESSIONAL SPECIALTY	14.93%	14.66%
TECHNICAL SUPPORT	5.03%	4.49%
SALES	13.57%	13.97%
ADMINISTRATIVE SUPPORT	18.62%	18.43%
SERVICE: PRIVATE HOUSEHOLD	0.20%	0.41%
SERVICE: PROTECTIVE	2.13%	2.10%
SERVICE: OTHER	12.02%	11.14%
FARMING FORESTRY & FISHING	1.52%	1.56%
PRECISION PRODUCTION & CRAFT	9.62%	9.66%
MACHINE OPERATOR	3.55%	3.91%
TRANS. AND MATERIAL MOVING	3.87%	3.99%
LABORERS	3.58%	3.75%

Wed Mar 17, 1999

Page 5

CUSTOM SUMMARY REPORT
(POP FACTS: FULL DATA REPORT)
BY NATIONAL DECISION SYSTEMS 800-866-6510
PREPARED FOR
Electronic Marketing

3 and 6 Mile Radii of U.S.F.

COORD:	2806296	8241321
DESCRIPTION	3.00 MILE RADIUS	6.00 MILE RADIUS
FAMILIES BY NUMBER OF WORKERS	20,213	59,283
NO WORKERS	10.50%	12.01%
ONE WORKER	30.17%	28.99%
TWO WORKERS	48.99%	47.52%
THREE1 WORKERS	10.34%	11.47%
HISPANIC POPULATION BY TYPE	88,175	234,511
NOT HISPANIC	89.76%	89.82%
MEXICAN	0.98%	0.72%
PUERTO RICAN	3.94%	3.23%
CUBAN	1.74%	2.30%
OTHER HISPANIC	3.59%	3.92%
1998 HISPANICS BY RACE: BASE	13,811	34,129
WHITE	74.79%	77.38%
BLACK	4.77%	4.64%
ASIAN	0.75%	0.60%
OTHER	19.69%	17.38%
POPULATION BY TRANSPORTATION TO WORK	46,303	118,244
DRIVE ALONE	75.17%	77.44%
CAR POOL	14.86%	13.90%
PUBLIC TRANSPORTATION	2.47%	2.20%
DRIVE MOTORCYCLE	0.44%	0.40%
WALKED ONLY	3.88%	2.62%
OTHER MEANS	1.71%	1.44%
WORKED AT HOME	1.47%	2.00%
POPULATION BY TRAVEL TIME TO WORK	46,303	118,244
UNDER 10 MINUTES/WORK AT HOME	17.85%	14.37%
10 TO 29 MINUTES	53.34%	56.75%
30 TO 59 MINUTES	25.93%	25.65%
60 TO 89 MINUTES	2.28%	2.53%
901 MINUTES	0.59%	0.70%
AVERAGE TRAVEL TIME IN MINUTES	20.46	21.22
HOUSEHOLDS BY NO. OF VEHICLES	37,024	95,243
NO VEHICLES	10.24%	10.05%
1 VEHICLE	45.15%	40.64%
2 VEHICLES	34.85%	37.14%
3+ VEHICLES	9.77%	12.17%
ESTIMATED TOTAL VEHICLES	54,090	146,541

Wed Mar 17, 1999 Page 6

CUSTOM SUMMARY REPORT
(POP FACTS: FULL DATA REPORT)
BY NATIONAL DECISION SYSTEMS 800-866-6510
PREPARED FOR
Electronic Marketing

3 and 6 Mile Radii of U.S.F.

	COORD: 2806296	8241321
DESCRIPTION	3.00 MILE RADIUS	6.00 MILE RADIUS
POPULATION 25+ BY EDUCATION LEVEL	52,205	148,629
ELEMENTARY (0-8)	6.16%	7.62%
SOME HIGH SCHOOL (9-11)	12.55%	15.17%
HIGH SCHOOL GRADUATE (12)	26.84%	27.84%
SOME COLLEGE (13-15)	20.58%	19.71%
ASSOCIATES DEGREE ONLY	9.50%	7.98%
BACHELORS DEGREE ONLY	16.10%	14.05%
GRADUATE DEGREE	8.27%	7.65%
POPULATION ENROLLED IN SCHOOL	27,592	63,279
PUBLIC PRE-PRIMARY	3.00%	3.46%
PRIVATE PRE-PRIMARY	2.81%	3.79%
PUBLIC ELEM/HIGH	35.59%	47.33%
PRIVATE ELEM/HIGH	4.62%	6.69%
ENROLLED IN COLLEGE	53.97%	38.74%
HOUSING UNITS BY OCCUPANCY STATUS	45,638	110,412
OCCUPIED	81.05%	86.25%
VACANT	18.95%	13.75%
VACANT UNITS	8,649	15,183
FOR RENT	75.25%	61.04%
FOR SALE ONLY	7.02%	12.95%
SEASONAL	3.23%	4.77%
OTHER	14.50%	21.24%
OWNER OCCUPIED PROPERTY VALUES	10,545	42,379
UNDER $25,000	2.39%	4.03%
$25,000 TO $49,999	22.78%	25.11%
$50,000 TO $74,999	34.42%	32.82%
$75,000 TO $99,999	15.14%	16.73%
$100,000 TO $149,999	12.28%	11.72%
$150,000 TO $199,999	6.88%	4.71%
$200,000 TO $299,999	4.43%	3.26%
$300,000 TO $399,999	0.92%	0.77%
$400,000 TO $499,999	0.31%	0.29%
$500,000+	0.46%	0.56%
MEDIAN PROPERTY VALUE	$68,030	$65,889
TOTAL RENTAL UNITS	23,230	43,256
MEDIAN RENT	$363	$359

Wed Mar 17, 1999

Page 7

CUSTOM SUMMARY REPORT
(POP FACTS: FULL DATA REPORT)
BY NATIONAL DECISION SYSTEMS 800-866-6510
PREPARED FOR
Electronic Marketing

3 and 6 Mile Radii of U.S.F.

	COORD: 2806296	8241321
DESCRIPTION	3.00 MILE RADIUS	6.00 MILE RADIUS
PERSONS IN UNIT	36,990	95,230
1 PERSON UNITS	31.86%	28.39%
2 PERSON UNITS	35.16%	34.45%
3 PERSON UNITS	16.23%	17.23%
4 PERSON UNITS	11.17%	12.55%
5 PERSON UNITS	3.83%	4.86%
6 PERSON UNITS	1.15%	1.54%
71 UNITS	0.59%	0.99%
YEAR ROUND UNITS IN STRUCTURE	45,638	110,412
SINGLE UNITS DETACHED	28.51%	48.37%
SINGLE UNITS ATTACHED	3.28%	3.27%
DOUBLE UNITS	7.49%	5.48%
3 TO 9 UNITS	22.63%	15.61%
10 TO 19 UNITS	18.34%	11.89%
20 TO 49 UNITS	9.75%	6.01%
501 UNITS	4.36%	2.83%
MOBILE HOME OR TRAILER	4.72%	5.56%
ALL OTHER	0.93%	1.00%
SINGLE/MULTIPLE UNIT RATIO	0.51	1.24
HOUSING UNITS BY YEAR BUILT	37,024	95,243
BUILT 1989 TO MARCH 1990	2.47%	1.97%
BUILT 1985 TO 1988	17.49%	13.40%
BUILT 1980 TO 1984	21.98%	17.74%
BUILT 1970 TO 1979	30.76%	26.38%
BUILT 1960 TO 1969	16.06%	17.08%
BUILT 1950 TO 1959	8.93%	13.79%
BUILT 1940 TO 1949	1.58%	4.67%
BUILT 1939 OR EARLIER	0.73%	4.96%

Wed Mar 17, 1999 Page 8

CUSTOM SUMMARY REPORT
(RETAIL TRADE POTENTIAL REPORT - CURRENT YEAR SALES BY STORE TYPE))
BY NATIONAL DECISION SYSTEMS 800-866-6510
PREPARED FOR
Electronic Marketing

3 and 6 Mile Radii of U.S.F.

	COORD: 2806296	8241321
DESCRIPTION	3.00 MILE RADIUS	6.00 MILE RADIUS
FAMILIES BY NUMBER OF WORKERS	20,213	59,283
TOTAL RETAIL SALES	$1,148	$2,840
APPAREL & ACCESSORY STORES	$45	$111
AUTOMOTIVE DEALERS	$307	$765
AUTOMOTIVE & HOME SUPPLY STORES	$18	$43
DRUG & PROPRIETARY STORES	$42	$107
EATING & DRINKING PLACES	$107	$263
FOOD STORES	$173	$428
FURNITURE & HOME FURNISHINGS STORES	$32	$81
HOME APPLIANCE, RADIO, & T.V. STORES	$36	$88
GASOLINE SERVICE STATIONS	$59	$146
GENERAL MERCHANDISE	$121	$296
DEPARTMENT STORES (INCLUDING LEASED DEPTS.)	$104	$254
HARDWARE, LUMBER & GARDEN STORES	$52	$127

($'S IN MILLIONS)

Wed Mar 17, 1999 Page 9

MicroVision AREA PROFILE REPORT

BY NATIONAL DECISION SYSTEMS 800-866-6510
PREPARED FOR
Electronic Marketing

3 and 6 Mile Radii of U.S.F.

COORD: 2806296 8241321

DESCRIPTION			6.00 MILE RADIUS 1998 HSHLDS.	PCT.	BASE 1998 HSHLDS.	PCT.	INDEX
MVG01	1	UPPER CRUST	482	0.5	3783	0.4	118
MVG01	2	LAP OF LUXURY	151	0.2	2893	0.3	48
MVG01	3	ESTABLISHED WEALTH	4190	4.2	11216	1.2	346
MVG01	4	MID-LIFE SUCCESS	1756	1.8	12402	1.3	131
MVG01	5	PROSPEROUS METRO MIX	439	0.4	10007	1.1	41
MVG01	6	GOOD FAMILY LIFE	414	0.4	7329	0.8	52
MVG06	7	COMFORTABLE TIMES	573	0.6	5338	0.6	99
MVG04	8	MOVERS AND SHAKERS	4739	4.7	18764	2.0	234
MVG03	9	BUILDING A HOME LIFE	66	0.1	490	0.1	124
MVG02	10	HOME SWEET HOME	7219	7.2	73762	8.0	91
MVG02	11	FAMILY TIES	1475	1.5	24022	2.6	57
MVG04	12	A GOOD STEP FORWARD	5077	5.1	44851	4.8	105
MVG09	13	SUCCESSFUL SINGLES	0	0.0	0	0.0	0
MVG01	14	MIDDLE YEARS	192	0.2	1690	0.2	105
MVG04	15	GREAT BEGINNINGS	9287	9.3	39111	4.2	220
MVG02	16	COUNTRY HOME FAMILIES	768	0.8	16206	1.7	44
MVG02	17	STARS AND STRIPES	0	0.0	3225	0.3	0
MVG02	18	WHITE PICKET FENCE	7908	7.9	40071	4.3	183
MVG03	19	YOUNG AND CAREFREE	43	0.0	642	0.1	62
MVG06	20	SECURE ADULTS	2024	2.0	55143	5.9	34
MVG06	21	AMERICAN CLASSICS	588	0.6	12094	1.3	45
MVG02	22	TRADITIONAL TIMES	2542	2.5	21801	2.4	108
MVG02	23	SETTLED IN	5002	5.0	119743	12.9	39
MVG08	24	CITY TIES	3189	3.2	13719	1.5	215
MVG03	25	BEDROCK AMERICA	3760	3.8	30839	3.3	113
MVG07	26	THE MATURE YEARS	78	0.1	638	0.1	114
MVG05	27	MIDDLE OF THE ROAD	240	0.2	2339	0.3	95
MVG03	28	BUILDING A FAMILY	2171	2.2	14501	1.6	139
MVG05	29	ESTABLISHING ROOTS	504	0.5	4214	0.5	111
MVG06	30	DOMESTIC DUOS	511	0.5	66480	7.2	7
MVG06	31	COUNTRY CLASSICS	46	0.0	3269	0.4	13
MVG04	32	METRO SINGLES	3269	3.3	9224	1.0	329
MVG07	33	LIVING OFF THE LAND	0	0.0	258	0.0	0
MVG04	34	BOOKS AND NEW RECRUITS	1394	1.4	1397	0.2	925
MVG02	35	BUY AMERICAN	2726	2.7	13890	1.5	182
MVG09	36	METRO MIX	0	0.0	193	0.0	0
MVG09	37	URBAN UP AND COMERS	0	0.0	10	0.0	0
MVG02	38	RUSTIC HOMESTEADERS	532	0.5	33107	3.6	15
MVG04	39	ON THEIR OWN	7383	7.4	115784	12.5	59
MVG04	40	TRYING METRO TIMES	7192	7.2	36247	3.9	184
MVG08	41	CLOSE-KNIT FAMILIES	202	0.2	2845	0.3	66
MVG08	42	TRYING RURAL TIMES	421	0.4	2940	0.3	133
MVG08	43	MANUFACTURING USA	1173	1.2	5963	0.6	182

BASE DEFINITION MSA/NEC: Tampa-St. Petersburg-Clearwater, FL

Wed Mar 17, 1999 Page 10

MicroVision AREA PROFILE REPORT

BY NATIONAL DECISION SYSTEMS 800-866-6510
PREPARED FOR
Electronic Marketing

3 and 6 Mile Radii of U.S.F.

COORD: 2806296 8241321

	6.00 MILE RADIUS		BASE		
	1998				
DESCRIPTION	HSHLDS.	PCT.	HSHLDS.	PCT.	INDEX
MVG08 44 HARD YEARS	242	0.2	972	0.1	231
MVG09 45 STRUGGLING METRO MIX	2985	3.0	5921	0.6	467
MVG08 46 DIFFICULT TIMES	4000	4.0	19306	2.1	192
MVG09 47 UNIVERSITY USA	1473	1.5	1551	0.2	880
MVG09 48 URBAN SINGLES	896	0.9	15064	1.6	55
MVG10 49 ANOMALIES	94	0.1	738	0.1	119
MVG11 50 UNCLASSIFIED	617	0.6	1296	0.1	441
TOTALS	100032	100.0	927288	100.0	100

BASE DEFINITION MSA/NEC: Tampa-St. Petersburg-Clearwater, FL

Wed Mar 17, 1999 Page 11

MicroVision AREA GROUP REPORT

BY NATIONAL DECISION SYSTEMS 800-866-6510
PREPARED FOR
Electronic Marketing

3 and 6 Mile Radii of U.S.F.

COORD: 2806296 8241321

DESCRIPTION	6.00 MILE RADIUS HSHLDS.	1998 PCT.	BASE HSHLDS.	PCT.	INDEX
MVG01 ACCUMULATED WEALTH	7623	7.6	49320	5.3	143
MVG02 MAINSTREAM FAMILIES	28171	28.2	345827	37.3	76
MVG03 YOUNG ACCUMULATORS	6039	6.0	46472	5.0	120
MVG04 MAINSTREAM SINGLES	38342	38.3	265378	28.6	134
MVG05 ASSET-BUILDING FAMILIES	744	0.7	6553	0.7	105
MVG06 CONSERVATIVE CLASSICS	3742	3.7	142324	15.3	24
MVG07 CAUTIOUS COUPLES	78	0.1	896	0.1	81
MVG08 SUSTAINING FAMILIES	9227	9.2	45745	4.9	187
MVG09 SUSTAINING SINGLES	5354	5.4	22739	2.5	218
MVG10 ANOMALIES	94	0.1	738	0.1	119
MVG11 UNCLASSIFIED	617	0.6	1296	0.1	441
TOTALS	100032	100.0	927288	100.0	100

BASE DEFINITION MSA/NEC: Tampa-St. Petersburg-Clearwater, FL

Wed Mar 17, 1999 Page 12

MicroVision AREA PROFILE REPORT

BY NATIONAL DECISION SYSTEMS 800-866-6510
PREPARED FOR
Electronic Marketing

3 and 6 Mile Radii of U.S.F.

COORD: 2806296 8241321

DESCRIPTION		3.00 MILE RADIUS HSHLDS. 1998	PCT.	BASE HSHLDS.	PCT.	INDEX
MVG01	1 UPPER CRUST	473	1.2	3783	0.4	287
MVG01	2 LAP OF LUXURY	18	0.0	2893	0.3	14
MVG01	3 ESTABLISHED WEALTH	790	2.0	11216	1.2	162
MVG01	4 MID-LIFE SUCCESS	713	1.8	12402	1.3	132
MVG01	5 PROSPEROUS METRO MIX	2	0.0	10007	1.1	0
MVG01	6 GOOD FAMILY LIFE	248	0.6	7329	0.8	78
MVG06	7 COMFORTABLE TIMES	155	0.4	5338	0.6	67
MVG04	8 MOVERS AND SHAKERS	1936	4.8	18764	2.0	237
MVG03	9 BUILDING A HOME LIFE	29	0.1	490	0.1	136
MVG02	10 HOME SWEET HOME	1674	4.1	73762	8.0	52
MVG02	11 FAMILY TIES	7	0.0	24022	2.6	1
MVG04	12 A GOOD STEP FORWARD	1915	4.7	44851	4.8	98
MVG09	13 SUCCESSFUL SINGLES	0	0.0	0	0.0	0
MVG01	14 MIDDLE YEARS	91	0.2	1690	0.2	124
MVG04	15 GREAT BEGINNINGS	5933	14.7	39111	4.2	348
MVG02	16 COUNTRY HOME FAMILIES	34	0.1	16206	1.7	5
MVG02	17 STARS AND STRIPES	0	0.0	3225	0.3	0
MVG02	18 WHITE PICKET FENCE	2754	6.8	40071	4.3	158
MVG03	19 YOUNG AND CAREFREE	28	0.1	642	0.1	102
MVG06	20 SECURE ADULTS	486	1.2	55143	5.9	20
MVG06	21 AMERICAN CLASSICS	425	1.1	12094	1.3	81
MVG02	22 TRADITIONAL TIMES	536	1.3	21801	2.4	56
MVG02	23 SETTLED IN	214	0.5	119743	12.9	4
MVG08	24 CITY TIES	102	0.3	13719	1.5	17
MVG03	25 BEDROCK AMERICA	1161	2.9	30839	3.3	86
MVG07	26 THE MATURE YEARS	16	0.0	638	0.1	58
MVG05	27 MIDDLE OF THE ROAD	96	0.2	2339	0.3	94
MVG03	28 BUILDING A FAMILY	970	2.4	14501	1.6	153
MVG05	29 ESTABLISHING ROOTS	227	0.6	4214	0.5	124
MVG06	30 DOMESTIC DUOS	122	0.3	66480	7.2	4
MVG06	31 COUNTRY CLASSICS	7	0.0	3269	0.4	5
MVG04	32 METRO SINGLES	2674	6.6	9224	1.0	664
MVG07	33 LIVING OFF THE LAND	0	0.0	258	0.0	0
MVG04	34 BOOKS AND NEW RECRUITS	1359	3.4	1397	0.2	2230
MVG02	35 BUY AMERICAN	296	0.7	13890	1.5	49
MVG09	36 METRO MIX	0	0.0	193	0.0	0
MVG09	37 URBAN UP AND COMERS	0	0.0	10	0.0	0
MVG02	38 RUSTIC HOMESTEADERS	29	0.1	33107	3.6	2
MVG04	39 ON THEIR OWN	5784	14.3	115784	12.5	115
MVG04	40 TRYING METRO TIMES	3228	8.0	36247	3.9	204
MVG08	41 CLOSE-KNIT FAMILIES	53	0.1	2845	0.3	42
MVG08	42 TRYING RURAL TIMES	9	0.0	2940	0.3	7
MVG08	43 MANUFACTURING USA	39	0.1	5963	0.6	15

BASE DEFINITION MSA/NEC: Tampa-St. Petersburg-Clearwater, FL

Wed Mar 17, 1999

Page 13

MicroVision AREA PROFILE REPORT

BY NATIONAL DECISION SYSTEMS 800-866-6510
PREPARED FOR
Electronic Marketing

3 and 6 Mile Radii of U.S.F.

COORD: 2806296 8241321

	3.00 MILE RADIUS		BASE		
	1998				
DESCRIPTION	HSHLDS.	PCT.	HSHLDS.	PCT.	INDEX
MVG08 44 HARD YEARS	203	0.5	972	0.1	479
MVG09 45 STRUGGLING METRO MIX	2958	7.3	5921	0.6	1145
MVG08 46 DIFFICULT TIMES	410	1.0	19306	2.1	49
MVG09 47 UNIVERSITY USA	1468	3.6	1551	0.2	2170
MVG09 48 URBAN SINGLES	133	0.3	15064	1.6	20
MVG10 49 ANOMALIES	26	0.1	738	0.1	79
MVG11 50 UNCLASSIFIED	617	1.5	1296	0.1	1091
TOTALS	40449	100.0	927288	100.0	100

BASE DEFINITION MSA/NEC: Tampa-St. Petersburg-Clearwater, FL

Wed Mar 17, 1999 Page 14

MicroVision AREA GROUP REPORT

BY NATIONAL DECISION SYSTEMS 800-866-6510
PREPARED FOR
Electronic Marketing

3 and 6 Mile Radii of U.S.F.

COORD: 2806296 8241321

DESCRIPTION	3.00 MILE RADIUS HSHLDS.	1998 PCT.	BASE HSHLDS.	PCT.	INDEX
MVG01 ACCUMULATED WEALTH	2336	5.8	49320	5.3	109
MVG02 MAINSTREAM FAMILIES	5545	13.7	345827	37.3	37
MVG03 YOUNG ACCUMULATORS	2188	5.4	46472	5.0	108
MVG04 MAINSTREAM SINGLES	22829	56.4	265378	28.6	197
MVG05 ASSET-BUILDING FAMILIES	323	0.8	6553	0.7	113
MVG06 CONSERVATIVE CLASSICS	1195	3.0	142324	15.3	19
MVG07 CAUTIOUS COUPLES	16	0.0	896	0.1	41
MVG08 SUSTAINING FAMILIES	815	2.0	45745	4.9	41
MVG09 SUSTAINING SINGLES	4560	11.3	22739	2.5	460
MVG10 ANOMALIES	26	0.1	738	0.1	79
MVG11 UNCLASSIFIED	617	1.5	1296	0.1	1091
TOTALS	40449	100.0	927288	100.0	100

BASE DEFINITION MSA/NEC: Tampa-St. Petersburg-Clearwater, FL

Wed Mar 17, 1999 Page 15

CUSTOM SUMMARY REPORT
(POP FACTS: FULL DATA REPORT)
BY NATIONAL DECISION SYSTEMS 800-866-6510
PREPARED FOR
Electronic Marketing

3 and 6 Mile Radii of U.C.F.

COORD:	2860080	8119870
DESCRIPTION	3.00 MILE RADIUS	6.00 MILE RADIUS
POPULATION		
2003 PROJECTION	42,032	162,017
1998 ESTIMATE	37,127	144,836
1990 CENSUS	26,003	105,659
1980 CENSUS	8,745	39,770
GROWTH 1980-1990	197.33%	165.68%
HOUSEHOLDS		
2003 PROJECTION	15,721	58,664
1998 ESTIMATE	13,856	52,386
1990 CENSUS	9,759	38,582
1980 CENSUS	3,218	13,905
GROWTH 1980-1990	203.27%	177.48%
1998 ESTIMATED POPULATION BY RACE	37,127	144,836
WHITE	86.75%	85.81%
BLACK	4.97%	6.45%
ASIAN & PACIFIC ISLANDER	4.94%	4.07%
OTHER RACES	3.34%	3.66%
1998 ESTIMATED POPULATION	37,127	144,836
HISPANIC ORIGIN	11.27%	13.29%
OCCUPIED UNITS	9,759	38,582
OWNER OCCUPIED	64.48%	66.84%
RENTER OCCUPIED	35.52%	33.16%
1990 AVERAGE PERSONS PER HH	2.54	2.68
1998 EST. HOUSEHOLDS BY INCOME	13,856	52,386
$150,000 OR MORE	2.44%	2.63%
$100,000 TO $149,999	5.36%	5.89%
$ 75,000 TO $ 99,999	8.97%	9.94%
$ 50,000 TO $ 74,999	20.91%	23.26%
$ 35,000 TO $ 49,999	20.54%	19.78%
$ 25,000 TO $ 34,999	12.05%	13.20%
$ 15,000 TO $ 24,999	12.44%	12.55%
$ 5,000 TO $ 15,000	13.83%	10.19%
UNDER $ 5,000	3.45%	2.55%
1998 EST. AVERAGE HOUSEHOLD INCOME	$51,104	$53,890
1998 EST. MEDIAN HOUSEHOLD INCOME	$41,007	$43,720
1998 EST. PER CAPITA INCOME	$19,196	$19,515

Wed Mar 17, 1999 Page 16

CUSTOM SUMMARY REPORT
(POP FACTS: FULL DATA REPORT)
BY NATIONAL DECISION SYSTEMS 800-866-6510
PREPARED FOR
Electronic Marketing

3 and 6 Mile Radii of U.C.F.

COORD:	2860080	8119870
DESCRIPTION	3.00 MILE RADIUS	6.00 MILE RADIUS
1998 ESTIMATED POPULATION BY SEX	37,127	144,836
MALE	51.49%	50.51%
FEMALE	48.51%	49.49%
MARITAL STATUS	21,529	83,653
SINGLE MALE	21.93%	16.82%
SINGLE FEMALE	15.37%	12.42%
MARRIED	50.63%	56.69%
PREVIOUSLY MARRIED MALE	4.55%	5.24%
PREVIOUSLY MARRIED FEMALE	7.51%	8.82%
HOUSEHOLDS WITH CHILDREN	2,930	14,640
MARRIED COUPLE FAMILY	80.13%	79.83%
OTHER FAMILY-MALE HEAD	5.38%	4.72%
OTHER FAMILY-FEMALE HEAD	12.88%	14.06%
NON FAMILY	1.61%	1.39%
1998 ESTIMATED POPULATION BY AGE	37,127	144,836
UNDER 5 YEARS	6.57%	7.29%
5 TO 9 YEARS	6.80%	7.32%
10 TO 14 YEARS	6.14%	6.96%
15 TO 17 YEARS	3.13%	3.82%
18 TO 20 YEARS	7.84%	4.99%
21 TO 24 YEARS	8.85%	6.56%
25 TO 29 YEARS	8.65%	8.73%
30 TO 34 YEARS	8.91%	8.73%
35 TO 39 YEARS	9.30%	9.10%
40 TO 49 YEARS	13.22%	15.61%
50 TO 59 YEARS	7.40%	9.18%
60 TO 64 YEARS	2.86%	3.18%
65 TO 69 YEARS	2.93%	2.72%
70 TO 74 YEARS	3.03%	2.42%
75+ 1 YEARS	4.38%	3.40%
MEDIAN AGE	31.13	32.48
AVERAGE AGE	33.56	33.54

Wed Mar 17, 1999

Page 17

CUSTOM SUMMARY REPORT
(POP FACTS: FULL DATA REPORT)
BY NATIONAL DECISION SYSTEMS 800-866-6510
PREPARED FOR
Electronic Marketing

3 and 6 Mile Radii of U.C.F.

	COORD: 2860080	8119870
DESCRIPTION	3.00 MILE RADIUS	6.00 MILE RADIUS
1998 ESTIMATED FEMALE POP. BY AGE	18,011	71,673
UNDER 5 YEARS	6.68%	7.18%
5 TO 9 YEARS	6.82%	7.24%
10 TO 14 YEARS	6.06%	6.84%
15 TO 17 YEARS	3.03%	3.73%
18 TO 20 YEARS	7.86%	4.79%
21 TO 24 YEARS	7.58%	6.18%
25 TO 29 YEARS	7.99%	8.22%
30 TO 34 YEARS	9.05%	8.54%
35 TO 39 YEARS	9.13%	9.15%
40 TO 49 YEARS	13.27%	15.91%
50 TO 59 YEARS	7.49%	9.19%
60 TO 64 YEARS	3.14%	3.34%
65 TO 69 YEARS	3.29%	2.91%
70 TO 74 YEARS	3.43%	2.68%
75+1 YEARS	5.19%	4.11%
FEMALE MEDIAN AGE	32.21	33.41
FEMALE AVERAGE AGE	34.51	34.35
POPULATION BY HOUSEHOLD TYPE	26,003	105,659
FAMILY HOUSEHOLDS	72.56%	81.43%
NON-FAMILY HOUSEHOLDS	22.94%	16.42%
GROUP QUARTERS	4.50%	2.14%
HOUSEHOLDS BY TYPE	9,759	38,582
SINGLE MALE	10.16%	9.18%
SINGLE FEMALE	8.81%	8.86%
MARRIED COUPLE	53.65%	58.87%
OTHER FAMILY-MALE HEAD	3.55%	3.38%
OTHER FAMILY-FEMALE HEAD	6.68%	8.26%
NON FAMILY-MALE HEAD	10.91%	7.15%
NON FAMILY-FEMALE HEAD	6.23%	4.30%
POPULATION BY URBAN VS. RURAL	25,984	105,627
URBAN	92.75%	90.74%
RURAL	7.25%	9.26%

Wed Mar 17, 1999 Page 18

CUSTOM SUMMARY REPORT
(POP FACTS: FULL DATA REPORT)
BY NATIONAL DECISION SYSTEMS 800-866-6510
PREPARED FOR
Electronic Marketing

3 and 6 Mile Radii of U.C.F.

DESCRIPTION	COORD: 2860080 3.00 MILE RADIUS	8119870 6.00 MILE RADIUS
FEMALES 161 WITH CHILDREN 0-17: BASE	10,241	40,737
WORKING WITH CHILD 0-5	5.02%	6.38%
NOT WORKING WITH CHILD 0-5	0.13%	0.44%
NOT IN LABOR FORCE WITH CHILD 0-5	3.79%	3.62%
WORKING WITH CHILD 6-17	9.65%	12.89%
NOT WORKING WITH CHILD 6-17	0.21%	0.44%
NOT IN LAB. FORCE WITH CHILD 6-17	2.43%	3.31%
WORKING WITH CHILD 0-5 & 6-18	3.12%	3.79%
NOT WORKING WITH CHILD 0-5 & 6-18	0.27%	0.27%
NOT IN LAB. FORCE W/CHILD 0-5 & 6-18	2.18%	2.51%
WORKING WITH NO CHILDREN	41.91%	41.69%
NOT WORKING WITH NO CHILDREN	2.28%	1.97%
NOT IN LAB. FORCE WITH NO CHILD.	29.00%	22.67%
HH BY AGE BY POVERTY STATUS	9,839	38,816
ABOVE POVERTY UNDER AGE 65	70.50%	79.93%
ABOVE POVERTY AGE 651	14.08%	10.36%
BELOW POVERTY UNDER AGE 65	14.38%	8.80%
BELOW POVERTY AGE 651	1.04%	0.91%
POPULATION 161 BY EMPLOYMENT STATUS	21,355	82,302
EMPLOYED IN ARMED FORCES	1.01%	1.07%
EMPLOYED CIVILIANS	65.27%	70.02%
UNEMPLOYED CIVILIANS	2.88%	3.19%
NOT IN LABOR FORCE	30.85%	25.72%
POPULATION 16 + BY OCCUPATION	13,938	57,624
EXECUTIVE AND MANAGERIAL	12.27%	13.91%
PROFESSIONAL SPECIALTY	16.83%	15.81%
TECHNICAL SUPPORT	4.14%	4.21%
SALES	13.75%	14.01%
ADMINISTRATIVE SUPPORT	18.54%	18.39%
SERVICE: PRIVATE HOUSEHOLD	0.23%	0.28%
SERVICE: PROTECTIVE	1.47%	1.74%
SERVICE: OTHER	11.17%	10.17%
FARMING FORESTRY & FISHING	1.18%	1.41%
PRECISION PRODUCTION & CRAFT	10.58%	10.74%
MACHINE OPERATOR	2.01%	2.60%
TRANS. AND MATERIAL MOVING	4.40%	3.62%
LABORERS	3.43%	3.09%

Wed Mar 17, 1999

Page 19

CUSTOM SUMMARY REPORT
(POP FACTS: FULL DATA REPORT)
BY NATIONAL DECISION SYSTEMS 800-866-6510
PREPARED FOR
Electronic Marketing

3 and 6 Mile Radii of U.C.F.

DESCRIPTION	COORD: 2860080 3.00 MILE RADIUS	8119870 6.00 MILE RADIUS
FAMILIES BY NUMBER OF WORKERS	6,345	27,281
NO WORKERS	11.10%	7.28%
ONE WORKER	25.85%	25.43%
TWO WORKERS	53.14%	54.34%
THREE1 WORKERS	9.91%	12.95%
HISPANIC POPULATION BY TYPE	26,003	105,659
NOT HISPANIC	91.60%	90.10%
MEXICAN	0.68%	0.59%
PUERTO RICAN	5.09%	6.12%
CUBAN	0.85%	1.13%
OTHER HISPANIC	1.78%	2.06%
1998 HISPANICS BY RACE: BASE	4,183	19,253
WHITE	69.84%	70.52%
BLACK	1.49%	2.13%
ASIAN	2.42%	2.32%
OTHER	26.25%	25.03%
POPULATION BY TRANSPORTATION TO WORK	13,938	57,430
DRIVE ALONE	80.37%	82.68%
CAR POOL	12.56%	12.76%
PUBLIC TRANSPORTATION	0.35%	0.34%
DRIVE MOTORCYCLE	0.53%	0.38%
WALKED ONLY	2.97%	1.31%
OTHER MEANS	2.08%	1.08%
WORKED AT HOME	1.15%	1.44%
POPULATION BY TRAVEL TIME TO WORK	13,938	57,430
UNDER 10 MINUTES/WORK AT HOME	12.46%	9.95%
10 TO 29 MINUTES	41.66%	46.93%
30 TO 59 MINUTES	41.55%	38.92%
60 TO 89 MINUTES	3.73%	3.69%
901 MINUTES	0.60%	0.50%
AVERAGE TRAVEL TIME IN MINUTES	25.87	25.28
HOUSEHOLDS BY NO. OF VEHICLES	9,761	38,564
NO VEHICLES	2.38%	2.92%
1 VEHICLE	33.45%	30.35%
2 VEHICLES	46.82%	48.41%
3+ VEHICLES	17.34%	18.32%
ESTIMATED TOTAL VEHICLES	17,824	71,650

Wed Mar 17, 1999

Page 20

CUSTOM SUMMARY REPORT
(POP FACTS: FULL DATA REPORT)
BY NATIONAL DECISION SYSTEMS 800-866-6510
PREPARED FOR
Electronic Marketing

3 and 6 Mile Radii of U.C.F.

DESCRIPTION	COORD: 2860080 3.00 MILE RADIUS	8119870 6.00 MILE RADIUS
POPULATION 25+ BY EDUCATION LEVEL	14,583	63,981
ELEMENTARY (0-8)	4.54%	4.23%
SOME HIGH SCHOOL (9-11)	11.80%	10.21%
HIGH SCHOOL GRADUATE (12)	29.78%	28.08%
SOME COLLEGE (13-15)	18.39%	21.59%
ASSOCIATES DEGREE ONLY	9.57%	9.20%
BACHELORS DEGREE ONLY	19.66%	19.35%
GRADUATE DEGREE	6.25%	7.35%
POPULATION ENROLLED IN SCHOOL	9,587	31,811
PUBLIC PRE-PRIMARY	2.21%	3.37%
PRIVATE PRE-PRIMARY	3.14%	4.06%
PUBLIC ELEM/HIGH	27.92%	44.89%
PRIVATE ELEM/HIGH	2.68%	4.70%
ENROLLED IN COLLEGE	64.05%	42.97%
HOUSING UNITS BY OCCUPANCY STATUS	10,704	42,085
OCCUPIED	91.17%	91.68%
VACANT	8.83%	8.32%
VACANT UNITS	945	3,503
FOR RENT	42.61%	44.57%
FOR SALE ONLY	18.77%	21.39%
SEASONAL	20.77%	10.72%
OTHER	17.85%	23.31%
OWNER OCCUPIED PROPERTY VALUES	4,090	20,551
UNDER $25,000	0.60%	0.52%
$25,000 TO $49,999	9.38%	5.45%
$50,000 TO $74,999	27.55%	23.23%
$75,000 TO $99,999	26.58%	35.17%
$100,000 TO $149,999	25.92%	23.88%
$150,000 TO $199,999	5.79%	6.79%
$200,000 TO $299,999	3.37%	3.85%
$300,000 TO $399,999	0.60%	0.76%
$400,000 TO $499,999	0.17%	0.23%
$500,000+	0.05%	0.13%
MEDIAN PROPERTY VALUE	$86,742	$89,784
TOTAL RENTAL UNITS	3,366	12,354
MEDIAN RENT	$450	$479

Wed Mar 17, 1999 Page 21

CUSTOM SUMMARY REPORT
(POP FACTS: FULL DATA REPORT)
BY NATIONAL DECISION SYSTEMS 800-866-6510
PREPARED FOR
Electronic Marketing

3 and 6 Mile Radii of U.C.F.

	COORD: 2860080	8119870
DESCRIPTION	3.00 MILE RADIUS	6.00 MILE RADIUS
PERSONS IN UNIT	9,759	38,582
1 PERSON UNITS	18.97%	18.04%
2 PERSON UNITS	39.88%	35.57%
3 PERSON UNITS	19.57%	20.37%
4 PERSON UNITS	14.14%	16.72%
5 PERSON UNITS	5.22%	6.41%
6 PERSON UNITS	1.51%	1.99%
7+ UNITS	0.70%	0.90%
YEAR ROUND UNITS IN STRUCTURE	10,704	42,085
SINGLE UNITS DETACHED	46.86%	58.87%
SINGLE UNITS ATTACHED	6.07%	5.70%
DOUBLE UNITS	2.36%	1.43%
3 TO 9 UNITS	12.84%	11.55%
10 TO 19 UNITS	4.51%	5.81%
20 TO 49 UNITS	5.91%	4.14%
50+ UNITS	0.00%	0.91%
MOBILE HOME OR TRAILER	20.94%	11.14%
ALL OTHER	0.51%	0.46%
SINGLE/MULTIPLE UNIT RATIO	2.07	2.71
HOUSING UNITS BY YEAR BUILT	9,761	38,564
BUILT 1989 TO MARCH 1990	9.05%	7.31%
BUILT 1985 TO 1988	36.08%	34.84%
BUILT 1980 TO 1984	25.47%	22.51%
BUILT 1970 TO 1979	17.34%	22.30%
BUILT 1960 TO 1969	6.56%	7.84%
BUILT 1950 TO 1959	4.99%	4.18%
BUILT 1940 TO 1949	0.37%	0.56%
BUILT 1939 OR EARLIER	0.15%	0.46%

Wed Mar 17, 1999 Page 22

CUSTOM SUMMARY REPORT
(RETAIL TRADE POTENTIAL REPORT - CURRENT YEAR SALES BY STORE TYPE)
BY NATIONAL DECISION SYSTEMS 800-866-6510
PREPARED FOR
Electronic Marketing

3 and 6 Mile Radii of U.C.F.

COORD: 2860080 8119870

DESCRIPTION	3.00 MILE RADIUS	6.00 MILE RADIUS
TOTAL RETAIL SALES	$462	$1,733
APPAREL & ACCESSORY STORES	$25	$92
AUTOMOTIVE DEALERS	$125	$470
AUTOMOTIVE & HOME SUPPLY STORES	$7	$25
DRUG & PROPRIETARY STORES	$14	$54
EATING & DRINKING PLACES	$59	$214
FOOD STORES	$66	$251
FURNITURE & HOME FURNISHINGS STORES	$13	$52
HOME APPLIANCE, RADIO, & T.V. STORES	$12	$49
GASOLINE SERVICE STATIONS	$24	$91
GENERAL MERCHANDISE	$60	$226
DEPARTMENT STORES (INCLUDING LEASED DEPTS.)	$48	$182
HARDWARE, LUMBER & GARDEN STORES	$23	$89

($'S IN MILLIONS)

Wed Mar 17, 1999 Page 23

MicroVision AREA PROFILE REPORT

BY NATIONAL DECISION SYSTEMS 800-866-6510
PREPARED FOR
Electronic Marketing

3 and 6 Mile Radii of U.C.F.

COORD: 2860080 8119870

DESCRIPTION		6.00 MILE RADIUS 1998 HSHLDS.	PCT.	BASE HSHLDS.	PCT.	INDEX
MVG01	1 UPPER CRUST	0	0.0	2379	0.4	0
MVG01	2 LAP OF LUXURY	0	0.0	2258	0.4	0
MVG01	3 ESTABLISHED WEALTH	1812	3.5	19515	3.5	99
MVG01	4 MID-LIFE SUCCESS	1733	3.3	12079	2.2	153
MVG01	5 PROSPEROUS METRO MIX	2464	4.7	15937	2.9	165
MVG01	6 GOOD FAMILY LIFE	2055	3.9	7566	1.4	289
MVG06	7 COMFORTABLE TIMES	600	1.1	3479	0.6	183
MVG04	8 MOVERS AND SHAKERS	0	0.0	4796	0.9	0
MVG03	9 BUILDING A HOME LIFE	553	1.1	981	0.2	599
MVG02	10 HOME SWEET HOME	9894	18.9	42210	7.6	249
MVG02	11 FAMILY TIES	6791	13.0	33543	6.0	215
MVG04	12 A GOOD STEP FORWARD	0	0.0	14409	2.6	0
MVG09	13 SUCCESSFUL SINGLES	0	0.0	0	0.0	0
MVG01	14 MIDDLE YEARS	31	0.1	1253	0.2	26
MVG04	15 GREAT BEGINNINGS	9311	17.8	68614	12.3	144
MVG02	16 COUNTRY HOME FAMILIES	2789	5.3	25864	4.6	115
MVG02	17 STARS AND STRIPES	112	0.2	13749	2.5	9
MVG02	18 WHITE PICKET FENCE	4317	8.2	37908	6.8	121
MVG03	19 YOUNG AND CAREFREE	57	0.1	585	0.1	104
MVG06	20 SECURE ADULTS	534	1.0	17131	3.1	33
MVG06	21 AMERICAN CLASSICS	131	0.3	3609	0.6	39
MVG02	22 TRADITIONAL TIMES	302	0.6	11616	2.1	28
MVG02	23 SETTLED IN	772	1.5	33317	6.0	25
MVG08	24 CITY TIES	196	0.4	11816	2.1	18
MVG03	25 BEDROCK AMERICA	2692	5.1	34007	6.1	84
MVG07	26 THE MATURE YEARS	14	0.0	309	0.1	47
MVG05	27 MIDDLE OF THE ROAD	51	0.1	1629	0.3	33
MVG03	28 BUILDING A FAMILY	906	1.7	13482	2.4	71
MVG05	29 ESTABLISHING ROOTS	207	0.4	3829	0.7	58
MVG06	30 DOMESTIC DUOS	656	1.3	20526	3.7	34
MVG06	31 COUNTRY CLASSICS	12	0.0	2449	0.4	5
MVG04	32 METRO SINGLES	0	0.0	3340	0.6	0
MVG07	33 LIVING OFF THE LAND	0	0.0	190	0.0	3
MVG04	34 BOOKS AND NEW RECRUITS	43	0.1	111	0.0	412
MVG02	35 BUY AMERICAN	30	0.1	4875	0.9	7
MVG09	36 METRO MIX	0	0.0	90	0.0	0
MVG09	37 URBAN UP AND COMERS	0	0.0	18	0.0	0
MVG02	38 RUSTIC HOMESTEADERS	57	0.1	17662	3.2	3
MVG04	39 ON THEIR OWN	595	1.1	30416	5.5	21
MVG04	40 TRYING METRO TIMES	37	0.1	13543	2.4	3
MVG08	41 CLOSE-KNIT FAMILIES	0	0.0	593	0.1	0
MVG08	42 TRYING RURAL TIMES	0	0.0	1417	0.3	0
MVG08	43 MANUFACTURING USA	0	0.0	2927	0.5	0

BASE DEFINITION MSA/NEC: Orlando, FL

Wed Mar 17, 1999 Page 24

MicroVision AREA PROFILE REPORT

BY NATIONAL DECISION SYSTEMS 800-866-6510
PREPARED FOR
Electronic Marketing

3 and 6 Mile Radii of U.C.F.

COORD: 2860080 8119870

DESCRIPTION	6.00 MILE RADIUS HSHLDS.	1998 PCT.	BASE HSHLDS.	PCT.	INDEX
MVG08 44 HARD YEARS	1	0.0	293	0.1	14
MVG09 45 STRUGGLING METRO MIX	0	0.0	1616	0.3	0
MVG08 46 DIFFICULT TIMES	0	0.0	11214	2.0	0
MVG09 47 UNIVERSITY USA	2342	16.9	3719	0.7	2533
MVG09 48 URBAN SINGLES	0	0.0	3741	0.7	0
MVG10 49 ANOMALIES	7	0.1	728	0.1	41
MVG11 50 UNCLASSIFIED	0	0.0	2	0.0	0
TOTALS	13856	100.0	557340	100.0	100

BASE DEFINITION MSA/NEC: Orlando, FL

Wed Mar 17, 1999 Page 25

MicroVision AREA GROUP REPORT

BY NATIONAL DECISION SYSTEMS 800-866-6510
PREPARED FOR
Electronic Marketing

3 and 6 Mile Radii of U.C.F.

COORD: 2860080 8119870

		3.00 MILE RADIUS		BASE		
		1998				
DESCRIPTION		HSHLDS.	PCT.	HSHLDS.	PCT.	INDEX
MVG01	ACCUMULATED WEALTH	1247	9.0	60987	10.9	82
MVG02	MAINSTREAM FAMILIES	7425	53.6	220744	39.6	135
MVG03	YOUNG ACCUMULATORS	1212	8.7	49055	8.8	99
MVG04	MAINSTREAM SINGLES	405	2.9	135229	24.3	12
MVG05	ASSET-BUILDING FAMILIES	57	0.4	5458	1.0	42
MVG06	CONSERVATIVE CLASSICS	1149	8.3	47194	8.5	98
MVG07	CAUTIOUS COUPLES	11	0.1	499	0.1	89
MVG08	SUSTAINING FAMILIES	1	0.0	28260	5.1	0
MVG09	SUSTAINING SINGLES	2342	16.9	9184	1.6	1026
MVG10	ANOMALIES	7	0.1	728	0.1	41
MVG11	UNCLASSIFIED	0	0.0	2	0.0	0
	TOTALS	13856	100.0	557340	100.0	100

BASE DEFINITION MSA/NEC: Orlando, FL

Wed Mar 17, 1999 Page 26

MicroVision AREA PROFILE REPORT

BY NATIONAL DECISION SYSTEMS 800-866-6510
PREPARED FOR
Electronic Marketing

3 and 6 Mile Radii of U.S.F.

COORD: 2860080 8119870

		3.00 MILE RADIUS		BASE		
		1998				
DESCRIPTION		HSHLDS.	PCT.	HSHLDS.	PCT.	INDEX
MVG01	1 UPPER CRUST	0	0.0	2379	0.4	0
MVG01	2 LAP OF LUXURY	0	0.0	2258	0.4	0
MVG01	3 ESTABLISHED WEALTH	81	0.6	19515	3.5	17
MVG01	4 MID-LIFE SUCCESS	359	2.6	12079	2.2	119
MVG01	5 PROSPEROUS METRO MIX	40	0.3	15937	2.9	10
MVG01	6 GOOD FAMILY LIFE	755	5.4	7566	1.4	401
MVG06	7 COMFORTABLE TIMES	305	2.2	3479	0.6	353
MVG04	8 MOVERS AND SHAKERS	0	0.0	4796	0.9	0
MVG03	9 BUILDING A HOME LIFE	344	2.5	981	0.2	1411
MVG02	10 HOME SWEET HOME	4519	32.6	42210	7.6	431
MVG02	11 FAMILY TIES	507	3.7	33543	6.0	61
MVG04	12 A GOOD STEP FORWARD	0	0.0	14409	2.6	0
MVG09	13 SUCCESSFUL SINGLES	0	0.0	0	0.0	0
MVG01	14 MIDDLE YEARS	13	0.1	1253	0.2	41
MVG04	15 GREAT BEGINNINGS	32	0.2	68614	12.3	2
MVG02	16 COUNTRY HOME FAMILIES	9	0.1	25864	4.6	1
MVG02	17 STARS AND STRIPES	1	0.0	13749	2.5	0
MVG02	18 WHITE PICKET FENCE	2318	16.7	37908	6.8	246
MVG03	19 YOUNG AND CAREFREE	3	0.0	585	0.1	20
MVG06	20 SECURE ADULTS	228	1.6	17131	3.1	53
MVG06	21 AMERICAN CLASSICS	40	0.3	3609	0.6	45
MVG02	22 TRADITIONAL TIMES	49	0.4	11616	2.1	17
MVG02	23 SETTLED IN	19	0.1	33317	6.0	2
MVG08	24 CITY TIES	0	0.0	11816	2.1	0
MVG03	25 BEDROCK AMERICA	645	4.7	34007	6.1	76
MVG07	26 THE MATURE YEARS	11	0.1	309	0.1	143
MVG05	27 MIDDLE OF THE ROAD	7	0.1	1629	0.3	18
MVG03	28 BUILDING A FAMILY	220	1.6	13482	2.4	66
MVG05	29 ESTABLISHING ROOTS	50	0.4	3829	0.7	53
MVG06	30 DOMESTIC DUOS	574	4.1	20526	3.7	112
MVG06	31 COUNTRY CLASSICS	1	0.0	2449	0.4	2
MVG04	32 METRO SINGLES	0	0.0	3340	0.6	0
MVG07	33 LIVING OFF THE LAND	0	0.0	190	0.0	0
MVG04	34 BOOKS AND NEW RECRUITS	43	0.3	111	0.0	1556
MVG02	35 BUY AMERICAN	0	0.0	4875	0.9	0
MVG09	36 METRO MIX	0	0.0	90	0.0	0
MVG09	37 URBAN UP AND COMERS	0	0.0	18	0.0	0
MVG02	38 RUSTIC HOMESTEADERS	2	0.0	17662	3.2	1
MVG04	39 ON THEIR OWN	329	2.4	30416	5.5	44
MVG04	40 TRYING METRO TIMES	1	0.0	13543	2.4	0
MVG08	41 CLOSE-KNIT FAMILIES	0	0.0	593	0.1	0
MVG08	42 TRYING RURAL TIMES	0	0.0	1417	0.3	0
MVG08	43 MANUFACTURING USA	0	0.0	2927	0.5	0

BASE DEFINITION MSA/NEC: Orlando, FL

Wed Mar 17, 1999 Page 27

MicroVision AREA PROFILE REPORT

BY NATIONAL DECISION SYSTEMS 800-866-6510
PREPARED FOR
Electronic Marketing

3 and 6 Mile Radii of U.C.F.

COORD: 2860080 8119870

DESCRIPTION	6.00 MILE RADIUS HSHLDS. (1998)	PCT.	BASE HSHLDS. (1998)	PCT.	INDEX
MVG08 44 HARD YEARS	2	0.0	293	0.1	7
MVG09 45 STRUGGLING METRO MIX	0	0.0	1616	0.3	0
MVG08 46 DIFFICULT TIMES	0	0.0	11214	2.0	0
MVG09 47 UNIVERSITY USA	2582	4.9	3719	0.7	739
MVG09 48 URBAN SINGLES	0	0.0	3741	0.7	0
MVG10 49 ANOMALIES	46	0.1	728	0.1	67
MVG11 50 UNCLASSIFIED	2	0.0	2	0.0	838
TOTALS	52386	100.0	557340	100.0	100

BASE DEFINITION MSA/NEC: Orlando, FL

Wed Mar 17, 1999 Page 28

MicroVision AREA GROUP REPORT

BY NATIONAL DECISION SYSTEMS 800-866-6510

PREPARED FOR

Electronic Marketing

3 and 6 Mile Radii of U.C.F.

COORD: 2860080 8119870

	6.00 MILE RADIUS		BASE		
	1998				
DESCRIPTION	HSHLDS.	PCT.	HSHLDS.	PCT.	INDEX
MVG01 ACCUMULATED WEALTH	8095	15.5	60987	10.9	141
MVG02 MAINSTREAM FAMILIES	25064	47.8	220744	39.6	121
MVG03 YOUNG ACCUMULATORS	4207	8.0	49055	8.8	91
MVG04 MAINSTREAM SINGLES	9987	19.1	135229	24.3	79
MVG05 ASSET-BUILDING FAMILIES	258	0.5	5458	1.0	50
MVG06 CONSERVATIVE CLASSICS	1933	3.7	47194	8.5	44
MVG07 CAUTIOUS COUPLES	14	0.0	499	0.1	30
MVG08 SUSTAINING FAMILIES	199	0.4	28260	5.1	7
MVG09 SUSTAINING SINGLES	2582	4.9	9184	1.6	299
MVG10 ANOMALIES	46	0.1	728	0.1	67
MVG11 UNCLASSIFIED	2	0.0	2	0.0	838
TOTALS	52386	100.0	557340	100.0	100

BASE DEFINITION MSA/NEC: Orlando, FL

MicroVision Segments/Short Descriptions

1 UPPER CRUST These are families with older children located in the suburbs. They have very high levels of income and education, work in executive and managerial, sales, and other white-collar occupations.

2 LAP OF LUXURY These are suburban family homeowners with children. They have very high levels of income and education, and work in sales and other white-collar occupations. Most of these households contain two or more workers, and three or more people.

3 ESTABLISHED WEALTH These are families with and without children. They are typically homeowners located in suburban areas. They have very high levels of income and education and work in white-collar occupations.

4 MID-LIFE SUCCESS These are households with very high incomes living in suburban areas. They are homeowners with very high property values, who primarily work in white collar occupations such as sales.

5 PROSPEROUS METRO MIX These are typically married couples with young children, living in suburban and urban areas. They have high income and education levels, are home owners and work in white collar occupations.

6 GOOD FAMILY LIFE These are typically high income, married couples with children. They live in owner-occupied, single family detached units in rural areas. They have a high level of education and work in white collar occupations.

7 COMFORTABLE TIMES These are typically high income households, with slightly older than average married couples, with and without children. They live in the suburbs, own their home, have a high level of education, and work in white collar occupations.

8 MOVERS AND SHAKERS These are typically households containing singles and couples, with two workers and no children. They live in the suburbs and in some urban areas, and have high levels of education and income.

9 BUILDING A HOME LIFE These are typically married couples with children, living in owner-occupied, detached single family units. They have a medium-high income level and live in suburban and some rural areas.

10 HOME SWEET HOME These households are typically married couples with one or no children at home. They have an above average household income, own their home, and are primarily concentrated in the suburbs.

11 FAMILY TIES These households are generally families with children, living in suburban areas in the West. They have a medium-high level of income, have attended some college, and live in houses built between 1960 and 1979.

12 A GOOD STEP FORWARD These are typically 25 to 39 years old living in non-family households with one or two people. They are concentrated in urban areas, are renters, have above average household and per capita income.

13 SUCCESSFUL SINGLES These are urban, renter-occupied, non-family households, usually containing one person and sometimes two. They have very high income and education levels, and work in white collar occupations.

14 MIDDLE YEARS This segment contains suburban, high income, white collar workers, with an above average concentration of people age 50 to 64 years

old. They rank slightly above average for home-ownership, and for having two people in the household.

15 GREAT BEGINNINGS These are typically households with one or two young adults, renting in urban and suburban areas. Their household income is slightly higher than average, as is the percent that have college degrees and white collar occupations.

16 COUNTRY HOME FAMILIES These are typically married families with children, located in rural areas. They have a household income just above the national average, are homeowners, and work in blue collar occupations.

17 STARS AND STRIPES These are typically young families with a relatively large number of children. They live in urban and suburban areas, have household incomes around the national average, work in blue collar occupations, and are more likely than average to be renters.

18 WHITE PICKET FENCE These are typically suburban families with one or two children. They have household incomes around the national average, live in owner-occupied housing, and work in blue collar occupations.

19 YOUNG AND CAREFREE This segment consists primarily of young adults without children. They are typically one and two person households renting in suburban and some urban areas. They have an average income level, and work in white collar occupations.

20 SECURE ADULTS Older singles and couples, living in the suburbs with no children and a household income just below the national average. They are typically home owners, living in single unit detached or mobile homes.

21 AMERICAN CLASSICS These are older singles and couples, living in suburban and rural areas. They are both home owners and renters, with incomes near the national average, medium-low education level, and a high percentage receiving retirement income.

22 TRADITIONAL TIMES This segment is comprised of singles and couples, some with one or two children. They have medium-low levels of income and education, and are primarily located in suburban areas. They live in owner-occupied units and work in blue collar occupations.

23 SETTLED IN These are primarily older couples, with no children in the household, or single person households. They live in suburban areas, have medium levels of income and education and a high likelihood of being retired.

24 CITY TIES These are families with a relatively large number of children. They primarily live in urban areas and have medium-low income and education levels. They tend to have blue collar occupations and take public transportation to work.

25 BEDROCK AMERICA This segment consists of families with children, located primarily in rural areas. They have low income and education levels, are home owners with low property value, and work in blue collar occupations.

26 THE MATURE YEARS These households are singles and couples, with and without children, located in suburban and some rural areas. They have low income and education levels, work in blue collar occupations, and have low property values and rent levels.

27 MIDDLE OF THE ROAD This segment primarily consists of family households with children, located in rural areas. They have medium-low income and education levels, and work in blue collar occupations, especially farming, forestry, and fishing.

28 BUILDING A FAMILY These households contain younger than average adults and their children, who live in older homes and located in rural areas. They have low income, property value, and education levels and work in blue collar occupations.

29 ESTABLISHING ROOTS These are primarily families with large numbers of children, located in rural areas, and living in older homes. They have low income, property value, and education levels and work in blue collar occupations.

30 DOMESTIC DUOS This segment consists primarily of seniors, with one or two people in the residence, located in suburban areas. They live in one-unit attached and multi-unit housing, have a medium-low income level and almost one-third receive retirement income.

31 COUNTRY CLASSICS These are owner-occupied households, containing mature couples and some children. They live in rural areas, have low household incomes, and work in blue collar occupations.

32 METRO SINGLES This segment consists of households containing relatively young singles, some couples and few children. They are typically urban renters, with medium-low income and education levels, who work in administrative support and blue collar occupations.

33 LIVING OFF THE LAND These are married couples, many with children, located in rural areas. They are typically low income home owners, living in older houses with a low property value.

34 BOOKS AND NEW RECRUITS This segment consists of young, single adults, living in rental or group housing, in urban and suburban areas. They have an above average education and medium-low income level and they are likely to work in white collar occupations.

35 BUY AMERICAN These are married families, many with children, living in suburban and rural areas. Most are home owners with low property value and household income, working in blue collar occupations. Relatively few have education beyond high school.

36 METRO MIX Typically young urban singles, living in non-family households. They are primarily renters with medium-low income, and little college education, which work in administrative support and service occupations.

37 URBAN UP AND COMERS This segment consists of singles, primarily living alone, in rental property. They live in urban areas, have a high level of education, medium-high income, and work in white collar occupations.

38 RUSTIC HOMESTEADERS These are primarily rural households, containing married, middle aged adults, with older children. They have little education beyond high school, low incomes, and work in blue collar occupations.

39 ON THEIR OWN These are typically young adults and seniors, living in renter-occupied households located in urban and suburban areas. These

households typically contain one to two persons, have a low level of income, and many contain white collar specialty and blue collar service workers.

40 TRYING METRO TIMES **This segment typically consists of younger, single adults with young children, and seniors, located in urban and suburban areas. They are typically renters, with very low income and education, working in blue collar occupations.**

41 CLOSE-KNIT FAMILIES **These are urban households with young adults and a large number of children. They are typically renters, with very low income and education levels, who work as laborers, machine operators, and in other blue collar occupations.**

42 TRYING RURAL TIMES **These are rural households with a large number of children. They are primarily home owners with very low incomes and little education, who work in blue collar occupations.**

43 MANUFACTURING USA **This segment consists of very low income households located in urban and suburban areas. They are young adults and seniors, many with children, living in renter-occupied housing. They have low levels of education and work in the service sector and other blue collar occupations.**

44 HARD YEARS **This segment contains primarily young adults and seniors renting in urban areas. They have very low income and education levels, live in multi-family dwellings and work in blue collar occupations.**

45 STRUGGLING METRO MIX **These households are typically young singles renting in urban areas. They have few children, low levels of income and education, with many employed in blue collar or administrative support positions.**

46 DIFFICULT TIMES **These are primarily families with a relatively large number of children. They have very low income and education levels, and are mostly renters who work in the service sector and other blue collar occupations.**

47 UNIVERSITY USA **These are typically young urban singles with very low incomes, which live in non-family households and group quarters. Almost all are currently in college, and live in one or two person households in multi-unit structures.**

48 URBAN SINGLES **This segment contains primarily young adults and seniors with few children, renting in urban areas. They have a very low level of income and a lower than average level of education. They are very likely to live in single person households in multi-unit structures.**

49 ANOMALIES & 50 UNCLASSIFIED **Non-homogenous segments which should not be included in a marketing plan.**

Appendix C: Web Resources

Internet Information

The Web itself is rich in resources to aid in marketing and doing business on the Internet. Many of these resources are offered free of charge by government units, universities, businesses, and individuals. Here are some sites that are worth exploring.

Some addresses are constantly changing due to the expansion and improvement of the Web, so try alternative addresses if they are listed.

Before you begin your specific research, you might want to check the MetaIndex at www.ncsa.uluc.edu/SGD/Software/Mosaic/MetaIndex.html, which is an excellent starting point for surfing the Web in general.

Web Marketing Information Center, www.wilsonweb.com/webmarket/

This is a list of high quality information sites that are germane to a variety of businesses.

WWW Virtual Library, www.w3.org/hypertext/DataSources/bySubject/ Overview.html

This virtual library maintains a distributed subject catalog, even attempting an experimental Library of Congress classification. The site covers much ground, from engineering and the sciences to commercial services, education, and more.

Open Market's Commercial Sites Index, www.directory.net/

What began as a small project at the MIT Laboratory for Computer Sciences has become one of the best listings of commercial services on the Web. It maintains the listings as the free public service for the Internet community. Open Market facilities commerce on the Internet through assisting in the creation of storefronts and other services involving store creation, account management, buyer authentication, and secure payment processing.

Internet Surveys

NUA Internet Surveys, www.nua.ie/surveys/index.cgi

Maintained by NUA, the Irish market research firm, this site has a searchable database of Internet reports and surveys from around the world. It is searchable by subject, geography, and date, with subjects including advertising, demographics, e-mail, automotive, infrastructure, online communities, and much more. NUA also offers a weekly e-mail newsletters, Internet surveys that describe the newest surveys that you can subscribe to on the site.

GVU's User Surveys, www.cc.gatech.edu/gvu/user_surveys/User_Survey_Home.html

The GVU's WWW User Surveys contain some of the most extensive data on consumer and commercial users on the Internet. This site contains the survey background and results of the ten WWW user surveys conducted by the Graphics, Visualization, and Usability Center at the Georgia Institute of Technology. The surveys cover a number of areas. The general section includes general demographics, Web and Internet usage, attitudes towards electronic privacy and spamming, and politics. The Consumer Survey covers security of transactions, information gathering behavior, purchasing behavior, opinions of vendors, and Internet banking. There are also special sections on Web mastering, HTML authoring, and Web/Internet Service Providers.

Hoffman and Novak, Owens Graduate School of Management at Vanderbilt University

Donna Hoffman and Tom Novak are premier Internet issues researchers and have published many valuable Internet studies. While permission is necessary to quote or cite findings of their research, the topics are rich for study. Among their Internet research includes papers on:

- Modeling the Clickstream: Implications for Web-Based Advertising Efforts, www2000.ogsm.vanderbilt.edu/papers/clickstream/clickstream.html (1998)

- Information Privacy in the Marketplace: Implications for the Commercial Uses of Anonymity on the Web, www2000.ogsm.vanderbilt.edu/papers/anonymity/anonymity2_nov10htm (1997)
- Diversity on the Internet: The Relationship of Race to Access and Usage, www2000.ogsm.vanderbilt.edu/papers...diversity.on.the.Internet.oct24.1997.html
- Internet and Web Use in the United States: Baselines for Commercial Development, www2000.ogsm.vanderbilt.edu/baseline/Internet.demos.july9.1996.html

  You might check their academic papers site, Project 2000, www2000.ogsm.vanderbilt.edu/papers, occasionally to see what Hoffman and Novak have produced research on. The team is most prolific.

The Internet Advertising Report, www.ms.com/insight/misc/inetad/index.html

This fourteen-chapter report is an extensive look at the Internet dated December 1996. An in-depth comparison for a year-to-year review, written by Mary Meeker of Morgan Stanley/Dean Witter.

J. P. Morgan Research Reports, www.jpmorgan.com/MarketDataInd/Research/

This site includes the 1995 report, "Online Services: A New Medium Develops," as well as 1996 and 1997 reports on the year 2000 problem.

The Gallup Organization, www.gallup.com

The world's premium source for public opinion data since 1935. Includes the most recent Gallup Polls, special, or the opportunity to take part in the active poll.

Netsurfer Digest Reader Survey, www.netsurf.com/surveys.html

This page has the results of the Netsurfer Digest Reader Survey for the periods June 1994 to May 1995 and November 1995 to June 1996. They show readership growing more diverse and less use of online services and Bulletin Board Services.

ActivMedia Market Research for Net Marketers, www.activmedia.com

This site contains table of contents and executive summaries from the many ActivMedia research reports, along with order forms for the full fee-based reports. Reports include the Real Numbers Behind Internet Service and Promotion Providers, The Real Numbers Behind Net Profits 1997, Understanding the Japanese Web User, and Chinese Consumer Markets, Web Transaction Processing.

Interactive Publications Alert Survey of Women Online, www.netcreations.com/ipa/women.htm

Executive summary. Order form and cost information for full report.

CommerceNet/Nielsen Internet Demographics Survey, www.commerce.net/nielsen/index.html

This survey is updated periodically. A brief description of the 1997 survey as well as executive summaries of older reports are available on the page. The full report is $5,000, and it is also available by section for lower fees.

American Internet User Study by Cyberdialogue, www.cyberdialogue.com/

Cyberdialogue offers a number of Internet studies, including this one that provides projectable information on the U.S. online population, based upon a random representative sample of the U.S. population. It is updated twice a year.

Jupiter Communications Market Studies and Syndicated Research, www.jup.com/

Studies from 1997 include the Revenue Prospects for Online Chat, 1998 studies include Online Advertising Report, Banners and Beyond: Strategies for

Branding, Driving Traffic and Sales, Music Industry and the Internet, and 1999 studies include European Online Markets and Consumer Internet Economy. Jupiter also offers a number of newsletters that track various online markets, including Digital Kids, Internet Business Report, Online Marketplace, Interactive Content, Interactive Home, WebTrack, and Digital Travel. An electronic weekly newsletter, Digital Digest, is free; check for costs of other materials.

NPD Group, www.npd.com

One of the nation's largest marketing information firms, NPD Group helps companies around the world answer their marketing questions, for existing and new product concepts and especially for research such as the fragrance industry and video game industry. NPD Insights newsletter is available. Check for costs.

Find/SVP Emerging Technologies Research Group, http://etrg.findsvp.com/index.html

Find/SVP has produced a number of Internet-related reports including the American Interactive Healthcare Professionals Survey, Internet Timeline, Children on the Internet, and Local Information on the Net User Demand, Industry Players, and Marketplace Outlook. The periodically updated American Internet User Survey is a random sample survey focusing on current adult Internet users. Current survey chapters include an overview, media trade-offs, personalizing of the Internet, top content choices, online ads are effective, and more Americans are interested, in the Net. A summary of the report from Spring 1995, is available on the site. Check for costs.

The Netcraft Web Server Survey, www.netcraft.co.uk/survey/

This is a monthly survey of Web Server software usage on Internet connected computers. Netcraft collects and collates host names providing HTTP service and systematically polls each one with an HTTP request for the server name.

Survey Net, www.survey.net/

This site conducts Internet surveys on a variety of subjects, including presidential polls, American comedy, shopping, shareware, demographic surveys, and more. You can both take the surveys and see the results.

Zona Research, www.zonaresearch.com/

This site has a number of fee-based studies. Recent reports include Java: Markets, Opportunities, and Trends; Internet and Intranet: 1997 Report (Third Edition); and Network Computers: Markets, Opportunities, and Trends. Summaries of the studies with lists of their tables and ordering information are on the site. Zona offers its clients daily alerts, analyses of industry trends, and white papers. Check for costs.

Killen & Associates, www.killen.com

This company produces a wide range of Internet-related reports. Some of the 1997 reports include Market Strategies for IT Providers, Global IT Market Perspectives Service, Online Value-Added Financial Services: The Next Revenue Generator, and Automotive Financing on The Internet: Opportunities and Threats. Check for costs.

Cowles/Simba Net, www.simbanet.com/

Cowles/Simba provides a variety of online-related research reports. Some of the current ones include Publishing for Professional Markets: 1997–98 Review, Trends & Forecast, Business Information Markets 1999: The Strategic Outlook, and Information Publishing: Business/Professional Markets & Media, 1996–97. Check for costs.

Internet Statistics

Internet Index, www.folio.com/intindex/
Edited by Win Treese. Interesting and odd Internet statistics; patterned after Harper's Index.

Network USA Internet Service Providers Catalog, www.netusa.net/ISP/
Number of ISPs by country and some lists by country.

Matrix Information and Directory Services, Inc., www.mids.org/
Internet Growth Graphs, weather report, demographic surveys, Plus By Matrix Information and Directory Services, Inc. (MIDS). Some free and some fee-based.

Internet Domain Survey, www.nw.com/zone/WWW/top.html
Compiled by Network Wizards, this periodical survey attempts to discover every host on the Internet by doing a complete search of the Domain Name System. The results are presented in both text and graphical formats. The site also links to related surveys at other Web sites.

Making Sense of Internet Statistics, www.boardwatch.com/mag/95/dec/bwm1.htm
In Editor's Notes, by Jack Rickard, Boardwatch Magazine, December 1995. You must register, free, to read this article about the inflation of Internet demographic statistics.

Internet Statistics—Estimated, www.netree.com/netbin/Internetstats/
Estimate of the current number of people and web sites on the Internet, derived from a number of sources. By Internet Solutions.

Yahoo: Computers and Internet: Statistics and Demographics Surveys,www.yahoo.com/Computers_and_Internet/Internet/Statistics_and_Demographics/RIP
E Network Coordination Centre, www.ripe.net/
Contains statistics on European connectivity, host counts, service providers, and more.

CyberAtlas: The Internet Research Guide, www.cyberatlas.com
CyberAtlas' mission is to provide a concise, data-based overview of the Web and the science of Internet marketing. Topics include marketing and demographics, Intranets, ISPs, online services, browsers, advertising, and more.

Internet Domain Name Database, www.Internet.org/
By The Internet Business Center. This site has a domain name database searchable by name, state, city, or zip code. It also offers related domain names and other Internet statistics and some survey information.

Larry Landweber's International Connectivity Table, ftp://ftp.cs.wisc.edu/connectivity_table
Chart of types of Internet/UUCP/BBS, etc. Service by country.

Internet Monthly Report, www.isi.edu/in-notes/imr/
Report by members to the Internet Research Group. Interesting tidbits of information by major connectivity providers.

Internet Society Internet connectivity charts and graphs, ftp://ftp.isoc.org/isoc/charts/ftpisoc.html

Browser Watch: Stats Station, http://browserwatch.Internet.com/stats.html
This site tracks the use of the various browsers, counted by visits to the browser watch site.

Other Internet-Related Demographic Reports and Statistics Services

Rand Report on Universal Access to E-Mail: Feasibility and Societal Implications, www.rand.org:80/publications/MR/MR650/

Summary available online. Document # MR-650-MF. Full report is $20.

I/Pro: Delivering measurability to the Internet, www.ipro.com/

I/Pro is a commercial service, working with A. C. Nielsen, that offers products to audit and measure Web traffic.

Falling through the Net: A Survey of the "Have Nots" in Rural and Urban America, www.ntia.doc.gov/ntiahome/fallingthru.html

U.S. Department of Commerce, July 1995. About universal service and the Information Age. Summary and list of charts.

Search Engine Watch by Danny Sullivan, http://searchenginewatch.com/

This site contains information about how search engines work, comparisons of search engines, recent news about changes in search engine, Web site design with search engines in mind, Web masters guide to search engines, and much more.

Creating Learning Communities: Practical, Universal Networking for Learning in Schools and Homes,
www.eff.org/pub/Groups/CITS/Reports/epie_cits_school_networking.report

By the EPIE Institute. ASCII version of the report contains hundreds of school networking tips gleaned from 670 references, contains over a hundred URLs relevant to school networking, and provides ways to strength home/school connectivity. A word processing version of the report is also available.

Web Compare, http://webcompare.Internet.com/

This site has the Web server comparison chart that compares features of Web servers. There are also links to other sites that have Web server benchmark studies.

The World Wide Web as a Universal Interface to Government Services, www.ctg.albany.edu/resources/htmlrpt/ittfnlrp.html

This report describes the results of a project to demonstrate the potential of the Web to become a universal interface between citizens and government.

SRI International iVALS survey, http://future.sri.com/ivals/

The SRI Values and Lifestyles program categorizes U.S. adult consumers into mutually exclusive groups based on their psychology and several key demographics. They have an online survey that people can fill out to be added to the sample population.

Appendix D: Situation Analysis Questionnaire for Business Interviews

Interviewer:

Date:

1. Product/service name:
2. Company/corporate name:
3. Industry/SIC code:
4. Summary of product/service:
5. Date of introduction:

   Brief history of product/company:

   What is the purpose of the promotional program?
6. What are the primary benefits?
7. What is the pricing strategy?
8. Who is the primary target? Any secondary prospect targets?

9. What is the geographic coverage area?

10. What is the manner/levels of distribution?

11. What is the organization of sales staff?

12. Who is the primary competition?

    What are the competitions primary advantages? disadvantages?

13. Is the competition using online communications? If so, for what purpose and how?

14. How is the marketing budget to be set (objective and task, percent of sales, or other method)?

15. What will be the measurement criteria for judging the success of the marketing effort?

    Comments/notes:

    Research strategy—prioritize sources/databases:

INDEX